Winter in America

Winter in America

*A Cultural History of Neoliberalism,
from the Sixties to the Reagan Revolution*

DANIEL ROBERT MCCLURE

The University of North Carolina Press
Chapel Hill

This book was published with the assistance of the Authors Fund of the University of North Carolina Press.

© 2021 The University of North Carolina Press
All rights reserved

Set in Minion Pro by Westchester Publishing Services
Manufactured in the United States of America

The University of North Carolina Press has been a member of the Green Press Initiative since 2003.

Library of Congress Cataloging-in-Publication Data
Names: McClure, Daniel Robert, author.
Title: Winter in America : a cultural history of neoliberalism, from the sixties to the Reagan revolution / Daniel Robert McClure.
Description: Chapel Hill : The University of North Carolina Press, 2021. | Includes bibliographical references and index.
Identifiers: LCCN 2021007908 | ISBN 9781469664675 (cloth ; alk. paper) | ISBN 9781469664682 (pbk. ; alk. paper) | ISBN 9781469664699 (ebook)
Subjects: LCSH: Neoliberalism—United States—History—20th century. | White nationalism—United States—History. | Male domination (Social structure)—United States—History. | Privatization—United States—History—20th century. | United States—Social policy—History—20th century. | United States—Economic policy—History—20th century. | United States—Race relations—History—20th century.
Classification: LCC HB95 .M3835 2021 | DDC 306.30973/09045—dc23
LC record available at https://lccn.loc.gov/2021007908

Chapter 1 was previously published in a different form as "Possessing History and American Innocence: James Baldwin, William F. Buckley, Jr., and the 1965 Cambridge Debate," *James Baldwin Review* 2 (2016): 49–74; I am grateful to *James Baldwin Review* and Manchester University Press for permission to reprint and adapt this material. Chapter 5 was previously published in a different form as "Go West and Turn Right: John Wayne's Vietnam Trilogy, the Culture Wars, and the Rise of Neoliberalism," *Journal of the West* 52, no. 1 (2013): 33–41; used here with permission. Chapter 8 was previously published as "Who Will Survive America? Gil Scott-Heron, the Black Radical Tradition, and the Critique of Neoliberalism," *National Political Science Review* 17, no. 2 (2016): 3–26; reproduced with permission of The Licensor through PLSclear.

To Jennifer, Ani, and Everett

and

To the army of academic adjuncts who give everything to their students and institutions, who create scholarship and perform service without institutional reward, and who receive the bare minimum in compensation for their vital role in sustaining the programs and departments of universities and colleges in the twenty-first century. This book is especially dedicated to one of the brightest souls of this army, Edward L. Robinson Jr., an inspiring scholar and teacher who left this world way too soon.

Contents

Acknowledgments, xi

Introduction, 1

Chapter 1 American Innocence through the Possession of History, 23
 James Baldwin, William F. Buckley Jr., and the 1965 Cambridge Debate

Chapter 2 Did You Ever See a Dream Walking?, 49
 Western Civilization, the Longue Durée, and the Culture of Neoliberalism

Chapter 3 The Jim Crow Welfare State and the Corporate Revolution, 88
 Postwar American Capitalism

Chapter 4 The Idea of Doing with Less so that Big Business Can Have More, 128
 The Culture and Ethos of Business Week

Chapter 5 Go West and Turn Right, 161
 Settler Colonialism, Neoliberalism, and John Wayne's Possession of History

Chapter 6 Blood, Breasts, and Beasts, 207
 The Feminist Liberation Gauntlet and Flexible Misogyny at the Dawn of Social Equality

Chapter 7 Does Militancy No Longer Mean Guns at High Noon?, 248
 Feminist Dialogues, the Corporate Woman, and the Dawn of Neoliberalism

Chapter 8 Who Will Survive in America?, 284
 The Black Radical Tradition and the Poetic Critique of Neoliberalism

Conclusion, 317

Notes, 327
Bibliography, 379
Index, 429

Tables

2.1 "In general, do you think Negroes are as intelligent as white people—that is, can they learn just as well if they are given the same education (and training)?," 60

2.2 "Do you think most Negroes in the United States are being treated fairly or unfairly?," 61

2.3 "Would you move if colored people came to live in great numbers in your neighborhood?," 62

3.1 Stock of accumulated foreign direct investment, 107

3.2 U.S. manufacturing exports/foreign sales of U.S. multinationals, 118

Acknowledgments

I would like to thank the Authors Fund of the University of North Carolina Press for providing support for the publication of this book. *Winter in America* took just over ten years to conceptualize and write. Two scholars provided early inspiration for a project examining the interaction of culture and economics: Mark Levine helped shape my theoretical, *longue durée* conception of modernity, whereas Sohail Daulatzai suggested some concise parameters: the neoliberal era. Driven by my interest in capitalism and popular media spanning the 1960s–'80s, I started organizing a variety of sources and voices to chart the curious ways culture seemed to inform the rise of neoliberalism at the same time neoliberal ideas influenced the evolution of culture. Through accident, conversations with colleagues, and a combination of old and new interests in popular media, my jumble of disconnected sources slowly cohered. On the initial voyage of the manuscript, Winston James offered critical guidance for my sometimes-erratic forays through a world-historical prism grounded by the "anvil of modernity": the post-1492 Caribbean and the intersecting processes emerging out of the plantation system and its setting for New World colonialism, the Atlantic slave system, capitalism, an Enlightenment balancing freedom atop slavery, the accumulation of wealth for European nations (including the United States), and later, the staging ground for the U.S. brand of economic imperialism. I am indebted to James for his critiques of the direction I took for my project, as well as the trust he held in what undoubtedly appeared, early on, to be too blurry of a vision to convert into an acceptable project.

With the first draft completed in 2013, I was surer of the direction I was taking, though the project still trembled under the weight of conceptual gaps holding the chapters together. I intuitively understood the patterns, but I did not quite have the concise language and knowledge to articulate what I saw. This uncertainty was reflected in the number of presses who passed on the proposal. With my first year of teaching, combined with some insight and encouragement from Jared Sexton, the manuscript entered a new stage of articulation. It took a few years, but the project finally found a home at the University of North Carolina Press. I would like to thank my editor, Brandon Proia, who recognized some worth in a slowly coagulating manuscript composed of crooked paths, potholed roads, and choked gutters, which, when viewed as a whole, argued that to understand the rise of neoliberalism, you had to understand the assumptions, policies, and material outcomes rooted in the deep history of settler colonialism, slavery and its anti-Black aftermath, as well as patriarchy—all of which found expression through the ideas of John Wayne, James Baldwin, William F. Buckley Jr., exploitation films, *Business Week* magazine, Black feminism, multinational corporations and the finance industry, Jayne Cortez, Gil Scott-Heron, and the usual suspects of neoliberalism, Milton Friedman and Friedrich von Hayek. Like a good music producer, Proia's guidance, encouragement, and insight helped immensely with the molding of often disjointed chapters into something acceptable to publish. I am very indebted for his confidence in my vision for the book.

Along with James, Sexton, Levine, and Daulatzai, *Winter in America* emerged through years of discussions with Emily Rosenberg, Victoria E. Johnson, Selamawit D. Terrefe, Bridget R. Cooks, Laura Mitchell, Tiffany Willoughby-Herard, Vinayak Chaturvedi, David Igler, Cécile Whiting, Ken Pomeranz, Steven Topik, Norman L. Rosenberg, Mike Davis, Touraj Daryaee, Sharon V. Salinger, Tina Bell Wright, Nahum Dimitri Chandler, James Kyung-Jin Lee, Jon Wiener, Glen Mimura, Adriana M. Johnson, Horacio Legras, Aaron James, Robert Chase, Robert Wood, Shanon Fitzpatrick, Mark Berlin, Teishan Latner, Tina Shull, Michael Koncewicz, David Wight, Eric Steiger, Erik Altenbernd, Ernesto Bassi, Angela Hawk, Christine Eubank, Liam O'Mara, and David Fouser. I also appreciate the time taken by Jeff Guinn, Gerald Horne, David R. Roediger, and Angus Burgin—and the two anonymous readers—to read through drafts of my manuscript. A big thanks to the welcoming atmosphere of Fort Hays State University, including my colleagues Paul Nienkamp, Kim Perez, Juti A. Winchester, Marco A. Macias, Hollie Marquess, David E. Goodlett, Christy Craig, Jay Steinmetz, Matthew Smalley, Perry Harrison, and Grady Dixon. Many thanks to Jochen Burgtorf, Natalie Fousekis, Nancy Finch, Gayle K. Brunelle, Jessica Stern, Volker Janssen, Benjamin Cawthra, Robert McLain, Maged S.A. Mikhail, Margie Brown-Coronel, Stephen Neufeld, Jasamin Rostam-Kolayi, and the other faculty members of the history department at California State University, Fullerton (CSUF). I would also like to thank Kenneth L. Shonk Jr., Lindsay Steiner, Nicholas Schlensker, Mary T. Anderson, Richard and Jessie McClure, Matt and Sandy Antenore, Chris Arnold, Travis LaMetterey, Terence Dobkins, and Donald Mahon for their encouragement over the years. A vital nonacademic foundation for my understanding of capitalism came from my experience working as a cost and field engineer for the Golden Gate Bridge Retrofit and the San Mateo Bridge Widening Project. Thus, I would also like to thank my ex-coworkers at Balfour Beatty Construction Inc.—particularly Mark Johnnie and Crandall Bates—who taught a history undergrad how to shoot foundations to grade, organize multimillion-dollar budgets, and schedule and oversee hundreds of yards of concrete. Finally, I would like to thank my family—Jennifer, Ani, and Everett—who had to endure the decade-long journey for the book's completion. Additional apologies to Jennifer, who suffered through screenings of untold numbers of films—some good, a few bad, and many awful.

A foundational prism for *Winter in America* included Fernand Braudel's *longue durée* (big picture) view of history and an understanding of the intersectionality binding together settler colonialism, slavery and its aftermath, and patriarchy. Although I discovered Braudel's framework at CSUF, my study of capitalism found new life in the interdisciplinary world of the University of California, Irvine's (UCI's) humanities' programs and departments, especially UCI's history department's emphasis on global perspectives and the critical race and gender theory of the African American studies department and the visual studies program. These approaches found additional stimulus as I entered the world of teaching after graduation in 2013. Chapman University proved to be a fertile space for instruction, initiating many vital conversations that solidified *Winter in America*'s connections between culture and economics. I would like to thank the folks in the master of arts in international studies program—particularly Lynn Horton, Crystal Murphy, and Allison DeVries—and the Department of History—particularly Jennifer Keene, Alexander Bay, and Stacy Laird. Although it was a brief stay, I would also like to thank members of the CSUF African American studies department, particularly Edward Robinson, Gwendolyn Alexis, and Siobhan Brooks, who welcomed me into the department during the 2019–20 academic year. I would also like to thank the history and African American studies departments at UCI, who offered an array of upper-division courses to teach—which both helped to further fill in the book's conceptual gaps, as well as filling the gaps of employment uncertainty.

The bulk of *Winter in America* was written and edited across five challenging years of adjuncting at six different university and college campuses in Orange County, California, where I ended up (at last count) prepping and teaching more than twenty-five different courses. As anyone who has experienced the life of an adjunct understands, one teaches through a labyrinth of part-time academic work (often on multiple campuses), existing within a perpetual tidal wave of prep work for courses one has never taught that are sometimes offered a few days before the beginning of a semester or quarter (and one needs to accept the course regardless of the lack of preparation time in the fear of being "passed up" the next cycle). These "states of emergencies," however, allowed me to work through an assortment of unfamiliar literatures outside my immediate twentieth-century U.S. field, which slowly filled in the *longue durée* gaps in *Winter in America*—from histories of film to the Atlantic slave system to courses on cultural diversity and race to international studies courses on the authoritarian populist present. Teaching four to five courses a semester/quarter while writing often took a toll, but the experience helped normalize an overwhelming and sometimes chaotic routine in tune with the chaos and uncertainty of the period I was writing about. This state of tension undoubtedly helped shape *Winter in America*.

In light of the long commutes, incessant anxiety haunting the procurement of classes, and the rootless life of an academic adjunct, I would also like to acknowledge the large army of part-time professors, instructors, and lecturers across the nation who subsidize their respective campuses with their cheap, apprehensive, and contingent labor that keeps "their" institutions running. This book on the rise of the neoliberal era—the era forming the backdrop of the contemporary moment of academic austerity—is dedicated to them.

Winter in America

Introduction

> Let me emphasize the quality that seems to me to be an essential feature of the general history of capitalism: its unlimited flexibility, its capacity for change and *adaptation*. If there is, as I believe, a certain unity in capitalism, from thirteenth-century Italy to the present-day West, it is here above all that such unity must be located and observed.
>
> —Fernand Braudel, *Civilization and Capitalism, 15th–18th Century, Volume II: The Wheels of Commerce* (1979)

> This overview serves to show the institutional embeddedness of the current conflicts. Opponents on whatever side and in whatever faith are not simply discontented; their discontent is organized, directed, and cumulatively speaking, very well funded. A cultural conflict this extensively entrenched will not simply fade away. Apart from the ideological passions that are at play, too much is at stake institutionally for that to happen.
>
> —James Davison Hunter, *Culture Wars: The Struggle to Define America* (1991)

After years of social justice activism, urban unrest, and federal legislation, the 1970s emerged as the first decade in U.S. history when white men, especially white men with property, were forced legislatively to compete with people of color and women regarding political and economic opportunities in the mainstream of American life. As this epochal alteration in the nation's fabric unfolded, the United States and much of the world entered an economic downturn related to the global restructuring of capitalism. As it had since the shift from Spain-Genoa to the Dutch Republic in the 1600s, and to the ascending British Empire in the late 1700s and 1800s and later the United States in the twentieth century, capitalism entered a new period of reorganization as decolonization created more nation-states with abundant markets and resources while civil rights legislation established legal equality between the descendants of the formerly enslaved and former slave masters, as well as between men and women. A driving element of the reorganization of capitalism included the evolution of multinational corporations and finance between the 1940s and 1970s. Pushing against the constraints of the New Deal–era regulations and banking reforms, these economic institutions imagined and implemented new routes for international investment across the 1950s and 1960s. Against this backdrop of an expanding globalization of capital, the postwar white male-centric American identity and its relationship to economic policies entered a period of flux as the changing ideas and policies related to civil rights–era reforms explicitly questioned the assumptions people of the United States had long taken for granted—from the success stories of the American dream, to legendary tales underlining American exceptionalism, to the 200-year promise of American equality and liberty finally extended to those previously deemed inferior. Ultimately, this historical conjuncture heralded the unraveling of the prosperous Keynesian-inspired regulatory welfare state at the dawn of liberation, guiding the United States—and much of the world—down the path of neoliberalism.[1]

Celebrated for creating the postwar economic boom, the welfare state grew out of the reforms of the Progressive Era, leading to the 1930s New Deal programs implemented during the Great Depression.[2] Finding tentative stability through the relationship between big business, finance, organized labor, and government, many characterized this era as the postwar liberal consensus. Reined in by regulations in the wake of the Depression, large corporations and finance grew out of the stability of the welfare state but soon chafed against its constraints as the 1950s turned into the 1960s. Despite the centrist-liberal foundations of the welfare state coalition driving the postwar economic boom, the needs of business increasingly found champions in the New Right as conservatism reawakened after decades of marginalization after the Great Depression. The national conservative swing right in the late 1960s and 1970s opened the space to dismantle the welfare state as "Keynesian logic appeared to have died in the maelstrom of 1970s inflation."[3] Conservative-libertarian journalist Henry Hazlitt articulated this sentiment in 1969, "The solution to our problems is not more paternalism, laws, decrees, and controls, but the restoration of liberty and free enterprise, the restoration of incentives, to let loose the tremendous constructive energies of 200 million Americans."[4]

Alongside the goal of unshackling free enterprise, conservative champions confronted an old threat: social equality across race, gender, and sexuality. Long a shadow haunting a nation founded on both liberty and slavery, the threat of social equality in the decades after the 1950s forced conservatives to confront founder John Adams's fear of the destruction of "all distinctions"—the nightmare of liberty *to all the masses*. As one of the fathers of American conservatism, Adams's conservation of the status quo implied "that every man should know his place and be made to keep it."[5] Long secured in the wake of the American Revolution through slavery, the cult of true womanhood, Indian Removal, exclusionary legislation (anti-Chinese laws and Jim Crow), white terrorism (both mob and paramilitary), and culture buttressing white, heterosexual male supremacy, these traditional values could no longer hold after the 1960s. For economists seeking to reverse federal intervention on behalf of the working and middle classes, this swelling culture war over social equality provided an important rhetorical route toward achieving their goal of an ostensibly laissez-faire economy.[6]

The sudden reality of treating people of color and women as equals after centuries of white male heteronormative supremacy stirred the deep impulses—*the traditions*—of American society, leading to what some have called a backlash. By the end of the 1960s, it was not politically feasible to overtly terrorize people of color through traditional forms of mob or vigilante violence aimed toward "socially conservative" goals of stripping away newly gained rights as white America did during Reconstruction up through the twentieth century in the forms of white pogroms against Black communities in cities such as Colfax, Wilmington, Atlanta, Springfield, Knoxville, Elaine, Chicago, Tulsa, Los Angeles, and Detroit.[7] Rather, "white rage"—as Carol Anderson notes—went to work in the wake of the 1960s in different ways.[8] Southern segregationists laid the bedrock of culture war as they attempted to elude the hypocrisy of "separate but equal": as early as 1949, state governments sought to defund education and redirect tax payer money to private schools, while also "using race-neutral language—'ability,'" as ways to negotiate funding.[9]

As neoliberalism ascended to dominance after the 1960s, two of its defining elements—privatization and color blindness—found common cause with the political language of resistance against social equality. Public facilities would be privatized, with these policies of access justified using the language of "rights of property" and anti-government rhetoric; color-blind language espousing analytical measurements would institutionally limit access.[10] Eluding the language of racism, these rhetorical shifts contributed toward the conservation of the status quo against the threat of social equality. Moreover, the new language established an affiliation with a corporate world bristling under what they perceived to be their own struggle to retain "rights of property" against New Deal–era government regulations. The postwar anti-labor conservative voting bloc grew tighter as segregationists and the reborn conservative movement within the Grand Old Party (GOP)—with its traditionally wealthy constituents—embraced the populist authenticity of the South and West to present a common folk image amid its elitist ranks.[11] The economic logic tying these elements together arrived in the manifestos of a group of economists seeking to re-create and institute pre-1930s classical liberalism: the neoliberals.

The ideas, policies, and organizations of anti–welfare state conservatives, Southern segregationists, big business, and neoliberals converged in the 1960s and 1970s, finding codification in the 1980s. As capitalism entered a period of adjustment at the same moment legislated social equality became a reality after the 1960s, the inability of Keynesians to address the 1970s economic crisis opened a vacuum filled by conservative and neoliberal economic policies, which ultimately restructured federal interventionist priorities away from the white working and middle classes (as had been the case with the postwar welfare state) and toward the needs of multinationals, finance, and the wealthy. To facilitate one of the greatest American ironies—convincing the white American public to vote away the economic system that shaped their postwar prosperity—economic policies drew on the language of old sentiments derived from the historical legacies of social inequality. Sparked to life in the 1960s, a conservative culture war pushed back against the hard-won gains of women and people of color using the populist-inflected language of neoliberalism to tap into the discontent toward social equality reforms. Culture war, writes James Davison Hunter, was—and still is—rooted in the "competition to define social reality" resulting from the history of "America's uneasy pluralism."[12] This conflict challenged the new structures of social equality, with conservatives aiming to "retain their advantage in defining the habits and meaning of American culture."[13] In short, the United States ventured into an era Dylan Rodríguez calls "White Reconstruction," a period in which racial whiteness reformed through the "process of nominally abolishing a formally racist national system (chattel slavery/Jim Crow apartheid) while forming the groundwork for a reformed—*and reinvigorated*—white supremacist patriarchal social ordering."[14] Ridding itself of overt racism, this new social order would harvest the residual feelings cultivated during the era of overt white nationalism via the culture war. Winning the culture war meant controlling the language and knowledge defining social and economic reality; for a moment in the 1960s, this control had briefly escaped the grasp of "tradition" as women and people of color gained legislated social equality with white men. A perfect storm brewed across the 1970s, however, as the raw emotions driving culture war sentiments and seething discontent conjoined with corporate reorganization, neoliberal economic ideas, and the ascending New Right to direct populist angst against the redistributionist welfare state as the era of neoliberalism took shape in the late 1970s and 1980s.

A driving force for this culture war was the belief that a "golden age" had passed. This sentiment found reflection at the time through popular media and calls for a renewal of "traditional values." In hindsight, a sharp break appears certain, as many scholars mark the 1970s as a significant shift in American history.[15] Woven through the fabric of the New Deal welfare state, this conjuncture burst to life at the pinnacle of legislated social equality and the onset of the 1970s economic downturn. The winds driving this conjuncture gestated across the *longue durée* of American history, particularly the aftermaths and legacies of settler colonialism, slavery, and patriarchy—erupting as centuries-old customs suddenly became legislatively censured across the turbulent decade of the 1960s. We see a surrealist glimpse of these gusts in the observations of musician-poet, Gil Scott-Heron, who noted in 1975:

> There is a revolution going on in America/the World; a shifting in the winds/vibrations, as disruptive as an actual earth-tremor, but it is happening in our hearts. . . . The seeds of this revolution were planted hundreds of years ago; in slave ships, in cotton fields, in tepees, in the souls of brave men. The seeds were watered, nurtured and bloom now in our hands as we rock our babies. It is mid-winter in America; a man-made season of shattered dreams and shocked citizens, fumbling and frustrated beneath the crush of greed of corporate monsters and economic manipulators gone wild. There are bitter winds born in the knowledge of secret plans hatched by Western Money Men that backfired and grew out of control to eat its own. We must support ourselves and stand fast together even as pressure disperses our enemies and bangs at our doors. We must all do what we can for each other to weather this blizzard.[16]

In highlighting the centuries-old processes of U.S. history, Scott-Heron suggests the mid-1970s conjuncture signaled an onset of calamity for citizens confused at the swiftly changing times and unable to access the rewards tied to the resurgence of corporate America. Other commentators across the political spectrum also noted the *longue durée* stakes of this moment, warning of civilizational collapse at the onrush of the expansion of democracy and social equality toward the historically marginalized. For conservatives and neoliberals, unfettered free enterprise—a return to the anti-labor classical liberalism of the 1920s—was offered as the healing agent for difficult times. A collision of various momentums driven by the inherited legacies of U.S. history, this conjuncture appeared to rekindle the racial, gendered, and economic struggles and antagonisms stretching back to the colonial era.

Winter in America investigates this convergence of deep cultural history with the rise of neoliberalism, when the second light of legislated social equality cast down upon the United States (the *first* light, the Civil War amendments, did not take—though corporations made good use of the Fourteenth Amendment to obtain the "rights" of personhood).[17] Treading through the era's complicated and interlaced chaos, the book seeks a systemic view, asking: What does the rise of the neoliberal era look like when placed against the centuries-spanning history of the United States? How might seemingly disparate processes and institutions such as popular film, music, television, business media, and global business institutions—filtered through the *longue durée* of American history—paint a cultural and economic portrait of the U.S.

in transition? And how do these expressions represent what it felt like to lose the omnipotence of white male supremacy after centuries of legislated entitlement? Finally, how might these cultural breadcrumbs lead us to a better understanding of the evolution of neoliberal ideas and policies after 50 years of implementation? Exploring the interconnections between the conservative culture war against newly gained social equality and the onset of neoliberal economics sheds needed light on the lingering *longue durée* shadows still haunting the interplay between culture and economics in the twenty-first century. In the years after the 1970s, neoliberalism advanced from a marginalized capitalist ideology to fusing its worldview "deep into everyday life, almost to the point of passing as the 'ideology of no ideology.'"[18] How might we see this course of change? How might we give language and knowledge to an era that has since melted into normalcy?

Unemployment and inflation across the 1970s offered a much-needed opening for neoliberal ideas to translate into federal and state government policies, facilitating what poet-musician Gil Scott-Heron called Winter in America. Upon leaving the decade of the 1970s, the middle and working classes witnessed a significant decline in earning power and wealth accumulation in the 1980s and 1990s.[19] The wealthy, on the other hand, did extremely well.[20] As the third decade of the twenty-first century unfolds, the resulting unrest from the failures of neoliberalism to foment economic prosperity beyond the wealthiest segments of society across the United States *and the world* has led to various brands of populist conservatism and authoritarian policies.[21] This uncertain atmosphere makes it vital to understand how the deep continuities of American history blended in the 1970s to foster an economic change that both reversed the postwar welfare state's economic focus on the working and middle classes as well as mobilized a culture war derived from a carefully cultivated memory of this welfare state.

Traditional histories of neoliberalism examine its evolution after the 1930s and 1940s as a transnational political philosophy and system of economic, political, and cultural relations.[22] In describing the U.S. variant of neoliberalism, scholarship notes the period of institutional consolidation in the 1950s and 1960s, the work of scholars at the Chicago School of Economics, and the growing dialogue with the New Right. As Keynesian economists failed to address the economic crisis of the 1970s, neoliberal ideas increasingly found acceptance in news magazines and political circles—and finally into a bipartisan arrangement between Democrats and Republicans, tying together the economic logics of Presidents Reagan, H. W. Bush, Clinton, W. Bush, Obama, and Trump.

As a successor to the classical liberal ideas from the late nineteenth and early twentieth centuries, the dominant theoretical premise of neoliberalism rests on a fundamentally free market unfettered by government intrusion. Far from the elimination of government, however, neoliberalism in practice has merely redirected the state's prerogatives away from the public welfare of Keynesianism and toward a state working on behalf of private capital through the protection of property, subsidies, tax breaks, hardline law enforcement practices, and sometimes military coercion abroad.[23] The primary theoretical features of neoliberalism include a combination of deregulation and privatization justified in the name of competition, the elimination of bureaucratic inefficiencies, and the unfettering of the market. The logic stems from Friedrich August von Hayek, who, asserts Philip Mirowski, declared that the market was the greatest "information processor" available for humankind.[24] In many ways this concept bypassed the Enlightenment's belief in rationality and planning to rectify the "debilitating consequences" of capitalism.[25] For neoliberals, the market acts as an unbiased allocator of knowledge—in short, "the market does the thinking for us that we cannot."[26] A notable deviation from the liberalism of Adam Smith includes neoliberalism's acceptance—or disregard—of concentrated or monopoly capital. With the knowledge-generating market guiding the ostensibly laissez-faire economic path, the reorientation of state functions away from social safety nets to a more pro-business approach to government regulation in the 1970s and 1980s favored the fortunes of American multinational conglomerates, the global financial services industry, and the wealthiest segments of society—contributing to a level of wealth inequality not seen since the years leading up to the Great Depression.[27]

Mirowski offers a succinct outline of neoliberalism's successful strategy for political and economic ascendancy: "Neoliberals aimed to develop a thoroughgoing reeducation effort for *all parties* to alter the tenor and meaning of political life: nothing more, nothing less. Neoliberal intellectuals identified their targets, which, in Fabian tradition, had been described as elite civil society. Their efforts were aimed primarily at winning over intellectuals and opinion leaders of future generations, and their primary tool was redefining the place of knowledge in society, which also became the central theme in their theoretical tradition."[28] The policy outcomes resulting from these ideas include: pro-corporate support of the free flow of capital, the redefinition of the state's prerogatives toward markets and capital, the freeing of markets from democratic interference, and the assertion that the market is better able to produce information and services than the state. Adding to their belief in the market as an information processor, neoliberals and conservatives presented these economic programs as "moral codes" grounded in the notion that "pronounced inequality of economic resources and political rights . . . [were] a necessary functional characteristic of their ideal market system."[29] This latter moralizing of economics found common cause with the conservative culture war over social equality.

One of the most powerful attributes of neoliberalism rests in its ability to cast a reformist image of capitalist society supporting the needs of big business and finance while articulating this program through the populist language of small-scale, small business community relationships.[30] This populist-conservative identity imagined the "small guy" seeking liberty against the tyranny of "big government," cementing the moral code of neoliberal economics as an economics for ordinary people against elite government intrusion. Draped in an outsider's garb (a duster, perhaps), neoliberalism's use of populist conservatism regenerated an American innocence disavowing the institutionally racist and sexist elements of American capitalism's recent past dramatically unveiled throughout the civil rights era—a stance that drew working- and middle-class white people, whose lives were battered by the Depression at the end of the GOP-led 1920s classical liberal era, into the ranks of post-1960s conservatism that ushered in a return to the policies of inequality they thought they had escaped after World War II.

The strained denial of New Deal–inspired welfare state policies contributing toward shaping "affirmative action for whites," including federal programs facilitating a "massive transfer of quite specific privileges to white Americans," is one of the many ironies of the post–civil rights era and its contemporary memory.[31] Jefferson Cowie notes the "pretax income of the bottom 60 percent of households more than doubled between 1949 and 1979, tracking neatly with rising productivity."[32] In describing the source of warm remembrance, Cowie continues, "Keynesian economics gave a shared logic to economic growth, and the modern industrial labor movement appeared to have finally solved the "labor question" for the indefinite future. As a result, more income, more equality, more optimism, more leisure, more consumer goods, more travel, more entertainment, more expansive homes, and more education were all available in the postwar years to regular people than at any other time in world history."[33] Although these programs "produced economic and social opportunity for favored constituencies," because of the racial calculus, they also "widened the gap between white and black Americans in the aftermath of the Second World War."[34] Finally, the gendered assumption guiding the welfare state was the "family wage," where men were envisioned as the breadwinner and women were seen as dependent on the man's income.[35] Women's independence from men was never a part of the welfare state's logic. Within this rhetorical denial of the cultural and economic logic of the welfare state, populist conservatism provided neoliberal policies with a potent mixture of familiar ruggedly individualistic American history—summoning images of the past to cast an innocence on the culture war against the social equality legislation that dismantled the racial and gendered policies of the 1950s and 1960s.

Balancing upon this tension, the cultural-economic characteristics of the rise of neoliberalism in the 1970s included two often-antagonistic ideas: "formal equality and complete faith in the marketplace."[36] The blend of color blindness and the rights of property aided the culture war's intention to deflect the race and gender-based criticisms of society and business. In particular, color blindness and the rights of property reconfigured racial antagonism toward Blacks and other people of color by censuring vulgar or overtly racist rhetoric positing the inherent biological inequality of African Americans and replacing it with a color-blind language espousing market guidelines, analytical measurements, or simply the "rule of law"—all important concepts for neoliberalism's argument against government intervention in matters of property and wealth.[37] Through this prism, inequality could be framed through the workings of a market or "quantitative analysis": an ostensibly race- and gender-neutral arena of commerce; discrimination might be attached to a lack of skills (a product of economics), while it thoroughly ignored the unequal access to acquiring skills (a product of an exclusionary cultural politics).[38] Thus, this color-blind framework focused on an abstract *equality of access* to theoretically free markets, with the invisible hand of whiteness finding concealment behind the abstraction of ostensibly impartial quantitative analysis, market efficiency, and the desire for a profitable enterprise.[39] In short, all faith was placed in the information processing power of the market.

The material outcomes associated with the decades—and centuries—of virtually white male-only access to the outlets of economic prosperity simply disappeared from debate when measuring how exactly markets would reform their logics whose origins lay within a racialized and gendered U.S./global capitalism. Unwilling to address this legacy, the faith in markets encouraged neoliberals to assume that all gains for white Americans in the postwar years were cultivated through a ruggedly individual work ethic and not a system adhering to the nation's centuries-old tradition of white male supremacy. Thus, in the absence of the history of racism, white homeowners after World War II simply made a market choice to live and work in the suburbs while Black people did not—racist federal and state policies, let alone white terrorism, appeared to have no hand in maintaining pure white neighborhoods.[40] David M. P. Freund notes that

> federal interventions did more than simply structure opportunity; paradoxically, they also helped popularize the idea that government interventions were *not* providing considerable benefits to white people. Public officials, their private-sector allies, and even federal appraisal guidelines assured whites that state interventions neither made suburban

growth possible nor helped segregate the fast-growing metropolis by race. They promoted a story that urban and suburban outcomes resulted solely from impersonal market forces. Not surprisingly, white homeowners, particularly in the suburbs, embraced this narrative and made it a central refrain in local debates about housing, race, and inequality.... [This disavowal of institutional racism] enabled countless white people to insist that their support for exclusion was not a racist act.[41]

As this market-centered ideology surfaced in tandem with legislated social equality in the 1960s and 1970s, the retrenchment of federal intervention in the Nixon era—what was called benign neglect—absolved the need to address the still-embedded inequalities untouched from 1960s civil rights legislation. Ibram X. Kendi describes the road to the Civil Rights Act of 1964 as one where "supporters of the act agreed on outlawing future discrimination, but disagreed on what to do about past discrimination"—a past now solidified with worker seniority, housing subsidies for all-white suburbs, and access to higher education.[42] There would be no compensation for African Americans who were legally held back from starting the race for the American dream—whether in the postwar years or Reconstruction or enslavement. Meanwhile, whites found solace in the new social equality by forgetting their centuries-long head start. More insidiously, the act helped to deregulate the way racial discrimination operated by defining racist policies via "public intent" versus "public outcomes."[43] Kendi adds, "By not principally focusing on outcome, discriminators had to merely privatize their public policies to get around the Civil Rights Act."[44] With newly legislated freedom, the 1970s could now be imagined as "year zero" for racial and gender equality. By the 1980s, federal enforcement of civil rights was thoroughly undermined by the Reagan administration under the guise that discrimination no longer was a factor in the lives of non-white people. One of Reagan's favorite theorists, George Gilder, offered this soothing announcement in 1981:

> The last thirty years in America . . . have seen a relentless and thoroughly successful advance against the old prejudices, to the point that it is now virtually impossible to find in a position of power a serious racist. . . . Problems remain, but it would seem genuinely difficult to sustain the idea that America is still oppressive and discriminatory.[45]

Neoliberalism thrived amid this backdrop, with various sets of cultural processes bridging the gap between a conservative reaction to social equality legislation and the arguments of neoliberal intellectuals.

Accordingly, a crucial avenue to understanding neoliberalism asks how we might map out the dialogue between the ascension of neoliberal ideas and policies and the *longue durée* existential jolt of the first decade of legislated social equality between white men, women, and people of color. As we understand culture to be a shared system of symbols, gestures, and communication passed generationally within societies, another larger question asks: What buried cultural roots were mobilized in reaction to legislated social equality?[46] And how did this conjuncture regenerate and reform language and knowledge from the American past in the service of contemporary policies designed to dismantle the welfare state and usher in neoliberalism?

Operating both consciously and unconsciously, culture organizes and makes sense of peoples' lives—including economic decisions measuring gendered, sexual, or racial difference. Learned through socialization, culture gains efficiency when people *think through* its tenets, operating as an unconscious prism—an ontology—interpreting the world through language and gestures deemed universal. In this sense, U.S. culture operates through frameworks Michel-Rolph Trouillot calls North Atlantic universals: the sets of language and knowledge established through the administrative and violent relationships derived from the legacies of colonialism, the Atlantic slave system, and capitalism, which coalesced into a Eurocentric interpretation of the world in the wake of European expansion. Out of these developments arose ostensibly neutral concepts, including "progress," "development," "globalization," and even the very idea of "modernity" itself.[47] North Americans inherited these ideas, influencing the culture of capitalism and naturalizing unequal power relationships demanded for the maintenance of colonial society and the United States. Across centuries, Trouillot writes, the cultural expressions interlaced through these activities fostered a particular way of seeing the world, an ontology anchored to ambiguously conscious and unconscious ways of remembering history to account for the present:

> They do not describe the world; they offer visions of the world. They appear to refer to things as they exist, but because they are rooted in a particular history, they evoke multiple layers of sensibilities, persuasion, cultural assumptions, and ideological choices tied to that localized history. They come to us loaded with aesthetic and stylistic sensibilities; religious and philosophical persuasions; cultural assumptions ranging from what it means to be a human being to the proper relationship between humans and the natural world; ideological choices ranging from the nature of the political to its possibilities of transformation.[48]

Winter in America peels back the intricate layers weaving through the centuries-old history of the United States and traces the various ways they manifested during the conjunctional crisis of the long 1970s and the rise of neoliberalism.[49] The outcome of settler colonialism and slavery, the first layer includes the status quo racial laws and culture of the United States and their intensification in the late nineteenth and early twentieth centuries through scientific racism and Jim Crow segregation, leading to a more formidable system of racial wealth inequality: the welfare state.[50] With the institutionalization of what I will refer to as the Jim Crow welfare state, whiteness regenerated its ability to accumulate wealth and opportunity, as it had since the seventeenth century, creating homeowners out of the white ethnic working classes and fostering an unprecedented prosperity and standard of living. The Jim Crow welfare state's primary constituency was white men, with the economic system designed to buttress the family wage—including the Cold War "containment" of women within the home.[51] Although this era is immortalized as a golden age of prosperity, for people of color the postwar years remained synonymous with the previous centuries of racial antagonism and second-class citizenship.[52]

A second layer included the political reawakening of multinational corporations and finance after a brief lull during the Depression and World War II. These large institutions of capital actively participated in creating American postwar hegemony, taking advantage of global decolonization to enter new markets while profiting from federal intervention in the economies of the United States, Japan, and Europe (the Marshall Plan).[53] Postwar libertarians often pointed to these federal interventions on behalf of big business as one of the significant reasons for the perpetuation of the welfare state.[54] However, despite suggesting that "big businessmen cannot necessarily be relied upon to be their allies in the battle against extension of government encroachments," conservative authors like Hazlitt really had nothing to fear—indeed they underestimated big business's approach toward reorganizing the state's prerogatives.[55] In short, corporations were hardly "confused" or full of "timidity" in their relationship with government; rather, they were good businessmen using government for their own ends.[56] Although the welfare state provided stability and a demand-side economic approach benefiting the spending power of ordinary Americans, the regulations associated with federal intervention increasingly became burdensome to multinationals and their financial partners in the 1960s and 1970s. The welfare state had saved capitalism from its Depression and created a strong consumer society around a secure white middle class, but a new economic framework was needed. In this sense, the evolving needs of big business conjoined with the economic prescriptions of neoliberals.

A third trend grew out of the reaction to the redistributive effect of the New Deal–derived, Jim Crow welfare state: the rebirth of conservatism after its crash in the Great Depression. The New Right, shaped by figures such as William F. Buckley Jr., sought to break apart the liberal consensus holding the Jim Crow welfare state together. The 1960s civil rights legislation dismantling—or, using the language of neoliberalism, "deregulating"—the racist and sexist laws upholding the centuries-old traditions of white male supremacy provided conservatives with a significant opportunity to break apart the liberal consensus through the mobilization of a "Southern strategy" (what Matthew D. Lassiter reimagines as the Sun Belt South "suburban strategy") targeting the very demographic who benefited from the Jim Crow welfare state.[57] Southern segregationist Democrats joined with the Republican Party, where a rejuvenated conservatism attacked federal intervention, particularly on issues of racial equality and the previous right to racially and sexually discriminate in the realm of culture and economics. The party of Lincoln initiated a long-term engagement in racial coding—using the deeply embedded American sentiment of anti-Blackness through color-blind language—to break white Democrats away from supporting pro–welfare state politicians. Although many saw their votes against the welfare state as votes taking away "welfare" payments to poor people (most often coded "Black" or "brown") this demographic shift away from the support of the welfare state represented a counterrevolution against a vibrant postwar American economic system that actively funded infrastructure, education, health care, and other "social spending" programs targeting white working- and middle-class Americans.[58] Seen through the prism of the culture war, whites now voted against the system largely responsible for shaping their postwar prosperity and opportunity. Viewing their federally subsidized, racially segregated suburbs as a "class-based outcome of meritocratic individualism rather than the unconstitutional product of structural racism," the suburban strategy imagined government intervention through social equality legislation as "an unconstitutional exercise in social engineering and an unprecedented violation of free-market meritocracy."[59] This populist-conservative reaction facilitated the political space for neoliberal ideas and policies to be woven into the nation's fabric. By the 1980s, the structures were in place to reverse the distribution of wealth away from the post–World War II downward trend. Moving in the opposite direction under the path charted by conservative and neoliberal economists, the redistribution of wealth upward returned the United States to the type of wealth and income inequality not seen since the 1920s classical liberal era.[60]

Neoliberalism, Modernity, and the *Longue Durée*

The conjuncture leading to the neoliberal era needs to be understood within the wider historical frameworks in which it developed—the way culture weaves through capitalism, allowing the economic system to present itself as an unquestioned, "natural" development.[61] More than just economic relationships born out of a market system based on private property and profits accumulated through trade, capitalism exists as an anchoring component of the cultural-economic system of modernity, the set of intersecting historical processes taking shape after the 1400s: colonialism, settler colonialism, the Atlantic slave system, capitalism, the Enlightenment, the nation-state, and imperialism.[62] Driven by European expansion, capitalism evolved through these material and ideological structures, leading to various sets of cultural institutions establishing the archive of language and knowledge shaping ideas ranging from nationalism to the Enlightenment, as well as the intersectional hierarchies of race, gender, sexuality, and class (among others).[63] Neoliberalism and the neoliberal era inherited the racial, gendered, sexual, and class assumptions and antagonisms derived from the previous 400 years of North American history, becoming the latest formation of this deep—what Fernand Braudel called the *longue durée*—outgrowth of the system of modernity, and not merely a set of ideas related to monetary systems and trade discussed in the isolation of twentieth-century economic textbooks.[64]

Situating these developments within long-term structures of thought, sets of policies, and their material outcomes, the *longue durée* is central for understanding the set of cultural-economic changes circulating through the United States as neoliberalism fused into American economic common sense after the 1960s. The *longue durée* sets the history of events—*histoire événementielle*—into a larger framework: one encompassing an analysis of history across centuries, noting economic, cultural, and environmental changes that evolve slowly, often imperceptibly, over time.[65] In this sense, the *longue durée* spurs important sets of questions for understanding the rise of neoliberalism. One way the deep past influences the justification of contemporary policies includes mobilizing Janus-faced "universals" to justify unequal relationships, including "Western civilization," an idea evoking a cultural or biological superiority of people of European descent (generally designated masculine) while simultaneously supporting abstract tenets of liberty and equality. Using the epochal righteousness of Western civilization as a justification for present policies summons a set of language and knowledge in which the present assumes an innocent relationship to the past: as universals, this language conveniently veils the crimes against humanity involved in the very material outcomes and ideological meanings shaping Western civilization from the processes of modernity. Out of earlier precedents defending slavery, segregation, and patriarchy, we see this continuity in the language of the culture war when policies target historically marginalized groups—women, people of color, or the LGBTQ community—and find justification through the familiar "defense of Western civilization" trope. From the perspective of 500 years of modernity, *Winter in America* outlines how the rise of neoliberal capitalism amid the first decade of legislated social equality found validation through carefully constructed *ideas* such as Western civilization.

From this *longue durée* vantage point, we may understand what historians call the "white backlash" as not a mere backlash—implying a level of unfairness forced on the "rights" of white people—but rather, a white re-entrenchment of long-embedded entitlements and privileges accumulated across centuries of American history (described by Anderson as "white rage," or what Rodríguez calls White Reconstruction, or what Richard Maxwell Brown calls the "socially conservative" goals of vigilante or mob violence).[66] In short, "massive resistance" against political and economic equality between people of European descent and people of color *defines* the *longue durée* of American history—it was not an aberration of the period but the legacy of the deep historical momentum of what Michael Omi and Howard Winant call the "racial dictatorship" of U.S. history.[67] Using the *longue durée*, we may appreciate the existential magnitude of the impact of social equality legislation upon the minds of those who historically could gain access to the fruits of the American dream since the 1600s: the civil rights era "dismantled," or deregulated, the legal frameworks upholding this centuries-old common sense. Further, we must add "male" to this historical entitlement, particularly "white males with property" to be fully accurate. Thus, if white males (especially those with property) were forced to compete for economic and political access for the first time with people of color and women after the 1960s, a cultural reassertion of power—informed by the specters of white nationalism—would inevitably appear as a reaction to the legislative dismantling of centuries-old norms, traditions, and economic relations. The reaction to social equality legislation, then, is also a crisis of identity, as deep customs of deference to white male authority slowly eroded in its ability to dictate norms in the face of social equality legislation. The loss of power that once seemed to be distributed through the laws of nature pressed into service the conservative culture war, as the loss of authority (to quote Hunter again) "to define social reality" led to a battle over the possession of language and knowledge to "retain their advantage in defining the habits and meaning of American culture."[68] The culture war took special aim at the government's failure to protect 300-year-old entitlements for white Americans, deeming social equality legislation as an infringement upon the rights of white citizens. While white masculinity found potency under the welfare state, social equality legislation presented government policy as a betrayal against deep American traditions, opening the door for white beneficiaries of the welfare state to begin voting against it.

The historical roots of American white masculinity emerged from the violence of frontier settlement and a slave–Jim Crow segregation economy. Greg Grandin characterizes the frontier in American society as "a proxy for liberation, synonymous with the possibilities and promises of modern life itself and held out as a model for the rest of the world to emulate."[69] However, the faith in believing the frontier could "shake off [Americans'] circumstances" was the exclusive reserve for white men in this myth.[70] The moment of liberation for formerly subjugated people—especially *all* women—presented white men with an existential crisis over an identity long defined through their entitlement to define their liberty and freedom through the subjugation of others—the frontier had, yet again, been closed as Jim Crow no longer protected the economic opportunities of white men. When people long-deemed inferior became legislated social equals, the traditional ideas of white masculinity trembled with impotent uncertainty—they no longer legally meant anything.[71] As James Baldwin noted in *The Devil Finds Work* (1976), the oppression of *Others* justified the freedom and autonomy of white men since the 1600s; however, "when the prisoner is free, the jailer faces the void of himself" as the prison in which the jailer guarded and historically found meaning in was dismantled, with the formerly caged and beaten now deemed legislatively equal.[72] The conservative culture war gave voice to this reaction to 1960s social justice movements as the more progressive forms of the civil rights and women's liberation movements constructed an intricate set of language and knowledge challenging the normalcy of white male supremacy and its relationship to capitalism. White masculinity often claimed "injury" in the wake of social equality legislation, a rhetorical maneuver that protested "the erosions of white men's historical advantage while denying that advantage ever existed."[73] Summoned to defend the status quo, the culture war aided in the reformation of the now-outdated language of domination with new color-blind, gender-neutral language, tying a large demographic of people uneasy about what would later be called multiculturalism or diversity to the rhetoric and logics of neoliberalism.

Gestures and statements from films, television, music, or business magazines often come filled with an inherited culture derived from the deep past.[74] A close examination of these *longue durée* layers unveils a genealogical dialogue tying cultural-economic eras together, what David Armitage calls transtemporal history.[75] Within these moments, we may glimpse the sequences of contexts framing the way agents operate, using language and knowledge to deploy ideas.[76] This vantage point encourages a "history *in* ideas—rather than history *of* ideas—where the "focal points of arguments shaped and debated episodically across time with a conscious—or at least a provable connection—with both earlier and later instances of such struggles."[77] Thus, as overtly racist or sexist language became censured, coded words connected to past meanings of inferiority took their place, resetting older ideas of inequality under new language acting as an umbrella of innocence denying past (or current) crimes.

Winter in America tells the story of this transition in capitalism and relationships between white men, people of color, and women in the United States, where the tension between the contemporary reforms of civil rights and white intransigence to social equality provided a cultural language coalescing with the rise of an economic system built around the needs of corporations, the finance industry, and the wealthy. The book outlines and theorizes how popular media projected these forces, creating a space where new language reinforced and rehabilitated old habits of thought. As the victories of 1960s social movements bore some fruit in the 1970s, the American paradox of inequality in the land of the free found kinship with the arrival of neoliberalism. On the one hand, the 1970s saw African Americans and (especially white) women make inroads within state and civil society after centuries of exclusion. On the other hand, new institutional forms and structural conditions of hierarchy adapted to hard-won gains through a process of "deregulated discrimination," not only reframing ideas of race, gender, sexuality and freedom itself, but also weaving progressive reforms into the logic of neoliberalism.

Taking Scott-Heron's title of his 1974 LP—*Winter in America*—as a metaphor for the onset of the neoliberal era, *Winter in America* analyzes and contextualizes the intersections of these micro-historical processes within the larger framework of the history of capitalism. The chapters consist of a series of case studies analyzing the intersections between the rise of neoliberalism, popular media, and the *longue durée* cultural language connected to slavery, settler colonialism, and patriarchy. The book takes seriously popular media as both a conscious and unconscious set of cultures re-creating and reimagining the present through the deep logics inherited from the past. Drawing from multiple popular media sites, *Winter in America* brings together the pages of *Business Week* with the late-period output of John Wayne; American exploitation movies produced in the Philippines to neoliberal envisioning of freedom through the weathered concept of Western civilization; the feminist politics of films such as *Nine to Five* (1980) and *Born in Flames* (1983) to the poetic performances of Gil Scott-Heron and Jayne Cortez and the early years of hip-hop. These sources provide windows into the careening culture representing the dawn of neoliberalism.

The first chapter of *Winter in America*—"American Innocence through the Possession of History: James Baldwin, William F. Buckley Jr., and the 1965 Cambridge Debate"—examines the 1965 debate between James Baldwin and William F. Buckley Jr. Setting a theatrical tone for the book, this chapter analyzes the performances of Baldwin and Buckley, focusing on the various ways different understandings of history were mobilized to engage with the debate's topic: "Has the American Dream Been Achieved at the Expense of the American Negro?" Baldwin specifically notes the curious way history is possessed in the service of those who dominate groups considered inferior. Embodying the "possession of history," Buckley's response to Baldwin's assertions justified the conditions of African Americans through a deployment of a selective past in order to secure an innocence for the present. As a representative of the centuries-old Black radical tradition, Baldwin framed the civil rights movement and its grand task of dismantling American racism through a *longue durée* framework underscoring the deep legacies of anti-Blackness inherited from slavery.[78] Buckley, a founder of the modern conservative movement, rallied a different *longue durée* view of history, utilizing conservatism's defense of Western civilization—and its notions of order and hierarchy—as a justification for downplaying the extent of racism in America. Buckley's use of Western civilization both denied its contribution to the construction of racial inequality as well as dismissed the need for any action of remediation in the name of social equality.

The arrival of neoliberalism against the backdrop of racial and cultural unrest appeared to mimic earlier eras of upheaval, including Reconstruction and Post-Reconstruction, which saw significant capital concentration and a sharp rise in white racial antagonism and racist legislation.

> Most of [Andrew] Johnson's northern and southern audiences had been raised in the church of Andrew Jackson's "primitive simplicity and purity," with its already racialized understanding of the federal government, when any publicly administered social program would be seen as but an opening for "extraneous corrupting influences." So their shared, already-understood animosity to the Freedmen's Bureau, which needed nothing but laughter and hisses to convey, made it easy for the president to shift all the many problems of post-Civil War America—its corruption, concentration of power, low wages, and inadequate housing—onto African Americans and their "blood-sucker" advocates in Congress, radical Republicans such as Thaddeus Stevens and Wendell Phillips, who were trying to fund the bureau.[79]

As neoliberalism replaced the economic system that helped shape the American middle class after World War II, these faint *longue durée* echoes surfaced. The language and policies of the federally directed welfare state primarily benefited white men, a pattern consistent with legal and cultural practices since the 1600s. The puzzle, of course, is how neoliberalism—born in reaction to the Jim Crow welfare state—was voted into place using language directed toward systematically dismantling the very framework sustaining the white middle class. It is in this political-cultural arena where we see the struggle over the possession of history as a critical attribute for understanding the culture war's usefulness for the rise of neoliberalism. Buckley's defense of Black inequality at the dawn of liberation helped shape a receptive audience for the language of neoliberalism: "privatization" connected to the deregulation of public space after civil rights legislation (pioneered, of course, by Southern segregationists); deregulation challenged government oversight of business *and the lives of whites uncomfortable with desegregation*; and a strict belief in a color-blind market obscured the federally directed welfare state spending that developed the white suburbs and concentrated people of color into impoverished inner-city public housing. Under privatization, deregulation, and color-blindness, failure in the face of an economic program redistributing capital upward would reinforce older ideas suggesting that some groups were inferior or incapable of competing in the post-1960s world. The meeting of Baldwin and Buckley neatly ties this struggle together, with the latter helping to establish the theoretical baseline linking the shift in discussions of race from overt ideas of white superiority to notions of "cultural pathology." For conservatives, this cultural turn replaced scientific racism with ideas assuming that some groups were not culturally equipped for full equality. Or as an earlier era of overt white nationalism might articulate, they were neither civilized nor ready for social equality with white people.

The defense of Western civilization, with its attendant ideas of liberty and freedom, arose as an important cultural argument mustered by neoliberals and conservatives to justify their critique against the welfare state. Titled "Did You Ever See a Dream Walking? Western Civilization, the *Longue Durée*, and the Culture of Neoliberalism," chapter 2 examines the way the processes of modernity wove through the cultural undertones of the writings of Friedrich August von Hayek and Milton Friedman. In particular, the chapter explores the intersections of twentieth-century conservatism, the New Right, and neoliberals, and how they summoned the history and ideas of Western civilization to vindicate their ideals. A close reading reveals a culture valuing both the ideas of liberty and freedom while assuming social equality outside the transnational community of white men was a cause for alarm (an echo back to the American conservatism of John Adams). The chapter establishes a brief history of neoliberalism's evolution in reaction to the welfare state, including the neoliberal "possession of history": the disavowal of the racial and gendered exclusions ignored by neoliberal writings in their discussions of freedom and tyranny. This disavowal of the extent to which racial and gendered antagonisms shaped American history—including European (or people of European descent) domination of the world in the early twentieth century—established the baseline cultural norms dominating conservative and neoliberal rhetoric after World War II.

Chapter 3, "The Jim Crow Welfare State and the Corporate Revolution: Postwar American Capitalism," outlines the economic evolution of multinational corporations, conglomerates, and the finance community after World War II. As a cultural interpretation of the institutional history of postwar big business, this chapter emphasizes an often-overlooked element contributing to the rise of neoliberalism: the actual economic policies developed by multinationals and finance across the postwar era to negotiate their way through the various regulations of the welfare state. These transnational policies brought to life the networks of economic activity neoliberal ideas conjoined with in the 1970s. Rather than envisioning the onset of neoliberalism leading to the expansion of corporate and financial power, this chapter underlines the extent to which the Jim Crow welfare state provided a secure space for the economic growth of big business. Adapting to the regulatory structures of Keynesianism, postwar corporate policies envisioned and implemented the new needs of capitalism for which neoliberal theory justified in the 1970s and 1980s. Once no longer useful, corporate America shed the hull of the welfare state like a snake sheds its skin. From this macro view of postwar capitalism, the next chapter changes to a micro view.

Using articles and editorials from *Business Week* as an entrepôt to the shift from the Jim Crow welfare state to neoliberalism, chapter 4, "The Idea of Doing with Less So That Big Business Can Have More: The Culture and Ethos of *Business Week*," traces the evolution of business culture between the 1960s and 1980s. In particular, this chapter places many of the assumptions and arguments advanced in the first three chapters into the language of the business world, including its interaction with the culture war, 1960s social justice movements, and the unfolding economic crisis of the 1970s. The chapter also notes how *Business Week* increasingly embraced neoliberal and conservative economic ideas and culture war tenets across the decade.

Through a reading of films involving John Wayne in the 1960s and 1970s, the fifth chapter, "Go West and Turn Right: Settler Colonialism, Neoliberalism, and John Wayne's Possession of History," explores the populist conservatism anchoring the culture war. Specifically, this chapter examines the connection between populist conservatism and one of the foundational processes defining American identity: the legacy of settler colonialism. The chapter highlights the paradox of celebrating the romantic heroism of settler colonialism while simultaneously silencing or disavowing the history of ethnic cleansing and gratuitous violence aimed toward people of color, including the policing of domestic "enemies" such as African Americans. These settler colonial white nationalist imaginings also revere the masculine patriotic "warrior" culture of the settler and *his* family—with the equation assuming that white women were in need of protection to preserve the home(land) from "savage"

Others. A vital anchor to this system includes the equation of feminine deference to masculine authority, a bond sealed through the anti-Black practices of lynching Black men accused of raping white women. This feminine deference implied a relinquishing of women's rights to men in the name of protection. Populist conservatism proved crucial for the American acceptance of neoliberalism, as its rugged individual, militant masculinity, pulled together the white working- and middle-class male demographic who equated patriotic righteousness with an American nation historically catering to their needs—from Indian Removal to the Homestead Act to the postwar white suburbs. The rugged toughness of this populist conservatism, moreover, acted as a balm for the existential crisis related to the relinquishing of legislative superiority and control toward people of color and women. The myths of rugged individualism and male heroism imbued much of the rhetoric pressing neoliberal ideas into policies, as they were defined against a so-called dependency-laden, feminized and racialized welfare state regulatory system—despite the its well-documented privileging of white men.

Chapters 6 and 7 focus on the various reactions to women's liberation and second-wave feminism in the 1970s and 1980s—including the way neoliberal ideas, corporate prerogatives, and the culture war formed a nexus. Chapter 6, "Blood, Breasts, and Beasts: The Feminist Liberation Gauntlet and Flexible Misogyny at the Dawn of Social Equality," outlines how women became convenient targets for those anxious about the legislative victories of 1960s social justice movements. Working through both feminist and misogynist representations, the chapter explores music and American exploitation films, especially those made in the Philippines by U.S. companies who outsourced production overseas and imported these movies back into the United States (a defining strategy for American corporations after the 1960s). Through this embodiment of an industry relocating overseas to a regulation-free environment, this chapter theorizes routes for women's liberation against centuries-old patriarchal systems, especially in terms of gendered violence. I utilize the concept of a "liberation gauntlet" to suggest that liberation for women in popular culture often took the form of violence or humiliation—rooted in old patriarchal patterns of violence against women's bodies—on the way to empowerment.

Chapter 7, "Does Militancy No Longer Mean Guns at High Noon?: Feminist Dialogues, the Corporate Woman, and the Dawn of Neoliberalism," examines the restructuring of boundaries for women's liberation, characterized in *Business Week*'s "Corporate Woman" column and the "acceptable assimilation" model seen in the film *9 to 5* (1980). In contrast, the Black feminist-inspired, independent movie *Born in Flames* (1983) offers a more systematic critique of capitalist patriarchy. Through the intersectional dynamics of these films—with *Network* (1976) added as a bridge between the liberation gauntlet and the corporate woman—the sixth and seventh chapters underscore the adaptability of capitalism, suggesting that the corporate reforms characteristic of neoliberalism enabled a narrow middle-class multicultural set of previously excluded people to find opportunity in the post–civil rights world, which blunted the most radical of systemic critiques emanating from 1960s and 1970s social movements.

Returning to the Black radical tradition embodied by James Baldwin, the final chapter analyzes the work of African American spoken-word artists—particularly Gil Scott-Heron and Jayne Cortez—and their contemporaneous critique and identification of the neoliberal economic system across the 1970s and 1980s. Alongside African American spoken word, the chapter connects this movement with its Black Atlantic offshoots in Jamaican sound system and DJ styles related to reggae and dub music as well as the ascendant 1970s hip-hop culture arising in decaying, capital flight-afflicted postindustrial urban spaces. In the post–Black Power United States, the Black radical tradition continued its centuries-old role in providing language and knowledge countering the coercive aspects of modernity as it entered its neoliberal phase.

Together, these chapters limn the evolution of American capitalism from the Jim Crow welfare state to neoliberalism between the 1960s and 1980s, addressing the question: What did the culture of the rise of neoliberalism *look* and *feel* like? The second frontier of postwar prosperity for white men had closed in the 1960s, leading to white Americans both defending a status quo constructed through the Jim Crow welfare state, while also reveling in nostalgia for the time of innocence before the end of the frontier; before the civil rights movement made white nationalism self-conscious; before it was *named* and condemned.[80] These are the cultural roots of the neoliberal era.

Chapter 1

American Innocence through the Possession of History

James Baldwin, William F. Buckley Jr., and the
1965 Cambridge Debate

> It was this Africanism, deployed as rawness and savagery, that provided the staging ground and arena for the elaboration of the quintessential American identity.... Autonomy is freedom and translates into the much championed and revered "individualism"; newness translates into "innocence"; distinctiveness becomes difference and the erection of strategies for maintaining it; authority and absolute power become a romantic, conquering "heroism," virility, and the problematic of wielding absolute power over the lives of others. All the rest are made possible by this last, it would seem—absolute power called forth and played against and within a natural and mental landscape conceived of as a "raw, half-savage world."
>
> —Toni Morrison, *Playing in the Dark* (1992)
>
> What one needs to consider is the individual who stands to suffer.
>
> —William F. Buckley Jr., "Pro-Negro Discrimination Encouraged" (1968)
>
> The nation's dual origins in slavery and freedom imbued modern conservatives with a deep sense of cultural authenticity, and northerners and southerners alike held fast against the quest for inclusion. They saw no contradiction between claiming to stand for liberty and opposing the black freedom movement because they revered a tradition that silenced and subordinated blacks.
>
> —Nancy MacLean, *Freedom Is Not Enough* (2006)

Nineteen sixty-five materialized as another year promising the continued economic growth of the preceding two decades. By then, the postwar Keynesian mixed-economy consensus—the set of welfare state policies developed out of the 1930s New Deal—had become the dominant economic and political norm for the nation.[1] Historian Kim Phillips-Fein asserts, "On the national level, the spring of 1965 was a high-water point for liberalism."[2] Indeed, as James T. Patterson described the year, "No people in the modern history of the world had had it so good."[3] Smoldering beneath these positive economic signs, however, was a range of discontent as African Americans and other people of color continued to navigate the restrictions and state-sanctioned violence defining Jim Crow America. Meanwhile, white America confronted the uneasy prospect of legislated social equality with the very targets of their Jim Crow America.

The title of Patterson's book, *The Eve of Destruction*—named after the folk-rock tune "Eve of Destruction," by Barry McGuire—aptly describes the cresting tidal wave about to flood through American society in 1965. Various flash points interrupted the celebrations of the good life anchoring the largely white suburban American dream: the assassination of Malcolm X in February, the violent setbacks for the civil rights movement in Selma, Alabama, in March (coinciding with the official invasion of Vietnam in the same month), and the Watts uprising in August just days after Congress passed the Voting Rights Act. Caught in both an inherited and self-made tragedy, the U.S. public at the very height of postwar prosperity continued to walk through a fog of exceptional innocence, failing to take responsibility and account for the racial antagonism sustaining an American dream atop anti-Black sentiments and institutions inherited from the days of slavery.[4] The material space in which to enact these dreams, of course, evolved through centuries of displacement of Indigenous peoples and Mexicans via settler colonial policies.[5] The reenactments of these historical processes of displacement and enslavement—generally framed as heroic white masculine deeds—found warm reception from radio, film, and television consumers across the nation, creating an imagined history where the violence of invasion was converted into the innocence of settlement, free from the wanton greed and hatred demanded to secure white American freedom and liberty across North America. These accumulated debts of history, however, appeared to come due in 1965.

The relationships between white America, material well-being, and a normalized oppressive society protecting this dream had found regeneration across the centuries. The ideas woven through settler colonialism and slavery and its aftermath rhetorically supported a sense of white innocence obscuring the legacy of violent racial antagonism defining American identity. Patricia Nelson Limerick charts how innocence was imagined via westward expansion, writing, "The dominant motive for moving West was improvement and opportunity, not injury to others. Even when they were trespassers, westering Americans were hardly, in their own eyes, criminals; rather, they were pioneers. The ends abundantly justified the means; personal interest in the acquisition of territory, and those interests overlapped in turn with the mission to extend the domain of Christian civilization. Innocence of intention placed the course of events in a bright and positive light; only over time would the shadows compete for our attention."[6] This identity of free, autonomous whiteness juxtaposed itself against unfree, enslaved Blackness, naturalizing ideas of "difference and the erection of strategies for maintaining it," as Morrison notes.[7] These ever-evolving centuries-old practices define an important part of the identity of American whiteness.[8] During the postwar years, welfare state policies reimagined this identity through federal intervention subsidizing white suburbanization and economic opportunities aimed toward white males (using the gendered language of the "family wage").[9] By the end of 1965, it was increasingly obvious that the deep currents of institutional, anti-Black racism interlaced into the framework of the welfare state and the postwar American dream clearly needed more than legislation to remediate the structural second-class citizenry of African Americans and other people of color in the United States.

One of the period's leading critics connecting the American dream to the nation's legacy of anti-Blackness was the African American author James Baldwin. Baldwin's systemic critique of the relationship between racial oppression and economics appeared in full force through his nonfiction writings between the 1950s and 1980s. He summarized the entanglement of culture and economics in his 1971 dialogue with poet Nikki Giovanni:

> It's very hard to recognize that the standards which have almost killed you are really mercantile standards. They're based on cotton; they're based on oil; they're based on peanuts; they're based on profits. . . . Because, you see, the reason people think it's important to be white is that they think it's important not to be black. They think it's important to be white because white means you are civilized, and being black means you are not civilized. . . . What I'm trying to get at is my apprehension of the crisis of this age. The crisis has something to do with identity, and that has something to do with buried history. . . . People invent categories in order to feel safe. White people invented black people to give white people identity.[10]

As an outgrowth of racial capitalism, anti-Blackness evolved through the twin dynamics of economics and culture, with the concepts and policies of slavery and freedom generating a sense of value in both human worth as well as profits (whether the value of the enslaved, or the value of the product produced by the enslaved).[11] As Jared Sexton writes, "If, in the economy of race, whiteness is a form of money—the general equivalent or universal standard value—then blackness is its gold standard, the bottom-line guarantee represented by hard currency."[12] Marked socially dead from the initiation of the United States of America, Black people were envisioned as noncitizens from the start—from the 1790 Naturalization Act to the Dred Scott decision in 1857 to the foundation of the Jim Crow welfare state: *Plessy v. Ferguson* (1896).[13] Slavery provided the labor demanded for sustaining European transnational enterprises, while the slaves themselves were converted into exchangeable currency and measurements of wealth: Black enslaved bodies were worth $3.5 billion in 1860, "making them the largest single financial asset in the entire U.S. economy, worth more than all manufacturing and railroads combined."[14] In short, social death for Blacks equaled massive wealth for white America later to be translated into the terrorism of "racial domination" marked by lynching and the rise of crime statistics justifying the criminalization of Blackness.[15] In the mid-1960s, a yawning gulf appeared through the celebrations of civil rights legislation, blatantly exposing the institutional racism hardwired into the very fabric of the infrastructure supporting the American dream. In response, the "buried history" long celebrated by white Americans in their popular media burst forth to defend the racial calculus still intertwined in the socioeconomic structures of U.S. society at the dawn of legislated social equality. The second Reconstruction had reached its bottleneck, as the crisis of identity—wrapped in the old spectral identities haunting American history—found renewed life amid the historic deviation from *Dred Scott* and *Plessy vs. Ferguson*. Baldwin confronted this shift head-on in 1965 when he debated William F. Buckley Jr., one of the major architects of the New Right and an important figure helping to shape the culture of neoliberalism.[16]

This chapter situates the 1965 debate as a crucial moment of dialogue reflecting the long-term contradictions of American society, as well as a preview of how the United States would address racial inequality as civil rights legislation reformed—or deregulated, to use the language of neoliberalism—the legal framework of Jim Crow. On one end, a man of Irish descent and the era's conservative standard bearer who steadfastly stood "athwart history, yelling Stop, at a time when no one is inclined to do so" during an era of civil rights activism.[17] On the other end, a descendent of formerly enslaved peoples who pressed his pen into service on behalf of the era's civil rights movement. Performing in the nation (England) that coordinated the destinies of both men's ancestors, Baldwin and Buckley operated as vessels of the larger historical conjuncture spanning the 1960s and 1980s.

Sponsored by the Cambridge Union Society, Baldwin's debate with Buckley on February 18, 1965, in England represented an important signpost reflecting the evolution of the ongoing American paradox of slavery and freedom 100 years after emancipation. The debate topic asked: "Has the American Dream Been Achieved at the Expense of the American Negro?"[18] With two Cambridge students debating the two sides and an audience of over 700 students filling the Cambridge Union's debating hall, the event touched on the core cultural intricacies of racial inequality, the history of the African American experience, and the intersection of these processes with American capitalism.[19] The program's host, Norman St. John-Stevas, MP, described the momentous event, exclaiming, "Hundreds of undergraduates and myself, waiting for what could prove one of the most exciting debates in the whole 150 years of the Union history.... I don't think I've ever seen the Union so well attended. There are undergraduates everywhere; they're on the benches, they're on the floor, they're in the galleries. And there are a lot more outside, clamoring to get in."

An excitement resounded through the Cambridge campus as one descendant of European ancestry and one descendent of African ancestry debated the legacies of slavery and its connection to economic opportunity within England's former settler colony, the United States. Taped by the British Broadcasting Corporation (BBC) and later broadcasted by the National Educational Television Network (the precursor to Public Broadcasting System), the setting was visibly claustrophobic, with a sea of students filling the television screen.[20] The debate's relevancy, in hindsight, signaled an important cultural shift stirring through American society in the mid-1960s. Marking the beginning of the end for institutional American racial reform, 1965 witnessed the initiation of significant challenges against the further erosion of institutional racism that had become the focus of the Black freedom struggle.[21]

Throughout the debate, the long shadow of slavery and its ideas of anti-Blackness pressed heavily on Baldwin's and Buckley's arguments, as their performances in front of the Cambridge crowd represented the oppositional dialogue defining the post-1960s conservative culture wars. Baldwin's critique of the American dream implicitly utilized the centuries-old Black radical tradition in his interrogation of the ideas, policies, and material outcomes of anti-Blackness rooted in the Atlantic slave system.[22] In his defense of the American dream, Buckley evoked a deep reservoir of language and knowledge rooted in the maintenance—the *conserving* element of "conservatism"—of the racial hierarchical system of order in the nation's institutions.[23] Both in their early forties, Baldwin and Buckley represented two different intellectual poles in 1960s America, as well as two distinct understandings of history.

Buckley, born into the white conservative Catholic family of an oil baron and lawyer, schooled in France and England, and later married to the daughter of a Canadian industrialist, developed the intellectual framework for the resurgence of conservatism with the establishment of the *National Review* in 1955 and later his television talk show, *Firing Line* (first airing in 1966).[24] Buckley was critical in bringing together the three major strands of the New Right: religious conservatism, libertarianism, and neoconservatism.[25] Buckley's patient persistence helped navigate the culture of capitalism away from the dominant set of ideas instilled by the Great Depression and the New Deal, World War II, and the postwar Keynesian economics up through the 1960s.

Rather than social welfare, Buckley's libertarian conservatism reimagined President Herbert Hoover's idea of a rugged individualism at odds with government intervention—ranging from low taxes to a renewal of state's rights regarding social relations. Moreover, Buckley's notion of individualism found root in what Nicholas Buccola calls inegalitarian libertarianism, a notion of freedom where "only some people were sufficiently 'advanced' to be free."[26] For Buckley, the attention toward an imagined individualism wrapped in an "inegalitarian libertarianism" helped deflect the collective power white men wielded for centuries, which disavowed the white male monopoly on political, economic, and social power that culturally and legally justified the exclusion of women and people of color. Historically, this sense of individualism sheltered the white nationalist collective nature of American society from charges of constitutional hypocrisy. Consequently, the idea of "human rights" arising out of the experience of World War II appeared antithetical to conservatives, as they understood the concept's potential to dismantle the second-class citizenship of people of color—or even justify the welfare state. Conservatives, on the other hand, embraced the color-blind notion of "individual rights."[27] This sentiment, of course, harmonized with the massive resistance of segregationists in the 1950s and 1960s who claimed federal intervention interfered with one's individual right to decide whom they wanted to associate with. Sensing an ideological partnership, Buckley not only hired one of the segregationist movement's greatest defenders (James J. Kilpatrick), but the father of modern conservatism also vehemently defended Southern segregation in his *National Review* and in other media outlets.[28]

Buckley and the segregationists' embrace of "individual" rights without mention of race—in short, color-blind language—represented one of the vital pillars of neoliberalism.[29] The embrace of color-blind individualism at the precise moment when the white nationalist structures of the nation confronted legislative censure provided a key anchor for the conjuncture leading to neoliberalism. In a rhetorical shift, the long-collective nature of white superiority dissolved into a pure individualism, shaking loose the "buried history" haunting the *longue durée* legacies of freedom and slavery as the language conserving hierarchies adapted to the new political context. Morrison, again, offers insight into the contradictions surrounding a rugged individualist American identity anchored to "inegalitarian libertarianism," writing "Autonomy is freedom and translates into the much championed and revered 'individualism.'"[30] White men (especially, white men with property) had always embodied autonomy within the American historical context—freedom of movement, speech, and access to institutions—out of which emerged an existential and material state of individual freedom perceived as a given norm—including the freedom to discriminate. Considering federal action on civil rights to be unconstitutional social engineering and an undermining of preexisting racial hierarchies, the conservative embrace of color blindness regenerated the reverence for individualism—with the racial and gendered discrimination squeezed out of the historical record as if it never happened. In the new world of color-blind individualism, there were no groups of people, only "individuals" abstractly isolated from the inherited legacies of racism and sexism. Through this imagining of the individual, innocence found regeneration—it was "born again," alongside the myth of rugged individualism—despite a catalogue of oppression. Meanwhile, the embedded ideas and material outcomes of settler colonialism and slavery would continue to inform American society. As white supremacy fell to social justice legislation, Buckley and his segregationist allies in the South began stressing this individual freedom just as the door of the welfare state opened for people of color and women. A post–civil rights world took shape: the welfare state, no longer exclusive to white males, was reimagined as a handout to those who just recently gained access. Now repelled by the economic system responsible for the postwar prosperity, discontented whites looked favorably upon the ideas of neoliberalism, its racial ideology of color blindness, and its reforming of American anti-Blackness through the language of "culture" and "individual responsibility."

As a best-selling novelist and essayist, Baldwin grew up poor in Harlem, eventually leaving the country to live and write in Europe.[31] As he gained international recognition from a series of novels and collections of essays, the civil rights movement pulled Baldwin back to the United States in 1957, where he quickly became a sought-after spokesman for the civil rights movement. A central Black intellectual of the time, Baldwin's rhetoric combined his working-class, Christian background from Harlem with his ability to "speak the language of the white intelligentsia."[32] In a series of nonfiction works, Baldwin's critiques during these years provided a counter to both the mainstream views of the civil rights movement as well as what would become Black Power. As an exemplar of the Black radical tradition, Baldwin's critique contributed to the centuries-old tradition of resistance against racial antagonism by people of African descent in the New World. Exploding to life with the first group of enslaved Africans brought to the New World, Cedric Robinson describes the Black radical tradition as "an accretion, over generations, of collective intelligence gathered from struggle. In the daily encounters and petty resistances to domination, slaves had acquired a sense of the calculus of oppression as well as its overt organization and instrumentation."[33] A genealogy of resistance rooted in slavery and maroon communities, and later post-emancipation forms of de jure and de facto segregation, informed this evolving tradition as it adapted to the changing process of racist oppression rooted in settler colonialism and slavery.[34] We see this tradition's presence in the thoughts of Benjamin Franklin, who voiced the blueprint of the soon-to-be republic when he asserted, "Every slave might be reckoned a domestic enemy."[35] Within a global sense, the *enslaved as insurgent to European expansion* formed the core of Paul Gilroy's counterculture of modernity.[36] Baldwin's rhetoric and oratory built off these centuries-old traditions, blending "the hope of Martin Luther King, Jr." with "the threat of Malcolm X."[37] In the 1960s, Baldwin increasingly brought arguments rooted in economics into his arguments.[38]

The Baldwin-Buckley debate represents an early glimpse of the dynamics shaping the historical conjuncture in which neoliberalism took root in the American political economy: the culture war between the demands of civil rights social justice movements and the so-called white backlash or states' rights advocates who bristled against anti-racist federal intervention.[39] The phrase *white backlash* too narrowly frames the historical ramifications of the era, as the concept obscures the deep contours of an American identity rooted in racism. In short, it implies a Black provocation against a white presence innocent of past and present crimes of racial antagonism and institutional discrimination, obscuring the fact that for many white Americans, especially white men, civil rights legislation represented a loss of centuries-old rights and entitlements over historically marginalized peoples as the new laws dismantled the restrictions on opportunity for women, African Americans, and other people of color. An epochal existential crisis of identity unfolded as this deregulation of hierarchies included a loss of normalized employment discrimination, whites-only housing (in the North and South), access to credit, voting, sitting on juries, and the cultural loss of deference to white male authority.

Unsurprisingly, this upsetting of deep hierarchies alarmed conservatives. In 1954, conservative intellectual Russell Kirk asserted, "What really matters is that we should accept the station to which 'a divine tactic' has appointed us with humility and a sense of consecration."[40] This cultural viewpoint mobilized various levels of "higher authority," from God ("a divine tactic"), to notions of Western civilization in its imagining of order. The defense of Western civilization became a core element of the conservative movement and especially the circle of intellectuals Buckley recruited for the *National Review*.[41] James Kilpatrick, a contributing editor to the *National Review*, echoed these sentiments in a 1963 essay arguing that social equality between white and Black was anti-American: "This precious right to discriminate underlies our entire political and economic system."[42] The proudly white supremacist essay—titled, "The Hell He Is Equal"—was held back by the *Saturday Evening Post* after the white nationalist terrorist bombing in Birmingham, Alabama, killed four African American girls: Addie Mae Collins (age 14), Denise

McNair (age 11), Carole Robertson (age 14), and Cynthia Wesley (age 14).[43] Through today, however, cultural war debates against the claims of social justice activists continue to evoke—indeed demand—an innocence toward the history of racial and sexual antagonisms, both disavowing the past and placing an emphasis on individuals rather than groups. Buckley made this clear in his attack on affirmative action in the late 1960s: "What one needs to consider is the individual who stands to suffer."[44] His assertion, of course, dismisses the collective nature of white supremacy's privileging of white males at the exclusion of African Americans. Moreover, in the wake of civil rights legislation, Buckley insists that it would be unfair to have legislation helping historically marginalized groups if this meant interfering with individual rights. This denial of historical context would incessantly haunt the culture war arguments of conservatives for years to come.

The Cambridge debate between Baldwin and Buckley underscores the two very different sets of language and knowledge anchoring the culture war. Mobilized in reaction to the demands of the civil rights movement, an ethos of anti-Black antagonisms outlines the historical experience of people of European descent in the United States, a state of being defining the overall post-1400s European encounters with the New World where the identity of whiteness, the West, or Western civilization found its binary in the Other, the enslaved, the Alien, the savage, the heathen, *the Black*.[45] The dominant American attitude constructed through the processes of modernity—including the Atlantic slave system, settler colonialism, and patriarchy—shaped a vision of the world translating the violence required to ethnically cleanse Native Americans from their land, enslave people of African descent, and objectify women as property of men into a system experienced as a naturally ordered and righteous (Western) civilization led by white men. The notion of civilization, as many have noted, melded together the idea of "progress" into a culture emanating from these experiences and structures that helped Americans navigate and define their history and identity.[46]

The Baldwin-Buckley debate provides a snapshot of the contestation of the culture war ideals, with the historical moment weaving a systemic tapestry outlining the relationship of power to language and the "possession of history."[47] While Buckley's ethos possessed the "progress"-laden language and history of Western civilization to defend his argument, Baldwin's approach, on the contrary, foregrounded the Black radical tradition's subaltern position of the enslaved, the oppressed peoples written out of history. This confrontation between systems of knowledge born out of the *longue durée* processes of settler colonialism and slavery represent the stakes of the 1965 debate at Cambridge, let alone the anchoring precepts of the post-1960s culture war and its struggle over "buried history" and its crisis of identity.⁴⁸ Critical to this culture war struggle was the possession of the meanings of history.

Framing of Debate through the Possession of History

Commenting in the last decade of his life on the nature of history, Baldwin discussed the inability of people trying to escape "history and the effects of history":⁴⁹

> I have been living with those questions for a long time. You see, the trouble I am having right now is with the word itself. History means one thing in a European head. It actually means something else in an American head, and yet again something else in a black man's head. To leave it at that is enough for openness. I am not sure any longer what the word means. Especially as the white world now is calling on what it calls history to justify its dilemma without having the remotest sense of how they got to where they are. . . . Because if history means something, it means that you have learned something from it. If you haven't then the word has got to be changed. History in England, or France, or Germany, or indeed in Europe is now meant as an enormous cloak to cover past crimes and errors and present danger and despair. In short, it has become a useless concept. Except that it can be used as a stick to beat the people without history, like myself, over the head. That worked as long as I believed that you had history and I did not. And now that it is clear that that is not so, another kind of dilemma, another kind of confrontation, begins. Perhaps history has got to be born for the first time. It is certainly true that all the identities coming out of history with a capital H are proven to be false, to be bankrupt. . . . And in terms of America, the Americans are even more abject than the Europeans who are stifling among their artefacts, their icons, which they call history. The Americans have never even heard of history, they still believe that legend created about the Far West, and cowboys and Indians, and cops and robbers, and black and white, and good and evil. . . . If the Europeans are afflicted by history, *Americans are afflicted by innocence*.⁵⁰

When Baldwin reflected on the inability to escape history and its effects, he identified an important component of the post–civil rights–era culture war: analyzing the present and past from within the language and knowledge inherited from years of oppression. Baldwin points to this bottleneck as an impediment toward articulating and reconciling the crimes of the past and their bearing on the present: one needed power over controlling the circulation of knowledge, which, in turn, determined the boundaries of debate. Like the walls of a frontier outpost, these boundaries of debate protected the sense of innocence veiling the coercive nature of American westward expansion and the atrocities of slavery and the maintenance of Jim Crow.[51] For Baldwin, this possession of history allowed a sort of cognitive dissonance to call on an established history justifying one's contemporary sets of systems, structures, and institutions, while simultaneously disavowing the material outcomes produced through these very systems, structures, and institutions. The result, of course, was a version of nationalist myth: "the white world now is calling on what it calls history to justify its dilemma without having the remotest sense of how they got to where they are." This knowledge and language of an *exceptional* American past is a significant element in national identity. As Geoff Eley and Ronald Suny note, "This reservoir of cultural meanings" is "at the heart of the process of building the nation. A common memory of belonging, borne by habits, customs, dialects, song, dance, pastimes, shared geography, superstition, and so on, but also fears, anxieties, antipathies, hurts, resentments, is the indistinct but indispensable condition of possibility. For nationalism to do its work, ordinary people need to see themselves as the bearers of an identity centered elsewhere, imagine themselves as an abstract community."[52] For Americans, this possession of history found expression through the legacy of slavery and its Jim Crow aftermath, the success of settler colonialism and westward expansion, and the patriarchal normalcy guiding relationships between men and women. Tom Engelhardt suggests that this desperate need to foster a "victory culture" stemmed from the settler colonial experience: "It was important that the arrival of the Europeans be a matter of 'settlement' not 'invasion,' and the move across the continent 'expansion' not 'conquest.'"[53] It was critical for the land to be imagined as unoccupied, empty of people, where the mythical idea of Manifest Destiny and rugged individualist settlers merely struggled against the elements—with Native Americans and the environment becoming one and the same. The real struggle over the possession of history, of course, rested in debates among the white settlers: "this was history as a success story, an ennobling tale of the growth of a powerhouse of goods and ideas, a land of natural abundance open to the emigration of 'free men' everywhere."[54] Americans consumed and celebrated this imagined past through cultural avenues such as historical textbooks, captivity narratives, popular media, and national holidays, all of which draped (as Baldwin suggested) an "enormous cloak . . . cover[ing] past crimes and errors and present danger and despair."[55]

An example of confronting this possession of history includes W. E. B. Du Bois's *Black Reconstruction of America* (1935), a work that condemned the history profession for its "propaganda" in retelling the history of Reconstruction. Du Bois takes aim at the rhetorical strategy designed to protect American innocence: "Our histories tend to discuss American slavery so impartially, that in the end nobody seems to have done wrong and everybody was right. Slavery appears to have been thrust upon unwilling helpless America, while the South was blameless in becoming its center."[56] Underlining the embeddedness of this historical innocence, up through the twenty-first century conservatives continued to "set out to 'strike a fair balance' on slavery by recognizing the 'benefits' blacks gained from it and the 'substantial advantages' they enjoyed as a result."[57] This possession of history long circulated through public education history books, most recently on egregious display in debates surrounding 2015 Texas high school textbooks.[58] Innocence demands constant maintenance to shore up its naturalness as it struggles for an identity beyond the shadow cast by crimes against humanity.

Consequently, the power to frame the debate, to possess history, is the ability to silence history that reflects an inconvenience to a traditional narrative shaping contemporary politics. In times of crisis, there is the necessity for the maintenance of this constructed past in which to shed light on contemporary policies aimed toward discrediting oppressed people's claims in the present (one of the primary functions of the Black radical tradition has been to reclaim this silenced past). This struggle between forgetting and remembering becomes especially relevant, as Baldwin notes above, when one is constantly beaten over the head by the very forces of institutionally remembered history. Forgetting or remembering help buttress contemporary rhetoric and policies, ultimately providing justification for material or economic processes while cultivating and renewing methods of oppression and privilege. Historically, violent oppression allows for the disciplining of this knowledge, leading to the ability to frame both contemporary reality and the historical record. This violence performs a "function," whereby acts coated with rhetoric subsume violence into prerequisite norms determining the manner different groups interact historically.[59] A few questions arise from this situation: when a relationship founded on violent antagonism is reformed by legislation, how does the oppressor reconcile their ostensible of loss of engaging in unencumbered violence toward those who helped shape—through violence—the very identity of the oppressor? What happens when historically marginalized people begin speaking out of turn, and refuse to defer; or what happens when the acts and language of African Americans fail to acquiesce to the controlling images of, for example, the Sambo, an image white Americans have trafficked in and revered since the antebellum era? As Baldwin asserted in his classic *The Devil Finds Work*, "That victim who is able to articulate the situation of the victim has ceased to be a victim: he, or she, has become a threat. The victim's testimony must, therefore, be altered."[60] As the victim becomes a threat, and attempts to present a counternarrative, a struggle over the possession of history ensues.

The power to dominate generally favors those with a recognized history, literally establishing a rhetorical legitimacy structuring the violent antagonisms toward those, as Baldwin asserts, "without history."[61] In his exploration of the history of capitalism, Fernand Braudel notes this power dynamic in explaining the perceived "superiority" of European markets versus other "populated regions of the world": "There is for one thing a "historiographical" inequality between Europe and the rest of the world. Europe invented historians and then made good use of them. Her own history is well-lit, and can be called as evidence or used as a claim. The history of non-Europe is still being written. And until the balance of knowledge and interpretation has been restored, the historian will be reluctant to cut the Gordian knot of world history—that is the origin of the superiority of Europe."[62] Although written through a Eurocentric lens—the rest of the world did have history—Braudel's observations may also be read as an earnest assessment of the unequal dynamic between those "with history" and those "without history." His admission of the power of a Eurocentric-historical methodology is correct in how it marginalizes non-European history as existing outside the acceptable boundaries of European-approved knowledge—and thus enjoys limited power for mobilization in the present to confront ongoing social justice issues. Hardly a controversial observation, the very contours of historical methodology and its truth-making ability developed during the era of imperialism and, for American historians, the final years of the centuries-old war against North American Indigenous peoples and the evolution of Jim Crow segregation in the late 1800s (Du Bois's *Black Reconstruction in America* also highlights this).[63] Institutionalized by the twentieth century, the silences haunting history become weapons for the powerful against the politically weak and historically marginalized.[64]

Remembering particular stories about the past, then, rhetorically extends the past into the present, shifting memories and impulses into conceptual, historically vindicated relationships within the current moment. As Morrison asserts, an American self is "not history-less, but historical; not damned, but innocent; not a blind accident of evolution, but a progressive fulfillment of destiny."[65] Consequently, traditional U.S. history operates through the recurring trope of innocence in its narrative defining the American identity as one of defending itself *after* an unprovoked, sudden ambush (e.g., the Alamo, the *Maine*, Pearl Harbor), with this identity wrapped in a thin shroud isolating innocence from the bloodied layers of crimes against humanity related to settler colonialism and slavery.[66] This well-worn innocence proved crucial for navigating the policies of neoliberalism into place as the conservative culture war struggled against the victims of the American dream in the 1950s and 1960s.

A certain level of performance is needed to profess innocence in the face of a well-documented history of brutal racial antagonism. Paraphrasing William Faulkner, Baldwin once asserted, "History is not the past, it's the present. One may even make an argument, in a couple of more weeks, that history is never the past, that everyone is always acting out history."[67] Baldwin suggests here that real history is performed every day by people who act out their historically inherited patterns of relations. We might call these performances "historical projections," the rhetorical deployment of possessed history. Here, conglomerated layers of inherited rhetoric, discourse, ideology, gestures, ontology, and the results of material power are summoned and regulated through one's positionality in society. More precisely, these interactions reflect Baldwin's concept of the balance of power between those possessing history and those supposedly lacking history. Historical projections in practice help facilitate the dominant common sense and historical calculation directing society's traffic through well-rehearsed paths justified with the aid of familiar stories of a prejudice either normalized or disavowed. Performance and adherence to these constructed traditions in everyday life culturally link the past to the present, with conflicts arising when an act of remembering challenges the dominant narrative of the past and present—a disruption creating noise. This memory trespass represents Baldwin's idea about the victim articulating their situation as the victim, including the outcome resulting in the containment of that noise from those seeking to conserve existing power relations. These conflict sites are the spaces of culture wars, where trespasses of unequal relationships are policed.

These culture war struggles over the possession of history take us back to the relevance of the *longue durée*. A narrowly remembered history—decades, for example—too often eludes the *longue durée* processes haunting sets of centuries-old norms, such as racism, sexism, and homophobia. Absent the larger context of history, the narrow conception leads to an ostensibly "clean slate" for future arguments to operate free from their tainted social, economic, and cultural connection to the "whole *longue durée* of racial dictatorship since the conquest."[68] The unpleasant past is quarantined like a virus, allowing the nationalist trope of "innocence" to be redeemed. For example, the twenty-first-century use of religious liberty imagines Christians (the dominant religion of the United States) as innocent victims of federal intervention overriding states' rights, which retroactively pardons the crimes of Southern segregationists whose use of the concept of religious liberty long justified Southern segregation, slavery, and the violence maintaining these institutions.[69] American exceptionalism amid innocence disavows the violent past's contribution to the present, placing a "silence" around ongoing, centuries-old practices enacted through a reformed language where explicit racism is removed, while the confrontation with difference finds justification through the color-blind moniker of "culture."⁷⁰ The performance of disavowal or silencing blankets the present with reinforced ideas of "progress" and the superiority of Western civilization. It is here, in "progress," where the very sense of "innocence" Baldwin and Morrison suggest afflicts the American idea of history obscures the violence of settler colonialism and slavery shaping the American dream.

At Cambridge, Baldwin represented the descendants of American ex-slaves, a status in 1965 bearing the racial antagonism represented by American history and its obsession with anti-Blackness. Baldwin's work—both fiction but especially nonfiction—examined these structures and ideas throughout the mid-twentieth century, addressing the ongoing anti-Black antagonisms Saidiya Hartman calls the "afterlife of slavery."⁷¹ The material and cultural aftermath of the colonial era and the nation's founding utilized the ideas of Enlightenment progress to form a contradictory existence between, on the one hand, recognition of the "rights of man," and on the other, a specificity of these rights that did not apply to those non-whites who were colonized or enslaved. Buckley, a descendent from Ireland—and a beneficiary of the Enlightenment's "rights of man"—represented the quintessential white ethnic. This identity, revived in the 1970s after a brief pause during the post–World War II years of white ethnic assimilation into suburban America, largely emerged as a response to the ethnic pride movements initiated with the civil rights–Black Power movements.⁷² Beginning publicly in the 1950s within his journal, the *National Review*, Buckley's attacks against the civil rights movement stressed the supposed cultural deficiencies of African Americans when compared to other ethnic Americans, such as the Irish, Italians, or Jews.⁷³ This shift in language from previous discussions based on racial science to ideas of culture formed a core component of the 1960s culture war.

The "Ethos" and Victims of the American Dream

Broadcast announcer, St. John-Stevas, described Baldwin as the "star of the evening" as the author rose and ventured his way through the crowded union to the podium amid an enormous applause.⁷⁴ Framed in a sea of white British faces, with a few Black Britons, Baldwin initially responded to the question of the American dream and its relationship to the Negro by calmly positing that the overarching, "deeper" question depended on "one's point of view," "on where you find yourself in the world, what your sense of reality is. That is, it depends on assumptions we hold so deeply as to be scarcely aware of them."⁷⁵ Baldwin outlined this notion of ontology by describing the dynamics of white interpretations of Black resistance to racial oppression. For whites, this resistance appeared as an irrational attack on "the system to which [the white man] owes his entire identity."[76] Culturally and economically, the status quo of the social structure fostered a white identity dependent upon the existence of Black and white social dispositions where the subjugation of Blacks by whites occurred "naturally." For example, Black enslavement was imagined as the inverse to white freedom, with the suppression of "African resistance," becoming, notes Gerald Horne, "a crucial component of forging settler unity—and the solidifying identity that was 'whiteness.'"[77] A few years after the debate, Baldwin described the intricacies of the relationship between whiteness and Blackness: whiteness was a set of attitudes permeating the system of oppression, whereas Blackness was the condition created by these antagonistic beliefs toward Black bodies.[78] Thus, this situation left resistance by Black people against American racism to be seen as an insurrection against the system whiteness utilized as a normative baseline, whether in the form of a lack of deference to breaching color lines to all-out rebellion. In short, a society premised on whiteness viewed Black agency as turning Western civilization on its head—an affront to nature, law and order, and the axioms of the conservatism espoused by Buckley and his *National Review*.[79]

During the debate, Baldwin also contextualized the economic contributions of African Americans to the economy—the "expense" of this system—noting the free labor Black people provided to build the ports, railroads, harbors, and other economic features that aided industrialization and the accumulation of capital. This weaving together of race and economics highlighted the way American racism operated, where the status of Black people circulated through both their connection to capitalism as living property and, after emancipation, cheap labor. Moreover, this relationship performed another role for those not benefiting from the accumulation of capital. Describing the minds of poor whites to his Cambridge audience, Baldwin outlined their frame of reference: "They have been raised to believe, and by now they helplessly believe, that no matter how terrible some of their lives may be and no matter what disaster overtakes them, there is one consolation like a heavenly revelation—at least they are not black."[80] An investment in anti-Blackness, then, is the reward for white acquiescence to an American dream you might or might not become a part of. In this sense, monetary value binds itself to a racially coded binary, where whiteness assumes the role of property—it can be possessed.[81] In the postwar years, the greatest asset driving the American dream for the majority of white Americans was the federally subsidized, racially exclusive housing in the white spaces of suburbia; for people of African descent, this aspect of the welfare state did not exist as a possibility.[82]

Moving his argument to the present, Baldwin announced to the Cambridge audience, "What we are not facing is the results of what we've done. . . . What is crucial here is that unless we can manage to establish some kind of dialogue between those people whom I pretend have paid for the American dream, and those other people who have not achieved it, we will be in terrible trouble." Here, we see Baldwin's notion of the operation of history at work, insisting on those living in the present to recognize the outcome of this centuries-old paradox anchoring the American dream. This recognition demands, however, an admission that the American dream embodied a white imagined space and existence and that it was created through an ethos built on the brutality of slavery and the exclusion of African Americans from the protections and opportunities of civil society.[83] Adding an ominous epilogue, Baldwin summed up:

> Until the moment comes, when we, the Americans, we the American people, are able to accept the fact, that I have to accept, for example, that my ancestors are both white and black, that on that continent we are trying to forge a new identity, for which we need each other. That I'm not a ward of America; I'm not an object of missionary charity. I am one of the people who built the country. Until this moment, there is scarcely any hope for the American dream, because the people who are denied the participation in it, by their very presence, will wreck it. And if that happens, it's a very grave moment for the West. Thank you.

The Cambridge Union hall awarded Baldwin's conclusion with a standing ovation.

A more subdued applause greeted Buckley's arrival, unlike Baldwin's raucous reception. Buckley began with a solemn appraisal of Baldwin's "indictments," with his rebuttal immediately embodying many of the attributes outlined by Baldwin's theorization of the American dream. In an attempt to disqualify Baldwin's testimony, Buckley began by normalizing the field of objectivity as a strict domain of "white rationalism," one of the signal attributes of Western civilization. Buckley asserted, "It is quite impossible in my judgment to deal with the indictment of Mr. Baldwin unless one is prepared to deal with him as a white man, unless one is prepared to say to him that the fact that your skin is black is utterly irrelevant to the arguments that you raise. The fact that you sit here as is [sic] your rhetorical device, and lay the entire weight of the Negro ordeal on your own shoulders, is irrelevant to the argument that we are here to discuss." Underlining the dichotomy between "those with history" and "those without history," Buckley demanded an erasure of Baldwin's Blackness—his history—from the debate while remaining silent about the inherent power of Buckley's own male whiteness (which, of course, was normalized into invisibility). The question at hand, according to Buckley, could not be judged objectively by someone who was Black. With the loss of an unapologetic white supremacy, the demand for color blindness wrapped in white normativity stressed Baldwin's bias as a Black man and underlined Buckley's innocence as a mere rational white man attempting to make a sober analysis of the era's upheavals. We may associate this reform, later embraced by neoliberalism, as a continuation of modernity's "scientific" objectivity so vital for the engineering of the dreams and truth statements of Europeans and white Americans.[84] The ability to be objective, especially for white Americans, established itself through a measurement of humanity that set people of African descent as the savage "race" furthest away from the "superiority" of rational European "stock."[85] Buckley's objectivity, or arguments grounded in the normality of whiteness to judge *things* exterior to it, offered a reassuring balm—a pledge of innocence—for those associated with parts of the system connected to the brutality toward non-whites in the name of maintaining Western civilization. Buckley's pronouncements mustered the historical projections still circulating in the mid-1960s mimicking this logic: the socially dead—enslaved or descendants of enslaved Africans—cannot speak their case as they are without history, and thus not reliable sources of knowledge. This rhetorical shift for Buckley, moreover, provides insight into the evolution of color blindness from its overtly racist origins. Indeed, eight years before the 1965 debate, Buckley rigorously defended the resistance of Southern segregationists against desegregation with a similar logic: "the White community is so entitled [to discriminate] because it is, for the time being, the advanced race."[86] Color blindness removed the explicit racial markers from language criticizing the civil rights movement, while retaining the implied white authority of the ideas justifying the policies.

The attempt to undermine Baldwin's credibility spoke to the mid-1960s anxieties surrounding the historically reflexive white fears of the formerly subjugated speaking back. These anxieties were tied to the dissolution of older ideas constructed to imply an innocence of white participation in anti-Black crimes against humanity. One of the oldest white-imagined caricatures of African Americans was the plantation Sambo.[87] The Sambo was the image of the passive Negro, whose childlike behavior needed direction and guidance, while clearly unable to exercise self-rule let alone be socially equal with white society.[88] In short, it both reinforced Black inferiority and emphasized white paternalism, or the benevolent slaveowner. In addition, notions of self-rule secured the truth statements insisting that African Americans were socially dead, outside civil societies' boundaries of decency and security. At the debate in 1965, the logic of self-rule emerged through an ad hominem attack aimed at Baldwin. Buckley suggested that "he [Baldwin] didn't, in writing that book [*The Fire Next Time*], speak with British accents that he used exclusively tonight"—painting Baldwin with another controlling image of African Americans from the mid-1800s, the caricature of Zip Coon: the awkwardly free Black who, despite trying, can never speak, act, or think like a white man.[89] Zip Coons made a mockery of the idea of social equality between whites and Blacks. In the same sentence, Buckley also charged Baldwin with threatening "America with the necessity for us to jettison our entire civilization." Again, for Buckley, the removal of the oppressive conditions connected to policing Blackness would turn the ethos of white America, specifically its putative "progress" narrative of innocence, on its head.[90]

In a full performance of the post–civil rights era's white defense of privilege, Buckley inverted the power dynamics between whites and Blacks. Suggesting Baldwin somehow had an advantage, Buckley presented himself as being unfairly matched—not against the intellect of Baldwin but against a presumed social power Baldwin possessed over Buckley, who was a mere white man. Buckley was the victim: "Tonight," Buckley announced, he was "going to speak to [Baldwin] without any reference whatever to those surrounding protections which [he was] used to in virtue of the fact that [he is] a Negro." This performance of powerlessness focused on a narrow moment of the present that stipulated an enhanced rhetorical power connected to Blackness despite centuries of white supremacy and anti-Blackness. Rhetorically excluding the *longue durée* history between people of European descent and African descent, Buckley sought allies in the Cambridge hall who might feel uncomfortable with an increased public criticism toward deep traditions that have now been condemned as racist. George Lipsitz labels this type of situation a "manifestation of privilege masquerading as powerlessness."[91] According to Buckley, Baldwin's Blackness simultaneously disqualified him from the engagement in civil society to make his own arguments, while at the same time Baldwin's Blackness was pronounced as an unfair power advantage over an innocent, white ethnic Buckley. In minutes, centuries of white supremacy and systemic anti-Blackness dissolved; race as an identity suddenly appeared as a discriminating rhetorical device against white people. Indeed, Buckley's performance is an early moment of color blindness when, as Nikhil Pal Singh notes, "race now means racism, especially when it is used to define or defend the interests of a minority community."[92] Color blindness solved the issue, leaving whiteness in its hierarchical position, unnamed and normalized, leaving an unspoken contempt toward Blackness to survive through acerbic charges of "using the race card" or in color-blind coded words such as *culture*.

Buckley's parries illustrated more than the modern fear of the enslaved striking back at the master. More importantly for the next decade's economic restructuring, these discursive strategies were employed for reconceptualizing the operation of power by historically erasing centuries of white privilege after a decade of embarrassing scenes transmitted globally of naked white brutality against Blacks whose crime was seeking the same protections of the Constitution enjoyed by white people. In his assessment of the unfairness of Baldwin's Blackness, Buckley helped to anchor a conceptualization of centuries of white antagonism toward Blacks as a process conceived of as reciprocal, insinuating that each "side" had equal ability to deliver "damage" to the other. In short, a system of "race relations" that imagines racial prejudice arising "out of a natural antipathy between groups on the basis of difference," rather than a system of "racial oppression," which "locates the source of the problem within the structure of society," where a "system of domination ... entails major political and economic institutions, including the state itself."[93] As a relationship decontextualized from history, one could innocently frame any support for African American equality as an unfair advantage against whites, a familiar binary in reverse imagining whiteness as an ethos, and Blackness as a condition. The so-called white backlash, then, reaffirmed a white innocence in order to counter the growing chorus of 1960s social movements questioning the violent norms of modernity and its language of Western civilization.

Alongside the rewriting of history, Buckley also deflected the criticisms of African Americans away from notions of structural racism. In attacking Baldwin's argument, Buckley dismissed the connection between capital accumulation and enslaved or Jim Crow–disciplined Black labor. A primary tool for Buckley's defense of the status quo lay in the arguments underpinning a book he suggested the students read to fully understand the situation in America: Nathan Glazer and Daniel P. Moynihan's *Beyond the Melting Pot: The Negroes, Puerto Ricans, Jews, Italians, and Irish of New York City* (1963).[94] Published the same year as Baldwin's *The Fire Next Time*, *Beyond the Melting Pot* embodies what historian Matthew Frye Jacobson calls "an inaugurating text" of the culture wars.[95] While acknowledging discrimination, *Beyond the Melting Pot* downplayed its impact upon African Americans by regenerating ideas of inferiority: "the 'weak' Black family" was to blame for the unequal status of African Americans in the United States.[96] In short, writes Ibram Kendi, "Blacks were not taking enough responsibility for their own problems."[97] Of course, this academic assessment was music to Buckley's ears. "My great grandparents worked too, presumably yours worked also," Buckley innocently proclaimed to the Cambridge audience, reciting what would become a familiar white retort to affirmative action after the 1960s.[98] In highlighting the "complicated" nature of the racial problem in the United States, Buckley suggested that the issue existing in America was individual discrimination against Blacks, not institutional—a problem for reform, not radical solutions.

Buckley's use of Moynihan, coauthor of *Beyond the Melting Pot*, is noteworthy as the latter was instrumental in developing white liberal, and later conservative, responses to Black critiques of institutional racism. Three significant interventions by Moynihan include *The Moynihan Report* (1965), his contribution to President Lyndon Johnson's commencement speech at Howard University in 1965, and his memo to President Richard Nixon in 1970 suggesting that the "issue of race could benefit from a period of benign neglect. The subject has been too much talked about."[99] Constructed through the racist sociological debates of the 1920s and 1930s—including the controlling image of Black women's so-called sexual depravity and the Black family's matriarchal structure—Moynihan's ideas expressed the *longue durée* thoughts white Americans cataloged to justify the very real sexual depravity connected to slavery's brutality.[100] The other coauthor, Glazer, later wrote *Affirmative Discrimination* in 1975 where he asserted that affirmative action policies were unfair for whites, who were innocent of the crimes of their descendants while Glazer denied the ongoing connection between racism and economic opportunity.[101] Building on his long-held civilizational beliefs, Buckley's second suggestion during the debate dismissed the idea that racism was the sole reason for the conditions of African Americans in the United States: a primary "failure of the Negro community itself [was in its inability] to make certain exertions which were made by other minority groups during the American experience." Noting the absence of the "particular energy ... so noticeable in the Jewish community and to a certain, and lesser, extent, into the Italian and Irish community," Buckley asserted, "we should focus on the necessity to animate this particular energy" in African Americans. In short, encourage them to develop an "ethos"—a particularly favorite word for Buckley when describing this situation throughout his television program, *Firing Line*.[102]

Buckley's use of the concept of ethos updated the racial science language of white superiority: rather than a biologically imagined Black inferiority, the new language suggested Black Americans lacked the proper cultural ability to adapt to mainstream white society. This new language amid the changing political landscape of the civil rights era was necessary to keep alive the sentiments of anti-Blackness through color-blind assertions coated in deeply rooted ideas of culture and ethos.[103] This is where the concept of Western civilization bears importance as an overarching transnational idea tying together the *longue durée* fraternity of European expansion throughout modernity. Buckley—wealthy, white, and brought up in a transnational world—naturally saw people of color, especially Blacks, as inferior, just as many elites and educated white men did in the early twentieth century.[104] Moreover, his anti-Blackness is better understood in light of his recurrent need to justify brutality and ongoing social inequality toward African Americans through the studies of Glazer and Moynihan, who debated the so-called Negro problem through the historical experiences of white ethnic assimilation. As Matthew Jacobson notes, "The historical weight of incorporation by conquest or by slavery, for instance, was of little account in this model, as *all* groups could expect to proceed along roughly the same lines of acceptance, mobility, and success as had the great waves of immigrants from Europe beginning in the 1840s."[105] Two outcomes occurred through this racial calculus: white ethnics became more white, especially after World War II, while Jim Crow helped shape their whiteness through the exclusion of Black people from postwar assimilation and economic opportunity. The result is that the forces of anti-Blackness obtained new allies at the precise moment when the flexible contours of cultural pathology replaced racial science as a justification for exclusion or a reason explaining the status of African Americans.

By contrasting differences between African Americans and white ethnic Americans, Buckley helped to outline the rhetorical contours of Martin Barker's notion of the "new racism," where theories of race are concealed in order to "provide form and structure to people's experiences and reactions, without displaying itself as a whole theory with big and dangerous implications."[106] Here, ideas of culture manifested historical ideas of civilization (and who is included in its protections), setting parameters where contemporary use of culture discursively links up to older embedded notions of science and biology. Meanwhile, culture-as-race pronouncements obscured the discredited assumptions of racial superiority through innocent language describing "a 'way of life'"—with the latter judged from the dominant cultural perspective.[107] As the authors of *The Empire Strikes Back: Race and Racism in 70s Britain* assert, "Once the argument has been couched in terms of 'alien cultures,' common-sense racism can be relied upon to provide the missing inflexions."[108] Rather than having racial matters weighted in biology and science, the dominant issue is "the insurmountability of cultural differences, a racism which, at first sight, does not postulate the superiority of certain groups or peoples in relation to others but 'only' the harmfulness of abolishing frontiers, the incompatibility of life-styles and traditions."[109] By the early twenty-first century, this rhetorical shift became the dominant frame of debate regarding what otherwise would be a discussion about race and the fears of integration.

For Buckley and many of his successors, culture replaced the explicit racial arguments justifying the conditions of African Americans, relieving white society of moral complicity in fostering, defending, and policing racial antagonism. The transition from overt racism to a cultural sense of inferiority gained momentum through the innovation of "crime statistics" at the dawn of the twentieth century, leading to a scientific measurement of difference fueling "gendered notions of black male pathology, and when linked to illegitimacy rates, doubly burdened black women by defining them as sexually deviant and undeserving of the protections of womanhood."[110] From this renewed position of innocence, Buckley's cultural approach ventured into sociological territory inhabited by Glazer and Moynihan, where a technocratic and "unbiased" study denotes the range of deficiencies allotted to African Americans. In *Nobody Knows My Name* (1961), Baldwin observed, "One of the reasons we are so fond of sociological reports and research and investigational committees is because they hide something. As long as we can deal with the Negro as a kind of statistic, as something to be manipulated, something to be fled from, or something to be given something to, there is something we can avoid, and what we can avoid is what he really, really means to us. The question that still ends these discussions is an extraordinary question: Would you let your sister marry one?"[111] This combination of statistical investigation and the sexualization of the so-called Negro problem—embedded into American crime statistics in the early years of Jim Crow—found mobilization alongside another set of self-rule tropes near the end of Buckley's speech.[112] Adding statistics from *Beyond the Melting Pot* to underline the inferior ethos of African Americans, Buckley confidently asserted the sexual distance between Blacks and whites, a trope deeply ingrained in American slavery and the American albatross of miscegenation fears.[113] Speaking this language, Buckley declared, "Fourteen times as many people in New York City born of Negros are illegitimate as of the whites." Building on this conception of Black deviancy, Buckley then connected the biological deviance of Blacks with that of the ignorance of poor whites in a response to an audience member's heckle demanding that Blacks be able to vote in Mississippi: "The problem in Mississippi isn't that too few Negroes can vote; it's that too many whites can." This remark conveniently laid the blame for racism on the poor and ignorant, erasing the origins of institutional racism while simultaneously creating a rhetorical bridge between Black inferiority and poor white ignorance. This *longue durée* gesture of conservatism brought traditional suspicion toward the poor and working class together with an inscription of poor whiteness—"white trash"—as a separate degraded race akin to people of African descent.[114] Buckley followed up the question paraphrasing the conservative Black thinker Booker T. Washington, who, strategically, sought education and training for African Americans over the need for political rights. Using the Black conservative's words as a shield against charges of buttressing white supremacy, Buckley suggested that mere voting rights or holding public office were not enough: "but that they be prepared to hold public office. Not that they vote, but they be prepared to vote.... It is much more complicated, sir, than simply just the question of giving them the vote." Through this logic, a so-called deviant or deficient culture—a culture lacking an "ethos"—justified the skepticism of civilized and rational people toward extending self-rule to African Americans.

A critical ontological anchor of modernity, Buckley's defense of white nationalism and Black inequality consistently embraced the civilization versus savagery mindset.[115] The primary difference between the 1960s and 1950s, however, lay in Buckley's more overtly racist language. An August 1957 issue of the *National Review* highlights a more honest, less subtle assertion of rational innocence guided by a sense of "progress" and the defense of Western civilization draped in the language of white supremacy. In the piece, Buckley contextualizes ongoing Jim Crow practices within the *longue durée* of the American experience:

> Reasonable limitations upon the vote are not exclusively the recommendations of tyrants or oligarchists (was Jefferson either?). The problem in the South is not how to get the vote for the Negro, but how to equip the Negro—and a great many Whites—to cast an enlightened and responsible vote. . . . The South confronts one grave moral challenge. It must not exploit the fact of Negro backwardness to preserve the Negro as a servile class. It is tempting and convenient to block the progress of a minority whose services, as menials, are economically useful. . . . So long as it [the South] is merely asserting the right to impose superior mores for whatever period it takes to effect a genuine cultural equality between the races, and so long as it does so by humane and charitable means, the South is in step with civilization, as is the Congress that permits it to function.[116]

The truth-making discourses of Western civilization, reason, and progress, so essential to justifying the processes of American history—from slavery to settler colonialism to the restriction of women's rights—provides Buckley with the rational and moral language and knowledge to save the South from criticism of its own "civilization." The assertion of "Negro backwardness" easily fit into its antithesis of white "superior mores," justifying Buckley's logic of inequality of power, delaying "genuine cultural equality," and helping shape the future dynamic of individualizing structurally racist institutions: African Americans merely needed to develop an ethos, like the Italians, Irish, and Jews, to gain access to the American dream—nothing else, apparently, stood in their way. For Buckley, American history leading up to the 1965 debate contained "reasonable" precedents in the anti-Black policies of the colonists and founders, and later, the segregationists who appeared to be unfairly tarnished as "tyrants" as they resisted desegregation in the 1950s and 1960s. For Buckley, order and respect for laws came before social equality and the guarantees of the Constitution.

The nonovertly racist defense against the criticisms of the American dream during the 1965 Baldwin-Buckley debate characterized the cultural shift responding to the overall deregulation of civil rights in the United States. If Jim Crow laws created a strict segregation of employment opportunities on the weight of anti-Black cultural logic, once these laws were removed, the now-embedded cultural logic would remain—though now wrapped in color-blind language. Economically, the post–civil rights era saw the Jim Crow welfare state replaced with the more laissez-faire system of neoliberalism in the late 1970s and 1980s. Contextualized within the *longue durée* of white nationalist privilege, the welfare state found itself dismantled—and condemned—at precisely the same moment African Americans and women gained access to it via 1960s civil rights legislation. All wealth and economic opportunities accumulated through the racially exclusive Jim Crow welfare state dissolved from view, obscured behind the veil of neoliberal color blindness. Along with the absence of reparations for slavery and the Jim Crow segregation years, nothing addressed the ongoing ontological features inhabiting institutional racism after the 1960s—leaving the reason for slavery and Jim Crow untouched, carefully buried in the language and knowledge of "culture." Working through the *longue durée* normalcy of Black inferiority and exclusion from the rights of civil society, these reforms deregulated the legislature and language of an unabashed white supremacy. Rather than explicit language, such as the "Negro problem," the path was cleared for new language, such as the "urban problem." The ability of language to disavow the knowledge of the crimes and injustices of the past helped make the American dream of the post–World War II era appear in line with the historical projection of American exceptionalism. The possession of history mattered, with Baldwin's debate with Buckley representing what was at stake in the 1960s culture war.

As an ideological-economic project of capitalism, neoliberalism thrived on, and gained momentum from, the tension produced through the culture war and its possession of history. Color-blind language displaced overt discrimination while at the same time retaining the same sets of impulses and historical projections Americans could still manifest to identify antagonists: people of color. With the new language came a new veneer; renewed innocence draped around the virtuous narrative of "progress" celebrating 1960s civil rights legislation. As conservative ideas ascended in the 1960s and 1970s, neoliberalism (and its application as Reaganomics) utilized the historical projections performed by Buckley (among others) to gain political leverage from the white working and middle classes in dismantling the Jim Crow welfare state, which, ironically, proved so crucial for their economic prosperity and the achievement of the American dream in the postwar years. As their economic opportunities dwindled, their source of warmth came primarily through conservative rhetoric scapegoating people of color and historically marginalized groups.

Baldwin, nonetheless, continued to work through these issues in the 1970s, publishing *No Name in the Street* (1972), the delayed follow-up to his book *The Fire Next Time*. *No Name in the Street* reflected a contemporary assessment adorned in pessimism and prophecy regarding the inability of U.S. society to come to terms with its legacies of modernity, particularly its inability to fully rid itself of anti-Black antagonisms born of slavery.[117] Reminiscing about the previous decade's civil rights activism and dialogue on race, Baldwin noted the ongoing haunting of America's past and the impossibility for closure without an adequate accounting of the layers of damage:

> [William Faulkner] is seeking to exorcise a history which is also a curse. He wants the old order which came into existence through unchecked greed and wanton murder, to redeem itself without further bloodshed—without, that is, any further menacing itself—and without coercion. This, old orders never do, less because they would not than because they cannot. They cannot because they have always existed in relation to a force which they have had to subdue. This subjugation is the key to their identity and the triumph and justification of their history, and it is also on this continued subjugation that their material well-being depends.[118]

Noting the difficulty of dismantling the new color-blind racism in the post–civil rights United States, in 1980 Baldwin remarked, "Another kind of dilemma, another kind of confrontation, begins."[119] That dilemma essentially involved wrestling with the ghosts of history guiding white privilege, which, in the wake of civil rights legislation, reset the playing field of the American dream, with its innocence renewed for future generations. At the very moment modernity's ideological construct of Western civilization fell under siege from anti-colonial liberation movements abroad, and various social justice movements within the United States, conservatives did more than occupy the barricades in defense of the status quo in the 1960s. They entered a period of organizing aimed toward "recovery and restoration" of the power of business after years of the left-liberal welfare state.[120] One important tool was the well-entrenched ideological construct of "civilized" versus "savage," with these embedded cultural symbols summoned as weapons to push back against the new diversity spreading through the United States at the dawn of the first decade of legislated social equality in U.S. history.[121]

Chapter 2

Did You Ever See a Dream Walking?
Western Civilization, the Longue Durée, *and the Culture of Neoliberalism*

How sharp a break not only with the recent past but with the whole evolution of Western civilization the modern trend toward socialism means becomes clear if we consider it not merely against the background of the nineteenth century but in a longer historical perspective. We are rapidly abandoning not the views merely of Cobden and Bright, of Adam Smith and Hume, or even of Locke and Milton, but one of the salient characteristics of Western civilization as it has grown from the foundations laid by Christianity and the Greeks and Romans. Not merely nineteenth- and eighteenth-century liberalism, but the basic individualism inherited by us from Erasmus and Montaigne, and Cicero and Tacitus, Pericles and Thucydides, is progressively relinquished.

—F. A. Hayek, *The Road to Serfdom* (1944)

So much for the present. What about the past? The closest approach to free enterprise we have ever had in the United States was in the 19th century. Yet your children will hear over and over again in their schools and in their classes the myth that that was a terrible period when the robber barons were grinding the poor miserable people under their heels. That's a myth constructed out of whole cloth. The plain fact is that at no other time in human history has the ordinary man improved his condition and benefited his life as much as he did during that period of the 19th century when we were the closest to free enterprise.

—Milton Friedman, "Which Way for Capitalism" (1978)

We must reassert and renew American civilization. From the arrival of English-speaking colonists in 1607 until 1965, there was one continuous civilization built around a set of commonly accepted legal and cultural principles. From the Jamestown colony and the Pilgrims, through de Tocqueville's *Democracy in America,* up to Norman Rockwell's paintings of the 1940s and 1950s, there was a clear sense of what it meant to be an American. Our civilization is based on a spiritual and moral dimension. It emphasizes personal responsibility as much as individual rights. Since 1965, however, there has been a calculated effort by cultural elites to discredit this civilization and replace it with a culture of irresponsibility that is incompatible with American freedoms as we have known them. Our first task is to return to teaching Americans about America and teaching immigrants how to become Americans. Until we re-establish a legitimate moral-cultural standard, our civilization is at risk.

—Newt Gingrich, *To Renew America* (1995)

The James Baldwin–William Buckley debate in 1965 embodied a momentary *longue durée* skirmish: a collision of inherited cultural and economic assumptions guided by two related scales of world-historical geography. Zoomed into a local-national level, the first scale involved the articulation of the post–World War II American dream. Imagined as a secure standard of living for white Americans (defined as a male, family wage-earning person), this scale historically found implementation through federally subsidized westward expansion, the racial-gendered hierarchy achieved through settler colonialism, slavery, and the Jim Crow aftermath, and after World War II, the federally subsidized suburbs (including infrastructure development and defense spending). The other, more global scale was the struggle over the meanings of the centuries-old project of "Western civilization," the world-historical commanding term embodying the ideas, policies, and material outcomes of modernity since the 1400s (including the processes of colonialism, settler colonialism, the Atlantic slave system, capitalism, the Enlightenment, the nation-state, and imperialism). Embodying Michel-Rolph Trouillot's North Atlantic universals, this term blanketed the processes of modernity with a benevolence—an innocence—that articulated the brutality of colonialism and slavery as progress, providing a righteous confidence to European and American power projection.[1] This confidence, moreover, was compounded by indifference and often celebration of the consequences of violence toward colonized or enslaved peoples. Viewed through the *longue durée* of modernity, we may situate Western civilization as an ideological and cultural agent of transnational white superiority, all of which justified Europe and people of European descent to essentially control the world through economic, cultural, or political means up through the 1900s.[2]

The performances and language of the Baldwin and Buckley debate reflected the different interpretations of the grand history of Western civilization. At the national, post–World War II scale, the contextual boundaries of the 1960s culture war drew from the tensions over the inherited racial hierarchy of whiteness and Blackness and its unequal distribution of freedom and economic opportunity in the United States. Those who embodied the imagined benefactors of the American dream confronted both civil rights and decolonization movements in the 1950s and 1960s, which troubled their entrenched norms of racism, sexism, heteronormativity, or xenophobia rooted in conceptions of Western civilization. What was once an assumed hierarchy paternalistically based off the natural superiority of people of European descent had suddenly become a relationship defined as oppression secured through brutal violence. Baldwin's notion of the "possession of history" highlights the stakes of the mid-1960s culture war: is there a glorious American past made up of heroes like Thomas Jefferson, Andrew Jackson, and Teddy Roosevelt, or are these heroes willing participants in crimes against humanity as sadistic slave owners, ethnic cleansers, and Anglo-Saxon supremacists? If these men are heroes of Western civilization, how did they extend and distribute the rewards of liberty and equality embedded in the constitution? At the dawn of liberation, many Americans were not ready to relinquish the honorable past shaping Western civilization, especially as the struggle—often referred to as a backlash—*against* social equality surfaced across the tumultuous 1960s and 1970s. Amid this uncertainty against the extension of civil rights, many desperately continued to justify their ideas and policies through the celebration of Western civilization, a grand history of European accomplishment cleansed of its sins and brought—again—into the light of innocence for the heavy ideological lifting required to dismantle the vastly popular Jim Crow welfare state.

Civil rights activist's and global liberation movements challenged the norms of white male supremacy, unsettling the righteousness of Western civilization. Suddenly, the confidence of the narrative faced serious questions: were the heroes of "the West"—whether a cowboy or overseas "adventurer"—tyrannical oppressors or rugged individualists building civilization? A paradox confronted the conservative mind: how does one celebrate Western or American civilization when it is conjoined with the brutal processes of colonialism and slavery; or, to use Newt Gingrich's words, how does the *longue durée* "spiritual and moral dimension" of American society come to terms with the crimes committed to create the quaint postwar banality of Norman Rockwell images comforting Americans across the twentieth century?[3] These were significant questions as the formerly colonized or segregated tore away the cloak of normalcy tied to racial and sexual domination, and charging those of European descent with securing their power through arbitrary, vindictive—savage—acts of greed and wanton violence while using the myth of biological supremacy and Western civilization as a protective façade to hide their crimes. Poet Gil Scott-Heron noted this post–civil rights, postcolonial change in outlook in 1970: despite the filmic majesty of content and loyal enslaved people—Sambos—depicted in *Gone with the Wind* (1939), Scott-Heron asserted that "slavery was no smiling happy-fizzy party; your ancestors raped my foremothers and I will not forget."[4] Those seeking to retain the privileges promised by racial discrimination (or sexual and gendered discrimination) quickly abandoned overt mentions of biological race for the color-blind concept of culture, while obstructing reforms to the status quo by wielding the ideological shield of Western civilization. Secure in their possession of history, the epigraphs above highlight just how important the concept of Western civilization—let alone conservatism's own use of the *longue durée*—was in pressing forward neoliberalism and conservatism by blanketing the history of their ideas with the comforting weight of order, tradition, and security connected to the long-celebrated idea of Western civilization.

Providing a key lubricant for structural adjustment, the grand vision of Western civilization established a bridge easing the transition from overt notions of racial supremacy defining the pre–World War II era to ideas of cultural difference after the war. We may situate this transition as an intimate partner in what William Davies notes is a salient feature of neoliberalism: the conceptual shift from policies based on "'fairness' of law" (which translated into a welfare state based on overtly white supremacist laws normalizing inequality out of fairness to the white "race's" superiority over people of color—and hence, a "fair" hierarchy) to a color-blind "quantitative analysis" *measuring* and *justifying* economic opportunity in an age where overt racism was censured.[5] This transition, of course, arose through the changing global context. As Quinn Slobodian suggests, the period of decolonization between the 1930s and 1970s shaped the evolution of neoliberalism just as much as the welfare state, including the construction of institutions aimed toward managing the expansion of democracy in the United States and newly independent, formerly colonized nations.[6] Now that blunt power based on coercion and the language of white superiority fell out of fashion, the simple enforcement of "the rule of law"—defined and constructed through the processes of modernity (i.e., colonial law)—found renewal as policies of the past synced with the abstract notion of "quantitative analysis." The outcome for neoliberals: the renewal of classical liberal language "separating politics from economics," and the removal of political notions of "fairness" from the visible equation of economic policy.[7] These rhetorical maneuvers, however, needed the conscription of the concept of Western civilization to provide a shield of justification for neoliberalism and its conservative allies.

The very need for a this *longue durée* defense lay in the fact that the road to neoliberalism could only be paved through the labor and support of the very demographic benefiting from the "fairness" of the welfare state. Thus, neoliberals looked to establish "cultural and social bonds" coated with a sense of lost traditions and a perceived collapse in the "rule of law" during the particularly anxious and turbulent period of the civil rights era.[8] Drawing on the epochal language of Western civilization, neoliberals and postwar conservatives reconceptualized the deep racial loyalties undergirding the institutions of the Jim Crow welfare state. A curious paradox characterized this transaction: the very white nationalism cultivated through the history of "Western civilization" both constructed the Jim Crow welfare state (and the creation of the prosperous white middle class) as well as dismantled the welfare state (at the expense of its primary beneficiaries). When this cultural bond combined with the abstract "rule of law" (a concept neoliberals deployed to protect capital from democratic passions), a smooth road redirected economic loyalties away from a politics connected to economics toward a politics separated from economics. Accordingly, the transition to neoliberalism also signaled a defense of Western civilization, which was visibly under attack by the civil rights movement, second-wave feminism, and Vietnamese peasants seeking independence. To defend Western civilization—as Friedrich August von Hayek, Milton Friedman, and Gingrich attempt in the epigraphs—meant voting for ideas and policies that not only liberated markets, but also, as Slobodian notes, encased and inoculated "capitalism against the threat of democracy, to create a framework to contain often-irrational human behavior, and to reorder the world after empire as a space of competing states in which borders fulfill a necessary function."[9]

Placing the evolution of neoliberalism within the language of Western civilization and the legacies of modernity provides a window into understanding how white Americans prospering under the Keynesian-inspired, federal interventionist welfare state shifted voting patterns toward politicians whose policies sought to dismantle the very welfare state shaping *their* postwar American dream. This chapter examines how neoliberals in the 1940s through the 1970s, particularly Hayek and Friedman, anchored their economic ideas to the celebrated concept of Western civilization. Although others have mapped out more detailed histories of the evolution of neoliberalism, this chapter offers a brief summary of its development as an ideological movement with an eye on contextualizing the language and knowledge within the *longue durée* cultural contours of modernity, including the dismissal of criticism toward capital concentration and monopolies. Finally, the chapter establishes the ideological links between the neoliberal thought collective and conservatism in the postwar years, particularly its cultural affiliation with the emerging conservative culture wars of the 1960s.

"Equality Is a Disorganizing Concept": Sentiments, Hierarchies, and the *Longue Durée*

Although unsuccessful at Cambridge, Buckley's efforts would eventually pay off. The United States moved to the right of the political spectrum between the 1960s and 1980s amid an uncertainty linked to the unsettling of traditional social and economic hierarchies. Between a white American anxiety over social equality with those previously deemed second-class citizens and a New Right conservative movement seeking the dismantling of the welfare state, a culture war proved an efficient path for this economic transition. Republican standard bearers like Gingrich would continue to gain traction from this *longue durée* possession of history in service to the culture war well into the 1990s and twenty-first century.[10] At the precipice of formal equality between Black and white in the United States, color-blind language displaced overtly racist language (at least within "respectable" political debate) with coded phrases long familiar to white Americans. This color-blind language found root in the concepts of the "rule of law," "rights of property," "deviant culture," and the relationships between the nation-state and its citizenry woven through the idea of Western civilization. The abstract legal framework of the American founding fathers—the sons of the Enlightenment—were summoned in the 1960s through the language of "law and order" to frame the debate about the proper roles of protest, dissent, and the validation of grievances.[11] The unconstitutional nature of systemic discrimination and unchecked violence across centuries would be redacted from the record and disavowed. A cynical year-zero arose at the end of the 1960s, imagining a world where equality between all people had always existed and where affirmative action programs or reparations appeared as unfair for whites who'd grown used to the Jim Crow welfare state.

The struggle over the possession of history and its mobilization in the present shaped the essence of this 1960s culture war. In his dialogue with Nikki Giovanni, Baldwin suggested that these were the deeper meanings underlining the vast shifts affecting the United States: "What I'm trying to get at is my apprehension of the crisis of this age. The crisis has something to do with identity, and that has something to do with buried history."[12] Unintentionally agreeing with Baldwin about the struggle over the possession of history, Gingrich—with his PhD in history—described the ongoing stakes in retaining the type of understanding of history embraced by the United States prior to the civil rights era: "From the Jamestown colony and the Pilgrims, through de Tocqueville's Democracy in America, up to Norman Rockwell's paintings of the 1940s and 1950s, there was a clear sense of what it meant to be an American. Our civilization is based on a spiritual and moral dimension. It emphasizes personal responsibility as much as individual rights. Since 1965, however, there has been a calculated effort by cultural elites to discredit this civilization and replace it with a culture of irresponsibility that is incompatible with American freedoms as we have known them."[13] For Baldwin, and inversely with Gingrich, the intersection between identity and buried history formed the root of the American racial dilemma—whether one is condemning the identities constructed through settler colonialism, slavery, and the afterlife of slavery, or celebrating them as the essence of civilization and freedom. An important aspect of the culture war delicately rested on this vital possession of history: the conservation of a social order based on the disavowal of the wanton violence sculpting American identity from the experience of invasion, the expulsion of Indigenous peoples, and the degradation and terrorism targeting enslaved and free people of African descent. Justified through the "rule of law" enforced by the nation-state and religiously sanctioned through a culture of white supremacy, American identity—*American civilization*—existed within the paradox of unbridled freedom and liberty within a racial dictatorship. Describing liberty, Dorothy Roberts notes the underlying liberal logic of its idealization: "The dominant view of liberty reserves most of its protections only for the most privileged members of society. This approach superimposes liberty on an already unjust social structure, which it seeks to preserve against unwarranted government interference. Liberty protects all citizens' choices from the most direct and egregious abuses of government power, but it does nothing to dismantle social arrangements that make it impossible for some people to make a choice in the first place. Liberty guards against government intrusion; it does not guarantee social justice."[14] When the victims of American liberty began articulating "the situation of the victim," they "ceased to be a victim" and instead became "a threat"—leading to liberty's calling for decisive action in altering the "victim's testimony" and conditions of inclusion into the liberal realm of liberty.[15] To confront this catalog of crimes against humanity voiced by the victims of the American dream, conservatives and neoliberals doubled down on the founder's rhetorical belief in individual rights and the embrace of the color-blind phrase, "all men are created equal," as the cliff of legislated social equality loomed ahead. In short, the dominant idea of liberty—the guarding against government intrusion—would be more than adequate to handle civil rights reforms.

Undermining the arguments of social justice activists was vital for conserving status quo white power and its possession of history. For conservatives, accepting Baldwin's critique would, as Buckley argued, entail "the necessity for us to jettison our entire civilization"; a zero-sum sentiment driven by the assumption that any deviation from the status quo meant the end of Western civilization and the end of relationships of order long treasured and revered by conservatives. Buckley's rhetorical power lay in the weight of traditional memories of American history learned in the classroom during the height of legislated white nationalism before the 1960s, a familiar space aiding his denial of Baldwin's outline of inequality regarding African Americans and an American dream enjoyed by white Americans.[16] Buckley's argument aligned with a past most Americans continued to—*needed to*—believe. For conservatives, this possession of history long justified denying a past built on violence and a defense of American social and economic inequality.[17]

Rooted in Auguste Comte's ideas of "order" and the "social subordination" of social classes, those basking in the pinnacle of Western civilization and enjoying the inherited legacies of European expansion found the reality of social equality with long-deemed racially inferior people as an unfathomable change, an antithesis to the very logics of a Western civilization constructed atop colonialism and slavery.[18] This concept of order and subordination filtered through the language of race and the restriction of social equality in the United States.[19] For example, during a weeklong filibuster against federal legislation prohibiting anti-lynching in 1938, Louisiana senator Allen J. Ellender prophesized that passage of the law would spell the end of civilization itself.[20] In his defense of the historical right of whites—*their liberty*—to freely and publicly engage in the murder of Black people outside the official justice system, Ellender asserted, "We draw the line with respect to legislation that will make it possible for the white and the colored to rub elbows together; because, I repeat, and I hope it will sink in, political equality leads to social equality, and social equality will eventually spell the decay and downfall of our American civilization."[21] As a salient anchor of American racism, the roots of this "white right" of gratuitous violence—what two scholars call "the endless ambushes of white populism"—toward people of African descent derived from the sexual language of miscegenation, long circulated through American literature and popular culture—including the iconic film celebrating this white nationalist vision: *Birth of a Nation* (1915).[22] Less than thirty years after Ellender's defense of anti-Black violence, and a year before the Baldwin-Buckley debate, William J. Simmons addressed the Greater Los Angeles Citizens' Council, on June 30, 1964, asserting, "We know that these two cornerstones—liberty and racial integrity or social separation of the races—provide the foundation upon which our system of social, political and economic values is built."[23] Again, liberty and racial antagonism become synonymous with the larger social system (or civilization).

It is useful to connect this twentieth-century language and knowledge against the backdrop of conservative thought from a century before. As asserted in James Henry Hammond's infamous 1858 "Cotton Is King" speech before the U.S. Senate:

> In all social systems there must be a class to do the menial duties, to perform the drudgery of life. That is, a class requiring but a low order of intellect and but little skill. Its requisites are vigor, docility, fidelity. Such a class you must have, or you would not have that other class which leads

progress, civilization, and refinement. It constitutes the very mud-sill of society and of political government; and you might as well attempt to build a house in the air, as to build either the one or the other, except on this mud-sill. Fortunately for the South, she found a race adapted to that purpose to her hand. A race inferior to her own, but eminently qualified in temper, in vigor, in docility, in capacity to stand the climate, to answer all her purposes. We use them for our purpose, and call them slaves. We found them slaves by the common "consent of mankind," which, according to Cicero, "lex naturae est." The highest proof of what is Nature's law.

Hammond offers a clear assessment of the ideas, policies, and material outcomes associated with slavery. What is revealed is an honest *longue durée* assessment of social conservatism based on a rigid social and class order justified through concepts such as "progress" and "civilization," the ontological gears of Michel-Rolph Trouillot's "North Atlantic universals."[24] Western civilization operates as a conceptual pivot offering cultural authority for conservatives such as Ellender and Simmons to base their claims: a possession of history aimed toward forestalling social equality toward African Americans in the twentieth century out of deference to a glorious past. For those anxious over the disruption of embedded hierarchies, the mobilization of Western civilization to attack the charges of social justice activists operated as an abstract, color-blind concept denoting and celebrating a white transnationalist vision of society under the cover of a *longue durée* embrace of modern and pre-modern thinkers who shaped the rhetorical foundations of Western thought.

The conservatism born out of the unstable racial and gendered constructs in the post–World War II era used the rhetorical weight of Western civilization—cleansed of its antagonisms—to reassert a defense of the status quo. Hierarchy within the existing social structure needed maintenance (as all social constructions do). In his 1948 book about the "dissolution of the West," conservative writer Richard M. Weaver offered an early postwar assessment of the clamor rippling through a world of decolonization and civil rights, where the normalcy of white supremacy increasingly became openly questioned after the defeat of the Nazis.[25] In his defense of "distinction and hierarchy," Weaver asserts:

> The most portentous general event of our time is the steady obliteration of those distinctions which create society. Rational society is a mirror of the logos, and this means that it has a formal structure which enables apprehension. The preservation of society is therefore directly linked with the recovery of true knowledge. . . . If society is something which can be understood, it must have structure; if it has structure, it must have hierarchy; against this metaphysical truth the declamations of the

> Jacobins break in vain. . . . Equality is a disorganizing concept in so far as human relationships mean order. It is order without a design; it attempts a meaningless and profitless regimentation of what has been ordered from time immemorial by the scheme of things.[26]

Equality, then, was a dangerous addition to the liberty and freedoms espoused by defenders of Western civilization—an irony still in motion in the twenty-first century. Of course, through their protest against creeping equality, conservatives implied that the very success of Western civilization rested on inequality and hierarchy—despite the rhetoric of "rights of man" and "all men are created equal." As such, one's position in the maelstrom of Western civilization determined one's possession of history. If one was near the top of the hierarchy, then one was able to deny the past centuries of human rights violations and systemic violence required to shape the present state of inequality one benefited from. From this position of authority, one could innocently assert truisms such as those espoused by one of Weaver's contemporary conservatives, Russell Kirk, whose *Program for Conservatives* (1954) stated the following:

> That some men are richer than others, and that some have more leisure than others, and that some travel more than others, and that some inherit more than others, and that some are educated more than others, is no more unjust, in the great scheme of things, than that some undeniably are handsomer or stronger or quicker or healthier than others. This complex variety is the breath of life to society, not the triumph of injustice. Poverty, even absolute poverty, is not an evil; it is not evil to be a beggar; it is not evil to be ignorant; it is not evil to be stupid. All these things are either indifferent, or else are occasions for positive virtue, if accepted with a contrite heart. What really matters is that we should accept the station to which "a divine tactic" has appointed us with humility and a sense of consecration.[27]

Kirk's possession of history and his power to summon this particular vision of the past allowed those seeking to halt the dismantling of historically unequal social or economic relationships to utilize the truisms of Western civilization—with a sprinkling of "divine" sanction—in their arguments to conserve the status quo. There would be no accounting for crimes against humanity, as the atrocities of settler colonialism and slavery disappear from discussion, allowing an untarnished Western civilization to set the terms of debate at the dawn of neoliberalism. More importantly, the possession of history would continue to pay its dividends.

The majority of Americans understood ideas of Western civilization and its American context through schooling, popular media, social interactions, holidays, nationalistic reverence, and, perhaps, the readings of Weaver and Kirk—or even from the apologetics of those defending the white mob murder of Black Americans. Examining the language of neoliberalism connects the conservatism of segregationists, Buckley, Weaver, and Kirk with the ideas of neoliberal economists. Culturally, this meeting facilitated a curious dialogue. The gaze back toward the era of free trade liberalism in the late 1800s and early 1900s simultaneously shines a light on the material outcomes of this era of industrial capitalism: Europe controlled 90 percent of the world through imperialism, and the United States was both constructing a Jim Crow apartheid state and wrapping up its 300-year ethnic-cleansing war against Native Americans. Postwar conservatism—reformed after the Great Depression shredded its economic credibility—continued to be skeptical of dismantling the hierarchies constructed through the *longue durée* of American history and were militantly intent on retaining this "traditional" order founded through settler colonialism, slavery, and patriarchy. A vital demographic needed to successfully implement conservative and neoliberal policies included the white middle- and working-class which prospered from the very set of welfare state policies condemned by neoliberals, conservatives, and anti–New Deal businessmen.[28] If middle- and working-class Americans could see their relationship with the federal government not as a beneficial one but an antagonistic one, then a new consensus could be built around dismantling the welfare state. Moreover, this dismantling did not necessarily remove government from the equation of economics. A crucial part of the neoliberal project included the construction of a protective, anti-democratic shell around economics: the welfare state would be reformed to suit the needs of business rather than providing a social safety net for the working- and middle class. Since most white working- and middle-class Americans grew up in a socially conservative society embracing laws, customs, and popular media portraying people of color as naturally inferior, legislated social equality was viewed with extreme unease. As 1950s and 1960s televised images recorded the brutalization of Black men, women, and children by white people seeking to halt the extension of social equality and broadcast these images into homes across the nation, the American white middle class confronted the very crisis haunting the Baldwin-Buckley debate: "Has the American Dream Been Achieved at the Expense of the American Negro?" The innocence of the postwar suburban paradise appeared to shatter, while, by the 1970s, the popular images of the 1950s had become camp.

Compounding the crisis was the Vietnam War, the rise of second-wave feminism, and the passage of civil rights legislation, pressing many white Americans into viewing the U.S. government through the prism of ideas espoused by conservatives and neoliberals: the welfare state unjustly interfered in the lives—the liberty—of Americans (and it unjustly interfered with the prosecution of the Vietnam War). More than this, once social equality became law through the series of civil rights legislation, the federal government was portrayed as unfairly aiding African Americans at the expense of white Americans.[29] In short, the anti–federal government language advocated by conservatives and neoliberals, which sought to reverse the New Deal redistribution of wealth downward, suddenly made sense to Americans whose lives—despite benefiting from the redistributionist policies of the welfare state—now appeared to be under siege from federal intervention they deemed unfair to hardworking white Americans. A new possession of history accompanied this revelation: federal intervention on behalf of white Americans melted away, a disavowed inconvenient history that planted the seeds of future ironies: as the conservative white children of the Jim Crow welfare state grew into retirement and demanded an end to "big government," this possession of history, the 1940s–1960s era of federal intervention, was labeled "when America was great."

The abstract, universal language and knowledge of Western civilization provided a key entry point as a way to tap into the sentiments of a white majority unsure about upsetting the *longue durée* American patriarchal, racial hierarchies. Indeed, as the public and private spheres increasingly found emancipation through civil rights and feminism, a rush to defend a concept of order—sometimes framed as "law and order," economic rights, anti-federal intervention, and by the 1980s, "family values"—became paramount.[30] Although measurement of this anxious white American sentiment is hardly an exact science, polls provide some insight into the various ways the postwar years reflected the *longue durée* legacies of settler colonialism and slavery and their accumulated habits of mind. When asked between the 1940s and 1950s if "Negroes are as intelligent as white people," the responses from whites and Blacks differed remarkably:

Table 2.1 "In general, do you think Negroes are as intelligent as white people—that is, can they learn just as well if they are given the same education (and training)?" (NORC, June 20, 1942; September 22, 1946; January 26 and April 20, 1956). From Hazel Gaudet Erskine, "The Polls: Race Relations," *Public Opinion Quarterly* 26, no. 1 (Spring 1962): 138.

	Yes	No	Don't Know
National Total	57%	37%	6%
Whites only			
June 1942	42%	48%	10%
May 1946	53%	40%	7%
January 1956	78%	19%	3%
Negroes only			
May 1946	92%	5%	3%

Although whites appeared to have less investment in the biological belief in Black inferiority, Cold War concerns within the long shadow of genocide connected to Nazi Germany might have helped dampen the respectability of overt racism—at least within the public sphere or in answers to pollsters. The national mood measured in these polls might also reflect the growing trend to *not appear racist* in the 1950s. Despite these shifts, racism still filtered through American society—from housing policies to popular culture to employment practices.[31] When asked if "most Negroes in the United States are being treated fairly or unfairly," answers from whites appeared to naturalize racial inequality by failing to recognize institutional racism at the same percentage Black Americans recognized it:

Table 2.2 "Do you think most Negroes in the United States are being treated fairly or unfairly?" (NORC, May 1944; May 1946; January 26, 1956). From Hazel Gaudet Erskine, "The Polls: Race Relations," *Public Opinion Quarterly* 26, no. 1 (Spring 1962): 139.

	Fairly	Unfairly	Don't Know
Whites only			
May 1946	66%	25%	9%
Negroes only			
May 1946	28%	66%	6%

In the 1950s, half of white adults did not believe "white students and Negro students should go to the same schools."[32] When asked if "a Negro family moved in next door to you," would you move?, 69 percent of white adults responded "yes."[33] This last question exemplified one of the critical elements of the culture war: the elimination of restricted housing measures *across the entire nation*. In California, Proposition 14 (1964)—which sought to nullify the Rumford Fair Housing Act of 1963 and legalize racial discrimination—united both white Democrats and Republicans, with polls showing a 58 percent bipartisan support.[34] It also provided Ronald Reagan with an early opportunity to color-blind his racial antagonistic appeals to white voters: "This has nothing to do with discrimination. It has to do with our freedom, our basic freedom."[35] White privilege in housing appeared to be the deal breaker for non-Southern whites extending civil rights to Black Americans—even for liberals. When asked, "Would you move if colored people came to live in great numbers in your neighborhood?," Gallup took note of white respondents' answers:

Table 2.3 "Would you move if colored people came to live in great numbers in your neighborhood?" (Gallup Poll). From Hazel Erskine, "The Polls: Negro Housing," *Public Opinion Quarterly* 31, no. 3 (Autumn 1967): 493.

	Yes, Definitely Move	Yes, Might Move	No, Would Not Move
1958			
North	45%	32%	23%
South	67%	21%	12%
National Total			
1963	49%	29%	22%
1965	40%	29%	31%
1966	39%	31%	30%
1967	40%	31%	29%

Between 1958 and 1963, the polls show a decline in "definitely" but a sustained 30 percent in the "might move" answer. If we understand the postwar trend of censuring overt displays of racism, we might contextualize the two columns of "yes" as a single answer, leading to an average of 70 percent "yes" answers through the mid-1960s as social equality legislation unfolded. As the authors of an article in 1981 noted, whites often faked not being prejudiced in polls, especially if the questions posed were readily seen as "old-fashioned racism" (school desegregation; having Black people come over to their home; keeping Black people out of white neighborhoods, and anti-miscegenation laws) versus the newer racism steeped in color-blind-coded racism surrounding housing and desegregation.[36] For conservatives, this was a godsend as they could frame issues for anxious Northern and Southern whites as a nonracist defense of property rights, states' rights, or discrimination against whites (especially regarding affirmative action or busing). Thus, the new color-blind racism allowed "any of their other opinions, beliefs, or actions that work to the detriment of blacks" as "not seen as prejudice; and since most white Americans either do not hold old-fashioned racist beliefs or they feel guilty about the ones they do hold, whites tend to think racism is a thing of the past. Hence, whites perceive the continuing efforts and demands of blacks as unjustified, while blacks see whites' resistance to these efforts as tangible proof of racism and hypocrisy, and the cycle of conflict continues."[37]

As a defense against contemporary intrusions into the postwar prosperity of the Jim Crow–era United States, conservatives like Buckley reformed the knowledge of the past by insulating it from post-1950s criticism. Most often, this took the form of discounting or disavowing assertions from spokesmen such as Baldwin that the legacy of the Atlantic slave system accounted for this ongoing antagonism in the present—including the still-used refrain, "my grandparents did not own slaves." At the same time, Buckley regenerated anti-Black antagonisms by infusing a new language cleansed of explicit racial designations with a less vulgar tone and rooted in the idea of different "cultures"—hence the use of the term Western civilization. A "'color-blind' strategy" summoned ideas of "cultural pathology" and "a lack of ethos"—what an earlier era simply called lazy, thieving, violent, and in need of direction or control—to account for the situation facing most African Americans in the 1960s.[38] For many white Americans, the old wine in new bottles underscored a continued sense that Black Americans were *still* not worthy of social equality. Or, as a leader of the Young Republicans declared in support for California Proposition 14, "Blacks 'haven't made themselves acceptable' for white neighborhoods" yet.[39]

In defending criticisms against Western civilization and the processes of modernity, performances such as Buckley's deployed *longue durée* historical projections to rhetorically justify structural inequalities between whites and Blacks in the present. Much like apologists of segregation, imperialism, genocide, colonialism, and slavery, those justifying a starkly unequal present rested their arguments on the possession of history rooted in the conceptual authority of Western civilization upon the common knowledge of American society. Highlighting how these sentiments wove through the ideas, and later policies, of neoliberals and their conservative allies presents a clearer picture of how our neoliberal era unfolded.

Market Freedoms and the Road (Back) to Laissez-Faire Economics

The origins and networks of neoliberalism stretch back to the transnational philosophical and economic circles of the 1920s and 1930s.[40] Dieter Plehwe characterizes neoliberalism as an evolving set of ideas, the product of a transnational historical "thought collective."[41] The concepts of neoliberalism surfaced in the work of Swedish economist Eli F. Heckscher—*Old and New Economic Liberalism* (1921)—while the first modern usage of the term *neoliberalism* appeared in 1925 in Swiss economist Hans Honegger's *Trends of Economic Ideas*.[42] An important seed included the Austrian school of economics, out of which Hayek arose from the tutelage of economist Ludwig von Mises.[43] Informed by the economic turmoil following World War I (especially regarding inflation), the Austrian school emphasized the role of money in the economy. Their conclusion: government intervention led to altering the "price mechanism," resulting in an unbalanced economy.[44] The Geneva school, on the other hand, sought to understand the business cycle through a project of economic data exchange.[45] A foundational premise for this project included: the "global economy was unknowable" and thus needed a type of structure allowing for the agency of global economics to be free from constraints—government intervention—and be allowed to naturally gravitate toward a rational equilibrium.[46] With the belief in an unknowable economy came another shift for neoliberal economists: an end to "a working faith in numbers," as "the use of numbers had become associated with those who believed in state action" in the 1930s.[47] Ironically, the neoliberal solution demanded an interventionist state guaranteeing no outside intervention in the economy.

Amid the European turmoil of the 1920s and 1930s, Hayek's neoliberal approach to economics clashed against the ideas of British economist John Maynard Keynes, particularly the latter's *The General Theory of Employment, Interest, and Money* (1936).[48] Hayek and Keynes would go on to frame the major economic debates defining twentieth-century economics. Nicholas Wapshott notes the basic logics of their theories: "Keynes believed that man had been placed in charge of his own destiny, while Hayek, with some reluctance, believed that man was destined to live by the natural laws of economics as he was obliged to live by all other natural laws."[49] In some ways, the debate suggested two realms of reality. From the Keynesian perspective, order arose from the balancing of social and economic worlds through human agency, with the unstable economic world regulated by the social-political world.[50] From Hayek's perspective, these realms operated outside the control of humans, existing as *a state of nature* where human interference—that is, regulation—within these quasi-spiritual realms would induce a level of disorder. Both lines of thought drew from the Enlightenment's rationalist thought and the economic science of the nineteenth century.[51] The policies of laissez-faire—meaning "allow to do"—economics informing neoliberalism, however, collided with the historical context of the 1930s.

In the wake of the Great Depression, public opinion veered away from a belief in laissez-faire economics as free market advocates struggled to convince a skeptical public that any policy leading the nation-state to interfere in the economy on behalf of working- and middle-class people was inimical to helping fix the economy. This argument proved difficult when a quarter of the population faced unemployment. The "free market" argument, moreover, trampled across the democratic voices of those who felt betrayed by the promises of Treasury Secretary Andrew Mellon's proto-supply-side economics, as well as the hesitancy of the Hoover administration to support "deficit-financed expenditures and easy monetary policies."[52] Troubled by the inability of the market to naturally rebuild itself, in late 1929 Herbert Hoover hesitantly called for public works money, a "no strike" pledge from organized labor, a loosened monetary policy from the Federal Reserve Board, and tariffs protecting agriculture.[53] Further inroads to federal intervention, such as expanding welfare, were deemed too extreme. As Ellis W. Hawley notes, conservative philosophy imagined too much federal intervention as undermining "the institutions essential to American freedom and progress."[54] For some, this logic led to both blaming the crash on too much government interference in the 1920s while simultaneously celebrating the "roaring" aspect of the 1920s as an example of what happens when capitalism is unfettered from the constraints of government.[55] These arguments about prosperity or federal overreach fail to account for the overall spread of growth in the 1920s, which hardly adhered to the laissez-faire promise: "a rising tide lifts all boats." The decade saw a 32 percent increase in productivity though only an 8 percent increase in wages.[56] Inequality rose substantially in the 1920s, with the top 10 percent drawing "45–50 percent of national income in the 1910s–1920s."[57] Hoover held fast to the conservative argument about self-help and adherence toward private charities over public relief and federal intervention, suggesting such actions would make government "master of [American] souls and thoughts."[58] At the same time, he did approve bailouts for Arkansas farmers' livestock ($45 million) while opposing "an additional $25 million to feed the starving farmers and their families."[59] For free market advocates, the aura of the market assumed its own agency as its "invisible hand" provided for the manipulation of goods and services—excepting livestock—outside the corrupting influences of bureaucrats. Viewed through the *longue durée*, the investment in the idea of the "invisible hand" regenerated a pre-Enlightenment view of "God's will" driving history, although this sentiment embraced the rational language of the Enlightenment. Whether it was "God's will" or the secular "invisible hand," it seemed both ideas operated more to buttress wealth and power than solve the instabilities of a market society. From this crucible of debate—along with the post-1932 U.S. government's response to the Depression—American neoliberalism took root.

Although one could theorize about the ideal state of the economy, the real world presented some complicated challenges. As a product of its time, neoliberalism blended the ideas of free markets with the changing needs of twentieth-century capitalism and, thus, was not just an update of classical liberalism.[60] Out of the momentum spurred by the work of Mises and Hayek, the term, neoliberalism, gained more frequent use in the 1930s—including the publication of Walter Lippmann's *(An Inquiry into the Principle of) The Good Society* in 1937. Echoing 1920s conservatism, "Lippmann's core message was the superiority of the market economy over state intervention," in obvious contrast to the Soviet Union and the prevailing logics developing out of the New Deal and the increasingly popularized economics developed by Keynes.[61] Although his work was celebrated by neoliberals, Lippmann was not blind to an ideology free from "the working faith in numbers."[62] Addressing the historical context of early twentieth-century industrial capitalism, Lippmann noted the oversight of conservatives and neoliberals: the lack of critique toward the "concentration of industrial power," and the collusion between industrialists and the nation-state to allow corporate concentration or monopolies.

> The concentration of control does not come from the mechanization of industry. It comes from the state, which began about a hundred years ago to grant to anyone who paid a nominal fee what had hitherto been a very special privilege. That was the privilege of incorporation with limited liability and perpetual succession. . . . For, without the privileges and immunities of the corporate form of economic organization and property tenure, the industrial system as we know it could not have developed and could not exist. So fundamentally true is this that we should do well to follow the suggestion of Messrs. Berle and Means and speak not of the capitalist system but of the corporate system. If that system exhibits a high degree of concentrated control, the cause is to be found not in the technic of production, but in the law.[63]

Lippmann's warning was dismissed, though his work was celebrated via the *Colloque Walter Lippmann*, an event held in Paris in 1938, out of which many of the attendees formed the neoliberal Mont Pèlerin Society almost ten years later.[64] Lippmann's ideas anticipated many of Hayek's, including a demand for serious revision of liberal theory using scientific methods.[65] For Hayek, the road to neoliberalism was a long-term project, aimed toward altering the fundamental way people viewed economics and its relationship to society and the state. It was a "battle of ideas," with the elite and "the active intelligentsia" being key points of struggle.[66] Slobodian describes Hayek's approach to the "long struggle" as mimicking the "example of socialists," who had "succeeded in shifting debates over time, thus capturing both public opinion and public power and making their vision reality."[67] This transnational conversation orbiting the evolving idea of neoliberalism included the coalescing of different theoretical approaches from different countries confronting both planned socialist philosophies as well as the welfare state.[68]

Within the United States, the rise of neoliberalism can be traced back to one institution: the Chicago school of economics.[69] "Joined at the hip from birth," the Chicago school and the Mont Pèlerin Society fostered a space in the United States for the development of a counterphilosophy against the Keynesian-inspired welfare state.[70] Here, American neoliberalism cast aside classical liberalism's critique of monopolies and large "concentrations" as stifling competition.[71] At the dawn of classical liberalism in the 1770s, Adam Smith sensed the volatility emerging with the growing concentration of capital and the growing pool of labor as cities filled with workers. He lamented the hypocrisy of "masters"—corporations, businessmen, monopolists, and so forth—whose charges of "labor combining" (i.e., workers organizing themselves against capital) reflected the very nature of the capitalist's own hidden activity:

> The masters . . . never cease to call aloud for the assistance of the civil magistrate, and the rigorous execution of those laws which have been enacted with so much severity against the combinations of servants, labourers, and journeymen. The workmen, accordingly, very seldom derive any advantage from the violence of those tumultuous combinations, which, partly from the interposition of the civil magistrate, partly from the superior steadiness of the masters, partly from the necessity which the greater part of the workmen are under of submitting for the sake of present subsistence, generally end in nothing, but the punishment or ruin of the ringleaders.[72]

For Smith, the relationship between capitalism and the nation-state was vital. Bound by the "rule of law," government protects private property and contracts, with the threat of state violence forcing workers to settle out of the necessity to subsist, with the leaders of workers submitting to the collective punishment of the nation-state protecting private property. Thus, different historical contexts insulated the concepts of classical liberalism. While the ideas of late 1800s classical liberals arose out of the environment of free trade imperialism (nestled in the coercive and racist structures of modernity's processes), neoliberals emerged through the material outcome of the internationalism and imperialism of industrial capitalism, including increased capital concentration, monopolies, and oligopolies in the 1920s and 1930s.[73] This moment of normalized concentration allowed the ethereal concept of the "invisible hand" to disavow the role of the state—and ignore the nuances of Smith's and Lippmann's distrust of concentration—as American neoliberalism conveniently shrugged off these warnings.

Funded largely by the conservative Volker Fund and the Olin Foundation, early American neoliberalism stressed the notion of a "freedom" that liberated corporations from the sets of regulations established during the New Deal and the welfare state after World War II.[74] Just as classical liberalism needed the nation-state to create the conditions for free trade—from imperialism to gunboat diplomacy—neoliberalism as outlined by the Chicago school admitted that its political program would only be successful if it was constructed *via the state*.[75] As Jamie Peck notes, "Neoliberalism, in its various guises, has always been about the capture and reuse of the state, in the interests of shaping a pro-corporate, freer-trading 'market order.'"[76] Neoliberals would redesign the laws of the state "and other institutions to protect the market."[77] Thus, rather than the "minimalist night-watchman state of the classical liberal tradition," neoliberalism's restructuring of the state acted to "impose the ideal form of society, which they conceive to be in pursuit of their very curious icon of pure freedom."⁷⁸ In his 1951 paper, "Neoliberalism and Its Prospects," Milton Friedman highlighted this crucial role of the state in constructing the system.⁷⁹ Friedman notes, "The state would police the system, establish conditions favorable to competition and prevent monopoly, provide a stable monetary framework, and relieve acute misery and distress."⁸⁰

Despite Friedman's assertion of preventing monopoly to protect free market competition, a salient aspect of American neoliberalism was its very indifference to the scale of market power between multinational big businesses and small businesses. The trend toward accepting the expansive role of multinationals bloated from the wartime government-interventionist economy and postwar rebuilding became a norm for both neoliberals as well as those defending the regulatory welfare state.⁸¹ This indifferent relationship to capital concentration helped establish a new moral code for measuring the scale of business. Rather than asserting an unfairness or unjustness toward large companies that dominate an industry, one used the rubric of efficiency or inefficiency as a measurement of whether a company was too large.⁸² Abstracted as such, one could now condemn the policies of the welfare state as restraining economic liberty—and thus personal freedom—regardless of the size of organizations or their ability to dominate markets. This new frame of debate spanned the spectrum of liberal to conservative, shaping American policy through the twentieth century. As neoliberals dismissed the criticisms of classical liberals regarding the ability of large companies to dominate markets, the articulation of their philosophy assumed that monopolies and the postwar conglomerate movement exemplified a natural state of capitalism and should be free from government interference. Discounting Lippmann's assertion of the nation-state's role in fomenting a culture of incorporation leading to concentration, a cursory history of the corporation in American life quickly outlines how these large organizations gravitated toward mergers, trusts, and monopolies to negotiate economic turbulence and secure markets in the late 1800s and early 1900s.⁸³ When one adds the era's rhetoric of social Darwinism, large concentrations appeared to *naturally* evolve into even larger concentrations.

The neoliberal break from classical liberalism largely stemmed from the reactionary nature of neoliberalism and its funding connection to businessmen and organizations struggling against the growing welfare state.⁸⁴ The influence of the Volker Fund, asserts Rob Van Horn, cannot be underlined enough in this reformulation of classical liberalism's hostility toward monopolies: "The Volker Fund went so far as to threaten to eject [Aaron] Director from his leadership role in the FMS [Free Market Study, a University of Chicago initiative] because the Volker Fund refused to accept certain tenets of classical liberalism."[85] In short, the Volker Fund—an early right-wing charitable foundation formed in the 1930s—dismissed the inconvenient elements of classical liberalism infringing on the rights of the corporate community to expand and dominate markets. William Davies asserts, "In many ways, the story of post-1945 neoliberal critiques is of its mutation from a *justification for markets* to a *justification for business*, where the former represents a check on public economic planning, but the latter produces freedoms for private economic planning."[86] Although initially critical of monopolies and large corporations in 1947, Friedman, too, had changed course by the early 1950s, despite his concerns in "Neo-Liberalism and Its Prospects."[87] For Friedman, private monopolies were more favorable than public monopolies, and suggested that deregulated free trade competition would stifle a monopoly's power.[88]

In 1947, Hayek, with a young Friedman and other like-minded academics, formed the Mont Pèlerin Society, representing "the inception of what is now commonly referred to as neoliberalism."[89] The organization's founding statement's pro–classical liberalism and anti-state views toward the market economy was aimed at communist countries as well as welfare states like the New Deal United States. The group, a prototype of the conservative think tank, also hinted at what neoliberalism would become after the 1960s. Their economic worldview drew justification from the weight of the grand authority attached to Western civilization and its attending processes of modernity. Using this possession of history, their assertions challenged the array of post–World War II issues, such as multiculturalism, decolonization, and the social equality of historically marginalized peoples. The 1947 statement read:

> Even that most precious possession of Western Man, freedom of thought and expression, is threatened by the spread of creeds which, claiming the privilege of tolerance when in the position of a minority, seek only to establish a position of power in which they can suppress and obliterate all views but their own.... The group [the Mont Pèlerin Society] holds that that these developments have been fostered by the growth of a view of history which denies all absolute moral standards and by the growth of theories which question the desirability of the rule of law. It holds further that they have been fostered by a decline of belief in private property and the competitive market; for without the diffused power and initiative associated with these institutions it is difficult to imagine a society in which freedom may be effectively preserved.[90]

The authors assert their claim of a timeless order driven by Western Man—the white agent of Western civilization—that has progressed through the centuries by adhering to freedom of thought and expression, superior moral standards, and adherence to the rule of law and the rights of property. In imagining this genealogy, we see the disavowal of the policies and material outcomes of the processes of modernity bestowed on "Western Man" at the expense of non-Europeans and women. Untroubled by the colonialism, imperialism, slavery, and the often-genocidal acts shaping the very meanings and material wealth of those nations within the Western civilization fold, the statement helps us understand the anchoring logic that silences the crimes of the West as it *became* the West, while simultaneously establishing a field of common sense in which nonelites—ordinary people—could identify with universal-sounding words such as *freedom of thought and expression*, *moral standards*, and the *rule of law*. Echoing Buckley's concerns, the statement also underlines a reactionary conservative view toward the unsettling of the social order amid the Great Depression and World War II and the rise of social democratic welfare states: (1) the so-called end-of-civilization fears (noted in various contexts above) connect neoliberalism to the fear of upsetting particular entrenched hierarchies (Western, white, male, property owning); (2) the "end of civilization" trope is also set against the very policies of redistribution that the Mont Pèlerin Society critiques, ironically resulting in the loss of the economic freedom *gained* by white working- and middle-class people who actually benefited from the redistributionist policies of the welfare state.

Using Western civilization as a justification, these ideas buttressed a particular understanding of the "rule of law." The rule of law, an ostensibly objective and neutral component of nature, allowed for the active construction of a free market society, where the rules of the game are outlined by the state through "legal procedures" designed to protect private property.[91] Along with racial and gendered contradictions infecting the history of the "rule of law" in the United States—from laws against miscegenation to institutional gender discrimination to Jim Crow—this deep tradition failed to recognize the economic disparities related to the concentration of capital taking place as industrial capitalism's monopoly and oligopoly tendencies foreclosed the existence of truly free markets in the wake of mergers.[92] With concentrated capital, one could buy the "rule of law." Echoing Lippmann's critique, George Orwell also noted this silence toward the realities of concentration in his review of Hayek's *Road to Serfdom* (1944) in the 1940s: "Professor Hayek... does not see, or will not admit, that a return to 'free' competition means for the great mass of people a tyranny probably worse, because more irresponsible, than that of the State. The trouble with competitions is that somebody wins them. Professor Hayek denies that free capitalism necessarily leads to monopoly."[93] Finally, the 1947 Mont Pèlerin statement imagines an ideal world innocent of the malevolence unleashed by modernity's policies and material outcomes guiding the rise of Western civilization. Through this disavowal, neoliberals could suggest capitalism was under siege, with those supporting the welfare state being labeled socialists.

For Friedman and Hayek, then, government should only intervene in civil society through the "rule of law." Notes Hayek, "Stripped of all technicalities, this means that government in all its actions is bound by rules fixed and announced beforehand—rules which make it possible to foresee with fair certainty how the authority will use its coercive powers in given circumstances and to plan one's individual affairs on the basis of this knowledge."[94] As a golden rule for an appropriate relationship between government and the economy, the "rule of law" would deny government the ability to redistribute the wealth of a nation for purposes other than defense, policing, or fire prevention (all organizations directed to protect property). In a society premised on institutional social inequality such as Jim Crow America, the federal government could only intervene to enforce constitutional laws safeguarding white supremacy or patriarchal containment of women—both concepts conservatives believed to be natural. Hence, the federal government should not interfere with the right of states (particularly the South) to enact these laws of inequality.

In the aftermath of World War II, it appeared to conservatives that democracy needed to be reined in at the very moment it was slowly being extended to historically marginalized peoples. Even though the wealthy and big business may use their wealth to shape laws aiding their economic interests, as the history of wealth and politics makes clear, when working- and middle-class people attempted a similar feat in their support of the welfare state, the political act becomes a deviation from the norms of Western civilization and economic order.[95] For Hayek, the unspoken inevitability of economic concentration in industrial capitalism acted, not as a component of business-state interactions but as a part of nature: "It cannot be denied that the Rule of Law produces economic inequality."[96]

Karl Polanyi foresaw this conception of freedom espoused by the trends leading to the Mont Pèlerin Society in his work *The Great Transformation*—published in 1944, the same year as *The Road to Serfdom*. Here, Polanyi pointed out what he considered the two types of freedoms in the twentieth-century market economy: (1) the freedom of speech, association, and choice of employment (among others) and (2) the freedom to exploit others under the veil of the market economy. Criticizing the nascent neoliberal model, he writes:

> Planning and control [Keynesian economics] are being attacked as a denial of freedom. Free enterprise and private ownership are declared to be essentials of freedom. No society built on other foundations is said to deserve to be called free. The freedom that regulation creates is denounced as unfreedom; the justice, liberty and welfare it offers are

decried as a camouflage of slavery.... This means the fullness of freedom for those whose income, leisure, and security need no enhancing, and a mere pittance of liberty for the people, who may in vain attempt to make use of their democratic rights to gain shelter from the power of the owners of property.[97]

Conjuring the very set of projections Polanyi noted above, Hayek's career-defining book, *The Road to Serfdom*, offered an economic theory counter to the ideas of Keynes and others he deemed "socialists" (those who advocated government intervention into market economies). In his possession of history, Hayek fashioned a grand narrative through the cultural authority of Western civilization. As this chapter's epigraph suggests, Hayek's need for justifying free markets utilized *longue durée* paths tying his positive vision for a free market social philosophy to the well-known minds shaping the genealogy of Western civilization. His construction of a morality in support of his economic vision of pursuing liberty through free markets attracted many supporters in the United States, particularly among those Americans fuming at the rise of the New Deal coalition and the redistributionist policies directly undermining older class hierarchies.[98] *The Road to Serfdom* contextualized American businessmen's struggle against the New Deal as a struggle to uphold the *longue durée* legacies of Western civilization.[99] In short, businessmen could portray themselves as victims of state tyranny and heroic defenders of humanity.

Hayek framed the struggle over market virtues as an ontological struggle between Western civilization and the chaotic alternative of state intervention. This was the spiritual war Gingrich spoke of, ultimately leading to apocalypse if the neoliberal-conservative movement failed to dismantle the welfare state.[100] Hayek's use of Western civilization and its zero-sum argument reflected the dilemma facing conservatives and budding neoliberals: they were struggling to negotiate the then-discredited culture and economics of turn-of-the-century laissez-faire capitalism into an ideology of freedom and liberty for an already economically stable postwar United States. This was obviously an uphill battle, as the discredited economic philosophy stumbled against its association with the Great Depression and the backdrop of the evolving mixed economy that, thanks to the success of World War II, legitimized government economic planning under the banner of the "good war."

On the other hand, a set of unintended consequences were about to aid the struggle of conservatives and neoliberals. Although the backdrop of the Cold War pressed the nation to the right, effectively marginalizing left-wing voices in American society, the Cold War also surprisingly aided the civil rights movement. The Soviet Union cast a glaring light upon the hypocrisy of a free nation steeped in the traditions of Jim Crow segregation, pressing the federal government to intervene into states refusing to recognize social equality legislation.[101] Foreign policy, then, helped open the door to the breakup of the postwar consensus by removing embarrassing domestic laws undermining relationships abroad, resulting in the social fractures caused by legislated social equality. The domestic unrest related to the Vietnam War provided yet another opening. This perfect storm bolstered the return of conservatism. Those critical of government intervention in social equality found common cause with neoliberals and conservatives who sold a more receptive package embodied by the colorblind rubric of free market capitalism: state's rights and resistance to federal oversight—in business or personal preference—*was* liberty.[102]

In *The Road to Serfdom*, Hayek awkwardly walked another *longue durée* path: the white supremacist assumptions woven through the conception of Western civilization. The still-lingering scent of the eugenic and the distinctly northern European brand of white supremacy—the ideal of the Nordic, and the basis for the dominant "race" in American nationalism—permeated Hayek's language in a similar manner as it had with turn-of-the-century apologists of ethnic cleansing, such as President Theodore Roosevelt.[103] Echoing his mentor Ludwig von Mises, Hayek suggested that a "change in moral values" supporting "collectivism" was rooted in the dismissal of the "virtues" of "Anglo-Saxons":[104]

> The virtues these people possessed—in a higher degree than most other people, excepting only a few of the smaller nations, like the Swiss and the Dutch—were independence and self-reliance, individual initiative and local responsibility, the successful reliance on voluntary activity, noninterference with one's neighbor and tolerance of the different and queer, respect for custom and tradition, and a healthy suspicion of power and authority. Almost all the traditions and institutions in which democratic moral genius has found its most characteristic expression, and which in turn have modeled the national character and the whole moral climate of England and America, are those which the progress of collectivism and its inherently centralistic tendencies are progressively destroying.[105]

The "sharp break" away from Western civilization and Anglo-Saxon virtues by the rise of the mixed economy rhetorically operated as a symbol of spiritual warfare; a market advocacy jihad against government intervention. In this sanitized version of Western civilization's linear path toward free markets and individualism across the millennia, Hayek revealed his possession of history: (1) his debates about contemporary economics continued to submit a supernatural quality to the operation of markets, absent the role of historical relationships between the nation-state and capitalism, capital concentration, and the overall intimate connection between economics, politics, and culture; (2) this spiritual support for noninterference from democratically controlled government institutions found rhetorical strength through the *longue durée* rhetoric of liberty emanating from the processes of modernity, despite the inherently unequal and undemocratic nature these processes embodied in relation to women and people of color since (at least) the 1500s; (3) the evoked qualities of self-reliance and individualism find themselves clearly quarantined from their material counterparts: European expansion, colonialism, settler colonialism, and the Atlantic slave system (similarly, the Atlantic slave system was quarantined from the history of celebratory discussions of the Enlightenment up through the twentieth century).[106]

Hayek's possession of history remained a key to his *longue durée* argument. In his chapter on "The Common Sense of Progress" in *The Constitution of Liberty* (1960), the previous centuries of coercion, subjection, and enslavement continue to be silenced in their role in the rise of the West: "Although the fact that the people of the West are today so far ahead of the others in wealth is in part the consequence of a greater accumulation of capital, it is mainly the result of their more effective utilization of knowledge. There can be little doubt that the prospect of the poorer, 'undeveloped' countries reaching the present level of the West is very much better than it would have been, had the West not pulled so far ahead."[107] Along with downplaying the global violence clearing the way for the rise of the West, the rhetorical use of the *longue durée* operated as a device marking any deviation from the cited logics of Western civilization as an inevitable venture to ruin.

Defenders of Hayek continue to redeem these concepts through a similar devotion to the idea that markets somehow operate through a knowledge transcending mere mortal appreciation, often denying or explaining away the violence complicating the celebration of capitalism. In his chapter on Hayek, historian Jerry Z. Muller writes, "The competitive market was not merely about exchanging information; it also served to create new knowledge about the potential use of resources. For discovering which goods are 'valueable' to the other members of society and how much value is actually placed on them is not something that can be known with certainty in advance."[108] Despite an uncritical explanation of the radical inequality inherent via the human agency required to broker a relationship between information, knowledge, and the economy, this enchanted hand of the market is the spiritual lifeblood of the ideas of Hayek and others within the "neoliberal thought collective."[109] In many ways, it is what humans thousands of years ago would call "magic," the will of the gods, or, just simply, the will of God—there is human agency involved, but the outcomes are imagined to be directed by otherworldly forces.

The seductiveness of these ideas leads to conclusions about capitalism clearly discredited by a glimpse at the history of modernity. When market optimism bleeds, it usually trickles down: "Though capitalism is sometimes blamed for racism, sexism, and chauvinism," writes Muller, "the most sophisticated analysts (whether of the left or the right) have noted that the market tends to break down barriers between groups."[110] In the twenty-first century, many groups of people across the global marketplace, unfortunately, continue to find themselves still violently marginalized in a global capitalism conceptually imagined, in part, by the legacy of Hayek and Friedman.[111]

Neoliberalism, the Individual, and Culture War

Informing Barry Goldwater's message of the reinvigoration of free market conservatism during the 1964 election campaign, the publication of Milton Friedman's *Capitalism and Freedom* (1962) became the harbinger of post-1960s neoliberalism.[112] A series of lectures from the late 1950s connecting unfettered capitalism with individual freedom, Rob Van Horn and Philip Mirowski characterize *Capitalism and Freedom* as the "corporate neoliberal version of *Road to Serfdom*."[113] Much like Hayek, Friedman's classic work deployed the ideal of Western civilization to imagine a relationship between the economy, the nation-state, and the ideas of Western civilization freed from the legacies of exploitation. Discounting the history of nineteenth-century American business and its influence on the political system (whether state or federal), Friedman asserts, "Economic arrangements are important because of their effect on the concentration or dispersion of power. The kind of economic organization that provides economic freedom directly, namely, competitive capitalism, also promotes political freedom because it separates economic power from political power and in this way enables the one to offset the other."[114] Friedman's assumption, of course, bears a normalized Eurocentric, white men–only characterization of historical reality.

Friedman's possession of history is an ideal, imagining only the abstract relationships between markets and white men (Black men could not obtain "political freedom" through "competitive capitalism"), while also ignoring the brutal class conflict (from workers to farmers) characterizing American history, Jim Crow legislation's effect on both white and Black employment, and patriarchy's effect on men and women's employment opportunities.[115] Friedman's rhetoric bolsters an American innocence toward racial and gendered antagonisms, and rescues American freedom and liberty and its connection to Western civilization from the harsh judgment of history. Much like Hayek in the epigraph, Friedman summons a *longue durée* characterization of the connection between nineteenth-century capitalism and freedom, asserting, "historical evidence speaks with a single voice on the relation between political freedom and a free market. I know of no example in time or place of a society that has been marked by a large measure of political freedom, and that has not also used something comparable to a free market to organize the bulk of economic activity."[116] For this to be a statement of truth, the coercive features of settler colonialism, the afterlife of the Atlantic slave system, the concentration of capital spurring the labor movement and populism, and patriarchy need silencing—let alone the scientific racism driving the imperialist, free trade era of laissez-faire capitalism of the late nineteenth and early twentieth centuries. Like a chessboard, one's positionality in the realm of Western civilization determined the freedom of movement, with the unequal distribution of movement options dampening one's ability to enjoy freedom or avoid oppression. To elude this visible history, neoliberals and their conservative allies emphasized the Enlightenment's ideal of abstract individuality versus the material reality of collectives protected or targeted by racial designations. Moreover, abstract individuality silenced the systemic role of white male supremacy in guiding the freedom of movement across the chessboard.

As the welfare state subsidies toward white working and middle classes began dissolving in the 1970s, the decades-old neoliberal-conservative emphasis on individualism arrived as a crucial philosophical concept targeting both the dismantling of the Jim Crow welfare and the disavowal of its white nationalist collective nature. This reawakened sense of color-blind individualism found renewed meaning among white folks who, for the first time in the history of the nation, were legislatively forced into social equality with people of color and women: the nation's promise of "all men are created equal" came due for the greatest generation, the silent generation, and the baby boomers. The polls cited above underline the level of anxiety related to the full deregulation of inequality. From a systemic, *longue durée* perspective, the gut-level reaction to social equality felt "wrong," a deviation away from the tradition of liberty. For those living in white suburbs, individualism equated to keeping African Americans out of their community—a sentiment fueling the national swing right as these voters sought to "punish the liberals" for interfering with segregation (particularly on display during the Boston school busing crisis).[117]

Although its disavowed or unacknowledged in most discussions of economic history, the racial aspect of American pronouncements of "individualism" in defense of the privileged is not to be underestimated. Cheryl Harris notes how this deep American identity and position in society has always rested on "the valorization of whiteness as treasured property in a society structured on racial caste".[118]

> In ways so embedded that it is rarely apparent, the set of assumptions, privileges, and benefits that accompany the status of being white have become a valuable asset that whites sought to protect and that those who passed sought to attain.... Whites have come to expect and rely on these benefits, and over time these expectations have been affirmed, legitimated, and protected by the law. Even though the law is neither uniform nor explicit in all instances, in protecting settled expectations based on white privilege, American law has recognized a property interest in whiteness that, although unacknowledged, now forms the background against which legal disputes are framed, argued, and adjudicated.[119]

In short, individualism in the United States historically upheld male whiteness as its normative anchor, an invisible standard underscoring the universality of American or Western civilization. This ontological sense of the world operated in much the same manner as the gendered and racialized image of the benevolent "settler," implying the right of white men to "discover" territory occupied by non-white groups and victoriously claim it in the name of progress or Western civilization. Indeed, the mythic "Promethean self-made man"—or the "autonomous selfhood"—in which individualism has been imagined throughout American history nestled neatly into the industrial capitalist age, including "its most forthright formulation in the economic theories spawned by classical liberalism."[120] Thriving through the era of scientific racism up through the 1920s, individualism projected the very essence of the American success story. In its disavowing of the coercive structures protecting white male entitlement—especially the legislative protections toward white male liberty, including the Naturalization Act of 1790, The Dred Scott Decision of 1857, or *Plessy v. Ferguson of 1896*—the privileges and protections of individualized whiteness found insulation through the "rule of law" comprising civil society and the nation-state, all historically dominated by propertied white men.

Propelled by the delusion of white supremacy and anti-Blackness, an irony smothers the evolution of postwar individualism, the welfare state, and neoliberalism. The initial barrier for the arguments of neoliberals and conservatives between the 1930s and 1960s lay in the policies of the Jim Crow welfare state and its successful construction of a prosperous white working and middle class (despite some white people left behind by these policies).[121] As individuals, the welfare state primarily allotted white people with economic opportunity, the "family wage," housing, and access to the American dream.[122] To sync with the historical legacy of American individualism, however, the collective aspects of the welfare state (its regulations and redistribution of wealth) were downplayed against the national security rhetoric of the Cold

War: a struggle against the collectivism of the Soviet Union.[123] While subsidized by the welfare state, the notion of rugged individualism—scattered culturally through Western films, crime thrillers, and other forms of popular culture—framed the success of the white working and middle classes. Federal intervention on behalf of white men vanished, obscured by the giant shadow of Cold War individualism. Once African Americans and other people of color gained legislated social equality, conservatives discovered their successful rhetorical path: federal spending on people of color would be framed as a collective redistribution of wealth coming at the expense of white people and their rugged individualism (an extension of the post-1930s argument of the wealthy: redistribution of wealth came at the expense of the rich).[124] The late 1960s white "silent majority" greeted conservative calls for liberty, equality, and less government interference enthusiastically.[125] Despite decades of federal intervention through housing, defense, and infrastructure spending, the white working- and middle-classes shifted to the right in the wake of social equality legislation, slowly voting away many of the redistributive elements of the welfare state that contributed to the environment in which white people could fully express their individualism. The concept of a "golden age" coincided with the unfolding conjuncture as the 1960s became the 1970s, resulting in a curious memory. On the one hand, the memory of simpler times gained popularity, depicting a pre-1960s era when white men were free of economic competition from women and people of color, including the memory of economic security rooted in full employment and good wages (i.e., the "family wage"). On the other hand, the memory of the federal intervention demanded to make this happen found itself safely warehoused in academia. For the majority of people, the age of American social democracy silently dissolved into air.

Cultivated by Richard Nixon on the road to his 1968 victory, the rhetorical strategy of the "silent majority"—or "the Southern strategy"—sought an imagined community made of the white working and middle classes who felt overwhelmed by the upheavals of the 1960s, especially the disturbances questioning racial and gendered hierarchies.[126] In that same year, Harold Cruse noted the future: "White America has inherited a racial crisis that it cannot handle and is unable to create a solution for it that does not do violence to the collective white American racial ego."[127] With the weight of the past bearing down on the reality of legislated social equality, conservatives produced the appropriate adhesive conjoining the culture war with the language of neoliberalism: individualism, liberty, and their genealogical connection to Western civilization. The concept of the silent majority focused "on people's resentments," allowing Nixon—along with other conservatives and neoliberals to create a political space for this demographic to be viewed as innocent victims of government overreach and its unfair attack on their individualism and liberty.[128] Perlstein notes, "Nixon made political capital of a certain experience of humiliation: the humiliation of having to defend values that seemed to you self-evident, then finding you had no words to defend them, precisely because they seemed self-evident. Nixon gave you the words. 'A great many quiet Americans have become committed to answers to social problems that preserve personal freedom,' he said. 'As this silent center has become a part of the new alignment, it has transformed it from a minority into a majority.'"[129] Characterizing the literal majority of the United States into a "minority" under siege proved to be a brilliant maneuver, as any action toward groups disrupting "self-evident" truths, such as white male entitlement and privilege, could be framed as a righteous defense of one's hard work, one's rugged individualism toward achieving the American dream. The sentiment seemed familiar: violent antagonism toward Native Americans found justification through the rhetoric of defending the settler family; and the freedom to lynch Black people was rooted in protecting white womanhood, an individual right celebrated by the segregationist Ellender. Indeed, Buckley's counterattack against Baldwin's criticisms of the American dream becomes the "silent majority's" defense. Humiliation in the face of social equality legislation renewed innocence, as the court decisions and legislation came from the interventionist federal government: the "silent majority," who were the primary recipients of the redistributionist welfare state, now viewed government intervention as betraying *their* civil rights by unfairly allowing people of color access to spaces and institutions designed specifically and traditionally for white Americans through the logic of white supremacy. Furthermore, the innocence of American individualism reinforced the disavowal of the legacies of racial and gendered violence buttressing the Jim Crow welfare state, let alone the ideological and material foundations of Western civilization.

Friedman's *Capitalism and Freedom* helped shape the reception of this renewed emphasis on individual freedom, as his once marginal thoughts now cohered with the anxieties of the silent majority: the enlarged New Deal state had concentrated too much power into the hands of government, becoming "a threat to freedom."[130] As the lecture was written in the mid-1950s, precisely the same moment when the civil rights movement started challenging institutional racism, one may safely assume that the "freedom" Friedman speaks of wholly belonged to those traditionally envisioned as having inalienable rights to the full fruits of citizenship: those classified as "white," and predominantly male. Government intervention on behalf of minorities and against the wishes or market desires of whites appeared as a threat to free institutions—and the liberty to choose. Friedman's thoughts on the civil rights movement hardly veered from this attitude.

Friedman condemned government interference in de jure segregation, writing that "fair employment practice commissions" bent on countering discrimination via religion, color, or race are a direct threat to the "freedom of individuals to enter into voluntary contracts with one another."[131] Friedman's conservatism held firm in the maintenance of the cultural-economic relationship characterizing U.S. capitalism under the Jim Crow/de facto segregation schemes. Friedman's ideas of freedom and the individual obviously disavowed the racial dictatorship and gendered exclusions cultivated through the processes of modernity. Skeptical of removing or even questioning these U.S. traditions, Friedman added quotation marks to "discrimination" in *Capitalism and Freedom*, implying that the word was merely an allegation and not based on evidence—further buttressing the white reader's presumed innocence in the *longue durée* practices of discrimination on the behalf of whiteness. The contours of this logic haunted conservative arguments and criticisms of the 1964 Civil Rights Act—from Goldwater to Reagan—including the racial conservatism of Buckley and James Kilpatrick's defense of segregation.[132]

Discrimination under the guise of markets found new legitimacy amid civil rights legislation, however. Neoliberal arguments highlighted market relations as the ultimate guide to freedom—Hayek's market as "information processor"—at precisely the same moment old forms of de jure exclusion collapsed after centuries of eluding constitutional censure.[133] The conjuncture between the development of neoliberal thought and the dismantling of the Jim Crow welfare state via civil rights legislation can be viewed as one of the earliest gestures toward systemic deregulation. On the one hand, the civil rights movement and legislation represented the legal reform of the racist and sexist structures guiding American society *and* economy; on the other hand, the rise of neoliberalism against the backdrop of civil rights reform provided neoliberals and conservatives with the language of freedom from coercive tyranny. Ironically, conservatives also embraced the color-blind rhetoric of civil rights activists such as Martin Luther King Jr. to innocently argue for a society based on content of character and not skin color as legalized white supremacy confronted dismantlement.

A few outcomes become apparent through this historical moment. First, the deregulation of civil rights represented not just a reform of social relationships but, crucially, a deregulation of economic-cultural designations denoting values measured through ideas of race: white skilled workers earned more than Black skilled workers (if, of course, someone of African descent was allowed into a union apprenticeship program). With civil rights legislation, this informal-formal relationship is ostensibly removed in the name of social equality; for business, the blending of the two previously segregated pools of labor—now also including women—created an ostensibly color-blind workforce, while the immense expansion of wage workers helped squeeze wages down at the same moment blue-collar jobs increasingly disappeared across the 1970s.[134] Added to the erosion of wages, the *longue durée* social construction of race would continue to act as a roadblock to solidarity *between racial and gender groups* as racial distrust disrupted organization drives; in the meantime, politicians associated with labor concerns were seen by the conservative white working class as only working on behalf of minorities to take *their* jobs.[135] In short, the 300-year aftermath of Bacon's rebellion continued to prove useful for the white economic elite.[136]

Although the removal of legislated racial hierarchies among the working class was hardly a conscious policy of neoliberal thinkers, the conjuncture of the civil rights movement and the ascension of neoliberal and conservative alternatives to the welfare state nevertheless intimately converge with a core tenet of neoliberalism: "a project of taking measures and principles from the marketplace, and using these to perform judgements across social and political spheres, including the state itself."[137] As the United States entered an era of legislated social equality, large-scale structural policies directed to correct centuries of inequalities tied to wealth or access to employment opportunities shriveled to half-hearted affirmative action policies which were immediately attacked by conservatives as reverse discrimination. The centuries-old momentum of racism and sexism pressed forward as resentments amid the collapse of the white labor movement in the 1970s found a voice in a rejuvenated conservatism long-practiced in the art of racial and gendered scapegoating.

In some ways, the deregulation of race proved fruitful for the allegiance of white working and middle classes, particularly men, who were most negatively affected by civil rights reforms. Discrimination could still influence social and economic relationships in the color-blind world of the post–civil rights era, where access to the full fruits of the American dream demanded capital and education, but also the enduring social connections based on prior access to opportunities before the civil rights era. Once free of the overt policies of the Jim Crow welfare state, the age of color-blindness and social equality legislation permitted a "born again" rugged individualism to flourish, now innocent of institutional racism based on white group identity, allowing decades of white male affirmative action to dissolve into the asphalt surfacing the road to neoliberalism. Conservative policies downplaying and ignoring civil rights violations—institutionalized by the Reagan administration—helped disavow ongoing discrimination as well.[138] As John McConahay et al. noted above, for whites in the 1970s and 1980s, racism was a thing of the past.[139] Accordingly, Friedman's abstract model of *Capitalism and Freedom* gained a wider, more receptive audience.

Business Week's review of *Capitalism and Freedom* illustrates the clear break between the dominance of the liberal consensus and the ascension of neoliberal ideas into the realm of American common sense.[140] Calling Friedman a "genuine radical" and his ideas "an extreme program," the magazine equated his philosophy to Adam Smith and the "hidden hand."[141] The charge of radicalism stemmed from the philosophical nature of Friedman's economic theories, equating economic freedom with political freedom. A brief description of the liberal consensus by *Business Week* underscores the challenges facing Friedman's neoliberalism: "These doctrines are virtually the antitheses of the ones that have dominated U.S. monetary and fiscal policy for the last 30 years. To most American economists, the Depression of the 1930s demonstrated once and for all that capitalism, whatever its other virtues, is inherently unstable. Since then they have been seeking the best ways for government to correct that instability and thus promote full employment and growth."[142] Listing the sets of institutions Friedman sought to privatize—from National Parks to the postal system—*Business Week* noted that there would be pain in surrendering to "the ruthless rule of impersonal market forces," but the economist saw these changes as being "in the public's best interests in the long run—and anyway, it's freedom, not economic security, that counts" for the neoliberal.[143] Friedman's fellow economist Theodore W. Schultz asserted at the time, "Some of Friedman's policy proposals are nonsense. But he is one of the great minds now at work in economics—and a man certain to be remembered 50 years from now when most of us will be forgotten."[144] Although dismissive of Friedman's radicalism, the winds appeared to be shifting toward Schultz's prophecy.

A few years after the review of *Capitalism and Freedom*, *Business Week* noted the comeback of "monetary policy" in the wake of the 1964 tax cut, where "a quiet revolution is brewing in economic theory."[145] Written at the height of postwar prosperity in 1965, the article examined the Third Annual University Professors Conference, sponsored by the American Bankers Association, which brought together fifty economists to debate the fiscal policy of Keynesianism and the monetary policy of the Chicago school. The argument centered on early 1960s economic growth, with monetarists arguing that the "money supply" in deposits, rather than the (Keynesian) fiscal policies of deficit spending, accounted for the exceptional economic growth.[146] The ideas framing this debate came from Friedman's work with economist Anna J. Schwartz on the Depression, where their argument asserted that a lack of monetary policy was the primary culprit for the Great Depression. The basic premise Friedman wanted economists to understand was that "fluctuations in the quantity of money offer a better statistical explanation of business cycles than does instability of investment."[147] This assertion of downplaying the demand-side argument of Keynesian economics and reframing the economic debate around monetary policies controlling money—whether through lowered taxes or the Federal Reserve's manipulation of interest rates—offered a preview to a future neoliberal supply-side economics policy.

By the late 1960s, Friedman increasingly found broader platforms for his message, including the January 8, 1968, televised meeting of Friedman and Buckley on *Firing Line with William F. Buckley Jr.*[148] In their criticism of the welfare state, the conservative and neoliberal anchored the debate on the trope of the "Negro problem"—the long familiar way to explain negative features of American life (historically, this involved the valorization of whiteness as the norm through the exploration of pathologies tied to Blackness). The conversation centered on the "urban problem" (the color-blind alternative referring to what in the early 1960s was called the Negro problem) and the coding of the welfare state as, literally, welfare for "dependent" African Americans. Buckley asked Friedman a question regarding the connection between government welfare programs and the "diminution of poverty," with Friedman answering, "Oh, there's no question about that. The major source of poverty has been the welfare programs of the government." The economist then brought out notions of supply and demand: the more programs and spending enacted, the more it would create welfare recipients. Underlining the familiarity of the concept of dependency to American viewers' minds, Friedman unpacked his equation using African Americans as the quintessential state burden:[149]

> Let's get down to specific details. Why is it that 25% of Negro teenage boys—male teenagers, young men between the ages of 16 and 19, are unemployed and walking the streets? Because of a government program supposed to be for welfare purposes, namely, the Minimum Wage rates. The government has legislated that it is far better for a Negro boy of 18 to be unemployed at $1.50 an hour, than to be employed at $1.00 an hour. That's the only reason why unemployment among Negro youngsters is 25%, instead of 7 or 8%, which is what it was before the minimum wage was raised so high.

Connecting minimum wage laws, welfare support rolls, and Blackness, Friedman's logic pointed to minimum wage laws as the primary culprit for Black unemployment. Institutional anti-Blackness and capital flight following white flight (to subsidized white suburbs) were invisible in this equation. Buckley then added his concern over those who "deserved" welfare—another legacy of American ideas surrounding dependence and poverty—and those who did not, again using African Americans as the focal point. Buckley eloquently stated:

Well, I see that point, and it certainly is a logical extension of the whole idea of rule by law, but in fact, don't we know from the evidence of our census that the poor really are divided into two categories: there are the poor who are victimized by circumstances—let's say a Negro who leaves the South and arrives in New York and finds that he is not in command of any negotiable skill, though he's anxious to work—that's one category. The other category, and it is generally estimated this would make up for about 50% are simply the disorganized poor—the people who are poor because they are completely unmotivated and because there is some sort of a neurotic block that keeps them from acting in the way that under—if you deal with universals—you would expect them to act. Now, you say, or do you say, that they should be treated alike. What are you going to do with the poor person who, having consumed his $3,000, or whatever it comes up to under the Negative Income Tax, spends all of that on the races, and then turns to the community and says, this is the 2nd of January, I have consumed my year's income. Now, meanwhile, I have four children.

These mundane meanderings fortifying existent anti-Black sentiment among Buckley's audience played on the *longue durée* sense of Black "savagery" derived from the era of slavery, the early twentieth-century mainstream belief in the racial science of eugenics, and the work of sociologists to construct "cultural pathology" as a replacement to overt racism: African Americans had too many children, were unmotivated and lazy like the Sambo whites consumed through popular culture since the 1800s, while government aid only made this "pathology" worse.[150] In addition, Buckley helped establish the identity of what Reagan would popularize in the mid-1970s as one of the key color-blind monikers of the culture war, the "welfare queen," which was code for unmarried Black women on welfare.[151] For a television program aimed toward middle-class whites, the scourge of the welfare state was placed on a small impoverished minority, a demographic long despised, and deemed a tax burden by those enjoying the economic opportunity of the postwar welfare state. Long a target of white discipline and control, Black women and their reproductive choices would remain an important pillar for the conservative culture war's deployment of white resentment.[152]

Exchanges such as these underline how the late 1960s culture war regenerated the *longue durée* sentiments of Western civilization and its struggle against savagery.[153] Through these interactions with one of the most important facilitators of the New Right (Buckley), Friedman brought neoliberalism into dialogue with the broader conservative movement and its obsession with anti-Blackness as a wedge issue for whites benefiting from the welfare state conservatives wished to dismantle. In the exchanges between Buckley and Friedman, one noteworthy aspect was Friedman's relative color blindness in the face of Buckley's blunt insertions of Blackness into the dialogue, ensuring that particular phrases such as "welfare" would be explicitly coded "Black" for viewers.

At the close of the decade, *Business Week* continually noted the increased respectability of Friedman's monetarist thinking in cracking through the dominant Keynesian model.[154] The debate came to a head under Nixon in 1969, with Keynesians and monetarists agreeing over easing the money supply.[155] By 1971, the combination of recession and inflation helped to further dent the reputations of Keynesians while the monetarists predicted the recession. As the decade progressed, the project of Hayek and Friedman thrived amidst the "economic dislocations of the 1970s," establishing "an environment in which neoliberal nostrums finally acquired real traction."[156] Support for neoliberal policies received further justification as the two economists won the Nobel Prize in Economics in 1974 (Hayek) and 1976 (Friedman). Although their strict brand of monetarism was never fully adopted—except between 1979 and 1982—the intricacies of the two economists' logic and the phrases connecting ideas to policy implementation would help to define the new economic common sense through the 1980s and beyond.

The evolution of neoliberalism's ideology anticipated and ultimately wove itself into the post-1960s culture wars. First, fear and anxiety—and later, resentment—accompanied the inclusion of historically marginalized groups into the public sphere, with old conservative dread toward overturning entrenched hierarchies evolving into market-based solutions to inequalities between groups (in other words, using Hayek's idea of the market as "information processor"). However, the success of this market-based solution more often than not demanded access to economic opportunity the previous system (the Jim Crow welfare state) firmly embedded into the "traditions" of society. For white Americans uneasy about casting expressions of overt racism (at least beyond the confines of the private sphere), the color-blind rhetoric of conservatives filled the rhetorical void. Now, criticism of African Americans could be veiled in the defense of one's "liberty," including the language of property rights. Buckley's "ethos" argument sunk in as well: white affluence was imagined as the fruit of individual responsibility—and not the Jim Crow welfare state—while a broken culture of deviance accounted for Black poverty. The rhetoric of "law and order" offered further reassurance by disqualifying civil disobedience as a form of legitimate protest as conservatives equated protest with street crime (a notion further reinforcing the idea of Black cultural pathology).[157] Second, as the field of democracy expanded, neoliberals proposed and embraced laws geared toward protecting private property and investment through the strict separation of democracy and the market. The place of lobbyists—funded by big business and labor unions—fail to appear in these equations designed to remove the possibility that the state can and should alleviate hardships resulting from free market capitalism. The bailout of the finance industry in the wake of the 2007–8 crash, and not the unemployed whose taxes bailed out bankers, underscores the extent of neoliberalism's normalization since the 1970s.[158] William Davies notes, as "economics techniques for measurement and evaluation" arose in the marketplace and these ideas were codified within late-nineteenth-century "neoclassical economics," these techniques were mobilized to critique the welfare state: quantitative analysis should guide policy, not ideas about "fairness" or "public ethos" or a social safety net.[159] Creating a just society free of wealth inequality, even if unemployment ripples through a quarter of the population, went against the nature of markets. And protecting markets was protecting Western civilization.

The reification of Western (white) man—or Western civilization—as embodying superior cultural norms operated as the bridge between the racial science-based white supremacy and the color-blind era of neoliberalism, providing white Americans steeped in the postwar Jim Crow welfare state with a universal concept to reform the language and institutions of American capitalism. This deregulation and reform of the crudely outdated overt racism of Buckley's 1950s white nationalist writings provided a color-blind cultural guideline for justifying ongoing racial discrimination. The concept of freedom envisioned by Friedman and Hayek coalesced around a theoretical model of the world in which the legacies of white supremacy, settler colonialism, slavery, or patriarchy had nothing to do with the ideas and policies shaping the material life of the United States in the twentieth century—despite the visibility of African Americans and other people of color facing de jure or de facto segregation or women being denied equal access and rights to the public sphere before social equality legislation in the 1960s.

The possession of history proved critical in procuring this common sense. It took decades for neoliberalism and conservative economics to reshape the American political-economic system into an invisible, normalized framework reoriented toward the wealthy and corporate community while summoning coded appeals to whiteness for the demographic that both voted for these changes and suffered economic contraction from their implementation. Patience was well rewarded, however, as the affluent made incredible gains in the share of American wealth after the 1970s. Meanwhile, those in the working and middle classes who benefited from the Jim Crow welfare state, including those who voted it away at the dawn of legislated social equality, would see their wages stagnate and purchasing power diminish in the years to come.[160] Resentment against the historically marginalized would expand in sync with wealth inequality. In many ways, the use of the *longue durée* for conservatives and neoliberals paid off handsomely: the possessive investment in whiteness continued to pay dividends for the economic elite, as the ghosts of Bacon's Rebellion helplessly looked on.[161]

Chapter 3

The Jim Crow Welfare State and the Corporate Revolution
Postwar American Capitalism

> The laws or so-called laws of economics probably last only as long as the desires and realities of the period they reflect or interpret more or less faithfully. A new age brings its own "laws."
>
> —Fernand Braudel, *Civilization and Capitalism, 15th–18th Century, Volume II: The Wheels of Commerce* (1979)

> The world of finance is now completely different from that of 1970. Money and flows of currency, commercial paper, bonds, and equities between the countries of the world now tie us all together in a manner that would have been impossible to foresee even 20 years ago. In this sense the economic system of the years since 1973 is quite different from that of the 1960s. Yet the seeds of the global financial system were sown in the 1950s and 1960s.
>
> —Michael J. Webber and David L. Rigby, *The Golden Age Illusion* (1996)

> Over a hundred-year stretch, from the 1860s through the 1970s, corporations learned the art of stability, assuring the longevity of businesses and increasing the number of employed. The free market did not effect this stabilizing change; rather, the way businesses were internally organized played a more significant role.
>
> —Richard Sennett, *The Culture of the New Capitalism* (2006)

A considerable ingredient paving the road to neoliberalism was public disillusionment with large obtrusive institutions such as government, labor, and corporations in the 1970s.[1] As the austerity of recession and deindustrialization set in, expanding transnational corporate entities became targets of populist rage against a globalizing world and a withering American dream. In Hollywood, populist contempt toward government and big business found expression in movies such as *Jaws* (1975) and *Nashville* (1975).[2] In the film *Network* (1976), the infamous television newscast character, Howard Beale, epitomized this burst of frustration, as he condemned the general decay of the United States in the 1970s: "I'm mad as hell, and I'm not going to take this anymore!"[3] However, a more telling speech later in the film articulated animosity toward the ever-growing power of multinational corporations/conglomerates and a globalized economy no longer benefiting the working and middle classes. On his nightly show, *The Mad Prophet of the Airwaves*, Beale turned his anger toward globalization, taking aim at multinational conglomerates (specifically the fictional company in *Network*, CCA—the Communications Corporation of America) and the fears of "foreign" ownership of American business:

> We all know that the Arabs control $16 billion of this country. They own a chunk of Fifth Avenue, 20 downtown pieces of Boston, a part of the Port of New Orleans, an industrial park in Salt Lake City, they own big hunks of the Atlanta Hilton, the Arizona Land and Cattle Company, part of a bank of California, the bank of the Commonwealth in Detroit, they control Aramco, so, that puts them into Exxon, Texaco, and Mobil oil. They're all over New Jersey, Louisville, St. Louis, Missouri. And that's only what we know about. There's a hell of a lot more we don't know about. Because all of those Arab petrodollars are washed through Switzerland and Canada and the biggest banks in this country. For example, what we don't know about is this CCA deal and all the other CCA deals. Right now, the Arabs have screwed us out of enough American dollars to come right back and with our own money to buy General Motors, IBM, ITT, AT&T, DuPont, US Steel, and 20 other American companies.[4]

The economic populism glimpsed in *Network* highlighted the growing omnipresence of multinational conglomerates and finance leading up to the 1970s—as they lit the path to the neoliberal era.

The history of neoliberalism is more than just an exploration of the ideological rhetoric and financial circuits of neoliberal thinkers. A conducive cultural-business environment needed to materialize for neoliberal ideas and policies to be taken seriously and implemented. In short, supply and demand: a moment of conjuncture needed to arise, when a vacuum of ideas could be filled by neoliberals, whose program could be implemented into policies and displace the previously dominant economic system. Two vital players helping to foster this vacuum included multinational corporations (MNCs) and the trend toward conglomeration, as well as the reawakening of finance after the Great Depression. These organizations emerged as the two defining capitalist institutions dominating the neoliberal era after the 1970s.

The economic dislocations of the Vietnam War, increased competition with Japan and Europe, and the oil crisis and recessions of the 1970s opened the space of conjuncture where the practices of MNCs and finance intersected with the ideas of the decades-old project of neoliberalism, pressing together the economic-political theory of Milton Friedman and Friedrich August von Hayek with the material needs of transnational capitalism. Developing through the welfare state (and its European extension via the Marshall Plan),

Geoffrey Jones notes, MNCs and finance began to structure "a new global economy" in the decades after World War II, but their efforts only "came to fruition during the 1980s and 1990s."[5] Building on the various techniques and strategies multinationals and finance developed in the postwar years to navigate the welfare state, by the 1970s the resistance against regulations—deemed federal intrusion into the rights of business—coincided with the conservative culture war rippling through American society after the 1960s. This conjuncture of institutional, economic, and cultural processes laid the groundwork for the rise of neoliberalism.

In the *longue durée* of economic change, this conjuncture represented an end to a cycle of accumulation driven by the rise and expansion of American capitalism—what Julian Go suggests was a similar feature of decline matched by Britain a century before.[6] Giovanni Arrighi asserts that since the 1400s, there have been four cycles of accumulation in the history of capitalism. The first cycle of accumulation arose through the combination of the Italian city-state of Genoa and the Iberian Peninsula. Barcelona's primary banks collapsed in the early 1380s, opening up opportunity for Genoese merchant bankers to step in and "become the most important financiers in the Iberian region."[7] The blending of the feudal aristocracy with the Genoese bourgeoisie ("which specialized in the buying and selling of commodities and in the pursuit of profit") initiated the birth of capitalism.[8] As the Spanish Empire struggled against its Dutch rebels to the north, the center of capital slowly shifted to Antwerp, as Genoese finance turned New World silver from Spain into "gold and other 'good money' delivered in Antwerp near the theater of operations."[9] Although beneficial to the Genoese, it also led to their eclipse by the Dutch. This second cycle of capital accumulation in the Netherlands led to the rise of mercantile capitalism (including joint-stock companies) in the 1600s and the beginning of modern capitalism.[10] The third cycle of accumulation unfolded as capital moved from its center in the Netherlands (between the 1600s and 1700s) over to the British—with London becoming the new center of capital. In all these cases, the rising cycle was characterized by production and trade while the descending phase switched to an emphasis on finance as investments in production failed to secure acceptable profits. As the fourth cycle of accumulation arose in the United States, investment capital found a critical outlet in production *and consumption*, as internal markets were soaked in productive output.[11] This dynamic in the United States—something the British and Dutch cycles could not achieve—existed because of the territorial expansion related to settler colonial policies, the fantastic wealth accumulated through the institution of slavery and cotton, and the massive amount of immigration into the United States that both provided labor to develop the bountiful resources of North America and acted as an outlet for the consumption of manufactured products. Robert J. Gordon describes this takeoff as an "economic revolution," leading to an ever-increasing standard of living that began slowing by the end of the 1960s.[12] Beginning with businesses related to railroads, oil, and steel, the modern corporation proved to be the most efficient form for the organization of capital. As Arrighi notes, "The integration of the processes of mass production with those of mass distribution within a single organization gave rise to a new kind of capitalist enterprise. Having internalized a whole sequence of subprocesses of production and exchange from the procurement of primary inputs to the disposal of final outputs, this new kind of capitalist enterprise was in a position to subject the costs, risks, and uncertainties involved in moving goods through that sequence to the economizing logic of administrative action and long-term corporate planning."[13] The U.S. cycle of accumulation eventually evolved from its nineteenth- and twentieth-century production phase into a financial phase after the 1960s, setting the stage for the conjuncture of MNCs, finance, the New Right, the culture war, and neoliberal economists to usher in the era of neoliberalism.

To help guide us through the postwar history of the business environment, this chapter leans on the voice of *Business Week* magazine (while also setting up a more focused exploration of the weekly journal in chapter 4). *Business Week*'s sets of commentaries and observations offer a glimpse of postwar economics and culture across decades: the evolution of business practices, the negotiation of government regulations, and the shifting language of business leaders. In defense of its immediate constituencies' political and economic prerogatives—and swimming within a similar field of argument as *Fortune*, *Forbes*, and *The Economist*—*Business Week* offered a central forum for the discussion of capitalism. Sociologist Herbert J. Gans describes the political economy of weekly news journals: "News is about the economic, political, social, and cultural hierarchies we call nation and society. For the most part, the news reports on those at or near the top of the hierarchies and on those, particularly at the bottom, who threaten them, to an audience, most of whom are located in the vast middle range between top and bottom."[14] *Business Week*'s value as a significant prism lies in its ability to give "voice" to the workings of capital on a week-by-week basis. The writers of *Business Week*—sometimes anonymous, sometimes with bylines—operated within the logic of American business, interpreting data and trends through an inherited set of common sense related to business, economics, and most often unacknowledged, their racial-gendered position in society. After the 1960s, *Business Week* helped foster the post-Keynesian consensus to establish a new path out of the cultural and economic issues of the 1970s.

First published in 1929 by McGraw-Hill, *Business Week* was explicitly created to interpret the events affecting the business world.[15] For decades, the pages of *Business Week* acted as a bellwether for the shift in economic patterns and ideas and as an exemplary site for business culture to manifest. In a 1974 survey of what U.S. leaders read, Carol H. Weiss discovered that along with *Fortune* magazine, *Business Week* was "read by almost all the economic managers and by at least half of the members of every other sector" (sectors included industrial executives, owners of large wealth, labor union presidents, government representatives, civil servants, political party officials, and mass media executives and professionals).[16] Matching the demographic of its subject matter, the magazine's perspective was an exceedingly white male reading space, seen in both its features and advertisements.[17]

Trade journals are important sources for outlining the intricacies of culture because of their detailed and specialized breakdowns—from representations to economic data—as well as interpretations of variously tracked commodities and trends. In short, they are sources of knowledge creation tied to economics. According to Glenn C. Altschuler and David I. Grossvogel, in reference to their work on the role of *TV Guide* in U.S. life, journals act as cultural mediators helping to shape and "define the possibilities and limitations" of their particular subject.[18] In terms of authorship, journals offer a spectrum of opinion determined by the editorship. Because of their intimacy with the wider outlines of capitalism, including downturns and adjustments, journals like *Business Week* also perform the service of fostering the dialectical processes connecting capitalism to culture, and culture to capitalism. *Business Week* made sense of their readers' world, tying familiar sentiments to contemporary events, while explaining emergent ideas as new circumstances arose in the business world. *Business Week* is an important site for understanding how economics evolved across the twentieth century, as the magazine's engagement with these social changes reshaped and regenerated deep cultural worldviews.

Fresh off the production stimulus of World War II, business in the postwar years discovered the value of the interventionist welfare state as it created a stable foundation to rebuild the United States after the Great Depression. As business ventured abroad, capital found ways to adapt to the constraints of the welfare state, essentially constructing an alternative transnational business world through adept negotiations of the rules of the welfare state's mixed economy. However, with economic growth slowing in the 1970s, business organized in a similar manner as the civil rights movement, using the language of "rights" to free business from postwar regulations. In this conjuncture, the needs of business, the forty-year-old project of neoliberalism, and the escalating culture war converged. The ferocity of the 1970s recession helped to shape the perfect storm needed by neoliberals to transition the United States away from the Jim Crow welfare state and reform the economic common sense of the nation.

Although more visible in the 1970s, American business had long negotiated its way through the boundaries and barricades of national and global capitalism. In a century filled with Marxist revolutions and anti-colonial liberationist movements, some saw the successes of transnational corporations to be more revolutionary. Adolf A. Berle presciently noted this underappreciated nature of American MNCs:

> The fact appears to be that from and after World War I the entire world was in revolution, and the base of that revolution was technical far more than it was social. Changes in human life and habits, modification of human institutions, and expansion of human horizons occurred everywhere. The philosophical and scientific discoveries of the nineteenth century were put to work in the twentieth, and whole civilizations changed as a result. The Russian revolution was nominally based on Communist dogma; but its significant struggle was to find some instrument by which a vast backward country could be mauled into industrialization. The capitalist revolution in which the United States was the leader found apter, more efficient and more flexible means through collectivizing capital in corporations. . . . Elsewhere the Marxist state seemed a brutal, blunt, and fumbling instrument; capitalism was evolving its own instruments, and accomplishing the twentieth-century revolution with infinitely more humanity and efficiency. The fundamental change was technical: the application to the everyday life of hundreds of millions of people of newly developed methods of production. Economics necessarily developed with that change; politics was modified by the economics; the social theory has yet to be written. . . . In this aspect, it is justifiable to consider the American corporation not as a business device but as a social institution in the context of a revolutionary century.[19]

Written in 1954, Berle's conception of the capitalist revolution and its influence on politics strikes an earnest chord for an optimistic future. An important driving force for this revolution was the Democratic Party's "final abandonment of the party's dominant anti-monopoly tradition"—monopolies would be regulated, not eliminated.[20] As a core member of Franklin D. Roosevelt's "brain trust," Berle epitomized the liberal consensus tying together business, labor, and government in the New Deal–derived Jim Crow welfare state—including coauthoring of *The Modern Corporation and Private Property* (1932).[21] Berle's reflections, however, also hint at a broader potential for MNCs. From the perspective of the twenty-first century, we might ask of Berle: what happens when the revolution outpaces the consensus, when labor and government move from economic partners to economic obstacles—or enemies?

At the conclusion of World War II, Americans feared sinking back into economic depression, continued to distrust big business, and supported unions.[22] A tentative consensus forged during the war balanced the needs of business with the needs of the American people who, after fighting for almost four years, continued to vote for legislators supporting the Keynesian-inspired welfare state constructed through the experience of the New Deal and World War II. Wartime nationalism helped justify the welfare state, with many in the business community supporting its premise of a mixed economy where government regulation offered the promise of stability.[23] Luckily for business, the Red Scare environment of the Cold War policed the more radical regulatory and redistributionist aspects of the welfare state.[24] The unprecedented wave of strikes across the nation in the year after August 1945 appeared to justify the Red Scare paranoia—workers were angry over "wartime sacrifices," "reverses in wages and working conditions," and "pursued policies designed to increase their control over production and to combat the centralized power of the corporate-liberal alliance."[25] Accusations of "communism," "socialism," and "collectivism" further disciplined the expansion of the welfare state, while helping to eradicate the left-wing elements of the labor movement, government, Hollywood, and other influential sectors of society.[26] The Taft-Hartley Act (1947) would severely weaken the power of labor, damaging "union solidarity by banning secondary picketing and reinforcing state right-to-work laws," as well as outlawing "members of the Communist Party" from union activities.[27] The mold was cast for a moderate mixed economy, reformed for both business and labor.

American business entered a golden age as they took advantage of the regulated markets shaping the 1950s economic boom. Put into place during the crisis of the 1930s, the logic of "controlled" capitalism, writes Harold James, resulted in a postwar consensus view "that the large short-term capital flows of the 1920s and 1930s as mediated through the financial system had led to disaster."[28] For the mixed economy, capital movements were channeled through "the official sector, rather than with banks and bond finance, and then the flows became increasingly privatized."[29] This regulation sought to control and direct, rather than succumb to unstable speculation. Writing in the early 1960s, Harold G. Vatter described this Keynesian feature of the postwar world as follows:

> The *guarantee of growth*, which was evolving as a corollary policy of the Federal government during the 1950's, implied the conversion of mere intervention into participation. The commitment to guarantee both stability and growth in an economy in which private, profit-oriented business firms made the basic production decisions meant that the

profitability of private business, in the aggregate, had to be guaranteed—not just agricultural business, but large corporate business in general. This was not clearly understood in 1946, and indeed it is by no means fully appreciated even today. However, the economy was more thoroughly "mixed" by 1960 than was envisioned when the Employment Act was passed.[30]

At the time of Vatter's writing in 1963, he noted the public's democratic desire for wealth redistribution: "a wide dispersion in the control of the nation's tangible wealth is a requisite for the maintenance of a healthy private enterprise economy."[31] For the working- and middle-class beneficiaries of the welfare state, the ideas of neoliberalism developing concurrently across the postwar years appeared to be antithetical to their vision of the American dream—a throwback to the instability of the teens and twenties which led to the Depression. A shaky consensus existed, nonetheless, balancing the needs of an anxious, Cold War–disciplined middle class against an empowered labor movement caught in a paradox where the very language of class conflict—a crucial source of unity for unions—led to accusations of "communism," political marginalization, and sometimes criminalization.[32] In addition, the specter of social equality slowly rose from the margins in the form of the civil rights movement.

Postwar wealth trickled-down to the white working and middle classes through the demand-side Keynesian Jim Crow welfare state, particularly through the Serviceman's Readjustment Act of 1944, or the GI Bill. A vital element contributing to the support of the welfare state by postwar Americans included the dramatic growth of "real disposable income per American."[33] While the 1950s saw about a 13 percent rise in real disposable income ("*after* subtracting for inflation and most taxes"), between 1965 and 1972 this number increased, "on an average, about 3 percent per year, or 24 percent over the seven years."[34] Consumerism formed the glue holding together the consensus—labor shelved its language of class, corporations negotiated and accepted government regulations, and many white Americans started down the path of regulated-redistributive prosperity. MNCs proved to be the most adept organizations for navigating this new American-led global system unfolding after the war, as they enjoyed a stable economic and political environment conducive to expansion overseas.

The era of New Deal–federal intervention proved ephemeral, however, for the newly emerging prosperity for working- and middle-class Americans. It was, asserts Jefferson Cowie and Nick Salvatore, the "long exception" in U.S. history, ending amid the uncertainty of the 1970s economic crisis.[35] The success of the postwar welfare state among white Americans and MNCs and finance ironically helped pave the road to the dismantling of the mixed economy and the ascension of neoliberalism. As the economic crisis of the 1970s deepened, neoliberals and conservatives proposed privatization rather than government intervention, deregulation rather than government regulation of often unstable markets. Significantly, the anti–welfare state language emphasized an active masculine response to the crisis, rather than an inactive reworking of a mixed economy increasingly characterized through the language of effeminate dependency: the socioeconomic life of the rugged individual was imagined through market competitiveness, rather than the collective New Deal–era ideas linked to notions of fairness and justness.[36] Although politicians and economists receive the lion's share of credit in tilting the nation away from the welfare state and toward neoliberalism, an unsung champion of this shift was private enterprise itself, or more accurately, the MNCs, conglomerates, and the financial industry that had been steadily growing in potency and reach throughout the postwar era. Their adaptation to the regulations of the postwar United States, Europe, Japan, and other nations encouraged transnational business to develop innovative ways to navigate American-led global capitalism. These innovations eventually found kinship with the ideas of neoliberalism in the 1960s and 1970s.[37]

The Corporation

Though precedents date back at least as early as the seventeenth- and eighteenth-century golden age of joint-stock companies, the modern corporation came of age in the mid-nineteenth century.[38] With the expansion of the federal government during the Civil War, many of the soon-to-be giants of big business earned large sums through wartime government contracts—an early hint at the profitability of Keynesian military spending. The modern corporation, moreover, arose within the production phase of the fourth cycle of accumulation as the United States edged its way to global economic dominance.[39] After the 1870s, an era of deregulated industrial capitalism operating through state and federal cooperation—the very era Friedman called "the closest to free enterprise"—led to the rise of the concentration of economic power in corporations, mergers, trusts, and Wall Street finance.[40] Violent battles between capital and labor movements characterized this era of economic expansion, spurring the rise of the populist movement as the imperial ambitions of the United States shifted from westward expansion to obtaining possessions in the Pacific Ocean in the late nineteenth and twentieth centuries.[41]

The revolution in management practices significantly influenced the development of the modern corporation, a practice first implemented by the far-reaching activities of railroads.[42] Along with railroads, other corporations who were involved in "capital-intensive operations" increasingly depended on both the evolving partnership with investment stocks via Wall Street and the legal framework of "limited liability," which protected the agents of the corporation from being "responsible for debts that exceeded the amount of their original investment."[43] Due to the increased scale of industrial capitalism, this divorcing of ownership from management helped reshape the social responsibilities of corporations: business became an abstract concept, with the needs of shareholders becoming the only legal responsibility of the manager (regardless of social cost).[44] Late-nineteenth-century industrial capitalism set the frame of debate for the cultural and economic world of the twentieth century, including the struggle between the imperatives of freedom and democracy on the one hand and the rapid growth and power of industrial capitalism, big business, and concentrated wealth on the other hand.[45] Of course, the most important partner for the modern corporation was the nation-state, as the Hamiltonian federalism of the post–Civil War era enabled the financing of large infrastructure projects such as the transcontinental railroad, as well as later technological advancements through defense spending and freeway expansion (at the expense of public transportation) in the twentieth century.[46]

Alongside their innovations in managing widespread activities, the railroad industry helped pioneer relationships between corporations and government, particularly the techniques for securing political power. Railroads operated at both the state level ("against agrarian politicians who believed that elected officials had not only the right but also the obligation to intervene in the workings of the economy") and the federal level, where intervention in the economy leaned toward the interests of big business.[47] With the rise of oil, these relationships evolved even further, including new ways of organizing corporate structures transnationally and integrating the needs of American foreign policy into the oil industry.[48] These connections between corporations, Wall Street, and the legal mechanisms of the nation-state would define the dynamics of American capitalism operating within and across national boundaries through the twentieth century.[49]

The multinational corporation, a term coined by New Dealer–turned–multinational corporate executive David E. Lilienthal, embodied the economic and bureaucratic bridge tying together the global economy with the domestic, deftly navigating "business-government relations" and various "regional associations."[50] Lilienthal theorized the MNC's mission as an extension of the nation-state diplomat: "another facet of internationalization," though ostensibly without the coercive baggage of nineteenth-century imperialism.[51] Alfred Chandler and Bruce Mazlish define multinationals as (1) "firms that control income-generating assets in more than one country at a time"; (2) have "productive facilities in several countries on at least two continents with employees stationed worldwide and financial investments scattered across the globe"; and (3) MNCs "are not mere economic entities but part of a complex interplay of factors."[52] In short, multinationals shaped capital networks spanning politics and culture through their global economic ventures.

The business strategy of conglomeration complemented the multinationals' overseas investment. *Business Week* noted the emergence of conglomerates in the mid-1950s, at first calling them polyglots. An article from 1956 describes a new "kind of corporation . . . is sprouting up with the postwar boom. Essentially they consist of a host of smaller companies tucked under one corporate umbrella. They muster a wide diversity of product lines, with no apparent logic or relation between them—and they have appeared so suddenly that businessmen still have no name for them. For want of a better name, call them polyglots."[53] According to *Business Week*, polyglots/conglomerates arose through the large amount of cash circulating in the early postwar years, especially as a result of federal defense spending, a slightly less-regulated finance industry, and the "development of management controls and techniques for handling decentralized operations."[54] Finally, conglomerates found it easier to negotiate around the "strict antimonopoly laws of the period"—it was legally easier to merge with an unrelated industry than to buy directly competing companies.[55]

These organizations operated through a variety of industries rather than the traditional Rockefeller-inspired monopoly that created concentrated and controlled markets. This new, diversified approach aimed toward escaping "from business-cycle profit squeezes, and the development of regular income."[56] Characterized as "a portfolio of investments rather than a unified operation," this buying of businesses outside their immediate specialty allowed multinationals a greater economic flexibility in a rapidly changing global economy.[57] The growth of mergers and acquisitions rested on "financial practices" pioneered by conglomerates in the 1960s, anticipating the "era of financial daring" of the 1980s, and the victory of neoliberalism through Reaganomics.[58] The first wave of mergers occurred between 1949 and 1955, while by the end of the second wave, 1964 to 1968, "four fifths of all mergers were conglomerate in nature."[59]

Global markets, according to *Business Week* in 1963, now distinguished the normative scope for U.S. business.[60] More than this, the overseas-domestic aspect of the multinational created an internal economy for the companies. As Ray R. Eppert of Burroughs Corp. asserted, "The net result of our investing abroad is that we have grown at both ends. . . . That's because our overseas subsidiaries serve as captive markets for the parent corporation."[61] "More than 80% of the U.S. parent's $25-million in exports," added *Business Week*, "goes to its own subsidiaries, mostly as parts for fabrication but also as finished machinery. Internal sales as well as total exports have nearly doubled since 1956."[62] Reporting on the National Industrial Conference Board's antitrust conference in New York City in 1965, *Business Week* observed that mergers continued to be seen "as a technique for growth," noting the "record 1,700 corporate consolidations last year," which were expected to "pick up speed, if company earnings keep up their present pace."[63] Market shares expanded with mergers: "100 largest manufacturing companies had grown from 23% in 1947 to 32% in 1962."[64] Rather than the traditional monopoly, conglomerates embodied the concept of concentrations Walter Lippmann warned of in his *Good Society* (1938). They would also become the archetype enterprise for the neoliberal era.

Throughout this evolution of multinationals and finance, an American public increasingly became a part of this expanding world of MNCs or within the employment sectors related to their growth. This new class of managers, technicians, academics, and journalists working in large corporate organizations also raised families in spacious, newly constructed, federally subsidized white suburbs.[65] Consequently, the new middle class, particularly in the West or Sun Belt or the "gun belt" shared "a technocratic culture, an acceptance of Cold War ideology, [and] a relatively conservative politics."[66] In the context of settler colonialism, the Sun Belt represented a new postwar ideological divide between a stagnant East and a rejuvenated West. Michael Ryan and Douglas Kellner characterized this geographic identity as "a place outside civility or urban civilization, a site associated with the male subject conceived as a private entity, the bearer of rights of property and propriety whose boundaries must be protected with violence. The exaltation of the male individual in conservative thought is always linked to nature for this reason. Nature is unconstrained. . . .The more 'natural' Sunbelt is thus a metaphor for the conservative ideal of individual freedom, the exaltation of individual rights over collective responsibility."[67] It would take until the passage of social equality legislation, however, for the Sun Belt to begin truly championing individualism over the collective nature of the welfare state.

Exemplary of the consensus politics at the time, "conservative politics" mostly policed social boundaries related to race, gender, and sexuality—safely secured by pre-1960s federal housing policies—rather than a retreat from federal intervention. Taking advantage of the welfare state, many Americans found prosperity and opportunity through the various housing programs, infrastructure developments (e.g., the interstate freeway system), educational investments, and defense spending—all of which aided the success of big business.[68] Shaping the institutions of federal intervention, of course, was the ongoing institutional racism of de jure and de facto Jim Crow discrimination.[69]

The South, the champion of free trade and states' rights ideology, fed lustfully at the trough of defense-spending capitalism, so much so that in 1956, William Faulkner noted, "Our economy is no longer agricultural. . . . Our economy is the Federal Government."[70] As the space race took hold, "southern leaders saw the space program as a conduit to a new 'New South' of science and technology-based enterprise," including a flood of money toward "scientific research in universities across the South."[71] As the civil rights movement targeted postwar discriminatory policies, a shift in political allegiances occurred and destabilized the consensus supporting the regulatory state. Meanwhile, corporations successfully operating through the welfare state increasingly bristled at regulations, finding common cause with the New Right and neoliberal economists.

Postwar America: "The Long Exception"

The reconversion of the nation from wartime status to "peacetime" was largely a matter of scale, as a permanent Cold War setting helped solidify the balance between retaining the "business-government cooperation" while "strengthening the demand side of the economy" in order to increase American purchasing power.[72] The bipartisan Employment Act of 1946 brought the long-desired concern of economic stability to the economy, realizing the dream of Rockefeller in the late 1800s—although a year later, Taft-Hartley put the brakes on further labor empowerment.[73] Built off the 1920s development of mass consumption, the logic of full employment included the construction of suburbs and the new industries related to this expansion. Moreover, in the age of jets, missiles, and television, technology developed exponentially. The computer both revolutionized how companies and, later, society operated, with the computer-based knowledge industry—born of federally subsidized "technological innovations"—emerging as the quintessential business of the neoliberal service economy.[74] Computers quickened the pace of change in capitalism, helping to generate what Alvin Toffler termed information overload in 1970, a concept that erupted after the big bang of the internet, the rise of big data, and what Shoshana Zuboff calls surveillance capitalism.[75]

We see the success of the welfare state's golden age through the development of corporations and the growth in wages related to the rise of productivity tied to the technological updating of machinery: increased wages equated to increased purchasing power, and a higher standard of living.[76] A crucial multiplier effect for this economic expansion came through the federal subsidization of newly constructed suburbs, resulting in "economic expansion throughout the whole economy," including public services, infrastructure, power, sewage, water systems, education, housing, and transportation.[77] In an early retort against the postwar alarmist neoliberal rhetoric from "Professor Hayek at the University of Chicago," Berle underlined the pervasive nature of this consensus in 1954, writing:

> Few of the major segments in a community really want a regime of unlimited competition in the modern community—neither the great corporations, nor their labor, nor their suppliers. Fundamentally, they all want, not a perpetual struggle, but a steady job—the job of producing goods at a roughly predictable cost under roughly predictable conditions, so that goods can be sold in the market at a roughly predictable price. Their reasoning has a solid basis behind it. Competition between thousands of people from time to time eliminating marginal groups of inefficient producers likewise produces only marginal hardship. A struggle between giants may wreck hundreds of thousands of lives and whole communities.[78]

Berle asserted that the mixed economy was "not the result of any creeping socialism," again, taking a jab at Hayek's "road to serfdom" warnings; "rather," Berle writes, "it is a direct consequence of galloping capitalism."[79]

Corporations benefited immensely from this system in the 1950s, as "corporate business accounted for 57.8 per cent of all income originating in business in 1929 and had grown to 62.5 per cent in 1950 (it rose again by 1957, to 65.6)."[80] Increasingly giant corporations—what Berle (and Lippmann) called concentrates—controlled "half of all American industry."[81] By the end of the decade, the leading corporate industries were chemicals, aircraft, motor vehicles, steel, and electronics—with those industries connected to federally funded research and development making the greatest gains (80 percent of aircraft sales were bought by the federal government).[82] Residential construction accounted for "one fifth to one fourth of aggregate gross private investment," as the white suburbs expanded, along with jobs increasingly leaving the city.[83] As a part of the mixed economy, real wage growth continued to expand with productivity without impinging on profits.[84] David Harvey notes the significance of this economic system, what many have since called Fordism (named after its originator, Henry Ford): "What was special about Ford (and what ultimately separates Fordism from Taylorism), was his vision, his explicit recognition that mass production meant mass consumption, a new system of the reproduction of labour power, a new politics of labour control and management, a new aesthetics and psychology, in short, a new kind of rationalized, modernist, and populist democratic society."[85] A dramatic rise in real disposable income defined the "age of compression," as the share of wealth spread across the middle and working class, including an expansion of benefits: holidays, paid vacations, health insurance, and pensions.[86] This welfare state arrangement continued to be balanced on a tentative relationship between domestic labor and business at the federal level: corporations could invest abroad while promising to create and sustain the standard of living for workers at home.[87]

Corporate expansion abroad relied on *Pax Americana* defining the post–World War II era. An anchor guiding this American-led capitalism was the Bretton Woods Agreement of July 1944, an arrangement holding the international financial system together through the creation of a gold standard tied to the U.S. dollar. Seventy percent of the world's gold reserves were in the United States in 1947, leading to foreign businesses and governments seeking American dollars, resulting in "US control over world liquidity."[88] As Michael J. Webber and David L. Rigby suggest, "Linking the dollar and gold was a boon to trade and the emerging postwar international financial system. Dollars could be produced more easily than gold, and thus international liquidity accelerated more rapidly than under a pure gold standard. Furthermore, unlike gold, dollar reserves could be invested to earn interest."[89] Finally, the arrangements supporting the Bretton Woods agreements included the "social democratic welfare state [as] an integral part."[90] While tying together the capitalist countries of the world, a new form of interdependence—a notion popularized by Richard Cooper in 1968—arose, whereas Keynesian policies in one country provoked "international ramifications."[91]

Alongside Bretton Woods, investment abroad found growth particularly through the Marshall Plan, a policy directed toward rebuilding Europe and acting as an offset to the drastic cuts in U.S. military spending after the war.[92] In helping to institutionalize U.S. capitalism abroad, these socialized investments operated like a New Deal "Works Progress Administration" for multinationals overseas.[93] Hardly critical of this brand of federal intervention on a global scale, businessmen and government eagerly capitalized on these Keynesian policies. Writes Kim McQuaid:

> The cold war, like the Depression and World War II, was a situation not considered in traditional American economic or political ideology. Many government and business leaders came to see the Marshall Plan as simple necessity, a down payment on the American century. They created a de facto Keynesian pump-priming program, which paid for 25 percent of all Western European imports between 1947 and 1950. They reduced destabilizing dollar shortages in world trade. They helped begin the thirteen-fold increase between 1950 and 1990 in inflation-adjusted trade in global goods and services.[94]

A part of this socializing included significant tax provisions for corporate write-offs of losses from federal spending due to cutbacks in military spending after World War II.[95] The Marshall Plan positioned American business to gain a foothold in Europe, presenting, as Victoria de Grazia notes, an opportunity to globalize America's consumer market, exporting the mores of the "premier consumer society" to the Old World.[96] Building off the Marshall Plan, foreign investment in the 1950s included Latin America ($361 million), Canada ($742 million), and Europe ($440 million), eventually leading to nearly 70 percent of American corporate expansion money going abroad by the end of 1960.[97]

Despite foreign investment, U.S. economic growth continued to rely on the prosperity of working- and middle-class Americans. For white Americans, the prosperity induced by the welfare state economy included the race-based entitlement of Jim Crow legislation and institutional segregation in the North and West. As a white male dominated framework, its economics centered on the concept of the male–wage earning "family wage."[98] In a stunning reversal of the 1920s era of GOP-led economics, the Jim Crow welfare state shaped what has been called the "Great Compression," an era characterized by the share of wealth of the top 1 percent shrinking after the 1940s and producing a "wage structure more equal than that experienced since."[99] The guiding white "middle-class ethos"—whose democratic practices politically supported both the liberal consensus guiding the welfare state *and* discriminatory Jim Crow practices—anchored the New Deal–Keynesian model so securely that the Republican president Dwight D. Eisenhower left the top income tax rate at 91 percent throughout his two terms.[100] Against this political consensus, the "extreme right wing"—what Richard Hofstadter described at the time as pseudo-conservatives—and their American business allies engaged in a nationwide campaign to restore the pre–New Deal American language of individualism, free enterprise, competition, and the overall prerogatives of business over the encroachment of the more democratic-led mechanisms of the welfare state.[101] This was the fertile ground for neoliberal economists, of course, who would find common cause with this right wing in the 1950s, including Friedman's economic advice to the political fortunes of Barry Goldwater.[102] Despite the burden of the mixed economy, the wealthy found ways around their enormous income tax, investing in municipal bonds, utilizing expense accounts, or benefiting from the lower-taxed capital gains (which did not count as income).[103] At the same time, moderate business leaders who worked in or with government during World War II understood the profitable benefits unlocked by the partnership between government, the military, and industry during the war years.[104]

The Cold War's anti-communist rhetoric helped immensely to downplay the reality of the redistributionist nature of the welfare state. The political rhetoric of individualism, liberty, and free enterprise provided the language and identity characterizing the U.S. struggle against the Soviet threat. In doing so, it fostered a cognitive dissonance obscuring the level of federal interventionist collectivism circulating through the American economy. In short, the redistributionist aspect of welfare state policies toward the white working and middle classes, such as the GI Bill, federal infrastructure projects, and other direct-indirect subsidies toward industry, disappeared from the equation that fostered American prosperity. Just as defense spending built Southern California and the Sun Belt while fostering an anti-welfare state conservative ideology, the dynamic of federal housing policies operated in a similar fashion.[105] David M. P. Freund notes that subsidized housing policies hid behind both the white supremacy policies constructing white neighborhoods as well as the popularization of "the idea that government interventions were *not* providing considerable benefits to white people. Public officials, their private-sector allies, and even federal appraisal guidelines assured whites that state interventions neither made suburban growth possible nor helped segregate the fast-growing metropolis by race. They promoted a story that urban and suburban outcomes resulted solely from impersonal market forces."[106] The private and public conjoining of the economy appeared natural after almost two decades of Depression and global war mobilization.[107] More than this, however, it reinforced the normality of white Americans seeing their access to the welfare state as an entitlement of citizenship and liberty. Just as government intervention was made invisible, whiteness, too, remained a policy submerged within "impersonal market forces," inevitably leading to anger toward both African Americans and the federal government as social equality legislation opened access to the benefits of the welfare state by people of color.

Appearing as an unfair intrusion into white space, this discord established a starting point for the conservative culture war and the shifting allegiance away from the welfare state. At the same time, a cognitive dissonance crept into the culture war: the post-1960s nostalgia for the 1950s and the absence of the economic reality of the welfare state contributing to the conditions for the "happy days" of the *fifties*.[108] Silence toward this intervention often includes an uncritical assessment of this golden age's thriving white supremacy, including the male-only prospects further narrowing competition for political and economic opportunities between white men (although this *remembered* experience, too, contributes to the embers of nostalgia's warmth). Against the backdrop of federal intervention into white America's centuries-old rights to discriminate against people of color, the attacks against the welfare state by the emerging New Right and neoliberals made more sense. Perhaps Hayek was correct when he insisted that the "collectivist" logic of the welfare state would inevitably lead liberal democracies down "the road to serfdom" and authoritarian communism? In the context of social equality legislation and the neoliberal critique of the welfare state, the charges of communism leveled at the civil rights movement by Southern segregationists suddenly became relevant to Northern and Western white suburbia.[109]

After years of popular disparagement during the Great Depression, corporate America came out of World War II with a rebuilt image capitalizing on the Cold War. In many ways, American business became an important defining symbol of capitalism, taking credit for building a mass culture responsible for the domestic revival of the "American way of life" (again, federal intervention was downplayed in the name of fighting communist "collectivism").[110] Many championed the modern corporation under the shadow of the mixed economy, concurring with Berle's suggestion that these institutions were "the outstanding achievement of our generation."[111] Of course, postwar U.S. hegemony abroad tied to the welfare state provided the ideal situation for American corporations: while domestically protecting the economy from the instability of economic depression, internationally, the U.S. nation-state sought to further open areas of the world for trade and investment as diplomacy targeted protective tariffs, tax laws, subsidies, and other barriers in the name of creating a "universal free trade" world.[112] In short, a contradictory quest for an international laissez-faire market organized by *Pax Americana* on behalf of a national regulatory mixed economy.

Odd Arne Westad describes the *Pax Americana* projection of power as lying in America's "symbols and images—the free market, anti-Communism, fear of state power, faith in technology."[113] Out of this "way of life," the United States sought to remake the world in its own liberal democratic image to counter the antagonistic forces of communism, and "bind all states to a new rule of law in the international economy."[114] Building off pre–World War II precedents, the postwar United States embraced a foreign policy where the government brokered foreign investment within "unstable" states through contracts between U.S. businesses and foreign nations. These practices ostensibly replaced old imperialism with "the use of loans to leverage fiscal supervision."[115] For internationalist liberals guiding *Pax Americana*, modernization theory brought up to date the ideas of progress inherent in Western civilization, with the imperial and technical experience of U.S. intervention in the early twentieth century translating into newly independent nations imagined as spaces for the exportation of American values—or, as Michael Latham notes, the blending of "national security and economic needs."[116] Thus, the dynamics of the Cold War created overseas business climates suitable for investment, including support for right-wing dictatorships and the undermining of labor movements (often through state-directed purges of left-wing activists).¹¹⁷ These postcolonial authoritarian environments also offered few regulatory controls on the environment and capital flows, which fell in line with the 1947 General Agreement on Tariffs and Trade (GATT). Anticipating the neoliberal logic of structural adjustment programs (SAPs) in the 1980s and 1990s, the United States sought the "liberalization of the world economy—not only free trade, but also the free movement of both long- and short-term capital— regardless of its effect on the displacement of labor as manufacturing moved to cheap labor and relaxed regulations in formerly colonized nations."¹¹⁸

A looming crisis began unfolding in the 1960s as President Lyndon B. Johnson extended the New Deal via the Great Society. As an increasingly anxious white population grew weary of the civil rights movement challenging de facto or institutional racism, this renewal of social spending collided with the growing costs associated with the Vietnam War, a creeping stagnancy of the economy, and the rhetorical momentum of the New Right conservative movement.¹¹⁹ The convergence of global competition between the United States, Japan, and West Germany led to overproduction and overcapacity. Moreover, the United States faced fixed costs of production (plant and equipment) as well as a regulated economy linking productivity with wage levels "that could not quickly be squeezed downward," whereas Japan and West Germany enjoyed cheaper labor.¹²⁰ As *Business Week* pointed out, 13 percent of U.S. equipment was obsolete by the end of 1968, leaving industry operating at more than 10 percent below the operating rate of up-to-date factories.¹²¹ The profit rate for U.S. manufacturing capital stock fell 43.5 percent between 1965 and 1973.¹²² With trade imbalances and the amount of dollars—Eurodollars— held abroad rising, the combination of the costs and "inflationary effects" of the Vietnam War and Great Society helped propel the U.S. economy into crisis.¹²³ To weather these changes, corporations utilized their two decades of experience negotiating the regulatory state and the international marketplace after World War II, and turned to the postwar merger trend for solutions.

Finance and the Growth of Multinational Conglomerates

With the global economy becoming more competitive, flexibility in business practices displaced the tentative alliance with labor characterizing the 1950s and 1960s "consensus." The intricacies of this new model took shape through the financial innovations of a rejuvenated Wall Street, including policies that increasingly found kinship with the neoliberal rhetoric of free markets and economic liberty against the regulatory welfare state as the 1970s dawned. Although the ties between finance, corporations, and the American state stretch back to the nineteenth century, this entwined relationship grew expansively in the postwar years.[124] Through postwar finance, mergers became a useful way to stay competitive in the world economy.[125] With the stable environment of American-led postwar capitalism, growth rates hovered around 5 percent annually up through the early 1970s (with slight downturns in 1954, 1957, 1967, and 1970).[126] The development of U.S. multinationals abroad operated through this system, moving capital investment, profits, and goods across vast networks spanning the American-led world economy. "An old tradition of U.S. business has been broken," asserted *Business Week* in 1959: since 1950 business had turned away from the nation and ventured overseas for markets, as U.S. companies poured a "huge dollar investment . . . into production facilities abroad."[127] The magazine went on to note that 99 out of 100 of the largest corporations in the United States were "involved today in one or another kind of overseas operation."[128] A headline a year later asserted, "Capital Spending: Flat at Home, Up Abroad."[129] Foreign direct investment grew rapidly from 1960 on:

Table 3.1 Stock of accumulated foreign direct investment. From Michael J. Webber and David L. Rigby, *The Golden Age Illusion: Rethinking Postwar Capitalism* (New York: Guilford, 1996), 33.

1938	$26 billion
1960	$70 billion
1971	$172 billion
1978	$400 billion

An important factor guiding postwar finance evolved drastically in the 1960s. Throughout the decade, a series of problems increasingly exerted strain on the Bretton Woods system as trade imbalances and an outflow of dollars—especially to Europe—from the United States weakened the economy. In an attempt to drive down the deficit in the 1960s, Johnson put a $1 billion curb on multinational overseas capital investment in 1968, leading MNCs to fear that they would lose "their competitive edge in world markets."[130] Compounding the problem, inflation surfaced as a critical issue, a long-term consequence of the perpetual expansion of Keynesian economics on top of the growing costs of the Vietnam War.[131] Speculators scrambled to buy gold as the outflow of U.S. dollars persisted as a result of the imbalance of payments.[132] The changing global economy made the regulatory state's controls over capital obsolete—at least in the minds of finance. Arrighi cites 1968 as the beginning of this shift, "when the growth of liquid funds held in the London-centered Eurodollar market experienced a sudden and explosive acceleration."[133]

Eurodollars entered Europe through the Marshall Plan, with the market exploding in the late 1950s as they became an important source of capital invested around the world from its trading center in London.[134] An example of this transaction includes a scenario where a German bank might have a surplus of dollars and deposits them in London, with London turning around and lending them to a Japanese company needing "payment in dollars."[135] Although the Federal Reserve regulated interest rates in the United States, overseas the situation was different. *Business Week* described the procedure: "Europeans—or even U.S. international oil companies—who find themselves holding dollar balances have an incentive to lend where rates are highest.... Thus, the Eurodollar market—and the satellite markets in Eurosterling and other Euromonies—reflect the evolution of a truly international money market. Eurodollars offer an avenue of escape from conventional methods of credit control, blurring the lines between national monetary systems and creating new problems of financial control."[136] U.S. banks jumped on the opportunity to trade in Eurodollars, setting up "numerous branches in London to participate."[137] This adaption by transnational economic organizations forged a patched-together standard for the freer flow of capital eventually enacted by neoliberal policies in the 1980s.[138]

In a February 1969 issue of *Business Week*, a special report on the Bretton Woods agreement argued for reforms and a more flexible system: "Unless the United States can halt inflation and enlarge last year's minuscule trade surplus, the dollar could come under attack. In the end, what happens to the dollar determines what happens to the system."[139] At the close of the nation's economy's successful run (the U.S. poverty line declined to 10 percent in 1973 from a high of one-third in 1950), *Business Week* noted one policy of note for the United States and Britain: the balance between "full employment" and "domestic deflation."[140] Becoming "'flexible' on the gold price question" was one answer, letting the free market set the price while nations' currencies would adjust accordingly.[141] Once the United States "shut the gold window" in 1971, rising prices would work to define the decade.[142]

Richard Nixon's dismantling of the Bretton Woods agreement in August 1971 provided a jolt to a system increasingly stifling U.S. economic expansion. The era of trade deficits had arrived. As the United States "posted its first postwar trade deficit in 1971," write Webber and Rigby, "it was clear that the international financial system was pegged to an overvalued dollar."[143] With the collapse of Bretton Woods, floating exchange rates replaced the convertibility of dollars to gold. With dollars held by foreign nations depreciated, a turning point had been reached: "Henceforth, the relatively high level of international economic cooperation that had been achieved against the background of the great post-war economic expansion would increasingly give way to intensifying international politico-economic conflict in the face of a much slower growing world economic pie, especially over the rules of the game for international investment, trade, and money."[144] As *Business Week* observed, "With the dollar floating—that is to say, exchanging for other currencies at fluctuating rates—there no longer is a system, rather a jumble of day-to-day exchange-rate quotations."[145] In terms of finance, a weakness of the welfare state regulatory system was the inability to predict and adjust to the "great surges of capital across national borders."[146] Spurred by technological advances in communication, the regulatory system could not keep up with the pace of change engaged in by multinationals and finance, resulting in a situation where the trading of dollars ventured into uncontrolled environments outside the United States (e.g., Eurodollars).[147] More than this, the unleashing of capital outside the regulatory restraints of the postwar Bretton Woods monetary system led to an even greater internationalization of capital as the "banking business transformed itself to cope with this cornucopia," including providing the capital for corporations to diversify through "mergers and acquisitions"; as Richard Sennett suggests, "The hostile takeover became a form of art, as money looked for ever new ways to install itself."[148]

The sort of global deregulation of capital flows characterizing national policy after the 1960s found root in these experiences of MNCs operating across multiple nations and currencies in the postwar years. The limitations of the welfare state arose as the regulatory networks failed to keep pace with the needs of expanding multinationals.[149] In 1971, *Business Week* noted how this strategy protected the capital of multinationals around the world "from currency losses," stating, "In doing so they can build up or relieve pressure on the exchange rates that relate the dollar to pounds, yen and deutschemarks."[150] These were the practices undermining the regulatory frameworks of nation-states. *Business Week* outlined this complicated process: "They play a complex game of money management, 'leading' and 'lagging' payments between far-flung affiliates for products that they sell each other and constantly hedging their operating funds in many currencies against parity changes.... There is no doubt that the massive corporate movements of short-term funds at high speed have helped to magnify recent monetary crises.... Such networks, extending into dozens of countries, give corporate financial officers great flexibility in designing protection against currency losses."[151] According to *Business Week*, the MNCs' greatest fear was the further growth of capital movement restrictions aimed toward regulating these innovations. As multinationals outgrew the regulatory welfare state, these contradictions pressed together the interests of MNCs and the anti-regulatory neoliberals: while the United States intervened in the economy in the name of middle-class economic stability via democratic passions, its very regulatory features increasingly interfered with the prerogatives of multinationals. The age of currency flexibility found expression through currency speculation, as MNCs benefited from the dismantling of Bretton Woods, reversing some trends away from foreign investment for U.S. corporations.[152] As currencies realigned, and the federal government began penalizing imports, some overseas companies expressed interest in reinvesting in the United States.[153]

In the summer of 1974, *Business Week* ran a special report titled "The World Economy."[154] With the collapse of the Bretton Woods agreement and the inability of governments to successfully grapple with the problems of inflation, unemployment, and the huge rise in the price of petroleum, the authors noted that central bankers in nations around the world were left to squeeze credit, resulting in slow growth. Mirroring the domestic situation, MNCs in foreign nations increasingly discovered that they were not necessarily welcomed but "reluctantly tolerated."[155] One point of contention for multinationals included the more frequent conflicts with "their host governments": from oil companies in the Middle East to aluminum companies in Jamaica.[156] Customs unions and monetary cooperation, the older mechanisms smoothing out overseas operations, were quickly "breaking down."[157] The paths for doing business abroad needed to be rethought to sustain the high profits from before 1973, especially as newly decolonized nations began asserting their sovereign rights (which often removed the favorable climate multinationals enjoyed during the colonial era). A delicate balance remained, as most of the companies operating overseas were "often major factors in key sectors of the economy."[158] Problems with profits created another stumbling block, especially for local government partners taking exception to MNCs pulling "out large dividends because it believed the local currency was about to be devalued."[159] Erratic capital flows quickly became an ongoing reality for poor nations in desperate need of stable, long-term investment capital.

This scenario, of course, personified the mission of neoliberals as the world decolonized. The expansion of democracy after imperial autocratic rule, let alone the popularly elected U.S. and European welfare state governments, trampled across the rights of private capital.[160] Contrary to Friedman's assertation that capitalism equated to freedom, the neoliberal mission sought to make the democratic voice of nations subservient to the needs of capital. As Quinn Slobodian notes, "Democracy might have to be restricted for certain peoples in order to preserve stability and prosperity. Restricting political freedom, as commonly understood, was necessary under some circumstances to preserve economic freedom."[161] Although this might be achievable through U.S.-led coups supported by MNCs (such as United Fruit in Guatemala or ITT in Chile) operating in newly decolonized nations or Latin American countries, for nations with a history of democratic participation, the stumbling block included fostering a new consensus away from the welfare state and toward a vision where the needs of finance and multinationals would find protection over the passions of democracy.

An important stimulus pressing the consensus away from the welfare state and toward the economic disciplining of neoliberalism was the 1974-75 recession and the deep waters of inflation.[162] Although U.S. industry suffered from overproduction before the oil crisis in 1973, the Organization of Petroleum Exporting Countries' (OPEC's) rise in oil prices influenced an already increasing inflation as it drastically raised the price of energy.[163] Amid the recession, the spike in oil prices spurred the trade in petrodollars out of the profits of OPEC. The Treasury department under Nixon and Ford sought to strategically secure "interdependence" through petrodollars passing between the U.S. and oil producing nations.[164] The Treasury's "free market ideology and disdain for New Deal or Great Society-esque programs," adds David M. Wight, set the federal government's policy toward petrodollars within the evolving framework of neoliberalism in the 1970s.[165] Prophetically, Treasury undersecretary, Paul Volcker, who was instrumental in these policies, would later become head of the Federal Reserve in 1979—and help steer the national economy toward the neoliberal era in the 1980s. Consequently, a small handful of multinational U.S. banks gained control of petrodollars seeking investment by OPEC nations in the wake of the 1973 oil crisis, channeling investment capital through Wall Street rather than through the International Monetary Fund as many U.S. allies sought. As exporting oil nations invested their earnings in Western banks, their petrodollars were recycled through these institutions, providing more capital to invest overseas as well as paying for the risings costs of the very source of their loans—oil.[166] The added capital for finance via petrodollars provided a key outlet for corporate restructuring as the Bretton Woods agreement collapsed and profits from manufacturing declined in the 1970s.[167] In addition, petrodollars helped to offset the indebtedness of the U.S. government as well.[168] With OPEC money routed through Wall Street and into investments in developing nations, banks pushed to open U.S. markets to exports from developing nations receiving petrodollar loans—and needing to repay banks.[169] "The new lending policies," writes Judith Stein, "created new conflicts between American finance and American manufacturing."[170] For those outside Wall Street, these years proved more painful as inflation diminished earnings, and unemployment eroded the gains of the blue-collar prosperity enjoyed during the height of the welfare state.[171]

Other financial innovations provided breathing space and flexibility for MNCs to reorganize their activities at home and abroad. The computer and telecommunication revolution created faster and cheaper avenues in which international financial trading took place, "so currency trading exploded in the early 1970s, destabilizing money markets."[172] The profits of this money market trading caught the attention of private investors, international banks, and MNCs, further destabilizing the dollar standard.[173] Tensions surrounding these innovations in the 1960s eventually culminated with transnational corporations and finance straining "against the compartmentalization laid down in the Glass-Steagall Act [1933]"—a measure enacted during the New Deal to separate commercial from investment banking.[174] The finance industry helped undermine capital regulation even more as government agencies were unable to access the "statistical information ... because of bank resistance."[175] The corporate-finance embrace of utilizing computers to navigate Toffler's information overload led to one of the most important revolutions related to the business world's growing relationship with technology. The critical change took place when the 1960s "applications approach"—a model "characterized by the programming of individual computer applications that satisfied a specific output requirement"—was displaced by the database management system of the 1970s, where rather than relying on a "pre-defined information need," computer systems would capture as much data as possible to create a more flexible model: "through a data model, data collection and storage could be approached completely independently from the output, the information product, and the ultimate use of such information for satisfying a managerial decision-making need."[176] The age of big data—and the increasing value of information *as private property*—had begun.[177] Significantly, innovation outpaced the tendrils of government regulation. These pressures found their release through the incremental deregulation of capital flows in the 1970s, helping to establish the political environment shaping the financial boom of the 1980s. Webber and Rigby write, "In the USA restrictions on capital flows were abolished in 1974, all restrictions on interest rates had been dropped by 1986, banking regulations were steadily relaxed through the 1970s, and in 1981 banks were permitted to offer international banking facilities within the USA."[178]

The quickened movement of data fostered by computers combined with the dismantling of Bretton Woods, opening the door to currency speculation. For example, "between 1971 and 1980 the US dollar depreciated 25% against a trade-weighted index of foreign currencies, whereas between 1980 and 1985 the US dollar rose by 67% against a share-weighted average of other OECD [Organisation for Economic Co-operation and Development] countries."[179] For developing nations borrowing capital through the flood of petrodollars, this had the expected effect: at the height of borrowing, the cheapening dollar made loans especially attractive; once interest rates linked to dollars rose, nations suddenly fell into debt far beyond the ability to repay. This instability of currencies and ensuing debt crisis opened the door for neoliberal-directed

SAPs in the 1980s and 1990s.[180] A big winner in these systemic shifts was finance, though even the U.S. government felt the effects of this restructuring as it emerged in 1983 as the "largest debtor nation in the world."[181]

With the infrastructure in place providing the foundation for freer trade and capital flows after the 1970s, and the acceleration of financial deregulation near the end of Jimmy Carter's presidency, finance not only helped reenergize multinationals, they also influenced trade relations and the economic policies of other governments on a scale not seen since before the Great Depression.[182] Indeed, the rejuvenated finance industry helped tremendously in providing capital for MNCs to merge or acquire small companies during the 1970s economic downturn. "Creative financing," writes Benjamin C. Waterhouse, facilitated the rise of conglomerates: "Rather than save up accumulated profits from the past to finance expansion, as they had traditionally, postwar executives borrowed and raised money more aggressively through private capital markets, bonds, or stock sales, all underwritten by investment banks."[183]

Characteristic of the quickening pace of economic change, conglomerates embodied what some observers began labeling the era of postmodernity.[184] The chroniclers of this often-ambiguous label offer some useful insights with regard to the cultural context of the rise of conglomerates. For example, Fredric Jameson notes postmodernity—or what he calls late capitalism—as materially manifesting itself through the dominance of "multinational capitalism," the "new international division of labor, a vertiginous new dynamic in international banking and stock exchanges . . . , new forms of media interrelationship . . . , computers and automation, [and] the flight of production to advanced Third World areas."[185] David Harvey's assessment also foregrounds the economic changes circulating through postwar capitalism, including the new system of "flexible accumulation" from the 1960s that embraced "[a] flexibility with respect to labour processes, labour markets, products, and patterns of consumption. It is characterized by the emergence of entirely new sectors of production, new ways of providing financial services, new markets, and, above all, greatly intensified rates of commercial, technological, and organizational innovation."[186] Of course, this flexibility depended upon the perpetual innovation of computer communication systems, allowing for a lean and diverse corporation to access finance capital in order to negotiate the buying and selling of businesses (acquisitions) as investments. In this framework, government regulations became anathema to an economy increasingly pressing toward free capital flows. In some ways, postmodernism embodied the Depression-era dreams of Hayek.

A key to the ongoing success of these large, transnational organizations lay in their ability to unify the "processes of mass production with those of mass distribution" under a single capitalist organization.[187] This centralization of all the dynamics of global trade achieved greater efficiency while reducing costs. Both size and strategic separation of duties created a flexible environment for MNCs operating across nation-states. *Business Week*, in a special report in 1970, underlined the role of these multinationals in creating the new global economy at the dawn of the 1970s—and the roadblocks presented by nation-states: "But as multinational companies reshape the patterns of production and marketing, they are also clashing with traditional interests of the world's basic political institution, the nation state. At home and abroad, their impact on established businesses, labor markets, and even cultural patterns is creating social strains. For businessmen and statesmen, a major challenge of the 1970s is to reconcile these conflicts."[188] Much of this tension between the U.S. government and the growing power of conglomerates centered on the uneasiness of acquisitions and mergers, pitting government regulation against an industry whose needs increasingly aligned with the neoliberal vision of deregulation and the disavowal of the dangers of capital concentration. In 1967, *Business Week* described the accelerating drive toward growth and the flood of new developments that accompanied the drive to diversify through conglomeration: "The same trends that brought the conglomerate into being have been running in the other big companies, too. They also are becoming more diverse, more oriented toward high technology, and more flexible. They are developing staffs of specialists relying more and more on professional management.... There's so much impetus—so steady a pattern of growth, so rapid an evolution in sophistication—that the corporation can only go ahead. It's changing the world rapidly now—and almost certainly will change it far more in the next 20 years."[189]

Much like the era of monopoly almost 100 years before, controversy shrouded the merger movement in the late 1960s. Conglomerates operated in an environment where they could not control the pricing of markets as monopolies could. However, they exerted a wide range of power as "concentrates," straddling various industries from mining to insurance to department stores to military contracts to Hollywood studios (e.g., *Paramount: A Gulf+ Western Company*). The identity of American business began to blur as they "lost any industry identification," while treating newly acquired businesses as often short-term investments.[190] With earnings slipping along with the overall economy in the late 1960s, both Wall Street and the Johnson administration looked warily at the growth of conglomerates.[191] With neither institution truly checking the growth of multinationals, this period was an important turning point for MNCs and the construction of global financial networks characterizing neoliberalism and the finance phase of the fourth accumulation cycle. Sprawling, flexible, and diverse, these institutions would not only weather the economic crisis of the 1970s, but they also came to define post-1970s capitalism.

The most alarming feature of these corporate organizations was their size, with investors questioning the control over such a wide array of divisions. The public, too, began "to conjure up images of ruthless capitalists practicing their black arts of high finance to their own ends."[192] Challenges to the conglomerate also came from the Securities and Exchange Commission's push to "eliminate some of the accounting and financial reporting loopholes that have been the conglomerators' stock in trade."[193] In defense of conglomerates and echoing the neoliberal defense of monopolies and large companies, *Business Week* offered a different take that aligned more with Friedman's nostalgic possession of history for the late-nineteenth-century brand of unregulated capitalism:

> All of this scrutiny tends to focus on the corporate octopus image of the conglomerates, but there's another aspect. At its best, the conglomerate style harkens back to the entrepreneurial spirit and daring that typified the early days of U.S. capitalism.... Creators rather than curators, the conglomerates often revive competition in settled industries by picking up marginal producers and energizing them with new capital, uninhibited ideas, and fresh expertise.... Shrewd, aggressive, and often charismatic, they excite and sometimes inspire the men around them. Their energy is contagious. And to many people, energetic business is healthy business.[194]

The price-earnings multiple was one of the keys to the success of conglomerates: "The higher a conglomerate's stock price relative to its earnings per share, the less it spends to buy another company."[195] With investors looking more toward future growth in profits, "growth expectations" form the perennial stock and trade for conglomerates as low-growth acquisitions shift into "high growth expectations" after purchase and renovation by the multinational.[196] From this logic, *Business Week* offered a solution to the highly regulated airlines industry in 1971: "Only mergers can bail out the airlines."[197] Consequently, the deregulation of the airline industry "became, almost overnight, the general model."[198] Trucking soon followed via the Motor Carrier Act of 1980.[199]

Although the growth of conglomerates slowed in the late 1960s—with most activity aimed at small and medium-size firms—a new model for weathering the uncertainties of the world economy had been established.[200] Unconsciously anticipating the new frontier of neoliberalism, *Business Week* imagined conglomerates as regenerating socioeconomic mechanisms ostensibly connected to late 1800s American settler colonialism. Culturally, these large corporations found protection against antitrust actions through Cold War celebrations of private enterprise and the welfare state's embrace of big business, as well as the ascending logic of the neoliberal view of big business and monopolies: "price and efficiency—rather than firm size or market share"—determined whether a corporation should be a target of antitrust suits.[201] So-called price-grounded antitrust doctrine would become the common sense in business legislation by the 1980s.

Business Week's special report on MNCs in 1970 outlined the threshold leading to the new culture of neoliberal globalization. Their strategy, noted the authors, was to be "in every single country there is."[202] With competition from Japanese and European companies, multinationals leaned on their flexibility and diversity to gain entrance into nations, creating affiliates, joint ventures, and coproduction arrangements with foreign governments. Defending large transnational companies, *Business Week* asserted that these MNCs were "unleashing new productive capacities around the world as they escape the confines of national markets"; in short, they "have in fact found the means of applying the Ricardian principle of comparative advantage more efficiently than ever before. The result is rising production of goods and services all over the world. The United States, which has contributed more than any other country to the creation of the multinational corporation, has a just claim to a share in the new wealth."[203]

Winter in America: Ending the Great Compression

By the 1970s, capital unwaveringly leaned toward larger companies whose increasingly diverse holdings lay far outside the original corporation's industry. Diversification offered greater stability navigating the fast-paced, unstable post-1973 global economy. The transition of the American economy from factories (production) to finance—to paraphrase Judith Stein—accelerated, reflecting the fourth phase of Arrighi's *longue durée* "cycles of accumulation."[204] Banking institutions and the evolution of finance combined with the new networks of multinational conglomerates, leading to what has been described as the postindustrial era of globalization, or what we may simply call the neoliberal era.[205]

Just as corporations conglomerated through acquisitions and mergers, banking also took similar steps in the late 1960s. Following the example of First National City Bank in 1968, banks increasingly became holding companies where, *Business Week* notes, the "world's financial assets are being concentrated in fewer and fewer hands, and this process of concentration is far from over."[206] Overseas assets for the largest U.S. banks accounted for 25–50 percent of their overall income. An important step toward this drive came from the Bank Holding Company Act of 1970, which "allowed holding companies to own more than one bank—and also to be in any business that the Federal Reserve Board deems to be 'closely related' to banking."[207] The latter included the leasing of equipment, finance companies, insurance, travel services, and data processing (which anticipated the big data revolution in the twenty-first century).[208] This momentum toward transnational diversification demanded the deregulation of increasingly obsolete welfare state regulations. A growing consensus at the Fed and among bankers targeted one critical measure curtailing the ascension of finance: the full repeal of the Glass-Steagall Act.[209] Although it would take until the 1990s to completely dismantle the Glass-Steagall Act, the law would be a primary target for the finance industry throughout the next few decades. Banking expansion did, however, help solve the problems of capital as U.S. banks, alongside access to petrodollars, used Eurodollars to finance MNCs abroad while shipping Eurodollars "home in quantity whenever the Fed tightened the domestic money supply."[210] After years of lobbying against regulations, the money market mutual fund was created and, after approval in 1972 by the federal government, increasingly became an alternative to regular bank savings accounts.[211]

A third round of mergers accompanied these changes in banking in the early 1970s.[212] In a June 1975 issue, *Business Week* noted Wall Street's new enthusiasm for conglomerates who had weathered the recession thus far through "both solid management and the sort of successful diversification that resists economic cycles."[213] Drawn to these large entities, capital found a new stable site for accumulation. Moreover, by the spring of 1976, foreign investors increasingly eyed the United States for investment, with *Business Week* noting the "depreciation of the dollar and depressed stock prices in the past year have made U.S. corporations a good buy for foreigners looking for acquisitions."[214]

An example of corporate conglomeration includes the Mobil Oil Corporation, a company that moved to diversify its capital holdings through the purchase of the chain department store, Montgomery Ward, rather than investing its post-1973 oil crisis profits into domestic oil production.[215] Exxon soon followed the trend as well, buying Compania Minera Disputada in Chile, in the Cold War market-friendly post-coup (U.S.-led) environment headed up by the dictatorship of General Augusto Pinochet.[216] Even steel companies transferred their profits away from capital stock and toward "the acquisition of chemical firms, shopping malls, and other activities; so much so that, by 1979, forty-six cents of every new dollar of U.S. Steel capital investment was going into the corporation's non-steel ventures."[217] Amid stagnation, mergers seemed to be the surest bet on surviving the economic turbulence of the 1970s. According to *Business Week*, by 1980 more capital was spent on acquisitions than research and development.[218] As Harvey documents, the dollars spent on mergers went from $22 billion in 1977, to $82 billion in 1981, to $180 billion in 1985.[219] Instead of creating new factories, two-thirds of "new" plants purchased were older ones. Falling victim to the process of "milking," profitable factories would often be bought by conglomerates, drained of its cash reserves, and then discarded, shut down, or sold again—in short, a "strategy of planned disinvestment in its recent acquisition."[220] As Barry Bluestone and Bennett Harrison note, throughout the 1970s these *Fortune* 500 companies "physically expanded only *one in seven* of the plants they owned at the start of the decade."[221]

To bolster profits, multinationals often sold exports to foreign affiliates in which they had a majority stake. This trade between different but financially connected corporations allowed for a manipulation of pricing—called transfer pricing—outside the so-called market price.[222] Significantly, "intra-firm transactions" grew from "20–30 per cent in the 1960s to something in the order of 40–50 per cent in the late 1980s and early 1990s."[223] Techniques such as these aided transnational business in negotiating various nation-state regulations as products and capital flowed across borders, including price controls, tax rates on profits, fluctuating exchange rates, and import duties.[224] The ratio between U.S. manufacturing exports and that of U.S. multinationals' foreign sales looked like the following across the 1960s:

Table 3.2 U.S. manufacturing exports/foreign sales of U.S. multinationals. From Andre Gunder Frank, "The Post-war Boom: Boon for the West, Bust for the South," *Millennium* 7 (1978): 156.

U.S. manufacturing exports
1961 $15 billion
1970 $35 billion
Foreign sales of U.S. multinationals
1961 $25 billion
1970 $90 billion

In total, U.S. direct foreign investment increased sixteenfold between 1950 and 1980, "from about $12 billion to $192 billion."[225] Three-quarters of the sales of MNCs were aimed toward the markets in which they operated, whereas the remainder was exported abroad (often to the United States). Indeed, in 1976 alone 29 percent of imports into the United States were from the overseas plants of American multinationals or their subsidiaries.[226] These trends marked both less-developed countries and industrialized Western nations: "fully 40% of 'Latin American' manufacturing exports in 1968 were in fact exported by U.S.-owned subsidiaries in Latin America; and U.S. multinationals also account for an appreciable share of 'British' and other countries' exports."[227] As the 1980s unfolded, the profits from overseas expansion reached "a third or more of the overall profits of the hundred largest multinational producers and banks in the United States."[228] In relation to domestic employment, some estimates suggest that 26,500 jobs were eliminated for every $1 billion of foreign investment by U.S. MNCs.[229]

As a result of overseas expansion and diversification, modernization of existing domestic factories suffered. Short-term diversification measures were embraced to weather the changing dynamics of global capitalism, replacing the long-term structural planning of the past. In their efforts to reduce costs through the disinvestment of capital stock domestically (such as machine tools and factories), by 1979 factories failed to keep pace in efficiency (they had an average age of 7.1 years).[230] *Business Week* pointed this out as early as 1972, criticizing the technological gap between the United States and its primary competitors, Japan and Europe.[231] The authors suggested that the root of the problem was management—an assessment *Business Week* would rearticulate through the neoliberal worldview by the end of the 1970s: government regulation costs accounted for inefficiencies.[232] In the early 1970s, however, *Business Week* noted that although companies in the 1950s and 1960s outpaced their competition, MNCs complicated this process as their "management, marketing, production, and development knowhow [had] spread rapidly outside the boundaries of the United States. At the same time, U.S. companies [became] less innovative, less willing to gamble on new products, and less adept at translating a scientific development into a commercial product."[233] Growth for U.S. companies rested more on acquisitions and overseas expansion rather than national reinvestment or channeling profits into innovations.[234] For the U.S. worker unable to access this fast-changing economic environment, the warm and prosperous 1960s summer of love quickly changed into a bitter winter of downsizing and outsourcing in the 1970s and 1980s.

Examples of outsourcing throughout the 1970s outline this trend. General Electric, for instance, expanded its capital stock overseas rather than in the United States, leading to 25,000 domestic jobs being replaced by 30,000 foreign jobs.[235] Ford and General Motors followed similar trends, divesting their obsolete plants and workforces domestically and expanding internationally.[236] In some extravagant cases, companies would invest in their overseas competition while simultaneously protesting foreign competition. In the case of U.S. Steel Corporation in the 1970s, it held shares in South African mining and mineral companies that worked closely with the state-owned South African Iron and Steel Corporation. Investment was further insulated as the South African company received loans from U.S. banks (Chase and Citicorp), which were also "among those banks ... refusing to provide investment capital to upgrade the domestic U.S. steel industry."[237]

This strategy of deindustrialization was macro in nature, as Arrighi's financial phase unfolded. With production in the United States failing to produce sufficient profits, capital moved to where it could find better returns. Through the moral prism of neoliberalism market logic, the social costs for American society became irrelevant to business decisions. A cultural precept of neoliberalism helped justify this cold turn away from the postwar idea of fairness and justness characterizing the redistributionist logic of the Jim Crow welfare state to the neoliberal logic of market efficiency and quantitative analysis.[238] Trends initiated in this era included the reformed regulatory framework of neoliberalism reemphasizing "the rise of 'shareholder value' as the legitimate goal of corporate governance during the 1980s and 1990s."[239] As managers lost the ability to organize their corporations in the long term, the new environment of "sophisticated shareholder power" pressed the concerns of big business toward "short-term rather than long-term results": "share price rather than corporate dividends was their measure of results."[240] Corporations moved away from the postwar regulatory logic of stability at the dawn of the neoliberal era: "stability seemed a sign of weakness," notes Richard Sennett, "suggesting to the market that the firm could not innovate or find new opportunities or otherwise manage change."[241] Technology (as noted above) signaled the avenues this new culture of capitalism would follow, with information and database management systems becoming vital in their ability to generate instantaneous and accurate assessments while leading toward a future where "data-centered concepts ... provided a conceptual grounding for the materialisation and growth of ideological beliefs concerning data's objectivity, truthfulness, and transparency."[242] In short, decisions based on the morality of quantitative analysis. The early fears of job displacement through technological advancement further eroded "the social element of social capitalism."[243] This reconfigured relationship between capital and labor shredded the remnants of the postwar consensus, provoking a return to the social Darwinist laissez-faire capitalism of the classical liberal era before the New Deal: the mere threat of factory relocation would discipline the demands of labor. The corporate responsibility era of "awareness" between 1953–67, "in which there became more recognition of the overall responsibility of business and its involvement in community affairs," dissolved amid economic restructuring and the ascension of neoliberal economics.[244] As Sennett suggests, "social capitalism" became "a nostalgic memory."[245] The shedding of the consensus era's social responsibility removed the moral constraints in reversing the wealth distribution of the postwar years: labor productivity continued to rise in this restructured environment, although wages began falling or stagnated across the 1970s and up through the twenty-first century.²⁴⁶ This conjuncture of economic restructuring became the foundation of neoliberalism and one of the pillars of the Reagan revolution. As conservative author Kevin Phillips observed in 1990, "From 1981 on, workers barely kept up with inflation and homeowners on average could stay only a bit ahead.... Corporate executives and investors were the prime 1980s beneficiaries. Their gains roared ahead of the consumer price index like a sonic boom."²⁴⁷

With the redistribution of wealth away from the middle and working classes came the effect of stripping political power away from organized labor—an important goal of big business since the 1930s.²⁴⁸ The high watermark of postwar capitalism, from the vantage point of the Reagan era, undoubtedly was the mid-1960s, as Keynesianism secured unprecedented low unemployment while unions became ever larger and bureaucratized like their corporate brethren. However, the decline of unions coincided with the onset of the culture war as strikes increased after the mid-1960s. For *Business Week*, unions became the source for growing inflation.²⁴⁹ The wave of labor unrest affected American domestic productivity, with strikes and absenteeism reducing the "average growth of production per worker between 1967 and 1970."²⁵⁰ In 1970, *Business Week* bluntly stated on its cover, "The U.S. can't afford what labor wants."²⁵¹ Companies such as RCA, who had already followed a well-worn path of relocating across the Northeast to the Midwest as labor consolidated gains, began in earnest to move outside the United States.²⁵²

Along with the increased labor discontent and attacks from the business press, three additional changes further widened the crisis for labor in the 1970s: (1) the rise of unemployment as industry relocated from older areas of production, (2) the entry of people of color and women workers into areas previously reserved for white males, and (3) the rise of contingent, part-time work, rather than full-time positions with benefits.²⁵³ Augmented with the fair employment provision of the Civil Rights Act of 1964, existing tensions between Black and white workers were exacerbated amid the panic over deindustrialization. For the most part, white skilled unions long practiced a masculine white supremacist exclusion of people of color and women.²⁵⁴ In 1972, *Business Week* explained why unemployment would grow, asserting, "Since the first quarter of 1971, employment has climbed by 2-million jobs, but the labor force has grown just as fast."²⁵⁵ Included in this expansion of the labor market, *Business Week* continued, were women, teenagers, and "discouraged workers" outside the job market.²⁵⁶ The authors cite the Labor Department's assertion that "the labor force appears to have grown more elastic."²⁵⁷ John E. Schwarz characterized this conjuncture as a "crushing avalanche of American workers entering the labor market," growing "40 percent" between 1965 and 1980.²⁵⁸ The normalization of underemployed or contingent labor set in, establishing a baseline for the arrival of the twenty-first-century gig economy.²⁵⁹

For finance and MNCs, this political momentum would unlock the regulatory world set in place by the New Deal and unleash the greatest expansion of wealth inequality in the nation's history. In his three-volume history of capitalism published in 1979, Fernand Braudel noted the rising influence of large MNCs and their transformation of global capitalism: "The laws of the market no longer apply to huge firms which can influence demand by their very effective advertising, and which can fix prices arbitrarily."²⁶⁰ More importantly, the structural relationship of multinationals and finance to nation-states adopting elements of neoliberalism facilitated the desired space for the corporate world to flourish. And the political actors of this era, too, found success as taxes on the wealthy dropped precipitously in the 1980s, based on the argument of trickle-down economics: if the wealthy and big business were given tax relief, the abundance of wealth would overflow their coffers and trickle down to the lower 90 percent. This promise sealed the new weather patterns, as winter in America firmly set in, establishing a norm of extended periods of a windy, cold draught.

Conjuncture: Capitalism and the Culture War

The conjuncture of neoliberal ideas, the New Right, and the evolution of MNCs and finance ultimately depended on key demographic voting shifts related to the evolution of American capitalism after World War II. A reorganization of the economy arose simultaneously with the movement of white people and capital from cities to suburbs just as postwar American foreign policy helped to further erode the geographical boundaries of business, pressing more and more corporations to be multinational.²⁶¹ As business relocated to the new American, Jim Crowed suburbs, production jobs increasingly moved overseas. Compounding this trend was the competition arising from a rebuilt Western Europe and Japan—just as the global economy began to slow in the 1960s. For white Americans able to access the benefits of the Jim Crow welfare state—including an education geared toward the new technology-knowledge industry or, in the case of the Sun Belt, a massive influx of federal spending—their hard work and embrace of the rhetoric of rugged individualism disavowed the role of federal intervention from, as James Baldwin and William F. Buckley Jr. debated, their access to the American dream.

The creation of white suburbs normalized the "right" of living in all-white spaces, with the dominant rhetoric imagining that it was a mere choice and not a result of federal policy wedded to the culture of white supremacy. In the age of the Jim Crow welfare state, new ways arose for white people to reimagine race. Before World War II, white supremacy expressed itself through the idea of racial superiority, a subset of the biological superiority of Anglo-Saxons driving the progress of Western civilization.[262] After the war, notes Freund, "most northern whites justified racial exclusion by invoking what they viewed as nonracial variables: protecting the housing market, their rights as property owners and, linked to both, their rights as citizens. Whites still actively kept blacks out of their neighborhoods, yet insisted, and many apparently believed, that they were merely exercising what they described as the prerogatives of 'homeowners,' 'property owners,' and 'law abiding citizens.'"[263] Thus, the federal government's subsidizing of white America helped secure a new market vision of race while simultaneously instilling the market logic neoliberals and conservatives championed in the wake of legislated social equality in the 1960s. Rather than institutional racism, the idea of "impersonal market forces" arose as a narrative explaining racial inequality.[264] As Black people posed a threat to the property values of white homeowners, the exclusion of Blacks merely represented sound investment advice. It was not about fairness; it was about quantitative analysis and the growing belief of the market as information processor, with data existing as objective, truthful, and transparent.

Supported by the real estate industry, residential builders, and politicians with an unflinching attachment to white supremacy, policies developed for the Jim Crow welfare state offered social safety nets to areas of employment dominated by white Americans. In this sense, as Ira Katznelson points out, Jim Crow welfare state policies in the postwar world created "affirmative action for whites," as federal programs constructed a "massive transfer of quite specific privileges to white Americans."[265] For example, while unemployment insurance covered most jobs, domestic and farmworkers—occupations dominated by people of color—were excluded. Only a small percentage of African Americans could access the benefits of the GI Bill, as the administration of the bill rested with the states. Thus, even though the bill was color-blind, its application through the states was racially based, working to the advantage of white veterans:[266] "In this aspect of affirmative action for whites, the path to job placement, loans, unemployment benefits, and schooling was tied to local VA centers, almost entirely staffed by white employees, or through local banks and both public and private education institutions."[267] As a result, housing and its regeneration of whiteness via suburbanization found kinship with the ideas of Friedman, whose *Capitalism and Freedom* denounced civil rights legislation and characterized it as a direct threat to the "freedom of individuals to enter into voluntary contracts with one another."[268] Freedom and liberty now demanded the white right—their historic entitlement—to both "choose their neighbors and to be free from government interventions that might interfere with the market mechanisms that had allowed them to prosper."[269] Rather than simple biological inferiority, the white imagination suggested that African Americans "were unable or unwilling to play by the rules of the marketplace. The debate over integration, whites insisted, no longer turned on questions about race, ideology, or personal preference. What counted was a person's relationship to places and to property, and a person's ability to function properly in what was assumed to be a free market for both."[270] In short, Buckley's statistical and racist argument over the inability of African Americans to pull themselves up by their bootstraps—like Irish or Jewish Americans—was warmly received by white Americans no longer comfortable with the overtly racist language of their youth.

Reality upset this postwar white innocence, as the urban uprisings after 1964 expressed a systemic Black reaction to white intransigence to extending the social equality ideals of the constitution to the descendants of the founding fathers' enslaved property. The corporate media framed the burning of cities and civil unrest on television as sensationalized events, including news documentaries deploying images of Daniel Patrick Moynihan's "broken family" thesis while underlining the prevalence of welfare programs.[271] Ignoring the findings of the Kerner Commission (including the revelatory claim "that white society is deeply implicated in the ghetto. White institutions created it, white institutions maintain it, and white society condones it"), the possession of history held firm: old ideas woven through the legacy of the American racial dictatorship recycled assertions assigning blame to African Americans.[272] Indeed, a lack of respect for property, community, and the "law" became a mantra for explaining away Black unrest for the post–civil rights era, justifying what became the post-1968 civil rights policy of "benign neglect" toward the Black community, as suggested to Nixon by Moynihan (setting the seeds for mass incarceration and the war on drugs in the 1980s).[273]

Business Week also ventured into the space of explaining the struggles of African Americans amid its discussions of multinationals and finance. For example, *Business Week* described the Kerner Commission as a "compelling" document in understanding the "details it provides of the riots and in its sweeping portrayal of the historical and social context in which the country's racial problem must be understood," supporting the liberal conclusion that "in any democratic society integration must be the final goal."[274] A month earlier, *Business Week* had outlined the need for business to take the lead in ending segregation, through jobs, housing, and education—asserting market solutions over government action (an attitude a few large corporations adopted in the 1940s and 1950s).[275] The effort toward desegregation in American business was daunting, as a poll in 1944 supported ongoing racial segregation (even as the nation fought against white supremacy in Europe).[276]

Setting a pattern at the dawn of social equality, the magazine was silent in mentioning the decades-long, federally subsidized housing discrimination—among other features of the Jim Crow welfare state—enjoyed by the primary demographic reading *Business Week*. Going back to the mid-1950s, innocence shrouded this distribution of racial wealth inequality through *Business Week*'s benevolent assessment of the North's attitude toward Negroes: "Though [the North] doesn't think of the Negro as a social equal, neither has it formally defined a place for him [as the Jim Crow South has]. And with a more liberal political tradition, it has at least paid lip service to the idea of equal opportunity, though it often amounts to little more."[277] A discussion of federal intervention in white suburban housing was beyond the boundaries of debate, let alone the targeting of federal intervention toward white people through programs such as defense, space, or infrastructure. Moreover, the magazine paternalistically described the situation facing African Americans in 1954, noting: "While it is true that the Negro in the United States is, to a great extent, what the white man made him, it is also true that the white man as a whole is ignorant of his creation. The facts about the Negro are still obscured by a cloud of mythology."[278] As W. E. B. Du Bois discussed the white historiography of slavery in the 1930s, "in the end nobody seems to have done wrong and everybody was right. Slavery"—or in this case, institutional racism—"appears to have been thrust upon unwilling helpless America."[279] Unlike the conclusion of the Kerner Commission, *Business Week* felt white America was innocent in its history of race relations.

By the early 1960s, *Business Week* took a more aggressive tone toward the civil rights movement. Writing defensively about the civil rights movement's criticism toward institutional racism such as housing in 1963, the magazine used older language denoting white fear of Black people constructed through decades of criminalizing Blackness, asserting, "Still there's trouble. Despite such concessions, trouble lies ahead. Part of the *menace* comes from Negro impatience."[280] The magazine offered a warning to its predominantly white readership, embodying an early justification for white backlash against the quest for social equality: "North and South, Negroes are stepping up the pace of their marches, picketing, and sit-ins, provoking mass arrests and sometimes violence on both sides. Negro willingness to risk violence shows up in a city such as Gainesville, Fla., where Negroes retaliated against a white attack by dragging a white man from his car and beating him. . . . Says Paul Anthony, field director of the moderate Southern Regional Council: 'You get a sense of real militancy and an anti-white feeling that we haven't experienced before.'"[281] Inverting the deep history of white rage and terrorism toward Black America, and obscuring the rank hypocrisy of condemning oppressed Americans who struggle for the rights taken for granted by white Americans, *Business*

Week's possession of history entered familiar avenues of anti-Blackness, trafficking well-worn representations and familiar images circulating through mass media. When African Americans marched assertively, often in directions well outside the boundaries of white acceptability, old fears of Blackness surfaced. *Business Week* highlighted that the confrontational tactics for achieving social equality went too far, as *moderates* who prayed and exhibited patience appeared to ease the concerns of whites—who grew up consuming the acceptable image of the Sambo caricature (content, dimwitted, loyal, and lazy) in literature and film.[282] The old threat of the slave rebellion surfaced when African American activists condemned the "all deliberate speed" of racial progress, which, of course, was the primary barricade for white resistance making its last stand against social equality one hundred years after the Emancipation Proclamation. For *Business Week*, the insistent Black demand for constitutional rights was at fault, not white intransigence:

> On the other side of the coin, Negro aggressiveness crystallizes white resistance. Even in cities with a reputation for moderation, some whites have lost sympathy with Negro tactics. After nine days of Negro mass demonstrations in Greensboro, N.C., Mayor David Schenck noted: "As a result of the large demonstrations, our group of moderates is shrinking".... Chamber of Commerce Pres. John Harden adds: "A few weeks ago, the directors of the Chamber of Commerce and the Merchants Assn. independently passed resolutions urging equal treatment of all people. Today I am sure the Chamber directors wouldn't pass such a resolution."[283]

By the end of the 1960s, a series of Gallop polls in May 1968 suggested that white people overwhelmingly denied there was ill-treatment of "Negroes" in "this community" (including discrimination by businesses) and that they disagreed with the Kerner Commission—58 percent of whites polled asserted that African Americans were "to blame for the present conditions in which Negroes find themselves."[284] Meanwhile, the "black-white income gap" remained faithfully unequal, more so in the South than in the North.[285] Centuries-old instincts found new life as white resentment in the post–civil rights era.

"What price will whites pay?" asked *Business Week*, addressing the most pressing cultural and economic question for white people about to experience their first decade of legislated social equality: "Money and emotions are inextricably mixed; fear of economic loss feeds the fear of Negroes.... Most white Americans limit their acceptance of Negroes in their neighborhood to those few Negro families with similar educational and economic backgrounds—those who can afford homes made accessible by the new federal open-housing law."[286] The authors, of course, shoveled more dirt on the grave of the Jim Crow welfare state, further obscuring the federal price associated with creating the white suburbs between the 1930s and early 1960s: $120 billion, with less than 2 percent going to people of color.[287] Desperate, the age of legislated social equality could only begin by burying the evidence of the racial dictatorship in order to foster the role of victim for a white America no longer protected by racist legislature. Through its invisibility, whiteness and its possession of history could disavow any set of past or present practices supporting white male supremacy. Baldwin spoke of this dilemma in *The Fire Next Time* (1963): "There is simply no possibility of a real change in the Negro's situation without the most radical and far-reaching changes in the American political and social structure. And it is clear [in 1963] that white Americans are not simply unwilling to effect these changes; they are, in the main, so slothful have they become, unable even to envision them."[288] The conspiracy of silence sheltering white innocence continued to tighten the Gordian knot.

Chapter 4

The Idea of Doing with Less so that Big Business Can Have More

The Culture and Ethos of Business Week

The standard of living of the average American has to decline. I don't think you can escape that.

—Paul Volcker (1979)

"Neoliberalism" is the term now used to describe the transformations capitalism underwent at the turning point of the 1970s and 1980s. One salient fact was the decision by the U.S. Federal Reserve Board to allow interest rates to rise as much as the fight against inflation required. But this emblematic action, whose consequences were dramatic for large portions of the world population, can only be understood as one of many components of a change whose principal trait was restoring many of the most violent features of capitalism, making for a resurgent, unprettified capitalism.

—Gérard Duménil and Dominique Lévy, *Capital Resurgent* (2004)

In early October 1974, *Business Week* issued a special report describing the United States as "the Debt Economy without peer."[1] The authors broke down what they called "a mountain of debt $2.5-trillion high": "$1-trillion in corporate debt, $600-billion in mortgage debt, $500-billion in U.S. government debt, $200-billion in state and local government debt, $200-billion in consumer debt."[2] According to the news magazine, perpetual borrowing based on the assumption of ongoing postwar growth finally stumbled in the late 1960s, crashing amid rising inflation, foreign competition, an expensive war, and the oil crisis in 1973. Although unable to see into the future, the structural deficit characterizing the years after the early 1970s had arrived.[3] With a recession emerging in the wake of skyrocketing oil prices in 1974, the Federal Reserve adopted measures to squeeze credit in an attempt to counter inflation. Postwar growth ground to a halt while inflation sliced into earnings.

The debate over an exit strategy from this economic pileup centered on what alternative path to take, a debate placing the welfare state squarely within its sights. After patiently waiting decades, conservatives and their neoliberal partners finally found their moment to sway opinion away from the welfare state. Although Richard M. Nixon resisted the counsel of his more neoliberal-friendly economic advisers, these voices gained ground in the Ford administration, eyeing avenues leading away from government intervention in social spending through an argument pitting inflation against recession. In his early days of presidency, Gerald Ford asserted, "Inflation is our domestic public enemy No. 1."[4] An economic paradox surfaced: the Federal Reserve's squeezing of credit might rein in inflation, but a recession would inevitably spread throughout the economy and payments toward debt would cease. On the other hand, inflation ate into the earnings of individuals and business, and thus hurt profits. As 1974 turned into 1975, productivity "plunged 2.7 percent."[5] A continuing decline in profits and more unemployment followed (9.2 by May 1975). According to the *Business Week* special report, the combination of economic woes could be traced back to the postwar welfare state consumption and an inefficient system of access to capital that forced corporations into the "debt markets": "This country's futile attempt at capital-export controls turned companies that had been modest suppliers to the international money markets into major international borrowers."[6] Transnational capital flows needed to be liberalized, deregulated from government regulations. Although the welfare state created the postwar environment for the growth of multinational conglomerates, the needs of these institutions now burst through the seams of the mixed economy.

In the commentary section of this "debt economy" issue of *Business Week*, John Carson-Parker prophesized the economic direction embraced by neoliberal economists and conservatives in the 1970s and 1980s:

> Some people will obviously have to do with less, or with substitutes, so that the economy as a whole can get the most mileage out of available capital. There will be fewer homes and more apartment houses built.... It will be harder to launch risky new ventures because the needs of existing businesses will be so great.... *Indeed, cities and states, the home mortgage market, small business, and the consumer, will all get less than they want because the basic health of the U.S. is based on the basic health of its corporations and banks: the biggest borrowers and the biggest lenders.* Compromises, in terms of who gets and who does without, that would have been unthinkable only a few years ago will be made in coming years because the economic future not only of the U.S. but also of the whole world is on the line today.[7]

As multinationals and banks went into debt through their borrowing, often for acquisitions expanding the size of conglomerates, the author of the commentary argued that Americans must give in to the prerogatives of big business. Considering how much depended on giant conglomerates, without healthy corporations, Carson-Parker warned, everything from cities to nations to world economies would collapse—they were too big to fail. Carson-Parker acknowledged this choice of austerity in exchange for supporting multinationals would be a "hard pill for many Americans to swallow—the idea of doing with less so that big business can have more," especially since "they [big business] are also in large measure the cause" of this crisis.[8] "Selling" this idea to "make people accept the new reality" would be difficult but needed in order to regain the profit margins of the postwar years.[9]

Carson-Parker did not lack suggestions for achieving this new reality. These included getting rid of the allocation of credit by the Federal National Mortgage Association; eliminating taxes on dividends and interest; depreciation write-offs on the cost of replacement rather than historical cost; making dividends tax deductible for corporations; and reducing capital gains.[10] The overall program was clear: a new economic ethos for the United States demanded shifting away from the welfare state provisions of the postwar Keynesian era in the name of stabilizing the economy. A primary focus included adapting a national economic program supporting the needs of multinational conglomerates and the finance industry directing capital around the globe. Although multinationals prospered under the regulatory welfare state, they had also developed creative strategies throughout the postwar years to negotiate alternative routes around regulations. By the early 1970s, conservative and neoliberal ideas coalesced with the existing policies of multinationals and finance, which, along with the culture war, helped shape the path forward out of the welfare state and into the era of neoliberalism.

The vision and medicine offered by *Business Week* fused with the coming of age of the New Right and neoliberal economists. As debt, inflation, and unemployment became a 1970s norm, an economic program usually tied to the interests of the wealthy—on display in the "roaring" twenties—regained legitimacy as its message attacked the inaction of Keynesian economists.[11] Envisioned by William F. Buckley Jr. in the 1950s, personified by the 1964 presidential candidacy of Barry Goldwater and the 1966 California governorship of Ronald Reagan, and culturally anchored by the reactionary populist conservatism of Southern Segregationist Democrats (who became Republicans in the 1970s), the New Right obtained the presidential prize through Nixon. While Nixon still held one foot in the postwar consensus, he was more than successful in deploying the newly articulated language of the conservative culture war—specifically a populist white resentment toward social equality legislation. With the liberal consensus buckling under domestic and foreign unrest after 1965, an ideological vacuum arose as the historical conjuncture unfolded. The ideas of the New Right, neoliberals, and the increasingly global needs of multinationals and finance filled his vacuum.

A shared cultural ethos for understanding the world—particularly ideas about the relationship between government and society—tied conservative thinkers together with multinational corporations. As a realm dominated by white men of property who were raised in a nation where Jim Crow segregation was as natural as baseball season, the outlooks of those managing multinationals and the finance industry could not be expected to fully embrace those in society considered inferior, such as people of color and women, let alone address the inequalities tied to institutional discrimination. Rather, this sentiment leaned toward a more familiar tradition: the deep historical arguments regarding states' rights over federal intervention, both an outgrowth of the legacies of settler colonialism (the settler versus the metropole) and the conservative Southern segregationist tactic championed by Goldwater: although he asserted he was against racism, he also voiced opposition toward the federal government enforcing constitutional rights for Black Americans. In other words, states controlled by their local constituents should have the right to adhere to their voting majorities' wishes in terms of regulating social equality. For Goldwater, federal intervention on behalf of enforcing the Constitution was—without irony—a landmark "in the destruction of a free society."[12] The white majority's voting power gravitated toward conservative voices criticizing the demands of civil rights activists, leaving Democrats with the image of doing too much for African Americans at the expense of white "rights of property" and "homeownership." In addition, conservatives and their Southern segregationist allies—including the nascent fundamentalist Christian Right—deployed anti-Black coded language to both demonize Democratic efforts at expanding the social equality promised through 1960s legislation while simultaneously presenting conservatives as grassroots protectors of white communities and families innocently being attacked by "big government" for achieving the American dream.[13] The neoliberal language of efficiency of markets pulled together the wide-ranging goals of these various economic, political, and cultural reactions to the upheavals of the 1960s. In wake of social equality legislation, quantitative analysis and market imperatives channeled through the "rule of law" should govern state action, rather than social justice fairness rectifying centuries of white supremacy.[14]

This emergent culture and ethos manifested itself through mass media, including news weeklies such as *Business Week*. Picking up where the previous chapter's history of American capitalism left off, this chapter provides a closer reading of *Business Week*'s language across the long 1970s, underscoring the various ways deeply embedded undercurrents of American history wove through the arguments supporting the legitimacy of multinationals, finance, and the policies of neoliberalism. In short, this chapter explores the cultural politics—its "ethos"—of the business interests espoused by *Business Week*. How did the political shifts related to the evolution of multinationals and finance, the New Right, neoliberals, and the deep shock of social equality in American society appear in *Business Week*? How did the magazine navigate the ascension of neoliberalism against the backdrop of the first decade in the history of the United States, when white men, especially white men with property, were forced to formally compete with women and people of color for political and economic opportunity for the first time?

The Structural Adjustment of Corporations

Many Americans had lost confidence in the U.S. corporate community by the early 1970s.[15] The alarm was sounded in 1971 by future Supreme Court justice Lewis Powell, a corporate lawyer, who warned the U.S. Chamber of Commerce about the growing skepticism against capitalism. To counter this trend, Powell suggested a massive "public relations campaign that would promote the idea of free enterprise."[16] The times, it seemed, had indeed changed. In the comfort of the 1950s welfare state, 75 percent of people polled supported big business after years of Depression-inspired skepticism: "Fewer than 10 percent believed that big business had too much control over government; almost 20 percent were fearful of government subjugating business."[17] Although corporations had steadily grown more popular in the 1960s, peaking in 1967, by 1972 they had hit a new low—with ITT epitomizing the target of anti-corporate sentiment. *Business Week* bleakly equated this mood as "turning sour on America—on its dreams, its promises, its leaders."[18] Pointing to non-American influences and summoning the *longue durée* American argument for explaining internal dissent ("outside agitators"), the magazine suggested that many Americans had adopted a new "European-style cynicism on the profits, prices, and policies of the country's largest corporations and on the workings of the entire economy."[19] These public sentiments, moreover, were expressed through the popularity of presidential candidates George Wallace and George McGovern. Using the work of the Opinion Research Corporation (ORC), also a McGraw-Hill subsidiary, *Business Week* cited ORC's call for greater communication to the public and an overcoming of misrepresentations by corporations—echoing Powell's suggestion. Facing an uphill battle, the study found that the public's anger at business ran second to the Vietnam War, with 21 percent of the respondents saying they were "cheated or deceived recently on a purchase of a service or product."[20] Unease about pollution and the environment added further concern. The authors concluded that, from the research, corporations definitely needed to reshape "the corporation around a system of social cost accounting" aimed not just at customers but at the public at large.²¹ A year later, the skepticism remained, with one headline reading, "Multinationals: The Public Gives Them Low Marks."²²

Organized labor, too, appeared out of step with public favor according to *Business Week* in October 1972. Although *Business Week* framed discontent toward corporations as misunderstandings and not the result of policies, for labor they took an opposite approach: the authors highlighted the power of labor and its "political aggressiveness" as a legitimate complaint of a public leery of "costly strikes, large contract settlements, disappointing worker productivity, and 'bossism' in unions."²³ Using ORC, *Business Week* pointed to the public's wariness toward the size of unions—much like their concern toward corporations. Other opinions mirrored the business critique: labor had priced itself out of world competition with its demands, strikes hurt the nation, and unions should be regulated. For RCA, strikes waves at its Bloomington, Indiana, plant in the late 1960s pressed the company into shifting production to Mexico—while their operation in Memphis, Tennessee, was closed after the 1970 strike.²⁴ Interestingly, with 1972 forming the "apex of earnings for male workers," the decade would play out as a blue-collar and white ethnic revitalization at the precise moment when the rise of neoliberal policies would incapacitate labor.²⁵ Meanwhile, in November 1972, *Business Week* announced: "Profits set still another record."²⁶

As the postwar labor-government-business partnership dissolved and the public connected corporate America to their discontented views on American institutions, an assortment of tactics and nongovernmental organizations arose seeking to create a more positive image for American capitalism and, most importantly, a route back to the prosperity enjoyed in the previous decade.²⁷ These organizations underscored the new political activism of business as a post–welfare state consensus defiantly surfaced. The "costs imposed on capital by labor and the state" needed addressing, particularly regulations and the strength of unions.²⁸ The complicated nature of the responses of corporations deserves quoting at length (from a *Business Week* article from 1975):

> The expanding role of government creates new imponderables. Inland Steel has a $1-billion (by 1984) capital expansion program under way, but [director of corporate planning Philip D.] Block says: "We are wondering just what it is really going to cost us. We are trying to pay for it out of profits, but they depend on adequate selling prices. It is difficult to factor in government interference on pricing and the impact of controls of any kind—including 'jawboning.'" Sun Oil is trying to factor into its planning such possibilities as postponement of certain Environmental Protection Agency regulations, removal of the oil depletion allowance

and tax incentives, and imposition of a windfall profits tax. . . . If political action is an imponderable in the U.S., it is doubly so abroad, and for some of the largest multinational corporations that is currently where the action is. . . . Thus companies are trying to cut their risks in countries considered "difficult" or unstable.[29]

The challenges facing multinationals demanded a new set of tactics and organizations to negotiate nation-state political processes adversely affecting business prerogatives. Although an initial beachhead of groups formed in the wake of the New Deal to fight against the rising welfare state, such as the American Liberty League, it was not until the 1970s when the intersection of a faltering economy and the 1960s culture wars created a seasoned field for a more sophisticated right-wing business organizing.[30] A resurgent Chamber of Commerce joined the newly established Business Roundtable, with the latter founded in 1972 by the leaders of General Electric and Alcoa "in order to find ways to improve the tarnished image of big business in both government and the media."[31]

Formed from a membership of *Fortune* 500 chief executive officers, the Business Roundtable "transformed the longtime agenda of business conservatism . . . by translating it into a pragmatic antirecession program."[32] Another push came in the form of the Supreme Court case *Buckley v. Valeo* in 1976, where the decision lifted restrictions on campaign contributions, further encouraging business to enter the political arena through lobbying and political action committees (PACs).[33] By the end of the 1970s, over 100 of the largest companies in the United States entered this alliance to reshape public opinion through cultural production and public relations, as well as within the political arena through an alliance with the New Right and increasingly conservative Democrats.[34] Other organizations would follow, ranging from the oil funds of Charles Koch, who would create the Cato Institute in 1977, to the founding of the Manhattan Institute in 1978.[35] One of the more controversial organizations included the Trilateral Commission, set up in 1973 by David Rockefeller, head of Chase Manhattan.[36] In reaction to the instability of Nixon's economic policies, the Trilateral Commission sought to reinforce ties between Europe, Japan, and North America, via figures from these respective areas of the world representing the global connections of the multinational corporations.[37] The Trilateral Commission offered an example of the sort of transnational politics multinationals helped pioneer throughout the postwar period. Their focus on "market-centered change" also placed them within a pre-neoliberal framework as many of future president Jimmy Carter's senior positions went to Trilateral members.[38] The infamous Trilateral Commission report on "the crisis of democracy" appeared in 1975, bluntly describing the organization's concern over American public apathy over U.S. institutions: "In recent years, the operations of the democratic process do indeed appear to have generated a breakdown of traditional means of social control, a delegitimation of political and other forms of authority, and an overload of demands on government, exceeding its capacity to respond."[39]

The primary target for the political organizing of business was the economic turbulence of the early 1970s. Inflation doubled from 7.8 percent consumer price inflation rates to 13.4 percent between 1973 and 1975; stocks and gross national product growth reversed from their previous levels, as production fell and unemployment rose.[40] Productivity plunged by 2.7 percent leading to the worst business profits in seventeen years, while labor suffered a fall in wages by 2.1 percent and a rise of unemployment to 7.2 in December 1974.[41] As Judith Stein notes, consumer confidence hit a low point as half the nation polled by Gallup expected another Great Depression.[42] In response to the crisis, a wave of strikes hit in 1974 as capital outflows went from zero in 1973 to over $18 billion by the end of 1974, routed to manufacturing investments in Mexico, Brazil, and East Asia.[43] A Gallup poll in July 1975 discovered that "people had less confidence in big business than in organized labor, Congress, the Supreme Court, or the president."[44] As Carson-Parker noted above, "selling" the idea of making "people accept the new reality" of shifting the nation's economic priorities to the needs of multinationals at a time of economic crisis proved to be a "hard pill for many Americans to swallow—the idea of doing with less so that big business can have more."[45] Obviously, a stronger narrative from the Business Roundtable and other think tanks was needed to navigate the 1970s economic storm.

Out of this early-to-mid-1970s crisis surfaced a new language and knowledge articulating the needs of business. In particular, two catch phrases framed the discussion of economic policies. The first was "business climate," a phrase describing the political conditions facing businesses in cities, states, or nations, including labor politics, tax rates, and regulations. A positive "climate" included the lowering of corporate taxes in states and cities in order to boost incentive to invest and increase profits. Facing decreased profits in the late 1960s, corporations sought to direct their investment to areas of the nation—or world—friendly to their needs.[46] This resulted in states vying against one another for corporations to build plants and create employment. For example, advertisements in *Business Week* in 1971 included the state of South Carolina's boast: "Business is good here"; in another ad, Georgia simply described itself in sexually gendered terms: "the unspoiled," a place "offering those who believe in—and practice—private free enterprise."[47] For the revitalized Chamber of Commerce and Business Roundtable, this was the new terrain of politics, as PACs established by business aimed their contributions toward "probusiness politicians."[48] Between 1974 and 1982, these committees grew from a mere 89 to 1,467.[49]

The concept of "business climate" stems partly from the Southern and Western (or Sun Belt) tradition of distrust in government and adherence to low taxes and free markets—despite the paradox of federal intervention paving the way for the Sun Belt's growth.[50] The impact of the 1974–75 recession spurred an even fiercer diffusion of what historians have called the Southernization of the U.S.[51] At a meeting of the American Economic Association held in San Francisco in 1975, *Business Week* reported that discussions centered on the amount of taxes to cut. The liberal economists aimed their cuts—ranging from $15 billion to $20 billion—toward cutting unemployment. Milton Friedman, however, asserted the more neoliberal position of tax cuts alongside cuts in federal spending (aimed toward fighting inflation): "What really matters to economic recovery is the rate at which inflation decelerates.... Anything that stops inflation from coming down will hamper recovery, and this includes any tax cut not matched by a cut in federal spending."[52] In a special report in 1976, *Business Week* described this deluge of corporate migration as the "second war between the states," with the South and West becoming prime locations for relocating industry, people, and foreign investment due to their less-regulated, anti-union environment.[53]

Barry Bluestone and Bennett Harrison note that by the late 1970s, a favorable business climate for states included "low taxes, low union membership, low workmen's compensation insurance rates, low unemployment benefits per worker, low energy costs, and few days lost because of work stoppages—in that order."[54] This model justified the migration of business away from the older industrial areas of the country, encouraging states to compete with one another for investment. Consequently, by 1975, only a single percentage point differentiated business tax rates between Sun Belt and Frost Belt states—with the policies of union power or regulations often deciding the final outcome.[55] Consequently, the race to the bottom created a new baseline for economic activity among states. By 1976, *Business Week* observed, "Despite evidence that special inducements such as tax abatement and low-cost loans play only a limited role in determining where businesses will move, the stage has been set for a rising spiral of government subsidies as companies play off city against city and state against state for the most advantageous terms."[56] As the celebrations of the bicentennial unfolded, corporations had found a winning formula to adjust government safety nets away from regular people and target business for subsidies in return for setting up shop in a state or city.

The second catch phrase from this era was "regulation" (or more appropriately, the call for "deregulation"). *Business Week* broached the subject in early 1970, calling the machinery of regulation "antique" and in vital need of reform and updating.⁵⁷ The Nixon administration even pondered the deregulation of transportation (roads, rails, and waterways) at the end of 1970.⁵⁸ Feeling besieged, executives from major multinationals held multiple meetings throughout 1974 and 1975 to discuss strategies for deregulation. *Business Week*, too, questioned the onrush of regulations that appeared to increase in the wake of the environmental and consumer movements in the early 1970s. Amid the "more sober climate of double-digit inflation, rising unemployment, and shortages of just about everything," the costs associated with these regulations began to be questioned, labeling them legislated values.⁵⁹ Companies passed on the increased costs of regulations to consumers, pointing their fingers toward government as the source of the further rise of inflation. Historian Robert Sobel noted that between 1976 and 1978, the price tag faced by corporations for environmental controls was $600 million while they spent $100 million on "occupational safety and health measures."⁶⁰ One vocal critic, Donald C. Cook (chairman for American Electric Power Co.) articulated the overall conservative perspective toward the welfare state: "I grew up as a New Dealer and was imbued with remaking America. I learned one thing: You get a liberal who has an idea he wants to push, that he believes is in the public interest, and he will stop at nothing, absolutely nothing, in order to push it. He believes the end justifies the means, period. I'm talking about the people at the Environmental Protection Agency."⁶¹ Cost-benefit studies took aim at evaluating whether government regulations were "worth the price."⁶² One spectacular measurement included a study on seat belts. A free market economist deemed that "precisely because auto seat belts have substantially reduced the risk of driver injury and death, they have caused motorists to take more chances."⁶³ These dual threats to profits—taxes and regulations—ushered in a trend leading many multinational corporations to locate much of their business offshore in sanctuaries such as the Cayman Islands.⁶⁴

The struggle against regulations also intersected with the outcome of social equality legislation. A growing outcry against affirmative action programs blended into this mid-1970s critique of government intervention. White Americans enjoyed an "affirmative action for whites" during the height of the Jim Crow welfare state, with subsidies ranging from education and housing to employment via federally funded programs, let alone white men only competing with other white men for white-collar employment.⁶⁵ However, the moment people of color obtained social equality, racial exclusion leaned on an argument draped in color-blind market imperatives determining whether one possessed skills or not. The legacies of white access to training in all-white programs, of course, failed to appear in these arguments. For conservatives, affirmative action provided another culture war front to critique the welfare state, despite its historic tilt toward white men. Nancy MacLean writes, "Whereas the old screeds against the New Deal state had tangled conservatives in trying to argue the majority of whites out of government help to which they felt entitled, the affirmative action attacks employed more favorable math. A large number of white males (and, thanks to shared racial attitudes, almost as many white women) could be persuaded that efforts at remedying exclusion had harmed them, their children, or their friends, however weak the empirical evidence. Conservative movement intellectuals encouraged such resentments."[66]

An early struggle against affirmative action took place in Atlanta, Georgia, in 1975. At a local level, the goals of the nation's "first minority business affirmative action plan" pressed further than federal mandates.[67] *Business Week* picked up this story stating, "The Atlanta mayor's plan goes beyond any federal affirmative action program."[68] The assumption for white business owners was that "the plan will increase costs by forcing them to take in unqualified partners."[69] Casting this plan as an impediment on their business practices, Maynard H. Jackson Jr.'s (Atlanta's Black mayor) policies were framed as an infringement of business freedom. This call for freedom, ironically, shed responsibility of the business community's participation in the centuries-old white male bias of private enterprise. Framing their dilemma within the post-1960s rhetoric of color-blind innocence after years of white male monopoly over economics, business interests asserted that Black contractors and engineers were "unqualified" and the white business community had no responsibility for rectifying their legacy of preference toward white men. The language of skilled versus unskilled labor when justifying the exclusion of unskilled workers of color into business mirrored *Business Week*'s usage from the late 1960s.[70] Together, these intersections of government interference into the affairs of business underscored the political usefulness of the color-blind coded language of the conservative culture war in creating a new politics that both disavowed a very recent past of white nationalist policies while simultaneously regenerating the *longue durée* antagonisms of anti-Blackness to mobilize whites against further welfare state interventions.

Debates over affirmative action represented one of the clearest intersections of the uneasiness whites felt over post–civil rights legislation aiming to create social equality after centuries of institutionalized racism and sexism. Just as polled whites during the 1960s could not quite blame white society for discrimination against African Americans, there was considerable unease about compensation for past injustices—not reparations for slavery, necessarily, but a program rectifying the immensely unequal distribution of economic opportunity (training and access to employment) given to white Americans during the exceptionally prosperous era of Jim Crow. *Longue durée* in nature, whiteness *as property* accounts for this unease, as race historically fused its way through ideas of property, from rights of property, relationships of property (including slavery), or the right of spatial exclusion in the name of property.[71] As group identity tied to the language of race was deregulated as a form of discrimination, its mobilization on behalf of historically marginalized peoples now appeared unfair to whites. Notes Harris, "Whites concede that Blacks were oppressed by slavery and by legalized race segregation and its aftermath, but protest that, notwithstanding this legacy of deprivation and subjugation, it is unfair to allocate the burden to innocent whites who were not involved in acts of discrimination."[72]

An example of this exercise in innocence is reflected in a March 1976 issue of *Business Week*, where labor editor John Hoerr reviewed Nathan Glazer's book *Affirmative Discrimination*. Although conceding some room for criticism of the work, Hoerr's analysis concluded with the suggestion that liberals seeking to carry out the struggle to help African Americans were wrong to think that the outcome rested on the dissolution of "merit." Of course, there was no question asking, "What does merit mean when employment opportunity was historically narrowed to white males only?" For Glazer, African Americans did not need affirmative action because the passage of laws against discrimination in the 1960s had already created "marked" economic progress. Conjuring the obsessions of William F. Buckley Jr., Hoerr continues: Glazer does contend that "poorly educated, low-income black families—especially those headed by women—were out of reach of antidiscrimination programs because they were largely unemployable."[73] In short, the natural mechanisms of the market and assumptions about race did not need interference by federal intervention, as institutional racism was a thing of the past after civil rights legislation. American equality reset to a "year zero" in the 1970s, as the material gains of white supremacy evaporated, leaving only a trace of innocence.

Buckley and other culture warriors found confirmation in their bigotry through Glazer and Daniel Patrick Moynihan's *Beyond the Melting Pot: The Negroes, Puerto Ricans, Jews, Italians, and Irish of New York City* (1963)—the book Buckley suggested to the Cambridge debate crowd in 1965—while the Moynihan report on "The Negro Family" in 1965 helped reinforce the new racism of cultural pathology.[74] Coded racism connecting Black women to welfare dependence became a stock-in-trade trope for conservatives trying to convince white voters of the evils of the welfare state. *Business Week* emphasized the so-called threats posed by families led by single Black women in the 1970s, including the cover of the January 17, 1977, issue depicting a drawing of a young Black woman sitting on a chair with her infant and young son; the background contained a cutout silhouette of a father (not) standing in the background.[75] Set as a patch within blue jean fabric, two other patches appear as well—one depicting milk rations and the other a "Food Coupon"—with the seams of the fabric coming unfurled in the center of the cover, reading: "The $60 Billion Welfare Failure: What Carter Could Do." Although the majority of recipients have historically been white, welfare's coding by mass media and conservative politicians (most infamously by Ronald Reagan, who helped popularize the coded racist trope "welfare queen" in 1976) tapped into still-seething white anxiety and resentment toward the civil rights movement in general by portraying the anti-poverty programs as helping undeserving Blacks.[76] To reinforce the dehumanization of Black people, the anti-Black coding of welfare emphasized the hypersexual stereotypes long believed in by white America—as noted in previous chapters, Buckley wielded this image with obsessive tenacity. These sentiments stretched back to the days of slavery and were historically used to justify white sexual violence toward Black women; moreover, the image of Black dependency amid economic decline further justified racial antagonism as whites equated affirmative action and welfare as unfair preferential treatment toward Black people.[77]

After decades of the Jim Crow welfare state's multibillion-dollar investment in the white suburbs, these concerns among white middle-income earners and the working class further encouraged support for tough-talking conservatives who challenged African American demands for a solution to an American dream in which whites enjoyed a centuries-long head start. This rhetorical wedge proved vital for reframing the political-economic debate of the United States, where the psychology of white resentment of perceived Black preferential treatment by liberals found its target in the welfare state.[78] Building on the unspoken benefits accrued to whites from the Jim Crow welfare state housing policies, race subsumed into the color-blind market language of neighborhoods. Moreover, this color-blind language aligned with the same language targeting business regulations, pulling corporate critiques of the welfare state together with white working- and middle-class critiques of government interference with institutional racism and the redistribution of wealth toward the poorer, non-white segments of society. For business, the free market should take precedence over the "have-nots."[79] "The businessmen believed that the government, responding to the have-nots, controlled and allocated too much of the nation's wealth," writes Stein, and "They feared that the trend toward government financing, subsidy, and control would end up socializing investment decisions. And, on the basis of the economic troubles of the utilities, airlines, and railroads, they concluded that government regulation always ignored the imperatives of capital accumulation. Many thought that only a sharp recession would sober up their fellow citizens."[80]

With this antipathy toward government in mind, an increasing number of the commentaries in *Business Week* framed the redistributionist policies of Keynesianism as socialist threats, echoing the language of far-right and neoliberal critics from the first decades of the New Deal and post–World War II welfare state.[81] One such case was published in a December 1975 issue without a byline: "Egalitarianism: Threat to a Free Market."[82] Criticizing the federal government's programs designed to "level goods and powers in the American society," the author condemned this redistribution of income and wealth that overrode "the classic principle that what a man consumes must be determined by what he produces or what he owns.... The egalitarian movement is essentially authoritarian. It is highly critical of business and contemptuous of *laissez-faire* economics."[83] The major difference from the 1970s and the early New Deal, according to the author, was that the latter accepted inequality and justified welfare programs as humanitarian, whereas in the 1970s, aid to the poor is seen "as a matter of right."[84] Of course, within this resentment of the present linking welfare to civil rights gains lay a convenient silencing of whites-only policies of housing, infrastructure, and defense spending that characterized the socio-economic world of the author of the essay. However, for whites resentful of the first few years of legislated social equality, their bitterness toward Black recipients of government aid gained renewed justification through the business press.

Even within the title of the piece—"Egalitarianism: Threat to a Free Market"—the author inadvertently underscores the *longue durée* ontology underlining American ideas of freedom, markets, and equality. The sheer inability to acknowledge the loss of white entitlement highlighted the emerging existential crisis facing white male Americans in the first decade of legislated social equality. The essay points toward those who interfered with the normalcy of white male dominance as the primary threat to the "free market" (again, without irony): the primary culprits demanding income redistribution were, according to the essay, "the blacks and other minorities—and lately from the women's movement.... The demand for equal job opportunities and equal pay for equal work has paved the way for the assertion of a right to equal housing, education, and enjoyment of life."[85] *Business Week*'s assessment of the mid-1970s underscored their possession of history, particularly their power to silence policies that prior to the 1960s were considered exclusive "rights" of white men. Adding more irony to their essay, the author then deployed a quasi-Marxist class argument warning that liberals were attempting to transfer the costs of these programs "to upper-bracket incomes."[86]

The commentary also quotes future Reagan cabinet member Caspar W. Weinberger, who, speaking at the Commonwealth Club of San Francisco, was quoted as saying, "Federal spending has shifted away from traditional federal functions such as defense and toward programs that reduce the remaining freedom of individuals"—again, a disavowal of the Jim Crow Keynesian society Weinberger came of age in.[87] Moreover, the focus on individuals pointed to the ideological mechanisms of Western civilization: the interpretation of social equality as the end of "freedom of individuals" further highlighted the anxiety faced by those adjusting to life after a long tradition of pro–white male discrimination. Following the conservative culture war script, Weinberger lists the usual suspects seeking unfair inclusion into the realm of economic opportunity historically reserved for white men: "from blacks, from women, from welfare workers who are now so numerous they constitute a power bloc on their own."[88] For good measure, the author also threw in the "leaders of the new unions of government employees."[89] Corporate America appeared to be under siege from the least powerful groups in the history of the United States who were only a decade into enjoying "civil rights." The framing of the business community as an innocent and powerless minority worked through the white masculine norm of its constituency—a wealthier shadow of the so-called white backlash. Of course, these arguments completely disavowed corporate America's role in engineering, funding, supporting, and profiting from racial and gender inequality since *at least* the dawn of the corporate era during Reconstruction and Post-Reconstruction.

The 1960s culture war found fertile ground in the anti–welfare state rhetoric of neoliberals such as Friedman, who won the Nobel Prize in 1976. In the wake of Friedman receiving the Nobel Prize, *Business Week* noted that the "timing of the award is particularly apt—Friedman proposals have suddenly become part of the international codes that govern the way in which governments make economic policy. And their practical success or failure will go a long way toward determining whether the anti-Keynesian revolution that Friedman launched over 25 years ago will carry the day."[90] The journal listed the array of institutions adopting Friedman's proposals, from Basel's Bank of International Settlements to the International Monetary Fund, with the latter agreeing "on a code of conduct permitting nations to let their exchange rates vary in accord with free market forces"—a policy Friedman had been proposing since "the onset of the Bretton Woods system."[91] The authors also pointed to the University of Chicago's belief that the free market private sector could always outdeliver government. Out of these pages, one can see the reframing of politics: government-expanding liberals are "authoritarian"; conservatives espousing less government are identified as "libertarians."[92] Noting his "radicalism of the right," *Business Week* wrote of Friedman's ties to Chile, where his policies corralled the nation's inflation by half while also creating an unemployment level of 18% and widespread starvation.[93] To charges that he fostered these conditions, Friedman countered, "If there is a ghost of a chance of democracy ever being restored in Chile, it will depend on a considerable improvement in the state of their economy.... I have no regrets except for the utter irresponsibility of American publications, including *Business Week*, in dealing with this."[94] This statement took aim at an article from January 1976, where the magazine, describing the application of the so-called shock treatment in curtailing inflation at the expense of social costs, quoted Friedman, who stated, "My only concern . . . is that they push it long enough and hard enough."[95] Friedman's Nobel Prize helped legitimate his brand of free market capitalism, regenerating the conservative economic counterrevolution originally stalled after Goldwater's loss in 1964.[96]

With the austere conditions of the 1970s recession and the government's reassessment of social spending, the labor movement suffered immensely as unemployment levels stayed around 5.5 percent between 1975 and 1978.[97] This environment provided business with the justification for downsizing their operations in the United States. Faced with another wave of profit squeezes, industry sought to cut costs through layoffs or uprooting their operations from older industrial sectors and moving South, West, or overseas, where lax labor laws forced wages down.[98] Although there was moderate expansion keeping the unemployment rate stable, most new jobs appeared in the service sector and were increasingly part time—a trend that had slowly gained traction between the 1950s and 1970s.[99] D. J. Frantzen notes that these tentative moves from industry reflected their "fairly pessimistic long-term demand expectations and tried to keep wage costs as low as possible by not recruiting employees on long-term Fordist contracts, especially unskilled labour."[100] More importantly, it set the stage for a revitalization of U.S. competitiveness in the 1980s by securing an increased reserve of labor, now disciplined into accepting lower wages and less job security.

Along with attacking and discrediting unions, another signpost pointing to the transition from the welfare state to neoliberalism included calls for a change in corporate planning. In an article from 1975, *Business Week* analyzed the "flexibility" and "speed" related to the decade's major business changes.[101] As noted in the previous chapter, flexibility meant outlining multiple contingency plans to negotiate the rapidly changing economy. Although forward planning took a back seat in the 1960s, by the 1970s it was crucial for survival.[102] As one prescient commentator said, "Many companies feel we are moving into a new era. . . . The 1950–70 assumptions probably will not be good guidelines for the 1970s on."[103] Executives noted the "period of transition" for Western economies, with the ability to "react quickly" becoming the norm for growth and survival.[104] Included in this strategy was the idea of "cutting back too much than in pruning too little."[105] The ability to navigate the unpredictability of the world economy in the 1970s helped to sculpt a vastly different business mentality than existed in the previous decade. *Business Week* also highlighted the role of the computer as a vital instrument in calculating variables for planning: "With a computer... not only can long-range and short-range plans be updated continuously, so whenever managers refer to them they are current, but any number of what-if questions can be asked."[106] Along with computers, the tactic of "group management" helped to make companies more flexible while continuing to control their diverse holdings.[107]

In a special issue from 1977, *Business Week* took aim at the Carter administration's increase in regulations, comparing statistics from 1970 and 1975 showing the spending by regulatory agencies and the "pages in *Code of Federal Regulations*."[108] The impetus toward attacking the "bigness" of government, especially the segments impeding corporate profits, grew in tandem throughout the decade with the rise of conservative voices demanding lower taxes. Further, *Business Week* blamed the technological gap with foreign competition on government interference and regulations—reversing their earlier observation from 1971 describing management's decisions as the primary culprit.[109] Nonetheless, this chorus of condemnation added fuel to the fires of the tax revolt during the summer of 1978, when middle-class Californians initiated a populist retreat, through Proposition 13, from high property taxes fueling the state's expenditures. The revolt of Proposition 13 also created a new stipulation about the state raising taxes: the legislature needed to have a two-thirds vote to pass new taxes. This tax revolt, notes Kevin Kruse and Julian Zelizer, "represented the dawn of a new era in American politics."[110] The significant year of 1978 also saw another harbinger of the future in the publication that helped define the Reagan revolution and the institutionalization of neoliberalism: Jude Wanniski's *The Way the World Works* (1978).[111] The middle classes of other states quickly followed California's example and found Wanniski's observations useful for their justification. Meanwhile, *Business Week* continued to defend large concentrations, arguing that antitrust charges against monopolies or oligopolies would hurt research and development.[112] The third quarter profits of 1978 rose to 5.6 percent from 5.2 percent the previous year, with steel companies doing especially well with 200 percent profit increases from U.S. Steel and Republic Steel.[113]

In its 1978 special issue on the "New World Economic Order," *Business Week* charged that the rise in oil prices, although hurting the United States, had nonetheless benefited the nation over its rivals in Japan and Europe through "a transformed economic relationship between the industrialized and the less developed countries."[114] The changes of the decade were related to shifts between old and new economic worlds: "The catalyst for the current upheaval in world economic power was the most jarring event of the 1970s—the quadrupling of oil prices in 1974 by the Organization of Petroleum Exporting Countries (OPEC)."[115] The resulting changes caused "a sharp slowing in world economic growth, a slowing in the rise of world trade, and an increase in the productivity of labor relative to capital that is strengthening the economies of advanced developing countries, such as South Korea and Brazil."[116] Recycled petrodollars circulated from oil developing nations to U.S. banks, who in turn loaned this capital to non-oil developing nations.[117] A fear remained, however, in this treading of water: aid merely kept countries afloat so they would not "default on their growing private obligations, a development that would have serious financial and economic repercussions for the developed countries. The upshot has been that the nonoil developing countries, like the U.S., have been able to finance their oil bill and continue to grow relatively rapidly."[118] Investment opportunities, in other words, outweighed the risks of systemic collapse tied to unsustainable debt—with petrodollars easing the path through the turbulent 1970s. In a welcome turn of events for multinationals, these nations would default in the 1980s, opening them up to structural adjustment programs which effectively removed the control of one's economy from national sovereignty as they proscribed privatization, deregulation, and low taxes on foreign businesses—long a dream of neoliberals since the 1930s.[119]

While the 1970s hurt most Americans, some weathered the storm better than others. In a September 1978 issue of *Business Week*, an editorial raised concern over the vast amounts of cash corporations had accumulated over the previous few years, as they held back capital spending out of concern for inflation and regulation.[120] Specifically, the authors criticized Carter's "populist and egalitarian proposals"—with the magazine overtly adopting the language of the New Right and neoliberalism (previously reserved for editorials) in reframing the last strains of the welfare state as oppressively socialistic against capital. The end result of "uncertainty and apprehension" is that "cash will continue to pile up in idle accounts."[121] With confidence in the Keynesian redistributive system shattered, solutions for economic growth called for the further freeing of private enterprise from regulations rather than government initiative. As the 1980 election loomed on the horizon, supply-side economists, neoliberals, and conservatives forcefully argued for slashed regulations and taxes, including deep cuts to welfare state social spending and civil rights enforcement.[122] These policies, it was argued, would unleash a torrent of cash back into the economy and revive the prosperity of the postwar years.

Heated arguments surrounding the redistribution of the tax burden accompanied the pileup of cash in the mid-1970s.[123] Poll readings noted "dissatisfaction reached a level in 1978 which, if not the historic high, lay fair claim to being the highest since survey data first became available."[124] At least 55 percent of respondents to one poll indicated that the tax system was "unfair."[125] The authors noted the increased criticism of "governmental performance" in the second half of the 1960s, leading to at least two-thirds of respondents saying they had "low trust" in government.[126] The lies about the Vietnam War, the Nixon Administration's criminal behavior related to Watergate, and the various revelations of government spying on the American people added to this distrust.[127] Even though negative views on welfare spending grew to 61 percent by 1978, most Americans continued to want "big government, if the latter means a high level of government-provided services."[128] In some Midwest cities and states, however, mayors and governors still convinced voters to raise taxes amid the fiscal crisis—underlining the incomplete transformation to neoliberal Reaganomics.[129] Thus, although conservatives were successful in placing the image of the "welfare state" in the minds of Americans as government handouts to the undeserved poor (most often imagined as people of color), for most, the actual workings of the welfare state enjoyed by Americans appeared to be something they were not ready to relinquish to the free market utopia of neoliberalism. This complicated relationship to the welfare state led to a majority of respondents to assert that it would be possible to reduce taxes without reducing services simply by cutting the "waste" and making government more efficient.[130]

The Revenue Act of 1978 aimed toward appeasing this economic anxiety. For Wall Street and financial interests, the justification for the act lay in its importance as a stimulus for encouraging investment—with fewer taxes, so the supply-side economics argument proposed, more money could be invested.[131] The Revenue Act slashed the tax on capital gains from 49 percent to 28 percent—with one commentator calling the legislation "the Millionaire's Relief Act of 1978."[132] Daniel Rodgers argues that "the supply-side publicists were anti-Keynesian more by conservative reflex than by analysis," thus bestowing a sentient aura around the concept of the market, propping up the neoliberal argument of the "invisible hand" as a supernatural, deity-like entity.[133] The real loss of revenue and declining standard of living pressed the middle class into supporting this infamous tax revolt of 1978. With the Revenue Act signed into law by Carter, the Democratic president effectively transferred the income distribution upward, while the tax burden shifted downward upon the middle and working classes. Although the bankruptcy of New York City and Wall Street's takeover of the city's budget arguably inaugurates neoliberalism in the United States, the Revenue Act provides another moment of "ground zero" for the era of neoliberalism, initiating the expansion of wealth inequality up through the twenty-first century.[134] In the meantime, notes Stein, benefits flowed toward businessmen and the wealthy, with "no guarantees that they would invest it in the United States."[135]

Caught in the logic of the neoliberal, supply-side order, wealth previously redistributed to ease the burden of unemployment and raise living standards now operated beyond the reach of government, in private hands, to be invested wherever business found an outlet for a profitable return. With this restructuring, the anchoring logic of the government-private partnership of the welfare state dissolved, leaving government to enforce "the rule of law" as capital flowed through the invisible hands of multinational conglomerates and a rejuvenated finance community. Moreover, this invisible hand increasingly pointed overseas for its trickle-down target. During the Carter years, "American banks and corporations almost tripled their foreign investments, to $530 billion."[136]

Alongside the 1978 tax revolt, the deregulation of industry coincided with high interest rates (the tightening of credit) that helped to further remove restrictions on wage relations with the intent on gaining more flexibility on labor costs and a "reduction in employers' contributions to national insurance schemes."[137] The shift from production to finance gained momentum, with Carson-Parker's prophecy turning into reality as winter in America set in: the "hard pill for many Americans to swallow" began absorbing into the American body, with democracy pressing forward with the "idea of doing with less so that big business can have more."[138] Although taxes proved an easy sell, making "people accept the new reality" continued to demand more effort at communicating the needs of business.[139]

As a result, a reinvestment in public relations by corporations accompanied this pro-business legislation in the late 1970s. In a special issue, *Business Week* described the setting faced by business at the end of the decade. In full culture war mode, the newsweekly argued that corporations continued to operate in "a 'pressure-cooker' environment," as they came "under siege from consumerists, environmentalists, women's liberation advocates, the civil rights movement, and other activist groups"—the now-familiar cohort purportedly engineering the demise of society in the post–civil rights era.[140] Culture, politics, economics, and social movements coalesced into an entity on par with what *Business Week* called the "unprecedented wave of intervention by federal and state governments into the affairs of business."[141]

In the face of this late 1970s anti-corporate sentiment among the public, *Business Week* again emphasized how corporations were "being forced to become a political animal as well as an economic machine."[142] Indeed, the business community deployed its already adept skills at communication to articulate "its positions more clearly and urgently to government agencies, legislators, shareholders, employees, customers, financial institutions, and other critical audiences."[143] The large profits from the previous year aided the plight of corporations who now understood that they "must get used to the human climate of political behavior, which is often the result of irrational acts."[144] In short, democratic measures directed toward insulating human welfare—whether aid to the poor or regulations against environmental degradation by corporations—were not rational in thought, unlike the information processor of the market.

An example of fighting back included the Bechtel Corp., who attacked the criticism toward its "delays and cost overruns on the Alaska oil pipeline and San Francisco's BART subway projects, the Arab boycott, nuclear safety, and alleged connections with the Central Intelligence Agency."[145] Bechtel's response followed Powell's public relations suggestion above, including a flooding of national media with institutional ads, inviting the press to speak with its executives, and participation "in political action committees to support friendly political candidates."[146] In light of these measures, Vice President Paul W. Cane hints at both the perceived loss of hegemony among multinationals as well as the resurgence of a virile John Wayne–like masculinity in response to the current crisis: "If this had happened five years ago, I doubt whether we would have done anything. But we're not a patsy anymore."[147] Securely knit into the public relations fabric, the masculine component of the culture war proved indispensable as a core element of the political-business nexus of multinational conglomerates: tough masculinity defined the new ascending neoliberal sentiment, while a dependent effeminacy defined support of the welfare state.

Contextualizing the regulatory framework of government within the rhetoric of culture war and color-blind market language helped highlight civil rights activists, feminists, unions, and environmentalists—all traditional targets of conservative Americans—as the primary scapegoats highlighted by conservative politicians to convince voters to support further policies of deregulation in the name of freedom. Meanwhile, the standard of living for the working- and middle-class constituents supporting these policies would continue to walk in the cold shadow of Carson-Parker's prophecy.

Passing the Threshold: The Dawn of the Eighties

Business suffered another round of bad news in 1979 (though not for oil companies) with the Iranian Revolution and the second oil crisis, precipitating a deep recession lasting through 1982. As oil prices rose, economic expansion halted in the West. Inflation and unemployment rose, with the latter starting at 5.5 percent in 1979 (from 3.2 percent in 1973) and rising to 8.6 percent in 1982.[148] Offering a nationalist slant to the malaise, the cover of the March 12, 1979 issue of *Business Week* featured a close-up picture of the Statue of Liberty, shedding a tear beneath the headlines: "The Decline of U.S. Power."[149] Linking the Vietnam War with the fall of the shah of Iran (who became head of state through a U.S.-directed coup in 1953), the authors asserted, the "erosion of power is the product of the failure of U.S. leaders to recognize the connections between political, military, and economic events and to develop coherent approaches that deal with them in an integrated fashion."[150] Characterizing the years after the Vietnam War as a retreat, *Business Week* condemned the debilitating atmosphere of political debate in Washington "over who gets what share of the economic pie."[151] In subtle anticipation of the next decade, the author observed that foreign and military policy will most likely be decade-defining topics, writing, "If the decline in U.S. power is to be arrested, the trend toward spending a smaller share of the federal budget on defense must be reversed, and economic policy must change in a way that encourages investment at the expense of consumption."[152] In short, neoliberalism: investment through free trade, pro-business policies, as well as the reining in of government social spending on a public entering an era of austerity. Federal spending for multinational defense corporations, however, would continue apace. As Michael Parenti noted a year later, the strategy of calling for an increase in defense spending in the name of national security and the decline of U.S. power—ranging from the press to the Pentagon to its "corporate supporters"—hinged on a particular silence: as the public sank economically, corporate profits were up during an economy "beset by stagflation, recession, overcapitalization, declining investment opportunities, and the ever-present threat of a falling rate of profit."[153] Parenti also noted that although these defense proposals were usually justified in the name of creating domestic jobs, in reality "arms spending [according to the Public Interest Research Group in Michigan] create[d] fewer jobs per billion dollars than any other Government expenditure except the space program," but these contracts did "create the greatest margin of profit."[154]

Blocking this path, according to *Business Week*, was the "parochialism" of the U.S. middle classes who were "hardly in a mood to take on additional international responsibilities."[155] Reasserting the problem outlined by the Trilateral Commission earlier in the decade regarding the "excess of democracy," the middle class created through the Jim Crow welfare state were framed as an obstacle to corporate prerogatives and the smooth transition to the polices of neoliberalism.[156] In a blunt admission of class warfare connected to overseas (neo-)imperialism, *Business Week* asserted, "Pitted against them in the debate will, of course, be the powerful military establishment and nearly all of the outward-looking multinational corporations that operate on a global basis."[157]

Obstacles to economic policies came from overseas as well. Illustrating the ways moments of crisis often provoke blunt admissions of one's ideology, the head of a large U.S. bank looked nostalgically back to the era of imperialism, "It was easy in the pre-Vietnam days to look at an area on the map and say, 'that's ours' and feel pretty good about investing there. That's no longer the case, as Iran has made so terribly clear. American investment overseas is going to happen at a reduced rate until we can redefine our world."[158] For multinationals, it seemed, the "American retreat from global activism" had made it harder for them to operate among greater risks and lower profits.[159] High on the list was the rise in nationalist policies from less-developed countries who recently gained independence, and now became "more forceful and sophisticated."[160] Although the United States (and Britain before) engaged in nationalist protectionism from the 1800s to present, developing nations attempting to achieve goals of economic independence through protectionist measures amid postwar American economic hegemony were imagined as being unfair to multinationals.[161]

The ever-growing competition from Japan and Western Europe added further weight to the dilemmas facing the relationship between multinationals and their government. Although the Business Roundtable found success in 1978's tax revolt, multinationals complained of the unfair relationships defining Japanese and European multinationals and their respective governments. A vice-president for Bank of America lamented, "Our multinationals get no Brownie points from the State Dept. for getting a piece of the action for the U.S."[162] A list of unfair advantages included U.S. rules for multinationals that covered anti-bribery, anti-boycott, and environmental laws, as well as "having to pay taxes on income earned overseas."[163] The solution sought by multinationals included giving them "a freer hand and more effective support, especially on financing, tax policy, and in exerting economic pressure to help spur U.S. sales and guard investments"; however, *Business Week* noted "few want any return to gunboat diplomacy or subversion of unfriendly regimes by the Central Intelligence Agency"—a list that included the nations of Iran (1953), Guatemala (1954), Congo (1960), Iraq (1963), Brazil (1964), and Chile (1973).[164] In the meantime, as corporate profits for 1978 were 16% higher than 1977, and rose through the second and third quarters of 1979, the unemployment rate hovered between 5.6 and 6.0 percent.[165]

In this context of unemployment, inflation, and multinational discontent against the "parochial" middle class, the United States opened the door to the monetarism espoused by Friedman.[166] With the appointment of economist Paul Volcker as head of the Federal Reserve Bank in August 1979, President Carter helped integrate an important logic of neoliberalism into the engine of the American economy. Favoring lower inflation at the expense of rising unemployment, Volcker tightened interest rates in hopes of stabilizing the dollar. Charles S. Maier suggests that this near final act of the 1970s corporate revolution was a lesson in protecting one's rights: "Just as liberal democracies had learned to protect civil rights against democratic passions, so now they moved to make stable currencies a basic right shielded from majority pressures."¹⁶⁷ The consequences of this policy favored business as real wages were depressed. Instigated by Volcker the recession generated double-digit unemployment. Combined with the decline in manufacturing jobs and the rise of low-wage service work, this cleansing shock process also took aim at older, more obsolete firms more closely connected to previous Keynesian policies, further exacerbating unemployment as these manufacturing facilities closed shop.¹⁶⁸ The steady leak of deindustrialization turned into a catastrophic flood of jobs leaving the American industrial sector, spreading precarious employment at the same moment the old pattern of government intervention on behalf of working-class voters ceased to exist (except, perhaps, through defense spending).

With their experience in manipulating foreign investment from abroad and their conjuncture of interests with neoliberals and supply-side conservatives, larger multinational corporations and finance institutions not only survived but also thrived in the new political-economic environment. Both recessions in the 1970s reinforced the reasoning and logic behind the large diversified conglomerate as small and medium-size firms felt most of the recession's bite—while businesses tied to the increasingly deregulated levers of finance found it easier to obtain credit for bailouts.¹⁶⁹ The emerging victor would be finance, for whom these policies helped to revitalize after being "hard hit during the 1970s by accelerating price increases and a plethora of loanable funds."¹⁷⁰ More importantly, as noted by Bruce Schulman, the American public, too, seemed to "tolerate draconian policies" in the name of taming inflation.¹⁷¹ As a result, the United States again became receptive for foreign investments. By the mid-1980s, manufacturing regained its competitiveness as exports out of the United States increased; the late 1970s "combination of industrial shakeout, wage repression, and dollar devaluation" served business well.¹⁷²

An intense year led up to the election of President Reagan in November 1980 as the neoliberal framework introduced by Carter continued to evolve. In response to crippling inflation, *Business Week* in a March 3, 1980 editorial impulsively reached back to Keynesian methods, bluntly stating, "The editors of *Business Week* have rethought this magazine's longstanding opposition to wage-price controls."¹⁷³ A month later, the unemployment rate went from 6.2 to 7 percent. Adding to the anxiety was the baldly racist, xenophobic cover of June 23, 1980, picturing an ambiguously drawn brown-skinned man stepping through a tear in the American flag: "The Economic Consequences of a New Wave: The World's Poor Flood the U.S."¹⁷⁴ Imagined through language portraying poor brown people as analogous to natural disasters, the framing of non-white immigration to the United States added another instrument in the conservative culture war. First, it reinforced the idea that white people were the only "real" Americans, a status conditioned through centuries of settler colonialism and the slave republic's logic of the "whites-only" Naturalization Act of 1790 and the 1857 Dred Scott decision.[175] Despite being former immigrants who displaced the original inhabitants through the *wave* of westward expansion, whiteness reinterpreted invasion as peaceful—and innocent—settlement. Second, this sentiment reinforced the idea that darker skinned people were invasive aliens, underlining this "racial" invasion as a key emotional factor explaining economic hardship to "middle Americans."[176] Immigrants, especially non-white, were added to the usual suspects of the conservative culture war after The Immigration and Nationality Act of 1965.[177] Despite people of color being blamed for the economic misery (from taking jobs to welfare dependence), the second oil crisis and price increases had led to large gains for Western oil companies: their "total corporate profits [were] mind-numbing," in the words of *Business Week*.[178] For total manufacturing profits, oil now accounted for a staggering 40 percent, against a mere 18 percent a few years previous, and from 15 percent in 1972. Indeed, "in the middle of one of the sharpest recessions on record oil companies increased their net after tax earnings in the second quarter by some 32% over the year-ago figure, while the rest of U.S. industry was suffering a profit decline of 18%."[179] Meanwhile, the national average unemployment rate reached over 8 percent, with African Americans hovering around a staggering 34 percent.[180]

In a 1980 campaign strategy to "woo workers," Reagan offered promises of trickle-down prosperity weened from Wanniski's *The Way the World Works*, delivering rhetoric heavy in symbolic "patriotism"—a crucial wedge issue culled from the 1960s—and ditching or modifying "some of his previous antilabor rhetoric."[181] After the political and social upheavals of the 1960s and the economic turbulence of the 1970s, for many workers the aura of whiteness and the renewed pledge of masculine patriotism spoken by Reagan embodied one of the last remaining privileges in the post–civil rights United States. This was especially true for white men weathering legislated social equality just as they experienced unemployment due to economic restructuring. In the South, this sentiment was given a boost as Reagan began his presidential campaign near Philadelphia, Mississippi, the site of the murder of three civil rights activists in 1964. Here, the former actor pledged his solidarity with state's rights—a not-so-subtle nod to white nationalism—as scores of white Mississippians waved Confederate flags in desperation for a past defined by the Jim Crow welfare state.

New Deal regulations on finance received a critical blow the same month Reagan won the presidency. *Business Week* proudly announced in a November 1980 issue: "The revolution in finance is now finally under way, helped along by the most sweeping piece of financial legislation in U.S. history, the

Depository Institutions Deregulatory and Monetary Control Act of 1980."[182] This law effectively deregulated banking, eliminated interest rate ceilings, and made subprime loans easier—"allowing originators to charge higher interest rates on borrowers with higher credit risks."[183] A month later, the December 15 issue of *Business Week* printed the concluding verdict of both the death of Keynesianism and the birth of the new economics from one of the architects of neoliberalism, Friedrich August von Hayek, who asserted, "People simply must understand that you cannot have moderate inflation, because a little inflation always generates higher inflation, and higher inflation leads to still higher inflation. I believe that a real depression for six months could break that cycle."[184] With inflation reaching 12 percent in mid-1980, Fed Chairman Volcker's policies of raising interest rates eventually brought inflation down to 5 percent by the end of 1982. At this point, the structural policies of neoliberalism and their ideological justifications were largely in place, with capital adjusting its prerogatives to the vastly changed shape of global capitalism.[185] The postwar "liberal consensus" of the Jim Crow welfare state had officially been replaced by the neoliberal "Washington Consensus."[186]

The conservative culture war was essential for generating a populist rhetoric convincing those who benefited most from the welfare state to support a political program dismantling the structure of government responsible for shaping the white middle class in the 1950s and 1960s. Carson-Parker's "hard pill" to swallow, it seems, worked, as voters embraced the anti-welfare state rhetoric and policies that exchanged intervention on behalf of working- and middle-class citizens for a policy tilted toward supporting the needs of big business, multinationals, finance, and the wealthy. In return for their allegiance to a conservative economic program, white Americans were treated to the color-blind coded language of the New Right, with the intent to cement in the minds of Republicans and former Democrats a new justification toward the historical resentment of African Americans and, after the 1960s, feminism and non-white immigrants.[187] In a 1981 recorded off-the-record comment, GOP campaign mastermind Lee Atwater explained the historical evolution of the Republican "Southern strategy" that underlined the culture war: "You start out in 1954 by saying, 'N****r, n****r, n****r.' By 1968 you can't say 'n****r'—that hurts you, backfires. So you say stuff like, uh, forced busing, states' rights, and all that stuff, and you're getting so abstract. Now, you're talking about cutting taxes, and all these things you're talking about are totally economic things and a byproduct of them is, blacks get hurt worse than whites. . . . 'We want to cut this,' is much more abstract than even the busing thing, uh, and a hell of a lot more abstract than 'N****r, n****r.'"[188]

These "dog whistle politics" built on Buckley's anti-Black "culture" argument as coded phrases replaced overt racism.[189] Acting as a safety valve for white people uneasy with legislated social equality with people of color and their rapid decline in economic fortunes, this political racial—and later, sexual—coding defined the conservative social policies of the neoliberal era.[190] Underscoring the uneasiness of white acceptance of social equality, the early 1980s saw more willingness in whites to "accept at least some contact with blacks in their own schools, neighborhoods, and homes," while there remained firm opposition to upsetting the *institutional* "racial status quo" from programs such as affirmative action, busing, welfare, and anti-poverty programs.[191] A perception among whites, long believed even at the height of Jim Crow, suggested that Blacks did not face discrimination and thus should not benefit from "preferential treatment or reverse discrimination."[192] For many whites in the mid-1980s, the twenty years since the Voting Rights Act had somehow erased the institutional racism embedded in virtually every institution across the 300-year history of the United States. By 1985, the work of culture warriors peddling anti–welfare state economics, color blindness, and a renewed American innocence amid civil rights legislation congealed into an American common sense, where the new "symbolic racism" rested on the belief that government aid for Blacks violated "cherished values embodied in the Protestant Ethic"—what Buckley labeled ethos.[193] Most significantly for African Americans, "symbolic racism and traditional prejudice" continued to inform white attitudes toward Blacks in the post–civil rights era.[194] Another barometer measuring these new realities was the response of Democrats and liberals, who "tacitly accepted their opponents' portrayals of such policies as programs that benefited 'special interests' (meaning black people) at other Americans' expenses."[195] These attitudes also shaped the broad acceptance of the type of federal intervention that was acceptable: the escalated war on drugs and mass incarceration, which took a large toll on Black and Latino communities.[196] The focus on these non-white communities, moreover, reinforced the criminality of Blackness and brownness in the white imaginary, as drug-offending whites often escaped the notice of an increasingly sensationalized media and were given lesser sentences in court for the same offenses.[197]

For labor, arguably one of the major pillars of the welfare state, its days of strength fizzled under a headline in *Business Week* in the early 1980s: "Labor Seeks Less."

> With unemployment rising, management has very much the upper hand at the bargaining table. Companies will use this leverage to demand concessions, such as eliminating COLAs [cost of living allowances], capping them, or diverting payments to pay for other benefits. Indeed, unions in the airline, auto, steel, rubber, and other industries have made major concessions in wages, benefits, and work rules over the past year.

And the trend will continue. In the airline industry, a bargaining source at the International Association of Machinists says: "I have never seen such an up-front takeaway attitude by the carriers as I have this year. They are saying: 'Give us, or we'll shut down.' It's an implied threat, and it is not just across the table but out in public."[198]

Squeezed from the top, labor also suffered a "deepening and exaggerating intra-class differentiation," increasing a wider range of inequality between different segments of the working class in similar ratios to the working-class and upper-class income and wealth differentials.[199] Mike Davis notes that during the 1970s, the "wage differentials (not including supplementals) between steelworkers and apparel workers virtually doubled; or in absolute terms, where the difference between their wages in 1970 was $83, in 1980 it was $277!"[200] The gulf between skilled and unskilled labor would continue to widen. This restratification also hit Democrats who were increasingly going "over to the supply side."[201] Beginning initially in the early 1970s, by the 1980s political survival pressed Democrats into leaning right in their economics, with many adopting the mantra of neoliberal economics as they continued to refrain from criticizing capital concentration (inherited by the era of the New Deal)—the payoff came through the new business-oriented Democratic Party that eventually elevated Bill Clinton to the presidency.[202]

Through the promotion of finance over industry, the explosion of inequality in the late 1970s wove itself into the U.S. fabric; African Americans especially felt this foreclosure to opportunity at the dawn of liberation, confronting both a stagnant economy as well as a white backlash paving the way to Reagan's election.[203] These national shifts also reflected international changes as well. To address the accumulated debts of countries such as Mexico and Brazil (who were loaned petrodollars across the 1970s), the International Monetary Fund and World Bank were given authority in 1982 "to negotiate debt relief" with the intent on "prioritizing the needs of the banks and financial institutions while diminishing the standard of living of the debtor country."[204] The era of "structural adjustment" had arrived for developing or newly decolonized nations. For countries like Jamaica, the results were devastating.[205] The work of the Business Roundtable seemed to pay off, however, with corporate tax rates lowered from 33.3 percent in 1980 to 4.7 percent in 1981 and then back up to 15.8 percent in 1982.[206] The redistribution of wealth reversed the gains made by the middle class during the era of the welfare state. Winter had arrived with full force.

As the Federal Reserve tamed inflation, unemployment and recession combined with the anti-labor strategy of Reagan to further discipline the wages of working- and middle-class Americans.[207] Indeed, as Volcker stated regarding the role of Reagan's policies, "The most important single action of the administration in helping the anti-inflation fight was defeating the air traffic controllers' strike.'"[208] From this disciplining, labor unions were "accepting modest long-term contracts months before their current agreements expire—and with almost no threat of strikes."[209] Although the working- and middle-class whites were hurt by Reagan's attack on labor, they found the Gipper's ideas and policies toward rolling back the gains of African Americans (by defunding civil rights enforcement) appealing, as Atwater noted above. Women's rights also became a target for the resurging conservatism in the 1980s, becoming a central focus for the culture war.[210] In contrast, the 1 percent benefited handsomely as they won an increase from 22 percent to 39 percent of the nation's wealth between 1979 and 1989.[211] While poor people's after-tax income fell by 10 percent between 1980 and 1990, the wealthiest 1 percent's income gained 87 percent through tax breaks.[212] This trend would only escalate: between 1980 and 2005, the top 1 percent raked in 80 percent of American income.[213]

"There are increasingly two Americas," noted Dennis Kucinich in the early years of Reaganomics: "the America of multinationals dictating decisions in Washington, and the America of neighborhoods and rural areas, who feel left out."[214] For conservatives, this suggested a return to a natural state of free markets, generating a paradoxical nostalgia for the cultural memory of the 1950s Jim Crow Keynesian America to blend with the economic and social policies of the laissez-faire 1920s. A new possession of history arose to make sense of the rise of neoliberalism, with this contradictory reimagining of the past expressing itself plainly in a 2013 poll by *The Economist*. When asked, "Which decade of the 20th century would you most like to go back to?," conservative Americans elected to return to the 1950s, when the Jim Crow welfare state created a cultural order phrased as "morally uncomplicated."[215] In describing the return of this ethos from the less-than-half-century deviation of Keynesian economics, Rodgers suggests, "Equality was a fatal ambition for a just society. . . . Equality was the authoritarian dream of the 'new class'; it was a denial of nature, which only a government-directed state could satisfy."[216]

In the twentieth-anniversary edition of Friedman's *Capitalism and Freedom* from 1982, the economist rather bluntly presented the ideological role of intellectuals, especially in the case of the shift from Keynesian economics to neoliberalism: "There is enormous inertia—a tyranny of the status quo—in private and especially governmental arrangements. Only a crisis—actual or perceived—produces real change. When that crisis occurs, the actions that are taken depend on the ideas that are lying around. That, I believe, is our basic function: to develop alternatives to existing policies, to keep them alive and available until the politically impossible becomes politically inevitable."[217] A year after this remark, *Business Week* outlined the thoroughness of the sort of revolutionary change Friedman celebrated in an article detailing the new crop of "neo-liberals." Defined without reference to the actual neoliberal movement, "neo-liberals" were described as "a young Democrat politician who wants to stop relying on government to redistribute income and assure equality of opportunity. Instead, the neo-liberal focuses on market mechanisms, high technology, international competitiveness, and economic growth to achieve these ends."[218] In short, rather than the justness and fairness of the New Deal welfare state–era Democrat, the neoliberal Democrat adopted the quantitative analysis of conservative-neoliberal market logic.

After a decade of contraction, benign neglect, and Reagan's wholehearted institutionalization of neoliberal logic via Reaganomics, business steadily recovered from the 1970s at the expense of workers.[219] Indeed, the corporate counterrevolution of the 1970s heralding the so-called Reagan revolution solidified and built off the "seismic shifts in national mood and political debate."[220] By 1989, the poverty level had reached 32 million Americans (out of a nation of 246,819,230, or 13 percent), with the rates distributed through the deep patterns established across the centuries-old racial hierarchies tied to settler colonialism and slavery: "10.1 percent for whites, 26.8 percent for Latinos, and 31.6 percent for African Americans."[221] For many Americans, "Morning in America"—Reagan's political ad campaign for 1984—never arrived; instead, the prophecies from 1973–74 grew into reality: the dream of Carson-Parker transformed into policy while the title of Gil Scott-Heron's 1974 record, *Winter in America*, originally characterizing the bleak moment in the mid-1970s, now became a metaphor embodying the era's material outcomes.[222] With Keynesian economics no longer profitable, or at least in their heavily regulated form (as Reagan was quick to learn through defense spending), business reached a new point of departure within a neoliberal economy.[223]

A vital aspect of this ascendance of neoliberal hegemony lay in the possession of history imagining the relationship between working- and middle-class whites and the popular memory surrounding the era of the Jim Crow welfare state and its distribution of material outcomes. The 1960s culture war summoned the sets of *longue durée* antagonisms driving the logic of the Jim Crow welfare state, including the legacies of slavery (anti-Black racism), settler colonialism (a belief in rugged individualism and xenophobic zero-sum violence against non-white "foreigners"), and patriarchy (the privileged rights of men over women). These legacies fashioned a set of language and knowledge to interpret the nation's problems and deflect them onto the traditional targets of white American men: women and people of color. This long-brewing culture war guided conservative rhetoric through the first decade of social equality and into the twenty-first century.[224] Without a "whites-only" Jim Crow welfare state, the working and middle classes desperately laid their faith in neoliberal and conservative calls for market imperatives and quantitative analysis to justify economic policies rather than a fairness and justness policy of the welfare state that shaped white working and middle-class prosperity after World War II. The patriotic promises of "freedom" and "liberty" accompanying neoliberal economics intersected with the left-liberal critique of the Vietnam War, further anchoring those working- and middle-class Americans who supported the Vietnam War into the conservative ranks of an economic system engineered more for those targeted by late-1960s songs such as Creedence Clearwater Revival's "Fortunate Son"—"I ain't no millionaire's son!"—than the folks whose standard of living declined as the conservative movement grew stronger. By the 1980s, the interventionist ladder of economic prosperity disappeared, choking off further expansion of the middle class just as women and people of color gained access to the welfare state. Through the twenty-first century, "Fortunate Son" continues to resonate: "It ain't me / It ain't me / I ain't no fortunate one, no!"—despite its ongoing use by those who *were* fortunate sons.

Memories of a past defined by both white male supremacy *and* a prosperity-generating welfare state has been obscured for good reason. The remembrance of the comforting material benefits of an economic system geared specifically toward white males seemed to clash with the American myth of liberty, equality, and rugged individualism, especially in light of the visible and institutional evidence aimed toward stabilizing the hierarchies of race, gender, and sexuality. Memories based on the conservative possession of history disavowed the white male supremacy and violence deployed to police this hierarchy. The result was a delusional construction of the postwar years signaling pre-1960s innocence, traditional values, and hardwork, a righteous and convenient possession of history projected across popular media and rife with the nationalist grandeur defending an American dream constructed atop an erased set of racial, gendered, and sexual antagonisms. By the end of the 1960s, this fantasy needed buttressing, as many young white Americans joined the civil rights movement, the antiwar movement, and vented against an American dream they considered a vast lie. The resulting culture war provided a balm for white Americans shocked at their children's insolence as they simultaneously grew anxious over legislated social equality with non-white Americans. It seemed, as Newt Gingrich wrote in 1995, that Western civilization was coming to an end in the mid-1960s.[226]

On the other hand, those living through these decades who were not insulated by the space of whiteness and its protections clearly saw the system for what James Baldwin suggested in the 1965 debate with Buckley: America's prosperity came at the expense of Black Americans, as well as other people of color and women. Critical for the emerging neoliberal conjuncture, this blunt recollection clashed with the white possession of history imagining a time of tranquil—*utopian*—American greatness projected through postwar film and television, only to be disrupted in the 1950s and 1960s by historically marginalized people yearning for social equality and constitutional rights. In 1972, Baldwin noted the dynamics of this historical-identity paradox when describing the difference between the militancy of the excessively romantic white New Left in the 1960s—newly introduced to the antagonisms shaping their world—and the realities of the American system African Americans faced:

> It is only very lately that white students, in the main, have had any reason to question the structure into which they were born; it is the very lateness of the hour, and their bewildered resentment—their sense of having been betrayed—which is responsible for their romantic excesses; and a young, white revolutionary remains, in general, far more romantic than a black one. For it is a very different matter, and results in a very different intelligence, to grow up under the necessity of questioning everything—everything, from the question of one's identity to the literal, brutal question of how to save one's life in order to begin to live it. White children, in the main, and whether they are rich or poor, grow up with a grasp of reality so feeble that they can very accurately be described as deluded—about themselves and the world they live in. White people have managed to get through entire life-times in this euphoric state, but black people have not been so lucky: a black man who sees the world the way John Wayne, for example, sees it would not be an eccentric patriot, but a raving maniac.[227]

Baldwin's use of John Wayne as a pivot for the popular imaginations and experiences in America is significant. For many white Americans, John Wayne epitomized the American dream through his five decades of making and acting in films that taught U.S. history—let alone American manhood—to multiple generations. Wayne represented the true American, the popular media equivalent to George Washington or Abraham Lincoln, anchoring a set of truths buttressing the defense of an exceptionalist American history. Wayne's conservative reaction to the onset of legislated social equality embodied Buckley's *National Review* slogan of standing "athwart history, yelling Stop, at a time when no one is inclined to do so."[228] From a populist-conservative perspective, these truths acted like the intellectuals Friedman spoke of in 1982: "When that crisis occurs, the actions that are taken depend on the ideas that are lying around."[229] By the time Baldwin published *No Name in the*

Street in 1972, Wayne had already asserted himself as a militantly masculine culture warrior, defending the fabled memory of pre–civil rights era America. Still a respected hero from the movies—even in his sixties—Wayne was an important voice in the conservative culture war, espousing truths against a world deemed too liberal as the age of legislated social equality unfolded in the 1970s. In short, Wayne represented a crucial ingredient to the conjuncture of the New Right, neoliberalism, multinationals and finance, and the culture war as *the* symbol of the American spirit of settler colonialism.

Chapter 5

Go West and Turn Right

Settler Colonialism, Neoliberalism, and
John Wayne's Possession of History

> In the long run civilized man finds he can keep the peace only by subduing his barbarian neighbor.
>
> —Theodore Roosevelt, *The Strenuous Life: Essays and Addresses* (1900)

> But you have there the myth of the essential white America. All the other stuff, the love, the democracy, the floundering into lust, is a sort of by-play. The essential American soul is hard, isolate, stoic, and a killer. It has never yet melted.
>
> —D. H. Lawrence, *Studies in Classic American Literature* (1923)

> [John Wayne] has become the essential American soul that D. H. Lawrence once characterized as "harsh, isolate, stoic and a killer." Superficially his films have been as alike as buffalo nickels. Only the date changes; even the Indian looks the same.
>
> —*Time* (August 8, 1969)

> An historical wheel had come full circle. The descendants of the cowboys, who had slaughtered the Indians, the issue of those adventurers who had enslaved the blacks, wished to lay down their swords and shields. But these could be laid down only at Sambo's feet, and this was why they could not be together: I felt like a lip-reader watching the communication of despair.
>
> —James Baldwin, *No Name in the Street* (1972)

Near the end of the chaotic year of 1968, *Business Week* attempted to defend multinational conglomerates from public condemnation by conjoining them with the history of the frontier experience and its regenerative character underlining American identity.[1] Placing these transnational business organizations within the post–Civil War history of "the West" and the rise of industrial capitalism, the magazine asserted, "At its best, the conglomerate style harkens back to the entrepreneurial spirit and daring that typified the early days of U.S. capitalism. . . . Creators rather than curators, the conglomerates often revive competition in settled industries by picking up marginal producers and energizing them with new capital, uninhibited ideas, and fresh expertise.... Shrewd, aggressive, and often charismatic, they excite and sometimes inspire the men around them. Their energy is contagious. And to many people, energetic business is healthy business."² The magazine's description suggested that multinational conglomerates manifested the culture of rugged individualism tied to the memory of 1800s capitalism and, ostensibly, appeared to be the redeemers of U.S. capitalism and society at the dusk of the 1960s. *Business Week*'s possession of history deployed sets of meanings inhabiting the idea of the American settler colonial experience, rebranding postwar capitalism at the very moment the public grew weary about the bigness and impersonal nature of multinational conglomerates. In some ways, the public's reaction reflected the warnings of capital concentration outlined by Walter Lippmann and George Orwell decades before the 1960s, which neoliberal philosophy had deemed irrelevant and the welfare state embraced. Nevertheless, *Business Week* projected the mythology of the West upon the large-scale and capital-intensive transnational corporation, now imagined as a ruggedly individual entity of preindustrial America despite its obvious resemblance to the Gilded Age's concentration of capital via trusts and monopolies. It seemed that the robber barons, by 1960s standards, had become "the people"—creating a strange echo to their late-nineteenth century ascension to "personhood" through the Fourteenth Amendment.³

The idea of unrestrained freedom in the late 1800s continued to be a successful branding tactic in the twentieth century: "the West" and its various characteristics defined what was American. The West was America's original story, constantly in motion, representing both an idea and experience imagined as a regenerating process for its people through the trials of the frontier. Stanley Corkin defines the myth of "the West" "as a condition that removes the artifices of civilization from social life. Within the resulting state of nature, individuals show their essential qualities of character. Those who succeed do so because they are made of better stuff than others. Those who fail do so as a result of their weakness. Such a view relies on a kind of biological determinism, as well as on a simplified concept of nature and civilization."⁴ The myth of the West matured through the processes of late nineteenth-century global imperialism, classical liberal free trade, ideas of racial science and social Darwinism, and the final push of settler colonialism. The historical moment of the West straddled a future bureaucratic industrial era of modern urban rationality and the last decades of a sense of self resting on a preindustrial spirituality, not yet moved by the arrival of consumer capitalism.⁵ As such, the West provided a sentimental veneer of a bygone era, a conceptual space for the present to weave laissez-faire economics back into American life without the baggage of complexities: a time imagined through hardworking small businessmen, ranchers, and farmers, and before the concentration of capital and the Great

Depression crushed its legitimacy. Resituating big business within the *longue durée* veneer of the American settler colonial identity, *Business Week* imagined multinational conglomerates as successors to this rugged individualist identity, now rippling through the anti–welfare state rhetoric of the New Right, segregationists, and neoliberals who sought to replace the economic populism of the New Deal era with a populist conservatism, driven by memories of the West and an ideological project striving to delegitimize government intervention into the lives and economy of the United States.[6]

The mobilization of the West's rugged individualism on behalf of multinational corporations conjoined traditionally elitist and wealthy segments of the American populace with the common folk's brand of populism. The New Deal era's economic populism derived from the reform language of late-1800s "populists" and early-1900s "progressives," who suspiciously viewed large capital-concentrated businesses as undemocratic forces in need of regulation, which most Americans supported through the decades of the welfare state as long as the benefits flowed toward white families.[7] During the civil rights era, the attitude of populism transferred its suspicion toward the federal government, placing its historic social conservatism ahead of the economic considerations driving late-nineteenth century populism and the New Deal (the New Deal welfare state, of course, downplayed or ignored the populists' critique of capital concentration to gain support from big business). The rise of this populist conservatism helped redirect American loyalties away from the federal government toward private enterprise and its desire to deregulate the welfare state. This anti-government sentiment drew its roots out of the settler colonial experience, a liberty embodied as "freedom from restraint" in eradicating the obstacles—Native Americans, Mexicans, and African Americans (enslaved or free)—to white American settlers and communities.[8] The concept of government intervention formed the pivot: whereas business wanted an end to government regulations, populist conservatives wanted an end to government intervention in the form of social equality legislation aimed toward the very people who were targets of American expressions of freedom from restraint. This shift away from economic populism toward populist conservatism helped shape the cultural path for the ascendance of neoliberalism and the collapse of the Jim Crow welfare state.

As the neoliberal era unfolded, ideas of the West's rugged individualism, freedom, and its populist underbelly acted as a precedent to counter government regulations and interference. In May 1978, for example, Milton Friedman stirred the romance of the late 1800s rugged individualism and the free market West in justifying neoliberal policies:

> So much for the present. What about the past? The closest approach
> to free enterprise we have ever had in the United States was in the

19th century. Yet your children will hear over and over again in their schools and in their classes the myth that that was a terrible period when the robber barons were grinding the poor miserable people under their heels. That's a myth constructed out of whole cloth. The plain fact is that at no other time in human history has the ordinary man improved his condition and benefited his life as much as he did during that period of the 19th century when we were the closest to free enterprise.[9]

Business Week sought to muster a connection between the idea of using nineteenth-century Western mythology and populism to champion technologically driven, capital-intensive conglomerates. In a society still remembering the impersonal, concentrated, and anti-labor environment of pre–New Deal capitalism, multinational corporations needed to appear just like the "small guy"—the people—inhabiting the Western genre, the heroic cowboy who worked hard, always did the right thing, and was on the side of justice.[10] In the late 1960s, one man, more than any other, represented these ideals: John Wayne.

During the postwar years, Wayne—or Duke—was one of the most popular actors in the United States. Wayne's insistent and public defense of an American past cleansed of racial and gendered antagonism provided a critical possession of history aiding the conservative movement in eluding responsibility for the ongoing legacies of settler colonialism, slavery and its Jim Crow aftermath, and patriarchy. In doing so, Wayne projected a populist-conservative sentiment throughout the United States as many Americans grew anxious about government interference on behalf of social justice movements. Emerging as a cultural leader of the silent majority against the dismantling of traditional racial and gendered hierarchies, Wayne also helped police the antiwar movement's attempt to bludgeon the righteous sheen of American exceptionalism and history. For neoliberals and conservatives seeking the reestablishment of a system of capitalism framed around the needs of business and the wealthy—with the twinkling-eye wink promising a trickling down of wealth—populist conservatism provided an important spark for a broad political mobilization against the welfare state. This people's call for wealth redistribution upward has since become a vital cultural-political lever for conservatism up through the present.

Born in 1907 in Winterset, Iowa, Wayne grew up and into the modern emergence of filmed representations of the West and, later, World War II.[11] Wayne's persona and his roles in historical epics—including his immortally brief stint as a Roman centurion at the crucifixion of Christ: "Truly, this man was the son of God" (*The Greatest Story Ever Told*, 1965)—as well as his outspoken conservatism generated an aura of paternal authority and trust in his retelling of American history through film and television. He initially forged his identity in late 1920s and 1930s "B" Westerns, leading to his success in *Stagecoach* (1939) and ascension to stardom during and after World War II (unlike his contemporaries, such as Ronald Reagan and Jimmy Stewart, Wayne did not serve).[12]

In the 1950s, Wayne's frontier aura was at its height. J. Hoberman labels this era as Wayne's "Goldwater Westerns": "*The Searchers* [1956], *Rio Bravo* [1959], and *The Alamo* [1960]—movies in which rugged individualism was prized above all, with inequality and aggression understood as the natural order."[13] Wayne's projection of masculinity during the postwar era of globalization and the rise of multinational corporations offered what Russell Meeuf called consumable "models of modern masculine subjectivity."[14] For the 1960s culture wars, this stance was a major pillar: Wayne championed a militant masculinity woven through an American past infused with an unapologetic stance toward the ideas, policies, and material outcomes of settler colonialism and Jim Crow legislation.[15] In the era of civil rights, his unflinching embrace of a white nationalist past placed his paternalistic certainty in the service of downplaying any parts of American history that, now, in retrospect, could be characterized as crimes against humanity. Wayne projected this possessed history through the various films he participated in that reenacted the Manifest Destiny experience of settler colonialism.

As a cultural guardian, Wayne's presence on and off screen justified the 1960s white silent majority's faith in American exceptionalism. He was an American hero ready to deny and deflect the flood of criticisms and protests unleashed by people of color, women, and antiwar protesters. Anticipating the history wars of the 1990s, Wayne's summoning of pre–civil rights historical narratives of settler colonialism—absent the documented systemic racism and violence—clashed with the research of contemporary historians who increasingly identified the American expansion west as an aggressive imperialism based on ideas of racial superiority and gender inequality.[16] Wayne championed the populist-conservative response to the multiple fronts of civil rights activists, antiwar protesters, and unpatriotic historians challenging the righteousness of American civilization.

This chapter outlines the genealogical links entwining Wayne's persona and film and television work with the culture war and its connection to the legacy of settler colonialism. The first section discusses the interaction of Hollywood with the Cold War, while the second section explores how Wayne's iconic films of the 1940s and 1950s blended the contours of settler colonial sentiments with the Cold War. Important films such as *Red River* (1948), *Fort Apache* (1948), *Sands of Iwo Jima* (1949), *Hondo* (1953), and *The Searchers* (1956) bestowed Wayne with a populist-conservative authority.[17] The next section of the chapter discusses Wayne's contribution to the evolution of the 1960s culture wars and the ways it intersected with the ideology of neoliberalism in the 1970s. In particular, these connections arose through his involvement in government-sponsored documentaries, his film, *The Green Berets* (1968), and his involvement in the patriotic television special *Swing Out Sweet Land* (1970), a tribute to American history through the story of westward expansion.[18] Wayne's late 1960s and early 1970s films, including *True Grit* (1969), solidified the frontier patriarch imagery as his movies increasingly contained overt references to contemporary issues Wayne considered detrimental to the potency of American civilization at the dawn of the 1970s: long-haired white radicals, feminists, Black Power, the American Indian movement, and antiwar liberals.[19]

Wayne operated as a multimedia public persona performing roles in films often not under Duke's control, although the films were driven by his larger-than-life personality. Although directors such as John Ford and Howard Hawks *directed* Wayne in their pictures, Duke's onscreen charisma burst through the control of these auteurs, making Wayne into what Meeuf labels a star text: Wayne embodied various meanings and symbols connecting the films and persona of Wayne.[20] Wayne especially symbolized America in the postwar years, with his talk and stride reflecting American masculinity and its connection to deep national myths. His embrace of conservative politics during the height of the Jim Crow welfare state between the 1930s and 1960s (coinciding with the golden age of Western film) offered a "traditional," Middle American–Heartland–Western rural commonsense baseline for an emerging populist conservatism driving the 1960s culture wars.[21]

Populist conservatism offered a rhetorical strategy situating white male-led middle-class families as victims of the interventionist welfare state—despite receiving the largest share of redistributed wealth in the 1950s and 1960s. The language celebrated through Wayne's populist conservatism aligned with the critiques of the welfare state by the New Right, segregationists, and the economic ideas of Friedman, establishing a post–welfare state equation: unregulated capitalism equals freedom; welfare state interference in business and the lives of Americans enjoying the fruits of their hard work was the antithesis of freedom. As a culture warrior, Wayne held the line during the turbulent 1960s, collapsing the ideas of populist conservatism into the political momentum of neoliberalism, a resurgent conservatism, and the dismantling of the welfare state.

The work of John Wayne formed an important cultural core to the defense and revitalization of a pre–civil rights American nationalism—a *white* nationalism—and nostalgia so crucial for the historical justification of conservatism. Anthony D. Smith describes this cultural work: "Through a community of history and destiny, memories may be kept alive and actions retain their glory. For only in the chain of generations of those who share an historic and quasi-familial bond, can individuals hope to achieve a sense of immortality in eras of purely terrestrial horizons. In this sense, the formation of nations and the rise of ethnic nationalism appears more like the institutionalization of a 'surrogate religion' than a political ideology, and therefore far more durable and potent than we may care to admit."[22] These generational transfers of knowledge and history reflected through textbooks or popular media possessed a history informed by righteous glory rather than wanton violence. In the 1960s, settler colonial ideas attached to American nationalism provided a bulwark for white resistance against the civil rights movement and its demands for an end to institutionally based racism linked to voting, housing, employment, and access to space previously reserved for white America.[23]

Shaping the Culture War: Hollywood and the Cold War

> There was no black list at that time, as some people said.
> That was a lot of horseshit.
>
> —John Wayne, 1971

If one wanted to trace a popular culture response akin to the work of Friedrich August von Hayek, Friedman, or William F. Buckley Jr. and his coterie at *National Review*, late 1940s Hollywood is a plausible place to start, as it increasingly steered films away from popular front causes of the 1930s and 1940s and into the right-leaning Cold War era.[24] The conservative shift in Hollywood included the tempering of pre–World War II, anti–big business film narratives stressing the small producer idealism of the late nineteenth century. In short, the Cold War removed the economic populism against big moneyed interests from the realm of debate. Although many of Wayne's "B" Westerns contained hints of populism, the most famous example of this anti–big business sentiment surfaces in *Stagecoach* (1939), whose primary villain—aside from the faceless menacing Apaches—was the nefarious banker.[25] In an era of postwar prosperity, newly constructed white suburbs and the rise of the (white) white-collar corporate man, the disappearance of this critique against big business echoed the development of the neoliberal Chicago school of economics' uncritical stance on concentrated capital as well as the liberal consensus's disregard of the political consequences of big business.[26] It also coalesced with the classless Cold War ideal of defending the "American way of life" in the face of communism.

The "American way of life" slogan breached the barrier between the "myths of collectivity" from the 1930s and the "individual heroism" forged during

World War II as a "classless, undifferentiated folk" fighting for the nation and embodying what it meant to be an American.[27] Corporate advertising and public relations reimagined the slogans disseminated by the left-wing popular front through mass consumerism, using the language of American populism to defend against now-outdated charges of encroachment on "local autonomy" by corporations.[28] The "values enshrined by the corporate sponsors of the American Way of Life" also played to deep sentiments of populist conservatism.[29] T. J. Jackson Lears explains: "'The American' was devoted to practical labor but fond of material comfort, jealous of his private independence but eager for the public approval of others; above all he (always 'he') was pragmatic and optimistic, not given to unproductive speculation or brooding. For many analysts, pragmatic optimism explained our economic success as well as our cultural failures. It promoted a can-do attitude but also a bland indifference to the darker dimensions of life."[30] Disciplined by the existential weight of the Cold War, the redirection of the populist critique of big business to a suspicion toward an interventionist federal government provided an important foundation for the decades-long siege against the welfare state between the 1940s and 1980s.

Hidden behind the "American way of life" rhetoric, of course, were legacies of settler colonialism and slavery and its Jim Crow afterlife. As an industry with a track record of adhering to the cultural tastes of white America, Hollywood played an important role in representing the "American way of life" and the "reshaping [of] American culture and political ideology" after World War II.[31] Alongside other "free enterprisers of the blacklist" such as the American Business Consultants and the American Legion, Hollywood's sense of the American way of life included a strong self-censorship compulsion helping to renegotiate American identity through the Cold War/Red Scare blacklisting of left-wing Hollywood in the late 1940s and 1950s.[32] Despite the paranoia, the House of Un-American Activities Committee (HUAC) found "little evidence of Communist influence in films . . . , [while finding] considerable evidence of the impact of HUAC."[33] Aside from finding communist subversion, Richard Slotkin writes, "The anti-Communist crusade directly affected the language of cinema by imposing limits on the expression of liberal ideas," which largely fell into line with the conservative ideology of big business after the war.[34] Hollywood's role included actively participating in the "revolutionary effort sparked by corporate leaders who hoped to convert national values and popular imagery away from doctrines hostile to modern capitalism."[35]

For the 1940s and 1950s, this pro-business ideology synced with the liberal consensus guiding the Jim Crow welfare state. From a business standpoint, Hollywood's compliance with HUAC countered the antitrust decision of *U.S. v. Paramount Pictures, Inc.* in 1948 (the decision ended the ability of studios to own production, distribution, and exhibition).³⁶ This dismantling of Hollywood monopolies signaled the unraveling of the studio system, creating opportunities for multinational conglomerates to purchase failing studios in the 1960s. The late-1940s anti-communist blacklist also disciplined pro-labor Hollywood messages in films at the very moment when labor had gained enough strength to influence the framework of the Jim Crow welfare state. Jon Lewis notes, "By monitoring those who worked and those who did not, the studios ruthlessly policed the post-Paramount decision workforce and as a result effectively stripped the various industry guilds and unions of their bargaining power. As a result, the unions fell victim to the patriotic fervor of the Red Scare, so much so that the Ronald Reagan–led Screen Actors Guild joined management in implementing the industry-wide ban against some of its members."³⁷ In this sense, Hollywood extended its wartime partnership with the government to the Cold War, aiding the fusion of an anti-labor, corporate ideology into the American way of life safely nestled in the Jim Crow welfare state.³⁸

Hollywood's contribution to postwar ideologies cannot be understated. Since 1934, Hollywood chose to regulate itself through the work of Will H. Hays and the so-called Hays Code after a public outcry against so-called immoral content during the pre-code years (1930–34).³⁹ These policies established a set of production codes to regulate material on the screen, with the following general principles:

1. No picture shall be produced that will lower the moral standards of those who see it. Hence the sympathy of the audience should never be thrown to the side of crime, wrongdoing, evil or sin.
2. Correct standards of life, subject only to the requirements of drama and entertainment, shall be presented.
3. Law, natural or human, shall not be ridiculed, nor shall sympathy be created for its violation.⁴⁰

Notably, and following the eugenic arguments of the prewar years, the code included another exclusion: "Miscegenation (sex relationship between the white and black races) is forbidden."⁴¹ As these sets of rules went into play during the Depression years, films sympathizing with workers' struggles against business, such as *Grapes of Wrath*, appeared; the public accepted this critique as business was blamed for the Depression. However, by the 1940s, studio heads retreated from these pro-labor portrayals.⁴² Former Chamber of Commerce president Eric Johnston replaced Hays as the industry's spokesman, signaling the conservative attitude underlining the "new prominence of respectable businessmen in Hollywood."⁴³

As the head of the Motion Picture Producers' Association, Johnston told the Screen Writers Guild after the war, "We'll have no more *Grapes of Wrath*, we'll have no more *Tobacco Roads*, we'll have no more films that deal with seamy side of American life. We'll have no more films that treat the banker as a villain."[44] The doubting of capitalism through the 1930s appeared to be over, with *Variety* admitting in 1948, "Studios are continuing to drop plans for 'message' pictures like hot coals."[45] From this movement arose Ayn Rand, a screenwriter and author of the best-selling libertarian works *The Fountainhead* (1943) and her later, more well-known book, *Atlas Shrugged* (1957). Her incessant struggle to find communist propaganda in Hollywood led her to write the *Screen Guide for Americans* (1950), demanding, "Don't Smear Industrialists... don't smear the Free Enterprise System.... Don't Smear Success."[46] Rand also declared, "Don't ever use any lines about 'the common man' or 'the little people.' It is not the American idea to be either 'common' or 'little.'"[47] This element of conservative libertarianism hardly synced with the sentiment of populism on display by those embracing *Grapes of Wrath*; however, by the 1960s, these elements came together through the conjuncture of the culture war and civil rights and the antiwar movements.

Social criticism in films in the late 1940s and 1950s mostly found expression through existential, individual, or "personal conflict" (e.g., *film noir* and films about juvenile delinquency and racial tolerance) rather than an attack on some larger system.[48] On the other hand, communist aggression was represented in film as *the system*, including abstraction through the metaphor of a virus (and often through science fiction).[49] The fear of accusations of subversion were such that even Warner Bros. felt leery of mentioning HUAC by name in a film designed to highlight and legitimate the committee's mission: Wayne's *Big Jim McLain* (1952). Warner Bros. commented, "While I appreciate that the writers' endeavor is to laud and not demean these activities..., I submit that this story could backfire in its present form—even to the possible extent of placing *us* in contempt of Congress."[50] Although proof often eluded accusations during the communist witch-hunt, the disciplining momentum made clear that even liberals needed to watch their step.[51] By 1956, Wayne and other Hollywood cold warriors were meeting with the Defense Department discussing ways of inserting "the theme of 'freedom' into American movies."[52]

Cold War discipline fused with patriotism dampened the undemocratic censorship enveloping Hollywood's creative output. Under the guise of family entertainment, these policies became acceptable forms of curtailed freedom of speech, normalizing the sentiments of an uncritical love of country at the same moment the civil rights movement began questioning the very institutions Cold War culture celebrated. With the rise of the antiwar movement, Wayne's rallying of patriotism in the 1960s functioned as a vital anchor of defense, raising a righteous shield against the criticisms of civil rights and antiwar activists. By the 1970s, this populist-conservative reaction also offered an outlet for many who faced the emasculation of deindustrialization and the collapse of the middle class across the last third of the century. As George Lipsitz notes, "Patriotism and patriarchy both ease the anxieties of powerlessness, humiliation, and social disintegration, offering us identification with the power of the state and larger-than-life heroes, or at least authority figures."[53] As the neoliberal era set in after the 1970s, this balm induced a reassurance of tradition, with filtered memories of conquering the frontier regenerating the performance of white patriarchal manhood.

In the early Cold War years, the 1948 film *Red River* (directed by Howard Hawks) exemplified the use of frontier mythology defining the textual girth of Wayne and his mobilization of settler colonial sentiments and performances. The Western changed in style at the end of the 1940s through a synthesis of the "conventions and concerns of the combat film and the Western in a single coherent fable."[54] Richard Slotkin explains, "By transferring the ideological concerns of the World War and its aftermath from the terrain of the combat film to the mythic landscape of the Western, [Director John] Ford proposed a mythic response to the crisis of postwar ideology that is at once a moral critique of our "victory" and an affirmation of the importance of the patriotic solidarity that made victory possible."[55] As a historical film, *Red River* tells the story of the Chisholm Trail and the first cattle drive from Texas to Kansas after the Civil War. Wayne's character, the patriarch rancher Thomas Dunson, his adopted son, Matt (played by Montgomery Clift), and Wayne's longtime trail hand, Nadine Groot (played by Walter Brennan), maneuver through the settler colonial drama of entering "empty" land, staking a claim on territory patrolled by Native Americans (implying previous ownership) and owned by a Mexican land baron, initiating a cattle business for regional distribution, and then eventually forced to herd this cattle north to a railroad connection in Kansas. Settler whiteness initiates the film and the protagonist's journey as Wayne decides to leave a settler wagon train heading to California and instead turns south toward Texas in the stated year of 1851.

The film embodies the Manifest Destiny baseline of the American myth: white settlers seeking their own land amid an "empty nation." Included in this depiction of divine access to land includes the disavowal of *invasion* and the foregrounding of peaceful settlement. As a narrative from the perspective of settler colonialism, the actions of Native Americans are criminalized intrusions rather than heroic acts of defense for their homeland, with white settler violence portrayed as self-defense despite the viewer literally watching *the act of appropriating land* unfold.[56] This baseline of assumptions characterizes the Western film genre. Cleared of Indigenous peoples, Wayne's next obstacle takes the form of colonialism against the more civilized, though still savage, Mexicans. As Wayne squats on territory north of the Rio Bravo River owned by a Mexican land baron, ideas of American citizenship and rights to land arise, leaving a Mexican messenger dead with the other charged with telling his boss across the border that the land north of the river now "belongs" to Wayne. Nothing is ever heard from the land baron, underlining his fear of Wayne and deference to the spread of white civilization. Cleared of non-white interlopers claiming prior possession of land, Wayne projects the necessary frontier masculinity, vigilance, and ideology demanded for nation building.

Wayne's "calm authority of his walk," noted by Garry Wills, developed between *Tall in the Saddle* (1944) and *Red River*, as well as his trademark conveyance of an "air of indomitable will."[57] Under the stress of moving cattle north to Kansas, Duke's agency—the energy and focus reenacting the frontier myth—eventually presses the other cowboys in *Red River* too hard, with Wayne's increasingly paranoid behavior leading to his removal from leadership by his own adopted son. The juxtaposition between his earlier negotiations between Indians, Mexicans, and successful business leadership and his later mid-film breakdown during the epic cattle drive is reconciled by the fact that the cowboys—with adopted son leading—in fact successfully do the previously impossible: they herd the cattle to the train station in Abilene, Kansas, receiving a hefty profit for their cows. A trope is formed: the hardship and discipline emanating from the patriarchal authority figure in the name of successfully completing a task, while harsh, is necessary to develop the character needed for white men to conquer the frontier. However, recalling this tale through Hollywood film denies the invasive nature of settler colonialism, as the meaning of westward expansion displaces *invasion* with *settlement*. This framing through language and knowledge, then, secures and normalizes the possession of history.

Not admitting that these acts of antagonism were invasions—conquering acts against Native Americans rather than defensive gestures protecting white settlements—comprises an underlining element of American masculinity and its desperate fear of appearing weak. "Don't apologize—it's a sign of weakness!," declared Wayne in *She Wore a Yellow Ribbon* (1949).[58] This settler colonial masculinity found a crucial precedent in Theodore Roosevelt, who both thirsted for the experience "out West" and wrote glowingly of its regenerating benefits for the nation. Cognizant of the political nature of the possession of history, Roosevelt criticized the anti-imperialists of the turn of the century, suggesting that if one presented American history as imperialist aggression, then one must "condemn your forefathers and mine for ever having settled in these United States."[59] Writing in his *The Winning of the West*,

Roosevelt celebrated the violence connected to invasion and the elimination of the native: "The most ultimately righteous of all wars is a war with savages, though it is apt to be also the most terrible and inhuman. The rude, fierce settler who drives the savage from the land lays all civilized mankind under a debt to him.... It is of incalculable importance that America, Australia, and Siberia should pass out of the hands of their red, black, and yellow aboriginal owners, and become the heritage of the dominant world races."[60] Settler colonial acts of ethnic cleansing extended to knowledge creation as well, to the point where "American Indians ... largely disappeared from racial calculation."[61] Even the esteemed historian Hubert Howe Bancroft, in yet another defense of the segregation of African Americans, blithely stated, "We do not need the negro for any purpose, and never shall. We did not need the Indian and so eliminated him."[62] American masculinity in the postwar years found it hard to question this deep sentiment of stoic determination to define American atrocities as grand victories of Western civilization. Weary of minorities protesting about civil rights in the 1960s and 1970s, Wayne projected this American settler colonial sentiment in his interview in *Playboy* magazine in 1971, asserting, "I don't feel we did wrong in taking this great country away from [the Indians].... Our so-called stealing of this country from them was just a matter of survival. There were great numbers of people who needed new land, and the Indians were selfishly trying to keep it for themselves.... What happened between their forefathers and our forefathers is so far back—right, wrong or indifferent—that I don't see why we owe them anything."[63]

This toughness proved an important metaphor in the Cold War, as "softness" and "hardness" toward communism regenerated the settler colonial zero-sum attitude determining one's masculinity. For example, in the iconic Wayne-starring *Sands of Iwo Jima* (1949; directed by Allan Dwan), the Cold War language of "hard" and "soft" abounded. An eluder of military duty during the global conflict, *Sands of Iwo Jima* nonetheless positioned Duke as a hero of World War II, sealing his image as the personification of masculine leadership and discipline for the Cold War generation.[64] Produced through the close supervision of the United States Marine Corps, this film provided one of the most important patriotic propaganda devices for the baby boom generation coming of age in the 1950s and 1960s—and anticipated Wayne's active support for military propaganda in the 1960s. Similar in form to *Red River*, the various lessons and relationships guiding the soldiers to their destiny at Suribachi—via Wayne's Sergeant Stryker's leadership—remain one of the more important elements in the regeneration of American exceptionalism after World War II.

The lessons of manhood set within *Sands of Iwo Jima* center on the primary character, actor John Agar's Conway. In terms of the political discourse of the late 1940s, Agar's character is caught between his "soft" Harvard-educated world and his deceased father's toughness (or "hardness"), who died at Guadalcanal serving with Wayne's character. Conway reconciles his dead father's hardness with the new surrogate father of Wayne. Agar asserts, "I'm a civilian, not a marine," establishing a classic postwar argument regarding the emasculating effects of mass culture—here, the faceless civilian is juxtaposed against the heroic individual as a marine.[65] In this sense, *Sands of Iwo Jima* takes on the role of rehabilitation in the aftermath of the actual war and dawn of the Cold War. K. A. Cuordileone describes this set of post–World War II anxieties: "the dualistic imagery [of hard and soft] was also the reflex of a political culture that, in the name of combating an implacable, expansionist Communist enemy, put a new premium on hard masculine toughness and rendered anything less than that soft, timid, feminine, and as such a real or potential threat to the security of the nation."[66] Wayne's role in *Sands of Iwo Jima* renegotiated the father-son relationship with Agar, leading to Agar assuming Wayne's assertive and hard persona as the squad moves on after mourning Wayne's character's death in battle.

Just as *Red River* rehabilitated Wayne's "tough-minded strength" in contrast with Clift's "more temperate leadership" drawn from Wayne's discipline, *Sands of Iwo Jima* reinforces the need for a sense of permanent war preparation for the protection of the homeland, with firm masculinity and determination pointing the way through Hollywood history.[67] With these and other films from the late 1940s and 1950s, the idea of Wayne as an exemplar of American exceptionalism solidified into a nexus synonymous with American history itself, resulting in "intertextual references" accumulated by Wayne after *Red River* and *Sands of Iwo Jima*.[68] These films demonstrated how Hollywood provided the needed cultural lessons to combat the "softness" toward communism and garner a "cult of toughness."[69] John Wayne topped the polls for the man most admired by American men throughout the 1950s and the early 1960s, as Westerns continued to pervade the movie theaters and enter the home through television—only slowing in the mid-1960s as the Western genre hit a decline at the moment of social equality legislation for women and people of color.[70]

From Settler Colonialism to Culture War: 1960–70

> Hard times aren't something I can blame my fellow citizens for. Years ago, I didn't have all the opportunities, either. But you can't whine and bellyache 'cause somebody else got a good break and you didn't, like these Indians are.

> We'll *all* be on a reservation soon if the socialists keep subsidizing groups like them with our tax money.
>
> —John Wayne, 1971

As the 1950s turned into the 1960s, the United States increasingly confronted the complicated legacies underlining the exceptionalism blanketing the "American way of life." By the late 1950s, the civil rights movement exposed America's "racial dictatorship" to the world, with violent Southern resistance escalating in the early 1960s.[71] The difference between this antagonism and the violence before the 1950s was simple: mass media now captured images of whites beating and humiliating Black people who simply wanted to sit at a lunch counter, or attend school, or enjoy rights protected by the Constitution. The proliferation of these images of anti-Black violence, along with antiwar protests and graphic footage from the war in Vietnam, increasingly dissolved the 1950s naive belief in the innocence of American history. With postwar American exceptionalism seriously damaged through the white resistance to legislated social equality, a surge of populist conservatism arose in an attempt at nullifying this disintegration. The conservative culture war began in earnest.

Wayne's response came with his first opportunity to direct a picture, *The Alamo* (1960), aiming to produce a film that would "reawaken American patriotism."[72] With his role of frontiersman Davy Crockett, "his idealized image of himself," Wayne again regenerated the ties binding the settler colonial frontier myth with postwar patriotic jingoism.[73] Released the same year as the civil rights movement student-led sit-ins across the South, the one Black actor in *The Alamo* is Jester Hairston, who portrays Jethro, the slave to Jim Bowie. The representation of Jethro played on the pro-slavery myths and tropes developed across American historiography and retold in Hollywood—including *Birth of a Nation* (1915) and *Gone with the Wind* (1939).[74] The most popular controlling images included the mammie (the loyal and happy servant of the white family), the Sambo (docile, childlike, and content with life as a slave), and the Uncle Tom (who knew the value instilled through the Southern way of life).[75] Fulfilling this idealized and reassuring white image of enslaved African American men content with their subservient status, after Bowie frees Jethro, the formerly enslaved chooses to stay behind with his ex-master out of loyalty—a loyalty extending to the point of throwing himself in front of Mexican soldiers bayonetting Bowie.[76] A significant weapon in the *longue durée* culture war of white supremacy, Blackface minstrelsy's Sambo character disavowed the psychological and physical terrorism defining slavery, with the character of Jethro regenerating Southern slavery paternalism at the same moment white Southerners defended Jim Crow segregation through white terrorism.[77] For postwar audiences, their familiarity with Sambos and mammies was well entrenched in popular culture—for instance, the popular Will Rogers film *Judge Priest* (1934).[78] Just as Sambo blunted the condemnations of slavery in antebellum America, this dynamic attempted to blunt the arguments of civil rights activists in the South who suggested that Jim Crow segregation was unjust.[79] Bowie's selfless act of freeing his slave and Jethro's ongoing loyalty exemplifies the conservative possession of history: Southern paternalism was real, and slavery in the United States was not as bad as unpatriotic folks suggest. Despite the jingoistic fervor of *The Alamo*, the film did little to foster Duke's new career as a director, with some Hollywood conservatives asserting that the "bad reviews" were "inspired by the Communists."[80]

The conservative culture war Wayne entered in the 1960s emerged from Northern and Western Republicans and Southern segregationist Democrats who vehemently took exception to federally administered social equality legislation. Social order, a key lever of conservatism, was being upset. As noted in the first chapter, northern conservatives had no problem defending the strategies Southern segregationists deployed to halt the advances of the civil rights movement. Tactics included asserting the defense of individual property rights to blunt charges of racial discrimination, equating the federal intervention needed to end discrimination as the gateway to communism, accusing Black activists of being communist agitators, and upsetting the hierarchy critical to American (and Western) civilization—the latter being a preferred justification for conserving hierarchies by conservative intellectuals.[81] Ending the right to discriminate against non-whites—especially the descendants of enslaved peoples—appeared as the antithesis of the core traditions of white liberty in America, a blasphemous deviation from the "American way of life." In their possession of history, conservatives tapped into the silent majority's "fears" of racial equality as the normalcy of white entitlement came into question by social justice activists and the federal government in the 1960s.[82]

By the mid-1960s, Wayne's conservatism entangled both his private and public life, as he felt "progressively more uncomfortable with prevailing values in late-twentieth-century America."[83] The possession of history traditionally reassuring the national ideas of normalized white supremacy and patriarchy were under siege by a growing set of social justice movements. In the early 1960s, Wayne briefly joined the Orange County, California, anti-communist group, the John Birch Society, whose views blended together "populism, nativism, and conspiracism."[84] Formed in 1958, the John Birch Society also summoned the trope of "Western civilization" as its core concern, combining a business nationalism with a virulent antipathy conjoining the civil rights movement and the welfare state, all of which founder Robert Welch described as collectivism: "both the Greek and the Roman civilizations did perish of the cancer of collectivism, and the civilization of Western Europe is doing so today."[85] As the white supremacist, populist-conservative Alabama governor George Wallace ascended to national prominence in the 1960s, Birchers were quick to support and aid the man Michael Kazin characterizes as "a veritable angel of deliverance from the political margins."[86] And although Wayne supported Richard Nixon in 1968, he also contributed $30,000 to Wallace's presidential campaign for president that year.[87]

Acting as a levee for the social equality flood against mainstream white America, Wayne told and retold stories from the past and present through the comforting prism of settler colonialism and patriarchy. The patriotic and whitewashed history texts of the pre-1960s years were at stake, as historically marginalized peoples increasingly gained access to media platforms to tell their own stories beyond the traditional narratives written by mostly men of European descent. Decades before the word "inclusion" ruffled the feathers of conservatism, the presence of non-whites in history books upset the tranquility of the homeland. As historian of school textbooks Joseph Moreau notes, African American

> presence almost anywhere in the texts . . . cast doubt on many of the patriotically uplifting sentiments that had sustained and given meaning to the American story. It was virtually impossible to integrate them into [textbooks] without a fundamental rethinking of text content. Other nonwhites posed challenges too, of course. American Indians, the target of often openly genocidal warfare, hardly served as a testament to the benevolent course of westward expansion. Mexican Americans, who had been incorporated into the country in 1848 and subsequently stripped of much of their lands through legal chicanery, fit awkwardly into tales of immigrant success.[88]

The past became a contested site of the culture war as the old narrative legitimizing the present confronted a revision of the narrative now written with the voices of the historically marginalized. Rather than a wholesome journey through an American exceptionalism citizens pledged allegiance to in school and consumed through popular media, the road to postwar prosperity for white Americans suddenly became littered with the historical victims of the United States. The spotlight on past white nationalist laws, traditions, and actions of the nation unsettled the patriotic history downplaying American racial violence: casting light on past oppression made it harder to deny oppression in the present. Exploring this reactionary culture war after the 1960s, Michael W. Apple explains, "Behind the conservative restoration is a clear sense of loss: of control, of economic and personal security, of the knowledge and values that should be passed on to children, of visions of what counts as sacred texts and authority."⁸⁹ Wayne's participation in government propaganda, war films, Westerns, and his urban crime films in the 1970s worked through this politics of possessing history amid the siege from social justice movements.

An often-unmentioned aspect of Wayne's output in the 1960s was what might be labeled his Vietnam trilogy. Duke's Vietnam trilogy—*A Nation Builds under Fire* (1967), *The Green Berets* (1968), and *No Substitute for Victory* (1970)—represented the conservative culture war version of Director John Ford's more famous Cavalry trilogy: *Fort Apache* (1948), *She Wore a Yellow Ribbon* (1949), and *Rio Grande* (1950). *A Nation Builds under Fire* was a pro-American involvement in Vietnam documentary produced by the Defense Department from 1967, while *The Green Berets* (produced through the aid of the Defense Department) was the only feature film to be made about the Vietnam War during the actual fighting.⁹⁰ Finally, his pro-war and John Birch-esque conspiratorialist anti-government documentary *No Substitute for Victory*, offered Wayne's voice and persona to an increasingly vocal segment of predominantly white, hard-right conservative Americans who were dismayed with what they felt was government inference in prosecuting the Vietnam War and being "soft" on protesters at home.⁹¹

Wayne visited Vietnam in June 1966, touring the country and entertaining troops for the Department of Defense and participating in the production of *A Nation Builds under Fire*.⁹² As part of the *Big Picture* series produced by the Defense Department for American television (broadcast on ABC between 1952 and 1971), *A Nation Builds under Fire* aired in 1967 and featured Wayne discussing the need to support the South Vietnamese government. Wayne had previously worked with the *Big Picture* series for the 1960 episode titled, "Challenge of Ideas," which examined "the conflict between the democratic and communistic philosophies."⁹³ The heart of *A Nation Builds under Fire* stressed how American training and aid would help the South Vietnamese build their nation. The program suggests that "the Vietnamese are running the show," asserting the idea that the notoriously corrupt U.S. government–dependent South Vietnamese government was noble while the anti-government forces of the Viet Cong find themselves presented as a static product of the fifty-year-old global communist plot to take over the world (and not an extension of the French-resisting Viet Minh, or an element of the wave of decolonization after centuries of European rule).⁹⁴ Wayne leaves the audience with a final thought linking the work of building a nation in Vietnam with the experience of the United States between 1776 and 1787: the Vietnamese are fighting a revolution and building a nation at once, not because they want to but because "history will not give them the luxury of the time that it once gave us." Ironically, Wayne's comparison literally described North Vietnam's Ho Chi Minh's own path toward creating a nation after helping to defeat the Japanese during World War II (as an Office of Strategic Services [OSS] asset), when he cited the American declaration of independence in his 1945 declaration of Vietnam's independence.[95]

After his official work with the Defense Department, Wayne went on to direct his Hollywood version of *A Nation Builds under Fire*, titled *The Green Berets*. Created with government support, the film drew its ideas and images from Robin Moore's book *The Green Berets* (a best seller in 1965) and Barry Sadler's hit song, "The Ballad of the Green Berets."[96] Echoing *A Nation Builds under Fire*, Wayne utilized the beginning of the film as a quasi-documentary where citizens learn about the tactics and skills of the Green Berets and why the United States was in Vietnam. The film replicated other images and themes from the documentary, such as nation-building exercises such as the creation of strategic hamlets and caring for refugees. All of these elements fused together the message of the documentary and the fictional film with the interconnected symbolism of Wayne's past war and Western film successes.[97] Released by Warner Bros. in 1968, it fell just beneath *Bonnie and Clyde* for earnings, underlining Wayne's continued draw at the theaters despite the growing antiwar sentiment.[98]

The Green Berets linked together the settler colonial processes reproduced in postwar World War II films and Westerns with official propaganda, providing viewers with a sense of seeing the war in Vietnam as essentially an American frontier conflict and not a foreign-interventionist civil war rooted in anti-colonial struggles. Harkening the American West, Wayne and his troops arrive at a Montagnard base camp labeled Dodge City. His crew is a mix of white ethnic soldiers as seen in his postwar films—offering an "assimilationist model of the Hollywood combat film."[99] These intersections of the melting pot mythology placed race at the forefront in the film. The result commented on both contemporary civil rights issues as well as deeper binaries of civilization and savagery historically used to define the frontier experience. One Green Beret is African American (played by Raymond St. Jacques) and is a medic (Sgt. Doc McGee) who is often seen curing sick children and other villagers' wounds. Although Wayne argued that his inclusion of an African American reflected his notion of the appropriate number of Blacks in films according to their "supposedly proportional . . . percentage of the population," the Special Forces explicitly discriminated against African American inclusion into their elite ranks at the time (i.e., they still adhered to Jim Crow despite Executive Order 9981).[100] By taking the propaganda of the Defense Department and creating a film loosely based on Wayne's past films, *The Green Berets* lent Duke's aura to the fictional account of the war that appeared to be real.

Wayne's final project in his Vietnam trilogy was *No Substitute for Victory*, released in 1970 as a documentary film by Alaska Pictures. The title was taken from Douglas MacArthur's letter to Representative Joseph W. Martin Jr. in 1951, which was read by Martin to the House of Representatives on April 5, 1951. The letter describes how diplomats were fighting the Cold War with words while the "Communist conspirators" had chosen Asia as the base of operations for "global conquest." The phrase "There is no substitute for victory" underlined the need to fight communism with every means necessary, a settler colonial zero-sum equation dismissive of Franklin D. Roosevelt's "peaceful coexistence."[101] More importantly for the populist-conservative critique of the welfare state, MacArthur's sentiment aimed toward the welfare state's diplomatic interference in soldiers trying to achieve victory. *No Substitute for Victory* was not produced by the Defense Department and, like *A Nation Builds under Fire*, is curiously absent from the literature discussing Wayne's career. With *No Substitute for Victory*, we see a progression away from government-sponsored patriotism in *A Nation Builds under Fire* and the government-private partnership of *The Green Berets*. By 1967, when *A Nation Builds under Fire* was broadcast, a growing portion of the American public had started questioning the war. The early 1968 Tet offensive undermined government credibility in prosecuting the war—a part of the larger dissolution of American exceptionalism in the 1960s. When *The Green Berets* was released in the summer of 1968, Lyndon B. Johnson had pulled out of the presidential race, stopped the bombing of North Vietnam, and looked for a way out of the war. In his presidential bid, Nixon used his "secret plan" to end the war to help him secure the presidency, underscoring an American public's exhaustion with the Democratic Party's prosecution of the war. Privately financed, *No Substitute for Victory* vigorously attacked these divisions using the widely disseminated talking points of the conservative culture war. Significantly, this documentary projected the more extreme, conspiracy-tinged populist-conservative anti-government politics hovering along the margins of the conservative culture war.

Underscoring Wayne's enduring potency, the documentary continued to resonate with right-wing conservatives in the twenty-first century. A reissue of the documentary by the Roan Group Interactive Entertainment in 2006 combined the original documentary with supplementary interviews and comments by contemporary conservative political figures such as Congressman Dana Rohrabacher and OSS–Central Intelligence Agency (CIA) Major-General John K. Singlaub (who both played a leadership role in the World Anti-Communist League and had a hand in the Iran-Contra scandal).[102] As a right-wing counter to the growing disillusionment toward the early 2000s Iraq War (Gulf War II), the re-release of *No Substitute for Victory* was labeled "A Wake-Up Call to the Cut-and-Run Crowd," linking the failure to fully prosecute the Vietnam War with Iraq and the so-called War on Terror.

The content of *No Substitute for Victory* outlined the maturing culture war imagery developed across the 1960s by right-wing conservatives who connected an intrusive government at home with its failure—implied to be treasonous—to prosecute a war and discipline an increasingly unpatriotic, "communist-inspired" citizenry at home. "It's time we spoke out about Vietnam," states Wayne at the commencement of the film, "and the most obvious, yet most ignored threat ever faced by free people in the history of the world." Assuming the apocalyptic tones rooted in the decades-long conspiracist right-wing resistance against the Jim Crow welfare state, Wayne's presence offered a reassuring populist facade to these concerns. Alongside "street demonstrators," the enemies of freedom included government interference with generals trying to successfully prosecute the war. Noting this lack of common sense in the war's prosecution, Wayne asserts, "And the way it is now, we're not programmed to win, because of the politicians and civilians that we've let stick their nose in it." Wayne then asks for an opinion of someone who was there, an army helicopter pilot, who states, "I was there to fight the communists, there to win. But our politicians wouldn't let us." Cutting back to Duke, Wayne then builds on the pilot's frustration, reframing the means and methods of the Cold War against communism through the previous few years of antiwar demonstrations: "It's a war we're losing. Not only on the battlefield, but out on street corners, college campuses, in the offices of some of our most influential so-called statesmen." His trifecta of treason pointed toward the three primary elements shaping the conservative culture war: criminalized Black protest against intuitional racism ("street corners" and its relation to the "law and order" mantra of "street crime"); effete, drug-taking white college students ("college campuses"), and the liberal establishment guiding the welfare state ("so-called statesmen"). Wayne then refers to his various expert witnesses who supported the theme of a "no-win policy." Famed radio and television personality Lowell Thomas traced the history of American warfare in the twentieth century, chiding Roosevelt for his slow approach to dealing with Hitler in Germany and later giving up Eastern Europe to Stalin. Wayne then charges U.S. government complicity in the rise of communism in China.

As these oversights underline, the possession of history continued to serve its ideological role in the culture war, framing history through a narrow Cold War prism disavowing a more complicated historical context. Much like *A Nation Builds under Fire* and *The Green Berets*, *No Substitute for Victory* highlights the atrocities of the Viet Cong while providing no history of Vietnam before the late 1950s—when the United States took over the failed French counterinsurgency against the anti-colonial Viet Minh. For the viewer, there is no historical examination of French colonialism, Japanese occupation, the betrayal of the Vietnamese people by the United States after allowing and aiding the French to retake Vietnam after World War II, and the dismissal of the Geneva Conference of 1954. Skirting the lines of historical accuracy, the post–Geneva Conference migration of Vietnamese out of the north is used as an example of "voting with their feet" and a rejection of the leadership of Ho Chi Minh. Wayne's assertion is consistent with American policy after the Geneva Agreement, although Duke does not add that OSS/CIA Edward Lansdale organized the spread of disinformation and encouraged the Catholic hierarchy to convince fellow Catholics in the north to migrate south by "following priests who told them Christ had moved south" and staging the "much-photographed arrival in the South."[103] If the fear of the loss of Christ did not scare Vietnamese Catholics from going south, then rumors from Lansdale's propaganda campaigns regarding the use of atomic weapons, less than ten years after the United States dropped two on Japan, might make nonbelievers pick up and leave.[104] In addition, Ho Chi Minh's refusal to seek aid from the Soviet Union (noted by Dean Acheson in 1946), contrary to Wayne's Vietnam trilogy's charge of the "communist conspiracy," or the Vietnamese leader's post–World War II request for ties to the United States immediately after the war fail to be mentioned, all issues the high-ranking generals in the documentary most likely knew of.[105]

No Substitute for Victory cites opposition and criticism to the hawkish approach to the war as traitorous, including attacks on the "liberal press" and "communist rioting." One commentator in *No Substitute for Victory* declares, "I think it is far better to stop them [the communists] at some far away distant shore, than wait for another Pearl Harbor, or perhaps try to stop them on the shores of the U.S." Unaware, perhaps, of the Viet Cong's lack of a naval fleet, the speaker nevertheless delved into Cold War axioms and the Manichean worldview of no compromise. In true Cold War gendering, actress Martha Raye (the only woman commentator) offered a critique of domestic resistance to the war in Vietnam and the effects on children and young adults.[106] As she speaks, the viewer sees footage of demonstrations, with demonstrators milling about, carrying signs such as "God Is an Impudent SNOB." The demonstrators consist of long-haired men and women, Black and white, subtly pointing to the deep anxieties of miscegenation long haunting white Americans.[107] Raye asserts, "The Reds have declared in no uncertain terms, that they are going to destroy the moral character of a generation of young Americans. And when they have finished, there will be nothing left for us to defend ourselves against them." The last shot shows a bearded white hippie, slunk down and framed by metal bars (a gate), eyes closed in a daze, possibly on drugs. Wayne concludes, "And they're doing a pretty thorough job on some of our kids."

For conservatives at the dawn of the first decade of legislated social equality and on the verge of losing a war, America needed a booster shot of patriotism—and refresher course on the exceptionalist history of the nation. On cue, Duke galloped to the rescue through the alter ego of *No Substitute for Victory*: the lighthearted television special, *Swing Out Sweet Land*. Produced by Wayne's own Batjac Productions in partnership with the National Broadcasting Company (NBC), *Swing Out Sweet Land* (renamed *John Wayne's Tribute to America* when released on DVD decades later) was broadcast on November 29, 1970: the year of the Kent State and Jackson State shootings, the "hard hat" counter demonstrations supporting the Vietnam War, the illegal invasion of Cambodia, and the beginning of far-left bombings of government and police buildings. In this moment of crisis, Wayne's television special sought to reinvigorate the flagging patriotism of Americans increasingly polarized by the multitude of issues coming to a head at the end of the tumultuous decade.

At the time, *Swing Out Sweet Land* was the most expensive television special ever produced, and it was sponsored by Budweiser (Anheuser-Busch, Inc.).[108] Released the same year Wayne was named one of the most admired entertainers by a Gallup poll, the Nielsen ratings were high enough to rebroadcast the special in April 1971. The eighty-minute program mixed together song-and-dance numbers, sketch comedy, and recorded on-location scenes to celebrate the history of the United States, winning an Emmy in 1971 for Outstanding Achievement in Music Direction of a Variety, Musical, or Dramatic Program (for music director Dominic Frontiere).

Less militant than his appearance in *No Substitute for Victory*, Wayne's introductory speech not only made light of his renowned version of patriotism but also addressed the real problem he thought affected the nation: "I guess what I'm trying to say is, some folks have the idea that patriotism has gone out of fashion." To rebuild this patriotism, Wayne focused on the immigration-assimilation story (the melting pot myth), stressing rugged individualism and an imagined color-blind economic opportunity granted to those coming to America.[109] In short, Wayne summoned the popular immigration story used by Buckley, Daniel P. Moynihan, and Nathan Glazer to downplay the role of institutional racism toward African Americans. The show's trajectory can be summed up with Wayne's pondering of America at the end of the program: "With little more than the clothes on their backs and hope in their hearts, and all they asked was for a chance to put their two hands to work in our free market place. Europe's poorest became America's middle class. Them willing to work found no limits on their ambition. So in our first two centuries in this God-given land, men with a dream had converted untold acres of forest, and lakes, and rivers, and plains, mountains and valleys into a land of opportunity." In shaping westward expansion as a color-blind masculine project of taming the land, Wayne reinscribed the myth tying together rugged individualism with the American middle class. Wayne's vision assumed an ideal past without racial, class, or gendered conflict, where opportunity and a free market society appeared to have existed since the revolution without blemish. It was the version of U.S. history the silent majority learned as children and so desperately needed to believe in as the simplicity of this story of American exceptionalism collided with the complexities of the 1960s. The program hardly alluded to violent conflict, whether between Native Americans and settlers or between enslaved African Americans and white people, subscribing to an idea of settler colonial nation building "characterised by the absolute or relative lack of violence; it is a fantasy of communities devoid of disturbances or dislocations."[110]

Premised on a history silencing the sets of deep legacies of antagonism toward people of color, the first scene depicted the European colonial contact with Native Americans. Implicitly addressing the charges of aggression of British settler colonial policy at the time, Wayne neutralized European settler belligerence by framing the relationship as one of naive innocence between Europeans and Native Americans rather than the driving force of settler colonial logic: "[At the time of colonization, the] only inhabitants were Indians. Since there were no rulebooks on how to get along in the new world, a lot of the early settlers went about it the wrong way. Like, for example, moving right in on the Indians without even asking their permission. On the other hand, some of our people went about it the right way." The next scene shows Peter Minuit buying the island of Manhattan with trinkets, beads, and cloth, with Wayne stepping in and suggesting that Indians were getting cheated. The Indians, led by white actor Dan Blocker performing in "red face" (white actors darkening their skin to play Native Americans—similar to Blackface), botch the deal—of course—with laughter ensuing as the enduring joke of ignorant "Injuns" cushions the reality of European invasion and settlers going about colonization "the wrong way."[111] This transaction, presumably, highlights Wayne's "right way." Limerick charts this long-enduring trope of innocence back to the very act of westward expansion:

> The dominant motive for moving West was improvement and opportunity, not injury to others. Few white Americans went West intending to ruin the natives and despoil the continent. Even when they were trespassers, westering Americans were hardly, in their own eyes, criminals; rather, they were pioneers. The ends justified the means; personal interest in the acquisition of property coincided with national interest in the acquisition of territory, and those interests overlapped in turn with the mission to extend the domain of Christian civilization. Innocence of

intention placed the course of events in a bright and positive light; only over time would the shadows compete for our attention.[112]

Swing Out Sweet Land imbues innocence on settler colonialism at the moment of invasion, mere seconds after admitting the mistakes of a few. Tellingly, this is the last time the viewer hears from Native Americans (or at least white men dressed as Native Americans), conveniently avoiding the final bloody century of conflict. With their only remaining presence as small teepees on the giant map of the continental United States Wayne lumbers across throughout the program, the myth of the disappearing Indian endured.[113]

Alongside the silencing of Native American resistance, the normalization of sexism pervades the program. For instance, at Valley Forge, in 1775, the viewer gets to hear Bob Hope relate sexist humor—"Let's remember why we're fighting this war, men. To get back home to our girlfriends. Remember that. You remember what girlfriends are? Those soft, sweet, tender, caress-able young things our wives were right up until the wedding." This fetishization of virgin femininity—a pillar of patriarchy—provides a disciplining model for female acceptability in a male-dominated world. The aftermath is a song-and-dance number combining one woman and twenty men dancing in suggestive movements, underscoring the binary between the ideal virgin and accessible whore. Later, in a sketch on Belva Lockwood (who ran for president on the ticket of the National Equal Rights Party in 1888), Phyllis Diller kids about her bust and proposes to paint the White House pink if elected. Although surrounded by placard-carrying women with signs reading "Women Power" and "Female Power," Diller's routine reinscribes traditional gender norms at the expense of the contemporary women's liberation movement.

As feminism was discounted, race essentially disappeared from discussion as white supremacy and slavery dissolved into a color-blind U.S. history lesson. Ironically, *Swing Out Sweet Land* inadvertently highlights the "free white" requirement for citizenship as representation unfolds through this virtually all-white history of the United States. For the generation of folks watching the special and who frequented movies between the 1920s and 1940s, this historical display of whiteness formed a continuous line with Hollywood's race-conscious product, particularly the industry's frequent use of the American catchphrase "I'm free, white, and twenty-one." Placed in scenes to emphasize a white character's sense of liberty and independence from overbearing authority, the phrase arose in the 1830s after the expansion of the right to vote for white men—thus, "free, white, and twenty-one"; the phrase was supposedly banished by Eric Johnston in the 1940s in the wake of fighting the white supremacist Nazis.[114] Amazingly, slavery and the economics of race disappeared in the program's tale of Eli Whitney Jr.'s invention of the cotton gin, despite slave-grown cotton driving the nation's economy during the antebellum era.¹¹⁵ Disavowal also extends to westward expansion, as the Louisiana Purchase of 1803 is recollected: "Yes, the Louisiana Purchase just gave all those restless Americans back east a new frontier, a new place to head to. Folks came from just about everywhere." Describing "restless" settlers as "folks" reinforced the innocence of westward expansion. Those who had been living in the "empty" Louisiana territory—Native Americans—disappeared as contemporary folks watching at home found reassurance in the settler colonial disavowal of zero-sum violence demanded to cleanse the land of the indigenous.

Safely cleansed of Native American and Mexican resistance (there is no mention of the Mexican American War), this North American open space shaped the backdrop for the story of Abraham Lincoln. The scene begins with a wagon train slowly moving across the land bearing a young Abe. Wayne announces, "So the child of destiny moved west, to grow into the man who would remind a later generation that an earlier generation had declared 'all men are created equal,' and who died trying to prove it." The Civil War is contextualized by Wayne as a "pretty rough argument. Because for the first time in our lives we were having a family fight"—the substance of the argument is never discussed. Contributing to the conservative culture war struggle over the memory of the Civil War, Wayne's rendition of the Civil War as family quarrel—absent the mention of slavery—played into contemporary concerns over Southerners who still felt the pangs of defeat—both a hundred years before with the end of slavery, and at the end of the 1960s with legislated social equality. Downplaying slavery as a cause of the Civil War in contemporary twentieth-century politics, Southern renditions of the Civil War depict the conflict as one involving "states' rights," rather than a struggle over keeping enslaved people who provided the coerced labor for profitable cotton production. W. E. B. Du Bois noted this silence during the golden age of Hollywood's romantic plantation genre of films in 1935: "Our histories tend to discuss American slavery so impartially, that in the end nobody seems to have done wrong and everybody was right. Slavery appears to have been thrust upon unwilling helpless America, while the South was blameless in becoming its center."¹¹⁶ As Southern conservative whites fought against federal intervention via civil rights legislation, states' rights became a color-blind vehicle guiding their arguments of resistance.¹¹⁷ Slavery's silence as a cause for the Civil War disavowed the centuries of violence and inhumanity shadowing Wayne's tribute to America, including the post–Civil War violence and terrorism toward African Americans by white people heading west and settling in America's "heartland."¹¹⁸

As the program reached the triumphant turn of the twentieth century, Duke mused on the millions of people who had come to the United States to take part in the American dream (that had not been achieved, it seems, at the expense of African Americans). To illustrate this progress, the program re-enacted a conversation between Mark Twain (played by Bing Crosby) and Frederick Douglass (played Roscoe Lee Browne) using, as Wayne asserts, "direct quotes"—a somewhat odd moment to embrace historical accuracy. Although strange, there was indeed a purpose. To deflect criticism by those offended by the Black stereotypes in his novels, Twain says to Douglass, "Sad to say, you know, that some of your friends object to the character of Jim and Huckleberry Finn. Of course I can only regret that they're behaving as stupidly as whites often do." Douglass replies, "I doubt that those who criticize you are aware, as I am, of two young men of my color you sent through college," with Twain responding, "I am so proud of those boys." Incredibly, the first mention of race appearing near the end of the hour-plus program explores a conversation centered on unappreciative Black folk upset at Twain's denigrating deployment of popular representations of Black people historically used to justify enslavement, second-class citizenry, and violence toward African Americans. Of course, Twain was hardly the only practitioner of American literature taking part in the culture of anti-Blackness.

The old Southern paternalistic tone of white benevolence deployed by the scene provided a balm for white anxiety over Black Power and the social justice movements shedding light on the depth of institutional racism in American life. Indeed, "ungrateful complainers"—or what Wayne would call whiners and bellyachers—at the dawn of liberation for African Americans replaced the previously quaint Southern paternalism sanctifying the racial dictatorship. After over a decade of witnessing the legacy of violent white racism broadcast into their living rooms as the civil rights movement unfolded, white Americans continued to refuse to take stock in their inherited legacy and postwar perpetuation of institutional racism via housing, employment (including unions), and education. Disavowal surfaced in polls from 1968: the treatment of African Americans in the United States (treated the "Same as Whites": 73 percent), the blame for "Racial Problems" (placed on "Negroes": 58 percent), and the idea that businesses did *not* discriminate against Black people ("No," they did not: 68 percent).[119] Wayne hardly veered from this sentiment in his 1971 *Playboy* interview: "I don't know why people insist that blacks have been forbidden their right to go to school. They were allowed in public schools wherever I've been."[120] At one hour and six minutes into the program, the word *slave* is finally uttered for the first time by Douglass, with little consequence for the previous hour's worth of content. The program concludes with an ensemble singing of "God Bless America."

Swing Out Sweet Land exemplifies Baldwin's notion of the "possession of history." In particular, the program disavowed the violent legacies of settler colonialism, slavery, and patriarchy, allowing the depiction of the material benefits of these processes to be innocent of antagonism. It's worth revisiting Baldwin's statement in the epigraph as well, when he notes, "Those adventurers who had enslaved the blacks, wished to lay down their swords and shields. But these could be laid down only at Sambo's feet, and this was why they could not be together."[121] The absolute forgiveness inhabiting Frederick Douglass's voice in his dialogue with Mark Twain—when slavery was finally mentioned—reflected the temperate Sambo in white America's imagination. This is a very different Douglass from his 1842 self: "The white man's happiness cannot be purchased by the black man's misery." The ongoing warmth of the reassuring history broadcast by *Swing Out Sweet Land* is underlined by a brief perusal of the comment section of the program posted on the popular website, Youtube.com, in the second decade of the twenty-first century.

Wayne concluded the program with another speech, one summoning populist conservative culture war tropes:

> I'm a lucky fella. For many reasons. Lucky that I was brought up to, believe in a lot of things I found worthwhile. I believe in common decency, without which no society or goodwill can exist. I believe in my country, my family, my fellow man and my God. I believe in straight talk, and freedom with an accent on the free. Which is still the best four letter word I know. . . . I believe your kids and mine are, just you and me getting a second crack at the world. And our job is to see that they don't make all the mistakes we did and don't invent too many of their own. I believe 99% of them are a credit to their folks, a pride to their country, and deserve a pat on their back from all of us for being what they are—and not waving a white flag at life. . . . *But equal opportunity is based on equal obligation.* . . . And I believe this, if tomorrow, all of us, every single one of us, gets out of bed and says, "this is my country, and I'm gonna do good for it," we'll make the greatest step forward since the pilgrims' foot found Plymouth rock.

Anticipating the rise of family values as a political issue, Wayne embraces the range of concepts felt to be under attack by the social upheavals of the 1960s: nation, family, community, and God. Wayne offers historical reassurance to quell the desperate trauma and denial of realizing one's American dream—experienced through the golden age of the Jim Crow welfare state—relied on a legacy of violence at once visible and disavowed (the very topic of the Baldwin-Buckley debate). In Duke's history lesson, patriotism resolves all disputes, removing the need to ask uncomfortable questions about a nation's unequal distribution of opportunity and freedom. He paints the choices of the other 1 percent of "kids" supposedly against his list of patriotic values as antithetical to civil society. In addition, Wayne's conclusion intersects with the increasing reliance on the immigrant-assimilation narrative related to Europeans coming to the United States, significantly downplaying the evangelical-like tenacity of American anti-Blackness shaping the "skewed life chances, limited access to health and education, premature death, incarceration, and impoverishment" of African Americans, who were forcibly brought to the nation and legally terrorized as public policy and, in cases of lynching, civic duty.[122] As the polls above noted, the disavowal of a well-documented past reinforced the prevailing white attitude blaming poverty on a lack of "ethos" among African Americans. The comforting simplicity of old prejudiced assumptions leaned mightily against the complex intrusions flooding this delusion far too many white Americans refused to relinquish. Finally, Wayne's project reinforced a growing sense among conservatives that a year zero for racial inequality had been established for the post–civil rights era, creating a new innocent national consciousness willing to embrace Glazer's suggestion in *Affirmative Discrimination* (1975) that affirmative action policies were racist against whites—despite a three-century head start in the American dream.[123] Everyone was now equal—all lives, apparently, mattered.

Wayne's notion of "equal obligation" equated to the "rugged individualist" idea that hard work and merit would act as an assimilating vehicle. This rhetorical strategy inverted the logic of racism as the color-blind society resisted "black calls for social justice on a defense of market individualism and national unity, rather than on claims of black inferiority."[124] Wayne's assumption suggests that those "complaining" merely had not worked hard enough: "equal opportunity" would eventually arrive "with all deliberate speed" when one's obligation had been fulfilled. The obscured shadow of Wayne's television speech calling for "equal obligation"—race, assumptions of inferiority, and ideas of self-rule—were in the forefront of Duke's thoughts in the 1970s.[125] In 1971, a year after *Swing Out Sweet Land*, he asserted, "With a lot of blacks, there's quite a bit of resentment along with their dissent, and possibly rightfully so. But we can't all of a sudden get down on our knees and turn everything over to the leadership of the blacks. I believe in white supremacy until the blacks are educated to a point of responsibility. I don't believe in giving authority and positions of leadership and judgment to irresponsible people."[126] Far from being marginal in this common sense, even Wayne's favored candidate in 1968 adhered to this anti-Black self-rule thesis. When commenting on college scholarship programs for Blacks, Nixon explained, "Well, it's a good thing. They're just down out of the trees."[127] Nixon even gave a hearty laugh to Governor Reagan's labeling of African leaders as "monkeys" in 1971—a racist trope centuries in the making.[128] In an alternate universe edition of *Swing*

Out Sweet Land, the producers would have stressed the founding fathers' racist ideas of self-governance. Greg Grandin writes, "The American Revolution advanced a theory of political self-governance based on an individual's ability to self-govern, to use capacities, virtues, strength, and reason to constrain passions and control vices. People of color—enslaved peoples within the United States or dispossessed peoples on its border—helped define the line between proper liberty, which justified self-governance, and ungovernable licentiousness, which justified domination."[129]

For Wayne, these connections between values and notions of self-rule bore a prominently anti-Black conception, a sentiment that appeared more flagrantly the moment social equality legislation removed the legal barriers of white superiority. Duke's film work took him around the world, including through colonialized areas of white-ruled southern Africa. Just as Buckley would defend white South Africa from criticism throughout the most brutal decades of Apartheid, Wayne, too, possessed a romantic view of white settler projects in Africa, particularly the British colony Tanganyika (today's Tanzania) where he filmed *Hatari!* (1962).[130] While calling for the need of irresponsible Blacks to be educated and made responsible before ascending to leadership positions in the United States, Wayne expressed a similar anti-Black opinion of sub-Saharan Africa in the January 1972 issues of *Life*. Here, he scolded the youth of the United States, Britain, and France for not pursuing the settler colonial mission Duke saw so clearly during his visit to eastern Africa in the early 1960s: "Your generation's frontier should have been Tanganyika. It's a land with eight million blacks and it could hold 60 million. We could feed India with the food we could produce in Tanganyika. It could have been a new frontier for any American or English or French kid with a little gumption! But the do-gooders had to give it back to the Indians!"[131] Equating Black people in Africa to "Indians," the implications of this settler colonial and anti-Black imperialist sentiment most certainly included the prerequisite of settler colonialism's zero-sum relationship to the Indigenous people whose land fell prey to colonists. And like the frontier experience with Native Americans, the disavowal of the level of violence required to clear away 8 million Black Africans to create room for 60 million white settlers of European descent is not a troubling concern. "Meanwhile," he explains to the interviewer, "your son and my son are given numbers back here and live in apartment buildings on top of each other."[132] This failure to reshape Tanganyika into a "white man's country" proved disappointing enough that even the authors of one of Wayne's biographies appeared to lament this emasculating moment for virile white men with gumption: "Up until the middle of the twentieth century, most Americans would have endorsed Wayne's view—and indeed, Tanganyika could quite possibly have served as a breadbasket to the world. But in the 1960s and 1970s, such thoughts could hardly have been farther from acceptance."[133]

The Regeneration of Racial Order

> I don't feel guilty about the fact that five or 10 generations ago these people were slaves. Now, I'm not condoning slavery. It's just a fact of life, like the kid who gets infantile paralysis and has to wear braces so he can't play football with the rest of us. I will say this, though: I think any black who can compete with a white today can get a better break than a white man. I wish they'd tell me where in the world they have it better than right here in America.
>
> —John Wayne, 1971

Wayne never appeared too concerned with the guilt over an American civilization shaped by a well-cataloged series of crimes against humanity buttressing the American dream for white citizens. And perhaps his information flow about the past never left the confines of Eugenics-era history textbooks. His statements, however, betray an incessant concern with downplaying the numerous ways American society had always been designed with the interests and opportunities of white men at the forefront. In short, he sought to erase the past legacies of white nationalism characterizing his lifespan. This hardly made Wayne unique, as he simply reflected a systemic response to his society's dominant narrative of the past, with his contempt reflecting the need to downplay centuries-old entitlements as social equality legislation highlighted the extent white nationalism had been normalized across politics, economics, and culture. Long-embedded anti-Black white supremacy formed the baseline of racial ideas guiding Wayne through his youth in the 1910s and 1920s, when the N-word flowed across respectable newspaper headlines and through Christian sermons, including the Tulsan reverend J. W. Abel's pulpit message in the wake of the 1921 Tulsa massacre. Evoking the heartland commonsense model suggesting slavery was beneficial for African Americans, Abel articulated a set of white paternalist ideas about Black Americans still in circulation today: "There are all too many of the so-called leaders of the negro race who habitually discredit the white race as to our willingness to give the negro a chance under all of the rights to American citizenship. What other nation in all human history has done as much . . . as the white race has done for the race which but a brief half-century ago emerged from slavery? A race which even in slavery was a thousand times better off than the black princes who ruled their race in Africa."[134] Although Wayne grudgingly accepted some facts of slavery, he adamantly disavowed the contribution of the Jim Crow welfare state to ongoing racial and gender inequality. Much like Reverend Abel's sermon and

Buckley's discounting of Baldwin's history of racism, Wayne took offense at the critiques of American history by African Americans, interpreting the charges of centuries-old oppression as an attack on the nation's innocence. Further, Wayne suggested that if racism did exist, it benefited African Americans more than whites: if Black and white compete, he confidently asserted, it is the person of African descent who will "get a better break," with a stress on "break"—that is, unearned opportunity. Buckley even mustered this phrase in the 1965 Cambridge debate, when he asserted that he was "going to speak to [Baldwin] without any reference whatever to those surrounding protections which [he was] used to in virtue of the fact that [he is] a Negro." This delusional fantasy of inverted white power was a vital driving force of post-1960s populist conservatism up through the 2016 presidential election, relying on a mythology of the persecuted white male developed from the embers of the 1960s conservative culture war.[135]

Wayne's last run of films in the early 1970s represented many of the sentiments binding together the New Right, populist conservatism, and the culture wars of the unfolding neoliberal era. His urban crime film *McQ* (1974) embodied the rising genre of the action film in the 1970s and 1980s, which reflected a populist conservative interpretation of a collapsing social order.[136] The action film genre encapsulated elements of *film noir*, the Western, and "police procedural" films, creating a new mix of violent fantasy engagement between good and evil. Eric Lichtenfeld notes this combination of attributes: "*Noir*'s urban, hard-bitten milieu was an appropriately cynical, disaffected stage for the pulverizing of human life, while the Western's mythos would ultimately cast violence as a force for the righteous taming of the 1970s' social wild."[137] Thus, noir offered a familiar urban landscape for the white hero (and Black, as the Black action film—or what is often referred to as Blaxploitation—genre also helped shape action film aesthetics) to navigate through an era of high crime rates, while elements of the Western brought the zero-sum settler colonial project to the city, where Blackened criminals became savage Indians in need of elimination. At the same time, the police procedural element cast a positive light on policing, with corrupt politicians offering examples of intrusive government—whether it was the welfare state's interference with social equality or not allowing the police (paraphrasing Wayne) "to win, because of the politicians and civilians . . . [were] stick[ing] their nose in it"—with "it" equating to the regulations of policing, including the rights of criminals. In many ways, the action film genre emerged as a desperate populist commodity focusing on (usually) heroic men from the working or lower-middle class who possess extraordinary abilities to do violence in the name of justice—a narrative gesture aimed to satiate the audience's concern over a trembling social order and the feeling of powerlessness.

The popularity of the 1970s action film drew on the previous decade's concern over social equality, along with the unrest over the Vietnam War. Expressed in a more polite color-blind, gender-blind sense, Frank S. Meyer's 1965 definition of conservatism points to this reactionary impulse, including the summoning of "civilization": "Conservatism comes into being at such times as a movement of consciousness and action directed to recovering the tradition of civilization"[138] To recover tradition, conservatives mobilize their possession of history outlining the knowledge justifying this tradition. As we have noted, the processes of modernity leading to the rise of what is labeled Western civilization constructed a naturalized hierarchy premised on an omnipresent Eurocentric white male view of the world. By the twentieth century, this white male supremacy defined *tradition*. According to anti–welfare state conservatives, federal intervention into assumed "natural" relationships led to the spread of chaos as its interference undermined a social order ostensibly based on nature's laws. A critical part of securing this knowledge and tradition included disavowing the legacy of explicit laws constructing a playing field tilted toward the benefit of white males. The action film star represented a desperate reaction to the unsettling of this tradition as the white heroes rectified the imbalance in nature through their violent agency—often reenacting the unflinching violence of settler colonialism and slavery. Finally, the action film's mobilization of populist-conservative language offered a dose of simplicity to dismiss the complexity of 1970s America, blaming social ills on an interventionist government enabling criminal conduct while justifying violence through the juxtaposition of a white-led law and order versus a savage urban Blackness.

The rise of the action film came on the heels of the Western film's evolution in the 1960s, a trend leaning toward a more pessimistic view of the West against the backdrop of decay implied by social equality legislation and the Vietnam War. This change in the Western genre, Paul Monaco describes, explored characters "through themes of alienation and resistance to modern authority," as well as the reinterpretation of the "western frontier West as a lost ideal"—ranging from old white cowboys of the *The Wild Bunch* (1969), which Wayne detested for its vulgar violence, to the more honest portrayal of settler violence against Native Americans in *Soldier Blue* (1970).[139] Although the theme of resistance to authority could work through the lens of the antiwar-counterculture, by the end of the decade and into the 1970s this theme could easily slip into a populist-conservative sneer toward the new government policies protecting historically marginalized people from the traditional hierarchies of settler colonialism. In short, what in the twenty-first century conservatives call "political correctness" and the rebellious thumbing of the nose at relinquishing older, derogatory language targeting historically marginalized groups. Many of these films, asserts Michael Ryan and Douglas Kellner, "undermined the mythology of the western hero and the generic idealization which legitimated the violence of the 'good' hero against 'bad' Native Americans, Mexicans, or villains."[140] The golden age of the Western came to an end as settler innocence succumbed to the history of the present, and its unlocking of the history of the past.

Wayne rode the theme of the decaying West (and the Western film) throughout the 1960s, including *The Man Who Shot Liberty Valance* (1962) and *McLintock!* (1963).[141] As if mirroring the trend toward both the loss of white male supremacy and deindustrialization, the themes of the decaying West saw the arrival of civilization as an impediment to the settler ideal of liberty unrestrained by legal bureaucracy. For white men in the 1960s, this meant civil rights legislation, as these potent themes postulated a connection between an America once seen as pure before the 1960s and an America in need of law and order heroes facing down the civil strife unleashed by the permissive welfare state.

Along with others such as Clint Eastwood and Charles Bronson, the work of Wayne in the 1970s offered masculine reassurance to those affected by the transfer of blue-collar work overseas, the greater visibility of people of color and women who challenged the traditional voice of white men, and the national mood after the Vietnam War and Watergate displaced early 1960s optimism with 1970s pessimism. For conservatives, the nation thirsted for an untethered essential (white) masculinism, to manifest the aggressive measures historically vital for frontier struggle and release this force to tame the chaos unleashed by big government. Representing Monaco's theme of "resistance to modern authority," Wayne's description of his character Rooster Cogburn from *True Grit* fit this archetype: "He feels the same way about life that I do. . . . He doesn't believe in pampering wrongdoers, which certainly fits into the category of my thinking. He doesn't believe in accommodation. Neither do I."[142] Wayne would attempt to address the "pampering of wrongdoers" in his 1970s films, where he was awkwardly set amid younger, more virile actors navigating through the refuge of urban crime and corruption. From the action film's simplistic point of view, cities were victims of enabling liberal bureaucracies; from the point of view of complex history, they were the outcome of racist housing policies leading to white capital flight ignited by the Jim Crow welfare state's redistribution of wealth toward the developing white suburbs.

McQ positioned Wayne in the postindustrial city as a culture warrior struggling against deviant criminals and bureaucratic liberal apologists. Through the prism of settler colonialism, films like *McQ* replicate the "triangular relationship" model defining the connections between "settlers, the metropole, and the indigenous population," with the metropole government (liberal apologists) keeping settlers (white silent majority) from moving into Indigenous peoples' land or regulating their relations with "savages." For the latter, the equation's update sees savages as darkened criminals, with the settlers/white silent majority claiming victimhood against the savages, while liberal government pampers the "wrongdoers."[143] In action films, these tensions amount to the description by Lichtenfeld of *Dirty Harry* (from which *McQ* took obvious cues): "In the film, Harry clashes with his superiors in the police department, the district attorney's office, and even the Mayor's, all in Harry's pursuit of a sniper, Scorpio (Andy Robinson), whose aim is to kill until the city pays him to stop. The triangle that comprises Harry, the politicians, and Scorpio parallels the one so familiar to viewers of Westerns, a triangle that comprises the hero, the civilized, and the savage, which in turn can include outlaws, Indians, and the wilderness itself."[144] Most often, the trope of the aggressive detective hamstrung by burdensome regulations drives the viewers to excuse the vigilantism of Wayne or Clint Eastwood in *Dirty Harry* in their apprehension or elimination of the "bad guys." The message is that it is okay if the "good guys" break the law when fighting the lawless "bad guys." Operating in a similar dynamic as the settler disavowal of massacres and ethnic cleansings, the bitter sympathy toward characters criticizing the rights of criminals disavows the legacies of racism rippling through frontier justice and extended into twentieth-century policing, from the abuse of power to racial profiling—the very set of misconduct leading to laws protecting the rights of the accused.[145] As always, innocence is restored through disavowal. Finally, the conflict facing the protagonists reflected the 1970s neoliberal conjuncture: characters in these films are most often over forty, representing the generation of police who enjoyed the pre–civil rights era of law enforcement where racial profiling and white supremacy were unquestioned norms. Thus, a part of the emotional draw toward Wayne's or Eastwood's thwarting of the "new" rights for criminals includes the imagined police force where only the "bad" cops are racist, as most of the police force do not ostensibly harbor the types of racist sentiments outlined in the 1968 Kerner Commission report.[146] The frontier had closed again it seemed, as "civilization" ended the freedom of the settler to effectively eradicate savages on their own terms on the frontier.

Set in Seattle, Washington, a city visibly showing signs of deindustrialization, Wayne's character McQ is a detective attempting to solve what develops into a police corruption case tied to his dead partner. A crucial piece of the puzzle comes after spending the night with an informant prostitute: in exchange for information, Wayne offers cocaine and a hundred-dollar bill for snorting (possibly a first in Duke's film oeuvre). McQ learns that his partner's wife is involved in the corruption as well. The film concludes through a predicable ending, though updated and urbanized: McQ gets his hands on a Mac-10 submachine gun, delivers justice to all the wrongdoers, and learns that the upper echelons of the department were onto the scandal and had thought Wayne a part of it. Final words from Duke before the credits: "There's a bar over there; let's get a drink."

As a performance of the culture war, the film relays conservative talking points through dialogue and juxtaposed nuance. One of the first interactions refers to the ideas of law and order, possibly the key rhetorical device for 1960s conservatism.[147] This sentiment is underscored by polls in the early 1970s showing concern that courts were "too lenient" with criminals and that support for the death penalty appeared to be growing.[148] The wife of Wayne's partner, Lois Boyle (played by Diana Muldaur), provides one avenue of contemporary critique. At the hospital where her (not-yet-known-to-be-corrupt) husband lay dying from a gunshot wound, Lois vents her frustration at being a policeman's wife, suggesting the cause: "Some crazy getting it off, a radical doing his number." Later in the movie, the women's movement is added to the list of social disorder. In a scene on Wayne's boat (where he lives), Lois suggests that Wayne should get a woman to "straighten up" the boat for him. Wayne responds, "Not enough for them anymore, Women's Lib, you know." The exchange is ripe: a white woman ideologically rooted in the silent majority (she detests the counterculture radicals and embraces women's subservience toward men) suggests Wayne obtain a woman *imagined as housekeeper-servant*. Wayne, who came of age when women and people of color were not legislatively equal with white men, is paralyzingly unable to understand why housework no longer satisfies the needs of women. Indeed, Wayne's ex-wife in the film personifies the problem: she is a successful lawyer, who remarried a wealthy man who, although wealthy, is visibly not as virile as Duke. The brief scene with the ex-wife underscores the connection between the persistent weight of masculinity, its deep need to imagine women as dependent on men (and thus not in need of "rights"), and the populist-conservative contempt toward elites and government bureaucrats. Liberated career women are presented as abnormal and the implied source of the breakup of families.

When Wayne requests to be on the case of his dead partner, his captain's response foregrounds the debates of law and order and the criminal rights regulations for cops: "Lon, I know you. I'm not going to stand for you making up your own rules. You're not going to play that Mickey Peters thing all over again," referring to a previous case. "Peters was a hood and everybody knew it," responds Wayne, justifying what the audience assumes to be procedures now deemed outmoded because of the recognition of constitutional rights for criminals.[149] The captain then outlines what Wayne did: "Yeah, and you weren't satisfied with throwing him up on the roof; you had to go up and throw him back down. Six months in the hospital, four lawyers screaming about his civil rights—" Wayne interrupts, "Well, it kept him off the street, didn't it?" How the sixty-plus-year-old Wayne threw a grown man "up on the roof" is not addressed.

Building off the "triangular relationship" derived from the genealogy of settler colonialism and the *Dirty Harry* archetype, Wayne's character exudes the righteousness of frontier justice against big city bureaucratic corruption. Only unrestrained—*unregulated*—police action separated the peaceful suburbs from the urban jungle. Vincent Canby noted the populist-conservative conjoining of the Western and "law and order" politics of the early 1970s: "The easy willingness with which it would suspend civil rights in the name of law-and-order, something it shares with most of the other cop films . . . may well be a true reflection of our times but it is also a philosophy inherited from one kind of narrative, the classic Western."[150] When Wayne is placed at a desk after a bout of police brutality, he turns in his badge and gun, asserting, "Too much politics," echoing the government interference argument of *No Substitute for Victory*. Wayne decides to work in the private sector as a private investigator, where his actions will be less regulated by a metropole interfering with his struggle against savagery. In a larger context, cinema in the 1970s regenerated the *film noir*–era private detective, the perfect genre for the era's collapse of trust in government and society in the wake of Vietnam and Watergate. As Jonathan Kirshner asserts, Watergate "was about the collapse of faith in institutions, a foreboding sense of the erosion of privacy, and a basic loss of trust: in one's president, in one's colleagues, in one's (presumed) friends."[151] For Wayne, betrayal came from his corrupt police officer friend as well as his superiors who seemed too eager to protect the rights of criminals.

McQ also foregrounded another theme for post-1960s law and order debates: the connection between urban space and Blackness. A lesson in negotiating race in the age of color blindness is offered: without the use of overt racism, how do whites separate the "good" Blacks (who embodied the white ideal of Blackness) from the "bad" Blacks (who embodied the negative stereotypes)? Building off the performances of Sidney Poitier in the 1960s, the film creates a juxtaposition between Wayne's Black subordinate, J. C. Davis (played by Jim Watkins), and Wayne's pimp police informant, Rosie (played by Roger E. Mosley). Mosley's hip street talk signified his status as a stock pimp character from this film era's explosion of Black action films.[152] A moral hierarchy is established between Mosley and Watkins, with Mosley's "traits and actions" characterized as criminal and familiar to the white imagination of Blackness; Watkin's demeanor, on the other hand, equates to Blackness in the service of whiteness or the state—much like the deferring Frederick Douglass in *Swing Out Sweet Land*.¹⁵³ As Martin Berger notes, representing "an individual's personal morality and public conduct as markers of racial belonging" aids in the audience's identification of characters as either white or Black.¹⁵⁴

Far from unique, the portrayal in *McQ* of this binary of Blackness—denoting acceptability and the condemnation of Blackness—was present in many urban crime films of the 1970s, notably in the Dirty Harry series. Juxtaposed against the delinquent Rosie, Watkins becomes the positively framed African American man, loyal to law and order *and* Wayne. For post-1960s film and following on the roles of Sidney Poitier, African American men portrayed in the service of the state increasingly became binaries in underlining both a "post-racial" society (anticipating the arrival of Black men in positions of authority) while simultaneously doubling down on Black criminal pathology defining American popular culture and twentieth-century sociology.¹⁵⁵ More than this, for white viewers uncomfortable with social equality, Black characters operating on behalf of the state implied something else: the loyal Sambo. As Baldwin notes, the symbolism helped shore up the innocence of whiteness. The camaraderie between Wayne and Watkins, much like Baldwin's assessment of Poitier's relationship to Rod Steiger in the film, *In The Heat of the Night* (1967), reassured "white people, to make them know that they are not hated; that, though they have made human errors, they have done nothing for which to be hated."¹⁵⁶ Unlike Mosley's character, Watkins speaks without the street language associated with popular culture representations of urban crime and Black Power, which resuscitated the threatening image of the Black brute from Post-Reconstruction stereotypes.¹⁵⁷ Watkins' professionalism offers maintenance and protection to white authority, offering those in the Black middle class a possible route for a more secure position in white society. Anchored to class and state power, this unspoken condition of acceptance included the renouncing of the presence of institutional racism in American life. To embrace Black culture, with its lumpen proletariat assertive street talk publicly associated with Black Power and urban unrest, was to set oneself up as a target of white supremacy's historical ghosts filling out the costumes of post-1960s color blindness and the militarization of the war on drugs after the 1960s.¹⁵⁸

"We Built a Nation on It"

> I think that the loud roar of irresponsible liberalism, which in the old days we called radicalism, is being quieted down by a reasoning public. I think the pendulum's swinging back. We're remembering that the past can't be so bad. We built a nation on it.
>
> —John Wayne, 1971

With his career in films concluding at the age of sixty-nine in 1976, Wayne's America had changed immensely since his early career in the 1920s and 1930s. His popularity never waned after *Stagecoach*, and despite an awkwardness of struggling against "bad guys" as a sixty-something-year-old, his 1970s film output still drew audiences eager for another rendition of Duke's negotiations through society (setting a model for today's baby boom action stars who are still delivering justice—*Wayne style*—well into their sixties and seventies). Holding aloft the populist-conservative banner from cold warrior to culture warrior, Wayne pressed the legacies of settler colonial sentiments into service against the array of threats facing the homeland. The culture war established what Vice-President Spiro Agnew called positive polarization in the late 1960s, seeking to "replace the New Deal alignment based on economic class and region with a new alignment based on subcultures."[159] Wayne's films and persona acted as a nexus diverting the economic populism related to the Jim Crow welfare state toward a populist-conservative antagonism toward federal intervention, social equality legislation, and the perception of social upheaval.

An important concept critical for keeping alive the culture war was/is the idea of a golden age and its destruction by internal or external enemies. As Karl Mannheim writes, generations unable to grapple with contemporary circumstances often reach back to "an earlier generation which may have achieved a satisfactory form": a golden age.[160] The component blocking the return of the Golden Age, according to Michael Lind, is the "devil theory"—a term coined by Charles Beard suggesting "that adverse trends in society or economics can always be blamed, not on economic changes or the unintended consequences of institutional designs, but on the machinations of sinister (and often hidden) conspirators."[161] In short, a simplistic answer derived from familiar scapegoats rather than a full accounting of the complexities contributing the adverse trends. Under the *longue durée* delusions instilled by settler colonialism and slavery—from the constructions of the civilized versus the savage, to the normalcy of white nationalism—coming to terms with these complexities would shattered the identities and possessions of history from those who benefited from westward expansion and the racial constructions derived from slavery. Addressing this paradox, Baldwin notes white Americans "have always existed in relation to a force which they have had to subdue. This subjugation is the key to their identity and the triumph and justification of their history, and it is also on this continued subjugation that their material well-being depends."[162] Wayne's persona and work represented this paradox, where the celebration of America's freedom and liberty came wrapped in the history of a white nationalist America, steeped in a mythical past of honor, courage, and righteousness free of the complexities of the postwar world. Aside from his role in *The Searchers*, his actions against Native Americans never appeared ill-intended, most often fitting the paternalistic nature of his character, such as cavalry captain Nathan Cutting Brittles in *She Wore a Yellow Ribbon*. For people born between 1900 and the 1930s, the height of racial science, eugenics, lynching, and the reawakening of the Ku Klux Klan, Wayne's films projected the familiar norm of white omnipresence in American history, in sync with a living memory informed by popular literature, school textbooks, politicians, presidents, and a Supreme Court that always happened to be white male dominated. For many, the white nationalist arrangements of this period of U.S. history coincided with the economic uplift of the Jim Crow welfare state: tradition and the pre-1960s social order equaled an uncomplicated prosperity.

An important element in shaping this "ascent of monolithic whiteness" was the halting of immigration from non-white nations (except Northern Europe and the Americas).[163] Between the Immigration Act of 1924 and the Immigration and Nationality Act of 1965, white Americans were not forced to deal with non-white immigration (except in the Southwest).[164] Free of non-white immigrants, Wayne's heroism guided Americans through the trauma of the Great Depression, World War II, and the Red Scare of the 1950s, bestowing on him a cultural authority whose resoluteness eased those unnerved about the shock of social equality with African Americans or between men and women. When *Playboy* magazine asked Wayne in 1971, "Contrasting the America you grew up in and the America of today, is it the same kind of country, or has it changed?," he invoked the devil theory in response: "The only difference I can see is that we now have an enemy within our borders fighting with propaganda and coloring events in a manner that belittles our great country. But all in all, it's practically the same."[165] Conservatives since the 1960s have struggled incessantly in their attempt to put the genie of American diversity and multiculturalism, as well as the voices critiquing racial and sexual antagonisms, back in the bottle of American exceptionalism.[166] For many white Americans, particularly male, this adjustment in relationships of power continues to invoke an existential crisis: the negative changes in the nation stem from a simple deviation from traditional frameworks, and not the constant unfolding of a complicated history driven by forces one is not taught about in school. Wayne would help articulate this bitter sentiment as the sun set on his life.

In a BBC interview in the mid-1970s, the narrator noted Wayne's disillusionment "with America" as Duke described these changes: "We're being represented by men who are kowtowing to minorities so they can get votes. And, uh, I think it's bad for our country, and I am sad to see minorities make so much of themselves as hyphenated Americans.... They were luckily born here, and couldn't be better off in any other place. There shouldn't be so much whining and bellyaching."[167] The interviewer then asks about the 1960s and early 1970s, describing the "period of considerable change: civil rights for Blacks, equal rights for women. Has this made America a better place?" Wayne: "I am saddened by the fact that, although we were a matriarchy [mistakenly saying 'matriarchy' instead of 'patriarchy'], I think we will not be any longer." Lamenting on his vision of a benevolent patriarchy, Wayne continues, "I think opening doors and tipping your hat to ladies is a, probably a thing of the past. The, uh, forerunners of women's liberation of today have, uh, taken that feeling away from the average American man." Wayne lamented the act of women taking away this patriarchal entitlement, quaintly described as a folksy process where men tipped their hats to ladies. Disavowed from this equation, and the primary driving force for feminism, was a bit more coercive: pre-1970s patriarchy normalized marital rape, control of their wives' assets, and fostered a pervasive environment of sexual harassment in the workplace—among other male entitlements.[168] Social equality appeared to be a threat to these traditions.

The interviewer then asked about civil rights for African Americans and was abruptly interrupted by Duke with a contemptuous, "*What about the civil rights?*"—as if the interviewer delved into a personal issue for Wayne. The interviewer suggests that these rights were needed because for almost 200 years African Americans were denied rights in "this free America." Wayne glances away in frustration and then turns back to the interviewer, his voice audibly more frustrated: "I guess that they've had a pretty tough break, but, uh, not quite as bad as, uh, you and your do-gooder friends would have them believe." Like a bubble being popped, the past was quickly disavowed with Wayne's trusty possession of history, safely grasped in Duke's hands. Ideas of self-rule and agency immediately surface to defend against white intransigence: liberals ("do-gooder friends") needed to *inform* Black people of their tough break; Black people, according to Wayne, were unable to analyze the situation themselves. He continues, "They live as well here as they live in any other country—*over* that 199 years. True, I think they do have a right to more rights; but it isn't a thing where the rest of the country should feel terribly guilty about anything because they've had a better life here and their fathers and mothers than they would have had any place else." Holding back the weight of history with the tattered shards of innocence, Wayne then used himself as an example of why minorities should not "squawk and cry baby" about their situation: "Jeez, I had to go without meals when I was 16 and 17 years old; it's a terrible thing."

As the United States celebrated its bicentennial, the existential crisis of legislated social equality proved ripe for the New Right's "Southern strategy" and its use of race and anti-feminism to gain the votes of former Democrats. By the presidential election of 1980, a year after Duke's death, Morton Kondracke articulated both the depth of the culture war logic as well as Wayne's role in its momentum. Kondracke noted that Reagan's message was "a simplistic world view, a John Wayne view, but it is thoroughly American and of obvious appeal: the United States can do anything it wants, if it has the will."[169] For Reagan, notes Walter I. Trattner,

> the nineteenth century was the golden age of American history—a time when individualism, localism, free enterprise, and the laissez-faire philosophy prevailed. This nostalgic view of the past and obsession with self-sufficiency precluded the President understanding not only the problems faced by the victims of systematic oppression—members of various racial and ethnic minority groups confined to ghettos and women—many of whom were jobless through no fault of their own, but the plight of millions others as well, including white men and women who were working but who could not support themselves and their families on their meager earnings.[170]

It is this idealized, simplistic conception of America—a possession of history stripped of oppression and inequality—Reagan capitalized on in 1980. With a wink toward white nationalism and the defense of segregation via his first campaign stop near Philadelphia, Mississippi, Reagan claimed the populist-conservative mantle cultivated by Wayne: "I still believe the answer to any problem lies with the people. I believe in states' rights." Wayne helped articulate the populist rage cheering Reagan's message of tax cuts for the wealthy and corporations amid an anxious white middle- and working-class demographic who would only capture intermittent drops of Reagan's neoliberal trickle-down economics. Luckily for conservatives, the simplistic scapegoating of historically marginalized groups would help keep their constituencies' focus away from the complicated set of issues facing the United States and the world.

The shift from the New Deal economic populism fueling the Jim Crow welfare state to the populist conservativism of Reaganomics cleared the path for the rise of neoliberalism. In 1984, GOP strategist Lee Atwater underlined the balancing act of courting the populist vote for conservative economic policies:

> Populists have always been liberal on economics. So long as the crucial issues were generally confined to economics—as during the New Deal— the liberal candidate would expect to get most of the populist vote. But

populists are conservatives on most social issues.... As for race, it was hardly an issue—it went without saying that the populists' chosen leaders were hardcore segregationists.... When social and cultural issues died down, the populists were left with no compelling reason to vote Republican.... When Republicans are successful in getting certain social issues to the forefront, the populist vote is ours.[171]

Fortunately for Atwater, Reagan, and the GOP, the economic populism supporting the New Deal appeared to drown during the baptism of neoliberal Reaganomics in the 1980s. For the white middle and working classes, however, the choice of populist conservatism led to a struggle through a cold winter in America as wealth (and racial) inequality expanded to the widest gap on record in the twentieth century.[172] Indeed, this shift was not kind to Wayne's audience, especially the men boisterously cheering on the dismantling of the welfare state and the coming of Reaganomics. Conservative author Kevin Phillips noted at the end of the 1980s:

> White males serving as their family's only breadwinner were, as a category, particularly conspicuous. By one calculation, their median inflation-adjusted income fell 22 percent between 1976 and 1984. After the 1983 recovery, many squeezed or depressed households discovered that their economic problems weren't simply recession hangovers. As domestic and global economic restructuring continued, well-paid manufacturing jobs and the purchasing power of manufacturing paychecks shrank. For *all* workers, white-collar as well as blue-collar, their real average weekly wage—calculated in constant 1977 dollars—fell from $191.41 a week in 1972 to $171.07 in 1986.[173]

The exorcism of the critique of monopoly capital from both the politics of the New Deal welfare state as well as the populism of populist conservatism further supported the incredible economic growth of finance and multinational conglomerates, embedding a new national economic system: "the richest 5 percent of households obtained roughly 82 percent of all the nation's gains in wealth between 1983 and 2009. The bottom 60 percent of households actually had less wealth in 2009 than in 1983."[174] If only Wayne's cowhand conscience in *Red River*, Walter Brennan, was there to pipe up, "That's too much land for one man. Why, it ain't decent."

Wayne's simplicity in dealing with "bad guys" in his action films had become policy provisions for zero-sum tolerance conservatism, institutionalized by Reagan and perfected by the George W. Bush administration during the settler colonial imagined: War on Terror.[175] Speaking volumes to the ongoing symbolic capital Wayne exudes, the conservative mobilization of Duke continued into the Obama era, with writers from the *National Review* conjuring up Wayne's ghost in the wake of the 2009 piracy incident in the Red Sea:

> When an American-flagged ship was besieged, the president might have been paralyzed by his solicitude for the Islamic world and his commitment against unilateral action. He might have subordinated the safety of Americans to the bridge-building he has dubiously claimed to be central to our security. As commander-in-chief, he could have handcuffed the Navy. But he didn't. Whatever his predilections, Obama unleashed John Wayne when that's what was needed. For that we should be pleased and acknowledge a job well done. Piracy and the Islamic radicalism with which it is entwined remain scourges. That will not cease to be the case as long as they are given safe haven. . . . Wars don't end until someone wins. And this one will have to be won by American leadership and American will. It won't take a village. It'll take John Wayne.[176]

Although Wayne did not link his support for the New Right and its alliance with multinationals as a contradiction to his own position as a worker in the film industry, he did sense that something was amiss in his reflections on the changes sweeping through Hollywood in the 1960s. At the forefront was the deregulation of the Hays Code in the 1960s and its unleashing of more realistic displays of violence, vulgar language, and nudity in film by the end of the decade. He found this change distasteful. Another structural component, however, briefly exposed Wayne's own economic populism and its critique of monopoly capital. When asked about the current state of Hollywood in the early 1970s, a decade after multinational conglomerates bought many of the studios, Wayne responded, "The men who control the big studios today are stock manipulators and bankers. They know nothing about our business. They're in it for the buck."[177] These sentiments underline Wayne's contradiction undergirding his hard work as a culture warrior battling through the neoliberal conjuncture of the New Right, populist conservatism, and the rise of finance and multinational conglomerates.

Duke's defense of abstract notions of equal opportunity and the rights of individuals deployed in the arguments of the New Right provided the neoliberal era with the vaunted badge of American masculine frontier traditionalism. Big business, finance, and other institutions benefiting from the concentration of capital were imagined by *Business Week* (in 1968) as mere extensions of frontier individualism. Economist Robert Reich noted this lean toward populist language in his 1985 review of various books written by or about CEOs:

> In their contempt for bureaucracy, formal process, and intellectual abstraction—and their passion for outspoken independence, direct dealing, and charismatic leadership—these CEOs seem perfectly in tune with the anti-establishment tendencies now found on both the right and left of the political spectrum. They are cowboy capitalists. . . . These stories therefore give comfort to Americans who harbor vague misgivings about the place of the large, sluggish corporation in American life—and about the faceless oligarchs who run them. The cumulative message of these books is that we are entering upon a new populist era in which the mavericks are in charge. . . . There is no reason to question the fundamental legitimacy of big business in America, or to flirt with economic populism, because the populists already have taken over—from the inside.[178]

As Reich suggests, corporate America cultivated an image of the rugged cowboy, and just like John Wayne, Americans should trust them.

Business Week's conjoining of these two eras, however, offers a window into the strange echoes connecting the culture and economics of the late 1800s to the late 1900s. Just as the ghosts of the West were haunted by the notion of the frontier's ending in 1890 (and the supposed end of "rugged individualism" of Turner's "frontier thesis"), the legislative end to white male supremacy in the 1960s closed another frontier for white men. All of these processes—from the end of the frontier to the legal loss of white male entitlement—provoked a similar existential crisis of identity for white men (Theodore Roosevelt called for the "strenuous life" at the turn of the century while others called for "muscular Christianity").[179] To compound the situation, the Western genre too went into decline, and the old innocent youth training ground of "cowboys and Indians," in the wake of social justice movements, became a game replicating ethnic cleansing. Economically, Kevin Phillips suggests that the late-nineteenth-century Gilded Age—including its "populist" politics—offered similar material outcomes as the arrival of neoliberalism in the 1970s and 1980s: "The new theology [of the 1980s] even had overtones of the Gilded Age. Much more overtly than the supply-siders and the antitax theorists, Law and Economics stalwarts flirted with a neo-Darwinianism that echoed Herbert Spencer and William Graham Sumner in its view that commercial selection processes in the marketplace could largely displace government decision-making."[180] This observation, of course, echoed Hayek's "market as information processor" model. Phillips even labeled the neoliberal law professor from the Chicago school of economics Richard Posner an "intellectual frontiersman," further conjoining images of the West with the onset of neoliberalism.[181] Friedman and his glorification of the "period of the 19th century when we were the closest to free enterprise," most likely would have agreed.[182] Although not a star of *Swing Out Sweet Land*, Friedman's autobiography mirrored the program's imagined past when he mustered the immigrant-assimilationist narrative in his discussion of the utopia of nineteenth-century free society and free market capitalism:

> Many of us, I venture to say, are beneficiaries of that period. I speak of myself. My parents came to this country in the 1890's. Like millions of others, they came with empty hands. They were able to find a place in this country, to build a life for themselves and to provide a basis on which their children and their children's children could have a better life. There is no saga in history remotely comparable to the saga of the United States during that era, welcoming millions of people from all over the world and enabling them to find a place for themselves and to improve their lives. And it was possible only because there was an essentially free society.[183]

Without a secure possession of history, Friedman's conception of "an essentially free society" collapses like a house of cards, as the simple delusion is confronted by a complicated fact: the Jim Crow policies targeting African Americans and other people of color created a category of exclusion and entitlement that either fostered pathways or barricades to opportunities. In the wake of his defense of white exclusion of Black Americans in *Capitalism and Freedom*—written at the height of the civil rights era—Friedman's ideas of a free society and the historical precedents he summons to defend this free society appear to depend on the exclusion of people of African descent.

Chapter 6

Blood, Breasts, and Beasts

The Feminist Liberation Gauntlet and Flexible Misogyny at the Dawn of Social Equality

> That victim who is able to articulate the situation of the victim has ceased to be a victim: he, or she, has become a threat. The victim's testimony must, therefore, be altered.... Once the victim's testimony is delivered, however, there is, thereafter, forever, a witness somewhere: which is an irreducible inconvenience for the makers and shakers and accomplices of this world. These run together, in packs, and corroborate each other. They cannot bear the judgment in the eyes of the people whom they intend to hold in bondage forever.... This remote, public, and, as it were, principled, bondage is the indispensable justification of their own: when the prisoner is free, the jailer faces the void of himself.
>
> —James Baldwin (1976)

> Institutionalized rejection of difference is an absolute necessity in a profit economy which needs outsiders as surplus people. As members of such an economy, we have *all* been programmed to respond to the human differences between us with fear and loathing and to handle that difference in one of three ways: ignore it, and if that is not possible, copy it if we think it is dominant, or destroy it if we think it is subordinate. But we have not patterns for relating across our human differences as equals.
>
> —Audre Lorde (1980)

> Feminism with aggressive women is not going to be palatable in a mass market without tits and ass.
>
> —Jane Schaffer (2010)

John Wayne's populist-conservative regeneration of rugged individualism timelessly wove together the ideas, policies, and material outcomes inherited from the processes of settler colonialism, slavery, and its aftermath. This populist-conservative reaction against the welfare state shaped the momentum of the conservative culture war against social equality legislation, coalescing fortuitously with the ideas of individualism and freedom emanating from neoliberals. A decisive component of this rugged individualism rested on the imagined norm of the white male settler citizen, assertively directing his righteous violence against those deemed threatening to his family, community, homeland, and civilization. As Wayne's contentious interviews in the 1970s make clear, rugged individualism made for a convenient identity to both defend against the intrusions of the welfare state—whether economic regulation or social equality legislation—as well as fuel an aggressive disciplinary gaze toward new internal threats, most often taking the shape of those historically marginalized who recently obtained equal status with white men. Alongside defending the legacies of slavery and settler colonialism, Wayne's work consistently tapped into the traditional patriarchal framework from which masculinity could express itself as American rugged individualism. In defining the male individual struggling through the rugged frontier, masculinity drew upon the *longue durée* traditions—stretching back millennia—of patriarchy to recreate and reinforce proper—or "traditional"—roles for women in society.

In Wayne's private life, he cherished the all-male environments of deep-sea fishing and drinking, where women—with the exception of actress Maureen O'Hara—were absent from masculine bonding over liquor.[1] His interviews underscored his anguish over legislated social equality toward women in the late 1960s and 1970s, particularly feminist demands for equal treatment and independence from men. Wayne was once asked why he had not learned Spanish, as he had married three Latinx women. Duke's response was: "I guess I never listened to what they were saying."[2] Something had changed between the height of his fame in the 1950s—coinciding with the height of an unacknowledged male, white nationalist social democracy—and the perceived undermining of social order in the 1960s.[3] Indeed, the final scene in Wayne's film *McLintock!* (1963) made clear the remedy for unruly and assertive women.[4] After an aggressive chase throughout the frontier town named after Wayne's character, McLintock publicly spanks his estranged wife, Maureen O'Hara's character Katherine. Laughter abounds from the townspeople watching this disciplinary spectacle. Through the prism of settler colonialism, the final scene underscores the vitality of frontier masculinity reasserting its "naturally" superior will: Wayne and O'Hara reconcile amid reestablished patriarchal order through the lighthearted symbolic violence of spanking a woman, reassuring the community of her status as a dependent, a child. For some, this equation amounted to a good family film. Writer Jimmy Grant observed: "All you gotta have in a John Wayne picture is a hoity-toity dame with big tits that Duke can throw over his knee and spank."[5]

In the 1970s, this deep ontological rudder in men's lives found its challenge from women's liberation as the second wave of feminism drew momentum from the Civil Rights Act of 1964. Emerging in the first decade in the history of the United States when white men, especially those with property, were forced into legislated social equality with women and people of color, this abrupt shift in *longue durée* gender relationships triggered an anxious, conflict-ridden dialogue.[6] As the oppressed mobilized the language and knowledge defining their Lockean "natural rights" *for all humans*, a new cultural reality slapped oppressors in the face, shattering the simplistic and delusional world of white male supremacy. With oppressors legislatively forced (they did not volunteer) to relinquish their hold on those they historically defined as inferior, a new dilemma arose: how would white masculinity define itself if the old meaning of masculinity—patriarchal dominance of women and all people of color—was now illegal? Historically, white masculinity defined itself through the practices of settler colonialism (rugged individualism and the vanquishing of "savages" whose lands were claimed by white men), slavery and its aftermath (white men's freedom defined against a degraded Blackness tied to perpetual enslavement or second-class citizenship), and a patriarchy justifying racial antagonism toward people of color in the name of protecting white womanhood (including a woman's choice to control their reproductive capacities). As James Baldwin points out, the dilemma presented in the wake of social equality legislation was simple: "when the prisoner is free, the jailer faces the void of himself."[7] The act of ceasing to defer to men's authority sparked a reaction best captured in the folksy phrase, "If you want to be treated like a lady, you need to act like a lady"; or if a woman failed to submit or defer to male authority (the patriarchal contract for protection), this breach of patriarchy's tradition could result in violence (male disciplining of unruly women). Wayne's spanking of O'Hara in *McLintock!* represented a quaint version of this disciplining. As the first decade of legislated social equality unfolded, a market appeared in popular media for rhetoric and images reclaiming this dissolving masculine identity, often using the older language of subjugating supposed inferiors while embracing the film industry's newly deregulated guidelines on violence and nudity.

This chapter explores the various contours of the exploitation film movement of the 1960s and 1970s, offering an unlikely, though useful, starting point for examining ways the conservative culture war interacted with the rise of neoliberalism. Economically, many producers of exploitation films transferred capital aboard much like multinational conglomerates, seeking cheaper labor and fewer regulations in developing nations overseas.[8] Exploitation films, however, were more than mere calculated investment ventures aimed toward low-budget productions and an expectation of a healthy margin of profit. Producers capitalized on the tensions surrounding the unsettling of American social norms and taboos in the 1960s, offering viewers explicit explorations of the unease surrounding the "free love" drug-taking counterculture and the conservative backlash against hippies. Taking advantage of Hollywood's deregulation of the production code and the implementation of the more flexible and demographic-specific ratings system, exploitation films' use of the new permissiveness of the counterculture focused primarily on the spectacle of nudity and violence toward women. To further heighten the tension, producers capitalized on the Western civilization-savagery binary connected to exotic overseas jungle settings. At the same time, these low-budget exploitation film formulas opened the way for the rise of women action stars in Hollywood.[9]

A flexible misogyny (or what Doreen Massey called flexible sexism) surfaced in the 1970s as exploitation films combined feminism, action films, and the newly deregulated use of nudity, sexuality, and violence.[10] The formula's exploitative anchor rested on balancing the language of empowerment with older forms of patriarchal discipline presented through uncensored camera lenses. On the one hand, these films provided space in popular culture for empowered women and feminism to breach the boundaries previously reserved for assertive men. On the other hand, although the result was an unprecedented entry of women into action films in the 1970s, the call for equality with men appeared to demand this empowerment be juxtaposed with an unprecedented display of violence and nudity. In doing so, exploitation films—and other popular culture expressions—offered new spaces for the renewal and reform of patriarchal language, gestures, and behaviors woven through the unease over women's liberation during the first decade of legislated social quality. The outcome: women would be punished for their insolence as the void in the jailer's identity (following Baldwin's argument) found renewal through the spectacle of achieving equality. The final product often magnified the array of racial and gendered representations associated with the violent procedures characterizing slavery, sexual exploitation, and misogyny. Viewed from the *longue durée*, captivity narratives—the recorded experiences of white women captured by Native Americans—between the 1600s and 1800s offer an early market precedent for the spectacle of punishment targeting women. Although toeing the line between dependent and assertive womanhood, these narratives were ultimately shaped into the deeply-embedded anchors upholding the "idea of white victimization," turning the "invader into the invaded," and portraying the aggressor as an innocent settler.[11] This precedent also shaped an acceptable space/context for violent women taking revenge. Popular media in the 1970s explored ways to curtail or discipline the more radical rhetoric arising out of second-wave feminism—particularly the redistributive, socialist argument for equality—while both empowering women in defeating their oppressors and casting a more positive light on the idea of "difference" (what later came to be called cultural diversity or multiculturalism after the 1980s).[12] Exploitation films embody a cultural manifestation of this impulse, a consumer commodity of flexible misogyny weaving together the empowerment of women via an equality imagined through the sadistic and sexualized violence of action films.

The flexible misogyny of exploitation films marked an important connection to the rise of neoliberalism as the production and technological apparatus of filmmaking found curious alignment with what David Harvey calls flexible accumulation.[13] In Harvey's account, flexible accumulation is a response to the Fordist model characterizing and guiding the Keynesian economics of the welfare state. Following the trends of American multinational corporations, overseas production and investment by the 1950s "had become essential elements in Hollywood's financial survival."[14] This global Hollywood generated more than "half of their total revenue" overseas by the 1960s.[15] As mostly independent productions, exploitation movies followed this economic trend at the height of the film industry's postwar restructuring when many studios were purchased by multinational conglomerates (e.g., Gulf & Western bought the Paramount Pictures Corporation in 1966).[16] With the rise of the merger movement, the studio system veered toward deregulation: Hollywood evolved from direct, in-house production to a more flexible role of financing and distributing films made by independent producers.[17] Mirroring the trends of Giovanni Arrighi's fourth accumulation cycle, this adjustment toward greater economic flexibility also represented the shift from production to finance.[18] Moreover, this deregulation included changes in marketable mores across various demographics and different forms of media as the cultural upheavals of the 1960s unraveled into post-1960s multiculturalism.[19]

Consequently, a second element connecting exploitation films with neoliberalism included the embrace of the cultural and fashion trends emanating from the upheavals of the 1960s and the negotiation of cultural conflict tied to newly legislated social equality. The radicalism of the 1960s social justice movements evolved into a marketing tactic for a post-1960s generation of consumption.[20] Exploitation films exemplified this trend, targeting the youth demographic traversing this cultural tension by highlighting "difference, ephemerality, spectacle, fashion, and the commodification of cultural forms."[21] This exploration of difference, however, needs qualification: the normative baseline for this exploration was the Jim Crow welfare state, when social inequality was securely institutionalized. "We have not patterns for relating across our human differences as equals," notes Audre Lorde, as the processes of patriarchy, settler colonialism, and slavery found renewal in the deregulations and reforms characterizing the 1960s and 1970s.[22] For exploitation films, then, the representation of difference tied together new ideas of liberation with old patterns of sexual and racialized violence—packaged into a flexible, demographically specific product at the dawn of second-wave feminism and the neoliberal era.

Second-Wave Feminism and Women's Liberation

Before exploring exploitation films, a brief accounting of second-wave feminism is in order. Feminism's early roots can be found in the writings of Mary Wollstonecraft's *A Vindication of the Rights of Woman* (1790), while first-wave feminism is cited as beginning with the First Women's Rights Convention at Seneca Falls, New York, in 1848.[23] Struggling for the right to vote and equal rights, by the mid-1800s the Married Women's Property Acts had been passed by states around the nation, giving rights to property for married women (who previously lost all rights of ownership to their property once they were married).[24] The ultimate victory of the first wave was the Nineteenth Amendment passed in 1920. A notable expression of pre-second-wave feminism came from Simone de Beauvoir's 1949 classic, *The Second Sex*, a work asserting that gender and sexuality was a social construction and that women need to challenge these constructions to escape oppression.[25] In much the same way abolitionism helped shape first-wave feminism, second-wave feminism found root in the resurgence of social justice activism connected to the civil rights movement, the labor movement, and the poignancy of the phrase, "The problem that has no name" (from Betty Friedan's *The Feminine Mystique*).[26] Although some interracial organizing occurred after the Civil War, white supremacy and anti-Blackness often split white and Black women during the first wave, fashioning a legacy plaguing second-wave feminism in the 1960s.[27] As the civil rights movement gained steam in the early 1960s, the Kennedy administration released *American Women: The Report of the President's Commission on the Status of Women and Other Publications of the Commission*. Although moderate in tone, the fact of its existence proved important for the women's movement.[28] Another unexpected boost came from segregationist representative Howard Smith's (D-VA) inclusion of "sex" in the Civil Rights Act of 1964 in a desperate bid to derail the bill.[29] The bill passed, and suddenly there was social equality legislation between white men, men of color, *and all women*. However, the Equal Employment Opportunity Commission (EEOC) set up to implement the legislation generally ignored complaints against gender discrimination.[30]

Feminism gained momentum out of the experiences of the civil rights movement, as women activists like Ella Baker often found themselves marginalized in male-dominated settings, despite often running the organization and forced to defer to the "decision-making authority of the exclusively male leadership group."[31] A revolution within a revolution was set in motion. In late November 1964, "Position Paper 24" was submitted anonymously (coauthored by Casey Hayden, Emmie Schrader Adams, Mary King, and Elaine Delott Baker) at a Student Nonviolent Coordinating Committee (SNCC) meeting in Waveland, Mississippi—subsequently called the Waveland memo.[32] The memo offered a critique of sexism within the SNCC, locating "the struggle for sexual equality within the new left tradition of dissolving the barrier between the personal and the political."[33] Representing the broader American patriarchal norms, male domination affected New Left organizations as well, leading to "women's issues" finding voice in the New Left during the 1967 National Conference for a New Politics in Chicago. Another feminist group, the National Organization for Women (NOW), formed in 1966 to target the gender discrimination the EEOC ignored.[34] The often-negative reception toward ideas of equality eventually pushed women to begin meeting on their own and engaging in women's demonstrations by 1968.[35] Women's liberation gained mass media attention in September 1968, when a group of activists protested the Miss America pageant. The gendered, racial, and sexual politics emanating from women's liberation added further tension to not only the conservative culture wars against desegregation in the 1960s but also within ostensibly more "progressive" groups such as social justice organizations, where patriarchal worldviews failed to attract the same level of analysis race or class received. In these early years, feminism even found expression in the Republican Party through pro-choice feminists such as Michigan state senator N. Lorraine Beebe.[36] In trying to legalize abortion, Republican feminists utilized a conservative precept of individual rights, arguing that "the right to control one's own body is a basic human and democratic right."[37] Republican feminist Lee Kefauver reflected years later about the underlining patriarchy pressing men to restrict women's choice to control their bodies: "Collectively they [the male legislature] hate you as a woman because they are insecure as men. . . . If you are black, they can deal with you and go home to a segregated neighborhood. But most of these white, male legislators go home to a woman—a wife, daughter or whatever. And they'll be damned if they'll give up any power to women."[38]

The reactions to the rise of feminism and social equality legislation between men and women reinvigorated and reimagined many of the gendered and sexual norms rooted in American identity. Popular media's response to women's liberation in the 1970s represented a convergence of culture and economics, helping shape the evolving contours of patriarchy for the neoliberal era. These impulses marked the work of John Wayne, the apprehensive and alarming language of *Business Week* toward "feminists," and the male imaginations of the conservative defenders of Western civilization. Facing legislated social equality with people of color and women for the first time, anxiety over upsetting centuries-old privileges and entitlements for white men bound these groups together.

The bureaucratic nature of the Jim Crow welfare state did more than encode a racial logic designating spaces white and Black. Gender also provided the rudder navigating federally subsidized postwar suburbanization.[39] Reinforced by Cold War anxiety, the normalization of this racial geography rested on the regeneration of the ideal of women naturally belonging within the private sphere where they fostered a safe home for their husband's children—and protected from the racial dangers of the public sphere.[40] For women, especially white women, the business world of the postwar years subscribed, for the most part, to the mantra of the popular book *Modern Woman: The Lost Sex* (1947), warning that women's transcendence of "nature's" role for women would upend civilization; women needed "to stay out of 'fields belonging to the male area of exploit or authority.'"[41] An echo of Russell Kirk's conservatism—"we should accept the station to which 'a divine tactic' has appointed us with humility and a sense of consecration"—and the well-worn "end of civilization" trope of conservatives and neoliberals, the racialized geography of white suburbs took the advice of *Modern Woman* at face value, mapping out the logical contours of white women's containment in federally subsidized communities.[42] Safely secured at home, with (white) men earning a family wage (that ostensibly included additional compensation for wife and children), the idealized white woman was wrapped in a twentieth-century update of the nineteenth-century model of the cult of domesticity.[43] The cult of domesticity, or the cult of true womanhood, represented the white middle-class ideal popularized in the nineteenth-century religious and popular literature outlining the proper roles for white women in American society as the market revolution took hold: "piety, purity, submissiveness and domesticity."[44] By the Gilded Age and the height of "laissez-faire individualism" (celebrated by Milton Friedman and Wayne), the buttressing of patriarchy coalesced with the onset of progressivism as "most states moved to restrict or outlaw common-law marriages, raised the age of consent, reestablished waiting periods for marriage, banned interracial unions, and criminalized abortion and contraception"—thus institutionalizing the guiding "moral order" of the Jim Crow welfare state.[45] The update for the postwar era arose through the instability of the Great Depression and the disruptions of World War II (especially married women working), with a vision of stability imagined through the reinstilling of "traditional gender roles" for "the 'modern' middle-class home" after the war.[46]

The rise of second-wave feminism in the 1960s placed these "norms" under siege, as the language articulating a proper woman's life experience within the protected patriarchal confines of the public sphere found translation as oppression. In short, Baldwin's "victim" articulated "the situation of the victim."[47] As the neoliberal era took shape across the 1970s, the argument describing the naturalness of free markets demanded a renewal of what social conservatives considered feminism to be dismantling: the naturalness of women's subjugation to men.[48] Thus, alongside similar attitudes toward business and government, yet another link in the partnership between conservatives and neoliberals formed. Melinda Cooper notes, "Neoliberalism and social conservativism are thus tethered together by a working relationship that is at once necessary and disavowed: as an ideology of power that only ever acknowledges its reliance on market mechanisms and their homologues, neoliberalism can only realize its objectives by proxy, that is by outsourcing the imposition of noncontractual obligations to social conservatives."[49] With the passing of the Civil Rights Act of 1964 and the mounting demand for equality, popular media adjusted portrayals of women in response to the changing politics. For the most part, these reforms ranged from the difficulties women faced trying to compete in a male-dominated world to the suggestion that feminism equated women's rights to women's domination of men—and the destruction of families. Both of these variations settled into the consensus of social conservatism, rather than the assertions of feminists merely asking for a choice in the matter.[50]

As a market for disciplining women's yearnings for social equality expanded in the 1970s, film representations of explicit violence toward assertive women grew more prevalent. These images provided warnings to women of the many dangers related to equality in the public sphere, with the rise of women's liberation navigating this uneasy tension between activists producing language and knowledge reflecting the concerns of women's equality with men and mass media's uncertain translation of this increasingly commodified dialogue. Patricia Bradley notes, "The desire to meet the demands of the postwar generation prompted commercial underwriters of mass media to seek an inclusive audience, which led to some expression of emerging ideas. The commercial base of media was not an iron curtain erected against the postwar feminist impulse; rather, the commercial base allowed for—even demanded—the inclusion of postwar feminism as part of a mix that aimed to please and to please as many as possible."[51] Although there was an unfolding market for representations of independent women, there was also a lucrative market for the demographic most uneasy with social equality between men and women.[52]

A renegotiation of the boundaries of acceptability characterized the changing historical context of the new era of legislated social equality. *Longue durée* impulses guided these reforms across the historical conjuncture of the neoliberal era. Social equality for women before the 1970s attempted to utilize the welfare state's logic of fairness and justness representing the redistributionist reasoning of federal intervention after World War II. Meanwhile, the arrival of legislated rights for people of color and women in the 1960s was accompanied by Hollywood's own deregulation of its censorship codes. Herein lies the complexity of the relationship between culture and economics: as the rise of neoliberalism after the 1960s shaped a marketplace governed by quantitative analysis rather than the fairness and justness of the welfare state, the deregulatory impulse usually attached to neoliberalism found life *through* the structures and cultural reaction to the welfare state. Thus, in the wake of social equality legislation, the film industry's end to censorship of graphic violence and sexual objectification through explicit nudity surfaced simultaneously with women's liberation.[53] In short, the deep history driving the neoliberal conjuncture witnessed both the arrival of legislated social equality (the deregulation of legally constructed social hierarchies) and the rise of a new market depicting women's subjugation (the deregulation of acceptable commodities). In this sense, the old adage "Act like a lady" came true: if women turned their back on deferring to men's authority (ironically under the "fairness and justness" mantle of the male-dominated welfare state era), then women who did not defer would not be treated like "ladies" on the screen. The public perception of women's liberation would be conditioned by the cultural and economic changes of the 1970s, setting the dynamics for future feminist debates over "the right to be equal" and "the right to be different" in the 1980s and 1990s.[54]

Popular media's relationship with women's liberation in the 1970s operated as a significant contributor to the culture war, representing one of the cultural contours of neoliberalism as the film industry deregulated the censorship rules erected during the era of the welfare state. At the dawn of women's liberation, films embodied Friedrich August von Hayek's proposition that the market acted as an "information processor," seeking to satisfy markets and customers who were drawn to newly uncensored depictions of nudity and violence, particularly against women. Returning to Baldwin's jailer analogy, as masculinity no longer could base itself on the legal subjugation of femininity, a new outlet filled the vacuum to regulate the freedom of the newly released prisoner—and the perfect vehicle for this regulation of freedom was the sexual and gendered violence of the liberation gauntlet in exploitation films.

Exploitation Films: Regulations, Realism, and the Liberation Gauntlet

Early exploitation films grew out of the regulatory Jim Crow welfare state era. Initially attracting a popular following in the 1930s, these films eluded the Hays Code regulations—Hollywood's self-regulatory system—by offering lurid images under the banner of educational cinema (such as sex hygiene, drugs, vice, or nudist films).[55] Hollywood studios implemented the Hays Code in the early 1930s to thwart intrusive government censorship into Hollywood, with the aim of keeping movies moral and uncritical of law or religion.[56] An important impetus for this censorship was the brief era of pre-code films (1930–34), when movies depicted assertive women participating in activities usually reserved for men, including engaging with multiple sexual partners without moral consequence. During the Great Depression, these liberated films, along with gangster and horror movies brought in much needed revenue for Hollywood: the audience reacted enthusiastically to the realistic depictions of the rebellious spirit of 1920s liberated women. Consequently, this disruption of patriarchal order came to the attention of social conservatives anxious about independent women like Mae West and Barbara Stanwyck and images deemed lurid on the screen.

For the most part, exploitation films were nonmajor studio movies, usually created with low budgets and produced to capitalize on popular genres, contemporary issues, taboos, and anxieties, or merely "milk an existing market success."[57] In some ways, exploitation films are related to their less controversial but similarly low-budget cousin: the B movie. B movies were the second billing to Hollywood productions, however, they did not venture into the controversial subject matter that defined the exploitation film.[58] John Wayne began his career acting in B movies, although he also played a minor role in the quintessential pre-code film *Baby Face* (1933), portraying one of Barbara Stanwyck's conquests.[59] Nonetheless, by the late 1950s and early 1960s, exploitation films embraced the blossoming youth market and left behind their educational documentary past.[60] Director Stephanie Rothman, who worked for legendary exploitation film producer-director Roger Corman, notes, "The reason audiences came to see these low-budget films without stars was because they delivered scenes that you could not see in major studio films."[61] This formula of sensation proved extremely profitable.

The slow collapse of the studio system after the 1948 *Paramount* decision coincided and influenced the easing of the Hays Production Code in the 1950s as major studios released films adopting more serious topics such as adultery and prostitution.⁶² Adjusting to the post–World War II demographic shift in the United States, the film industry sought to contend with the growth of suburbanites watching television (and not going to the movies).⁶³ A new form of exploitation emerged during these years to lure in the youth market, inaugurated by the "nudie-cutie" films of director Russ Meyer, beginning with *The Immoral Mr. Teas* (1959).⁶⁴ Meyer's exploitation films in the 1960s—notably *Faster, Pussycat! Kill! . . . Kill!* (1965) and *Mudhoney* (1965)—depicted the objectification of women through sex role reversals where women dominate men.⁶⁵

Capitalizing on the success of mid-1960s exploitation films (what Peter Krämer calls youth-oriented taboo breakers), these policy adjustments in business and culture materialized out of the 1960s as representative commodities defining the arrival of the multinational media conglomerate and the embrace of the new cultural mores of the 1960s.⁶⁶ In a metaphoric sense, the studio system (ostensibly a Fordist institution) evolved into the conglomerate system (the defining institution of the neoliberal era) leading to a more flexible environment to create films. Important to this rearrangement was the intersection of the social revolutions of the 1960s, the dismantling of the Hays Codes, and the rise of the Code and Rating Administration system Hollywood utilized to review and rate films.⁶⁷ Together, these policies helped to deregulate the film industry from its pre-1960s form, with the added bonus of keeping their ratings system—the Motion Picture Association of America (MPAA)—under the control of Hollywood rather than an arm of government regulation.⁶⁸ Like the welfare state for multinationals, the film industry had outgrown the regulations of the Hays Code as the tastes of 1960s audiences had drastically changed from the 1950s. A "new" liberated Hollywood arose out of the rebelliousness of the 1960s, capitalizing on realistic depictions of sex and violence.⁶⁹ Realistic violence appeared initially in 1960s exploitation films, whereas mainstream productions picked up on the trend largely after 1966. Political unrest also found an outlet in film, as the rhetoric of Black Power, the counterculture, and women's liberation entered popular culture expression in the late 1960s and early 1970s, representing another set of exploitable material.

Black Power and feminism took shape at the same time the "new cinema of sensation" arrived, stemming from director Alfred Hitchcock's *Psycho* (1960), as well as the taboo-breaking films such as *Bonnie and Clyde* (1967), *The Dirty Dozen* (1967), *The Graduate* (1967), *Up Tight!* (1968), and *The Wild Bunch* (1969).⁷⁰ Richard Slotkin describes how these sensations pushed the realist envelope: "Part of our excitement and terror comes from realizing that what is normally and traditionally concealed will at last be explicitly displayed."⁷¹ Realism, Annette Kuhn notes, situates the viewer in a space where they are unaware that "she or he is making meanings: meaning seems to be there already in the film, the spectator's only task being to sit back and take it in."[72] Unfolding with the turbulent events of the decade, realism both represented the deregulation of the film industry's code of restrictions as well as that industry's competition with television, as the reality of violence connected to the civil rights movement, the wave of urban uprisings, antiwar confrontations, and the Vietnam War was broadcasted into the homes of Americans on a nightly basis. The saturation of these events across various forms of media expanded the concept of experience. One could obviously experience their everyday life, including face-to-face interaction with the various 1960s movements. However, with its omnipresence, one could also vicariously experience these movements through the flow of television.[73] Film productions across the 1960s failed to reconcile this new oversaturation of information-based reality and the everyday experience projected into homes every night: the outdated fantasies of Hollywood now became comparatively unrealistic when juxtaposed against the conflict and violence of the evening television news.

The rise of violence, nudity, and sex in full color—and rated R—became a new norm for post-1960s Hollywood in serving the growing demand for realistic film narratives.[74] For the most part, elements of Black Power and women's liberation entered movies as simplistic caricatures of angry Black men denouncing "the man" or women complaining of male chauvinists (with each character summoning older stereotypes set against the new politics). Containable within the film format, these representations of political movements became new commodities of spectacular "difference" to a public increasingly numb from the decade's turmoil.[75]

Although the initial response to the lowering of censorship posited a new liberated era, the baggage of patriarchy resituated itself in a similar manner as the reformation of race when confronted with the ideal of color blindness. In the name of realism, the incorporation of contemporary themes of women's liberation by directors often suffered from their own deep-rooted patriarchal ideas, sometimes becoming more amplified and fantastic under the less regulated measures outlining what could be shown in films. Furthermore, the deregulation of film coincided with another trend: the most profitable movies between 1967 and 1976 marginalized women and focused primarily on male protagonists, with women forming only 26 percent of characters in movies (both major and minor).[76] Noting this systemic response to social equality legislation, Krämer adds, "It would appear, then, that male filmmakers in their productions, and male cinemagoers in their film selections, went against the trend of increasing support for women's rights. Films seem to have fulfilled a compensatory function here. In the cinema, men could withdraw from social reality, in which they acknowledged the demands that women could legitimately make on them, into a world in which women were quite marginal or altogether absent."[77]

With some exceptions, the market for film realism and the filmmakers' satisfaction of this market narrowed itself to a much more sensationalist vision of realistic depictions of sex and violence from a male perspective, invoking what appeared to be a reinvigoration of the "experiences of men in contemporary America."[78] In short, the trend toward realism fixated on the rugged individual male, reaffirming the "male gaze" at the same moment women gained social equality with men.[79] Long an institutional norm in filmmaking history, the "male gaze" defined and contained women in film "as erotic object[s]."[80] Although the gaze characterizes the entire history of Hollywood film, once censorship was deregulated and the door was opened to the visual representation of violence and nudity, misogynist sentiments found greater and more explicit expression. Much like the limitations of the civil rights movement in significantly altering structural inequality, women's liberation, too, operated from largely a symbolic base of power in the face of male-dominated institutions. It was easier to change the facade facing the street—removing explicit signs of racism and sexism—than to adequately address the *longue durée* ontological sentiments of a society wired to imagine women as naturally inferior. Mirroring the feminist criticisms toward the so-called sexual revolution, the freedoms of the 1960s in film more often equated to the freedom of male (and some female) filmmakers to further objectify women's bodies through gratuitous nudity (without the comparable objectification of men) and graphic sexual violence rather than exemplifying some type of "revolution" confronting older patriarchal morals.[81] Although a few films portrayed empowered women overcoming life obstacles—for example, *Alice Doesn't Live Here Anymore* (1974) and *Claudine* (1974)—Hollywood's dominant responses to feminism more often took shape in the form of disciplinary punishment, either in erasure or what I call the liberation gauntlet.[82]

Exploitation movies drew on youth audiences' identification with political-cultural concerns, generating the sort of excitement, relevance, and interest from audiences that stars once brought to larger budget Hollywood productions. The budget for these films allowed for no stars, notes director-producer Roger Corman, leaving filmmakers to "exploit the subject material" instead.[83] Squeezing out the surface essence inscribed in the manifestos and voices from social movements, exploitation films deployed the feminist rhetoric (however caricatured) of empowerment and engagement with patriarchy (the subject matter) through a narrative mixed with the violence and nudity desired from the target audience (the exploitation). As an alternative market to mainstream films primarily based upon the experiences of men, female-centered exploitation films wrapped stories of assertive women together with the threads of objectification and brutalization while simultaneously securing a feminist sense of empowerment through cathartic revenge sequences at the climax of the film.[84] The resulting commodity was a patchwork of images conjoining the spectacle of liberation manifested through caricatured representations of Black Power and feminism with the renewal of the very patriarchal violence the feminist movement sought to challenge. As Pam Cook notes, although there appears to be empowerment in "the possibility of woman becoming the subject rather than the object of desire, that desire is seen totally in terms of male phantasies and obsessions."[85]

Much like early 1970s sitcoms of single women, these works denoted the structural market limits of cultural productions depicting feminism in the post-1960s era.[86] At the same time, however, many films from this era offered an unprecedented array of lead roles for women in action films. A few exceptions to this rule occurred, particularly with Stephanie Rothman's *Terminal Island* (1973), where a more egalitarian relationship exists within a prison setting despite the brutalizing images of women enslaved to the whims of the male inmates.[87] *Switchblade Sisters* (1975), a nonprison movie by exploitation film stalwart, director Jack Hill, offered glimpses of interracial solidarity against a misogynist white male gang.[88] As the films were intended to be drive-in "date movies," a mixed audience separated these films from the male viewership of "grindhouse" movies.[89] The novelty for exploitation films, particularly those produced by Roger Corman, was the focus on "the actions, desires, goals, and interests of women."[90] From this premise, filmmakers erected a liberation gauntlet filled with the vestiges of gender and racial violence to establish a path for their actresses to attain empowerment.

In defining the liberation gauntlet, the latter describes the end goal: to achieve liberation. The gauntlet, however, is the means by which one achieves the ends: it is the material and symbolic set of instruments, institutions, and obstacles framing the coercive path toward liberation through a series of public punishments and humiliations structuring one's ordeal. To survive the gauntlet is to achieve liberation, but the body is marked and/or recorded with scars of the ordeal, reminding the viewer of the cost and punishment of liberation. Thus, an important component of the liberation gauntlet is its public process, a spectacle of calculated humiliation aimed toward disciplining women's desire to be autonomous, at once violent and titillating. In 1983, film critic Richard Meyer noted the libidinal dynamics of exploitation films and their connection to realistic experience. "Exploitation films are the price we pay for, essentially, living a lie. Many would like to think that they are well-adjusted, considerate, intelligent people who would never enjoy—even revel—in the suffering of others. I know I would. . . . Like it or not, many receive a guilty, sometimes secret thrill out of witnessing savage action and titillating topics. I know I do. . . . In this case, exploitation films perform a much-needed service; they allow one to receive all of the perverted pleasure of looking at a car wreck without the guilt of knowing that the victims are real."[91] Realism now encompassed a cathartic flexible misogyny for filmgoers in the 1970s. Taking shape alongside other reforms as neoliberalism emerged in the 1970s, films projected what the conservative culture war rhetoric could never utter: equality would never be handed out as an inherent right (as John Locke suggested); women would need to earn their independence from men. Thus, if women sought to enter spaces previously reserved for men (the masculine genre of actions films), then the "protections" promised by patriarchy would be reversed: there would be a physical cost for women who sought liberation. Consequently, the liberation gauntlet provided men with their own revenge sequence by fostering a series of events showing women attempt to define a life outside the control of men but forced to negotiate a liberation gauntlet prescribed and under the control of men. As neoliberalism found implementation within institutional policies after the 1970s, the liberation gauntlet established itself as a profitable paradigm and a useful device during the Reagan era's backlash against women, forming the contours of anti-feminist films throughout the 1980s.[92]

When discussing 1970s exploitation films, attention to the most popular subgenre is required: Black action films, or so-called Blaxploitation.[93] Stephane Dunn's approach to this genre underlines how these films often centered on a "hypermasculine machismo," "envisioned in part through the accepted naming and treatment of women, black women in particular, as 'bitches' and 'hos.'"[94] Although many of these films contained elements of Black Power, the "films never radically upset either the racial patriarchal politics implicit in their making . . . nor popular contemporary and historical notions about race."[95] Fitting into the general film trend outlined by Krämer, the majority of these movies explored ways Black men fought back against organized crime, corrupt police, or simply becoming successful gangsters—often relegating women to roles as objects of the protagonist's desires. A few films, however, did utilize strong women leads, such as Tamara Dobson in *Cleopatra Jones* (1973) and Nichelle Nichols in *Truck Turner* (1974).[96] For the most part, however, the protagonists of these films engaged in sensual violence that activated a misogyny that "defined the spectacle of race, sexual, and gender power"—resulting in the reinforcement of "traditional hierarchies."[97]

The biggest star to emerge from this early period of women action stars was undoubtedly Pam Grier, who first made her name starring in Roger Corman–produced exploitation films coming out of the Philippines in the early 1970s. Grier would often be cast as a lower-class Black woman, sexualized via the guise or disguise of a prostitute—and thus conjuring the myths and controlling images of the Jezebel (the oversexed Black woman) and the Sapphire (the scheming and deceptive Black woman)—which allowed for her empowerment or agency against villains in films such as *Coffy* (1973) and *Foxy Brown* (1974).[98]

Unfortunately, these images often did appear empowering when placed in contrast to more masculine movies such as *Shaft* (1971) and *Super Fly* (1972).[99] Just as the sexually violent liberation gauntlet outlined the path for films exported from the Philippines, Grier's characters were often "raped, beaten, and degraded along the path to 'winning.'"[100] In other words, to attain empowerment, Grier's characters traversed a liberation gauntlet lined with an inventory of sexual violence and humiliation.

The feminist liberation gauntlet embodied a range of methods and routes of punishment and disciplining received by women in popular culture in the 1970s for declaring either freedom, equality, or in the final instance, demanding an end to racist patriarchy. Different versions of these gauntlets appeared in media as narrative devices, providing counterpoints to proposed empowerment and often espousing the reinscription of oppression. Unlike male empowerment themes stressing contemporary constraints in the protagonist's search for empowerment—bureaucratic meddling, male competition, repressive bosses, liberals being soft on crime, or castration by women—women's constraints in popular media worked through ideas geared toward naturalizing the concept of gender. This included (1) underlining the notion that women were naturally weak (2) and thus are shown to be susceptible to violence in the outside world (public sphere), and (3) leaving the viewer with an impression that the public sphere, as it had under the cult of domesticity, was naturally male. Although the path toward empowerment offered white males a distinct security in the fact that the structures and institutions operated from the power base of the white male, women faced an intersecting set of challenges, largely determined through gender, race, class, and sexuality, as they sought to navigate through the white male–dominated structures and institutions relatively undisturbed by the gains of 1960s social movements.

In many ways, the liberation gauntlet operated as a device to assimilate the ideology of feminism into images more easily incorporated into the broader framework of post-1960s identity politics. If a woman seeks liberation, she must submit to a fantastic level of brutality to underscore the unnaturalness of this liberation and social equality. Rather than a systemic critique of capitalist patriarchy, the liberation gauntlet channeled the quest for equality and empowerment through a male-defined set of obstacles—a misogynist version of the masculine hero's journey, where the hero negotiates various obstacles to achieve their goal.[101] Although made to traverse similar gauntlets on their way to becoming the hero in films, male protagonists were hardly made to traverse the soul-destroying experience of sexual violence—with perhaps *Deliverance* (1972) being a notable exception. No one could have imagined Clint Eastwood or John Wayne being raped on their way to victory. Consequently, the liberation gauntlet acted as both a set of commonsense parameters by predominantly male directors and creators of popular culture, as well as a set of structural impediments identified by feminists as obstacles in their quest for liberation (a regeneration of patriarchal violence disciplining demands of social equality). Hardly the creation of producers and directors, the liberation gauntlet represented versions of patriarchal disciplinary measures associated with the *longue durée* history of gender inequality.[102]

The liberation gauntlet embodied the updating of modernity's ideas and ontology connected to gender and its intersections. An anchor of this logic is rooted in the Enlightenment's social contract theory and its often-silenced sexual contract. Although the social contract theorizes a gender-blind concept of universal freedom—the same universalism attached to the concept of Western civilization—within the confines of abstraction, notes Carole Pateman, exists the embedded patriarchal notion of men's rights over women's bodies via the sexual contract. Men are born free—as a natural condition—and are thus able to enter contracts as the embodiment of freedom and equality. However, since the sexual difference assigned to women denotes the binary of men, women represent the antithesis of freedom and equality (an intersection directly related to the dynamics of whiteness and Blackness). Accordingly, women are not born free, as they belong to their father and future husband—and thus cannot claim the same natural rights as individuals defined as men. Or as Bruno Latour described the ontological conception of modernity, European men belonged to the category of human (and, thus, free) while women (and people of color) were placed within the unfree and physically exploitable category of nature: the object for human agency.[103] Therefore, women's relationship to men is one of naturalized subjugation, falling under the contractual rights of other men—of *individuals* who either purchase a woman via dowry or "give their daughter's hand away in marriage." Pateman writes:

> The original contract constitutes both freedom and domination. Men's freedom and women's subjugation are created through the original contract—and the character of civil freedom cannot be understood without the missing half of the story that reveals how men's patriarchal right over women is established through contract. Civil freedom is not universal. Civil freedom is a masculine attribute and depends upon patriarchal right. The sons overturn paternal rule not merely to gain their liberty but to secure women for themselves. Their success in this endeavor is chronicled in the story of the sexual contract. . . . [T]he contract establishes men's political right over women—and also sexual in the sense of establishing orderly access by men to women's bodies.[104]

This contractual access to women's bodies formed the ontological core guiding white American civil society, ideas of rights and liberty, and access to space and political-economic opportunity. The intersectional aspects of race and sexuality compound this equation. Developed through centuries of colonialism, the Atlantic slave system, capitalism, the nation-state, and imperialism, the intersections of race and sexuality utilized differently categorized women as defining elements buttressing the norms of patriarchal culture through the 1960s and beyond.[105] These *longue durée* norms reacted swiftly when provoked in the 1970s, as "all the old habits of thinking and acting, the set patterns which do not break down easily" were "a long time dying."[106] These norms found themselves abruptly challenged by the onrush of social justice movements in the 1960s, with previously legal—or legally ignored—practices such as discrimination, harassment, and violence articulated as injustice and crimes against humanity by the historic victims of American white male supremacy. As Baldwin noted above, once the victim articulated their condition *as a victim*, they ceased being a victim and now became a threat as the dominant and righteous ideas of liberty and equality celebrated in history textbooks were questioned. A reaction ensued as the voices of women and people of color made this condition self-conscious to the world.

The rekindling of violence toward women in popular culture both reinforced a sense of danger for women while simultaneously disciplining demands for equality through the spectacle of physical punishment. This ritual gesture underscored the deep contours of patriarchy, and the construction of the centuries-old cult of true womanhood, where women relinquished claims of equality and civil rights in exchange for male protection. According to Susan Faludi, this sentiment goes to the heart of anti-feminism: "women are better off 'protected' than equal."[107] At the same time, precedents of violence against white women in popular media—*and their fighting back*—stretch back to the colonial era and the very construction of American identity. Returning to colonial captivity narratives mentioned earlier, in the wake of describing spectacular violence dealt by Native Americans on the bodies of white women—with scenes describing their children's brains "dash'd out . . . against a tree"—women were given license to take on "warlike roles" to redeem themselves: "only in this way could women be hailed as 'amazons' for accomplishing murderous deeds in the wilderness."[108] A gauntlet constructed through white male imaginations, then, has always set the conditions for liberation. And patriarchal discipline would police the line.

Sensibilities such as this were/are ingrained across the so-called generation gap and assorted ideologies. Many of the early debates of the women's liberation movement included a conscious avoidance of "repeating the left's pattern of routinely invoking egalitarianism, while often ignoring it in practice."¹⁰⁹ An example of this contradiction inevitably arose during a New Left anti-inauguration rally sponsored by the National Mobilization Committee in 1969. As Marilyn Salzman Webb made a speech describing the oppression of women, scuffles broke out in the crowd, including taunts and threats toward the stage: "Fuck her! Take her off the stage! Rape her in a back alley," followed by taunts such as "Take it off!"¹¹⁰ Underlying the patriarchy of the New Left, the articulation of the condition of sexism within the movement found immediate resistance among many men steeped in the traditional patriarchy of their families and communities.

The soundtracks of these students' youth also operated through the logic women's objectification. Since its inception, rock 'n' roll borrowed the overbearing "figure of the matriarch as the chief organizer of conformism and mediocrity" from the 1950s.¹¹¹ This domineering matriarch trope neatly fit the women attempting to reframe the New Left struggle. Popular songs by the Rolling Stones, with titles such as "Under My Thumb" and "Stupid Girl," fostered new appreciation for implicit violence toward women while providing the lucratively nostalgic soundtrack of the decade.¹¹² In their 1971 release, "Brown Sugar," the Rolling Stones take a *longue durée* view of the intersectional violence against enslaved African American women:

> Gold coast slave ship bound for cotton fields
> Sold in a market down in New Orleans
> Scarred old slaver knows he's doing alright
> Hear him whip the women just around midnight
> Brown sugar
> How come you taste so good?
> Brown sugar
> Just like a young girl should¹¹³

Once past the images of capitalism, the Atlantic slave system, and the sexualizing of the enslaved, the listener was greeted with the song, "Bitch," on the B-Side. Even the countercultural icons, the Grateful Dead, sang of patriarchal free love in "Jack Straw" (1971), where the lyrics discuss the communal distribution of possessions: "We can share the women. We can share the wine."¹¹⁴ The sexual revolution appeared more like a license for men's lascivious behavior than overturning possessive ideas about men's control over women.¹¹⁵

Country music, as well, was a bastion of popular culture patriarchy mixed with conservatism and often-racist populism.¹¹⁶ Despite this link to tradition, glimmers of feminism appeared as the style developed in the 1920s and 1930s, including the Carter Family's "Single Girl, Married Girl" (1927).¹¹⁷ Although

Loretta Lynn marked the beginning of a more assertive, liberated voice for women in country music during the 1960s, the symbolic radicalism of women's liberation found itself in the sights of many country artists chafing at the criticism toward what would emerge after the 1970s as "traditional values" (or "family values") based upon patriarchy. Major labels like RCA records released works like Billy Edd Wheeler's "Woman's Talkin' Liberation Blues," which described a fight between the singer's parents after his mother threw down her apron and joined the women's liberation movement.[118] The song includes the singer's father offering equality through a punch in the face of his mother. Following a scuffle on the ground, the song's resolution finds his mother relenting, conceding "you wear the pants," and volunteering to get back in the house to take care of the kids. "Woman's Talkin' Liberation Blues" was on Wheeler's album titled *Love*, and pictured him lovingly holding his child.[119] "Thanks to women's liberation, we men are no longer free," sing the Willis Brothers on their song "Women's Liberation." Co-opting the centuries-old slave-freedom metaphor, the Willis Brothers interpret women's independence and critique of male dominance as an attack on men: "women are taking over this ol' nation enslaving innocent guys like you and me."[120] The language of innocence, the default stance of white male patriarchy at the dawn of liberation, disavowed the *longue durée* violence of patriarchy. Complaining about his wife's night job, the singer notes that he has to not only drop off the children at school, but when he comes home, there is only a frozen dinner waiting for him. Like most of this subgenre, the songs usually end with the women reconsidering women's liberation as a farce. Indeed, "the good Lord made a woman to fulfill the needs of man," and filling his shoes is not in "nature's plan."[121] The Willis Brothers' innocent demand for subjugated labor and sexual access is finally restored. Not to be outdone, women country singers such as Lana Roush joined in as well:

> I believe in having babies, and making apple pie,
> and I like the way men look at me when I wiggle by.
> Girls let's tell it like it is, we don't feel oppressed.
> The good Lord knew what he was doing when he made the weaker sex.
> Don't liberate me, please dominate me.[122]

The language of patriarchy and its naturalization of gender equality litters the common sense of these works, underscoring the cultural efforts to reinstill a sense of inequality based on "nature." For Roush—and conservative women following Phyllis Schlafly's lead in fighting against the Equal Rights Amendment—the role of the submissive, deferent housewife protected women. Indeed, as many evangelical Christians suggested, patriarchy was God's plan—and formed the essence of civilization.[123]

As noted by the song "Brown Sugar," Black women found themselves caught within this patriarchal network with the additional weight of racial antagonism. In 1960s social justice movements, Black women (much like white women in the New Left) ran into difficulties with male activists who embraced the dominant forms of patriarchal understandings of the place of women.[124] As Black Panther Party member Chaka Walls asserted in 1969, "The way women contribute is by getting laid," a more bluntly updated assertion of the persistently misconstrued thoughts (by activists and historians) about the position of women in SNCC echoed a few years earlier by Stokely Carmichael: "prone."[125] Although joking, Carmichael's comment reflected much of the sentiment across a significant portion of the New Left and Black Power social justice movements. As Brian Ward points out, with repression escalating in the late 1960s toward Black Power groups, an outlet of frustration formed against Black women, who had been hugely important in organizing and strategizing the civil rights movement.[126] Antagonism toward Black women gained federal backing in 1965 through the myth of the Black matriarch in Daniel Patrick Moynihan's "The Negro Family: The Case For National Action" (aka the Moynihan Report).[127] Circulated and constantly highlighted by conservatives like William F. Buckley Jr., this theme continued to place Black women within their historic role as symbols anchoring ideas of race and anti-Blackness—and assigning blame to them for the effects of institutional racism.

Much like the sexism permeating other popular culture, R&B and soul utilized tropes sexualizing women at the same time a new militancy entered music after 1968. Epitomizing this trend was James Brown.[128] Along with his mid-1960s frank notion, "It's a Man's Man's Man's World," in a track from 1970 Brown adopted a similar defense of patriarchy as country music in the wake of the new demands of women (a year noted for an increased gap in the pay ratio between men and women since 1960):

> Fellas, things done got too far gone.
> We gotta let the girls know what they gotta do for us!
> It's done gotten to be a drag, man, a man can't do nothin' no more!
>
> Girl, let me tell you what you got to do,
> T.C.B. so mellow, so nobody can get through.
> When he has to do your lovin', smile and kiss his cheek,
> Walk away and twist your hip, make sure you keep him weak.
> Don't let nobody take care o' your business better than you do,
> Do what he wants, give what he wants, expect 'em come to you.
>
> And then you can hold your men, you can hold your men, you can hold your men.[129]

The guiding assumption in most of these songs (from country to rock 'n' roll to soul and funk) imagines women already possessing power over men—a situation magnified for Black women confronted with the state-sanctioned matriarchy myth and the reality of *longue durée* intersectional antagonism. Through this conservative male-centric worldview, the idea of legislative social equality between men and women immediately conjures images of women replicating the patriarchal relationship of men dominating women, a similar idea fueling white fears over Black Power.[130]

Representations of women in television presented a subtler reaction. Strong, independent women appeared in sitcoms, including Mary Richards of the *Mary Tyler Moore Show* to Maude Findlay in *Maude* to Florida Evans of *Good Times*. However, in early 1970s film, strong women occupying traditionally male spaces most often appeared as caricatures of man-hating women who would see their family, and thus children, suffer for the sake of a career or personal empowerment. An exemplary illustration of this was Faye Dunaway's character Diana Christensen in *Network* (1976), the television producer whose ruthless, cold-hearted drive replicated the older lessons of femmes fatales from the *film noir* era: alienation and loneliness (or death in most *film noirs*).[131] With men's loss of control over women's sexuality, these charges sometimes linked second-wave feminism to homosexuality.[132] These homophobic indictments came from the backlash outside the women's movement as well as from within.[133] For example, Friedan's declaration of a "lavender menace" echoed the persecution of gays and lesbians by the federal government in the 1950s, though NOW disavowed Friedan's position in 1971 after vigorous efforts by lesbians.[134] Even women-in-prison exploitation films used lesbianism as an ultimate personification of villainy and the upending of civilizational norms.[135] Women connected to domesticity continued to operate as a normative value, as independent women became amoral, masculine corporate villains (like in *Network*) or selfishly confused about their identity as in *Kramer vs. Kramer* (1979).[136] Finally, the assertion of women's agency surfaced most spectacularly in the violent genre of revenge fantasy films featuring the psychotic murder of males after abuse or sexual assault, such as the made-for-TV movie *The Girl Most Likely to . . .* (1973), *Hannie Caulder* (1971), *Rape Squad* (1974), *I Spit on Your Grave (1978)*, and *Ms. 45* (1981).[137] The ratings system allowed producers to force viewers to sit through the liberation gauntlet of sexual assault as it unfolded.

This symbolic disciplining from the film industry arose in various forms, though frequently assuming a similar rhetorical shape as the anti–women's liberation narratives in music. Films most often established a sense of equality by equating equal treatment through a masculine-directed test of violence. Adriana Cavarero outlines how "modern political thought" modeled the "male subject" as the universal, allowing two paradigms: exclusion, which films during this period did, or "a homologizing, assimilating inclusion," where women are included through the model of men and thus have their difference silenced or magnified through the spectacle of ritually inscribed violence (symbolic or physical).[138] An equation of equality emerged: if women wanted equality, then the baseline of male-imagined equality—the coercion and violence shaping patriarchal relations—is highlighted and placed in the path of women seeking liberation. Since the rules of agency within film still adhere to the male gaze and dominance over narrative and production decisions (with a few exceptions), equal physical punishment on par with men extended into the masculine-driven dimension of sexual assault. Within the "liberated" bargain of equality is the relinquishing of the promise of male protection denoted in the "act like a lady" maxim. With patriarchy's romantic bargain in tatters, open season on women commenced.[139] The result for women in action films released amid the deregulation of censorship: a hypersurreal assault on body and mind wrapped in titillation.

Second-wave feminism's work against, and theorization of, sexual violence helped to pave the way for a broader understanding of the intersections between gender, sexuality, class, and race, particularly the publication of Susan Brownmiller's *Against Our Will* and Angela Y. Davis's "Joan Little: The Dialectics of Rape" in 1975 (as well as Davis's later work criticizing the "racist ideas" pervading Brownmiller's arguments regarding Black men).[140] Previously framed as an issue where "women are said to invite rape and murder and abuse by not being submissive enough, or by being too seductive, or too . . . ," feminists in the 1970s reframed the "she asked for it" commonsense response to sexual violence: theorized as a male social act, rape projected control and power by men over women's bodies.[141] As Maria Mies points out, "Women began to understand that rape, wife-beating, harassment, molestation of women, sexist jokes, etc., were not just expressions of deviant behaviour on the part of some men, but were part and parcel of a whole system of male, or rather patriarchal, dominance over women. In this system both direct physical violence and indirect or structural violence were still commonly used as a method to 'keep women in their place.'"[142] Rape operated as both an acquaintance-driven, though sometimes random, selection of victims acting as a reinforcement of a particular hierarchy through extralegal measures. Indeed, these acts are intimately linked through their intersectional relationships to the various hierarchies embedded in patriarchy—race, class, sexuality, and so forth. The long history of white men raping women of African descent often failed to be classified as a crime, acting as another tool of domination in the arsenal of slavery.[143] In the name of realism, then, the sets of policies unveiled in post-censorship Hollywood brought previously censored depictions of explicit violence to the fore as exploitative marketing gestures to attract audiences.

These depictions grew graphic within cinema as the Hays Code ceased to exist. Rape within popular culture, what Tanya Horeck calls public rape, is represented in sexual assaults that "serve as cultural fantasies of power and domination, gender and sexuality, and class and ethnicity."[144] These filmed fantasies of sexual violence by men against women served—as it always has— "as a means of forging social bonds, and of mapping out public space."[145] For exploitation films in the 1970s, especially the less campy horror pictures like *Rape Squad* or *I Spit on Your Grave*, the act of rape is the ultimate motivating factor for women's empowerment toward the end of the film. Operating as a trigger for role reversals with men, these scenes reinforced the idea that women could not achieve liberation without the violent body and soul assault of sexual violence. Examples of this dynamic include *Jackson County Jail* (1976), which initiates the literal liberation of a woman prisoner after she kills a sheriff's deputy who raped her; more disturbingly grotesque, *I Spit on Your Grave* contains a gratuitous twenty-five-minute rape scene preceding the protagonist's violent spree against her male assailants.[146]

To make sense of these 1970s gestures and representations, American masculinity's patriarchal drive needs to be contextualized within the *longue durée* legacies of settler colonialism and slavery. Settler colonialism's contribution to patriarchy included the masculinity associated with men's protection of women and children from so-called savages on the frontier.[147] Thus, an equation infused with intersecting sexual, gendered, and racial ideas guiding the violent displacement of Indigenous people from their land while controlling women through the language of "protection" became a vital part of the defense of the homeland. Sexual violence against Indigenous women, moreover, formed a counterpoint to the "protection" of white settler women, with rape actively aiding the process of ethnic cleansing within the zero-sum nature of settler colonialism.[148] Slavery and the ideas of race and anti-Blackness formed yet another pillar of American patriarchal masculinity: from seventeenth-century laws forbidding Black men to possess firearms to the barring of people of African descent from testifying against white people, the law carried swift verdicts establishing the inflated worth of white men, especially white men with property.[149] Working off the white ideal of citizenship inscribed in the Naturalization Act of 1790, the *Dred Scott* decision consolidated these customs under a Supreme Court ruling, with Chief Justice Roger B. Taney arguing, "[African Americans] had for more than a century been regarded as beings of an inferior order, and altogether unfit to associate with the white race, either in social or political relations, and so far unfit that they had no rights which the white man was bound to respect."[150]

Meanwhile, lynch law extended these practices in the wake of emancipation after the Civil War through the twentieth century, specifically the threat of Black men raping white women justifying the "festivals of violence."[151] The white American embrace and defense of the lynching of Black Americans extended to the perverse commodification of the image of Black death through the selling and circulation of postcard photos of lynchings sent around the nation by white Americans in the late nineteenth and early twentieth centuries.[152] Science provided a new "objective" justification for racial antagonism through eugenics and statistics in the early twentieth century, codifying the criminalization of Blackness up through the twenty-first century.[153]

These dynamics legitimized violence against African Americans via the guise of the Black rapist or brute as well as reinforcing the curtailment of white women's rights in the name of white male protection.[154] For Black women within the structures of slavery, anti-Black patriarchal ideology foreclosed equality from the positions of both race and gender—with sexuality, moreover, adding yet another layer to the gauntlet of the American "racial dictatorship."[155] Within the legacy of slavery, anti-Black patriarchal ideology suggests multiple, simultaneously occurring acts. First, the notion erases the role of sexual coercion as "an essential dimension of the social relations between slave master and slave. In other words," as pointed out by Angela Y. Davis, "the right claimed by slaveowners and their agents over the bodies of female slaves was a direct expression of their presumed property rights over Black people as a whole."[156] Furthermore, the outcome of this sexual underpinning of race, class, and gender buttressed the unstable category of the cult of true womanhood developed during the height of slavery's profitability (the era of "cotton is king"), becoming a critical component of the rise of bourgeois patriarchy.[157] Other spectacles of violence toward women preceding the nineteenth century include the rituals of witch burning after accusations of witchcraft.[158] These early modern ideas expressed themselves in colonial North America, where the concept of rape defined the sexual relations between a Black man and a white woman—and not white men and Black women.[159] Finally, controlling images such as the Jezebel justified the act of rape, alongside a host of other oppressive institutionalized features of racial slavery, including "medical experimentation . . . and unwanted childbearing."[160] Within this contradiction, where Black women were raped in act (not by definition) only, this power relationship undoubtedly spilled into practices between white men and white women. In short, sexual coercion under the weight of racial slavery formed an important pillar upholding American patriarchy. Davis writes, "For once white men were persuaded that they could commit sexual assaults against Black women with impunity, their conduct toward women of their own race could not have remained unmarred. Racism has always served as a provocation to rape, and white women in the United States have necessarily suffered the ricochet fire of these attacks. This is one of the many ways in which racism nourishes sexism, causing white women to be indirectly victimized by the special oppression aimed at their sisters of color."[161]

Another element of the liberation gauntlet for Black women and men included the expanded use of the racial epithet n****r on screen.[162] The word's value for the United States translated to immense wealth for the new nation, a psychological boost for poor whites—fomenting a dependable safety valve for class conflict—and a license for the murder of Black people without retribution.[163] The word also proved important in achieving direct realism in entertainment, with many exploitation and 1970s action movies setting the term loose into public discourse against the backdrop of films set in the inner city, intermingled amongst representations of Black criminality and other spectacles of violence and nudity. Successful films such as *The Godfather* (1972) and *The French Connection* (1971) utilized the word as a sign of street authenticity and the blunt racism of the films' white protagonists. In *The French Connection*, for instance, the roughhewn protagonist, Doyle, represents the conservative mantra of law and order, wielding blatantly anti-Black views— "Never trust a n****r," he tells his more liberal partner. Although the viewer cheers the antihero Doyle on in his chase after a heroin supplier, his mundane racism is a literal depiction of the policing mindset the Kerner Commission outlined in their 1968 report as being one of the most prescient reasons for "riots."[164] Indeed, actor Roy Scheider remembers sitting in a Black theater in Manhattan and listening to the audience cheering after the utterance, as their charges of racism from the police were voiced on the big screen.[165] Moreover, these views were deployed in the name of artistic aesthetics and creating a realistic depiction of policing that even the liberal Gene Hackman came around to see as necessary in society (he won an Academy Award for playing the protagonist).[166]

In some cases, like *Across 110th Street* (1972) and many films that fell into the Blaxploitation category, white cops or authorities who used the epithet often signified their corruption.[167] Ideologically, this isolates the blunt post-1960s racism to working-class people, corrupt police, or criminals, rather than the actual power structure creating legislation and enforcing policies—who do not need epithets to assert power. In short, films ignored the sort of institutional racism buttressing the Northern or Western white suburbs, reassuring viewers that only individual racism survived after the 1960s, as institutional racism ostensibly disappeared with civil rights legislation. This equation helped reinforce the new paradigm of color blindness in the mainstream (ostensibly uncorrupted by "ignorant" white working-class prejudices toward inner-city Blacks) while signaling the individualistic racism associated with the use of the racial epithet as atypical in the new post–civil rights era. Finally, the term operated simultaneously as a reinforcement of anti-Black attitudes unacceptable within polite (or public) society, a reformed controlling image aimed toward inner-city African Americans caught within a desperately bleak postindustrial America. The new film realism allowed audience members to vicariously utter the epithet through white movie characters—reestablishing the fraternal ties of American anti-Blackness. As an important element of the liberation gauntlet, the resuscitation of the word $n^{****}r$ into renewed use in the public sphere of entertainment underlined the term's ongoing importance to white American identity creation.

Utilizing the new range of acceptable representations in film such as mixing sexual violence with female empowerment, assertive Blackness alongside feminism, and the renegotiation of anti-Black imagery, exploitation films in the early 1970s offered both a preview of life after the collapse of the Hays Code and provided an exaggerated path of possibilities for 1970s popular culture. As David A. Cook notes, "The replacement of the Production Code by the MPAA ratings system, led the majors to embrace exploitation as a mainstream practice, elevating such previous B genres as science fiction and horror to A-film status, retrofitting 'race cinema' as 'blaxploitation,' and competing with the pornography industry for 'sexploitation' market share."[168]

American-Philippine Exploitation Films and the Liberation Gauntlet

American directors in the late 1960s found the Philippines to be a lucrative site for low-budget exploitation movies. The sometimes gruesome, often titillating flood of films fashioned a powerful phalanx capitalizing on youth demand for the deregulated social mores of the post–Hays Code film industry: it was "what the market wanted," noted legendary Filipino director Eddie Romero.[169] The jungle setting of the Philippines added a turn-of-the-century imperialist aura to the imagery defining the binary between Western civilization (the Global North) and the savagery of the jungle (the Global South).[170] Thus, filming in the Philippines involved both an economic motive in relocating production overseas as well as Grace Kyungwon Hong's "fetishization of difference," where the jungle location provided a type of setting conducive to the story and cast of characters in Corman's movies.[171] Finally, the American production of exploitation films in the Philippines also marked the way cultural production comingled with the economic shifts of multinationals and the rise of neoliberalism.

After almost half a century of colonial ties to the United States, the film industry in the Philippines had established deep roots by the end of World War II.[172] Even John Wayne visited the Philippines to film *Back to Bataan* (1945), an homage to the heroism of Philippine resistance to the Japanese occupation that both downplayed the brutality of U.S. colonization and emphasized "the benefits of U.S. colonialism."[173] Beginning in the late 1950s, Philippine filmmakers such as Romero, Cirio Santiago, Gerardo de Leon, along with American expatriate Kane Lynn (who, with Romero, would form Hemisphere Pictures to distribute films in the United States) actively sought an international audience.[174] Most of these films—including *Brides of Blood* (1968)—were horror exploitation pictures, filled with violence and gore intended to shock audiences.[175] One of the important precedents these late-1960s films set included the use of white American actors—particularly actor John Ashley—set against the exotic jungles of the Philippines. The primary market for these films was the Midwestern drive-in movie theaters.[176] As Henry Jenkins notes of the drive-in, "People don't typically go to drive-in to watch a story. They go to see moments of spectacle, particularly erotic and violent spectacle."[177]

Although made in the Philippines (with Filipino crews), the films, as Filipino director Eddie Romero suggests, "were American pictures made by Filipinos, financed entirely by Americans."[178] Mirroring the strategic outsourcing of American multinationals, the relocation of U.S. filmmakers to the Philippines led to increased profit margins through low costs, nonunion labor, and nonexistent regulations (e.g., safety or pay scale). Directors could also count on the close cooperation of the nation's pro-American authoritarian government (especially after the 1972 coup) looking for foreign investment.[179] For many American directors who produced movies in the Philippines, the culture and economics went hand in hand. A blunt Jon Davison (producer) reminisced, "Human life was cheap, film was cheap. It was a great place to make a picture," while director John Landis unabashedly exclaimed, "You've got jungles, you've got girls who you can exploit. You've got everything and you get it cheap."[180]

The momentum of American capital transferring overseas and the exploitation of women represented a global trend for multinational corporations whose policies created the networks for the rise of Philippines-produced American exploitation films.[181] An Intel Corporation personnel officer echoed John Landis's excitement about exploiting women in developing nations: "We hire women because they have less energy, are more disciplined and are easier to control."[182] One advertisement for investment in Malaysia said this about its women workforce: "The manual dexterity of the oriental female is famous the world over. Her hands are small and she works fast with extreme care.

Who, therefore, could be better qualified *by nature and inheritance* to contribute to the efficiency of a bench-assembly production line than the oriental girl."[183] Accordingly, this overseas setting established a baseline imagination in sync with the ideas emanating from imperialism and the postwar American brand of orientalism built on the sentimental bridging of differences.[184] Based off these popular perceptions, exploitation films offered a blunt, sensational, facetious, and campy fantasy, often relying on Filipino "Otherness" to drive the tension even further.[185] Effectively provoking a slew of gendered violence crucial to the anchoring processes of patriarchy, these films wove together the brutalizing techniques of racial slavery via the prison context with the agency of multicultural casts espousing liberationist rhetoric. In short, the "three Bs" of Philippines-made horror pictures from the 1960s—"blood, breasts, and beasts"—made their way into 1970s American Philippines-made movies, underlining the intersectional politics of both the American culture war and the relocation of multinationals overseas, where women were viewed as "disposable" and the ideal labor source.[186]

One of the first exploitation movies inaugurating the flood of American-Philippine productions was *The Big Doll House* (1971), a film by Roger Corman.[187] Corman helped convert the content of exploitation movies of the 1950s and 1960s into the era of ratings and the incorporation of feminist and Black Power rhetoric into film. Corman's range of pictures included sci-fi and horror, biker and counterculture films, and even a foray into Black action films: *The Final Comedown* (1972).[188] Corman started making movies for Allied Artists and American-International Pictures in the late 1950s through the 1960s. In 1970, he started his own company, New World Pictures, Ltd. Besides making cheap films, Corman also provided opportunities for women to direct, produce, and write scripts in the infamously male-dominated film industry. Not necessarily "altruistic," notes Jenkins, "these women would work long hours for little money, hoping to get the film credits needed to break into Hollywood."[189] Corman's style has been compared to the older Hollywood studio system, churning out more than four cheap and quickly made films a year between the late 1950s and 1960s.[190] Although his work mirrored the old ways of Hollywood, putting out "raw 'product' devoid of any personal stamp or unique vision," Corman did create a style of his own by the time he started New World Pictures.[191]

The majority of Corman's movies were shot in the United States, but his pictures produced in the Philippines point to the larger shifts occurring in the film industry. When asked about the reason for shooting films in the Philippines in 1973, Corman described two main factors: "the look for an interesting, unusual location, and the economics as well."[192] These films also cast a significant number of Filipino extras, whose racial presence against the threatening jungle backdrop foregrounded the danger faced by the American cast. As Amy K. King writes, "These films exploit images of Filipinos as 'the subaltern' in the context of US imperialism, which is essential to the films' strategies to export 'deviant' US women for punishment in the Philippine prison-plantation system."[193] *The Big Doll House*'s enormous success revived the women-in-prison movie genre, a film trend rooted in the 1920s and taking modern shape in the 1950 film *Caged*.[194] In an interview, Corman comments on the economic morality of producing women-in-prison films overseas: "At first, I didn't like *The Big Doll House*. I thought it had gone a little too far with the sex and the violence. It cost about $100,000 and it grossed something like $4 million. When I saw the grosses, I have to admit, my scruples faded away and I said, 'Let's make another one.'"[195] Outsourcing and the raw material of the liberation gauntlet produced impressive profits. Other projects set in the Philippine jungle—and often preoccupied with a prison setting—quickly fell into production, including *Women in Cages* (1971), *The Big Bird Cage* (1972), *The Hot Box* (1972), *Night of the Cobra Woman* (1972), *Black Mama, White Mama* (1972), *The Woman Hunt* (1973), *T.N.T. Jackson* (1974), *Savage Sisters* (1974), and one of the first action films to use four Black female lead actresses, *The Muthers* (1976).[196]

The core trends of women-in-prison films include scenes of women arrested, violently stripped, tortured and raped, and then, as was often the case, a sequence of revenge acts by the brutalized women against their tormentors. Women antagonists sometimes played the tormentors running the prison, often coded as "lesbian" and interested in sadistic torture (the "predatory lesbian" caricature).[197] As the films take place in the Philippines, the ideas associated with the culture of imperialism highlight the "danger" the white American actresses face in the context of jeering Filipino men.[198] The tension of interracial sexual violence—long a Western civilization and American barometer fueling racial antagonism—occurred as the plot unfolded amid humorous, ironic, and campy banter as women were brought together in cells.[199] At the same time, male characters also sometimes appear as buffoonish or comic fodder in light of the obstacles facing the women; in a gesture toward camp, sometimes the guards were represented as homosexual men. In further role reversals—and production cost cutting—the roles of guards were often played by Filipino women.

Some observers suggest that there was the presence of feminism in the women-in-prison film genre, as it offered "spectacles of female bonding, female rage, and female communities, with strong doses of camp and irony."[200] In these settings, women gain empowerment through homosocial bonding under oppressive conditions, leading to a mobilization against their oppressors. In retrospective interviews, this flexible feminism is on display. For example, director Jack Hill (*The Big Doll House, The Big Bird Cage, Coffy, Foxy*

Brown, and *Switchblade Sisters*) notes that "some people started to see feminist messages in these movies. I was certainly a feminist, but I can't really say it was intentional. They were exploitation movies where you're basically exploiting women sexually. But I just felt that, in this case, it was going to work because the women were kind of in control—they were turning on the men."[201] Actress Cheri Caffaro (*Savage Sisters*) explicitly underlines the flexibility of using women leads in exploitation action films: "Women were never looked upon as the lead role in a movie. It was always the guy first, and the woman maybe two or three down the line. Having women do action was unusual then. And it became a craze, thanks to Roger [Corman]. Movies like the one I did, *Too Hot to Handle*, and Pam's movies, they became couples' movies. Guys got to see women fighting and nude scenes, which I never minded doing, and the girls got to see a heroine. It made them stronger to see another woman portrayed like that. It empowered them."[202] Undoubtedly empowering, there is, however, a logic guiding women through the liberation gauntlet on the way to empowerment. According to Hill, the structural requirements for women-in-prison films demanded certain scene obligations: (1) "Naked Girls in a Shower," (2) "Girls Fighting in the Mud," (3) "Women Being Tortured," and (4) "Hosing Scene (optional)"—note the change in description from "Girls" to "Women" according to the punishment.[203] The actresses of these films, for the most part, interviewed almost forty years later, attest to the excitement and thrill of the location of the Philippines and the various trials and tribulations their characters maneuvered through.[204]

In reinscribing the historical legacy of misogynist images, sexual assault is a continuous theme in these exploitation films. Often, these acts include women sexually violating other women—particularly early scenes when inmates are brought to the prison and female wardens call for full-body searches. Rape is also used in *The Big Doll House* as a reversed threat, with tongue-in-cheek lines spoken by actor Sid Haig regarding the possibility of being raped in the prison by the women inmates. Haig's business partner in the film faces this reality, when his female attacker threatens him: "Get it up, or I'll cut it off!"[205] One line from *The Big Bird Cage* echoed the racist logic of the controlling image of the hypersexual Black women and the patriarchal imagination that rape was not about the control and disciplining of women: "You can't rape me; I like sex."[206] The logic of this display of sexual and violent titillation on screen illustrated the paradox of women's liberation, as producer Jane Schaffer remarked: "Feminism with aggressive women is not going to be palatable in a mass market without tits and ass."[207] Nevertheless, the women-in-prison genre was so successful that even the family-friendly feminism of the hit television program *Charlie's Angels* contained an episode in its first season (1976) that took place in a women's prison in the South. Titled "Angels in Chains," the episode adapted these attributes for prime time, including scenes (censored through camera angles and props) of strip searches, shower scenes, being hosed down (with antiseptic), work in the (potato) fields, and forced prostitution.[208]

Taking a closer look at *The Big Doll House*, Corman and director Jack Hill's successful film tells the story of six women planning their escape from a brutal prison controlled by a sadistic female warden in an unnamed, ostensibly Latin American banana republic (in the Philippines with Filipino actors and actresses). The women prisoners' crimes ranged from killing their philandering husband, to infanticide (possibly code for abortion), to drug addiction and prostitution, as well as being a political prisoner whose love interest was a revolutionary figure fighting the government. The conjoining of the charges of prostitution with lesbianism by the only African American character in the film, Grear (played by future Black action film star Pam Grier), adds a racialized sexual "deviance" to the film through the performance of the historical controlling image of the Jezebel filtered through the newer construction of the hip street swagger of Black Power (Grier would also play a prostitute in *Black Mama, White Mama*).[209] Incidentally, Grier's character in the script did not originally call for an African American actress. Another white character, Alcott (played by Roberta Collins), offered a second set of sexual "deviance" as the nymphomaniac who attempts to rape a civilian male supplier. All of these ideals form a wide-ranging critique of the outcome of women's liberation. The prison embodied the necessary space for the viewer to watch the disciplining of these women back to the patriarchal fold at the same time they are allowed to see them make empowering gestures against their captors.

These "crimes" regenerated certain norms for audiences, as the women's flight from patriarchal authority had led them to the criminal justice system. By establishing the binary between normal and deviancy, a "cognitive framework" performs a disciplining function across race (white normativity), gender (masculinity dominates; femininity submits), and sexuality (heterosexuality = normal; homosexuality = abnormal), resulting in "the core hegemonic White masculinity."[210] Despite the unplanned casting, anti-Blackness designates the character of Grear to manifest the most symptoms of deviancy and, by association, savagery: she not only is the predatory lesbian seeking control of her women—first, Harrad, the heroin-addicted cellmate who committed infanticide, and second, the new inmate, Collier—but Grear is also the source of betrayal for the others in their escape scheme. With *The Big Doll House* as the successful archetype, Corman (with Hill) helped to popularize profitable films highlighting the "aggressive positive heroine obsessed with revenge."[211]

With the juxtaposition of caged, dehumanized, and disciplined Black, white, and Filipino women's bodies, these films conjured a selection of libidinal images mapped across the processes of modernity. Within the setting of a foreign prison in a non-white nation with predominately white female inmates, the historical association of torture and rape woven through the processes of settler colonialism (women's captivity narratives) and the Atlantic slave system (both the abuse of Black women, the Black rapist brute, and the white slavery scare of the early twentieth century) were turned on their head for 1970s exploitation cinema.[212] The violence of slavery is deployed through role reversal, allowing the very set of gendered and sexual power relations marking settler colonialism and the Atlantic slave system—including the incessant fear of white women being raped by men of color—to operate as the corrupting driving force for the film. Rather than using slavery as a means to understand contemporary oppressions, the system's coercion merely acted as a theater set for the objectification of an attractive, multicultural cast performing in a space filled with the mechanisms of violence associated with slavery, further enhancing the spectacle of role reversals, gratuitous nudity, violence, and torture/rape.

Women-in-prison films set within jungle-like prison plantations twisted the use of racial slavery as the white female members of the cast assume yet another role reversal when juxtaposed with their Black counterparts: they are presented as slaves within a plantation setting, an ahistorical impossibility adding to the films' spectacular nature.[213] The resurrection of plantation imagery is a striking element. In films ranging from *Big Doll House* to *The Big Bird Cage*, work regimes include harvesting rice, cutting sugarcane, and working sugar trapiches. They also highlight the wardens' and overseers' perverse fascination over the control of imprisoned and enslaved bodies, with many women forced to trade their sexual submission for lighter duties, while replicating the historical framework defining the master-slave dialectic for Black women.[214] Torture devices are sexualized, with fire, steam, and poisonous snakes encompassing various punishments. Finally, whips or batons are frequently used in mobilizing prisoners within chain gang settings.

Alongside the slave plantation-prison motif in these films, the background of the jungle stirred anxieties long defining its space as the antithesis of civilization and the target for taming via imperialism and resource extraction—as well as reminding audiences of the ongoing war in Vietnam. Associated with the jungles of sub-Saharan Africa or Southeast Asia, in many ways these films revived the 1920s and 1930s imperialist jungle film genre (with its conjoining notions of Africa and savagery), providing titillating spectacle of nudity and violence to the consumers occupying the movie genre's primary audience space: Midwestern drive-in theaters in the United States catering to a mostly white audience.[215]

The jungle films of the first third of the century and the exploitation films shot in the Philippines share a patchwork of intergenerational, historical projections.[216] First, during the early part of the twentieth century, U.S. imperialism—ranging from the conquest and occupation of the Philippines to the cultural-economic ties with nations such as Liberia—helped create a U.S.-derived fantasy of the "white man's burden" disseminated through literature, films, and photography.[217] During this era, the jungle film genre worked in tandem with the plantation film genre in representing Blackness on the big screen. Although differentiating the plantation genre from the jungle film genre of the 1930s, Cedric Robinson suggests that the two types "collaborated in general and differed in particulars."[218] Robinson continues, "The jungle film fashioned the present and the quite distant past into a racial pageant. The plantation genre policed the civic body and domestic labor; the jungle film patrolled the frontier."[219] In short, the two models provided viewers with dominant controlling images of Blackness at the height of Jim Crow. Coming of age in the aftermath of these multilayered tropes—raised on *Tarzan the Ape Man* (1932) and *King Kong* (1933)—filmmakers built on these ideas, updating the exotic sexual tension with the contemporary circumstances of the 1970s. The women-in-prison genre, then, deftly tapped into the libidinal energies and historical projections encompassing the desires mapped throughout the twentieth century's fascination with the gendered and sexual civilization-savagery binary and transnational whiteness.[220] Through the combination of ticket sales and low budgets, the Philippines provided an ideal location to produce films based around the exploitation of young, mostly white women and a lurid jungle setting with "exotic" peoples—a sort of *Playboy* magazine photo shoot twisted through the imperialist visions of a Rudyard Kipling tale and the demented fantasies of dominating women through the techniques and practices of slavery and patriarchy.

The physical relocation of filmmaking to the Philippines offered a material analogy to the economic shifts occurring in American business expansion overseas during the 1960s and 1970s. At the same time, the depictions of women in these films represented key manifestations of the culture war—and shaped the cultural contours of the ascending logics of neoliberalism. As the nation entered an identity crisis related to the Vietnam War, civil rights–Black Power, and second-wave feminism, the culture war found raw material for selling antiestablishment political rhetoric as the emerging reality of social equality between men and women unfolded in the 1970s.

Liberation Gauntlets and Mainstream Masculinity

There is an admitted absurdity in using low-budget exploitation films to explain the culture of neoliberalism. However, the cultural and economic context of 1970s exploitation films represent an exaggerated comment on, and reaction to, the particular moment in which they were created: the film production followed the trends of multinational corporations, outsourcing their production to unregulated nations with cheap labor, while its aesthetic content conjured the ghosts of cultural and economic processes from the past in an attempt to tap into the desires and anxieties of the present. In short, exploitation films offer cultural-economic signposts marking the historical conjuncture of neoliberalism's ascension to dominance in the 1970s and 1980s.

In their ability to provoke sensibilities, exploitation films represented a balancing act between "radically divergent potentials for pleasure and fantasy" and their depictions of liberation.[221] These products catered to the thirst for the taboo, the violent, the sexual—all elements weaving through the polarizing nature of the culture war. Although Richard Meyers's thoughts above about exploitation films are unsettling, there is a sad truth to his words: the suffering of others, especially those defined against one's identity, all too often provides meaning or an outlet for frustration—most grotesquely illustrated in early-twentieth-century lynching photos, or the staged Abu Ghraib prisoner photos during the Iraq occupation in the early 2000s. As Baldwin astutely noted, it's difficult for those who have obtained power through subjugation and oppression to suddenly relinquish this unequal relationship that comprises the very basis for one's identity: "They cannot because they have always existed in relation to a force which they have had to subdue. This subjugation is the key to their identity and the triumph and justification of their history, and it is also on this continued subjugation that their material well-being depends."[222] As the portrayal of violence and sexuality found deregulation amid the end of legislated white male supremacy, an anxious audience thirsting for catharsis appeared as they negotiated the onset of social equality with those who were formerly contained and seen as dependent on men. This juggling of titillating and violent subject matter based on deep historical antagonisms made exploitation films a perfect match for the new ratings system, helping to create a more efficient marketing device catering to increasingly segmented popular markets. Mainstream Hollywood quickly took notice. If women's independence found expression through the liberation gauntlet of exploitation films, mainstream cinema found an inversion to this via the rise of a more explicit masculine violence portrayed in the action film genre.[223]

White men have always dominated mainstream Hollywood, as Krämer noted, with male-centric films being the norm up through the 1970s.[224]

Against the backdrop of the deregulated mores of Hollywood, many male-centered action films in the late 1960s and 1970s depicted male protagonists *administering* the liberation gauntlet to women who, apparently, were no longer "ladies." The result unleashed misogynist contempt toward the social justice challenge against patriarchal legal constraints and social norms. For many conservatives and liberals, this offense against "tradition" and its romanticized "patriarchy" demanded contestation. And much like the way the welfare state found itself imagined as unfairly benefiting people of color, the culture war against women associated the undermining of patriarchy with a political challenge toward men, family (code for patriarchy), and of course, Western civilization.

Just like Wayne's *McQ*, culture war films wove "law and order" into narratives focused on the breakdown of urban spaces in conjunction with the rise of the civil rights movement and Black Power.[225] One aspect drew on the newly established "rights of criminals," particularly *Miranda v. Arizona* (1966). For many Americans criticizing boisterous social justice movements, marchers were no different than street criminals, and thus felt that the authorities were "coddling" protesters and criminals. These were the impulses driving Wayne's frustration with American society, as he, along with those identifying with the "silent majority," felt like they—white men—were losing the country they previously held a legislatively-sanctioned monopoly on before 1964.

As a pivotal anchor in the Southern strategy of Nixon, this reframing of the civil rights debate replaced the legacy of white nationalist ideas, policies, and material outcomes with a veneer of innocence: law and order implied equal protection under the law if you adhered to the law. As a truism, law and order also implied that there was never unequal discrimination in the criminal justice system—past or present—or at least not as much as Wayne's liberal "do-gooders" suggested. Indeed, "all men were created equal." This possession of history cast the innocent light of Manifest Destiny on those holding the line against social justice. In cinema, this law and order sentiment justified the cinematic unleashing of Wayne-inspired white masculine retribution against the "bad guys" hiding behind the liberal protections of the welfare state. With the rise of deregulated trends in Hollywood, these frustrations grew to embrace elements of the liberation gauntlet, including titillating nude and sexual scenes highlighting the permissiveness of the post-1960s counterculture.

In the early years of legislated social equality, these intersections of "law and order" and misogyny came together as themes in mainstream films, becoming a balm for an increasingly impotent white masculinity no longer legally able to generate their identity through the subjugation of others. Films such as *Coogan's Bluff* (1968), *Joe* (1970), *Dirty Harry* (1971), *The French Con-*

nection (1971), *Death Wish* (1974), as well as an array of Black action films tapped into the contemporary anxieties orbiting discussions of "law and order" and masculine (white) control.[226] To represent power, directors melded the application of explicit violence—guns, raping, hand-to-hand struggles, explosions, and car chases—in neat alignment with sexual analogies: phallic power, domination of women, bodily contact, orgasms, and courtship. The thrill of these action films—the inversion of the liberation gauntlet—traced an imagined ideal for sullen men newly equalized with women (especially those facing the loss of skilled labor jobs as multinational corporations relocated production overseas). The result: desperate caricatures of individual heroism based off an earlier era of confidence and power—what Tom Engelhardt calls victory culture.[227] Although these distressed images of lonely brooding men arose from the confident symbolism of Wayne riding the tide of "victory culture," within the context of legislated social equality these feats of masculinity could only unfold through the guise of the antihero. The antihero appeared as a populist-conservative avatar for the culture war's antipathy toward an interfering bureaucratic government overly regulating the character's ability to save society. Clint Eastwood's Dirty Harry personified this archetype:

> *District Attorney:* Where the hell does it say you've got a right to kick down doors, torture suspects, deny medical attention and legal counsel. Where have you been? Does *Escobedo* ring a bell? *Miranda*? I mean, you must have heard of the Fourth Amendment. What I'm saying is, that man had rights.
> *Harry Callahan:* Well, I'm all broken up about that man's rights.

Molly Haskell calls this reaction the "virility cult," a response to a range of social disruptions to a white male–dominated nation. The "virility cult," explains Haskell, was composed of men who worried "far more about assuring the world and one another of their masculinity than John Wayne ever felt called upon to do."[228] Wayne's career peak, of course, was during the height of the Jim Crow welfare state, when patriarchal white nationalism was the "American way of life."

Coogan's Bluff and *Joe* represent two early examples exhibiting the embrace of the new realism to help reconstitute white masculinity through the inversion of the liberation gauntlet. Both films offered responses to Black Power, the sexual revolution of the counterculture, and independent women. In particular, the white male counterculture became a target, with both films framing the movement as depraved, drug-addled, and effeminate (men wearing sandals and having long hair). As a crucial marker of the culture war, the counterculture challenged the Cold War patriarchal nuclear family structure with its embrace of alternative living situations (i.e., communal living). The protagonists in each film search for their respective fugitives within these counterculture circles: *Coogan's Bluff*'s white male Arizona deputy (Clint Eastwood) going after a criminal hiding away in New York City; in *Joe*, an angry white working-class man (Peter Boyle) aids a white upper-middle-class man's (Dennis Patrick) search for his daughter—an updating of the captivity narrative (e.g., Wayne's *The Searchers* [1956]).[229] Both films exploit an encounter with the "free love," sexual revolution aspect of the counterculture as an Odyssey-like waypoint on their journey. The protagonists in each film engage in sexual intercourse with young women, allowing audience members critical of 1960s sexuality to engage vicariously in an elicit fantasy involving casual sex and participation in the sexual revolution they despise. With sin, however, comes repentance: in both films, these sexual encounters quickly turn violent, as the protagonists attack the women they just had sexual intercourse with in order to obtain information for the protagonist's search. Acts of classic misogyny—slaps, violent grabbing, cold interrogation—reinstills proper social order. Unlike exploitation films, however, the gauntlet these women traverse fails to provide liberation.

A viewer sympathetic to the conservative culture war might interpret the episode as a corrective disciplinary device aimed toward punishing the "loose" women of the counterculture: "If you want to be treated like a lady, you need to act like a lady." Haskell notes the logic of these moments in the early 1970s: "When women were 'liberated' on the screen—that is, exposed and made to be sexually responsive to the males in the vicinity—it was in order to comply with male fantasies or . . . to confirm men's worst fears."[230] Older men conquering younger women underscores the hypervirility of the individual protagonist while simultaneously reinforcing the patriarchal notion of men controlling women's bodies as the aftermath of sexual intercourse turns to a violent interrogation. Though suggesting hypervirility, Christopher Lasch suggests something else is at work: "As male supremacy becomes ideologically untenable, incapable of justifying itself as protection, men assert their domination more directly, in fantasies and occasionally in acts of raw violence."[231] Thus, the "rape-in-reverse" performance helps the viewer to understand the encounter as consensual—a romantic seduction even—between an older male protagonist and his younger female opposite. Once sexually satisfied, however, the protagonist engages in physical and psychological violence to extract the information he requires: a combination of power and lust connected to the so-called sexual revolution, with patriarchal anger triggered by the need for control—to gain information as well as punishing the women for sexually misbehaving. This desperate act for Hollywood's leading men pointed to the existential crisis confronting American masculinity in the 1970s.

These acts pose a critical question for men at the dawn of liberation: could social equality with women really mean relinquishing control over their bodies? As the inheritor of Wayne's symbolic presence as the personification of the American settler, Clint Eastwood embodied the model for treating liberated women in the 1970s. Eastwood's character in *The Enforcer* (1976)—the third film of the Dirty Harry series—inhabits a film that punishes his "affirmative action" partner, white female detective Kate Moore (Tyne Daly), for an intrusion into an all-male world of policing. Unlike other partners from the Dirty Harry film series who get hurt but not killed in their lesson on who is "fit" to be a cop in San Francisco (mirroring culture war resentment, the first two partners in the series were Chicano and African American men), Detective Moore is brutally gunned down *saving* Harry Callahan from an ambush attack.[232] The lesson here is that the stakes were too high for social equality—especially artificially applied through a political bureaucracy— as these performances underline the dangers of women, despite bravery, transgressing the older boundaries of American patriarchy so thoroughly unsettled by second-wave feminism. In *High Plains Drifter* (1973), directed by and starring Eastwood, the film's protagonist (Eastwood) teaches a lesson to a woman who deliberately bumps into him (to highlight her impulse to infidelity) by raping her within minutes of entering town.[233] The frontier, it appeared, continued to be too violent for women, as films renewed the patriarchal pledge of security for women over social equality. As Wayne told his love interest in *Red River*, it's "too much for a woman."[234]

This virility cult masqueraded as therapy for those uneasy about social equality, a new baseline narrative for men's behavior in the post–civil rights, post–Vietnam War world. As neoliberal policies coalesced with the culture wars, the liberation gauntlet operated as a visual narrative, an emotional-libidinal mechanism outlining the constraints in depicting how independent, liberated women challenged patriarchy. As Pateman outlines this disciplining secured a post-1960s cultural pact or contract, where one may enter the arena of (public) masculine conflict if one is prepared to pay the ultimate cost of entering the space: sexual objectification and/or violence.[235] For emerging neoliberalism, this disciplining in popular culture helped frame what exactly women could expect from women's liberation: either a place within the system acceptable to an anxious male status quo or exile from the "protections" of patriarchal capitalism and into a realm of social equality defined through explicit sexual violence and humiliation in the name of post-1960s sexual freedom.

The relationship of feminism to the early 1970s culture wars was a *longue durée* extension of the series of debates and policies shaping the national identities and hierarchies since the foundation of the colonies in the seventeenth century. As John Adams wrote to Abigail Adams bemoaning the advancement of liberty beyond white men of property (and politely denying Abigail's request to "Remember the ladies, and be more generous and favorable to them than your ancestors"), "We have been told that our struggle has loosened the bands of government everywhere; that children and apprentices were disobedient; that schools and colleges were grown turbulent; that Indians slighted their guardians, and negroes grew insolent to their masters."[236] In short, freedom extended beyond white men with property removed the very core defining both "order" and an American identity rooted in a hierarchy of white male supremacy. It is this array of patriarchal essence cultivated through the Atlantic slave system and settler colonialism that informed the militia-like "virility cult" patrolling and policing the liberation gauntlet as it converged with the 1970s conjuncture: overseas outsourcing, the wider trend of U.S. business mergers (including Hollywood studios), the emasculation of working-class men losing their factory jobs, and the rise of neoliberal economic policies. These intersectional views of the products created within the context of the rapid expansion of multinational capitalism in relation to music, films, and television is the cultural shadow accompanying the ideas and policies of neoliberalism.

Chapter 7

Does Militancy No Longer Mean Guns at High Noon?

Feminist Dialogues, the Corporate Woman, and the Dawn of Neoliberalism

So, this concept analysis report concludes, "The American people want somebody to articulate their rage for them." I've been telling you people since I took this job six months ago that I want angry shows. I don't want conventional programming on this network. I want counterculture, I want anti-establishment. I don't want to play butch boss with you people, but when I took over this department, it had the worst programming record in television history. This network hasn't one show in the top twenty. This network is an industry joke, and we'd better start putting together one winner for next September. I want a show developed based on the activities of a terrorist group, "Joseph Stalin and His Merry Band of Bolsheviks," I want ideas from you people. This is what you're paid for. And by the way, the next time I send an audience research report around, you'd all better read it, or I'll sack the fucking lot of you. Is that clear?

—Diana Christensen, *Network* (1976)

Oh, now we're getting at it. I lose a promotion because of some idiot prejudice, the boys in the club are threatened, and you're so intimidated by any woman that won't sit at the back of the bus. You understand zilch. . . . I'll tell you what I'm talking about: I'm no girl, I'm a woman. You hear me? I'm not your wife, or your mother, or even your mistress. I am your employee. And as such I expect to be treated equally, with a little dignity and a little respect.

—Violet Newstead, *9 to 5* (1980)

We will continue to fight, not against the flesh and blood, but of the system that names itself falsely. For we have stood on the promises far too long now, that we can all be equal, under the cover of a social democracy. Where the rich get richer, and the poor just wait on their dreams.

—Honey, *Born in Flames* (1983)

By the mid-1970s, a significant number of Americans felt the effects of global capitalism's structural adjustment away from postwar regulatory system. Under the weight of the Nixon administration's Watergate corruption, corporate mergers and downsizing, unemployment, inflation, and an oil crisis, the imagined serenity of the early 1960s—when "no people in the modern history of the world had had it so good"—now felt like a very distant past, pressing many Americans to long for its simplicity and economic growth.[1] Markets for nostalgia flooded the nation's entertainment outlets, including rock 'n' roll's return to the simple authenticity of country music with releases from Bob Dylan, the Band, and the Byrds in the late 1960s, or films set before 1964 like *American Graffiti* (1973) and *Grease* (1978) or television's *Happy Days* (1974–84).[2] Radio of the 1970s also had hits reminiscing about a less complicated, more *innocent* era, particularly the work of Bob Seger in songs such as "Old Time Rock & Roll" or "Night Moves":

> I woke last night to the sound of thunder
> How far off I sat and wondered
> Started humming a song from 1962
> Ain't it funny how the night moves
> When you just don't seem to have as much to lose
> Strange how the night moves
> With autumn closing in[3]

Winter quickly overtook autumn by the mid-1970s, however, as the first light of the 1980s appeared on the horizon. In its black-and-white televised form, the James Baldwin and William F. Buckley Jr. debate about the American dream in 1965 appeared as if it occurred more than a generation earlier. Pressed into austerity, Americans angrily sought answers for a "way of life" disintegrating in their hands like wet sand as they desperately failed to comprehend the history around them—their good jobs dissolved from the momentum of multinational restructuring and outsourcing, the concentration of capital drew available resources away from more decentralized locations and an economy based on information and service rather than production ascended confidently to the tune of *growth*. The increasingly deregulated, laissez-faire system left many Americans treading water in the economic decay floating in the wake of what came to be called globalization.

In the early 1970s, screenwriter Paddy Chayefsky set out to tap into the anger and discontent of Americans weathering the onset of winter's avalanche of economic anxiety and the jarring experience of legislated social equality. The final product was *Network* (1976), a film earning Chayefsky an Academy Award for his screenplay, as well as Best Actor (Peter Finch), Best Actress (Faye Dunaway), and Best Supporting Actress (Beatrice Straight). Considered a classic, the movie was also nominated for Best Director, Best Picture, Best Film Editing, and Best Cinematography. *Network* follows a set of characters working at a fictional television network (UBS) with historically poor ratings. Desperate for higher ratings, they capitalize on the unhinged tirades of an older news host, Howard Beale, who, after being told he was to be fired, melts down on live television and begins asserting honest truths about the nation, the news media, and life in general. The ratings soar. The main characters act quickly to capitalize on the instability of Beale and its translation into company profits. *Network* concludes with a chaotic crescendo of low ratings, broken careers, and an assassinated anchorman. As a case study, *Network* ties together the rapidly changing economic landscape of multinational conglomerates and the complex layers of post-1960s frustrations, including the collision between a faltering masculinity and the rise of the independent corporate woman.

Multinational conglomerate trends of the postwar period cast a deep shadow across *Network*: the viewer learns that UBS was recently acquired by the fictional Communications Corporation of America (CCA), and to compound the sense of capital concentration and the new era of globalization, there is news that CCA was about to be bought by an even larger Saudi Arabian conglomerate. This narrative element sought to link the early 1970s oil crisis with the larger contours of a nation struggling to regain its masculine composure after the previous decade's setbacks. Rooted in traditional populist suspicion toward non-white foreigners, the shock of Saudi Arabia owning an American news network shapes the context for Beale's populist cry calling for America to wake up.[4] In one of his unhinged prophetic sermons, Beale, now stripped of the veneer of nightly news respectability, bluntly states to the camera:

> I don't have to tell you things are bad. Everybody knows things are bad. It's a depression. Everybody's out of work or scared of losing their job. The dollar buys a nickel's worth, banks are going bust, shopkeepers keep a gun under the counter. Punks are running wild in the street and there's nobody anywhere who seems to know what to do, and there's no end to it. We know the air is unfit to breathe and our food is unfit to eat, and we sit watching our TVs while some local newscaster tells us that today we had fifteen homicides and sixty-three violent crimes, as if that's the way it's supposed to be. We know things are bad—worse than bad. They're crazy. It's like everything everywhere is going crazy, so we don't go out anymore. We sit in the house, and slowly the world we are living in is getting smaller, and all we say is, "Please, at least leave us alone in our living rooms. Let me have my toaster and my TV and my steel-belted radials and I won't say anything. Just leave us alone." Well, I'm not gonna leave you alone. I want you to get mad! I don't want you to protest. I don't want you to riot—I don't want you to write to your congressman because I wouldn't know what to tell you to write. I don't know what to do about

the depression and the inflation and the Russians and the crime in the street. All I know is that first you've got to get mad. You've got to say, "I'm a HUMAN BEING, God damn it! My life has VALUE!" So I want you to get up now. I want all of you to get up out of your chairs. I want you to get up right now and go to the window. Open it, and stick your head out, and yell, "I'M AS MAD AS HELL, AND I'M NOT GOING TO TAKE THIS ANYMORE!"[5]

Beale's rant against the doldrums of the 1970s touched on the suffocating omnipresence of a perceived loss of control over one's life and country—and the apparent crumbling of "the will of the people." Unlike the ambiguous populist insurgency rippling through Kevin Phillips's *The Emerging Republican Majority* (1969) or the populist conservatism of Wayne, however, the blunt earnestness of Beale's populism embraced the critique of concentrated, monopoly capital—long ignored by conservatives, neoliberals, and New Deal Democrats—as the television host mixed assessments condemning corporate greed with cynical American institutions weighed down by the bureaucracy and elitism of the liberal welfare state.[6] Alongside Beale's rant, the film caricaturized social justice movements, encouraging the idea that social justice was merely a cynical political ploy for power and prestige. By the mid-1970s, the vestiges of 1960s radicalism appeared much like other American institutions: opportunistic and delving into desperate political terrorism—a theme driving the third Dirty Harry film, *The Enforcer* (1976). Much like the flexible viewership of the liberation gauntlet, both conservatives and liberals could sympathize with Beale's populist rant.

Although less obvious, the liberation gauntlet also haunted *Network*. This was particularly true for the character of Diana Christensen (played by Faye Dunaway), the young television executive whose passion for ratings transcends morality and manages Beale's rise to populist prophet. Christensen represented the dawn of the corporate woman in the 1970s—the material outcome of social equality legislation leading to a trickle of women executives into the ranks of corporate America. Although there were women executives before the 1970s, the decade of second-wave feminism shed more light on businesswomen and their struggles. As the movie opens, the camera circles around a table where executives work through the scheduling of the evening news. Seven executives sit at the desk, six white men and one white woman. Surrounding their busy bantering is a cast of administrative assistants, mostly represented by women—both white and Black. Even though the assistants dress in reserved business attire, they still appear traditionally feminine, including at least shoulder-length hair. It is interesting to note that the lone woman executive at the table with the six men wears a more masculine business suit and has very short hair (especially when compared to the assistants in the background). In portraying a realistic multicultural corporate workspace, the tentative inclusion of women into management demands female leadership to be coded masculine (as masculine is the universal).[7]

Empowered as an executive, Christensen's character represents an updating of one of the original liberation gauntlets in Hollywood: *film noir*'s femme fatale.[8] According to Jans B. Wager, the femme fatale "fights against male economic and social domination, usually at the cost of her life or her freedom. She is murdered, tortured, jailed, or at the very least contained by marriage in the final reel of the film."[9] Building off this older model, post-1960s corporate women characters also represented extreme forms of masculinity—from the first woman executive represented in *Network* to the cold, calculating, and rational Christensen—to make up for their sexual difference in a male-dominated environment. Dunaway's connection to this archetype included her recent femme fatale role in *Chinatown* (1974). In her review of *Network*, film critic Pauline Kael pointed out this updated version of the femme fatale: "The trick in *Network* . . . is to use a woman's drive toward fame or success as the embodiment of the sickness in the society."[10] In short, old wine, new bottles.

The consequence of the corporate woman's drive for success mimicked the Faustian bargain of *film noir*: women's success foreclosed romantic, loving relationships, and a family—the underlying promises of patriarchy—in return for success in business. Of course, the broad cross-section of represented businessmen do not face these predicaments, unless they use their masculine agency to cheat on their spouses. The lesson is that there was a price to be paid for women attempting to leave the private sphere and enter the masculine world of corporate America in the early years of legislated social equality. Self-aware of her "condition" in the film, Christensen explains her life to her lover through the language of psychoanalysis:

> I was married for four years, and pretended to be happy; and I had six years of analysis, and pretended to be sane. My husband ran off with his boyfriend, and I had an affair with my analyst, who told me I was the worst lay he'd ever had. I can't tell you how many men have told me what a lousy lay I am. I apparently have a masculine temperament. I arouse quickly, consummate prematurely, and can't wait to get my clothes back on and get out of that bedroom. I seem to be inept at everything except my work. I'm goddamn good at my work and so I confine myself to that. All I want out of life is a 30 share and a 20 rating.[11]

Unfolding like a conservative culture war talking point, Christensen fulfilled the anxious fears of those who saw feminism and liberated women as destroying families in pursuit of an activity that *appeared* to thwart biological norms. At the same time, reform appeared in Network as well: there were other women executives as background characters, mostly white, despite the primary agents in the film being white males. Moreover, although other male characters in Network displayed these self-destructive, amoral characteristics dismissing morality in the name of profit, there was a wider representation of white male characters that also embodied the antithesis of this nature (let alone the broader postwar public image of the corporate man). And true to the character's *film noir*'s femme fatale quality, Christensen has an affair with the protagonist, Max Schumacher (played by William Holden, veteran of the classic *film noir Sunset Boulevard* [1950]), the voice of reason who also falls from grace as he becomes obsessed with Christensen and leaves his wife of twenty-five years. As a quintessential 1970s film, the conclusion sees most of the characters sink into ruin—with Howard Beale assassinated on live television by a radical underground left-wing terrorist group modeled off the Symbionese Liberation Army (SLA).

While Christensen represented the empowered white woman in the corporate world in Network, Laureen Hobbs (played by Marlene Warfield) represented the radical Black woman modeled after the popular image of Angela Y. Davis.[12] As a member of the Communist Party, Hobbs is situated as an opportunistic radical who makes a deal with Christensen to produce a show called *The Mao Tse-Tung Hour* for UBS. The network will pay Hobbs for weekly features of the exploits of an extremist underground left-wing group: the Ecumenical Liberation Army (ELA). Despised by the disciplined Communist Hobbs, the ELA is led by the Great Ahmet Khan (played by Arthur Burghardt), a caricature of the hypermasculine Black radical modeled off the leader of the real SLA, General Field Marshal Cinque (Donald David DeFreeze). Anticipating the omnipresence of filmed spectacular deeds in the twenty-first century, the terrorist group film their exploits—robbing banks, for example—and proceed to sell them through Hobbs to UBS. The crimes are political and economic (robbing a bank), but true to the arising information economy, the filmed adventures of the ELA provide more revenue and publicity for their cause than the actual theft. As their taped product is sold to UBS for broadcast and enters into syndication, American viewers are allowed to vicariously live out the exploits of a political terrorist group in an age of crumbling austerity and a sense of powerlessness. In short, the final product represents another form of populist agency—or insurgency. Radicalism of the 1960s, it appeared, had succumbed to cynical commercial spectacle by the mid-1970s: radical chic as reality television, with Hobbs representing the alternative corporate woman selling revolution to an angry audience.

As Beale's rage increasingly targets the multinational merger scheme, executives of UBS decide to silence Beale's criticism by paying the ELA to assassinate Beale on live television. In an added layer of 1970s cynicism, Hobbs mirrors Christensen as she sells out her revolutionary soul to a conglomerate-owned network paying her and the Communist Party for radical content. Through the Black radical caricature of Hobbs, the challenge against the ongoing institutional racism untouched by 1960s civil rights legislation is now sidelined. Caught in the maelstrom of cynical corporate machinations, *The Mao Tse-Tung Hour* pressed Hobbs into the role of corporate executive, including a monologue similar in nature to Christensen's speech in the epigraph: "Don't fuck with my distribution costs! I'm making a lousy two-fifteen per segment and I'm already deficiting twenty-five grand a week with Metro! I'm paying William Morris 10 percent off the top, and I'm giving this turkey ten thou per segment, and another five to this fruitcake! And Helen, don't start no shit about a piece again! I'm paying Metro twenty-thousand for all foreign and Canadian distribution, and that's after recoupment! The Communist Party's not gonna see a nickel of this goddamn show until we go into syndication!" Under the avalanche of bureaucratic accounting, social justice succumbed to bickering over capital flows and percentage points derived from selling revolution. For the future market-driven world of neoliberalism, this "generalized practice of 'economizing' spheres and activities heretofore governed by other tables of value"—or the economizing of the social and political sphere—pressed radicalism into a game of market shares.[13] *Network* personified the way popular media both blunted the protest against ongoing racial-economic oppression and tapped into the frustrated desires of mainstream Americans who connected with Beale's color-blind populist critique.[14]

Whether it is in the white world of corporate America or the smoldering afterlife of 1960s New Left–Black Power radicalism, women executive characters offered a focal point of critique aiding in the reform of patriarchal organizations which started opening doors to women and people of color during the first decade of social equality legislation in the 1970s. Through caricature and long-rooted binaries imagining women as weak, dependent, and irrational, corporate women faced inclusion through a new archetype that, while ostensibly inclusive, problematized women's capacity to compete in spaces defined and controlled by men. Both Christensen and Hobbs reflected this trend. Near the end of *Network*, Max Schumacher summarizes the wake of damage Christensen has left:

It's too late, Diana. There's nothing left in you that I can live with. You're one of Howard's humanoids. If I stay with you, I'll be destroyed. Like Howard Beale was destroyed. Like Laureen Hobbs was destroyed. Like everything you and the institution of television touch is destroyed. You're television incarnate, Diana: indifferent to suffering; insensitive to joy. All of life is reduced to the common rubble of banality. War, murder, death are all the same to you as bottles of beer. And the daily business of life is a corrupt comedy. You even shatter the sensations of time and space into split seconds and instant replays. You're madness, Diana. Virulent madness. And everything you touch dies with you. But not me. Not as long as I can feel pleasure, and pain . . . and love.

For the viewer, corporate women like Christensen seemed to embody the worst instincts of a consumer-driven media selling revolution and pain for profit. Old white men like Schumacher, who came of age during an earlier, pre–civil rights era, appeared as a helpless herald narrating the nation's downfall. His wisdom, of course, represents the sober insight of the golden age of the Jim Crow welfare state—a hallmark of 1970s and 1980s films comparing the pre-1960s to the post-1960s United States.

Capitalism's adjustment to legislated social equality during the rise of neoliberalism incorporated the gains of women and people of color by deploying its own gauntlet stressing the deeply entrenched notions suggesting women were irrational and were unable to lead because of their "nature." Films like *Network* underscored the catastrophic outcome when these so-called natural qualities were unleashed in the public sphere of the corporate world. The gauntlet erected what appeared to be a catch-22 in the new bargain of assimilation into the masculine corporate world. For example, although male leadership might evoke a stoic, dictatorial style of governance tied to rugged individualism and the cold calculation of profit, women engaging in this behavior discovered themselves to be trapped in the gender binary: although needing to lead through strength and assertiveness to qualify for entrance into the corporate world, these attributes reflected different qualities in women than in men. Thus, women leaders were deemed heartless, with a string of gendered epithets defining their leadership style. As Schumacher asserted above, Christensen was "indifferent to suffering; insensitive to joy. . . . War, murder, death are all the same to you as bottles of beer." Even though this was typical behavior for any successful businessman in the corporate world, for women, this presented an impossible dilemma weighing down their ability to be accepted in the business world. Worse, the downfall of civilization could be blamed on women acting like men. At the same time, the drive of second-wave feminism collided with corporate reform, shattering the language of systemic critique in the name of procuring opportunity amid an increasingly austere economy characterized by the onset of neoliberal policies.

Moving from the spectacle of exploitation films as a prism for understanding the initial reaction to second-wave feminism, this chapter examines the economic integration of women into the workplace at the end of the first decade of legislated social equality. In particular, two main contours of feminism are examined: the mainstream liberal, corporate-friendly *9 to 5* (1980) and the Black feminist institutional critique of *Born in Flames* (1983).[15] A key concern for this chapter revolves around the way feminist discourse intersected with the adjusting economy, and how neoliberalism benefited from the reforms of a corporate version of feminism and multiculturalism while the radicalism of the Black feminist critique of American society found itself marginalized due to its systemic analysis of the intersections of race, gender, sexuality, and class. For women entering the corporate world, one needed to adhere to masculine corporate norms established by white men, who historically tolerated—indeed, often celebrated—decades of discrimination and sexual harassment until the legal challenges of the 1960s. Thus, women seeking the corporate route to success had to adhere to what essentially was/is a modified liberation gauntlet: women must engage with only market-oriented aspects of corporate life, leaving existing biases or sexual harassment to the traditional conspiracy of silence.

The reform of capitalism reflected an adjustment within the corporate world for the entrance of women into its executive sphere, rather than consigning them to secretaries and assistants.[16] Gender stereotyping operated as a critical obstacle, an ongoing sticking point for women up through the 1980s and 1990s (and beyond) as more and more women entered corporate management.[17] For exploitation films, the assimilation of women into action films bound independence to gratuitous nudity and violence, resuscitating the raw anchoring elements of patriarchy related to the framing of the new corporate woman of the 1970s. Social equality within the corporate world, then, confronted a similar backlash, though the reaction grew subtler as the 1970s turned into the 1980s.[18] During this conjuncture, an array of women did seek common cause across race to confront the intersectional oppression buttressing the system's maintenance.[19] At the same time, popular culture, in most cases, utilized elements of feminism most beneficial to the overall system's ability to create consensus and stability: a white, mainstream feminism deemed universal. In *Network*, Christensen's presence—along with the other women characters in the background—was seamlessly integrated into the corporate structure. However, setting Christensen up as a primary pillar of social corruption during the first decade of social equality between men and women operated as a disciplinary warning. Inclusion was possible but only on the terms of the masculine organization. And success would always come with a cost. Adriana Cavarero describes this dynamic: "When it becomes advantageous for the market, women are admitted to it, at opportune moments, at fixed times and in specific sectors. They are admitted, homologized to the male paradigm and subjected to the established conditions of productivity at all costs, merciless competition and will to power. This homologizing paradigm constrains women to become uniform with the male subject by erasing female sexual difference to such an extent that female sexual difference, even at its most biological level, comes to be regarded as an obstacle to homologization."[20]

For women in the corporate world, there would be no suggestion of ongoing discrimination nor a critique of the white masculine nature of the corporation—color blindness and gender neutrality marked the new unspoken economic culture of neoliberalism. The so-called unbiased rhetoric of *quantitative analysis*—strict adherence to efficiency, profitability, and trackable data—replaced the Keynesian era's notion of fairness and justness tied overtly to white male domination.[21] In effect, this reform embraced moderate demands from feminists and people of color for assimilation into the American capitalist dream and exorcized the more radical elements of feminism and Black Power from the frame of debate now centered on *equality of opportunity* rather than rectifying decades of systemic oppression and *exclusion from opportunity*. In short, reform, not revolution. By the end of the 1970s, this dilemma played out in feminist tracts seeking to reconcile the aftermath of the feminist–Black Power–New Left social movements.[22] From this viewpoint, second-wave feminism's critique of patriarchal capitalism dissolved into cordoned-off sections of class, race, and sexuality, with each position arguing for different forms of inclusion or structural critique.

The business world in the 1970s also coalesced around its own forms of solidarity against the welfare state via an assortment of lobbyists, think tanks, and structural adjustment austerity policies in an effort to carve a path out of the welfare state experiment and into the new frontier of neoliberalism. As if a movie script, the fragmentation of social justice movements formed an antithesis to the (upper-)class consolidation of American business. In 1979, *Business Week* noted this aggressive business counterattack, stating, corporations were "being forced to become a political animal as well as an economic machine."[23] The politics now, however, favored the abstract rhetoric of assessing candidates through ostensibly color-blind or gender-neutral measurements of merit, or William Davies's quantitative analysis, with opportunity still able to be patrolled by long-entrenched white male gatekeeping traditions—now innocently denied—in the corridors of legislated social equality.[24] To find opportunity, people of color and women entering this world of obscured intersectional antagonisms were encouraged to model their behaviors on the new corporate culture. With the systemic language of social justice removed, old patterns adjusted to new realities, as some women were able to move higher than others, often depending on the set of positionalities one inherited.

Just as white men found it difficult to recognize their unfair and unconstitutional advantages in the United States, for Black women struggling against both Black and white patriarchy, white feminism represented a similar case of unacknowledged privilege.[25] Alongside racism and a lack of racial critique of patriarchy, white feminism often utilized the metaphors of Black suffering and enslavement to describe the position of (white) women in patriarchy.[26] Viewed through a prism of universality—and thus invisible—the privilege of whiteness sometimes obscured white feminists' ability to see the circumstances faced by women of color. Audre Lorde noted this in 1980: "Some problems we share as women, some we do not. You fear your children will grow up to join the patriarchy and testify against you, we fear our children will be dragged from a car and shot down in the street, and you will turn your backs upon the reasons they are dying."[27] A paradox for Black women surfaced in the face of a predominantly white women's liberation, which, consciously and unconsciously, projected white second-wave feminism as universal.

The difficulty in recognizing difference within the second-wave feminist movement resulted in a simmering tension between white women and women of color. As the civil rights movement exemplified the model of activism for women's liberation (and other social movements), the slave-master dialectic provided an essential metaphor for explaining oppression. Indeed, this metaphor is arguably the urtext of American identity, inaugurated at the founding of the nation: the American founding fathers used slavery to both denote the unfair treatment by England *and* exclude enslaved persons from the freedoms and liberties of the Constitution.[28] The source of rhetoric for radical change grasped the language of suffering experienced by people of African descent caught in the processes of modernity. An example of these summoned metaphors in the 1970s includes the blunt usage by John Lennon and Yoko Ono in their "Woman Is the N****r of the World" from *Sometime in New York City* (1972) and Patti Smith and Lenny Kaye's "Rock N Roll N****r" from their album *Easter* (1978)—with Smith's lyrics underscoring the system's paradox: "Outside of society, that's where I *want* to be" (emphasis added).[29] These symbols of degraded Black bondage mobilized a rhetorical device for white feminism to challenge the same white male authority fueling anti-Blackness. Repeating mistakes from women suffragists in the nineteenth century, the white middle-class experience underpinned the identity of feminism while simultaneously appropriating the experience of anti-Blackness buttressing the hierarchical status of white women in American society.[30]

Popular Media and Second-Wave Feminism in Black and White

> We who are Black are at an extraordinary point of choice within our lives. To refuse to participate in the shaping of our future is to give it up. Do not be misled into passivity either by false security (they don't mean me) or by despair (there's nothing we can do). Each of us must find our work and do it. Militancy no longer means guns at high noon, if it ever did. It means actively working for change, sometimes in the absence of any surety that change is coming. It means doing the unromantic and tedious work necessary to forge meaningful coalitions, and it means recognizing which coalitions are possible and which coalitions are not.
>
> —Audre Lorde, "Learning from the 60s" (1982)

Popular culture depictions of feminism found its largest expression in U.S. mass media through working- and middle-class whiteness, appearing in television programs like *The Mary Tyler Moore Show* (1970–77), *Maude* (1972–78), *Alice* (1976–85), and *One Day at a Time* (1975–84), as well as films such as *Stand Up and Be Counted* (1972), *Alice Doesn't Live Here Anymore* (1974), *The Stepford Wives* (1975), and *An Unmarried Woman* (1978).[31] Included in this list of films and television are popular songs such as Helen Reddy's "I Am Woman," which reached number one on the Billboard charts in December 1972 after being popularized in the film *Stand Up and Be Counted*. In the latter hit song, Reddy deploys metaphors of oppression and resistance.

> I am woman, hear me roar
> In numbers too big to ignore
> And I know too much to go back an' pretend
> 'Cause I've heard it all before
> And I've been down there on the floor
> No one's ever gonna keep me down again
>
> Oh yes, I am wise
> But it's wisdom born of pain
> Yes, I've paid the price
> But look how much I gained[32]

Pointing toward the "conviction in my soul," this anthem's tone and avoidance of pointing out the source of oppression—white patriarchy—gives the song a reformist thematic quality intersecting with the goal of social equality for mainstream feminism.³³ This positive pronouncement of empowerment implied that men's patriarchal privileges constructed a network of "floors" and "pain" that women had to pay a "price" to "gain." In short, Reddy outlines a liberation gauntlet.

Another more radical feminist expression on LP came in the independent release, *Mountain Moving Day*, by two bands formed into a collective, the New Haven and Chicago Women's Liberation Rock Band.³⁴ Both groups started in 1969, organized by white women activist musicians and nonmusicians in the Chicago Women's Liberation Union and members of New Haven Women's Liberation who were either tired of the male dominance in most bands or simply wanted to create music within an all-women environment.³⁵ In the accompanying collectively written liner notes to the album, the artists outlined their approach to playing rock 'n' roll without the baggage of "insulting lyrics, battering-ram style and contempt for the audience."³⁶ Citing "Under My Thumb" (the Rolling Stones) and "It's a Man's Man's Man's World" (James Brown) as examples of the celebration of women's degradation, the authors note, "We had to think of some other way to make a hit besides bumping and grinding like Mick Jagger, raping and burning our guitars like Jimi Hendrix, or whacking off on stage like Jim Morrison."³⁷ Seeking a "radical, feminist, humanitarian vision," the bands assert that they were "the 'agit-rock' arm of our respective women's movements."³⁸ In a song charting the travails of women working in an office environment, the lyrics of "Secretary" announce: "Men's eyes / Fantasize / Memorizing thighs and getting off on you," with the band asserting, "Sister, I believe you when you say you hate."³⁹ Other songs include "Ain't Gonna Marry" and "Abortion Song" in which—a year before *Roe v. Wade* (1973)—the band framed the issue around control of their bodies while providing the historical background of the practice:

> We're talkin' about abortion it's as old as time
> Hidden in fear and pain
> The witches began it, they were burned at the stake
> For helping sisters break their chains
> Next came the butchers with their bloodstained hands
> We've lost too many sisters that way
> Now you go to the doctors and ask them to help
> They say come back another day⁴⁰

As the examples of both Helen Reddy and the New Haven and Chicago Women's Liberation Rock Band suggest, the white women's perspective signaled strength through the numbers of white women who could potentially become a powerful bloc. The New Haven and Chicago Women's Liberation Rock Band added a more systemic critique targeting the patriarchy of marriage, the sexist corporate life of an office, and the politicization of women's control of their bodies. In addition, both metaphors associated women's oppression with New World slavery. Reddy summoned the image of women occupying the lowest rung of society—"I've been down there on the floor"—while the New Haven and Chicago Women's Liberation Rock Band cite burnings, the breaking of "chains," and the coercive history of the white male medical profession's misuse of power. As forms of patriarchal violence, these practices were also connected to the history of Black men and women in the United States ranging from sexual violence to lynching to actual bondage to early medical experiments on slaves, with many of these antagonisms—from the Tuskegee syphilis experiment to the sterilization of women of color—continuing through the 1970s, and becoming one of the core issues of Black feminism.[41]

Mainstream feminism's deployment of the slave-master dialectic as a route toward escaping the authoritarianism of patriarchy finds kinship with another set of universals related to the European Enlightenment: Michel-Rolph Trouillot's "North Atlantic universals," the set of Eurocentric ideals believed to be universal as well but weighted down by a projection of European experience deemed universal.[42] For mainstream feminism, the result of this use of images offered an outlining of violence assumed to be universal for all women though failing to account for the protections afforded by whiteness. These blind spots underscore the historical relevance of Black feminism's concept of "intersectionality," the theoretical framework for understanding the ways various forms of power and antagonisms strike at different positionalities (e.g., race, gender, sexuality, class) in different ways.[43] An intersectional reading of the blind spots of white feminism operates in a similar fashion as the way "modern political thought" models the "male subject"—coded white—as the universal.[44] As Cavarero noted above, this model allows two paradigms to exist for women's entrance into previously all-white male spheres: exclusion or "a homologizing, assimilating inclusion" where women are included through the model of men.[45] With women's difference from men silenced, men's experience continues to be imagined as universal. Meanwhile, the cultural legacies assigned to women—based on their binary with men—continue *manning* the rudder.[46] Accordingly, the early expressions of feminism through the prism of white women, although a critique of male normative aspects of agency, retained a white normative framework exemplifying an early form of neoliberal color blindness. Moreover, a stress on women's unity helped police the inherent divisions along lines of race, class, and sexuality. As Benita Roth has noted, second-wave feminism had always been "organizationally distinct from one another ... along racial/ethnic lines."[47] These feminist universals found expression in exploitation films that generally cast a majority of white women as lead actresses (according to Midwest drive-in marketing demographics). Consequently, the slave metaphor proffered by white feminists emphasized the aspect of gender as the most important qualifier for women's oppression while neglecting the intersectional complexities that white feminists in day-to-day experience could elude out of privilege and, often, legal protection from the state.

The outcome of focusing solely on gender and deploying metaphors culled from the civil rights movement in the 1950s and 1960s resulted in a stultifying movement bound to elicit criticism and distrust from women of color.[48] Paula Giddings notes that white women's comparison of their situation with Blacks created resentment as it utilized the oppression of anti-Blackness for a cause of a purely gendered critique of oppression.[49] Mainstream white feminism's neglect of the particular situation faced by Black women—the "double jeopardy" of being Black and female—made the demands of social equality meaningless: why would Black women demand to be as powerless and reviled in American society as their Black men?[50] This alienation of Black women also grew out of the organizational structure of the women's liberation movement, as its often gender-specific critiques of oppression too often elided systemic examinations of the intersections of race, class, or sexuality.[51] Although there did exist some coalition building, the mainstream media's commodification of feminist imagery as white further narrowed the movement's diversity.[52]

The 1960s conservative culture war against the civil rights movement easily assimilated the women's movement into an antagonistic foe, defining feminism as anti-male and anti-family against the imagined and naturalized setting of postwar domesticity.[53] Significantly, this color-blind conservative attack on feminism pursued its own intersectional logic, attracting anti-feminist allies among men of color (who waded through the same masculine language as white men). In the face of these barriers, a weakness of second-wave feminism was its failure to bring all women together through an ideology or program addressing the diverse ways women encountered forms of oppression. Black feminist critics like Audre Lorde presciently noted that without an intersectional critique of patriarchy, "only the most narrow perimeters of change are possible and allowable."[54]

Caught in a one-dimensional or single-axis analysis of patriarchy using gender as the only position, the complexities of the past weighed heavily on second wave feminism. Within the *longue durée*, the slave-master dialectic as a symbolic baseline of gendered oppression reinforced the articulation of Black subjecthood as existing outside the civic body. In a similar way older ethnic groups adopted anti-Black attitudes to obtain a white identity—most notably the Irish in the nineteenth century—this mobilization of imagery for women's liberation offered a foundation to legitimize an ostensibly color-blind feminism.[55] In effect, this rhetorical strategy demanded an end to treating (white) women like Black people, effectively abandoning Black women in the transaction.[56] For (white) women, gaining access to power at the dawn of social equality and neoliberalism often demanded adhering to this unfolding political-economic dictate of color blindness blended with a gender neutrality absent of radical, systemic critique.[57] Entry might be possible, but the terms of entry still were contingent on the institutional norms shaped across decades of the Jim Crow welfare state (let alone centuries before).

By the end of the 1970s, the momentum of Black Power and women's liberation had begun to take shape more as a marketable nostalgic entity rather than embodying a threat to the system. Christensen and Hobbs from *Network* operated as a clarion call for this shift—the recognition that the seasons had changed, with radical analysis increasingly viewed as a naively romantic view of a world where white baby boomers now entered the workforce and were required to swim through the increasingly austere post-1960s economy. It was time to stop complaining, adopt color blindness and gender neutrality, and embrace the merit-driven mantra of an American capitalist evolving toward neoliberalism. For women, slow gains trickled toward the more reformist, mainstream goals of mainstream feminism: incremental access to job opportunities and political power. Although more visible in the late 1970s, the business community had already begun taking some tentative steps in addressing its white male dominance.[58]

Commenting on the integration of people of color and women in the corporate workplace in 1969, *Business Week* described some of the growing trends taking place in corporations regarding the inclusion of "Negroes and women."[59] Although suggesting it was "no longer true of Negroes"— civil rights legislation, ostensibly, had eliminated centuries of cultural and economic marginalization—the barriers excluding entry into corporate positions for women remained: "A Business Week survey of women in business found that, except for a few oases of female acceptability, American industry produces almost as few top women executives as it did four years ago—or 10 years ago."[60] The magazine also cited employers who dismissed "Women's Lib as irrelevant claiming that they employ more women in higher positions— and take greater care to pay them equally with men—than they did five years ago."[61] Employers cited the Equal Employment Opportunities Act of 1964 as reason for these changes and dryly noted that they would hire women according to their qualification—an early pronouncement of gender neutrality and neoliberalism's emphasis on quantitative analysis.[62] None of these announcements by corporate America ever mentioned the decades of affirmative action for white men who might not have been qualified but could more easily enter the corporate world because the labor pool was narrowed down to white, male, and college educated. The possession of history, as always, secured innocence. *Business Week*'s own institutional sexism surfaced two years later in the title of an article on the dearth of applicants for secretary positions in corporations around the nation: "Secretaries Play Hard to Get."[63] In 1972, the magazine noted the shifts Wall Street had made toward women as consumers and investors, as women began making gains working on "Wall Street where males have long dominated the scene and discounted women's financial prowess."[64]

The flirtation with women as legitimate businesspeople evolved from "playing hard to get" to a bit more respectable dialogue in the frequent column titled "Corporate Woman"—first appearing in November 1975. The inaugural column reported, "The Corporate Woman: Up the ladder, finally."[65] By 1976, "top 100" lists of corporate women appeared, as well as articles on the gender neutrality of stress, career couple conflicts, and challenges such as "how men adjust to a female boss"—arguably a key element in masculinity's existential crisis in the 1970s.[66] However, the fervor and rhetorical promise of equality from 1969 to hire women appeared to dampen, indeed reverse, in the middle of the decade, underlined by a 1976 headline: "A Double Standard for Women Managers' Pay."[67]

The combination of economic austerity in the 1970s, alongside the affirmative action programs aiding white women and the Black middle class into higher positions of power, reset the mainstream feminist agenda to sights aimed primarily toward obtaining equality with men—rather than the radical revolutionary idea of overthrowing the entire hierarchical system. The retreat from the intersectional critiques of power informing the more progressive feminist groups in the 1970s further solidified divisions between women unable to enter the corporate world and those who now attained some level of access. Significantly, those making gains in the corporate world provided counterexamples for those suggesting that the system was inherently unfair. The quest for equality with white men, moreover, reformed the tools of patriarchy—situating the neoliberal emphasis on quantitative analysis measuring individual success and merit as progressive reform (control over the rubric governing success and merit, of course, would be crucial in defining who was successful and who would be rewarded). Black feminist author Audre Lorde presciently noted this in the early 1980s, writing:

> Today, with the defeat of ERA [Equal Rights Amendment], the tightening economy, and increased conservatism, it is easier once again for

white women to believe the dangerous fantasy that if you are good
enough, pretty enough, sweet enough, quiet enough, teach the children
to behave, hate the right people, and marry the right men, then you will
be allowed to co-exist with patriarchy in relative peace, at least until a
man needs your job or the neighborhood rapist happens along. And true,
unless one lives and loves in the trenches it is difficult to remember that
the war against dehumanization is ceaseless. . . . But Black women and
our children know the fabric of our lives is stitched with violence and
with hatred, that there is no rest. We do not deal with it only on the
picket lines, or in dark midnight alleys, or in the places where we dare to
verbalize our resistance. For us, increasingly, violence weaves through
the daily tissues of our living—in the supermarket, in the classroom, in
the elevator, in the clinic and the schoolyard, from the plumber, the
baker, the saleswoman, the bus driver, the bank teller, the waitress who
does not serve us.[68]

This mainstream perspective of white feminism regenerated the patriarchal ideology of "liberal individualism" derived from the Enlightenment—one of the baseline assumptions guiding Trouillot's "North Atlantic universals."[69] In some ways, this sense of hierarchy arose both out of the early 1970s arguments about diversity within second-wave feminism and the incorporation of the ideal of equal opportunity—rather than systemic critique—guiding the activism of white middle-class woman. As bell hooks explains, the inability of white women and Black men (caught within a masculine vision of race) to see the interconnections between race, class, gender, and sexuality resulted in a feminism viewed strictly through gender and a Black liberation viewed strictly through race, resulting in movements defining "liberation as gaining social equality with ruling-class white men."[70] Obtaining a position did not necessarily alter the institution, rather, activism on behalf of social equality with white men actually strengthened the institutions, illustrating how the gendered, sexual, and racial reforms of the neoliberal era placed a progressive veil on capitalism while blunting the radical critique.

Pressed through multiple levels of oppression, the tendency of social justice movements struggling against complicated structures too often anchored their unity through an easily identifiable category or target—including recognizable binaries like male-female, oppressor-oppressed, rich-poor. The single unifying category more easily consolidates a solidarity against the binary opposite the movement attempts to question or dismantle. However, the hierarchical pluralism of U.S. society has always channeled agency through sets of complicated positionalities such as race, gender, sexuality, and class. These often conflicting positionalities historically operated as silver bullets hamstringing mass social justice activism through the *longue durée* intersectional weight of the settler colonial, slavery, Jim Crow, and patriarchal nexus. After World War II, these legacies, buttressed by Cold War anti-communism and white federal intervention, helped slay the "greatest age of equality in the United States" across the 1930s and 1970s, as intersectional differences became obstacles for solidarity at the precise moment conservatives, the corporate-finance community, and neoliberals found unity in their attack upon the liberal welfare state.[71]

The containment of social justice critiques demands a firm possession of history. As noted earlier, the pages of *Business Week* were filled with examples across the 1970s, as women's liberation, civil rights groups, environmentalists, and unions were grouped together as scapegoats, creating a readily identifiable target that various shifting industries could unify around during the economic instability of the period. As capital resides within both industry *and* its primary projection of ideals, advertisements, and imaginations, the ability to frame the public debate makes it easier to contain (though not always) aspects of racial, gendered, or class critiques derived from social justice movements.[72] Moreover, even those radical messages making their way into mainstream expression are themselves commodified as caricatures *to be sold*. Viewers literally see this process of co-optation in *Network*.

The consequence of this is the notion that mainstream guises of second-wave feminism—as Nancy Fraser has pointed out—served as a cultural benefactor to neoliberalism.[73] Feminism's critique of the postwar Keynesian state-led economy (and Black Power's critique as well) challenged the notion of the citizen as a male breadwinner, the unequal economic distribution between sexes, as well as other deeply embedded structures of subordination.[74] Between the early 1970s and the 1980s, however, the structural assessment of patriarchy in mainstream discourse slipped from questions of redistribution of wealth and power (the reformist aspect of the welfare state) to the recognition of difference, an idea dissolving feminism into an identity politics easily coexisting within the expanding fragmented consumerism defining neoliberal individualism. Moreover, as women and people of color demanded equality, the rhetoric of an inclusive workplace found root (labeled multiculturalism or cultural diversity after the 1980s), allowing capitalism to rebrand itself through the color-blind and gender-neutral quantitative analysis logic of "merit" as a slow trickle of non-white males gained acceptance into corporate America after the 1970s.[75] These reforms, in turn, constructed a new neoliberal set of divisions rooted in wealth inequality—especially racial wealth inequality.[76] Of course, women of color continued to shoulder most of the burden of inequality through the twenty-first century.[77]

With the structural critique sidelined, feminist difference could strengthen capitalism by cloaking the system as a politically progressive response to 1960s social movements—as the pages of *Business Week* noted about the strenuous efforts of corporations to recruit women. At the same time, the new consciousness of neoliberalism recognized the value of women's labor in a previously male-dominated workplace, especially the radical pay differentials between male and female secretaries (family wage logic) as well as the cheap unskilled labor overseas and within the United States.[78] Nonetheless, the result consisted of a broader labor pool pressing wages down: the deregulation of the Jim Crow welfare state translated into increased profits by incorporating a previously excluded, and institutionally devalued, workforce.

"They Just Use Your Mind, and They Never Give You Credit"

> It is not only the story of women's oppression, it is the story of sexism, racism, bigotry, nationalism, false religion and the blasphemy of the state-controlled church, the story of environmental poisoning and nuclear warfare. Of the powerful over the powerless, for the sake of sick and depraved manipulations that abuse and corner the human soul like a rat in a cage. It is all of our responsibilities as individuals and together to examine and to re-examine everything, leaving no stones unturned. Every word that we utter, every action and every thought. We are all, women and men, the prophets of this new age. And for those of us who would be safer in the sensibilities of racism, separatism and martyrdom: if you can't help us towards building this living church, then step out of the way. The scope and capabilities of human love are as wide and encompassing as this vast universe that we all swirl in.
>
> —Isabel, *Born in Flames* (1983)

In her essay on second-wave feminism and neoliberalism, Nancy Fraser makes what she considers a "disturbing" observation about the evolution of the women's movement: "The diffusion of cultural attitudes born out of the second wave has been part and parcel of another social transformation, unanticipated and unintended by feminist activists—a transformation in the social organization of postwar capitalism.... The cultural changes jump-started by the second wave, salutary in themselves, have served to legitimate a structural transformation of capitalist society that runs directly counter to feminist visions of a just society."[79]

As the second wave analyzed the culture of exclusion and demanded the "recognition of identity and difference," critiques over political economy and its unequal distribution of wealth outlined by radical feminists and social justice movements in the 1960s and early 1970s dissolved into a renegotiated acceptance of American capitalism.⁸⁰ With capitalism turning away from white male (and family wage) working- and middle-class redistribution logics characterizing the Jim Crow welfare state and reorienting government and business toward an ostensibly quantitative analysis (color blind and gender neutral) approach to economics, the very welfare state facilitating phenomenal economic growth and the "Great Compression" increasingly found itself characterized as governmental overreach.⁸¹ *Network* captured this evolution away from the radical political economic critique to pro-business reform through the juxtaposition of the comic absurdity of Hobbs's cynical radical caricature and the aggressive actions of the visibly empowered—though heartless—Christensen navigating her way through white male corporate culture. The film underscores the seemingly obsolete nature of social justice movements and illustrates how neoliberalism could recuperate the feminist and Black Power ideas of identity and difference to strengthen its cultural center of gravity as the Jim Crow welfare state and the energy of 1960s radicalism were swept into dustbin of history.

Two films from the early 1980s explore this dialogue between a radical feminist approach—from socialist feminism to Black feminism—and the more corporate-friendly, mainstream feminism. The first film, the hit comedy *9 to 5* (1980) directed by Colin Higgins, represents a triumph of neoliberal multinational corporate feminism and multiculturalism. The movie depicts three white women office workers struggling for social equality within a capitalist framework. Here, office reform centers on understanding difference as well as a quantitative approach to merit-derived advancement free of sexism, with the film's conclusion underlining how eliminating sexual harassment and male chauvinism leads to satisfied and productive workers.⁸² The second film, *Born in Flames* (1983) directed by Lizzie Borden, offers a counterargument about feminism and empowered women. As an independent science fiction film, *Born in Flames* underlines the importance of Black feminism in outlining the intersections of gender, race, class, and sexuality as American neoliberalism unfolded. *Born in Flames*'s alternative present brought together a conglomeration of feminisms that took to task the contemporary reforms taking shape under neoliberalism so readily on display in films such as *9 to 5*.

The successful Hollywood production of *9 to 5* embodied feminist reform in popular culture, released when "for many, 'feminism' had already turned into a dirty word."⁸³ The film emerged a few years after the so-called return of women to Hollywood films in the late 1970s, after a near-decade of "a long siege of male bonding films in which women were marginal."⁸⁴ The name of the film came from a women's labor group in Boston, Nine to Five, an organization that grew "out of Boston's socialist-feminist organization Bread and

Roses."[85] The original trailer to the movie presented a series of fast cut scenes of women typing, filing, making coffee, hearing the boss, hitting their legs on open desk drawers, and getting slapped on the behind—the corporate office liberation gauntlet. The voice-over asserts, "So long as he's [the boss] alive, from 9 to 5, they'll take it all they can. But what will go on, when the light finally dawns, that it's time to get back at that man"—a desk drawer opens showing a handgun.[86] From the perspective of the trailer, it appears *9 to 5* is more revolution than reform, more exploitation film than mainstream comedy. The actual film, however, only encourages the revolution toward the halfway point of reform.

The film grew out of celebrity feminist—and ultimate villain in the culture war—Jane Fonda's vision (she coproduced) of a movie about the "real experiences—and revenge fantasies—of women office workers."[87] Patricia Resnick and director Higgins scripted the film. The dominant message placed an emphasis on mainstream feminist expression, including the notion of "liberal or equity feminism" through an individualist framework of difference, while reinforcing acceptable feminism as a "white, middle-class, heterosexual" experience.[88] This neoliberal feminism provided viewers with an update of feminist ideas within the business world since the mid-1970s.[89] As a feminist film, *9 to 5* makes so-called good girls into assertive, "women-identified women" collaborating together, and mocking "the high drama of the lone male hero by setting it against the triumph of a female-centered community."[90]

The film's narrative involved a small revolt initiated in the office of the fictional Consolidated Companies, Inc. The instigators of the revolt were three white middle-class women in various states of marriage: the widowed Violet Newstead (played by Lily Tomlin), recently divorced Judy Bernly (played by Jane Fonda), and the happily married Doralee Rhodes (played by Dolly Parton). These latter categories legitimize the characters' ability to lead feminist reform as their positionality of whiteness, heterosexuality, and commitment to the institution of marriage (Judy's husband leaves her) elude the usual popular media caricatures of radical, anti-male women. The three women encounter different elements of discrimination at the company through the patriarchal and sexist persona of their boss, Franklin M. Hart Jr. (played by Dabney Coleman). At the beginning of the movie, Violet fails to get a promotion—Hart gives it to a man because he has a family, despite Violet being a widow with kids. Gaining access to positions above middle management thwarted Violet's merit (an echo of the headline of a *Business Week* article).[91] Bumbling through her tasks, Judy is the new office assistant, new to the work world after being a housewife (her husband left her for his secretary). She is constantly belittled. Doralee is the secretary to Hart and has to negotiate his insistent attempts at instigating an affair with her. In some ways, the film follows the revenge sequence offered by the exploitation films of the 1970s. In their attempts at acquiring a position in the corporate ladder, the women suffer setbacks that are constantly blamed on their "natural" inferiority to men.

Intersectional dynamics are at play, notably at the beginning when Violet is showing the new hire, Judy, around the office on the latter's first day. As Violet and Judy wait for one elevator, another opens and an African American office mail delivery person, Eddie Smith (played by Ray Vitte), exits, saying "hello" to Violet. After asking Violet about her expected promotion, Violet introduces Eddie to Judy, saying she was recently hired. "What?" exclaims Eddie. "Look, how am I ever going to get out of this mailroom prison if they keep hiring people from the outside?"[92] Consciously or unconsciously, the film denotes some of the conflicts surrounding the integration of women (white and Black) and Black men into corporate society in the 1970s, with the dialogue between Eddie and Violet underlining the gendered and racial contours of access to particular positions in the company. In the context of affirmative action in the 1970s, white women made markedly more progress than African Americans (women and men) throughout the decade, illustrated here with the dynamic between Violet, Eddie, and Judy—with Eddie's familiarity with the company not enough to gain a position over Judy's inexperience.[93]

As corporations operated through their leadership of predominantly white males socialized in twentieth-century white patriarchal norms, assimilation of women came slowly and cautiously.[94] As *9 to 5* depicts, it was easier for women to ascend in the corporate hierarchy as long as the space below them was filled with other women. Although Black women could gain from this arrangement, usually as an office assistant or secretary, Black men such as the character of Eddie might have a harder time gaining a foothold as his gender blocked his entry into the gender-coded "woman's" position as administrative assistant or secretary; his race and class foreclosed his entry into the predominantly white realm of corporate management. The producers of the film, however, did integrate women of color into the office, though they were relegated to extras or minor characters. The cosmetic inclusion and portrayal of an "integrated" office—much like *Network*—presented the film as realistic, favoring the framework of corporate multiculturalism. On the other hand, with Black women in corporate settings a rarity in 1970s and 1980s film, the movie establishes a new paradigm of possibilities in representation virtually absent from pre-1970s films. Thus, through the presence of women of color in *9 to 5*, the filmmaker's liberal social consciousness adheres to the white-led reformism associated with the corporate restructuring in the 1970s, as the model of flexibility included women—though often at a reduced set of pay despite civil rights legislation (as *Business Week* also noted).[95]

Targeting their male chauvinist boss, Hart, the subsequent flurry of reforms after the initial overthrow, in some ways, became a model of reform for the new corporate office environment of the post-1970s—"diversity management" in hiring was the future.[96] Legal frameworks also aided in this shift, as sexual harassment slowly became censured in the corporate world (reflecting yet another *Business Week* article).[97] The corporate structure is also given credit for *initiating* these reforms—in short, the corporation, as an organization, is deemed flexible enough to accommodate the needs of difference. Rhetorically, corporations embraced the individualist notions of mainstream feminism, where equality of opportunity into the capitalist system bypassed the radical roots of the critique of patriarchy. Thus, corporate reform in the wake of legislated social equality is presented as good business, providing viewers the sense that (1) not only is blatant sexism in the workplace wrong, but (2) if one creates a harassment-free workplace, then production—and thus profits—will rise. Finally, these reforms establish a sense of empowerment for employees that had come to be seen as a crisis in the 1950s and 1960s.[98] This embrace of a gender-neutral, anti-sexual harassment corporate environment—at least in rhetoric—allowed the silencing of the structural concerns of sexual violence, ongoing sexual harassment and discrimination, the inequalities of housing and education, or issues concerning women unable to gain higher management positions in the corporate world. Reform via corporate feminism, it seemed, eradicated sexism.

A quasi-revolution addressing these concerns is set in comedic motion in *9 to 5*, as the three women kidnap Hart, confine him to his house (they forcibly domesticate him), and begin implementing reforms over a period of six weeks. Doralee types up a memo to the office (forging Hart's signature), allowing plants and family pictures on desks, coffee cups, more individualistic expressions such as custom pen and pencil holders, and even permitting signs requesting "No Smoking." Violet then suggests they make even more "changes that really count." Here, we see many of the mainstream feminist goals unveiled. A montage showcases a series of memos laying out the changes:

EFFECTIVE IMMEDIATELY, EMPLOYEES WILL BE ... PAID EQUAL SALARIES FOR EQUAL JOB LEVELS; RE: DAY CARE CENTER.... A BREAKDOWN OF FEASIBILITY STUDIES DONE IN THE UNITED STATES AND EUROPE, INCLUDING ... THE U.S. GOVERNMENT'S ... COST EFFICIENCY ...: RE: PART-TIME WORK.... IT HAS COME TO MY ATTENTION THAT EMPLOYEES WOULD PREFER TO WORK ... SCHEDULE. ALL EMPLOYEES DESIRING ...

These reforms—equal salaries for equal jobs, the cost efficiency of day care centers, and flexible work hours and part-time work—also include the removal of a punch-in time clock. This is notable because removing the time clock detached administrative assistants from the working-class identity associated with the very use of the time clock: in some ways, the reform creates more hierarchy among workers (do those serving the administrative assistants at lower levels, like Eddie, continue to punch in?). Indeed, the humane reforms displayed in *9 to 5* proved productive for the company's bottom line, with the visiting chairman of the board hailing the reforms, though scoffing at the idea of equal pay. These reforms, although empowering to women in the corporate sector, also demanded the erasure of the critique of capitalist patriarchy forming an important part of radical feminism. As Jefferson Cowie observes, its inability to critique capitalist class relations makes *9 to 5* into a "modern Human Resources Department."[99] The deregulation of social relations through social equality legislation helped shape a more flexible hiring space for the corporate woman. The culture of neoliberalism wove together this material outcome of social justice movements with the adjusting needs of business and the emerging conservative-neoliberal economic philosophy. Recognition of difference—corporate women possessed a different set of needs and out-of-office responsibilities than corporate men—proved a critical equation for human resource departments now on the hunt for a more diverse workforce during the age of legislated social equality.

Director Lizzie Borden confronted these neoliberal corporate reforms through the fictional alternative present of *Born in Flames*.[100] Setting this film against the office reforms of *9 to 5* foregrounds the tensions between the different variants of second-wave feminism and their relationship to neoliberalism. By offering surface reforms for middle-class white-collar women at the expense of those hit hardest by the economic shifts of neoliberalism in the 1970s and 1980s—including working-class women, especially women of color—capitalism reformed its patriarchal image by opening opportunities for women, which further weakened already tenuous alliances with other women outside their class, race, or sexuality.[101] Following Milton Friedman's mantra of "capitalism and freedom," the new corporate woman sought women's empowerment through the marketplace. As *Business Week* pointed out in 1978, corporate women's groups had begun meeting as "old girl networks," with the leader of one group demanding a purely marketplace-centered group for women: "Members are not allowed to talk about their kids, their husbands, or their emotional crises.... We don't want people who are finding themselves or searching out new lifestyles. We are interested in people who can contribute to each other in the marketplace."[102] Denying the realities of women's lives—including their disproportionate role in caregiving for children *and* husbands—channeled the ostensibly gender-neutral logic of the marketplace into a normative masculine corporate framework: discussions of families and experiences with misogyny had no place in corporate culture, despite both issues being relevant to corporate women. Of course, men's experiences in family, or talk of sports or outdoor activities, were part and parcel to the corporate social life—it was positively labeled: male bonding.[103] In short, *Network*'s Diana Christensen, however much a caricature, signaled the model demanded for successful women in the corporate world.

If *9 to 5* suggests a revolt in the name of reform, then the politics of unrest in *Born in Flames* (1983) demanded revolution in the face of reforms. Born Linda Elizabeth Borden in 1958, at the age of eleven Borden told her parents that she wanted to change her name to the "accused murderess" Lizzie Borden—who in 1892 was tried for murdering her father and stepmother with an ax (later acquitted).[104] After graduating from Wellesley College, Borden relocated to New York City where she worked for artist Richard Serra as an editor and began to slowly produce *Born in Flames*. Work on the film started slowly in 1977 as a pseudo-documentary, science fiction vision of the United States ten years after the "social-democratic war of liberation"—an alternative present seen through the imagined victory of the 1960s New Left. Utilizing "disjunctive" collages of fast-paced edited scenes, the film primarily focuses on the collective and individual work of different feminist groups.[105] Ostensibly a critique of the limitations of the patriarchal New Left, the film also alludes to the contemporary situation facing women in the late 1970s and early 1980s.[106] The movie played sparsely in small art house theaters in New York City in the early 1980s and was criticized by *New York* magazine in November 1983: "This radical film could use more visual style and a little common sense. *What* socialist revolution? There isn't even a shred of plausibility to the film's premise."[107] Regardless, the strength of *Born in Flames* lies in its assessment of capitalist patriarchy and the critique of the neoliberal adjustments affecting women in the early 1980s—all under the guise of an alternative science fiction present viewed through the intersectional lens of Black feminism.

Rhetoric from various feminist groups weaves through the film's narrative. The resulting dialogue forms a conversation about reform and revolution, including the patriarchy associated with both socialism (in the science fictional sense of the film) and capitalism (in the actual present background of the film's production).[108] The primary protagonists are two pirate radio broadcasters. The first group is led by white punk rocker Isabel (played by Adele Bertei, an active member of the No Wave music scene), who runs a station called Radio Regazza and asserts cries of anarchy against the current regime. Another station, Phoenix Radio, is led by Honey (played by Honey), an African American woman representing an aspect of Black feminism.

Although not a member, Honey is sympathetic to a third group called the Women's Army. The Women's Army is a young activist/revolutionary group composed of a multiracial alliance of women—with a strong Black lesbian presence—that questions the so-called progress of the Social Democratic government with regard to women's rights. Led by African American Adelaid Norris (played by Jean Satterfield) and a white woman named Hillary Hurst (played by Hillary Hurst), the Women's Army is mentored by an older Black woman, Zella Wylie (played by pioneering Black feminist lawyer Flo Kennedy) who, as a former revolutionary, has now become an activist against the ruling government.[109] In the film, Norris travels to the western Sahara where she receives training from women guerrillas who are also struggling against patriarchy in the wake of their own revolution, signaling a connection between Muslim women and Black American women.[110] A fourth group is composed of three white women interns at the *Socialist Youth Review* newspaper—representing the bourgeois intellectual face of feminism. Finally, the Federal Bureau of Investigation (FBI)—represented by white men—is shown throughout the film discussing the workings of the Women's Army through a series of intelligence briefings and surveillance pictures. When Norris is arrested and found dead in prison, Radio Regazza and Phoenix Radio come together to create an alliance with the Women's Army, who, in turn, escalate their attack against the state.

Borden's production and film aesthetics embodied a significant example of coalition building for second-wave feminism.[111] In making the film, the director sought an explicitly collective effort, using real activists and incorporating their ideas into the movie. Kennedy's important role in the film as a mentor to young women evolved as the film progressed, including convincing Borden to create the martyred heroine character Adelaid Norris.[112] This level of collaboration, in part, was a reaction to Borden's experience seeing so much division among feminists in New York City in the late 1970s.[113] Significantly, *Born in Flames* reversed the "frequent invisibility of black women in white women's films and feminism" and addressed the heteronormativity of mainstream feminism.[114] For Borden, the primary rhetoric driving the film is anchored in the intersectional approaches of Black feminism espoused by groups such as the Combahee River Collective, one of the preeminent Black feminist organizations coming out of the 1970s and a particular leader in targeting heterosexism.[115] Borden also emphasized the strength of coalitions of difference versus small, unified fronts. In one telling scene, Flo Kennedy's character explains this tactic: "If you were the army, and the school, and the head of the health institutions, and the head of the government . . . and all of you had guns, which would you rather see come through the door: one lion, unified, or five hundred mice. My answer is five hundred mice can do a lot of damage and disruption."

Much of *Born in Flames* consists of juxtaposed scenes relaying the critiques of feminism, the mundane sexist practices in everyday life, and their translation through mass media. At times jarring for viewers, these rapid cuts nonetheless emphasize the differences in relationships of power between network programs aligned to the ruling party and mainstream feminism, and the more radical conversations occurring outside institutional frameworks. Borden's use of intersectionality involved a layered, dialogue-driven critique of patriarchy through discussions of sexism, racism, and homophobia in living rooms, interactions on the street, television talk shows, and news programs. The first dialogue is mainstream white feminism seeking equality with men and solidarity with the Social Democratic ruling party (the counterpart to the neoliberal feminism in *9 to 5*). The second is the more radical groups inspired by intersectional understandings of oppression and their assertions of hypocrisy toward the fictional social democratic government. A third set of power relations exist as well in the relationship between actions on the street and their translation through television. Much like the way *Network* criticizes the representational influence of television, Borden highlights the power of media in relaying legitimacy via the institutional networks of television, which by the 1970s was the major source of news for Americans.[116] Explaining this approach in an interview, Borden asserted, "It allowed me to show pieces of something happening so that we could believe this was not only how the world *was* but more important how it was being *interpreted*."[117]

One example of intersectional critiques of patriarchy in *Born in Flames* is a set of scenes beginning with a speech against inequality by radio host Honey. The host signs off with, "For we have stood on the promises far too long now, that we can all be equal, under the cover of a social democracy. Where the rich get richer, and the poor just wait on their dreams."[118] The immediate scene following this broadcast foregrounds the routine inequality underlined in Honey's speech as a young woman walks past a group of working-class men who, in turn, harass her. This clip is then followed by a news program outlining the celebratory festivities occurring in the city, including marches by unions, who are said to provide the "cornerstone of today's liberation"—a liberation put to question by the previous scene. Although feminists targeted corporations for their discriminatory practices, unions were also a target for their history of sexist and racist practices aimed toward protecting their white male skilled workers.[119] The next scene follows a Puerto Rican woman walking down the street, getting harassed by two men, and then shown fighting off the two men who attempt to sexually assault her. During the struggle, a group of women on bicycles (the Women's Army) ride toward the scene blowing whistles, making the assaulters scramble away in panic. Highlighting the media's power of framing, Borden then cuts to a television news report of the incident. Unable to address the oppression toward women, the white male anchor describes the Women's Army's actions through tropes of primitivism and violence. Characterizing the Women's Army as "well-organized bands of fifteen to twenty women on bicycles attacking men on the street," he suggests that men were assaulted, later adding that these claims were countered by accusations that the men were assaulting women. The hierarchy of recount tilts the balance of legitimate claims in favor of the first group claiming victimhood in the news story: the men were assaulted by the Women's Army, while instilling a sentiment of doubt in the "accusations" that these men were indeed assaulting women. Deemphasizing the violence against women, the Women's Army, instead, is criminalized as the newsman continues, "Officials have condemned the lawlessness of such vigilante groups, and ask for information leading to the arrest of the women involved." And then with a snarky smile he adds, "Maybe even their telephone numbers." At the end of these scene cuts—Honey's political speech, the harassment of women, the evening news celebration of the present, the depiction of a sexual assault, and the analysis of this assault by the news media—Borden links together a set of cultural codes meant to evoke the underlying relevance rape plays in patriarchal societies and the way the masculine corporate media normalizes or dismisses such actions.[120]

To address the rising militancy of the women, one of the FBI agents in a voice-over suggests putting some pressure on them in their jobs—in short, utilizing intersectionality to fragment the movement. This covert approach to neutralizing the threat of the Women's Army exasperates the wave of discontent already incipient to society. The scene following examines a riot by "angry young men" who perceived their situation as unfair within the "workfare"—instead of welfare—program of the social democracy. Feeling that they have been assigned "meaningless jobs," they accuse the program of favorable treatment toward women and people of color at the expense of white men. The next scene shows Norris being laid off from her construction job with no apparent reason, followed by a voice from the editors of the Socialist Youth Movement newspaper explaining the situation through the patriarchal party line:

> Many of the construction and steel workers laid off in the past few weeks have been the women. . . . The industries have been overburdened recently by the enormous number of minority workers who are applying to a limited number of jobs. Only a small percentage of this group can be

accommodated in these trades. The rest will receive alternative placement through the workfare program. We feel that women who immediately cry "sexism" are being selfish and irresponsible. Any move toward separatism, the demand for equal rights for one group alone, hurts our struggle for the equal advancement of all parts of society.[121]

Calling protesters of this structural inequality "selfish and irresponsible" highlighted the dominant category of male-privileged class. Indeed, this mirrored the gender-only critique of the mainstream feminist movement in the 1970s. Simultaneously, the remarks also highlighted the real concerns facing the blue-collar industries in the 1970s and 1980s that struggled to equitably include women and people of color after more than a century of exclusion, pitting blue-collar white males against women and people of color rather than the actual system allocating access to resources.[122] With the deregulation of the Jim Crow welfare state and its discriminatory laws against women and people of color, combined with the arrival of a large generation of baby boom workers, labor markets became overcrowded in the 1970s just as the economy entered recession and production transferred overseas.[123] A later newscast in the film discusses another wave of riots, this time by Black men protesting "racism in workfare," and—like the angry young white men—the newscaster asserts that "Blacks are given meaningless jobs that don't pay enough to support their families." Both of these broadcasts anchor the moral weight of the argument on the patriarchal, heteronormative family unit—that is, the family wage.[124] Thus, while the government promised to severely punish the rioters, they also address the systemic problems in relation to patriarchy, asserting, "In the future priority will be given to male heads of family."[125] In short, party-line solidarity rests on the concerns for issues most problematic to males, especially white and married males. The so-called gains of the revolution must be secured in light of continuing oppression of women.

Another example drawing out intersectional debates through the mundane includes Borden's links between mainstream issues brought up in *9 to 5* and broader issues addressed by Black feminism. One scene shows women putting up posters listing the political demands of the Women's Army in an attempt to highlight the reversal of state policies affecting women (both in the fictional and real sense):

Cutbacks in daycare centers
Ending of free abortions
Forced sterilization of minority women
Discrimination against single women lesbians in housing
Firing of single women in favor of families[126]

As another nexus attempting to facilitate dialogue between feminisms, this scene critiqued the decline in social spending tied to the austerity of actual neoliberal policies and the conservative culture war against women controlling their bodies. It is useful here to examine the similarities and differences between 9 to 5 and *Born in Flames*. For example, both speak in favor of day care for working mothers—an issue that made a brief appearance during World War II but had been espoused by the National Organization of Women since 1966.[127] Moreover, the oppression of corporate women provides a point of continuity between the two films. In one segment covering a General Secretarial Strike for office working women in *Born in Flames*, a white woman's response echoes the concerns of *9 to 5*: "Office wives, they expect a wife at home in the bedroom and a wife on the job. You're expected to make his coffee, get his lunch, do all these things for him that are not your responsibility on the job." However, whereas *9 to 5* addresses the treatment of women in the office, *Born in Flames* critiques the systemic attack on women beyond the narrow issues permeating white-collar professions. The coercive role of the state and its institutions is emphasized through the critique, as the list addresses issues of health care for poor women, from access to abortions to the forced sterilization of women of color. In short, Borden's intersectional breakdown established links between the mainstream issues of day care—which affected *all* blue- and white-collar working mothers—with matters influencing the lives, literally, of women of color, the poor, single women, and lesbians. *Born in Flames* suggests that these issues should be addressed as a systemic whole; to do otherwise is to compromise with moderate reform reinforcing the new hierarchies evolving through the first decade of legislated social equality.

The film concludes with a television commentary by a white male executive, representing both the television station and the conservative faction in the film (and the contemporary New Right). Borden's message from her alternative present mirrored that of contemporary reality of the pro-business policies taking shape under neoliberalism. In the commentator's outline of a way out of the situation facing the ruling party and the nation, it is interesting to note key terms expressed in the dialogue and their connection to New Right critiques of the welfare state in the late 1970s and 1980s, including the characterization of social spending in terms of economic inefficiencies (quantitative analysis) rather than in terms of providing a social net designed to blunt the adverse effects of capitalism (fairness and justness). Speaking into the camera, the newsman asserts:

> But have we gone too far? Is it time to ask if the politics and programs of yesterday's liberation have become the stagnation of today? We cannot ignore the monumental inflation with which we are burdened. Nor can

we condone the widespread abuse rampant in our social programs. At home, we are being trapped in bureaucracy and throughout the rest of the world our influence wanes. The management of this station fears that over-socialization has transformed our democracy into a welfare state. If we are to survive our ideals, we must carefully consider their implications. This, in the midst of our celebration, is the opinion...[128]

The broadcast abruptly stops—cutting to a scene of the twin towers of the World Trade Center, where an explosion destroys its broadcasting antenna. The first shot is fired in the feminist revolution against the socialist government. Its target is the representative core of capital and its networks dictating the flow of information and knowledge. Credits roll. At the dawn of neoliberalism, *Born in Flames* took to heart the French revolutionary Louis Antoine de Saint-Just's declaration: "Those who make revolution halfway only dig their own graves."

In the Name of the "Tyranny of the Status Quo": A "Half-of-a-Revolution"

> And true, sometimes it seems that anger alone keeps me alive; it burns with a bright and undiminished flame. Yet anger, like guilt, is an incomplete form of human knowledge. More useful than hatred, but still limited. Anger is useful to help clarify our differences, but in the long run, strength that is bred by anger alone is a blind force which cannot create the future. It can only demolish the past. Such strength does not focus upon what lies ahead, but upon what lies behind, upon what created it—hatred. And hatred is a deathwish for the hated, not a lifewish for anything else.
>
> —Audre Lorde, "Eye to Eye: Black Women, Hatred, and Anger" (1983)

"Anger is useful to help clarify our differences," notes Audre Lorde, echoing Howard Beale's call for people to become angry.[129] Lorde wrote about anger as clarifying difference but reminds the reader that this anger-driven clarification might also lead to blind destruction, a blundering brute strength making it impossible to construct a peaceful, post-oppression existence. For Beale, this anger, too, became a cul-de-sac of impotent rage at a world moving too fast. Too much power resided in the halls of capital-concentrating conglomerates, while a vaguely defined, exhausted, and apathetic civil society appeared too busy trying to survive. An unspoken specter haunting this quintessential fog of 1970s dreariness was the inability to escape the nation's history of antagonisms and the ideological detachment of democracy from economics. The populist element of Beale's comments portrays the flexibility of representation after the civil rights era: employment insecurities could be directed at mergers and downsizing or they could target people of color and women "taking" jobs historically reserved for white men. Meanwhile, rising crime rates demanded the quintessential color-blind coded phrase of the 1960s conservative mantra of "law and order," directed at both social justice movements *and* street crime. With historically marginalized people demanding social equality—and simultaneously coded as criminal—a righteous anger is stoked and justified. This anger, moreover, finds fuel from the inability to understand and effectively engage with the historical legacies that only recently—the Civil Rights Act of 1964—were deemed "wrong." With the United States tied together through the globalization of labor markets and capital investment, familiar scapegoats surfaced as a way to manage unrest to these changes as the seemingly endless complexities flooded an American society unprepared for a precipitous drop in the standard of living. Scapegoats offered a simple reassurance that the economic institutions becoming increasingly more powerful than government were not responsible for the turmoil; responsibility lay with groups of people one was raised to distrust or despise. For conservatives, this was a wise and successful political tactic leading to the simple, reassuring rhetoric of Ronald Reagan.

With the omnipresence of television by the 1960s and 1970s, consumer citizens found themselves held hostage in their living rooms by the flashing glow of television projecting this incessant escalation of history. As a "conversation in images, not words," however, the understanding of complex situations is drowned out by television's embrace of entertainment and simplicity, where "credibility" overshadows facts and "reality."[130] As television overtook print news in an age of anxiety, Neil Postman noted in 1985, the equation of fragmented images over words helped shape a new paradigm: "all political problems [had] fast solutions through simple measures—or ought to. Or that complex language is not to be trusted."[131] In this world of impatience and a thirst for explanation that ignored complexity, the discourse of television prophets like *Network*'s Beale anticipated an entire genre of televangelists, talk show hosts, and eventually, cable news commentators after the 1970s. Once the fairness doctrine was eliminated—or deregulated—in the 1980s, the world of radio opened to "sharper, more partisan hosts to dominate the airwaves" (reviving the memories of the 1930s conservative anti-Semitic radio host, Father Charles Coughlin).[132] Anger sold, giving one a sense of agency and control in a world that made one seem helpless. For men, angry conservatives rekindled the masculinity made impotent by social equality legislation. *Network*'s Diana Christiansen sensed this rage: "The American people want somebody to articulate their rage for them. . . . I want angry shows. . . . I want counterculture. I want anti-establishment." Historically, however, anger emanating from white men was normal and articulated the violently twisted meanings of civic duty tied to mob violence and vigilantism—the very definition of assertions of liberty and freedom in a world of settler colonialism and slavery. On the other hand, anger from a Black woman or man represented the antithesis of civilization, and further justification for white mob violence. Positionality defined who could be publicly angry at American society. How would *Network* be read and remembered if Laureen Hobbs of the Communist Party recited the lines of Beale? In some ways, Borden fulfilled this alternative history of righteous anger at a system and not scapegoats. As neoliberalism emerged, some images found more market value than others.

Although the consciousness of women changed between 1970 and 1983, with the latter year registering a third of women seeing "male chauvinism, discrimination, and sexual stereotypes ranked as their biggest problem," new openings into public life also meant a fragmenting of the women's movement.[133] Ruth Rosen notes, "As some middle-class women captured meaningful and well-paid work, ever more women slid into poverty and homelessness, which, on balance, the women's movement did too little, too late, to change."[134] Celebrating this arrival of women to the corporate world, *Business Week* offered the headline, "Women: The New Venture Capitalists."[135] A shuffling of hierarchies directly associated with the two major social movements of the 1960s most critical of American society took shape amid the onset of neoliberalism. On various levels, business culture—from *Business Week* to the entertainment industry—adapted to the representational presence of these movements by incorporating cosmetic change rather than addressing the more radical charges leveled at the Jim Crow welfare state. Capitalizing on deeply embedded patriarchy and anti-Black racism, old ideas occupied new contexts. With radicalism replaced by corporate-defined reform, "compensation for past injustice" for African Americans and women, as Michael Lind writes, was changed "to the promotion of 'diversity'" to include people of color, women, and the new immigration beginning after the 1965 immigration reform (much like civil rights legislation, immigration reform also embodied an early gesture toward deregulation before the onset of neoliberalism).[136] This neoliberal reform only tepidly attacked ongoing discrimination and harassment in predominantly white male workspaces, allowing these practices to continue under a cloud of power only recently becoming dispersed through the #MeToo movement—more than forty years after legislated social equality. For the LGBTQ community, there is still a long road to liberation, while admitting "Black Lives Matter" continues to be a struggle over the possession of history.

This narrowed frame of debate illuminates the political logic of the feminist struggle represented in *9 to 5*, as the actresses embodied various phases of white feminist expression: single ex-housewife, widowed middle management, working-class married woman. Equal access to the benefits of a system based on continued exploitation of those caught within the corporate hierarchy proved the decisive expression of feminism—until the so-called third wave of feminism in the 1990s arguably breathed some life into what was a solidly middle-class movement.[137] *Born in Flames* depicts the fantasy of taking the last step open for those falling outside the boundaries of whiteness or, however tentatively, connected to the networks of capitalism. The film tapped into Frantz Fanon's rush of liberation violence targeting oppressors represented in films such as *The Battle of Algiers* (1966) or *The Spook Who Sat by the Door* (1973).[138] The images eventually stop, however, and the viewer is forced to reconnect with the world outside the theater. For the neoliberal system, this was more than enough: revenge fantasies could safely remain contained within the profitable realm of fantasy. Sometimes, to the chagrin of conservatives, a "half-of-a-revolution" is what the system needs to regenerate itself and harness the energies of dissent to trudge past the "tyranny of the status quo" (in Friedman's words), creating yet another frontier of possibilities for those who can keep their heads above water long enough for winter to eventually change to spring.[139]

In the late 1960s and early 1970s, poets from the Black Power and Black arts movements recorded their observations of the era and identified what they recognized as the various post-civil rights political-economic developments. One poet, Jayne Cortez, brought a Black feminist perspective to the issues of gender, violence, and their globalized connections. In a poem from the early 1980s, Cortez noted:

> If the drum is a woman
> then understand your drum
> your drum is not docile
> your drum is not invisible
> your drum is not inferior to you
> your drum is a woman[140]

Striving for empathy and respect, Cortez's poetry outlined the contours of the interaction of Black men and women in the capitalist system, and how the anxieties, inequalities, and violence of everyday life stirred frustrated relationships between Black people.[141] "Recognizing the scars they share," Kimberly N. Brown adds, "Cortez appeals to rather than accuses black men [of abusing Black women] in order to include them in the dialogue."[142] Cortez continues:

I know the ugly disposition of underpaid clerks
they constantly menstruate through the eyes
I know bitterness embedded in flesh
the itching alone can drive you crazy
I know that this is America
and chickens are coming home to roost
on the MX missile[143]

The frustrations outlined in "If the Drum Is a Woman" were also translated into a defense against a defining aspect of the liberation gauntlet: sexual violence. In the poem "Rape" (a poem not recorded for her LP *There It Is*), Cortez describes two women rape victims from the 1970s—Inez Garcia and Joanne Little—and their resistance against sexual assault through the killing of their perpetrators.[144] Using these two cases to create a structural understanding of the act of rape, Cortez asks, what were they "supposed to do for // the man who declared war on her body"? Expanding the rape-as-war metaphor, Cortez compares the acts of Garcia and Little to "what a defense department will do in times of war." Against the declaration of war on women's bodies, Cortez asks, "Just what the fuck else were we supposed to do?"[145]

The poetry of the Black radical tradition offered another outlet for feminist resistance in U.S. popular culture across the 1970s. Coming out of the Black Power movement in the late 1960s, this poetry brought an uncompromising commentary to the rise of neoliberalism in the 1970s, bolstered by the *longue durée* critique of the Black radical tradition. Far from being extremists or exceptions in the history of people of African descent, Black Power advocates, according to Julius Lester (former field secretary of SNCC), were rather "the inheritors of a proud tradition of resistance to America and what it stands for."[146] The upheavals in the 1960s, what Baldwin called the "last slave uprising," stood as a resistant correlative to the Jim Crow welfare state structurally abetting Black inequality.[147] The intricate analysis developed within the diverse pockets of Black Power, however, evolved in the 1970s into a formidable critique of the postwar welfare state's successor.

Chapter 8

Who Will Survive in America?

The Black Radical Tradition and the Poetic Critique of Neoliberalism

> Parades
> what do we care for parades
> beggars boot lickers bugles
> motorcycle cops uniforms and
> civil servants
> I mean why should we slobber over a priest
> the benevolent society
> racketeers
> whiskey salesmen and
> the red cross
> What the fuck do we need with the
> corroded culture of colonialism
> Parades
>
> —Jayne Cortez, "Watching a Parade in Harlem 1970" (1971)

> Which brings me back to my convictions
> and being convicted for my beliefs
> 'cause I believe these smiles
> in three piece suits
> with gracious, liberal demeanor
> took our movement off the streets
> and took us to the cleaners.
> In other words, we let up the pressure
> and that was all part of their plan
> and every day we allow to slip through our fingers
> is playing right into their hands.
>
> —Gil Scott-Heron, "The New Deal" (1978)

Over a year before his untimely death in May 2011, sixty-year-old musician-poet Gil Scott-Heron released his anticipated comeback album, *I'm New Here: Gil Scott-Heron*, after a decade of struggle with substance abuse and bouts of incarceration.[1] The first official video for his 2010 release featured the song

"Me and the Devil Blues," with his spoken-word piece "Your Soul and Mine" added as an epilogue. The lyrics for "Me and the Devil Blues" derive from prewar country bluesman Robert Johnson's 1937 saga portraying a "Faustian bargain" with the devil which begat the artist's pleasures.[2] In the video, the Faustian bargain finds expression through the images of a vibrant Manhattan night with folks walking hurriedly against the background of prospering businesses. The sense of purpose and apparent economic status of the pedestrians mingling through assorted sidewalks contrasts sharply with occasional shots of poverty and homelessness, situating the latter as misplaced specters from a bygone era. Another set of ghostly characters traverse the streets as well, navigating their way through twenty-first-century wealth: young skateboarders, painted up as skeletons or figures of "death," vigorously skating through the concrete and steel paradox of wealth and homeless squalor. The juxtaposition of the footage and lyrics in the video for "Me and the Devil Blues"/"Your Soul and Mine" (aka "The Vulture") encapsulates the results of the economic transformation spanning Scott-Heron's recording career since the 1970s.

The use of New York City in 2010 as the background for the video is fitting as the metropolis marked both Scott-Heron's origin as a performing artist but also a key structural space where the rise of neoliberalism took root in the United States.[3] Like other urban centers in the 1960s, New York City increasingly faced budget issues emanating from the effects of deindustrialization and white flight.[4] Alongside Richard Nixon's federal aid cuts to cities, the 1973–74 recession aggravated an increasingly desperate situation: the urban crisis of the 1960s became the "urban *fiscal* crisis" of the 1970s.[5] From this predicament, solutions coalesced around austere budgeting measures primarily affecting municipal workers, racial minorities, the poor, and the governing liberal politicians; less was said regarding overdevelopment, the relationships between municipal borrowing and financial institutions, or planners overlooking industrial development.[6] The crisis of New York City provided an entry point for the adoption of what *Business Week*'s John Carson-Parker had offered in 1974 as a way out of the "debt crisis": "cities and states, the home mortgage market, small business, and the consumer, will all get less than they want because the basic health of the U.S. is based on the basic health of its corporations and banks: the biggest borrowers and the biggest lenders."[7] The resulting bailout deal between the New York City government and the financial industry replaced the prerogatives of publicly accountable political institutions with those of private capital, as the latter dictated the city's budget: social services (public health, education, transportation) were cut, wages frozen, and public employment downsized. The outcome of this restructuring writ large in the 1970s through today opened the door to neoliberalism, generating an ever-expanding inequality gap, particularly the racial wealth gap.[8] Reversing the postwar trends through the adoption of neoliberal policies mirroring Carson-Parker's suggestions, "The share of total income going to the top 1 percent of earners, which stood at 8.9 percent in 1976," writes Robert H. Frank, rose to 23.5 percent by 2007, but during the same period, the average inflation-adjusted hourly wage declined by more than 7 percent."[9] Amid newly gained legislated freedoms for women and people of color, the reform of overt sexism and racism took the shape of the economic logics of a color-blind "quantitative analysis" weighted toward those already integrated into the economy, while institutionalizing Nixon's "benign neglect" against those unable to escape the material outcomes of the Jim Crow welfare state.[10] Through the convergence of the culture war, the regulatory needs of multinationals and finance, and the political strategies of the New Right, the road to neoliberalism shaped a distaste for government spending through the familiar targets articulated by William F. Buckley Jr. and *Business Week* (among many others): poor people of color, especially African Americans, or their color-blind referent, the "undeserving" poor.[11]

The spoken-word epilogue in Scott-Heron's video for "Me and the Devil Blues"/"Your Soul and Mine" describes the onset of the coercive processes of the neoliberal mindset. Against the backdrop of footage of Scott-Heron in a recording studio speaking into a microphone, the poem built on the earlier scenes of Manhattan, conjuring the image of a vulture circling its urban victims within the video. Originally released on his debut record from 1970 as a song titled "The Vulture," "Your Soul and Mine" embodies a metaphoric partner of the "devil," reappearing in 2010 as a phantom from the Black Power era as well as a spoken summation of the ideological struggle of neoliberalism in the post–civil rights era.[12] Scott-Heron warns the listener of the philosophical ramifications of this circling beast: "So if you see the vulture coming, flying circles in your mind, remember there is no escaping, for he will follow close behind. Only promised me a battle, a battle for your soul and mine." Just as the *longue durée* processes of capitalism adjusted to legislated social equality, Scott-Heron's use of his early Black Power–era poetry to comment on the contemporary moment points toward the legacy and relevancy of the Black radical tradition and its *longue durée* confrontation with the processes of modernity. Along with Jayne Cortez and others, Scott-Heron's analysis carried on the 500-year global critique of colonialism, the Atlantic slave system, capitalism, the nation-state, imperialism, and the Eurocentrism of Enlightenment-inspired notions of Western civilization.[13] The neoliberal era represented an updating of these policies, including its approach to accommodate social equality legislation and newly independent, formerly colonized, nations. The most significant element of neoliberalism's accommodation to the new era of legislated social equality included removing the democratic hand over the economy the moment historically marginalized peoples were given rights to self-determination after years of colonialism and Jim Crow legislation.

As prescient observers and critics of the transition from the Jim Crow welfare state to neoliberalism, African American spoken-word artists continued the tradition of dissent pioneered by David Walker, Frederick Douglass, Harriet Jacobs, Sojourner Truth, Ida B. Wells, Anna J. Cooper, W. E. B. Du Bois, and many others across the twentieth century.[14] Scott-Heron's revisiting of "The Vulture" circa 2010 resurrects an important moment of this radical expression in the late 1960s and 1970s when many Black Power artists, activists, and intellectuals identified and resisted the evolving economic accommodation to the civil rights era as the limits of liberal reform for civil rights succumbed to the New Right's ascension.[15] Focusing primarily on the recorded work of Scott-Heron and poet Jayne Cortez, this chapter examines the spoken-word vinyl records and their challenge to the rise of neoliberalism in the 1970s.

Using the framework developed from 1960s Black radicalism, Black Power, and the Black arts movement, Scott-Heron and Cortez utilized popular culture to draw connections between the experience of people of African descent and the evolving networks of neoliberalism.[16] In particular, these poets found expression through popular media as "subaltern counterpublics," especially on long-playing (LP) vinyl albums as state violence against Black activists escalated in the late 1960s.[17] Building off the centuries-old "counterculture of modernity," they developed an "antisystemic position" culled from the Black radical tradition, producing albums charting the evolving sets of policies spilling over the "color line" into a wider populace experiencing the effects of 1970s austerity and the "age of diminishing expectations."[18] Noting the contours of the unfolding system of neoliberalism in the 1970s and 1980s, artists such as Scott-Heron and Cortez built off the long history of the Black radical tradition's critical memory.

In viewing the historic relationships between socioeconomic trends and racial oppression within a similar time frame as Fernand Braudel's *longue durée*, critical memory plays an important part in maintaining the Black public sphere. As Houston A. Baker Jr. writes:

> Critical memory . . . is the very faculty of revolution. Its operation implies a continuous arrival at turning points. Decisive change, usually attended by considerable risk, peril or suspense, always seems imminent. To be critical is never to be safely housed or allegorically free of the illness, transgression and contamination of the past. Critical memory, one might say, is always uncanny; it is also always in crisis. Critical

memory judges severely, censures righteously, renders hard ethical evaluations of the past that it never defines as well-passed. The essence of critical memory's work is the cumulative, collective maintenance of a record that draws into relationship significant instants of time past and the always uprooted homelessness of now.[19]

Critical memory sets the instances of the present within the context of the past and its material and spectral legacies, collapsing time and space into a compact entity of analysis. Critical memory, in many ways, is an elementary component in the struggle over the possession of history. As noted across these chapters, the conservative possession of history too often silences the experiences of women and African Americans (and other historically marginalized people). On the other hand, the compression of time and space in critical memory helped facilitate a possession of history both historically deep as well as broad, aiding the formation of the U.S. third world left by the 1960s as technology disseminated its ideas across the nation and globe.[20] Recognizing these trends as a coherent system, critical memory demands the recognition of the continuity and evolution of oppressive apparatuses across space and time (e.g., from the 1600s terrible transformation to slavery to Jim Crow to mass incarceration).[21]

Building on the Black radical tradition, Black spoken-word poetry artists conceptualized the present through the *longue durée* critical memory of Black history, communicating the possession of history and its accounting of the legacy of anti-Black racism, resistance, and the exploitation of labor evolving through the formations of modernity.[22] Tracing the evolution of Black Power through the unfolding of neoliberalism helps underline how the energy and critiques of Black Power and the Black arts movement (BAM) blended into the anti-globalization (i.e., anti-neoliberalism) movements of the 1980s through to the present day—accentuating the connections between the 1969 release of the Watts Prophets' "Saint America" and the 1982 recording of Grand Master Flash's "The Message."[23]

Spoken Word, the Black Aesthetic, and the Surrealist's Challenge

> These bloodthirsty people
> They're brooding in North Dakota with grenades in
> their hands
> brooding in the Carolinas with torches in their ears
> brooding in Alabama with water hoses still under
> their hoods

> brooding in Louisville with gasoline in their beer cans
> Brooding in New York City with long nails shooting
> from their hockey sticks
> brooding in Puerto Rico with sterilization on their
> minds
> brooding in South Africa with cactus missiles perched
> on their thighs
> just brooding brooding brooding brooding brooding
>
> —Jayne Cortez, "Brooding" (1977)

Gil Scott-Heron was born in 1949 in Chicago, Illinois.[24] Upon his parents' divorce—Bobbie Scott, a librarian, and Giles Heron Sr., a Jamaican professional soccer player—Scott-Heron moved to Jackson, Tennessee, where he lived with his grandmother, Lily Scott. In his poem "Coming from a Broken Home," a tribute to not only the women who raised him but also a critique against the so-called failures (as suggested by the Moynihan Report and later, the myth of the welfare queen) of Black families without the patriarchy of a strong father, Scott-Heron celebrates the strength of his grandmother:[25]

> Lily Scott claimed to have gone as far as the 3rd grade
> in school herself,
> put four Scotts through college
> with her husband going blind....
> And she raised me like she raised four of her own
> who were like her
> in a good many good ways.
> Which showed up in my mother
> who was truly her mother's daughter
> and still her own person.[26]

After his grandmother passed, Scott-Heron moved to New York City with his mother where he finished high school at the prestigious Fieldston School of Ethical Culture.

Upon graduation from high school, he attended Lincoln University—the alma mater of his hero Langston Hughes—where he went on to receive the Langston Hughes Creative Writing Award in 1968. Upon seeing the Last Poets perform at Lincoln in 1969, Scott-Heron formed a similar spoken-word group.[27] By his second year of college at Lincoln University in 1970, Scott-Heron had published his first novel, *The Vulture*, a book of poetry, *Small Talk at 125th and Lenox*, and an LP (titled after the book of poetry). As Joyce Joyce emphasizes, Scott-Heron's first LP personified the 1960s Black Power voice that bridged art with the needs of the community, embodying what

BAM defined as the "black aesthetic."[28] Scott-Heron's main influences were Hughes, J. Saunders Redding (whom he studied under at Lincoln), Richard Wright, and James Baldwin, as well as Black arts poets such as Amiri Baraka, Nikki Giovanni, and musician-poet Stanley Crouch. After Lincoln University and during his first few years as a recording artist, Scott-Heron received a fellowship to Johns Hopkins University, where he earned an MA in 1972. His second novel, *The N****r Factory*, also released in 1972, coincided with an appointment at Federal City College in Washington, D.C., where he taught creative writing until 1976.[29] Scott-Heron's increasing success with his music eventually provided him a full-time career in the recording industry as his records regularly entered the Billboard 200, Jazz, and R&B charts, with artists such as Esther Phillips, Penny Goodwin, and LaBelle covering his songs. Although the spoken-word components of his early records were increasingly edged out in favor of his soul jazz–inflected songs (written with creative partner Brian Jackson), across the thirteen albums recorded between 1970 and 1982 Scott-Heron continued to include spoken-word pieces that served as evolutionary signposts of the new socioeconomic system.

On the West coast, poet Jayne Cortez also personified the convergence of the Black aesthetic and community activism with her work in Los Angeles during the 1960s. Achieving more literary and academic achievements than Scott-Heron's commercial success, Cortez was a vital figure of the avant-garde jazz circles of Los Angeles.[30] Passing away on December 28, 2012, Cortez occupies an important place in the canon of literature, poetry, and spoken-word albums.[31] Born in 1936 in Arizona, Cortez moved to Los Angeles as a child, where she attended Manual Arts High School, an educational institution specializing in music and art. She later enrolled at Compton Junior College and studied painting and drawing, as well as theater for the Ebony Showcase Theater in Watts.[32] Cortez also took part in the Southern civil rights movement as a member of the Student Nonviolent Coordinating Committee (SNCC), going to Mississippi to work with Fannie Lou Hamer on voting drives in 1963 and 1964.[33] Between 1964 and 1970, Cortez was the artistic director and cofounder of the Watts Repertory Theatre Company, a group that helped to create an activist/poet community, including the spoken-word group the Watts Prophets.[34] Along with her family's vast collection of jazz and blues and exposure to music theory, these formative experiences congealed in her synthesis of jazz and poetry.[35] In addition, Cortez's evolving poetic voice tied together her time spent working in factories and her civil rights activism, leading to her "*Black* worker–oriented" critique of class.[36] She asserts, "I mean—I wasn't just Jayne, you know, picking daisies and then she goes to Mississippi. I was Jayne facing the everyday routine in the factories with the bosses and the unions and with police brutality in the city of smog, suppression, and racism."[37]

Like Amiri Baraka, Cortez's connections to the jazz scene in Los Angeles—she was once married to saxophonist Ornette Coleman and worked with pianist Horace Tapscott—informed her approach to poetry, in particular the musical nuances and the surrealist nature of free jazz.[38] Upon moving to New York City in 1967, she published her first work of poetry, *Pissstained Stairs and the Monkey Man's Wares* (1969), a work containing links to the tradition of Black music as well as the conjoining of the "power and creation of nature" with "everyday experience."[39] Cultivated from her experience in the factory and organizing in Mississippi for SNCC, the impetus for her work was grounded in her day-to-day life: "Yes. Being unemployed and without food can make you very sad. But you weren't the problem. The problem is the system, and you can organize, unify, and do something about the system. That's what I learned."[40] Cortez exemplified the self-sufficiency tract of Black Power, as she sought complete financial control over her artistic endeavors by setting up Bola Press after moving to New York City from which she published and released her poetry and records.[41] Cortez received various awards in the 1970s and 1980s for her work, including Creative Artists Public Service Awards, National Endowment for the Arts fellowships, a New York Foundation for the Arts award, as well as the Before Columbus Foundation American Book Award for excellence in literature in 1980.[42] As writer in residence at Livingston College of Rutgers University between 1977 and 1983, Cortez delivered lectures at different universities and colleges as a professor of literature.[43]

Cortez's surrealist—what she calls supersurrealism—poetry linked her to other Black poets utilizing surrealism as an anti-imperialist, anti-racist tool, with her primary inspirations being Aimé Césaire, Léon Damas, Langston Hughes, Margaret Walker, Nicolás Guillén, and Sterling Brown.[44] Black surrealism arose from the 1920s European movement, whose artists sought to undermine Western civilization by taking aim at colonialism.[45] The surrealist's approach to literature and poetry involved the techniques of automatic writing in composition, an aesthetic seeking to invoke an alternative "state of mind" to confront the staid rational thought of Enlightenment-derived modernity.[46] As Robin D. G. Kelley writes, "Automatism was a struggle against the slavery of rationalism, a means to allow the imagination to run free."[47] Cortez's approach to spoken word is intensely visual, where sentences summon a collage-like relay of images, instilling a sense of timeless connection between phrases, people, actions, and power structures. Like the jazz instrumentation accompanying Cortez's recorded work, the delivery sounds strategically improvised, making cadential twists and turns. Describing her approach, Cortez notes:

I use dreams, the subconscious, and the real objects, and I open up the body and use organs, and I sink them into words, and I ritualize them and fuse them into events. I guess the poetry is like a festival. Everything can be transformed. The street becomes something else, the subway is something else. Everything changes: the look of the person changes, their intentions change, the attitudes are different, experiences become fiercer. Voices become other voices. So that's what I do in my poetry. I keep making connections. I try to not wade in the shallow water of shallowness and I try to not get stuck in the mud of art council standards and the spectators' demand for messages. It's called multiplication, subdivision, and subtraction.[48]

Both Cortez and Scott-Heron drew much of their immediate inspiration from the fertile BAM scenes across the nation, where "a new genre of post-Beat, black avant-garde" statements influenced both free jazz and the "postwar experiments in black poetics."[49] Baraka's vernacular shift in his spoken word between the 1964 recording of "Black Dada Nihilismus" and "Black Art" in 1965 set the tone for BAM's "black aesthetic," merging the Black avant-garde with the street-level discontent of northern, urban Blacks (who the Black Panther Party called the lumpenproletariat) unaffected by civil rights reforms.[50] As Amy Abugo Ongiri suggests, "In developing the African American urban vernacular as an aesthetic, BAM attempted to reclaim the artistic merit of the poetics of a people for whom, as Don L. Lee put it, 'poetry on the written page . . . was almost as strange as money.'"[51]

Alongside the centuries of African oratory and storytelling traditions, the toast (also known as the dozens or spiels) formed one of the foundations for this "street aesthetic."[52] Bruce Jackson notes, "Along with black folk sermons and lyrics of work-songs, spirituals, and blues, the toasts comprise an extraordinary body of folk poetry matched hardly anywhere in the world."[53] Toasts are a form of poetic verbal jousting between participants, where one-upmanship marks the winner, while the loser is left humiliated. The boastful quality in a communal setting is often male dominated, aiming to affirm worth "in terms of physical strength, sexual prowess, and the ability to inflict harm."[54] Toasts and the dozens are a sort of "street theater" where a stress is placed on developing an individual style.[55] As T. J. Anderson points out, writers Amiri Baraka, James Baldwin, and Sonia Sanchez all underlined the importance of playing the dozens as children, as it "allowed them to develop an attention toward some of the most inventive and innovative qualities of rhythm and language."[56] Cortez reminisced about the education she gained from playing the dozens in her childhood: "We did it constantly. It was an everyday ritual. Oral poetry in an oral atmosphere."[57] The convergence of the street aesthetic of toasts and the dozens with the political consciousness of the Black working class, the avant-garde experimentation of BAM poets, as well as the critical memory of Black radicalism set the stage for an analysis of the white reaction to the rise of legislated social equality and the subsequent economic restructuring of the nation during the first decade of legislated racial and gender equality in U.S. history.

An array of spoken-word albums appeared in the late 1960s and early 1970s incorporating diverse musical backgrounds, and, in turn, laid the groundwork for the rise of hip-hop a decade later.[58] What might be considered the dawn of the golden age of Black Power popular culture, these spoken-word albums formed an important corollary to Baldwin's possession of history as they addressed issues ranging from racism and the history of white supremacy and anti-Blackness, to love and prison, to drug addiction and the links between the economy and anti-Black antagonism.[59] The early works of Black Power spoken word at the height of state oppression often aimed their arguments toward calls for racial solidarity, critiques of radicalism and Blackness, discussions of tactical aesthetics versus material action, and discontent toward white liberalism: the Watts Prophets' "I'll Stop Calling You N****rs" and "Response to a Bourgeois N****r," the Last Poets' "N****rs Are Scared of Revolution" and "Wake Up, N****rs," Sonia Sanchez's "Welcome Home My Prince" and "We Can Be," or Gil Scott-Heron's "Brother," Maya Angelou's "On Working White Liberals," and the Watts Prophets' "Saint America." The latter works by Angelou and the Watts Prophets highlight what Widener suggests is less a political gap between "right and left than the gulf between American liberalism and its radical detractors."[60] Drug abuse represented one of the many problems facing urban communities after years of cultural, economic, and legal segregation created a de facto barrier to escaping underemployment and the collapse of social services, with the Last Poets' "Jones Comin' Down" and "O.D." highlighting this condition. Scott-Heron's "Paint It Black" offered a picture of claustrophobic poverty with the only outlet for hope lying in shining shoes or cleaning toilets, as a family is stuffed in "a Harlem house" and told "how bad things [were] down South."[61] Out of this cultural front of Black poets, Scott-Heron's and Cortez's poetry across the 1970s charted the changing shape of the American economy and sociopolitical framework.

Black History, "Freedom," and the Liberated Message

> We're used to having white people try to rob us,
> Why don't they try stealing some of this poverty,
> Ain't no new thing.

> Anything they can't understand they try to destroy,
> Anything they can't understand they try to control.
> ... Ain't no new thing.
>
> —Gil Scott-Heron, "Ain't No New Thing" (1972)

Rooted in the masculine (and sometimes homophobic) veneer of Black Power rhetoric, *Small Talk at 125th and Lenox* critiqued the legacy of 400 years of slavery and oppression, linking these processes to the ongoing antagonisms of the 1960s. Mirroring the style of other groups such as the Watts Prophets and the Last Poets, Scott-Heron's work bridged the Black radical tradition with a critical engagement with the unfolding of neoliberalism. The black-and-white album cover of *Small Talk at 125th and Lenox* positions Scott-Heron within an isolated, urban labyrinth, staring at the camera, and surrounded by walls pasted with weathered postings, with long alleyways and streets containing random, scattered debris. The crumbling brick and mortar highlights the urban decay of the late 1960s and 1970s, as cities turned into postindustrial wastelands as capital relocated to state-subsidized white suburbs—or overseas.[62] Wearing a long-sleeved work shirt (cuffs rolled up to the elbow) and jeans, Scott-Heron conveys the image of the Black working class.

A key track from *Small Talk at 125th and Lenox*, "Enough," represents Scott-Heron's possession of history, an outline of the Atlantic slave system, Post-Reconstruction terrorism and the implementation of Jim Crow segregation, and the postwar Jim Crow welfare state. Scott-Heron highlights what Saidiya Hartman calls the "racial calculus and ... political arithmetic" still imperiling and devaluing Black lives in the introduction to the piece. He begins with: "Because, every once in a while, a brother gets shot somewhere for no reason; a brother gets his head kicked in for no reason. And you wonder just exactly what in the hell is enough."[63]

> It was not enough that we were
> bought and
> brought to this
> home of the slave;
> locked in the bowels of a
> floating shithouse, watching those
> we loved eaten away by plague and
> insanity—flesh falling like strips
> of bark from a termite infested tree.
> bones rotting, turning first to brittle
> ivory, then to rosin.
> [that was not enough][64]

Scott-Heron's description of slave owner's sadistic brutalization of people of African descent ensnared in the Atlantic slave system underlines the importance of critical memory and the naming of legacies still in play. Noting the system's adaptation from slavery to emancipation to the postwar white resistance against civil rights activists, he notes:

> Every time I see a rope or gun, I remember.
> And to top it all off, you ain't through yet.
> Over 50 you have killed in Mississippi, since 1963.
> That doesn't even begin to begin all of those you have maimed, hit and run over, blinded, poisoned, starved, or castrated.[65]

Here, the critical memory infusing Scott-Heron's possession of history ties together the symbols of coercion, the techniques of terrorism, and the murderous intent to protect white supremacy through any means necessary. The implication, of course, is that the institutions of civil society allowing and encouraging anti-Black terrorism find approval from the state, which had always disrupted, regulated, and suppressed "the development of black social space."[66]

In the song, "Comment #1," Scott-Heron targets the possession of history buttressing white innocence and its denial of racial antagonisms in the postwar world. Noting the relativity and contingent nature the concept of freedom historically embodies for the United States, he suggests that "freedom" for African Americans is more often "known az freedom. (*freedoom*)"[67] Revising "freedom" with the more accurate "freedoom," Scott-Heron highlights the paradox governing the different interpretations of "freedom": for whites, freedom denoted special entitlements tied to institutional oppression and exclusion of Blacks. This spotlight on one of the original binaries of American history—freedom = white; slavery = Black—helped provide the context explaining why social equality legislation for people of color (and women) proved to be a difficult concept to comprehend for white Americans who continued to see race through the prism of the Founding Fathers.[68]

White anxiety grew with each civil rights victory and periodic expressions of urban unrest as the 1960s drew closer to the 1970s.[69] Long a psychological powder keg, Rod Bush asserts, "White America's fear of 'slave revolts' is widespread. This fear has underwritten a fortress mentality, which closes many whites off from a more objective assessment of the status and nature of race relations in the United States."[70] Rooted in concerns over the extension of social equality to historically marginalized people, the post-civil rights era demanded a reconceptualization of freedom. At the forefront of this redefining of freedom, of course, stood the conservative culture war and the neoliberal embrace of quantitative analysis: the new freedom aimed toward reversing the welfare state's redistribution of wealth downward now that legislated social equality had entered the picture. Those still caught in the poverty of centuries of white supremacist policies, or those unable to access the benefits of social equality legislation, surfaced in the 1970s as ongoing threats to the newly defined "freedom."

Scott-Heron also targeted government policies benefiting corporations at the expense of ameliorating the poor living conditions of urban Blacks. "Whitey on the Moon" juxtaposed the federal spending tied to the 1969 moon landing with the perspective of a Black tenet trapped in a rapidly decaying urban housing project. Weaving together the unkempt building maintenance, inflation, unaffordable health care, drug abuse, and an income diminished from taxes, Scott-Heron connected these economic and de facto segregation policies to the nationalism generated by the American space race. In addition, the link between Cold War defense spending for corporations and the increasingly dilapidated safety net for impoverished Americans prophesized—much like John Carson-Parker—the economic future of the nation in the decades after the 1970s.

The economic austerity of the 1970s helped discipline the meaning of freedom under neoliberalism. In the liner notes for his second album, *Pieces of a Man*, from 1971, Scott-Heron suggested, "Be no bargain-day xtras on freedom and / ain't nobody givin it away."[71] This LP contained only one spoken-word piece, though arguably it is his most well known: "The Revolution Will Not Be Televised." Although previewed on his debut LP, the version from *Pieces of a Man* reset the expectations of those seeking revolution three years into the Nixon administration. In addition, the song provided one of the templates for hip-hop—the music of young Black and Puerto Rican teenagers in mid-1970s postindustrial South Bronx. Anticipating his suggestion in 1978 that liberals helped push the movement off the streets with a handshake (see opening epigraph), Scott-Heron highlighted the brash omnipresence of corporate advertising and branding inundating people's lives through television, pointing out how the rebellious energies of the 1960s had been channeled into commodity markets revolutionizing identities through consumer products—rather than the previous decade's activism. The revolution must come from within, he asserted, and would "put you in the driver's seat."[72]

"The Political Deck Has Been Restacked": The Black Atlantic and the Neoliberal Road to Globalization

> And in the name of god & progress &
> stuffed pockets

after so much torture
& so many invasions in the blood
your veins are
air strips for
multi-national corporations

—Jayne Cortez, "They Came Again in 1970 in 1980" (1984)

After publishing three poetry books between 1969 and 1973, Cortez released her first LP, *Celebrations and Solitudes* (1974) on the Black-owned Strata-East records, reciting her poetry to the accompaniment of jazz bassist Richard Davis.[73] The album drew connections between the internationalization of violence shaping the neoliberal landscape in the 1970s—from the U.S.-backed coup in Chile to civil wars across Africa to the winding down of the American war in Vietnam. For listeners, *Celebrations and Solitudes* presented a world of images in constant motion, slipping through history, geography, ontology, urban idiosyncrasies, murder, love, the celebration of cultural heroes, and remembrances of wars for liberation. Although different from Scott-Heron's recorded work in its use of string bass accompaniment, Cortez identified, made sense of, and proposed solutions to the onset of what Scott-Heron labeled: *Winter in America*.[74]

In the liner notes to *Celebrations and Solitudes*, Bob Rogers highlights Cortez's Black internationalism (or Pan-Africanism), stating, "In Jayne Cortez the line from Watts to Africa to New York vibrates underground setting off sensual waves of violent currents that sear the cold granite that is Manhattan, but feel soothingly cool to the freshly cast bronze of the Benin [*sic*]." This imagining of the Black Atlantic weaves through the poems Cortez wrote in the early 1970s, including the piece "Song for Kwame 1972," a track celebrating Kwame Nkrumah, the Ghanaian independence leader and noted Pan-Africanist who died in 1972. "Festivals and Funerals 1970" rhetorically connected the fate of Malcolm X with that of the Central Intelligence Agency (CIA)–Belgian–sponsored death of Patrice Lumumba: "Who killed Lumumba, what killed Malcolm"; with "what" perhaps being the political ideology Malcolm X had embraced in the years up to his death: the internationalization of "the condition of Black peoples in the United States"—an anticolonial, anti-Western problem of "human rights" rather than a nation-centric problem of "civil rights."[75] Nkrumah's contemporary, Amilcar Cabral from Guinea-Bissau, also received mention in Cortez's "Remembrance 1973," a commemoration of Cabral's death in the struggle against Portuguese colonialism in 1973. The naming and commemoration of these figures of resistance to the processes of modernity were summoned as possessions of history to reinvigorate the struggle in Black America in the 1970s:

> Our struggle continues in your guiding spirit
> the armed struggle for the complete freedom of
> our people
> . . .
> Long Live The Liberation Movements
> Long Live Our Warrior Hearts[76]

Anticipating the twenty-first-century movement Black Lives Matter, Cortez also gives name to those who fell victim to police brutality and would fail to reach the history books. In "Homicide 1973," she recites:

> He died from
> a bullet wound
> in the back
> fired by a plainclothes
> policeman
> in Queens New York
> don't forget 10 year old
> Clifford Glover[77]

Cortez's surrealistic outlines of heroes, memories, and anonymous bystanders caught in the traffic of anti-Black violence attempted to keep pushing forward the activism of the previous decades, tracing and naming the changing shape of economics and culture as the shadow of neoliberalism grew larger.

The pessimistic gloom of the early 1970s lay at the heart of Scott-Heron's (and partner Brian Jackson's) 1974 album *Winter in America*.[78] Released on the same label as Cortez's 1974 record, Strata-East, *Winter in America* embraced a transnational, Pan-Africanist view of Black oppression, commenting on an array of developments: war and capitalism, the increasingly obscured networks of imperialism through multinational business media framing, and the formative economic principles taking shape under neoliberalism. Mostly composed of sung songs rather than spoken-word pieces, *Winter in America*'s title added to the aesthetic aura of a rusting, hollowed-out city, where desperation filled the void of capital flight. The title of the album, "Winter in America," christened an insightful metaphor embodying the cold procedure of austerity marking the birth of neoliberalism.

"Just how blind, America?" Scott-Heron asks in "H2O Gate (Watergate) Blues" (the only spoken-word track on *Winter in America*), questioning the United States' role in Vietnam and America's failure to conquer a "people determined to be free."[79] Connecting foreign policy to Wall Street, he notes, "And when the roll was called it was: Phillips 66 and Pepsi-Cola plastics, Boeing Dow and Lockheed—ask them what we're fighting for and they never mention the economics of war."[80] He adds, "How long, America, before the consequences of: allowing the press to be intimidated; keeping the school system segregated; watching the price of everything soar; and hearing complaints 'cause the rich want more?"[81] After Scott-Heron's recounting of the present, he contextualized these deeds with other undemocratic moments in recent American history:

> The obvious key to the whole charade
> Would be to run down all the games that they played:
> Remember Dita Beard and ITT, the slaughter of Attica,
> The C.I.A. in Chile knowing nothing about Allende at this time, in the past, as I recollect.
> The slaughter in Augusta, G.A.
> The nomination of Supreme Court Jesters to head off the tapes,
> William Calley's Executive Interference in the image of John Wayne,
> Kent State, Jackson State, Southern Louisiana,
> Hundreds of unauthorized bombing raids,
> The chaining and gagging of Bobby Seale—somebody tell these jive Maryland Governors to be for real!
> We recall all of these events just to prove
> That Waterbuggers in the Watergate wasn't no news!
> And the thing that justifies all our fears
> Is that all this went down in the last five years.[82]

Scott-Heron's poetic stringing together of these moments foregrounded the various processes of modernity constructing the road to neoliberalism, including capitalism: the ITT [International Telephone & Telegraph] and Dita Beard scandal regarding bribes for the dropping of antitrust lawsuits; imperialism: the cynical foreign policy of the CIA, and Nixon's illegal war outside the borders of Vietnam; the nation-state: the violent state reaction to student antiwar unrest, and the pardoning of war criminal Calley (and noting the symbolic role of John Wayne).[83] In this possession of history, Scott-Heron's juxtaposition ties these processes together as a singular, though complex, network: the domestic shooting of protesters finds contrast with the illegal bombing of Indochina, while he conjoins the settler colonial symbolism of Wayne as a justification for pardoning the war crimes of Calley.

An important component driving these relationships in "H2O Gate (Watergate) Blues" includes the relationship of private corporations to government interventions abroad. In particular, Scott-Heron took aim at the workings of Dita Beard (ITT lobbyist in Washington, D.C.), the connections of the multinational ITT with the coup d'état in Chile (with aid from the CIA).[84] The Cold War built on earlier precedents for U.S. intervention into nations not aligning with American objectives—from the 1953 coup in Iran to the 1954 coup in Guatemala to the coup and assassination of Patrice Lumumba, the first prime minister of the Democratic Republic of the Congo in 1961.[85] This fusing of public and covert government policies led to alliances with right-wing authoritarian governments overseas, enabling the implementation of U.S.-led economic reforms more conducive to the needs of multinational corporations—and often in direct opposition to local peasant or worker demands for social and economic reforms.[86] These interventions (with U.S. involvement often obscured in the public eye), and the coercively imposed financial reforms via the International Monetary Fund and the World Bank, set the baseline for neoliberalism's global application, inaugurating what simply became known as "globalization."[87] The 1973 coup in Chile led to the nation becoming the test case for neoliberal doctrines in the 1970s by a group of Chilean economists educated at the University of Chicago.[88] Chile emerged as a celebrated model for neoliberal policies (despite its disastrous consequences across the 1970s) as well as a renewed commitment toward American support of dictatorships—including President Ronald Reagan's "constructive engagement" with white supremacy governments such as South Africa.[89] With right-wing fascist states winning the debate through torture and disappearances, this double standard helped shape the callous needed to install unpopular economic policies against a resisting public. In short, this double standard made it easier to normalize the coercive edge of domestic policies of "benign neglect," as support for police states abroad transferred domestically via an intensified police state and prison-industrial complex aimed at disciplining poor people of color in the United States.[90] By the 1980s, the privatization impulse of neoliberalism extended to both the privatization of foreign policy via the proto-military contractor (mercenary) structure engineering the illegal Iran Contra policy of the Reagan administration, as well as the rise of privately operated prisons.[91] In his description of Iran Contra in the 1980s, Harold Hongju Koh essentially outlines the proto-neoliberal practices of multinationals in the 1960s and 1970s and the transition toward deregulation: "After the Boland amendments restricted any official U.S. funding to the contras, military aid was privatized. In short, Congress's postwar efforts to enact legislation that would stop the last war simply channeled executive action into new, unregulated forms of warfare. In a familiar regulatory pattern, each succeeding congressional effort to catch up with executive evasion of its legislative controls served only to shift executive activity into a new pattern of evasion."[92] For Scott-Heron, these patterns of deregulation and the reliance on private institutions (publicly unaccountable) to carry out governmental (publicly accountable) duties had roots in the 1970s, a solid decade before Iran Contra.

Postindustrialism hit Black America especially hard as the global economy tilted toward finance and Nixon's "benign neglect" and the federally directed assault against Black Power organizations dispersed leadership through counter-intelligence, sabotage, and assassinations.[93] Scott-Heron noted this crisis in the liner notes to his 1975 album *First Minute of a New Day*, emphasizing the ramifications of U.S.-led economic globalization—including the potential for collective resistance as "mid-winter in America" set in:

> There is a revolution going on in America/the World; a shifting in the winds/vibrations, as disruptive as an actual earth-tremor, but it is happening in our hearts. . . . The seeds of this revolution were planted hundreds of years ago; in slave ships, in cotton fields, in tepees, in the souls of brave men. The seeds were watered, nurtured and bloom now in our hands as we rock our babies. It is mid-winter in America; a man-made season of shattered dreams and shocked citizens, fumbling and frustrated beneath the crush of greed of corporate monsters and economic manipulators gone wild. There are bitter winds born in the knowledge of secret plans hatched by Western Money Men that backfired and grew out of control to eat its own. We must support ourselves and stand fast together even as pressure disperses our enemies and bangs at our doors. We must all do what we can for each other to weather this blizzard.[94]

A turning point seemed to have taken place in the early 1970s. Although marking a singular year as a distinct moment when "everything changes" is more of a historian's narrative device than reality, 1973—in retrospect—marked a crucial time for the cultural production defining Scott-Heron's winter in America and the rise of neoliberal globalization.[95] One element of globalization included the Black radical tradition outside the United States expressing itself through various forms of popular culture challenging the legacies of slavery, colonialism, and capitalism.[96] Awakened by the civil rights and decolonization movements in the Caribbean and Africa, a rejuvenation of Pan-Africanist sentiment emerged through these global intersections of Black popular culture in the 1970s, spurring commercial connections and aesthetic exchanges tying Cortez and Scott-Heron to the the African diaspora.[97]

African American R&B and soul music from the 1960s helped initiate this exchange throughout the commercial networks (recordings and radio) of the twentieth century.[98] For example, the Black protest songs of Curtis Mayfield and the Impressions (among others) influenced the evolution of Jamaican music in the 1960s, especially ska, rock steady, and reggae music, combining with Caribbean music like Calypso and Mento, and older percussion traditions shaped by the African diaspora.[99] In particular, the globalization of reggae music, most notably through Bob Marley and the Wailers' *Catch a Fire* (1973) and the soundtrack to the film *The Harder They Come* (featuring Jimmy Cliff and others) occurred in the years after 1973.[100] Reggae's popularity arose simultaneously with many of the musicians embracing Jamaica's expression of Black Power: the Rastafarian religion.[101] Reggae channeled the folk music roots of the Rastafarian communities such as Burru drumming performed at Nyahbinghi gatherings in the mountains of Jamaica (vestiges of the old Maroon colonies from the dawn of the Atlantic slave system).[102] Synthesizing these traditions for the global market, alongside Rastafarianism's anti-colonial, anti-imperialist, and Black pride message, reggae linked the critical memory of slavery and resistance to the contemporary era of multinational domination of the Jamaican economy (a subject that the film *The Harder They Come* uses as a background to the narrative).[103] Song subjects ranged from opposition to South African Apartheid, the celebration of Africa, and contemporary issues facing people of African descent, such as poverty, segregation, and police brutality—in short, survival in Bob Marley's "concrete jungle."[104] As the popularity of reggae and its possession of history spread, Western artists covered songs by the Wailers and other Jamaican artists.

In terms of spoken-word connections between the United States and Jamaica, a long history exists of Caribbean peoples well versed in the art of "public oratory" as much as "street-corner orators of New York City."[105] Jamaican singer/DJ Big Youth brought his toasting skills to his second release, *Chi Chi Run* (1973), where he sung a version of the Last Poets' "When the Revolution Comes" (1970), titled "When Revolution Come."[106] Big Youth adapted the geography of the original song to the streets of Kingston, Jamaica, while retaining the same imagery: "When revolution comes, the preacher, and his bible, will be running up King's Street; when the revolution comes: Jesus Christ will be standing on the corner of Duke Street and Bisa Street, trying to get the first taxi to get him the hell out of here."[107]

Just as the influences of American R&B and soul music traveled to Jamaica in the 1960s, Caribbean migration to the United States also transferred musical aesthetics from Jamaica to New York City, providing an important seed for the arrival of another form of spoken word: hip-hop. Eighteen-year-old Jamaican immigrant Clive Campbell (adopting the name Kool Herc) brought the Jamaican sound systems of his youth to his neighborhood in the South Bronx, where he helped initiate the creation of hip-hop during the summer of 1973.[108] After realizing his young audience was not interested in dancing to reggae or rock steady, Herc incorporated soul, funk, and Latin music, with a particular emphasis on the drum breaks in songs. Contributing to the development of the Bronx MC style, Herc primarily shaped the musical backdrop for synthesizing Jamaican-inspired toast interludes with African American traditions of spoken word, street-corner oratory, and BAM poetry legacies inspiring the work of the Last Poets and Scott-Heron.[109]

Another contribution to hip-hop arriving the same year as young Kool Herc's creation was the release of the Last Poet Jalal Nuriddin's *Hustlers Convention*.[110] Here, Nuriddin adopted the persona of Lightnin' Rod and took the street-corner toasts about hustling and pimps as the theme for a full-length LP. The record reflected both an early precedent for hip-hop records as well as a nod toward the marketability of urban tales arriving in theaters via Black action films in the early 1970s.[111] In addition, *Hustlers Convention* became a source for breakbeats used by hip-hop DJs in the late 1970s.[112] This conjuncture of northern Black Atlantic styles and modes of expression in the early 1970s against the backdrop of the creeping austerity of postindustrial New York City combined with a range of influences helping to shape hip-hop—from R&B, soul, funk, jazz, rock, and blues.[113] As a hybrid cultural expression, hip-hop further compressed the notions of space and time for Black critical memory, though it would take until 1979 for commercial record releases to appear. From Jamaican dance halls and sound systems to Black Power–inspired spoken word, the seeds of the Black radical tradition found renewal in the 1970s for the children of Black Power, who would go on to generate a new form of spoken word built around the "technological terrain" of 1970s postindustrial America.[114]

By the mid-1970s, Scott-Heron's commercial success led to an album deal with Clive Davis's Arista Records in 1975. Fittingly, Scott-Heron now entered the world of the multinational conglomerate: Arista Records was a subsidiary of Columbia Pictures, the owner of other Columbia labels, such as Bell Records, Colpix Records, and Colgems Records.[115] During this period, Scott-Heron foregrounded his internationalist, Pan-Africanist perspective, including albums titled: *From South Africa to South Carolina* and *The First Minute of a New Day*.[116] Embracing a global approach to racism and economics, Scott-Heron envisioned a resistance against "globalization" (i.e., neoliberalism) as well as the growing anti-apartheid movement against South Africa.[117] As stated in the liner notes to a later compilation of spoken-word pieces, Scott-Heron wrote, the "focus of the struggle has shifted in the '70s, [and] become more aware of Pan Africanism and international responsibilities. If we recognize that it's all part of the same battle more will be accomplished. Different fronts, the same battle."[118] For the neoliberal age, it would be virtually impossible to separate the global from the domestic. Scott-Heron's expanding popularity enabled him to appear on an episode of NBC's *Saturday Night* (called *Saturday Night Live* after 1976), where he performed "Johannesburg" (an anti-apartheid song) and "A Lovely Day."

Based on poems written in the mid-to-late 1970s, Cortez's second release, *Unsubmissive Blues* (1980), also exhibited anti-apartheid sentiments.[119] On the album, Cortez celebrated the 1976 student uprising in South Africa and connected the South African government to the legacies of anti-Blackness in the United States.[120]

> and Soweto
> when i look at this ugliness
> and see once again how we're divided and
> forced into fighting each other
> over a funky job in the sewers of Johannesburg
> divided into labor camps
> fighting over damaged meat and stale bread in
> Harlem
> divided into factions fighting to keep from fighting
> the ferocious men who are shooting
> into the heads of our small children

In this globalized connection, Cortez links the material conditions connecting African Americans with Black South Africans and the outgrowth of Steve Biko's Black Consciousness Movement on the students of Soweto.[121] Cortez's global perspective tied the malnutrition of children and the products of South African Black labor, "pellets of uranium," with the nations buying the South African products for domestic comfort: France, Israel, and Japan. Moreover, she remarks on the timelessness of slave quarters "in Miami" (anticipating the uprising in 1980) with the ongoing diamond industry in Europe, asserting, "the gold market still functioning on wall street / and the scar tissues around our necks / swelling with tumors of dead leaves."[122]

These *longue durée* connections spanning space and time entered Scott-Heron's last album of entire spoken-word pieces: *The Mind of Gil Scott-Heron: A Collection of Poetry and Music* (1978). "The Ghetto Code (Dot Dot Dit Dot Dit Dot Dot Dash)" traced the relationship between foreign intervention with domestic oppression, outlining the international activities of the CIA, the waste of federal tax dollars, and U.S. interference in Congo and Chile.[123] On "The New Deal," Scott-Heron juxtaposes the past New Deal with the new political-economic situation of the mid-1970s, noting that the poem "is not to be confused (because of its title) with previous New Deals as set forth by FDR [Franklin D. Roosevelt], DDE [Dwight D. Eisenhower], JFK [John F. Kennedy], or LBJ [Lyndon B. Johnson]. It is the conclusion of an era of stagnation presided over by the Mill House and the Out House."[124]

Although Scott-Heron and Cortez outlined the ongoing oppression toward African Americans, some elements of the Black community gained a foothold: the tentative assimilation of middle-class African Americans (primarily men) into the American dream by the mid-1970s. As Marable writes, "the traditional income margin of racial inequality, at least for many of the black élite, had been almost eliminated by the mid-1970s."[125] Able to benefit (along with white middle-class women) from the brief moment of programs such as federal grants, affirmative action, and the "desegregation of corporate middle management positions," this assimilation implicitly demanded a relinquishing of criticisms toward systemic racism that traditionally bound together the Black working and middle classes during the Jim Crow era.[126] Prosperity for some often resulted in a divide between Black workers and a Black middle class that, due to the weight of intersectionality, posed a wider gap than between "white workers and the white petty bourgeoisie."[127] Scott-Heron noted this division in 1974 with his song "Peace Go with You, Brother," off *Winter in America*:

> Peace go with you brother
> Recognition don't come cheap anymore
> You're my lawyer, you're my doctor
> Yea, but somehow you've forgot about me
> And now, now when I see you
> All I can say is: Peace go with you brother[128]

These moments, transitions, and consolidations strengthened the arguments guiding neoliberalism's ascendance (with its color-blind philosophy) by tying together taxes, discrimination, and William Julius Wilson's arguments in *The Declining Significance of Race*—published in 1978—which supported the idea that the 1960s had finished off the last vestiges of racism.[129] The results of this so-called moment of a color-blind society further opened the door for coded racism articulated as cultural pathology—enthusiastically put into play by Nathan Glazer, Daniel Patrick Moynihan, and William F. Buckley Jr. at the dawn of legislated social equality.[130] If one was charged with racism, one could point to Wilson's findings as proof that their arguments based on culture were free of racist sentiment. As economists, corporations, think tanks, and legislators consolidated these culture war arguments alongside the dismantling of the welfare state, Black and Puerto Rican teenagers in urban spaces—in particular the South Bronx—dealt with the staggering unemployment of the 1970s and the surfacing class division with a new form of music and spoken-word style that both looked back to its roots and into the future.

A Perfect New Loop: Hip-Hop and Postindustrial America

> Rap's forebears stretch back through disco, street funk, radio DJs, Bo Diddley, the bebop singers, Cab Calloway, Pigmeat Markham, the tap dancers and comics, The Last Poets, Gil Scott-Heron, Muhammad Ali, a cappella and

doo-wop groups, ring games, skip-rope rhymes, prison and army songs, toasts, signifying and the dozens, all the way to the griots of Nigeria and the Gambia.[131]

—David Toop, *The Rap Attack* (1984)

The rise of hip-hop evolved through the sets of policies, politics, and the changing economic of the 1970s.[132] As New York City sank into bankruptcy in 1975, areas such as the South Bronx personified the era of hyper-postindustrialization, capital flight, and decaying social services. Hip-hop also represented the evolution of the spoken-word practices of the Black Power era to the children raised amid the challenges confronting continued institutional oppression in an emerging neoliberal age celebrating color blindness.[133] Kool Herc's creation from 1973 blossomed into a cultural revolution by the early 1980s. Jeff Chang describes Herc's work as embodying the concept explored across this book: the possession of history. As a new culture, hip-hop "seemed to whirl backward and forward—a loop of history, history as loop—calling and responding, leaping, spinning, renewing."[134] If jazz defined the arrival of modern American urbanization in the early twentieth century, hip-hop anchored the musical and cultural ferment of postindustrial America—a *longue durée* synthesis by Black and Puerto Rican teenagers of the last 500 years of African diaspora history.

In the wake of the crisis of capital in New York City and the 1977 blackout, the Bronx entered yet another level of postindustrial sprawl intersecting with waves of arson and neglect.[135] One aspect of the subsequent looting led to a new surge in practitioners of hip-hip music. Hip-hop pioneer Grandmaster Caz noted, "So when the blackout happened in '77, I mean, they broke into everything in the city, especially the electronic stores. . . . And so many DJs popped up the next day and week after that blackout, it was ridiculous."[136] The aftermath produced an even larger scene of musical expression built around the various strands of oral traditions, BAM, and Jamaican toasts combined and layered on pre-recorded music from the Black Power era of funk (and its offshoot, disco), jazz, soul, and rock 'n' roll.

Hip-hop's initial expression was as performance art showcased at parties or clubs rather than a recordable, sold product. The only "product" was tapes of performances passed around and collected. However, by 1979 hip-hop moved from an art of practice to a commodified form through vinyl recordings. Sixteen-year-old Spoonie Gee, raised by an uncle who owned a record store on 125th Street (Bobby's Records) in New York City, recorded one of the earliest hip-hop records called "Spoonin' Rap" in 1979 (the same year as the hugely successful, "Rappers Delight" by the Sugar Hill Gang).[137] Across more than six minutes, Spoonie Gee rhymes about various travails with women, boasting, and the subject of law enforcement, setting an early model for a broad range of subject matter. Along with numerous romantic and "party" themes, artists such as Kurtis Blow and Grandmaster Flash and the Furious Five carried the Black radical tradition torch into the 1980s, commenting on the ongoing "benign neglect" conditions facing urban America.[138]

The hip-hop generation came of age in the aftermath of state violence against civil rights and Black Power movements just as deindustrialization and recession deepened the urban crisis.[139] In place of the fantastic abundance of materialism fostered on the white suburban youth of the 1950s and 1960s, a concentration of policing complemented the vacuum of economic opportunity.[140] Finally, hip-hop also arose just as the trend in Black-themed films from the early 1970s subsided. Although the most radical of Black action films featured critiques of American institutional racism—ranging from *Up Tight!* (1968), *The Final Comedown* (1972), and *The Spook Who Sat by the Door* (1973) to lesser known independent drama releases such as *Bush Mama* (1976) and *Killer of Sheep* (1977)—these motifs were replaced with summer blockbuster movies such as *Jaws* (1975), *Rocky* (1976), and *Star Wars* (1977), where Black Americans either did not appear, or they portrayed a villain. As studios recovered from their late-1960s recession through the aid of Black action film profits, Hollywood no longer needed Black heroes fighting against American racism, especially in the climate of neoliberal color blindness and the conservative culture war. Driven by the criminalization of Black activism, a variant of older stereotypes arose through the new racism of cultural pathology, justifying the heavy policing of inner-city Blackness. New film productions from the mid-1970s on depicted crazed, urban gang members viciously attacking police stations, supporting the prevailing sense that poverty in Black ghettos stemmed from dysfunctional, amoral culture rather than the legacies of the Jim Crow welfare state. Examples of these films include *Assault on Precinct 13* (1976), *The Warriors* (1979), *Fort Apache: The Bronx* (1981), and the dystopian *Escape from New York* (1981).[141] Reassuring white Americans' deep fear of Black men, popular media appeared to delight in converting the censured jacket of white supremacy into the cloak of "cultural pathology" Moynihan and Buckley discussed in the early 1960s—in short, films exploiting this *longue durée* sentiment of anti-Blackness continued to pay dividends.

Regenerating anti-Blackness proved easy in the first decade of legislated social equality. Using cultural pathology, the conservative culture war tapped into the Post-Reconstruction's idea of the Black "brute," converting this image into the 1970s "thug."[142] Aligning with the sentiment of John Wayne, the culture war continued to paint the collapsing welfare state as too soft on inner-city Black youth.[143] The demand for more aggressive policing characterized this era—what Loïc Wacquant calls the "irruption of the penal state"—including the reinstating of the death penalty by states in the mid-to-late

1970s.¹⁴⁴ Consequently, a crucial point of attack against liberal spending policies associated with the welfare state helped define "blacks, Latinos, and immigrants as political enemies" in the first decade of legislated social equality.¹⁴⁵ Hip-hop's birth through these policies led rappers to address the issues head on, becoming the definitive soundtrack of the neoliberal era.

An early political hip-hop song reviving the ideas of Black Power was "How We Gonna Make the Black Nation Rise?" by Brother D with Collective Effort.¹⁴⁶ Released by Jamaican-born Lister Hewan-Lowe on his Clappers record label, this multigendered effort contrasted partying with organizing the Black community: "People, people, can't you see? What is really going on? Unemployment's high, housing's bad, and the schools are teaching wrong. Cancer from the water, pollution in the air, but you're partying hard like you just don't care." Along with the environmental and structural collapse associated with deindustrialization, the lyrics note the ominous role of the state and its historic connection to Black imprisonment. Brother D states, "America was built, understand, by stolen labor on stolen land. Take a second thought . . . can you rock the house from inside the can? As you're moving to the beat in the early light, 'cause you're moving to, moving to the right. Prepare now, all, get high and wait. 'Cause there ain't no party in the police state." Black Power is celebrated as well, with other verses connecting Martin Luther King Jr., Elijah Muhammad, John Coltrane, and Marcus Garvey in their various methods of struggle.

With President Jimmy Carter seemingly unable to gain control over the economy, Ronald Reagan offered a glimmer of hope through a large dose of pre–civil rights era nostalgia, leading to the inauguration of Reaganomics after the 1980 election.¹⁴⁷ Reagan adopted many of the ideas of neoliberalism, changing the prerogatives of the state toward using the private market to shape public policy—what Ruth Wilson Gilmore calls the anti-state state.¹⁴⁸ With his grandfatherly, easy demeanor in front of the camera, Reagan's white paternal image of Jim Crow–era American heroes from film and television helped project an air of calm as winter in America arrived in force.

A spoken-word piece from Scott-Heron's 1981 album *Reflections* challenged the spectacle of Reagan: "And when America found itself having a hard time facing the future they looked for one of their heroes. Someone like John Wayne. But unfortunately John Wayne was no longer available, so they settled for Ronald the Raygun. . . . And it has turned into something that we can only look at like a 'B' movie."¹⁴⁹ Revisiting the meaning of freedom in the post–civil rights years, Scott-Heron underlined the role Reagan played in redefining the notion of freedom from a conservative perspective, where the discrediting of the "rights" movements of the 1960s played into the hands of the white reaction to legislated social equality. After a decade of the conservative culture war, many white Americans perceived big government intervention as the reason for their loss of status and income, while negative attitudes toward affirmative action—according to a 1978 survey—betrayed the ongoing roll of racism.[150] As the first white male generation to face substantial competition in the workplace from half the population (women) and people of color, the nostalgia for a pre–civil rights America embodied by Reagan made sense. Paraphrasing John Adams's conservative fear of expanding liberty, Scott-Heron continues:

> Civil Rights. Gay Rights. Women's Rights. They're all wrong! Call in the cavalry to disrupt this perception of freedom gone wild. First one of them wants freedom and then the whole damn world wants freedom! Nostalgia. That's what America wants. The good old days. When we "gave them hell!" When the buck stopped somewhere and you could still buy something with it! To a time when movies were in black and white and so was everything else.[151]

The legislated social equality gained through the struggle against the cultural *and* economic structures barring people of color and women from American opportunity are, in the post–civil rights era, reframed as attacks against the older white entitlement now evoked through the image of "the good ol' days" (of constitutional social inequality). Reagan's easy nature offered a soothing, familiar balm for the still-seething (or as Cortez would say, "brooding") white reaction to legislated social equality, a sentiment extending to the belief that the Democratic Party had "been too concerned with blacks."[152]

Moving from the connections between the criticism of the 1960s liberation movements and the loss of white entitlement, "'B' Movie" also addresses the transition of global capitalism. Noting the economy's turn from production to finance, Scott-Heron points to the new barometer of American well-being: Wall Street.[153]

> So much for the good news. As Wall Street goes so goes the nation and here's a look at the closing stocks:
> Racism is up. Human rights are down. Peace is shaky. War items are hot. The house claims all ties. Jobs are down, money is scarce and Common Sense is at an all-time low with heavy trading.[154]

Scott-Heron aptly described the culmination of free market and a federal government alignment to the needs of big business: the expansion of unemployment was an acceptable trade-off for controlling inflation.[155] Despite conservative calls for small government, government continued to grow under Reagan (with defense spending edging out social spending) as deindustrialization finalized the transition from a production-oriented economy to a finance-driven economy more conducive to multinational conglomerates. The outcome of these policies positioned Wall Street as the focal point of late-twentieth- and early-twenty-first-century capitalism. The 1974 prophecy of *Business Week*'s Carson-Parker was fulfilled in the 1980s as winter in America appeared to be firmly set in place.

One inheritor of Scott-Heron's conception of winter in America was the hip-hop song "The Message," released in the summer of 1982 at the height of a severe recession that pushed the national unemployment rate to 10.8 percent ("higher than at any time in post–World War II history").[156] Credited to Grandmaster Flash and the Furious Five, "The Message" gave voice to the material outcomes of the transition to neoliberalism. Born in 1958 in Barbados, Grandmaster Flash (Joseph Saddler) exemplified the long trend of Caribbean migration to the United States. His family immigrated to the Bronx when he was a child where he grew up fascinated with electronics, dissecting and repairing old radios and washing machines. His youthful curiosity led him to the evolving world of hip-hop DJing made popular by Kool Herc. Beginning in 1975, Grandmaster Flash would develop a DJing technique that led to him becoming part of "the trinity of hip-hop," alongside DJ Kool Herc and Afrika Bambaataa.[157] Grandmaster Flash and the Furious Five created "Freedom" in 1980 (coming in at number nineteen on the R&B charts). The follow up release led to one of the first gold records for socially conscious rap: "The Message." A product of Grandmaster Flash and the Furious Five, "The Message" was actually created by the record label Sugar Hill's songwriter Ed "Duke Bootee" Fletcher, with Melle Mel the only group member on the record.[158] The accompanying video for the song contained a skit at the end mimicking the conclusion of Stevie Wonder's "Living for the City" (1973), where, to underscore the racist criminal justice system, the members of the group are arrested by the police for no reason.[159]

"The Message" ties together images of the impoverished inner city as an environment in perpetual breakdown, with the lyrics commenting on unemployment, apathy, and drug addiction—what Chang calls the "culmination of fifteen years of benign neglect."[160] The chorus repeats the phrase

> Don't push me 'cause I'm close to the edge
> I'm trying not to lose my head.
> It's like a jungle sometimes it makes me wonder
> How I keep from going under.[161]

Here, the psychic toll on the Black working class wrestles with the staggering decline in the standard of living, the loss of jobs to deindustrialization, and the collapse of social services due to capital flight.[162] What was once a flourishing neighborhood now became a de facto slum, susceptible to arson and arson insurance schemes that capitalized on fire insurance policies covering abandoned buildings unable to attract renters.[163] Economic and other related ulcers of neoliberalism swamped those left behind.

> The bill collectors they ring my phone
> And scare my wife when I'm not home.
> Got a bum education, double-digit inflation
> Can't take the train to the job, there's a strike at the station.

Although "The Message" outlined the systemic evolution of neoliberalism as it spread through the Bronx, by the 1980s and 1990s, the decline of living standards for most middle and working class people reflected the inverse world of the concentration of wealth upward.

Fear, anxiety, and austerity replaced the American dream debated by Baldwin and Buckley in the 1960s, as neoliberalism foreclosed on the welfare state like the government and banks foreclosed on family farms across the Midwest.[164] Meanwhile, the "war on drugs" established a social context where, in the early 1980s, African Americans were "seven times more likely to be killed by the police than whites."[165] This "counterrevolution against the New Deal" and the institutionalization of "benign neglect" politically represented a return to the American norm, or as Reagan announced in 1984, "Morning in America."[166] "Morning" turned to "mourning," however, as Reagan's charming description of the economic promised land of Reaganomics proved a false dawn for a return to prosperity for those unable to adapt to the new information-financial economy of neoliberalism.[167]

> I speak here of poetry as a revelatory distillation of experience, not the sterile word play that, too often, the white fathers distorted the word *poetry* to mean—in order to cover a desperate wish for imagination without insight.... For women, then, poetry is not a luxury.... Poetry is the way we help give name to the nameless so it can be thought.
>
> —Audre Lorde, "Poetry Is Not a Luxury" (1977)

In the same year "The Message" reached number eight on the Billboard R&B Albums chart and fifty-three on the Billboard 200, Cortez released the album *There It Is* (credited to Jayne Cortez and the Firespitters).[168] The song "There It Is" articulated the diverse techniques of oppression in the early 1980s, stating, "They will try to exploit you / Absorb you confine you / Disconnect you isolate you / or kill you."[169] Here, Cortez emphasizes the ways the post–civil rights era of neoliberalism disciplines people into individuals rather than a part of collective movements defining 1960s activism.[170] Submerged into individualism, Cortez outlines the bipartisan nature of neoliberalism:

> The ruling class will tell you that
> there is no ruling class

> as they organize their liberal supporters into
> white supremist lynch mobs
> organize their children into
> ku klux klan gangs[171]

In a surrealist depiction of the nation's conservative lean right and the culture war against Black Americans (and other people of color), Cortez nuances the connection between post-welfare state individualism and the discontent toward those who continued to participate in social justice movements. As racial justice organizing called into question the color blind delusion of the new socio-economic system, resentment renewed against this trespass, preparing the ground for a return of Carol Anderson's notion of "white rage" directed toward the victims of oppression who are—as Baldwin observes—"able to articulate the situation of the victim" and have now "become a threat."[172]

The class consciousness developed across the 1930s now found replacement by a culture war conflict pressing white American's attention toward individual identities—race, gender, sexuality—rather than class. The liberal retreat from addressing structural inequality stemmed largely from the fear of losing the Democratic Party's base: the white working and middle classes.[173] With this wedge, Cortez suggests liberals were more than mere pawns or innocent onlookers driving the rise of neoliberalism, as their talk of reform morphed into lynch mobs (demands for law and order) and support for the dismantling of the federal intervention on behalf of white working- and middle-class people. In their inability to address the structural conditions linked to the republic's system of racial slavery and its extension of inequality through the Jim Crow welfare state era, liberals closed ranks with their conservative white allies in the midst of urban uprisings after 1965 and the rise of Black Power in the late 1960s and 1970s. Scott-Heron noted this cynical shell game in 1978:

> 'cause I believe these smiles
> in three piece suits
> with gracious, liberal demeanor
> took our movement off the streets
> and took us to the cleaners.
> In other words, we let up the pressure
> and that was all part of their plan
> and every day we allow to slip through our fingers
> is playing right into their hands.[174]

Embracing the solutions and discourse of "law and order" and "benign neglect"—which foreclosed any reforms beyond social equality legislation—

Democratic liberals helped chart the path away from the welfare state toward the economic visions of neoliberals, conservatives, multinationals, and finance.

At the same time, the project of "racial" reform via civil rights legislation helped assimilate the entire decade of Black revolt into the American exceptionalist narrative of ever-expanding equality and freedom. Insidiously, Martin Luther King Jr.'s "I Have a Dream" statement, "they will not be judged by the color of their skin, but by the content of their character," was embraced as a civil rights reform benefiting the quantitative analysis, ostensibly color-blind-driven logics of the post-1960s U.S. The "content of their character" refocused protections upon individuals, moreover, rather than group oppression. Color-blind markets governed the actions of individual people after legislated social equality, suggesting that government intervention based off race or gender or sexuality infringed on an individual's freedom. In other words, capitalism (whether the Jim Crow welfare state or neoliberalism) need only remove overtly racist signs while the governing logics of markets would override the "natural" cycles of the supply and demand for racism, sexism, and other centuries-old antagonisms. Of course, the demand and market prerogatives developed across the centuries and decades of slavery and Jim Crow continued to inform the traditional cultural-economic logic driving racial capitalism. It would be a *longue* road for social equality legislation to divert the momentum of centuries-old anti-Black antagonism. Inoculated with the reformism of civil and women's rights (cleansed of both the Black radical tradition and radical feminist critiques), the silent majority consolidated the gains made across the era of the Jim Crow welfare state. In the name of individualism and color blindness, the socio-economic opportunity access ladder was pulled up behind those benefiting from the Jim Crow welfare state, as the redistributionist policies of the postwar years became unfair to whites the moment they were extended to people of color and women. In a true display of Baldwin's possession of history, this brief experiment, what Jefferson Cowie and Nick Salvatore call the "long exception," floundered into the memory hole of American history.[175]

Released in 1983 and set in the heart of the Reagan revolution, the film *Black Wax* presented Scott-Heron's ideas and music in concert, on the streets of Washington, D.C., and in a wax museum filled with a collection of historical figures.[176] As he did with his 2010 release, Scott-Heron resurrected two spoken-word pieces from his early albums, including "Paint It Black" and "Billy Green Is Dead" off *Free Will*.[177] The last poem in *Black Wax* was "Whitey on the Moon," recited beneath a wax astronaut. Scott-Heron's original statement from 1970 criticizing the space race/defense spending at the time of expanding inner-city poverty assumed even greater saliency in the Reagan years as the federal government transferred the tax burden to the middle and working classes, cut social spending on poverty, and attempted to outspend the Soviet Union in the final round of the Cold War.[178] Meanwhile, the poverty rate rose from 11.7 to 15.3 percent between 1980 and 1983, "the highest rate, and the greatest number (some 35.3 million), since the mid-1960s."[179] Here lay an important outcome of the 1960s and the rise of neoliberalism: the new economic system of the 1980s created a generous Keynesian stimulus to Southern and Western defense and aeronautical industries and their mostly white skilled or college-educated workers, many of whom lived in federally subsidized suburbs. At the same time, government economic policy proscribed austerity measures on Northern cities, particularly those hit by deindustrialization and populated by African Americans. A reformed Keynesianism channeling capital to large multinational corporations—whether in the form of defense, energy, or the prison industrial complex—existed without contradiction under the guise of neoliberal free markets. Leaving the wax museum during the closing scene of *Black Wax*, Scott-Heron reflected on a comment he made in an earlier performance in the film, "B Movie": "the odds are," glancing at a wax statue of John Wayne in the fake saloon, "we would've been better off with John Wayne." Scott-Heron then playfully patted Wayne's face as if he was an old friend, whispering, "Take care, big fella," and then exited through the fake saloon doors into the darkness.

The ideas circulating through the 1965 debate between Baldwin and Buckley continued through the rest of the twentieth century. Although Buckley might have lost the argument in 1965, his ideology eventually won the war. The 1980s were bleak years for Black Americans unable to escape inner-city poverty. The election bargains struck by white American working and middle classes in the 1970s and 1980s for tough, populist conservatives paved the road toward a contraction of their standard of living. The wealthy, however, did extremely well. By 1984, the reelection campaign of Ronald Reagan asserted, "It's morning again in America." The golden age of prosperity Reagan promised in 1980 had, it seemed, returned—at least for the wealthy. For those outside the new information-service economy or finance, the Reagan era represented a neo-gilded age. For the GOP, the successful polarizing wedges developed by the Nixon administration had become permanent fixtures in Republican strategies through today.[180] By the 1990s, the New Democrats arose to power under the leadership of President Bill Clinton: socially centrist, fiscally neoliberal, and ready to be tougher on crime than conservatives.[181] Hardly fazed by the bipartisan rightward shift in economics since the 1970s, conservatives found further momentum by demonizing Clinton as a "leftist," pressing populist conservatism even further to the right amid the so-called Republican revolution of 1994 and the mission to make tax cuts permanent, dismantle welfare even further, and disable "big government" for good. In other words, the neoliberal reforms of the 1970s and 1980s found aggressive institutionalization.

Scott-Heron's album *Spirits*, released in 1994, addressed this apparatus on the track "Work for Peace," a critique of the First Gulf War.[182] The opening lines cite the astute premonitions of Eisenhower, who "mumble[ed] something about a Military Industrial Complex." Linking what becomes the song's chorus—"The Military and the Monetary"—Scott-Heron observes, "Americans no longer fight to keep their shores safe, just to keep the jobs going in the arms making workplace. Then they pretend to be gripped by some sort of political reflex. But all they're doing is paying dues to the Military Industrial Complex." Citing the influence of the financial world of Wall Street, multinationals, and military industrialists, Scott-Heron asserts, "The Military and the Monetary, use the media as intermediaries, they are determined to keep the citizens secondary, they make so many decisions that are arbitrary." In linking the public-private collusion, Scott-Heron punctures the free market idealism of neoliberalism, with the implication that the military Keynesian policies of Reagan merely reproduced the state-sponsored support of capitalism under the guise of corporate welfare rather than social welfare. Scott-Heron also traces the routes of propaganda leading to the First Gulf War:

> The Military and the Monetary, they get together whenever they think it's necessary. War in the desert sometimes sure is scary, but they beamed out the war to all their subsidiaries. Tried to make 'So Damn Insane' [Saddam Hussein] a worthy adversary, keeping the citizens secondary, scaring old folks into coronaries.
> The Military and the Monetary, from thousands of miles in a Saudi Arabian sanctuary, kept us all wondering if all of this was really truly, necessary.

Scott-Heron's analysis emphasizes the way multinationals utilized media conglomerates to manufacture and reinforce a common sense, tying neoliberal economics to Americanism, and foreign policy abroad with job production at home: "The only thing wrong with Peace, is that you can't make no money from it." In an offer of hope and resistance to the leviathan, Scott-Heron reveals skepticism among the public, reminding the listener that the system, however powerful, was not absolute.

Almost ten years later, Scott-Heron's "Work for Peace" eerily gained a second life in similar context. Named "Operation Iraqi Freedom"—another play on the word *freedom*—the Second Gulf War added further credence to Scott-Heron's astute ability to identify and critique the political landscape. By the early 2000s, neoliberalism transformed into the dream child of neoconservative theoreticians who, after the 9/11 attack on New York City, implemented their update of Henry Luce's "American Century"—"Project for the New American Century."[183] Through the harnessing of media-instilled fear, ultrapatriotism, and a neo-McCarthyism, their neoliberal economics found new (oil) fields for cultivation in an occupied Iraq, under the contractual guise of the Coalition Provisional Government—with Paul Bremer proving folk singer Woody Guthrie's adage, "Some will rob you with a gun; And some with a fountain pen."[184] The political outcome of 9/11 provided the federal government with a mandate to not only propose a national purpose but also (as David Harvey suggests) The war with Iraq "was a grand opportunity to impose a new sense of social order at home and bring the commonwealth to heel.... The evil enemy without became the prime force through which to exorcise or tame the devils lurking within."[185]

The struggle over devils brings us back to "Me and the Devil Blues"/"Your Soul and Mine" (aka "The Vulture") from *I'm New Here: Gil Scott-Heron*, where the devil embodies the Faustian bargain for the pleasures of the marketplace at the expense of poverty. Scott-Heron's juxtaposition of the devil and New York City alludes to the structural evils analyzed in his 1970s work as well as his, Cortez's, and others' critical poetic paths since then. Mixing the devil with his metaphorical vulture places Scott-Heron's critique into a more existential realm. However, when situated within his canon, "Me and the Devil Blues"/"Your Soul and Mine" points back to the listener for solutions. "Me and the Devil" walking hand in hand is the result of a pact. And the vulture, while circling above and seeking a battle for your soul, still suggests a front on which one may put up resistance. His first video for *I'm New Here* puts the burden of societal change back on the people instead of charismatic figureheads. More than fifteen years earlier, Scott-Heron's "Work for Peace" warned listeners that peace would not be "easy" or "free"—let alone televised. It was complicated, not simple. In the wake of the Second Iraqi War in the 2000s, Scott-Heron sings over the black-and-white video for his 2010 comeback album: "Woke up this morning, me and the devil, walking side by side." Exceptional homelessness and ever-expanding poverty in Manhattan, walking side-by-side with fantastic wealth: although it has been a long morning in America, winter does not seem to end.

Conclusion

> In the three short decades between now and the twenty-first century, millions of ordinary, psychologically normal people will face an abrupt collision with the future. Citizens of the world's richest and most technologically advanced nations, many of them will find it increasingly painful to keep up with the incessant demand for change that characterizes our time. For them, the future will have arrived too soon.
>
> —Alvin Toffler, *Future Shock* (1970)

As this project went through draft after draft, one person's words grew in saliency with each pass: John Carson-Parker, writer for *Business Week* and *Fortune* magazine. As an articulation of neoliberal policies before neoliberalism ascended to its position of dominance in the Reagan era, Carson-Parker's words appear as a fever dream premonition. In the October 12, 1974, issue of *Business Week*, Carson-Parker prophesized the arrival of neoliberal austerity for the vast majority of Americans. Conceptually mapping out the post-1970s economic path of the United States, Carson-Parker presciently noted the radical changes the nation would make as it shifted from the Keynesian welfare state to the supply-side, neoliberal policies of the 1980s:

> Some people will obviously have to do with less, or with substitutes, so that the economy as a whole can get the most mileage out of available capital. There will be fewer homes and more apartment houses built.... It will be harder to launch risky new ventures because the needs of existing businesses will be so great.... Indeed, cities and states, the home mortgage market, small business, and the consumer, will all get less than they want because the basic health of the U.S. is based on the basic health of its corporations and banks: the biggest borrowers and the biggest lenders. Compromises, in terms of who gets and who does without, that would have been unthinkable only a few years ago will be made in coming years because the economic future not only of the U.S. but also of the whole world is on the line today.[1]

Underlining the stakes involved, Carson-Parker imagined a difficult struggle in convincing citizens to vote away the welfare state and implement an economic policy geared more toward the wealthy and big business than working- and middle-class Americans: "It will be a hard pill for many Americans to swallow—the idea of doing with less so that big business can have more. Nothing that this nation, or any other nation, has done in modern economic history compares in difficulty with the selling job that must now be done to make people accept this new reality."[2] The unraveling historical conjuncture between the 1960s and 1980s made this seemingly difficult job easier, as the transformation of the American political economy drew much of its popular momentum from the cultural anxiety many white Americans experienced under the specter of legislated social equality with historically marginalized groups they had long treated and understood as second-class citizens or inhuman objects whose lives did not matter. Culturally accustomed to the *longue durée* legacies and practices of settler colonialism, slavery and Jim Crow, and patriarchy, resentment toward legislated social equality regenerated the American tradition of populist-conservative sentiment in white voters, gracing the sale of neoliberal policies with a populist veneer designating the economic system as representing ordinary people and not just the wealthy and powerful.

As a set of economic ideas conceived in reaction to the economically populist and social democratic Jim Crow welfare state arising out of the New Deal and World War II, intellectuals such as Milton Friedman and Friedrich Hayek propagated neoliberalism within two protected spaces. Culturally, the centuries of anti-Blackness, racial science, and eugenics continued to firmly embed conceptions of liberty and freedom within the realm of whiteness, a material and psychological outcome based on settler colonial practices and the institutions of slavery and Jim Crow. The other protected space included, ironically, the welfare state itself, which fashioned the very economic setting that not only molded the prosperity of white working- and middle-class people, but more importantly, facilitated the ascent of multinationals and finance within the United States and abroad. Finally, the welfare state gave meaning to the neoliberal project, acting as a binary from which neoliberal economists could define their ideas against, allowing neoliberalism to be a viable alternative once the welfare state lost legitimacy. For white working- and middle-class people, particularly men, an artificially insulated space of prosperity arose across the 1950s and 1960s. Reflected in the content of images consumed as nostalgia after the 1960s, this protective bubble fostered a delusion of expectations from government and society, provoking a populist-conservative reaction against the inclusion of people of color and women after social equality legislation deemed this delusion both racist and sexist. As the white nationalist traditions of the welfare state faced censure and found itself challenged by social justice movements, the language of neoliberalism and the conservative culture war against the disruption of this postwar ideal began appealing to weary white voters who longed for the era of unquestioned white male dominance.

The market for pre-1960s nostalgia expanded dramatically in the 1970s, selling images and sounds of simpler, less complicated, times, before federal intervention through civil rights legislation dismantled the exclusivity of the federally subsidized American dream.

The possession of history conjured by nostalgia consisted of a pre–civil rights movement U.S. dominated by white male heroes from the ostensibly ordered Jim Crow era. Draped in the cloaks of rugged individualism, these heroes performed feats of American innocence with the racist fury captured by photography, film, and polls across the twentieth century removed from the story. Hardly unique, this disavowal of unseemly ideas and policies in American life aligned neatly with previous generations' histories of settler colonialism and slavery, where atrocities were scraped clean to provide justification for the politics of the present. From settler colonialism emerged the insistent suspicion of government intervention into the settlers' desire to extend their liberty on the frontier by obtaining land previously occupied by Native Americans or Mexicans. Liberty, in this sense, was the freedom to "do as one pleases" in territory newly conquered from groups deemed inferior, and in need of—or doomed toward—extinction.[3] From the perspective of Native Americans and Mexicans, of course, this liberty and freedom equaled invasion and ethnic cleansing, underlining the value of the possession of history and the ability to define and articulate one's history (in other words, James Baldwin's idea of the victim articulating their situation). From the 1960s to the present, the conservative culture war has taken aim at "history from below"—and the denouncement of "revisionist history"—that unveiled the politically incorrect narratives of violence and racist sentiment traditionally scrubbed clean from school textbooks. An honest and blunt history of the U.S. underscores the zero-sum process of white American settler colonialism, which constructed an identity through the appropriation of land in the name of liberty and freedom while reserving the right to administer violence toward those resisting these claims to space or government representatives seeking to regulate the settlers' use of land. Meanwhile, the possession of history safely characterized these policies as "settlement" and virtuous defensive measures protecting the liberty and freedom of the settlers. For the institution of slavery and its Jim Crow aftermath, the white settler derived another possession of history: the anchoring concept of freedom imagined and conditioned through the institution of slavery and the ongoing post-Emancipation oppression and violence targeting people of African descent. If settler colonialism embedded a xenophobic distaste for people deemed foreign and who were not white—and, thus, unable to assimilate—slavery firmly embedded social death upon the Blackness of the enslaved, emboldening a simmering anti-Blackness marking African Americans as enemies within the

United States, and convenient targets for new immigrants seeking assimilation into whiteness. Enhancing ideas of race through violent antagonism, these processes cultivated a white American masculinity, setting the foundations for the triumphal framework of Western civilization and its transnational white racial superiority.[4]

Patriarchy, long a part of human history, found a peculiar renewal through North American settler colonialism and slavery as well. By highlighting the masculine power of white male guidance in leading the settlers/invaders across the continent (and overseas) and defending against resisting Indigenous peoples (whether it was Tecumseh, Geronimo, or the American Indian movement in the 1970s), frontier threats and vilification of people of African descent helped inscribe a white paternal community leadership whose rule over women (including possession of their bodies) was branded as protection from Native Americans, Mexican Americans, and Black Americans—all of whom, it was imagined, zealously sought to rape white women. The experience of these antagonisms produced heroic stories of rugged individualism and manhood defined against Black or Native American laziness, cowardice, or treachery, while liberty and freedom translated into the aggressive expression of white community violence against enemies on the frontier and within—from white vigilante policing of "sundown towns" to racial mob violence such as the Tulsa massacre of 1921. These markings of race were hardwired into cultural assumptions, laws, institutions, and economic opportunity. The possession of history evoked by William F. Buckley and John Wayne translated the omnipresence of this white nationalism into an invisible coincidence of white male domination of American life—with the historical baggage of white violence removed from the histories and popular culture consumed by the public. The civil rights era legislatively ended this entitlement, unsettling the delusion of universal freedom and liberty bound to the legacies of white nationalism. This disruption of the traditionally wholesome stories of brave frontiersmen, innocent settlers, and benevolent slave owners provoked a bitter reaction. An existential crisis flared up in this vacuum of uncertainty as the long dependence on an often unacknowledged white supremacy for identity and opportunity felt the pangs of withdrawal, particularly anxiety and irritability, as the age of legislated social equality unfolded. For James Baldwin, this sobering era of the 1960s lay bare the *longue durée* consequences of an identity based off subjugation: "when the prisoner is free, the jailer faces the void of himself."[5]

Neoliberals, conservatives, the writers of *Business Week*, and John Wayne, among many others, filled this desperate void with a nostalgic renewal of an older possession of history. The archive of this constructed past lay in the popular media memories of the golden age of Jim Crow mass culture between the 1870s and 1950s, when white men dominated popular culture, Black Americans were either marginalized in media representation or made to play the fool or servant, assertive men could virtuously brutalize overemotional women, and Native Americans appeared as ghosts from a primeval past or embodied threats to "peaceful" settlements. While the social justice zeitgeist of the 1960s exposed these myths of innocence, the backlash of nostalgia provided a desperately needed balm for white Americans still pondering the haunting question of the Baldwin-Buckley debate and the larger meanings of the civil rights movement: did the American dream come at the expense of African Americans; or was the reassuring pre-1960s history books and popular culture correct in suggesting that anyone working hard in the United States could obtain the American dream—regardless of race or gender? While many desperately clung to the sanitized history, the legacies of settler colonialism, slavery, and patriarchy continued to cast a large shadow over the language many white Americans used to dismiss claims of the past and press their shoulders to the wind: the liberty and freedom enjoyed in the postwar years was now under siege by those who were *beneath them* just a decade before. A failed foreign adventure in Vietnam, a resigning president on the verge of impeachment, and the worst economic crisis since the 1930s added even more confusion and disruption to the stability of the grade school stories gracefully recounted by Walt Disney—all of which were questioned by the supporters of social equality legislation. With white Americans no longer able to legally capitalize on their whiteness via the Jim Crow welfare state, the ascending color-blind mantra of neoliberal quantitative analysis and the coded racism of the New Right appeared as an answer to their dilemma. White resentment toward legislated social equality took solace in Nixon's "southern strategy" (or Lassiter's "suburban strategy") and the arrival of a politics targeting Black people while never *saying* Black people.[6] Urban crime dramas and actions films both regenerated the criminality of urban Blackness and reawakened the white masculine vigilante fantasies expressed through *Dirty Harry* (1971), *Death Wish* (1974), and *Taxi Driver* (1976). With overt racism no longer publicly acceptable, the quantitative analysis of neoliberalism re-created Jim Crow structures in business and higher education through standardized testing without standardized equalization of education—with the latter resulting from the geographic relationships related to the policies and material outcomes of the Jim Crow welfare state.[7] The result: ideas of cultural pathology pontificated by conservatives and Hollywood replaced biological arguments legitimizing racist assumptions and policies.

Mirroring the settler colonial reclamation of freedom from government intervention, neoliberals, conservatives, and anxious white Americans fell within an ideological alliance with multinational conglomerates and finance who had for decades sought the deregulation of the welfare state. With the conjuncture of 1960s social equality legislation and the 1970s economic crisis, the stage was set for working- and middle-class white Americans to help dismantle the very economic system redistributing wealth toward their demographic by voting into place a system geared toward big business and the wealthy. In hindsight, Carson-Parker's fear of the public's resistance toward these policies now seems quaint. Adding to the irony, working- and middle-class white Americans found it hard to fully acknowledge the extent to which their economic fortunes were tied to the political economy of the Jim Crow welfare state's government intervention on their behalf. Thus, it only took a mere promise of conservative moderation in the form of trickle-down economics and a defense of "traditional values" (coded as white, patriarchal, and heterosexual norms) to ease white working- and middle-class concerns as they voted their way down a road leading toward massive wealth inequality and a significant decline in their standard of living.

Although quantitative analysis seemed a rational, and ostensibly fair, route to follow, a vague promise continues to haunt the idea of lowering taxes on the wealthy so that the benefits might splash down upon the working and middle classes. In the 1960s, Hayek attempted to negotiate this thin line: how do you convince working and middle-class voters to replace the welfare state—which was responsible for their postwar prosperity—with an economic system that is expected to bring back pre-Great Depression wealth inequalities?

> There is no practicable measure of the degree of inequality that is desirable here. We do not wish, of course, to see the position of individuals determined by arbitrary decision or a privilege conferred by human will on particular persons. It is difficult to see however, in what sense it could ever be legitimate to say that any one person is too far ahead of the rest or that it would be harmful to society if the progress of some greatly outstripped that of others. There might be justification for saying this if there appeared great gaps in the scale of advance; but, as long as the graduation is more or less continuous and all the steps in the income pyramid are reasonably occupied, it can scarcely be denied that those lower down profit materially from the fact that others are ahead.[8]

In asking for the removal of the redistributionist policies of the welfare state, Hayek's discussion of the anticipated extremes of economic inequality neoliberal policies most likely would produce entered the uncharacteristically subjective arena of "we'll know it when we see it—trust us." Here, quantitative analysis cannot judge wealth inequality in the same way it might judge the economics of deregulation, cuts in social spending on the poor, or the legal separation of politics from economics. This vague sentiment—in some ways the inverse of the welfare state's fairness and justness logic—would define the neoliberal defense of wealth inequality through the twentieth century. Is it fair that there is so much wealth inequality?—not according to the "rule of law" and free market capitalism. In their quantitative analysis studies on wealth inequality, economists such as Thomas Piketty and Emmanuel Saez could not break this dogged faith, as their scholarship appeared to be (using Hayek's words above) an impractical "measure of the degree of inequality," especially for those on the receiving end of the benefits of neoliberalism.[9] In the sixty years after Hayek's promise of moderation, winter now appears permanent—with various avenues of resentment exploding in directions unanticipated by the architects of wealth inequality. Many of those formerly benefiting from the welfare state now find themselves safely locked outside the keep, as the last hopes for a thawing spring find refuge through the numbing escape of opioids, ever-increasing culture war resentments, and the mobilization of paramilitary militias—all of whom found catharsis on January 6, 2021, when conservative supporters of President Trump revisited the mob violence of previous eras of white nationalism and stormed the Capitol building in the hopes of stopping the Electoral College count—leading to five U.S. Capitol police officers killed during the siege, with scores injured.[10]

Winter in America offers a cutaway rendering of the cultural-economic transition into the neoliberal era. Whether popular culture, news media, academic works, or general public political discussions, the road to neoliberalism was strewn with various streams of language and knowledge caught in the conjuncture of massive social change and economic uncertainty between the 1960s and 1980s. In the face of legislated social equality, a rhetorically blunt systemic reset of history to "year zero" unfolded, a strategy designed to silence the decades, *and centuries*, of white nationalist policies related to the Jim Crow welfare state and the overall history of the nation. Unable to reckon with the past, this possession of history desperately sought to redeem a tattered American innocence stripped bare of its righteous "exceptionalism," the comforting history Americans learned through the lens of twentieth century popular images of white Americans under siege. As participants in the culture war, conservatives became the settler family in television and film, under siege from Native Americans, and defending their homestead against the social justice movements seeking the legal enforcement of constitutional protections white Americans took for granted. The burden of history weighed heavily as the bills came due.

Beginning as a project in 2010, *Winter in America* took form as the children of the first recipients of the welfare state—the babyboomers, the last generation to come of age through legislated Jim Crow white nationalism—adopted the imagery of the founding fathers (the Tea Party) in reaction to the election of the first Black president. In 2016, they finally discovered a champion to restore their traditional status in the United States—enthusiastically embracing the hero's promise to "make America great again," forty years after voting away the very economic system responsible for their memories of the 1950s and 1960s. Grabbing the reins of populist conservatism (without asking establishment Republicans), Donald Trump intuitively understood the deep psychology fueling the festering resentment of those who formerly benefited from the Jim Crow welfare state and who dutifully voted for conservatives on cultural issues after the 1960s. Many, however, were unable to adapt to the swift changes characterizing the neoliberal economy. Rather than an appraisal of the neoliberal, trickle-down economic system, this constituency continued to knead the ever-evolving culture war resentments—immigration, women's rights, LGBTQ rights, criminal justice inequality, science, and sometimes just "the liberals"—into a bleak sustenance feeding their explanation of why their standard of living had declined since the 1980s. President Trump's campaign strategy wove a tapestry of antagonisms, all rooted in the deep processes of settler colonialism, slavery, and patriarchy. He demonized people of Latin American descent, Muslims, and Black protesters while praising representatives of white supremacy ("very fine people, on both sides")—even to the extent of refusing to condemn white nationalist groups when directly asked on national television.[11] Trump also surrounded himself with white men who celebrated the white supremacist eugenics-based Immigration Act of 1924, including the idea that excluding the Chinese, Italians, and Jews was "good for America."[12] At the same time, Trump directed the Department of Homeland Security to downplay the growing threat of white nationalism while highlighting the violence of antifa and Black Lives Matter. For strong women opposed to him, misogynist arguments and blunt celebrations of his sexual assaults and conquests—the disciplinary anchors of patriarchy—drew applause from populist conservatives, particularly from white evangelical groups whose more fundamentalist subsets explicitly call for women to be submissive to men ("submission theology").[13]

Viewed across the *longue durée*, this moment in history is hardly shocking. White masculine resentment steadily festered after the 1970s, the first decade in the nation's history when white men, especially white men with property, were legislatively forced into social equality with women and people of color. Now entering the third decade of the twenty-first century, the contingent nature of this brief fifty years of legislated social equality staggers on, still suffering symptoms of withdrawal from the distant days of legislated white nationalism. From the language of those inheritors of the conservative culture war, it is clear that the 1970s presented an existential threat to white America, as legislated social equality interrupted the innocent possession of history populist conservatives grew up with during the Jim Crow era. As the opioid crisis and the armed rage of paramilitary groups underscore, winter in America continues to provoke a desperate need to numb the austerity of neoliberal economic policies, whose populist-conservative roots have since evolved into a resurgence of overt white nationalism derived from the centuries of settler colonialism, slavery and Jim Crow, and patriarchy.[14]

The struggle over the possession of history continues to be a flashpoint of contention in the twenty-first century, a prize still sought to justify contemporary policies on ideas about the past. For conservatism, this is the function of the culture war: to defend and shelter a past built on rampant racism, sexism, classism, xenophobia, and other antagonisms, while rehabilitating an idealized history free of these trespasses. What is left is the simple story of American innocence with the complexities of settler colonialism, slavery, and patriarchy quarantined from view. Prior to the 1960s, these histories found divine sanction—an American exceptionalism, or manifest destiny glossing the official narratives spanning education, entertainment, and politics across the white nationalist era of Jim Crow (1870s–1950s). As the civil rights movement unfolded, scholars dug beneath this glossy history of the American past and started cataloging a less-celebratory history against the background of a contemporary present where women and people of color continued to struggle for social equality. For Americans experiencing the 1960s—from the Vietnam War to civil rights to the counterculture—the meanings of U.S. history came unmoored.

To help us conceptualize this collapse in meaning, we might revisit the work of historian Hans Kellner, who focused on the intricacies of language and text and its structuring of ontology.[15] Writing in the late 1980s, Kellner asserts, "Historians mistrust language; to speak of it is disturbing.... It is tempting to reject this strain of criticism as old-fashioned, resistant to change, or just lazy, but that would be to miss an important point. Conservatives (as Eugene Genovese has shown of slaveholders) foresee the consequences of change more clearly than others because their 'antennae' sense things before they can articulate them. This uneasiness before 'the language thing' is a genuine fear of losing the heavy but comforting 'burden of history' that has told us Westerners who we are for quite a while."[16] This passage offers some insight into the neoliberal era's existential crisis for white America and its relationship to history. Kellner suggests that as new threats arose (the foreseeing of "the consequences of change") from previously subjugated people, the conservative's "antennae" sensed the ramifications of this liberation, especially those whose subjugation defined the very identity of people benefiting from their oppression. A conservative reaction targets this new threat, as the subjugated is able to articulate their situation as "subjugated"—and thus, as James Baldwin notes, they "become a threat."[17] This is the context for the reinforcement of one's possession of history "that has told us Westerners who we are for quite a while."[18] If Michel-Rolph Trouillot is correct in describing ontological universals as "not describ[ing] the world" but "offer[ing] visions of the world," then this act of ontological salvaging engages in a struggle over the possession of history: it attacks the new language and knowledge describing the subjugated and their historical relationship to a nation-state defined by a legacy of white nationalism.[19] This reaction simultaneously continues to celebrate an American history made possible only through the subjugation of those designated to be naturally inferior—and calls the critics of this whitewashed past "unpatriotic" to invalidate histories documenting the words and deeds of white nationalism. This is not, of course, a contradiction in American history: the conservative's concept of social "order"—going back to at least John Adams—found root in the naturalization of hierarchy at the very moment when liberty and freedom justified a new republic governed by white men whose property often included enslaved people of African descent. For centuries, this cultural contradiction normalized the meanings and material outcomes of American economics. As a norm, the white nationalist character of the nation became obscured in American minds through the stories and histories told about liberty and freedom.

Culture provides purpose for humanity. It makes sense of a chaotic world through an exchange of symbols, language, and gestures that, through acceptance and repetition, embeds itself into a "traditional" way of interpreting reality. Anything interrupting this familiar signal becomes a disrupting noise—a threat to social order demanding containment. Culture also interprets the economic world, and economic policies often cohere through ideas inspired by various understandings of humanity and tradition. When the innocence surrounding the prosperous postwar socioeconomic world found itself under siege by the very targets of oppression helping to shape that prosperity, a powerful culture war phalanx not only pushed back against the disruption of innocence and exceptionalism but also obliterated from popular memory the economic structures framing the prosperity of postwar Jim Crow America: the welfare state. As the burden of the past was dumped into an unmarked grave at the dawn of neoliberalism, a new historical memory surfaced through the conservative culture war to delegitimize economic avenues leading back to a time of less-capital concentration while simultaneously—and ironically—highlighting the simple and refreshing moments of this golden age of welfare state white nationalism, when, ostensibly, "America was great." Looking back from the twenty-first century, this dynamic appears as a tragic paradox, a downward spiral of the American public screaming "Why?" as the nation desperately continues tightening the vise of its own making with the expectation of breaking free.

Notes

Introduction

1. For "conjuncture," I use Lawrence Grossberg's definition (influenced by Stuart Hall): "A conjuncture is a description of a social formation as fractured and conflictual, along multiple axes, planes and scales, constantly in search of temporary balances or structural stabilities through a variety of practices and processes of struggle and negotiation." See Grossberg, "Does Cultural Studies Have Futures?," 4. See also Paige, "Conjuncture, Comparison, and Conditional Theory in Macrosocial Inquiry."

2. See Trattner, *From Poor Law to Welfare State*; Gordon, *Pitied but Not Entitled*.

3. Cowie, *The Great Exception*, 202.

4. Hazlitt, *Man vs. the Welfare State*, 220.

5. See Adams, *The Works of John Adams*.

6. For a deep history of the conservative war against the New Deal welfare state on behalf of the wealthy, see Fones-Wolf, *Selling Free Enterprise*; Phillips-Fein, *Invisible Hands*; MacLean, *Democracy in Chains*.

7. Brown, *Strain of Violence*, 4. See also Williams, *Anatomy of Four Race Riots*; Mitchell, *Race Riots in Black and White*; Lumpkins, *American Pogrom*; Krehbiel, *Tulsa 1921*.

8. See Anderson, *White Rage*.

9. Anderson, *White Rage*, 74. See also Lewis, *Massive Resistance*; Webb, *Massive Resistance*.

10. See Kruse, *White Flight*.

11. Katznelson, *When Affirmative Action Was White*, 61–62. See also Patterson, "A Conservative Coalition Forms in Congress."

12. Hunter, *Culture Wars*, 39. Hunter writes, "Through the nineteenth and early twentieth century cultural discord was kindled, in general, by two competing tendencies. On one hand, there was the quest on the part of various minority cultures to carve out a space in American life where they could each live according to the imperatives of conscience and the obligations of community without harassment or reprisal. Such a space would provide the base from which to expand their own legitimate interests as a distinct moral community. On the other hand, there was the endeavor of Protestants and a largely Protestant-based populism to ward off any challenges—to retain their advantage in defining the habits and meaning of American culture."

13. Hunter, *Culture Wars*, 39.

14. Rodríguez, "Goldwater's Left Hand," 32–33. See also Rodríguez, *White Reconstruction*.

15. See Schulman, *The Seventies*; Jenkins, *Decade of Nightmares*; Berkowitz, *Something Happened*; Zaretsky, *No Direction Home*; Wilentz, *The Age of Reagan*; Stein, *Pivotal Decade*; Rodgers, *Age of Fracture*; Borstelmann, *1970s*; Self, *All in the Family*; Kruse and Zelizer, *Fault Lines*.

16. Liner notes for Scott-Heron and Jackson, *Midnight Band*. See also Scott-Heron, *Now and Then*, 69.

17. Phillips, *Wealth and Democracy*, 237. See also McCurdy, "Justice Field and the Jurisprudence of Government-Business Relations."

18. Mirowski, *Never Let a Serious Crisis Go to Waste*, 28.

19. See Phillips, *The Politics of Rich and Poor*; Piketty and Saez, "Income Inequality in the United States"; Noah, "The United States of Inequality." See also Hacker and Pierson, *Winner-Take-All Politics*; Congressional Budget Office, *Trends in the Distribution of Household Income*.

20. Piketty, *Capital in the Twenty-First Century*, 15. See also Phillips, *Wealth and Democracy*.

21. Lentin and Titley, *The Crises of Multiculturalism*; Bruff, "The Rise of Authoritarian Neoliberalism"; Müller, *What Is Populism?*; Milanovic, *Global Inequality*; Tansel, *States of Discipline*; Stiglitz, *Globalization and Its Discontents Revisited*; Judis, *The Nationalist Revival*.

22. For example, see Foucault, *The Birth of Biopolitics*; Blyth, *Great Transformations*; Duggan, *The Twilight of Equality?*; Duménil and Lévy, *Capital Resurgent*; Harvey, *A Brief History of Neoliberalism*; Prasad, *The Politics of Free Markets*; Goldberg, *The Threat of Race*; Mirowski and Plehwe, *The Road from Mont Pèlerin*; Peck, *Constructions of Neoliberal Reason*; Burgin, *The Great Persuasion*; Jones, *Masters of the Universe*; Mirowski, *Never Let a Serious Crisis Go to Waste*; Davies, *The Limits of Neoliberalism*; Cooper, *Family Values*; Slobodian, *Globalists*.

23. Goldberg, *The Threat of Race*, 333; Slobodian, *Globalists*, 6. See also Weiss, "Globalization and the Myth of the Powerless State"; Wacquant, *Punishing the Poor*; Grandin, *Empire's Workshop*; Springer, Birch, and MacLeavy, eds., *The Handbook of Neoliberalism*; Philip, "Hell Is Truth Seen Too Late."

24. Mirowski, *Never Let a Serious Crisis Go to Waste*, 79. See also Hayek, "The Use of Knowledge in Society."

25. Mirowski, "Hell Is Truth Seen Too Late," 8.

26. Mirowski, *Never Let a Serious Crisis Go to Waste*, 79.

27. See Hacker and Pierson, *Winner-Take-All Politics*; Congressional Budget Office, *Trends in the Distribution of Household*; Piketty, *Capital in the Twenty-First Century*.

28. Mirowski, "Postface," 431.

29. Mirowski, "Postface," 438, 440.

30. Reich, "The Executive's New Clothes."

31. Katznelson, *When Affirmative Action Was White*, 23.

32. Cowie, *The Great Exception*, 154.

33. Cowie, *The Great Exception*, 154.

34. Katznelson, *When Affirmative Action Was White*, 23.

35. See Gordon, *Pitied but Not Entitled*; Cooper, *Family Values*.

36. Borstelmann, *1970s*, 4.

37. For "rule of law," see Hayek, *The Road to Serfdom*.

38. Davies, *The Limits of Neoliberalism*, 27.

39. Kruse, *White Flight*; Lassiter, *The Silent Majority*; Lewis, *Massive Resistance*; de Jong, *Invisible Enemy*; Borstelmann, *1970s*; Davies, *The Limits of Neoliberalism*.

40. For a description of the white struggle against civil rights activism in the North, see Sugrue, *The Origins of the Urban Crisis*.

41. Freund, *Colored Property*, 9.
42. Kendi, *Stamped from the Beginning*, 385.
43. Kendi, *Stamped from the Beginning*, 386.
44. Kendi, *Stamped from the Beginning*, 386.
45. Gilder, *Wealth and Poverty*, 128.
46. My definition of culture comes from Geertz, *The Interpretation of Cultures*; Williams, *Marxism and Literature*; Hall et al., *Culture, Media, Language*.
47. Trouillot, "North Atlantic Universals," 847.
48. Trouillot, "North Atlantic Universals," 847.
49. For "long 1970s," see Schulman, *The Seventies*.
50. For violence shaping the culture and laws of Jim Crow, see Litwack, *Trouble in Mind*; Tolnay and Beck, *A Festival of Violence*; Allen, *Without Sanctuary*; Bay, *To Tell the Truth Freely*; Campney, *Hostile Heartland*; Brown, *Strain of Violence*.
51. MacLean, *Freedom Is Not Enough*, 16. See also May, *Homeward Bound*; Gordon, *Pitied but Not Entitled*; Fraser, *Fortunes of Feminism*; Cooper, *Family Values*.
52. See Omi and Winant, *Racial Formation in the United States*.
53. Arrighi, *The Long Twentieth Century*, 73.
54. Hazlitt, *Man vs. the Welfare State*, 207.
55. Hazlitt, *Man vs. the Welfare State*, 207.
56. Hazlitt, *Man vs. the Welfare State*, 208.
57. See Phillips, *The Emerging Republican Majority*; Lind, *Up from Conservatism*; Carter, *The Politics of Rage*; Lind, "Conservative Elites and the Counterrevolution against the New Deal"; Lassiter, *The Silent Majority*; McGirr, *Suburban Warriors*.
58. See Lowndes, *From the New Deal to the New Right*.
59. Lassiter, *The Silent Majority*, 1–2.
60. Piketty, *Capital in the Twenty-First Century*, 15.
61. For an especially deep history of neoliberalism, see Leshem, *The Origins of Neoliberalism*.
62. My concept of modernity originally arose out of Mark Levine's "modernity matrix" in Levine, *Overthrowing Geography*. Other conceptions influencing my modernity framework include Berman, *All That Is Solid Melts into Air*; Habermas, "Modernity—an Incomplete Project"; Huyssen, *After the Great Divide*; Harvey, *The Condition of Postmodernity*; Latour, *We Have Never Been Modern*; Beckles, "Capitalism, Slavery and Caribbean Modernity"; Hall et al., *Modernity*; Knauft, *Critically Modern*; Trouillot, "North Atlantic Universals"; Cooper, *Colonialism in Question*; Beckert, *Empire of Cotton*.
63. See Gay, *The Enlightenment*; Porter, *The Creation of the Modern World*; Curran, *The Anatomy of Blackness*; Anderson, *Imagined Communities*; Lake and Reynolds, *Drawing the Global Colour Line*; Horne, *The Counter-revolution of 1776*; Heller, *The Birth of Capitalism*.
64. For a biography on Fernand Braudel, see Dursteler, "Fernand Braudel." See also Wallerstein, *The Modern World-System in the Longue Durée*; Lee, *The Longue Durée and World-Systems Analysis*; Guldi and Armitage, *The History Manifesto*.
65. For work on the *Annales* school, see Burke, *The French Historical Revolution*.
66. See Anderson, *White Rage*; Rodríguez, *White Reconstruction*; Brown, *Strain of Violence*, 4.
67. For "massive resistance," see Lewis, *Massive Resistance*; Webb, *Massive Resistance*; Omi and Winant, *Racial Formation in the United States*, 70.

68. Hunter, *Culture Wars*, 39.
69. Grandin, *The End of the Myth*, 3.
70. Grandin, *The End of the Myth*, 3.
71. See Carroll, *Affirmative Reaction*.
72. Baldwin, *The Devil Finds Work*, 563.
73. Carroll, *Affirmative Reaction*, 5.

74. Braudel, *On History*, 32. As Braudel notes, "mental frameworks" often come loaded with "all the old habits of thinking and acting, the set patterns which do not break down easily and which, however illogical, are a long time dying."

75. Armitage, "What's the Big Idea?," 498. Armitage writes: transtemporal history "links discrete contexts, moments and periods while maintaining the synchronic specificity of those contexts.... It also stresses the mechanisms of connection between moments and is therefore concerned with questions of concrete transmission, tradition and reception, again unlike the traditional history of ideas which assumed but did not investigate how ideas travelled materially and institutionally across time."

76. Armitage, "What's the Big Idea?," 498.
77. Armitage, "What's the Big Idea?," 499.
78. See Robinson, *Black Marxism*.
79. Grandin, *The End of the Myth*, 105.

80. Gerald Clarke's *Time* magazine article, "The Meaning of Nostalgia," described this onset of intense nostalgia at the dawn of social equality legislation from May 1971, anticipating the political and cultural pull nostalgia would produce in the late twentieth century and continuing into the twenty-first.

Chapter 1

1. See Patterson, *The Eve of Destruction*.
2. Phillips-Fein, *Fear City*, 31.
3. Patterson, *The Eve of Destruction*, 18.

4. For anti-Blackness and the institutions of white supremacy, see Omi and Winant, *Racial Formation in the United States*; Hartman, *Scenes of Subjection*; Fredrickson, *Racism*; Davis, *Inhuman Bondage*; Sexton, *Amalgamation Schemes*; Wilderson, *Red, White & Black*; Kendi, *Stamped from the Beginning*.

5. For settler colonialism, see Wolfe, *Settler Colonialism and the Transformation of Anthropology*; Elkins and Pedersen, *Settler Colonialism in the Twentieth Century*; Jacobs, *White Mother to a Dark Race*; Veracini, *Settler Colonialism*; Lloyd et al., *Settler Economies in World History*; Hixson, *American Settler Colonialism*; Veracini, *The Settler Colonial Present*.

6. Limerick, *The Legacy of Conquest*, 36.
7. Morrison, *Playing in the Dark*, 44.
8. See Harris, "Whiteness as Property"; Roediger, *The Wages of Whiteness*; Painter, *The History of White People*.
9. See Gordon, *Women, the State, and Welfare*; Katznelson, *When Affirmative Action Was White*; Freund, *Colored Property*; Cooper, *Family Values*.
10. Baldwin and Giovanni, *A Dialogue*, 19–20, 70–72, 88–89.
11. For racial capitalism, see Robinson, *Black Marxism*; Cox, *Caste, Class, & Race*.
12. Sexton, *Amalgamation Schemes*, 30.

13. See Patterson, *Slavery and Social Death*; Kendi, *Stamped from the Beginning*.

14. From David Blight's "The Civil War and Reconstruction" course, quoted in Coates, "Slavery Made America." Course available at http://oyc.yale.edu/history/hist-119/lecture-11. See also Horne, *The Deepest South*; Johnson, *River of Dark Dreams*; Waterhouse, *The Land of Enterprise*.

15. Bay, *To Tell the Truth Freely*, 7; Muhammad, *The Condemnation of Blackness*; Campney, *Hostile Heartland*.

16. For an in-depth discussion of the debate, see Buccola, *The Fire Is upon Us*.

17. Buckley, "Our Mission Statement."

18. *Debate: Baldwin vs. Buckley*. The transcription of the debate appeared in the *New York Times*. However, the transcription was most likely the written speeches, whereas both Baldwin and Buckley deviated substantially from their prepared statements. All citations of the debate are from the actual debate, and not from the printed speeches from the *New York Times*. "The American Dream and the American Negro."

19. See Weatherby, *James Baldwin*, 273–75; Leeming, *James Baldwin*, 244–45; Schultz, *Buckley and Mailer*; Buccola, *The Fire Is upon Us*.

20. For the National Educational Television Network, see Hendershot, *Open to Debate*, xxiv.

21. See Steinberg, *Turning Back*.

22. For the Black radical tradition, see Robinson, *Black Marxism*; Taylor, "'Read[ing] Men and Nations'"; Kelley, *Freedom Dreams*; Davies, "Sisters Outside"; Rabaka, *Africana Critical Theory*.

23. As Corey Robin suggests, conservatism is "a meditation on—and theoretical rendition of—the felt experience of having power, seeing it threatened, and trying to win it back." See Robin, *The Reactionary Mind*, 4.

24. Bogus, *Buckley*, 13. See also Hendershot, *Open to Debate*.

25. Bogus, *Buckley*, 21.

26. Buccola, *The Fire Is upon Us*, 105.

27. Grandin, *The End of the Myth*, 219.

28. See Buckley, "Desegregation," 21–22.

29. Buccola, *The Fire Is upon Us*, 327; Lewis, *Massive Resistance*, 180; Webb, *Massive Resistance*.

30. Morrison, *Playing in the Dark*, 44.

31. For background on James Baldwin, see Weatherby, *James Baldwin*; Standley and Pratt, *Conversations with James Baldwin*; Porter, *Stealing the Fire*; Leeming, *James Baldwin*; Balfour, *The Evidence of Things Not Said*; Boyd, *Baldwin's Harlem*; Kaplan and Schwarz, *James Baldwin*; Field, *All Those Strangers*; Buccola, *The Fire Is upon Us*.

32. Aanerud, "Now More than Ever," 57.

33. Robinson, *Black Marxism*, xxx.

34. For maroon communities, see Price, *Maroon Societies*; Genovese, *From Rebellion to Revolution*; Robinson, *Black Marxism*. For more on the Black radical tradition, see Gilroy, *The Black Atlantic*; Kelley, *Race Rebels*; James, *Hold Aloft the Banner of Ethiopia*; Bush, *We Are Not What We Seem*; Collier-Thomas and Franklin, *Sisters in the Struggle*; Woodard, *A Nation within a Nation*; Kelley, *Freedom Dreams*; Bogues, *Black Heretics, Black Prophets*; Edwards, *The Practice of Diaspora*; James, "The Wings of Ethiopia."

35. Horne, *The Counter-revolution of 1776*, 19.

36. Gilroy, *The Black Atlantic*.

37. Schultz, *Buckley and Mailer*, 100.

38. See Werner, "The Economic Evolution of James Baldwin."

39. The "white backlash" grew out of the Southern anti-segregation movement as well as Northern liberal reforms, with white communities across the nation condemning local and federal government of interfering in the lives of white citizens. See Sugrue, *The Origins of the Urban Crisis*; Avila, *Popular Culture in the Age of White Flight*; Kruse, *White Flight*; Moye, *Let the People Decide*; Countryman, *Up South*; Lassiter, *The Silent Majority*; Lewis, *Massive Resistance*; Hughey, "White Backlash in the 'Post-racial' United States."

40. Kirk, "The Problem of the New Order," 367.

41. Curtis, "'Will the Jungle Take Over?'"

42. MacLean, *Freedom Is Not Enough*, 63.

43. MacLean, *Freedom Is Not Enough*, 63.

44. Buckley, "The Brownsville Affair and Old Discrimination Policy," 4.

45. By ethos, I mean an argument or vision of the world based on authority, with the latter woven through the "virtues most valued by the culture to and for which one speaks." Halloran, "Aristotle's Concept of Ethos, or If Not His Somebody Else's," 60.

46. See Davis, *Slavery and Human Progress*; Patterson, *Inventing Western Civilization*; Lepore, *The Name of War*; Trouillot, *Global Transformations*.

47. For "possession of history," see McClure, "The Possession of History and American Innocence."

48. Baldwin and Giovanni, *A Dialogue*, 72.

49. Standley and Pratt, *Conversations with James Baldwin*, 191.

50. Standley and Pratt, *Conversations with James Baldwin*, 191–92, my emphasis.

51. For more on Baldwin and "innocence," see Balfour, *The Evidence of Things Not Said*.

52. Eley and Suny, "Introduction," 22.

53. Engelhardt, *The End of Victory Culture*, 21.

54. Engelhardt, *The End of Victory Culture*, 22.

55. See Anderson, "History TV and Popular Memory"; Moreau, *Schoolbook Nation*.

56. Du Bois, *Black Reconstruction in America*, 714.

57. MacLean, *Freedom Is Not Enough*, 49.

58. See Hinckley, "Texas." See also Moreau, *Schoolbook Nation*.

59. Grandin, "Living in Revolutionary Times," 8.

60. Baldwin, *The Devil Finds Work*, 562.

61. Standley and Pratt, *Conversations with James Baldwin*, 192.

62. Braudel, *Civilization and Capitalism*, 134.

63. See Popkin, *From Herodotus to H-Net*; Novick, *That Noble Dream*.

64. See Trouillot, *Silencing the Past*.

65. Morrison, *Playing in the Dark*, 52.

66. For memory and history, see Trouillot, *Silencing the Past*; Rosenberg, *A Date Which Will Live*.

67. Baldwin and Mead, *A Rap on Race*, 197–98. For the Faulkner quote, see Faulkner, *Requiem for a Nun*, 73.

68. Omi and Winant, *Racial Formation in the United States*, 70.

69. See Lewis, *Massive Resistance*; Webb, *Massive Resistance*; Dailey, "Sex, Segregation, and the Sacred after Brown."

70. For the use of "culture" in place of overt racism, see Lentin and Titley, *The Crises of Multiculturalism*.

71. See Hartman, *Lose Your Mother*, 6.

72. See Jacobson, *Roots Too*.

73. Shultz, *Buckley and Mailer*, 118.

74. See Buccola, *The Fire Is upon Us*.

75. *Debate: Baldwin vs. Buckley*.

76. *Debate: Baldwin vs. Buckley*.

77. Horne, *The Counter-revolution of 1776*, 240.

78. "An Interview with James Baldwin," 52.

79. See Curtis, "'Will the Jungle Take Over?'"; Muhammad, *The Condemnation of Blackness*.

80. *Debate: Baldwin vs. Buckley*.

81. See Harris, "Whiteness as Property." See also Lipsitz, *The Possessive Investment in Whiteness*.

82. See Freund, *Colored Property*.

83. For the relationship to civil society, see Wilderson, "Gramsci's Black Marx."

84. Trouillot, "The Otherwise Modern," 220.

85. See Painter, *The History of White People*.

86. "The Week," 149. As Curtis points out, Buckley's views of "white, Western civilization" extended toward African in the 1960s as well, highlighting its transnational nature. See Curtis, "'Will the Jungle Take Over?'"

87. For Sambo, see Bogle, *Toms, Coons, Mulattoes, Mammies, & Bucks*.

88. For "self-rule," see Wiebe, *Self Rule*.

89. For Zip Coon, see Bogle, *Toms, Coons, Mulattoes, Mammies, & Bucks*.

90. Omi and Winant, *Racial Formation in the United States*, 66.

91. Lipsitz, *The Possessive Investment in Whiteness*, 50.

92. Singh, *Black Is a Country*, 10.

93. Steinberg, "'Race Relations.'"

94. Glazer and Moynihan, *Beyond the Melting Pot*.

95. Jacobson, *Roots Too*, 177.

96. Kendi, *Stamped from the Beginning*, 373.

97. Kendi, *Stamped from the Beginning*, 373.

98. Jacobson, *Roots Too*, 177.

99. Perlstein, *Nixonland*, 459–60.

100. Roberts, *Killing the Black Body*, 15. See also Muhammad, *The Condemnation of Blackness*.

101. Glazer, *Affirmative Discrimination*.

102. See transcript to "Black Power." For example, on a 1967 episode of *Firing Line* where Buckley interviewed Nat Hentoff about Black Power, Buckley questioned whether access to power was the only thing holding back African Americans: "Well, one of the reasons that I am perhaps as baffled as other people in trying to understand your critique, and that of so many other people, is I am never quite sure whether Black Power means that the desiratum [sic] is simply the use of a lever, with a maximmization [sic] of the lever inferred, or whether there is built into that some sort of concept; for instance, there is Black Power in Ghana, isn't there—not a hell of a lot of progress from your standards or mine—so, pure

political power isn't of itself enough. It is political power united with certain concepts, a certain ethos, that you and I feel we want to push. We hear from somebody like James Baldwin who says that the only thing the white man has that the Negro should want is power—meaning that he explicitly disdains the criteria, the value system of the white community."

103. See Sugrue, *Sweet Land of Liberty*.

104. See Lake and Reynolds, *Drawing the Global Colour Line*; Muhammad, *The Condemnation of Blackness*; Kendi, *Stamped from the Beginning*.

105. Jacobson, *Roots Too*, 178.

106. Barker, *The New Racism*, 3.

107. Barker, *The New Racism*, 10.

108. Lawrence, "Just Plain Common Sense," 82.

109. Balibar, "Is There a 'Neo-Racism'?," 21.

110. Muhammad, *The Condemnation of Blackness*, xiv.

111. Baldwin, *Nobody Knows My Name*, 219–20.

112. See Muhammad, *The Condemnation of Blackness*.

113. See Davis, *Women, Race & Class*; Giddings, *When and Where I Enter*; Jones, *Labor of Love, Labor of Sorrow*; Morgan, *Laboring Women*.

114. Isenberg, *White Trash*, 135–36.

115. See Curtis, "'Will the Jungle Take Over?'"

116. "The Week," 149.

117. Baldwin, *No Name in the Street*.

118. Baldwin, *No Name in the Street*, 46.

119. Standley and Pratt, *Conversations with James Baldwin*, 191–92.

120. Robin, *The Reactionary Mind*, 59.

121. See Patterson, *Inventing Western Civilization*.

Chapter 2

1. See Trouillot, "North Atlantic Universals."

2. See Fredrickson, *Racism*; Lake and Reynolds, *Drawing the Global Colour Line*; Kendi, *Stamped from the Beginning*.

3. Gingrich and Pious, *To Renew America*, 7.

4. Scott-Heron, *Small Talk at 125th and Lenox*.

5. Davies, *The Limits of Neoliberalism*, 27. See also Lentin and Titley, *The Crises of Multiculturalism*.

6. See Slobodian, *Globalists*.

7. Slobodian, *Globalists*, 143.

8. Slobodian, *Globalists*, 58.

9. Slobodian, *Globalists*, 2.

10. Gingrich and Pious, *To Renew America*, 7.

11. Flamm, *Law and Order*.

12. Baldwin and Giovanni, *A Dialogue*, 19–20.

13. Gingrich and Pious, *To Renew America*, 7.

14. Roberts, *Killing the Black Body*, 294.

15. Baldwin, *The Devil Finds Work*, 562.

16. See Moreau, *Schoolbook Nation*; Du Bois, *Black Reconstruction in America*.

17. See Newby, *The Development of Segregationist Thought*; Sigler, *The Conservative Tradition in American Thought*; Buckley, *American Conservative Thought in the Twentieth Century*.

18. Patterson, *Inventing Western Civilization*, 44.

19. Fredrickson, *Racism*; Horne, *The Counter-revolution of 1776*; Kendi, *Stamped from the Beginning*.

20. Newby, *The Development of Segregationist Thought*, 129.

21. Newby, *The Development of Segregationist Thought*, 130.

22. Martinot and Sexton, "The Avant-Garde of White Supremacy," 180. See also Pascoe, *What Comes Naturally*; Lewis, *Massive Resistance*; Lake and Reynolds, *Drawing the Global Colour Line*.

23. Newby, *The Development of Segregationist Thought*, 155.

24. See Robin, *The Reactionary Mind*, 24; Trouillot, "North Atlantic Universals."

25. Weaver, *Ideas Have Consequences*, 1.

26. Weaver, *Ideas Have Consequences*, 32, 38.

27. Kirk, "The Problem of the New Order," 367.

28. See Fones-Wolf, *Selling Free Enterprise*; Perlstein, *Before the Storm*; Phillips-Fein, *Invisible Hands*.

29. See Hancock, *The Politics of Disgust*.

30. See Flamm, *Law and Order*; Kruse, *White Flight*; Cooper, *Family Values*; Sugrue, *Sweet Land of Liberty*.

31. See MacLean, *Freedom Is Not Enough*; Freund, *Colored Property*; Bogle, *Toms, Coons, Mulattoes, Mammies, & Bucks*.

32. Erskine, "The Polls: Race Relations," 139.

33. Erskine, "The Polls: Race Relations," 146.

34. Perlstein, *Before the Storm*, 342.

35. Perlstein, *Nixonland*, 91.

36. McConahay et al., "Has Racism Declined in America?," 578.

37. McConahay et al., "Has Racism Declined in America?," 578.

38. Buccola, *The Fire Is upon Us*, 192.

39. Perlstein, *Before the Storm*, 342.

40. Foucault, *The Birth of Biopolitics*; Blyth, *Great Transformations*; Mirowski and Plehwe, *The Road from Mont Pèlerin*; Peck, *Constructions of Neoliberal Reason*; Wapshott, *Keynes Hayek*; Burgin, *The Great Persuasion*; Jones, *Masters of the Universe*; Eagleton-Pierce, "Historicizing the neoliberal spirit of capitalism"; Nik-Khah and Van Horn, "The ascendency of Chicago neoliberalism"; Slobodian, *Globalists*.

41. Plehwe, "Introduction," 4.

42. Plehwe, "Introduction," 10.

43. Wapshott, *Keynes Hayek*, 2–3.

44. Wapshott, *Keynes Hayek*, 29.

45. Slobodian, *Globalists*, 64–65.

46. Slobodian, *Globalists*, 84.

47. Slobodian, *Globalists*, 86.

48. Keynes, *The General Theory of Employment, Interest, and Money*. See also Eatwell and Milgate, *The Fall and Rise of Keynesian Economics*.

49. Wapshott, *Keynes Hayek*, 44.

50. Burgin, *The Great Persuasion*, 3.

51. See Jacob, *Scientific Culture and the Making of the Industrial West*; Muller, *The Mind and the Market*.

52. Ferguson, "Industrial Conflict and the Coming of the New Deal," 13.

53. Hawley, *The Great War and the Search for a Modern Order*, 166.

54. Hawley, *The Great War and the Search for a Modern Order*, 168.

55. See Shlaes, *The Forgotten Man*.

56. McElvaine, *The Great Depression*, 39; Badger, *The New Deal*, 30.

57. Piketty, *Capital in the Twenty-First Century*, 23.

58. Trattner, *From Poor Law to Welfare State*, 277.

59. Trattner, *From Poor Law to Welfare State*, 277.

60. Plehwe, "Introduction," 2.

61. Plehwe, "Introduction," 13.

62. Slobodian, *Globalists*, 86.

63. Lippmann, *An Inquiry into the Principles of the Good Society*, 13.

64. Plehwe, "Introduction," 13.

65. Plehwe, "Introduction," 13.

66. Peck, *Constructions of Neoliberal Reason*, 49–50.

67. Slobodian, *Globalists*, 124.

68. See Blyth, *Great Transformations*; Slobodian, *Globalists*.

69. For early work on the Chicago school of economics, see Miller, "On the 'Chicago School of Economics.'"

70. Van Horn and Mirowski, "The Rise of the Chicago School of Economics and the Birth of Neoliberalism," 159. See also Harvey, *A Brief History of Neoliberalism*, 19–20.

71. See Smith, *The Wealth of Nations*; Lippmann, *The Good Society*; Polanyi, *The Great Transformation*.

72. Smith, *The Wealth of Nations*, 94–96.

73. See Phillips, *Wealth and Democracy*; Dawley, "The Abortive Rule of Big Money."

74. Van Horn and Mirowski, "The Rise of the Chicago School of Economics and the Birth of Neoliberalism," 157; Leitner et al., "Contesting Urban Futures," 6.

75. Van Horn and Mirowski, "The Rise of the Chicago School of Economics," 161. See also Fligstein, "States, Markets, and Economic Growth."

76. Peck, *Constructions of Neoliberal Reason*, 9.

77. Slobodian, *Globalists*, 6.

78. Mirowski, *Never Let a Serious Crisis Go to Waste*, 40.

79. Van Horn, "Reinventing Monopoly and the Role of Corporations," 216–17.

80. Friedman, "Neo-Liberalism and Its Prospects."

81. See Berle, *The 20th Century Capitalist Revolution*.

82. Davies, *The Limits of Neoliberalism*, 76.

83. See Chandler, *The Visible Hand*; Trachtenberg, *The Incorporation of America*; Heilbroner and Singer, *The Economic Transformation of America*; Sobel, *The Age of Giant Corporations*; Brands, *American Colossus*; Lind, *Land of Promise*.

84. See Fones-Wolf, *Selling Free Enterprise*; Phillips-Fein, *Invisible Hands*.

85. Van Horn, "Reinventing Monopoly and the Role of Corporations," 208.

86. Davies, *The Limits of Neoliberalism*, 50.

87. See Birch, "Financial Economics and Business Schools."

88. Van Horn, "Reinventing Monopoly and the Role of Corporations," 220. See also Friedman, *Capitalism and Freedom*.

89. Burgin, *The Great Persuasion*, 72. See also Wapshott, *Keynes Hayek*, 211–14; Hayek, *The Road to Serfdom*; Mirowski and Plehwe, *The Road from Mont Pèlerin*.

90. Quoted in Harvey, *A Brief History of Neoliberalism*, 20

91. Foucault, *The Birth of Biopower*, 174.

92. See, for example, Pascoe, *What Comes Naturally*; Cobble, *The Other Women's Movement*; Giddings, *When and Where I Enter*; Katznelson, *When Affirmative Action Was White*.

93. Wapshott, *Keynes Hayek*, 202.

94. Hayek, *The Road to Serfdom*, 112.

95. See, for example, Phillips, *Wealth and Democracy*; Fraser and Gerstle, *Ruling America*; MacLean, *Democracy in Chains*.

96. Hayek, *The Road to Serfdom*, 117.

97. Polanyi, *The Great Transformation*, 265.

98. See Fones-Wolf, *Selling Free Enterprise*; Perlstein, *Before the Storm*; Phillips-Fein, *Invisible Hands*; Blyth, *Great Transformations*; Wapshott, *Keynes Hayek*; Burgin, *The Great Persuasion*.

99. Phillips-Fein, *Invisible Hands*, 36–46.

100. Burgin, *The Great Persuasion*, 103.

101. For civil rights and the Cold War, see Dudziak, "The Little Rock Crisis and Foreign Relations"; Skrentny, "The Effect of the Cold War on African-American Civil Rights"; Dudziak, *Cold War Civil Rights*; Berg, "Black Civil Rights and Liberal Anticommunism."

102. For government intervention in the economy, see Vatter, *The U.S. Economy in the 1950s*; Schulman, *From Cotton Belt to Sunbelt*; Hooks, "The Rise of the Pentagon and U.S. State Building"; Armstrong et al., *Capitalism since 1945*; Hooks and Bloomquist, "The Legacy of World War II for Regional Growth and Decline."

103. See Lake and Reynolds, *Drawing the Global Colour Line*; Brands, *American Colossus*; Painter, *The History of White People*; Gerstle, *American Crucible*.

104. See Von Mises, "How Liberty Defined Western Civilization."

105. Hayek, *The Road to Serfdom*, 219.

106. For a critique of this silencing of Enlightenment's "dark side," see Sala-Molins, *Dark Side of the Light*; Buck-Morss, *Hegel, Haiti, and Universal History*; Dubois, "An Enslaved Enlightenment."

107. Hayek, *The Constitution of Liberty*, 100.

108. Muller, *The Mind and the Market*, 365.

109. Plehwe, "Introduction," 4.

110. Muller, *The Mind and the Market*, 401.

111. See Wacquant, *Punishing the Poor*; Ferguson, *Global Shadows*; Carmody, *The New Scramble for Africa*; Tansel, *States of Discipline*; Stiglitz, *Globalization and Its Discontents Revisited*.

112. See "Theorizing for Goldwater?"; Friedman, *Capitalism and Freedom*.

113. Van Horn and Mirowski, "The Rise of the Chicago School of Economics," 166.

114. Friedman, *Capitalism and Freedom*, 9.

115. Du Bois, *Black Reconstruction in America*; Wiebe, *The Search for Order*; Davis, *Women, Race & Class*; Trachtenberg, *The Incorporation of America*; Goodwyn, *The Populist Moment*; Gilmore, *Gender and Jim Crow*; Norwood, *Strikebreaking & Intimidation*;

Kessler-Harris, *Out to Work*; Brands, *American Colossus*; Kendi, *Stamped from the Beginning*.

116. Friedman, *Capitalism and Freedom*, 9.
117. Sandbrook, *Mad as Hell*, 119.
118. Harris, "Whiteness as Property," 1713.
119. Harris, "Whiteness as Property," 1713–14.
120. Lears, *No Place of Grace*, 18.
121. See Harrington, *The Other America*.
122. See Katznelson, *When Affirmative Action Was White*; Lipsitz, *The Possessive Investment in Whiteness*; Cooper, *Family Values*.
123. See Freund, *Colored Property*.
124. See Roberts, *Killing the Black Body*.
125. For "silent majority," see McGirr, *Suburban Warriors*; Perlstein, *Before the Storm*; Kruse, *White Flight*; Lassiter, *The Silent Majority*; Lewis, *Massive Resistance*; De Jong, *Invisible Enemy*; Borstelmann, *1970s*.
126. For "Southern strategy," see Phillips, *The Emerging Republican Majority*; Lowndes, *From the New Deal to the New Right*; Farber, "The Silent Majority and Talk about Revolution."
127. Cruse, *Rebellion or Revolution?*, 104.
128. Perlstein, *Nixonland*, 277.
129. Perlstein, *Nixonland*, 277–78.
130. Friedman, *Capitalism and Freedom*, 2.
131. Friedman, *Capitalism and Freedom*, 111.
132. For race and the New Right, see Lind, *Up from Conservatism*; Carter, *From George Wallace to Newt Gingrich*; Marable, *Black Liberation in Conservative America*; Webb, *Massive Resistance*; Lewis, *Massive Resistance*; Kruse, *White Flight*; Lowndes, *From the New Deal to the New Right*; Buccola, *The Fire Is upon Us*.
133. See De Jong, *Invisible Enemy*.
134. Schwarz, *America's Hidden Success*, 116.
135. See Davis, *Prisoners of the American Dream*; Cowie, "Nixon's class struggle."
136. See Breen, "A Changing Labor Force and Race Relations in Virginia 1660–1710." See also Berlin, *Many Thousands Gone*; Horne, *The Counter-revolution of 1776*.
137. Davies, *The Limits of Neoliberalism*, 153–54.
138. De Jong, *Invisible Enemy*, 55.
139. McConahay et al., "Has Racism Declined in America?," 578.
140. "Free Enterpriser—without Any Strings."
141. "Free Enterpriser—without Any Strings," 76.
142. "Free Enterpriser—without Any Strings," 76.
143. "Free Enterpriser—without Any Strings," 78.
144. "Free Enterpriser—without Any Strings," 78.
145. "Money Theory Comes Back in Style," 110.
146. "Money Theory Comes Back in Style," 112.
147. "Money Theory Comes Back in Style," 112.
148. *Firing Line*, "The Economic Crisis."
149. See Fraser and Gordon, "A Genealogy of Dependency."

150. See Fredrickson, *The Black Image in the White Mind*; Roberts, *Killing the Black Body*; Muhammad, *The Condemnation of Blackness*.

151. Hancock, *The Politics of Disgust*.

152. Roberts, *Killing the Black Body*.

153. See Moreau, *Schoolbook Nation*.

154. "Chicago School Builds a Model"; "Monetarists Dent Conventional Wisdom"; "A Classical Look at the 'Real Cost' of Money."

155. "Advice and Dissent on Monetary Policy," 32.

156. Peck, *Constructions of Neoliberal Reason*, 69.

157. Muhammad, *The Condemnation of Blackness*.

158. See Mirowski, *Never Let a Serious Crisis Go to Waste*.

159. Davies, *The Limits of Neoliberalism*, 27.

160. For post-1970s wealth inequality, see Hacker and Pierson, *Winner-Take-All Politics*; Congressional Budget Office, "Trends in the Distribution of Household Income"; Piketty, *Capital in the Twenty-First Century*.

161. See Lipsitz, *The Possessive Investment in Whiteness*.

Chapter 3

1. For distrust in large institutions, see Sandbrook, *Mad as Hell*.
2. Hoberman, *Make My Day*, 44.
3. Lumet, *Network*.
4. Lumet, *Network*.
5. Jones, "Multinationals from the 1930s to the 1980s," 90.
6. Go, *Patterns of Empire*.
7. Arrighi, *The Long Twentieth Century*, 7.
8. Arrighi, *The Long Twentieth Century*, 123.
9. Arrighi, *The Long Twentieth Century*, 135.
10. Heller, *The Birth of Capitalism*, 157–58.
11. Arrighi, *The Long Twentieth Century*, 224.
12. Gordon, *The Rise and Fall of American Growth*, 1, 7.
13. Arrighi, *The Long Twentieth Century*, 248.
14. Gans, *Deciding What's News*, 284. Originally published in 1979.
15. See http://www.mcgraw-hill.com/site/about-us/corporate-history. I chose *Business Week* over *Fortune*—first published by *Time* magazine cofounder Henry Luce in 1930—because the latter is a weekly news magazine whereas the former was published monthly (and published twice monthly after 1977).
16. Weiss, "What America's Leaders Read," 7.
17. Like most mainstream media in the postwar years, especially one geared toward the masculine-defined efforts of private enterprise, *Business Week* sometimes offered gratuitous sexism in their advertisements in their 1960s issues; interestingly, this did not appear in the 1950s. Examples of this sexism included showing young white women in seductive poses with a look of confusion about the technological wonder being advertised, including advertisements with provocatively positioned women with captions such as, "She's wearing our latest plasticizer. You can see right through it. Exactly what we were after" (see advertisement

from Enjay Chemical Company in *Business Week*, January 20, 1968). This objectification and sexualization of women in a business magazine might be explained through the sexual revolution of the counterculture in the mid-to-late 1960s, as advertisers took the lead in the dissemination of many of these ideas. See also Frank, *The Conquest of Cool*; Bailey, *Sex in the Heartland*.

18. Altschuler and Grossvogel, *Changing Channels*, xi

19. Berle, *The 20th Century Capitalist Revolution*, 23–24.

20. Cowie, *The Great Exception*, 95.

21. Lemann, *Transaction Man*, 38.

22. See Lipsitz, *Rainbow at Midnight*; Frieden, *Global Capitalism*; Heilbroner and Singer, *The Economic Transformation of America*.

23. See May, "Making the American Consensus"; Hodgson, "The Foreign Policy Establishment."

24. Latham, *The Right Kind of Revolution*, 38.

25. Lipsitz, *Rainbow at Midnight*, 100. See also Fraser, "The 'Labor Question'"; Cowie, *The Great Exception*.

26. Phillips-Fein, *Invisible Hands*, 31. See also Stepan-Norris and Zeitlin, *Left Out*; Schrecker, *No Ivory Tower*; Navasky, *Naming Names*; Denning, *The Cultural Front*; Whitfield, *The Culture of the Cold War*.

27. Panitch and Gindin, *The Making of Global Capitalism*, 83.

28. James, "Finance Capitalism," 150.

29. James, "Finance Capitalism," 150.

30. Vatter, *The U.S. Economy in the 1950s*, 30.

31. Vatter, *The U.S. Economy in the 1950s*, 34.

32. See Cowie, *The Great Exception*; Von Eschen, *Race against Empire*; Stepan-Norris and Zeitlin, *Left Out*.

33. Schwarz, *America's Hidden Success*, 26.

34. Schwarz, *America's Hidden Success*, 26.

35. See Cowie and Salvatore, "The Long Exception"; Cowie, *The Great Exception*.

36. Fones-Wolf, *Selling Free Enterprise*; Phillips-Fein, *Invisible Hands*; Burgin, *The Great Persuasion*; Davies, *The Limits of Neoliberalism*.

37. James, "Finance Capitalism," 150.

38. See Braudel, *Civilization and Capitalism, 15th–18th Century*; Robins, *The Corporation That Changed the World*; Chandler, *The Visible Hand*; Sobel, *The Age of Giant Corporations*.

39. Arrighi, *The Long Twentieth Century*, 277–308.

40. See Dawley, "The Abortive Rule of Big Money"; McCurdy, "Justice Fiend and the Jurisprudence of Government-Business Relations"; Friedman, "Which Way for Capitalism."

41. See Goodwyn, *The Populist Moment*; McMath, *American Populism*; Bernstein, *The Lean Years*; Wiebe, *The Search for Order*; Chambers, *The Tyranny of Change*; De Santis, *The Shaping of Modern America*; Kazin, *The Populist Persuasion*; Go, *Patterns of Empire*.

42. Waterhouse, *The Land of Enterprise*, 83. See also Chandler, *The Visible Hand*.

43. Waterhouse, *The Land of Enterprise*, 57–58, 92–93.

44. Brands, *American Colossus*, 24.

45. Brands, *American Colossus*, 5.

46. See Schulman, *From Cotton Belt to Sunbelt*; Wolfe, *Competing with the Soviets*; Edwards, *The Closed World*; Gordon, *The Rise and Fall of American Growth*.

47. Nasaw, "Gilded Age Gospels," 124.

48. Panitch and Bindin, *The Making of Global Capitalism*, 103. See also Yergin, *The Prize*; Black, *Crude Reality*.

49. See Wilkins, "Multinational Enterprise to 1930."

50. Smith, "The Liberal Invention of the Multinational Corporation," 117.

51. Smith, "The Liberal Invention of the Multinational Corporation," 117–18.

52. Chandler and Mazlish, *Leviathans*, 3–4. See also Caves, *Multinational Enterprise and Economic Analysis*.

53. "A New Breed of Company Has Sprung Up with the Boom," 61.

54. "A New Breed of Company Has Sprung Up with the Boom," 61.

55. Hyman, "Rethinking the Postwar Corporation," 196.

56. "A New Breed of Company Has Sprung Up with the Boom," 62.

57. Hyman, "Rethinking the Postwar Corporation," 196, 202.

58. Hyman, "Rethinking the Postwar Corporation," 196.

59. Bluestone and Harrison, *The Deindustrialization of America*, 124.

60. "Special Report: Multinational Companies."

61. "Special Report: Multinational Companies," 75.

62. "Special Report: Multinational Companies," 75.

63. "New Look in Mergers Frowned on by FTC."

64. "Merger Tide Is Swelling," 28.

65. Lears, "A Matter of Taste," 50–51.

66. Markusen, "Cold War Workers," 51.

67. Ryan and Keller, *Camera Politica*, 91.

68. See Schulman, *From Cotton Belt to Sunbelt*; Hooks, "The Rise of the Pentagon and U.S. State Building."

69. For postwar institutional racism, see Katznelson, *When Affirmative Action Was White*; Freund, *Colored Property*; Feagin, "Excluding Blacks and Others from Housing."

70. Schulman, *From Cotton Belt to Sunbelt*, 135.

71. Schulman, *From Cotton Belt to Sunbelt*, 148.

72. Cohen, *A Consumers' Republic*, 116.

73. See Brands, *American Colossus*.

74. Vatter, *The U.S. Economy in the 1950s*, 10. See also Appleby, *The Relentless Revolution*, 317–20; Wolfe, *Competing with the Soviets*; Edwards, *The Closed World*; Sobel, *The Age of Giant Corporations*; Marcus and Segal, *Technology in America*.

75. Toffler, *Future Shock*; Mandel, *Global Data Shock*, 5–6; Zuboff, *The Age of Surveillance Capitalism*. See also Gordon, *The Rise and Fall of American Growth*; Baldwin, *The Great Convergence*; Gleick, *The Information*; Kerssens, "The Database 'Revolution.'"

76. Armstrong et al., *Capitalism since 1945*, 154.

77. Vatter, *The U.S. Economy in the 1950s*, 23. See also Schulman, *From Cotton Belt to Sunbelt*.

78. Berle, *The 20th Century Capitalist Revolution*, 51–52.

79. Berle, *The 20th Century Capitalist Revolution*, 109.

80. Vatter, *The U.S. Economy in the 1950s*, 41.

81. Berle, *The 20th Century Capitalist Revolution*, 27.
82. Vatter, *The U.S. Economy in the 1950s*, 166. See also Hooks and Bloomquist, "The Legacy of World War II for Regional Growth and Decline."
83. Vatter, *The U.S. Economy in the 1950s*, 49.
84. Brenner, *The Boom and the Bubble*, 9.
85. Harvey, *The Condition of Postmodernity*, 125–26.
86. Stein, *Pivotal Decade*, 2.
87. Bluestone and Harrison, *The Deindustrialization of America*, 133.
88. Arrighi, *The Long Twentieth Century*, 284.
89. Webber and Rigby, *The Golden Age Illusion*, 27.
90. Frieden, *Global Capitalism*, 299.
91. Maier, "'Malaise,'" 43.
92. Armstrong et al., *Capitalism since 1945*, 74.
93. Arrighi, *The Long Twentieth Century*, 305.
94. McQuaid, *Uneasy Partners*, 47.
95. See Wilson, "The Advantages of Obscurity."
96. de Grazia, *Irresistible Empire*, 4.
97. Vatter, *The U.S. Economy in the 1950s*, 171.
98. For "family wage," see Cooper, *Family Values*.
99. Goldin and Margo, "The Great Compression," 1.
100. Phillips, *Wealth and Democracy*, 76.
101. Hofstadter, *The Paranoid Style in American Politics and Other Essays*, xi.
102. Phillips-Fein, *Invisible Hands*, 136.
103. Phillips, *Wealth and Democracy*, 77.
104. Kolko, *Main Currents in Modern American History*, 311.
105. See Schulman, *From Cotton Belt to Sunbelt*; Hooks and Bloomquist, "The Legacy of World War II for Regional Growth and Decline."
106. Freund, *Colored Property*, 9.
107. McQuaid, *Uneasy Partners*, 22.
108. Marcus, *Happy Days and Wonder Years*; Dwyer, *Back to the Fifties*.
109. See Webb, *Massive Resistance*; Lewis, *Massive Resistance*.
110. Fones-Wolf, *Selling Free Enterprise*, 7–8; Lears, "A Matter of Taste," 41; May, "Making the American Consensus."
111. Berle, *The 20th Century Capitalist Revolution*, 9.
112. Panitch and Gindin, *The Making of Global Capitalism*, 67.
113. Westad, *The Global Cold War*, 9.
114. Panitch and Gindin, *The Making of Global Capitalism*, 74.
115. Rosenberg, *Financial Missionaries to the World*, 257. See also Rosenberg, *Spreading the American Dream*.
116. Latham, *Modernization as Ideology*, 9. See also Latham, *The Right Kind of Revolution*.
117. See Grandin, *Empire's Workshop*; Bevins, *The Jakarta Method*.
118. Brenner, *The Boom and the Bubble*, 13.
119. Harvey, *The Condition of Postmodernity*, 142. For Great Society, see Blum, *Years of Discord*; Schulman, *From Cotton Belt to Sunbelt*; Farber, *The Age of Great Dreams*; Steigerwald, *The Sixties and the End of Modern America*.

120. Brenner, *The Boom and the Bubble*, 16.
121. "Industry Still Needs Updating," 141.
122. Brenner, *The Boom and the Bubble*, 17.
123. Blyth, *Great Transformations*, 129; Brenner, *The Boom and the Bubble*, 17.
124. Brine and Poovey. *Finance in America*; Konings, "The Construction of US Financial Power."
125. "Merger Pot Is Boiling Over," 32.
126. Webber and Rigby, *The Golden Age Illusion*, 15.
127. "U.S. Industry Migrates Abroad to Tap Markets of the World," 28.
128. "U.S. Industry Migrates Abroad to Tap Markets of the World," 29.
129. "Capital Spending: Flat at Home, Up Abroad."
130. "Not Much Pain for Big Business," 17.
131. "Mounting a Long War on Inflation." See also Mandel, *The Second Slump*, 12.
132. "Gold Fever Rises to Record Heat."
133. Arrighi, *The Long Twentieth Century*, 310. See also Schenk, "The Origins of the Eurodollar Market in London."
134. "Eurodollar Works for Both Sides," 108.
135. "Eurodollar Works for Both Sides," 108.
136. "Eurodollar Works for Both Sides," 108.
137. Jones, "Multinationals from the 1930s to the 1980s," 93.
138. See Stiglitz, *Globalization and Its Discontents Revisited*.
139. "When a World Money System Is Out of Date," 70, 72–73.
140. "When a World Money System Is Out of Date," 76.
141. "When a World Money System Is Out of Date," 80.
142. Phillips, *Wealth and Democracy*, 86.
143. Webber and Rigby, *The Golden Age Illusion*, 28.
144. Brenner, *The Boom and the Bubble*, 27.
145. "The Deadlock over the Dollar," 82.
146. "The Deadlock over the Dollar," 82.
147. "The Deadlock over the Dollar," 94.
148. Sennett, *The Culture of the New Capitalism*, 38–39.
149. Panitch and Bindin, *The Making of Global Capitalism*, 111.
150. "The Deadlock over the Dollar," 101.
151. "The Deadlock over the Dollar," 101.
152. "The Multinationals Reap a Windfall," 22.
153. "New View: Build Here and Export," 29.
154. "The World Economy," 65.
155. "The World Economy," 73.
156. "The World Economy," 73.
157. "The World Economy," 73.
158. "The World Economy," 73.
159. "The World Economy," 74.
160. Slobodian, *Globalists*, 13.
161. Slobodian, *Globalists*, 150–51.
162. Mandel, *The Second Slump*, 22.
163. Mandel, *The Second Slump*, 26; Harvey, *The Condition of Postmodernity*, 145.

164. Wight, *Oil Money*, 89.
165. Wight, *Oil Money*, 89.
166. Webber and Rigby, *The Golden Age Illusion*, 29; James, "Finance Capitalism," 151.
167. "Petrodollars: Easing the Pressure on Western Banks," 34.
168. Spiro, *The Hidden Hand of American Hegemony*.
169. Stein, *Pivotal Decade*, 95.
170. Stein, *Pivotal Decade*, 95.
171. See Cowie, *Stayin' Alive*.
172. Webber and Rigby, *The Golden Age Illusion*, 29. See also Bluestone and Harrison, *The Deindustrialization of America*, 115; Harvey, *The Condition of Postmodernity*, 159; Mayer, *The Bankers*, 19–20.
173. Webber and Rigby, *The Golden Age Illusion*, 29.
174. Panitch and Gindin, *The Making of Global Capitalism*, 120.
175. James, "Finance Capitalism," 151.
176. Kerssens, "The Database 'Revolution,'" 13–14.
177. See Kerssens, "The Database 'Revolution'"; Mayer-Schönberger and Ramge, *Reinventing Capitalism in the Age of Big Data*.
178. Webber and Rigby, *The Golden Age Illusion*, 30.
179. Webber and Rigby, *The Golden Age Illusion*, 31.
180. See Stiglitz, *Globalization and Its Discontents Revisited*.
181. Webber and Rigby, *The Golden Age Illusion*, 31.
182. Harvey, *The Condition of Postmodernity*, 160–64. See also Rosenberg, *Financial Missionaries to the World*. For examples of this process in Africa and Latin America, see Ferguson, *Global Shadows*; Grandin, *Empire's Workshop*.
183. Waterhouse, *The Land of Enterprise*, 170.
184. For writers discussing postmodernity in the 1970s, see Hassan, *The Postmodern Turn*; Lyotard, *The Postmodern Condition*; Foster, *The Anti-aesthetic*.
185. Jameson, *Postmodernism*, xviii–xix.
186. Harvey, *The Condition of Postmodernity*, 147.
187. Arrighi, *The Long Twentieth Century*, 248.
188. "A Rougher Road for Multinationals," 57.
189. "Corporations: Where the Game Is Growth," 120.
190. "Time of Testing for Conglomerates," 38.
191. "Conglomerates: The Corporations That Make Things Jump."
192. "Conglomerates: The Corporations That Make Things Jump," 74.
193. "Conglomerates: The Corporations That Make Things Jump," 74.
194. "Conglomerates: The Corporations That Make Things Jump," 75.
195. "Conglomerates: The Corporations That Make Things Jump," 76.
196. "Conglomerates: The Corporations That Make Things Jump," 76.
197. "Only Mergers Can Bail Out the Airlines," 37.
198. Rodgers, *Age of Fractures*, 62.
199. See Robyn, *Braking the Special Interests*.
200. "Is the Merger Fever Really Cooling Off?," 35.
201. Rodgers, *Age of Fracture*, 56.
202. "A Rougher Road for Multinationals," 58.
203. "Guiding Growth toward a Global Economy," 146.

204. See Stein, *Pivotal Decade*; Arrighi, *The Long Twentieth Century*.
205. Bell, *The Coming of Post-industrial Society*.
206. "The New Banking," 89.
207. "The New Banking," 89.
208. Kerssens, "The Database 'Revolution,'" 24.
209. "The New Banking," 89.
210. "The New Banking," 92.
211. Schulman, *The Seventies*, 136–37.
212. "The New Diversification Oil Game," 76.
213. "Conglomerates Start Looking Good Again," 77.
214. "Why Foreign Companies Are Betting on the U.S.," 50.
215. Bluestone and Harrison, *The Deindustrialization of America*, 156.
216. "The New Diversification Oil Game," 77.
217. Bluestone and Harrison, *The Deindustrialization of America*, 41. See also "Diversification That Offsets the Slack in Steel," 99; "A Steelmaker Pushes into Lending," 77.
218. "The Reindustrialization of America," 78.
219. Harvey, *The Condition of Postmodernity*, 158. See also Stearns and Allan. "Economic Behavior in Institutional Environments."
220. Bluestone and Harrison, *The Deindustrialization of America*, 152.
221. Bluestone and Harrison, *The Deindustrialization of America*, 41.
222. Webber and Rigby, *The Golden Age Illusion*, 34.
223. Arrighi, *The Long Twentieth Century*, 73
224. Webber and Rigby, *The Golden Age Illusion*, 34.
225. Bluestone and Harrison, *The Deindustrialization of America*, 42.
226. Bluestone and Harrison, *The Deindustrialization of America*, 44.
227. Frank, "The Post-war Boom," 156.
228. Bluestone and Harrison, *The Deindustrialization of America*, 42.
229. Bluestone and Harrison, *The Deindustrialization of America*, 45.
230. Bluestone and Harrison, *The Deindustrialization of America*, 6.
231. "Why U.S. Technology Lags," 80.
232. "The Right Way to Spur R&D," 112.
233. "Why U.S. Technology Lags," 80.
234. "Why U.S. Technology Lags," 80.
235. Bluestone and Harrison, *The Deindustrialization of America*, 6.
236. Bluestone and Harrison, *The Deindustrialization of America*, 6–7.
237. Bluestone and Harrison, *The Deindustrialization of America*, 147.
238. Davies, *The Limits of Neoliberalism*, 27.
239. Davies, *The Limits of Neoliberalism*, 107.
240. Sennett, *The Culture of the New Capitalism*, 39–40. See also Sobel, *The Age of Giant Corporations*, 269.
241. Sennett, *The Culture of the New Capitalism*, 41.
242. Kerssens, "The Database 'Revolution,'" 24. See also Marcus and Segal, *Technology in America*; Haskel and Westlake, *Capitalism without Capital*; Baldwin, *The Great Convergence*.
243. Sennett, *The Culture of the New Capitalism*, 44.
244. Crane et al., *The Oxford Handbook of Corporate Social Responsibility*, 25.

245. Sennett, *The Culture of the New Capitalism*, 37.

246. See Phillips, *Wealth and Democracy*, 155–56; Western and Rosenfeld, "Unions, Norms, and the Rise in US Wage Inequality"; Bivens and Mishel, "Understanding the Historic Divergence between Productivity and a Typical Worker's Pay"; Bluestone and Harrison, "The Great American Job Machine"; Juhn et al., "Wage Inequality and the Rise in Returns to Skill."

247. Phillips, *The Politics of Rich and Poor*, 165–66.

248. See Fones-Wolf, *Selling Free Enterprise*; Phillips-Fein, *Invisible Hands*.

249. "Labor Woes Cloud Outlook for Economy."

250. Frantzen, *Growth and Crisis*, 142.

251. "The U.S. Can't Afford What Labor Wants," 104.

252. See Cowie, *Capital Moves*.

253. Webber and Rigby, *The Golden Age Illusion*, 52. See also Schwarz, *America's Hidden Success*; Cowie, *Stayin' Alive*; Davis, *Prisoners of the American Dream*.

254. See Davis, *Prisoners of the American Dream*. See also Maloney and Whatley, "Making the Effort"; Sundstrom, "The Color Line"; Nelson, *Divided We Stand*; Hill, "The Problem of Race in American Labor History"; Hill, "Racism within Organized Labor."

255. "Why Joblessness May Stay High," 44.

256. "Why Joblessness May Stay High," 44.

257. "Why Joblessness May Stay High," 44.

258. Schwarz, *America's Hidden Success*, 116. See also Gordon, *The Rise and Fall of American Growth*, 628.

259. Friedman, "Workers without Employers"; De Stefano, "The Rise of the Just-in-Time Workforce"; Aloisi, "Commoditized Workers."

260. Braudel, *Civilization and Capitalism, 15th–18th Century*, 229.

261. See Beauregard, *Voices of Decline*.

262. See Lake and Reynolds, *Drawing the Global Colour Line*.

263. Freund, *Colored Property*, 8.

264. Freund, *Colored Property*, 9.

265. Katznelson, *When Affirmative Action Was White*, 23.

266. Katznelson, *When Affirmative Action Was White*, 128.

267. Katznelson, *When Affirmative Action Was White*, 128.

268. Friedman, *Capitalism and Freedom*, 111.

269. Freund, *Colored Property*, 19.

270. Freund, *Colored Property*, 18–19.

271. Acham, *Revolution Televised*, 39. See also *Report of the National Advisory Commission on Civil Disorders*; Platt, *The Politics of Riot Commissions*.

272. *Report of the National Advisory Commission on Civil Disorders*, 2.

273. Singh, *Black Is a Country*, 5.

274. "The Warning of the Riot Commission," 143.

275. "Business and the Urban Crisis," C1.

276. Delton, *Racial Integration in Corporate America*, 21.

277. "Economically the Negro Gains but He's Still the Low Man," 80.

278. "Economically the Negro Gains but He's Still the Low Man," 78.

279. Du Bois, *Black Reconstruction in America*, 714.

280. "The Race Crisis Coming to a Head," 24, italics added. For criminalizing Blackness, see Muhammad, *The Condemnation of Blackness*.

281. "The Race Crisis Coming to a Head," 24.

282. For stereotypes, see Bogle, *Toms, Coons, Mulattoes, Mammies, & Bucks*.

283. "The Race Crisis Coming to a Head," 24.

284. Erskine, "The Polls: Recent Opinion on Racial Problems." See also Campbell, *White Attitudes toward Black People*.

285. Schulman, *From Cotton Belt to Sunbelt*, 178.

286. "What Price Will Whites Pay?," 75.

287. See *Race: The Power of an Illusion*, Episode 3. See also Freund, *Colored Property*; Feagin, "Excluding Blacks and Others from Housing."

288. Baldwin, *The Fire Next Time*, 335.

Chapter 4

1. "The Debt Economy," 45.

2. "The Debt Economy," 45. For a history of consumer debt, see Calder, *Financing the American Dream*.

3. Stein, *Pivotal Decade*, 49.

4. Stein, *Pivotal Decade*, 112.

5. Stein, *Pivotal Decade*, 115.

6. "The Debt Economy," 48.

7. Carson-Parker, "The Options ahead for the Debt Economy," 120, emphasis added.

8. Carson-Parker, "The Options ahead for the Debt Economy," 120.

9. Carson-Parker, "The Options ahead for the Debt Economy," 120.

10. Carson-Parker, "The Options ahead for the Debt Economy," 123.

11. Schui, *Austerity*, 140–41.

12. Carter, *The Politics of Rage*, 218.

13. Williams, *God's Own Party*, 70–71.

14. Davies, *The Limits of Neoliberalism*, 88.

15. Silk and Vogel, *Ethics and Profits*.

16. Kruse and Zelizer, *Fault Lines*, 33.

17. McQuaid, *Uneasy Partners*, 103–4.

18. "America's Growing Antibusiness Mood," 100.

19. "America's Growing Antibusiness Mood," 100.

20. "America's Growing Antibusiness Mood," 100.

21. "America's Growing Antibusiness Mood," 100.

22. "Multinationals: The Public Gives Them Low Marks," 42.

23. "Trouble Plagues the House of Labor," 66–67.

24. See Cowie, *Capital Moves*.

25. Cowie, *Stayin' Alive*, 12.

26. "Profits Set Still Another Record," 87.

27. See Kerr, "Creating the Corporate Citizen."

28. Akard, "Corporate Mobilization and Political Power," 601.

29. "Corporate Planning: Piercing Future Fog in the Executive Suite," 54.

30. See Phillips-Fein, *Invisible Hands*; MacLean, *Democracy in Chains*.
31. Cowie, *Stayin' Alive*, 231. See also Blyth, *Great Transformations*; Harvey, *A Brief History of Neoliberalism*.
32. Phillips-Fein, *Invisible Hands*, 194.
33. Kruse and Zelizer, *Fault Lines*, 18.
34. Cowie, *Stayin' Alive*, 231.
35. Borstelmann, *The 1970s*, 130.
36. Carroll, *It Seemed Like Nothing Happened*, 134.
37. Frieden, "The Trilateral Commission," 69.
38. Gill, *American Hegemony and the Trilateral Commission*, 99, 166.
39. Crozier et al., *The Crisis of Democracy*, 8.
40. Frantzen, *Growth and Crisis in Post-war Capitalism*, 147–48.
41. Stein, *Pivotal Decade*, 115.
42. Stein, *Pivotal Decade*, 114.
43. Stein, *Pivotal Decade*, 117–18. See also "A Loud Dissent from Blue Collars," 26–27.
44. Stein, *Pivotal Decade*, 121.
45. Carson-Parker, "The Options ahead for the Debt Economy," 120.
46. Brenner, *The Boom and the Bubble*, 17.
47. *Business Week*, April 17, 1971.
48. Fones-Wolf, *Selling Free Enterprise*, 289.
49. Borstelmann, *The 1970s*, 131.
50. See, for example, Vatter, *The U.S. Economy in the 1950s*; Schulman, *From Cotton Belt to Sunbelt*; Hooks and Bloomquist, "The Legacy of World War II for Regional Growth and Decline."
51. Schulman, *The Seventies*, xiv.
52. "A Consensus for a Tax Cut," 30.
53. "The Second War between the States," 92.
54. Bluestone and Harrison, *The Deindustrialization of America*, 182.
55. Bluestone and Harrison, *The Deindustrialization of America*, 185.
56. "A Counterattack in the War between the States," 71.
57. "The Regulators Can't Go On This Way," 60.
58. "White House Eyes Deregulation Route," 29; "'Deregulation' Is Off to a Halting Start," 26.
59. "Government Intervention: Regulation," 103.
60. Sobel, *The Age of Giant Corporations*, 249.
61. "Donald Cook Takes on the Environmentalists," 67.
62. "Are Government Programs Worth the Price?," 114.
63. "Are Government Programs Worth the Price?," 116.
64. Borstelmann, *The 1970s*, 137.
65. See Katznelson, *When Affirmative Action Was White*.
66. MacLean, *Freedom Is Not Enough*, 233.
67. Boston, *Affirmative Action and Black Entrepreneurship*, 1.
68. "White Business Balks at Sharing the Work," 47.
69. "White Business Balks at Sharing the Work," 47.
70. "Business and the Urban Crisis," C1. See also Delton, *Racial Integration in Corporate America*.
71. See Harris, "Whiteness as Property."

72. Harris, "Whiteness as Property," 1767.

73. Hoerr, "An Argument against Preferential Hiring," 21.

74. See Glazer and Moynihan, *Beyond the Melting Pot*.

75. *Business Week*, January 17, 1977.

76. Perlstein, *The Invisible Bridge*, 603–4.

77. For work on this image, see Hancock, *The Politics of Disgust*; Roberts, *Killing the Black Body*; Morgan, *Laboring Women*; Collins, *Black Sexual Politics*; Block, *Rape & Sexual Power in Early America*; Fischer, *Suspect Relations*.

78. See Carter, *From George Wallace to Newt Gingrich*; Anderson, *White Rage*.

79. Stein, *Pivotal Decade*, 123.

80. Stein, *Pivotal Decade*, 123.

81. See Phillips-Fein, *Invisible Hands*.

82. "Egalitarianism: Threat to a Free Market," 62.

83. "Egalitarianism: Threat to a Free Market," 62.

84. "Egalitarianism: Threat to a Free Market," 62.

85. "Egalitarianism: Threat to a Free Market," 62.

86. "Egalitarianism: Threat to a Free Market," 63.

87. "Egalitarianism: Threat to a Free Market," 63.

88. "Egalitarianism: Threat to a Free Market," 65.

89. "Egalitarianism: Threat to a Free Market," 65.

90. "The World Tests Friedman's Theories," 73.

91. "The World Tests Friedman's Theories," 73.

92. "The World Tests Friedman's Theories," 73.

93. "The World Tests Friedman's Theories," 75.

94. "The World Tests Friedman's Theories," 75.

95. "A Draconian Cure for Chile's Economic Ills?," 72.

96. See Jenkins, *Decade of Nightmares*; Wilentz, *The Age of Reagan*.

97. Frantzen, *Growth and Crisis*, 151.

98. Bluestone and Harrison, *The Deindustrialization of America*, 36.

99. Stein, *Pivotal Decade*, 17.

100. Frantzen, *Growth and Crisis*, 153.

101. "Corporate Planning: Piercing Future Fog in the Executive Suite," 46.

102. See Cowie, *Capital Moves*.

103. "Corporate Planning: Piercing Future Fog in the Executive Suite," 46.

104. "Corporate Planning: Piercing Future Fog in the Executive Suite," 47.

105. "Corporate Planning: Piercing Future Fog in the Executive Suite," 48.

106. "Corporate Planning: Piercing Future Fog in the Executive Suite," 49.

107. "Group Management to Control Diversity," 98.

108. "Government Intervention," 42–47.

109. "The Right Way to Spur R&D," 112; "Why U.S. Technology Lags," 80.

110. Kruse and Zelizer, *Fault Lines*, 103.

111. Wanniski, *The Way the World Works*.

112. "Vanishing Innovation," 46, 48.

113. "A Surprising Rally for Profits," 81.

114. "New World Economic Order," 68.

115. "New World Economic Order," 68.

116. "New World Economic Order," 68.

117. See Wight, *Oil Money*.

118. "New World Economic Order," 69.

119. See Chang, *Bad Samaritans*; Stiglitz, *Globalization and Its Discontents Revisited*; Slobodian, *Globalists*.

120. This moment foreshadowed the aftermath of the 2007–8 economic crisis. See Lahart, "U.S. Firms Build Up Record Cash Piles."

121. "Why the Cash Piles Up," 174.

122. Wilentz, *The Age of Reagan*, 121.

123. Zucker, "The Fallacy of Slashing Taxes without Cutting Spending," 62; "Why Business Needs Two Tax Cuts," 14; Roth, "How Tax Cuts Can Pay for Themselves."

124. Ladd et al., "The Polls: Taxing and Spending," 126.

125. Ladd et al., "The Polls: Taxing and Spending," 127.

126. Ladd et al., "The Polls: Taxing and Spending," 129.

127. See Mieczkowski, *Gerald Ford and the Challenges of the 1970s*.

128. Ladd et al., "The Polls: Taxing and Spending," 131–32.

129. See Rowe, "Local and Regional Countercurrents."

130. Ladd et al., "The Polls: Taxing and Spending," 134.

131. Stein, *Pivotal Decade*, 177–202.

132. Borstelmann, *1970s*, 157.

133. Rodgers, *Age of Fracture*, 70.

134. See Phillips-Fein, *Fear City*; Noah, "The United States of Inequality"; Congressional Budget Office, "Trends in the Distribution of Household Income between 1979 and 2007"; Piketty, *Capital in the Twenty-First Century*.

135. Stein, *Pivotal Decade*, 204.

136. Stein, *Pivotal Decade*, 204.

137. Frantzen, *Growth and Crisis*, 159.

138. Carson-Parker, "The Options ahead for the Debt Economy," 120.

139. Carson-Parker, "The Options ahead for the Debt Economy," 120.

140. "The Corporate Image," 47.

141. "The Corporate Image," 47.

142. "The Corporate Image," 47.

143. "The Corporate Image," 47.

144. "The Corporate Image," 47.

145. "The Corporate Image," 47.

146. "The Corporate Image," 47.

147. "The Corporate Image," 47.

148. Frantzen, *Growth and Crisis*, 156.

149. *Business Week*, March 12, 1979.

150. "The Decline of U.S. Power," 36. For history of U.S. role in Iran, see Blum, *Killing Hope*.

151. "The Decline of U.S. Power," 37.

152. "The Decline of U.S. Power," 37.

153. Parenti, "More Bucks from the Bang," 27.

154. Parenti, "More Bucks from the Bang," 28.

155. "The Decline of U.S. Power," 37.

156. See Gill, *American Hegemony and the Trilateral Commission*.
157. "The Decline of U.S. Power," 37.
158. "An Urgent Need for New Ties to Government," 74.
159. "An Urgent Need for New Ties to Government," 76.
160. "An Urgent Need for New Ties to Government," 76.
161. See Chang, *Bad Samaritans*.
162. "An Urgent Need for New Ties to Government," 76.
163. "An Urgent Need for New Ties to Government," 76.
164. "An Urgent Need for New Ties to Government," 82. For U.S. interventions abroad, Kinzer, *Overthrow*; Westad, *The Global Cold War*.
165. "How 1,200 Companies Performed in 1978," 89; "Profits Hold Up under a Threat of Recession," 25; "Profits Stay Surprisingly Strong," 87.
166. Rodgers, *Age of Fractures*, 55.
167. Maier, "'Malaise,'" 37.
168. Brenner, *The Boom and the Bubble*, 35. See also Klein, *The Shock Doctrine*.
169. Mandel, *The Second Slump*, 80–81.
170. Brenner, *The Boom and the Bubble*, 35.
171. Schulman, *The Seventies*, 132.
172. Brenner, *The Boom and the Bubble*, 64.
173. "Shock Treatment for Inflation," 96.
174. *Business Week*, June 23, 1980.
175. For the history of racism, see Kendi, *Stamped from the Beginning*; Fredrickson, *Racism*.
176. See Ngai, *Impossible Subjects*.
177. See Ngai, *Impossible Subjects*.
178. "The Implications of Oil Company Profits," 84.
179. "The Implications of Oil Company Profits," 84.
180. "Black Unemployment: Bad, and No Quick Fix," 17.
181. "Reagan's Plan: Sidestep Unions, Woo Workers," 148.
182. "America's New Financial Structure," 138.
183. Duménil and Lévy, *The Crisis of Neoliberalism*, 132–33.
184. "Interview with Friedrich von Hayek," 114.
185. Stein, *Pivotal Decade*, 262.
186. See Stiglitz, *Globalization and Its Discontents Revisited*.
187. Wilentz, *The Age of Reagan*, 122.
188. Perlstein, "Exclusive: Lee Atwater's Infamous 1981 Interview on the Southern Strategy."
189. See Lopez, *Dog Whistle Politics*; Edsall and Edsall, *Chain Reaction*.
190. For race and the New Right, see Lind, *Up from Conservatism*; Carter, *From George Wallace to Newt Gingrich*; Marable, *Black Liberation in Conservative America*; Lowndes, *From the New Deal to the New Right*; De Jong, *Invisible Enemy*.
191. McClendon, "Racism, Rational Choice, and White Opposition to Racial Change," 214–15.
192. McClendon, "Racism, Rational Choice, and White Opposition to Racial Change," 215.
193. McClendon, "Racism, Rational Choice, and White Opposition to Racial Change," 215.
194. McClendon, "Racism, Rational Choice, and White Opposition to Racial Change," 230.

195. De Jong, *Invisible Enemy*, 51.

196. See Wacquant, *Punishing the Poor*; Alexander, *The New Jim Crow*.

197. See Reinarman and Levine, "The Crack Attack"; Muhammad, *The Condemnation of Blackness*; Alexander, *The New Jim Crow*.

198. "Labor Seeks Less," 82–83.

199. Davis, *Prisoners of the American Dream*, 178.

200. Davis, *Prisoners of the American Dream*, 178.

201. Beman, "The Democrats Go Over to the Supply Side," 38.

202. Perlstein, *The Invisible Bridge*, 316–17; Schulman, *The Seventies*, 251; Kruse and Zelizer, *Fault Lines*, 128.

203. Phillips, *The Politics of Rich and Poor*, 207. See also Marable, *Race, Reform, and Rebellion*.

204. Harvey, *A Brief History of Neoliberalism*, 73. See also Stiglitz, *Globalization and Its Discontents Revisited*; Chang, *Bad Samaritans*; Klein, *The Shock Doctrine*.

205. See James, "The IMF and Democratic Socialism in Jamaica."

206. Stein, *Pivotal Decade*, 265.

207. "Where the Recession Really Hurts," 32.

208. Stein, *Pivotal Decade*, 267.

209. "The Payoff of Wage Moderation," 22.

210. See Faludi, *Backlash*.

211. Phillips, *Wealth and Democracy*, 92.

212. Edsall and Edsall, *Chain Reaction*, 23.

213. Noah, "The United States of Inequality."

214. Carroll, *It Seemed Like Nothing Happened*, 348.

215. See http://www.economist.com/blogs/graphicdetail/2013/08/daily-chart-12. See also Marcus, *Happy Days and Wonder Years*.

216. Rodgers, *Age of Fracture*, 189.

217. Friedman, *Capitalism and Freedom*, xiv.

218. "The Neo-liberals Push Their Own Brand of Reform," 96.

219. Schulman, *The Seventies*, 232.

220. Schulman, *The Seventies*, 239.

221. Marable, *Race, Reform, and Rebellion*, 204.

222. Scott-Heron and Jackson, *Winter in America*. For resistance against 1980s conservatism, see Martin, *The Other Eighties*.

223. Zucker, "Reaganomics II," 25.

224. See Lind, *Up from Conservatism*; Hunter, *Culture Wars*.

225. Creedence Clearwater Revival, *Willy and the Poor Boys*.

226. Gingrich and Pious, *To Renew America*, 7.

227. Baldwin, *No Name in the Street*, 128.

228. Buckley, "Our Mission Statement."

229. Friedman, *Capitalism and Freedom*, xiv.

Chapter 5

1. For regeneration, see Slotkin, *Regeneration through Violence*.

2. "Conglomerates: The Corporations That Make Things Jump," 75.

3. Phillips, *Wealth and Democracy*, 237. See also McCurdy, "Justice Field and the Jurisprudence of Government-Business Relations."

4. Corkin, "Cowboys and Free Markets," 67.

5. See Lears, *No Place of Grace*.

6. For "populist conservative," see Lind, "The Five Worldviews That Define American Politics."

7. For populism, progressivism, and the New Deal, see Goodwyn, *The Populist Moment*; McMath, *American Populism*; Wiebe, *The Search for Order*; Chambers, *The Tyranny of Change*; De Santis, *The Shaping of Modern America*; Kazin, *The Populist Persuasion*; Cowie, *The Great Exception*.

8. Grandin, *The End of the Myth*, 58.

9. Friedman, "Which Way for Capitalism."

10. For a structural breakdown of the Western, see Wright, *Sixguns & Society*.

11. For histories of John Wayne, see Roberts and Olson, *John Wayne*; Wills, *John Wayne's America*; Davis, *Duke*.

12. Ford, *Stagecoach*. See also Simmon, *The Invention of the Western Film*.

13. Hoberman, *The Dream Life*, 103.

14. Meeuf, *John Wayne's World*, 10.

15. For culture wars, see Hunter, *Culture Wars*; Kelley, *Yo' Mama's Disfunktional!*; Lepore, *The Whites of Their Eyes*.

16. For one of the early works on viewing American expansionism before 1898 as imperialism and the role of white supremacy, see Williams, *The Tragedy of American Diplomacy*; LaFeber, *The New Empire*; Berwanger, *The Frontier Against Slavery*. For other works discussing nineteenth-century American empire, see Beisner, *Twelve against Empire*; Jacobson, *Barbarian Virtues*; Greenberg, *Manifest Manhood and the Antebellum American Empire*; Blackhawk, *Violence over the Land*; Hixson, *American Settler Colonialism*.

17. Hawks, *Red River*; Ford, *Fort Apache*; Dwan, *Sands of Iwo Jima*; Farrow, *Hondo*; Ford, *The Searchers*.

18. Harris, *Swing Out, Sweet Land*.

19. Hathaway, *True Grit*.

20. Meeuf, *John Wayne's World*, 2.

21. See Johnson, *Heartland TV*; Lauck and Stock, eds., *The Conservative Heartland*.

22. Smith, "The Origins of Nations," 362–63.

23. See Lind, *Up from Conservatism*; McGirr, *Suburban Warriors*; Lewis, *Massive Resistance*; Freund, *Colored Property*; Lowndes, *From the New Deal to the New Right*.

24. See Denning, *The Cultural Front*.

25. Simmon, *The Invention of the Western Film*, 160.

26. May, "Introduction," 2. See also Cowie, *The Great Exception*; Horn, "Reinventing Monopoly and the Role of Corporations"; Birch, "Financial Economics and Business Schools"; Lind, *Land of Progress*.

27. Lears, "A Matter of Taste," 41.

28. See Denning, *The Cultural Front*; Wiebe, *The Search for Order*, 84. See also McMath, *American Populism*.

29. Lears, "A Matter of Taste," 51.

30. Lears, "A Matter of Taste," 51.

31. May, "Making the American Consensus," 72. See also Dick, *The Star-Spangled Screen*.

32. See Sklar, *Movie-Made America*.

33. Navasky, *Naming Names*, 85, 337. See also Sayre, *Running Time*, 17–24.

34. Slotkin, *Gunfighter Nation*, 367. For conservatism and big business, see Phillips-Fein, *Invisible Hands*; Phillips-Fein and Zelizer, *What's Good for Business*.

35. May, "Movie Star Politics," 127.

36. Lewis, "Money Matters," 88.

37. Lewis, "Money Matters," 89.

38. For World War II and Hollywood, see May, "Making the American Consensus"; Harris, *Five Came Back*.

39. See Black, *Hollywood Censored*; Leff and Simmons, *The Dame in the Kimono*; Doherty, *Pre-Code Hollywood*; Pollard, *Sex and Violence*; Steinmetz, *Beyond Free Speech and Propaganda*.

40. Lewis, *Hollywood v. Hard Core*, 303.

41. Lewis, *Hollywood v. Hard Core*, 304.

42. Walsh, "The Films We Never Saw." See also Zaniello, *Working Stiffs, Union Maids, Reds, and Riffraff*.

43. Sklar, *Movie-Made America*, 257.

44. May, "Making the American Consensus," 71–72. May quotes from Schumach, *The Face on the Cutting Room Floor*, 129.

45. Quoted in Sayre, *Running Time*, 48.

46. Whitfield, *The Culture of the Cold War*, 130.

47. Whitfield, *The Culture of the Cold War*, 131.

48. See Silver and Ursini, *Film Noir Reader*; Wager, *Dames in the Driver's Seat*; Wallace, "Race, Gender and Psychoanalysis in Forties Film"; Medovoi, *Rebels*; Doherty, *Teenagers and Teenpics*; Nickel, "Disabling African American men".

49. Sayre, *Running Time*, 140.

50. Davis, *Duke*, 164. See also Briley, "John Wayne and *Big Jim McLain* (1952)"; Ludwig, *Big Jim McLain*.

51. Sklar, *Movie-Made America*, 266.

52. Saunders, *The Cultural Cold War*, 284.

53. Lipsitz, *The Possessive Investment in Whiteness*, 84.

54. Slotkin, *Gunfighter Nation*, 334.

55. Slotkin, *Gunfighter Nation*, 334.

56. For Native Americans in film, see Kilpatrick, *Celluloid Indians*; Simmon, *The Invention of the Western Film*; Aleiss, *Making the White Man's Indian*; Raheja, *Reservation Reelism*.

57. Wills, *John Wayne's America*, 139. See Marin, *Tall in the Saddle*.

58. Ford, *She Wore a Yellow Ribbon*.

59. Quoted from Slotkin, *Gunfighter Nation*, 53.

60. Quoted in Bederman, *Manliness & Civilization*, 182–83.

61. Painter, *The History of White People*, 256.

62. Bancroft, "A Historian's View of the Negro," 83.

63. "*Playboy* Interview: John Wayne," 82.

64. Gibson, *Warrior Dreams*, 23-5.

65. Cuordileone, *Manhood and American Political Culture in the Cold War*, xxiii. For the feminization of mass culture, see Modleski, "Femininity as Mas(s)querade."

66. Cuordileone, *Manhood and American Political Culture in the Cold War*, viii.

67. Ray, *A Certain Tendency of the Hollywood Cinema*, 170–71.

68. Corkin, "Cowboys and Free Markets," 73–74. See also Meeuf, *John Wayne's World*.

69. Filene, "'Cold War Culture,'" 161.

70. Filene, "'Cold War Culture,'" 162. For Westerns on television, see Edgerton, *The Columbia History of American Television*, 196–97; MacDonald, *Who Shot the Sheriff?*; Taylor, *Prime-Time Families*.

71. Omi and Winant, *Racial Formation in the United States*, 65. See also Webb, *Massive Resistance*; Lewis, *Massive Resistance*.

72. Davis, *Duke*, 220. Wayne, *The Alamo*.

73. Wills, *John Wayne's America*, 221. A family-friendly, Walt Disney version of Davy Crockett's history appeared on television in 1954–55, depicting the Andrew Jackson–led cleansing campaigns—with Crockett providing militia leadership—across the Southeast as westward expansion opened the South to the expansion of slavery and cotton cultivation. Accordingly, this celebration, true to the settler colonial project, disavowed the ethnic cleansing campaigns structuring this aspect of westward expansion—with cleared Indian land turning into slave-grown cotton wealth. There is also a display of patriarchal ownership of women, when, in the wake of saving Davy's life, his partner, George, is promised a kiss from Mrs. Crockett. After riding for days, the first thing George does when riding up to Crockett's homestead is to dismount, grab Polly Crockett, and passionately kiss her without warning. This display of sexual assault by Walt Disney Productions, at the time, would have been viewed as "quaint" and family friendly.

74. See Novick, *That Noble Dream*; Foner, *The New American History*; Guerrero, *Framing Blackness*; Robinson, *Forgeries of Memory and Meaning*.

75. See Bogle, *Toms, Coons, Mulattoes, Mammies, & Bucks*; Collins, *Black Feminist Thought*.

76. Slotkin, *Gunfighter Nation*, 518.

77. See Genovese, *Roll, Jordan, Roll*. Genovese writes, "A paternalism accepted by both masters and slaves—but with radically different interpretations—afforded a fragile bridge across the intolerable contradictions inherent in a society based on racism, slavery, and class exploitation that had to depend on the willing reproduction and productivity of its victims. For the slave-holders paternalism represented an attempt to overcome the fundamental contradiction in slavery: the impossibility of the slaves' ever becoming the things they were supposed to be. Paternalism defined the involuntary labor of the slaves as a legitimate return to their masters for protection and direction. But, the masters' need to see their slaves as acquiescent human beings constituted a moral victory for the slaves themselves. Paternalism's insistence upon mutual obligations—duties, responsibilities, and ultimately even rights—implicitly recognized the slaves' humanity" (5).

78. Ford, *Judge Priest*.

79. See Lott, *Love and Theft*.

80. Slotkin, *Gunfighter Nation*, 227; Davis, *Duke*, 231; Roberts and Olson, *John Wayne*, 471–79.

81. See Kruse, *White Flight*; Lewis, *Massive Resistance*.

82. Perlstein, *Before the Storm*, xii.

83. Davis, *Duke*, 276.

84. Berlot and Lyons, *Right-Wing Populism in America*, 175.

85. Berlot and Lyons, *Right-Wing Populism in America*, 178.
86. Kazin, *The Populist Persuasion*, 237.
87. Kazin, *The Populist Persuasion*, 239.
88. See Moreau, *Schoolbook Nation*, 265.
89. Apple, "Rebuilding Hegemony," 107.
90. "A Nation Builds under Fire"; Wayne and Kellogg, *The Green Berets*. See also United States, *Catalog of the Big Picture Films*.
91. Slatzer, *No Substitute for Victory*.
92. Hoberman, *The Dream Life*, 148–49.
93. "Challenge of Ideas."
94. For the Vietnam War within the framework of anti-colonialism, see Young, *The Vietnam Wars*; Hahn and Heiss, *Empire and Revolution*; Westad, *The Global Cold War*; Hunt and Levine, *Arc of Empire*.
95. Westad, *The Global Cold War*, 89.
96. Wills, *John Wayne's America*, 229.
97. Wills, *John Wayne's America*, 234.
98. Hoberman, *The Dream Life*, 213.
99. Slotkin, *Gunfighter Nation*, 522, 526.
100. Slotkin, *Gunfighter Nation*, 526–27.
101. Gaddis, *The United States and the Origins of the Cold War*, 7.
102. See Marshall, Scott, and Hunter, *The Iran Contra Connection*.
103. Young, *The Vietnam Wars*, 45.
104. Young, *The Vietnam Wars*, 45.
105. Young, *The Vietnam Wars*, 22.
106. For gender and the Cold War, see May, *Homeward Bound*.
107. See Pascoe, *What Comes Naturally*.
108. Fairbanks, *Writings: Film*Literature*Music*Society*, 458.
109. For the white ethnic revival of the 1970s, see Jacobson, *Roots Too*.
110. Veracini, *Settler Colonialism*, 77.
111. See Lindsay, "Humor and Dissonance in California's Native American Genocide."
112. Limerick, *The Legacy of Conquest*, 36.
113. See Mohawk, "The 'Disappearing Indian.'"
114. Murrin et al., *Liberty, Equality, Power*, 362. See also Heisel, "The Rise and Fall of an All-American Catchphrase."
115. See Baptist, *The Half Has Never Been Told*; Beckert, *Empire of Cotton*; Kendi, *Stamped from the Beginning*.
116. Du Bois, *Black Reconstruction in America*, 714.
117. See Fahs, "Remembering the Civil War in Children's Literature of the 1880s and 1890s"; Blight, "Decoration Days."
118. See Campney, *Hostile Heartland*; Berwanger, *The Frontier Against Slavery*; Brown, *Strain of Violence*.
119. See Erskine, "The Polls: Recent Opinion on Racial Problems," 696–703.
120. "*Playboy* Interview: John Wayne," 80.
121. Baldwin, *No Name in the Street*, 185.
122. Hartman, *Lose Your Mother*, 6. For lynching, see Litwack, *Trouble in Mind*; Tolnay and Beck, *A Festival of Violence*; Allen et al., *Without Sanctuary*; Campney, *Hostile Heartland*.

123. Glazer, *Affirmative Discrimination*.
124. Singh, *Black Is a Country*, 10.
125. For "self-rule," see Wiebe, *Self Rule*.
126. "*Playboy* Interview: John Wayne," 80.
127. Lind, *Up from Conservatism*, 191.
128. Mervosh and Chokshi, "Reagan Called Africans 'Monkeys' in Call with Nixon, Tape Reveals." See also Jordan, *White Over Black*; Pieterse, *White on Black*.
129. Grandin, *The End of the Myth*, 64.
130. Hawks, *Hatari*. For white settler projects in Africa, see Elkins and Pedersen, *Settler Colonialism in the Twentieth Century*; Cavanagh and Veracini, *The Routledge Handbook of the History of Settler Colonialism*.
131. Kluge, "First and Last, a Cowboy," 46.
132. Kluge, "First and Last, a Cowboy," 46.
133. Roberts and Olson, *John Wayne*, 487.
134. Krehbiel, *Tulsa 1921*, 123.
135. Sirota, "The Legend of the Persecuted White Guy"; De Jong, *Invisible Enemy*, 109–110.
136. See Lichtenfeld, *Action Speaks Louder*.
137. Lichtenfeld, *Action Speaks Louder*, xviii.
138. Meyer, "The Recrudescent American Conservatism," 76.
139. Monaco, *The Sixties*, 179; Kluge, "First and last, a cowboy," 46.
140. Ryan and Kellner, *Camera Politica*, 80.
141. Ford, dir., *The Man Who Shot Liberty Valance*; McLaglen, dir., *McLintock!*.
142. Monaco, *The Sixties*, 179; David, *Duke*, 285.
143. Hixson, *American Settler Colonialism*, 5.
144. Lichtenfeld, *Action Speaks Louder*, 19.
145. See Hoefle, "Bitter Harvest"; Brown, *Strain of Violence*; Reiss, "Police Brutality—Answers to Key Questions"; Davis, *City of Quartz*; Johnson, *Street Justice*; Alexander, *The New Jim Crow*; Taylor, *Fight the Power*.
146. *Report of the National Advisory Commission on Civil Disorders*.
147. See Flamm, *Law and Order*.
148. See Erskine, "The Polls: Politics and Law and Order," 623–34.
149. Lichtenfeld, *Action Speaks Louder*, 174.
150. Quoted in Lichtenfeld, *Action Speaks Louder*, 26.
151. Kirshner, *Hollywood's Last Golden Age*, 135.
152. Guerrero, *Framing Blackness*; Massood, *Black City Cinema*; Dune, *"Baad Bitches" and Sassy Supermamas*.
153. Berger, *Sight Unseen*, 135; Sexton, "The Ruse of Engagement."
154. Berger, *Sight Unseen*, 135.
155. See Sexton, *Black Masculinity and the Cinema of Policing*; Muhammad, Khalil Gibran. *The Condemnation of Blackness*.
156. Baldwin, *The Devil Finds Work*, 528.
157. See Bogle, *Toms, Coons, Mulattoes, Mammies, & Bucks*.
158. For militarization of policing and harsher sentences, see Davis, *City of Quartz*; Wacquant, *Punishing the Poor*; Alexander, *The New Jim Crow*.
159. Lind, *Up from Conservatism*, 138.

160. Mannheim, *From Karl Mannheim*, 385.
161. Lind, *Up from Conservatism*, 140.
162. Baldwin, *No Name in the Street*, 46.
163. Jacobson, *Whiteness of a Different Color*, 93
164. See Ngai, *Impossible Subjects*.
165. "*Playboy* Interview: John Wayne," 92.
166. See Linethal and Engelhardt, *History Wars*.
167. Interview with John Wayne, *The Great American Picture Star*.
168. See Hoff, *Law, Gender, and Injustice*; Pateman, *The Sexual Contract*; Brownmiller, *Against Our Will*.
169. Jenkins, *Decade of Nightmares*, 174.
170. Trattner, *From Poor Law to Welfare State*, 363–64.
171. Edsall and Edsall, *Chain Reaction*, 221–22.
172. See Piketty and Saez, "Income Inequality in the United States." For an analysis of Reaganomics, see Phillips, *The Politics of Rich and Poor*. For the cultural-political path toward Reagan, see Phillips-Fein, *Invisible Hands*.
173. Phillips, *The Politics of Rich and Poor*, 18.
174. Mishel, "Huge Disparity in Share of Total Wealth Gain since 1983."
175. Engelhardt and Brown, "The War on Terror as an Indian War."
176. McCarthy, "John Wayne to the Rescue."
177. "*Playboy* Interview: John Wayne," 76.
178. Reich, "The Executive's New Clothes," 26–27.
179. For crisis of masculinity, see Kimmel, *Manhood in America*; Bederman, *Manliness & Civilization*; Lears, "The Managerial Revitalization of the Rich."
180. Phillips, *The Politics of Rich and Poor*, 65.
181. Phillips, *The Politics of Rich and Poor*, 65.
182. Friedman, "Which Way for Capitalism."
183. Friedman, "Which Way for Capitalism."

Chapter 6

1. See Davis, *Duke*, 149.
2. Davis, *Duke*, 307–8.
3. For masculinity in the 1950s, see Gilbert, *Men in the Middle*.
4. McLaglen, *McLintock!*
5. Wills, *John Wayne's America*, 278.
6. See Carroll, *Affirmative Reaction*.
7. Baldwin, *The Devil Finds Work*, 562–63.
8. See Ward, *Women Workers and Global Restructuring*; Frieden, *Global Capitalism*.
9. See Sims, *Women of Blaxploitation*.
10. See Massey, "Flexible Sexism."
11. Engelhardt, *The End of Victory Culture*, 23. See also Demos, *The Unredeemed Captive*; Lepore, *The Name of War*. The counterpart to white women's captivity narratives, of course, were the slave narratives written by enslaved women such as Harriet Jacobs. However, these narratives inverted the "white victimization" sentiment—white men terrorized

Black women—leaving these narratives in the shadow of the more marketable transgression of violated white womanhood. See Hartman, *Scenes of Subjection*.

12. For a history of multiculturalism, see Lentin and Titley, *The Crises of Multiculturalism*; Frey, *Diversity Explosion*.

13. Harvey, *The Condition of Postmodernity*, 147.

14. Sklar, *Movie-Made America*, 276.

15. Monaco, *The Sixties*, 10.

16. See Kunz, *Culture Conglomerates*.

17. Monaco, *The Sixties*, 30–39. See also Cook, *Lost Illusions*.

18. See Arrighi, *The Long Twentieth Century*.

19. See Sklar, *Movie-Made America*, 289–90.

20. For work on business appropriation of counterculture, see Frank, *The Conquest of Cool*.

21. Harvey, *The Condition of Postmodernity*, 156.

22. Lorde, *Sister Outsider*, 115.

23. See Hole and Levine, *Rebirth of Feminism*; Davis, *Women, Race & Class*.

24. Shammas, "Re-assessing the Married Women's Property Acts."

25. De Beauvoir, *The Second Sex*.

26. See Rosen, *The World Split Open*; Collier-Thomas and Franklin, *Sisters in the Struggle*; Kessler-Harris, *Out to Work*; Roth, *Separate Roads to Feminism*; Cobble, *The Other Women's Movement*; Springer, *Living for the Revolution*; Friedan, *The Feminine Mystique*; De Beauvoir, *The Second Sex*.

27. See Davis, *Women, Race & Class*; Gilmore, *Gender and Jim Crow*; Kopacsi and Faulkner, "The Powers That Might Be."

28. Hole and Levine, *Rebirth of Feminism*, 24. See *American Women: The Report of the President's Commission on the Status of Women and Other Publications of the Commission*.

29. Hole and Levine, *Rebirth of Feminism*, 30.

30. Kruse and Zelizer, *Fault Lines*, 68.

31. Collins, *Black Feminist Thought*, 8. For the 1960s and "women's liberation," see Echols, *Daring to Be Bad*; Echols, "Nothing Distant about It."

32. Rosen, *The World Split Open*, 107. See also Baxandall, "Re-visioning the Women's Liberation Movement's Narrative."

33. Echols, *Daring to Be Bad*, 34.

34. Kruse and Zelizer, *Fault Lines*, 68–69.

35. Hole and Levine, *Rebirth of Feminism*, 114–17.

36. See Wambeke, "Politics Makes for Strange Bedfellows."

37. Wambeke, "Politics Makes for Strange Bedfellows," 116.

38. Wambeke, "Politics Makes for Strange Bedfellows," 117.

39. See Gordon, *Pitied but Not Entitled*.

40. See May, *Homeward Bound*.

41. Amott and Matthaei, *Race, Gender, and Work*, 132. See also Lundberg and Farnham, *Modern Woman*.

42. Kirk, "The Problem of the New Order," 367.

43. See Cooper, *Family Values*, 36.

44. Welter, "The Cult of True Womanhood," 152. See also Cott, *The Bonds of Womanhood*; Ryan, *Cradle of the Middle Class*.

45. Cooper, *Family Values*, 88.

46. May, *Homeward Bound*, 24.

47. Baldwin, *The Devil Finds Work*, 562.

48. Bailey, "She 'Can Bring Home the Bacon.'"

49. Cooper, *Family Values*, 63.

50. Hole and Levine, *Rebirth of Feminism*, 228.

51. Bradley, *Mass Media and the Shaping of American Feminism*, 11.

52. For mainstream representations of feminism in television, see Dow, *Prime-Time Feminism*; Lehman, *Those Girls*.

53. Davies, *The Limits of Neoliberalism*, 27.

54. See Bock and James, *Beyond Equality and Difference*; Fraser, *Fortunes of Feminism*.

55. Schaefer, *"Bold! Daring! Shocking! True!,"* 3–4, 150–64.

56. See Black, *Hollywood Censored*; Jacobs, *The Wages of Sin*; Doherty, *Pre-code Hollywood*; Leff and Simmons, *The Dame in the Kimono*; Pollard, *Sex and Violence*; Wittern-Keller, "All the Power of the Law"; Steinmetz, *Beyond Free Speech and Propaganda*.

57. Thrower, *Nightmare USA*, 12. See also Meyers, *For One Week Only*.

58. Schaefer, *"Bold! Daring! Shocking! True!,"* 2, 44–46.

59. Green, *Babyface*.

60. Schaefer, *"Bold! Daring! Shocking! True!,"* 326.

61. Jenkins, "Exploiting Feminism." See also Smukler, *Liberating Hollywood*.

62. Schaefer, *"Bold! Daring! Shocking! True!,"* 327.

63. Hilmes, *Only Connect*, 227.

64. Schaefer, *"Bold! Daring! Shocking! True!,"* 337. See also "Interview: Russ Meyer" and Morton et al., "Russ Meyer: Biography."

65. See Morris, "Roger Corman on New World Pictures"; Cook, "Film Culture," 126.

66. Krämer, *The New Hollywood*, 47. See also Frank, *The Conquest of Cool*.

67. Krämer, *The New Hollywood*, 49.

68. Belton, *American Cinema/American Culture*, 337–38; Harris, *Pictures at a Revolution*, 183–84.

69. See Biskind, *Easy Riders, Raging Bulls*; Krämer, *The New Hollywood*; Lewis, "'American Morality Is Not to Be Trifled With.'"

70. See Monaco, *The Sixties*, 2; Krämer, *The New Hollywood*, 47–66; Sieving, *Soul Searching*.

71. Slotkin, *Gunfighter Nation*, 597.

72. Kuhn, *Women's Pictures*, 127.

73. Williams, *Television*, 86.

74. See Krämer, *The New Hollywood*.

75. Ongiri, *Spectacular Blackness*.

76. Krämer, *The New Hollywood*, 72.

77. Krämer, *The New Hollywood*, 72.

78. Krämer, *The New Hollywood*, 86.

79. Mulvey, "Visual Pleasure and Narrative Cinema."

80. Kaplan, *Women and Film*, 2.

81. See Piercy, "The Grand Coolie Damn"; Rosen, *The World Split Open*. For "sexual revolution," see Bailey, *Sex in the Heartland*.

82. See Kuhn, *Women's Pictures*; Haskell, *From Reverence to Rape*. My conception of the liberation gauntlet comes from the work of Stephane Dunn on Black action films. See Dunn, *"Baad Bitches" & Sassy Supermamas*.

83. Hartley, *Machete Maidens Unleashed!*

84. Other films of this nature not produced in the Philippines, though affiliated with Corman, include Demme, *Caged Heat!*; Miller, *Jackson County Jail*. See also Rothman, *Terminal Island*. For Italian versions of the women-in-prison films, see Di Silvestro, *Women in Cell Block 7*; Mulargia, *Escape from Hell*. For French versions of the women-in-prison films, see Franco, *Women behind Bars*. See also Tohill and Tombs, *Immoral Tales*.

85. Cook, "Film Culture," 126.

86. See Dow, *Prime-Time Feminism*; Lehman, *Those Girls*.

87. Rothman, *Terminal Island*. See Jenkins, *The Wow Climax*, 102–24.

88. Hill, *Switchblade Sisters*.

89. Jenkins, *The Wow Climax*, 109.

90. Jenkins, *The Wow Climax*, 109.

91. Meyers, *For One Week Only*, xiii. It is interesting that the introduction of the revised edition of Meyers's book did away with his admission of desiring to see the "suffering of others" and "witnessing savage action and titillating topics" with subsequent expressions such as "I know I would" and "I know I do." See Meyers, *For One Week Only*, 11.

92. See Faludi, *Backlash*.

93. For Black action films, see Guerrero, *Framing Blackness*; Martinez et al., *What It Is . . . What It Was!*; Massood, *Black City Cinema*; Sims, *Women of Blaxploitation*; Dunn, *"Baad Bitches" & Sassy Supermamas*.

94. Dunn, *"Baad Bitches" and Sassy Supermamas*, 2.

95. Dunn, *"Baad Bitches" and Sassy Supermamas*, 5.

96. Starrett, *Cleopatra Jones*; Kaplan, *Truck Turner*.

97. Dunn, *"Baad Bitches" and Sassy Supermamas*, 108. See also Reid, *Redefining Black Film*, 86–88.

98. Hill, *Coffy*; Hill, *Foxy Brown*. For controlling images, see Collins, *Black Feminist Thought*; Bogle, *Toms, Coons, Mulattoes, Mammies, & Bucks*.

99. Parks, *Shaft*; Parks, *Super Fly*.

100. Dunn, *"Baad Bitches" and Sassy Supermamas*, 121.

101. See Campbell, *The Hero with a Thousand Faces*.

102. See Lerner, *The Creation of Patriarchy*.

103. See Latour, *We Have Never Been Modern*.

104. Pateman, *The Sexual Contract*, 2.

105. See McClintock, *Imperial Leather*; Stoler, *Carnal Knowledge and Imperial Power*; Morgan, *Laboring Women*.

106. Braudel, *On History*, 32.

107. Faludi, *Backlash*, 23.

108. Engelhardt, *The End of Victory Culture*, 23.

109. Echols, *Daring to Be Bad*, 67.

110. Rosen, *The World Split Open*, 134; Gitlin, *The Sixties*, 364.

111. Reynolds and Press, *The Sex Revolts*, 7.
112. The Rolling Stones, *Aftermath*.
113. The Rolling Stones. "Brown Sugar/Bitch/Let It Rock."
114. Grateful Dead, *Europe '72*.
115. See Bailey, *Sex in the Heartland*.
116. DiMaggio et al., "Country Music"; Blair and Hyatt, "Meanings of the Home in Popular Song Lyrics"; McCusker and Pecknold, *A Boy Named Sue*; Willman, *Rednecks & Bluenecks*; La Chapelle, *Proud to Be an Okie*; Wade, "Johnny Rebel and the Cajun Roots of Right-Wing Rock"; Mann, "Why Does Country Music Sound White?"
117. See *Flowers in the Wildwood*; Bufwack and Oermann, *Finding Her Voice*.
118. Wheeler, "Woman's Talkin' Liberation Blues"/"Little Lucy."
119. Wheeler, *Love*.
120. The Willis Brothers, "Women's Liberation."
121. Shannon, "Women's Liberation's for the Birds."
122. Roush, "Don't Liberate Me." See also Wynette, "Don't Liberate Me (Love Me)."
123. See Kruse and Zelizer, *Fault Lines*.
124. See Giddings, *When and Where I Enter*; Sugrue, *Sweet Land of Liberty*.
125. Ward, *Just My Soul Responding*, 382; Joseph, *Waiting 'til the Midnight Hour*, 271; Carmichael with Thelwell, *Ready for Revolution*, 431–35.
126. See Giddings, *When and Where I Enter*; Collier-Thomas and Franklin, *Sisters in the Struggle*.
127. Ward, *Just My Soul Responding*, 382. For the matriarchy thesis, see Davis, "Reflections on the Black Woman's Role in the Community of Slaves"; Giddings, *When and Where I Enter*, 325–30; Steinberg, *Turning Back*, 119–23; Roberts, *Killing the Black Body*, 15–17.
128. Vincent, *Funk*, 316.
129. Brown, *It's a New Day—So Let a Man Come In*.
130. See Van Deburg, "Villains, Demons, and Social Bandits."
131. Lumet, *Network*.
132. Bradley, *Mass Media*, 124.
133. See Echols, *Daring to Be Bad*.
134. Rosen, *The World Split Open*, 83. See also Johnson, *The Lavender Scare*.
135. See Mayne, *Framed*, 115–45; Russo, *The Celluloid Closet*.
136. Benton, *Kramer vs. Kramer*.
137. Philips, *The Girl Most Likely To . . .*; Kennedy, *Hannie Caulder*; Kelljan, *Rape Squad* (aka *Act of Vengeance*); Zarchi, *I Spit on Your Grave* (aka *Day of the Woman*); Abel Ferrara, *Ms. 45*. See also Heller-Nicholas, *Rape-Revenge Films*.
138. Cavarero, "Equality and Sexual Difference," 37.
139. For a discussion on romance and patriarchy, see Ebert, "The Romance of Patriarchy."
140. Brownmiller, *Against Our Will*; Davis, "Joan Little"; Davis, *Women, Race & Class*, 178.
141. Lorde, *Sister Outsider*, 61; Rosen, *The World Split Open*, 182.
142. Mies, *Patriarchy & Accumulation on a World Scale*, 27.
143. Roberts, *Killing the Black Body*, 29–31.
144. Horeck, *Public Rape*, 3.
145. Horeck, *Public Rape*, 4.
146. For an extensive breakdown of *I Spit on Your Grave*, see Clover, *Men, Women, and Chain Saws*.

147. See Veracini, *Settler Colonialism*; Hixson, *American Settler Colonialism*.

148. Smith, "Not an Indian Tradition."

149. Harris, "Whiteness as Property"; Roediger, *The Wages of Whiteness*; Kendi, *Stamped from the Beginning*.

150. Kendi, *Stamped from the Beginning*, 204.

151. See Litwack, *Trouble in Mind*; Tolnay and Beck, *A Festival of Violence*; Campney, *Hostile Heartland*.

152. See Allen et al., *Without Sanctuary*.

153. Muhammad, *The Condemnation of Blackness*.

154. See Davis, *Women, Race & Class*, 172–201; Bogle, *Toms, Coons, Mulattoes, Mammies, & Bucks*, 13–14.

155. Omi and Winant, *Racial Formation in the United States*, 70.

156. Davis, *Women, Race & Class*, 175.

157. Rothman, "The 'Slave Power' in the United States"; Cott, *Bonds of Womanhood*; Beckert, "Merchants and Manufacturers in the Antebellum North"; Lind, *Land of Promise*; Baptist, *The Half Has Never Been Told*.

158. See Mies, *Patriarchy & Accumulation on a World Scale*.

159. See Block, *Rape & Sexual Power in Early America*; Fischer, *Suspect Relations*.

160. Collins, *Black Sexual Politics*, 59. See also Collins, *Black Feminist Thought*; Washington, *Medical Apartheid*.

161. Davis, *Women, Race & Class*, 177.

162. I use the bowdlerized n****r so as not to replicate the violence associated with the word. It should be read or pronounced "N-word" by non-Black readers who do not endure the legacies of violence the word historically commands and articulates.

163. See Beckert, *Empire of Cotton*; Lott, *Love and Theft*; Kendi, *Stamped from the Beginning*.

164. See *Report of the National Advisory Commission on Civil Disorders*.

165. Demme and LaGravenese, *A Decade under the Influence*.

166. See documentary for Friedkin, *The French Connection*.

167. Shear, *Across 110th Street*.

168. Cook, *Lost Illusions*, 4.

169. Hartley, *Machete Maidens Unleashed!*

170. See Bederman, *Manliness & Civilization*.

171. Hong, *The Ruptures of American Capital*, 110.

172. See Yeatter, *Cinema of the Philippines*; Capino, *Dream Factories of a Former Colony*.

173. Hawley, "You're a Better Filipino than I Am, John Wayne," 414. See Dmytryk, *Back to Bataan*.

174. Yeatter, *Cinema of the Philippines*, 84.

175. See Meyers, *For One Week Only*; Cook, *The Cinema Book*.

176. For a history of drive-in theaters, see Segrave, *Drive-In Theaters*.

177. Jenkins, *The Wow Climax*, 120.

178. Lim, "American Pictures Made by Filipinos," 24.

179. Hartley, *Machete Maidens Unleashed!* Corman's interest in overseas productions ventured into Argentina after 1982. See Falicov, "U.S.-Argentine Co-productions, 1982–1990." For U.S. support of the 1972 coup, see Gerson, "US Foreign Bases and Human Rights."

180. Hartley, *Machete Maidens Unleashed!*

181. See Grossman, "Women's Place in the Integrated Circuit"; Elson and Pearson, "'Nimble Fingers Make Cheap Workers'"; Safa, "Runaway Shops and Female Employment"; Wright, *Disposable Women*; Ward, *Women Workers and Global Restructuring*; Lim, "Women's Work in Export Factories"; Mies, *Patriarchy & Accumulation on a World Scale*; Standing, "Global Feminization through Flexible Labor"; Standing, "Global Feminization Through Flexible Labor: A Theme Revisited."

182. Grossman, "Women's Place in the Integrated Circuit."

183. Elson and Pearson, "'Nimble Fingers Make Cheap Workers,'" 93, emphasis added. See also Adelman, dir., *Controlling Interest*.

184. Klein, *Cold War Orientalism*, 15.

185. See King, "'Just like Back Home—Only Different!'"

186. See Wright, *Disposable Women*.

187. Hill, *Big Doll House*.

188. Williams, *Final Comedown*.

189. Jenkins, *The Wow Climax*, 105.

190. Morris, "Roger Corman," 63. See also Corman with Jerome, *How I Made a Hundred Movies in Hollywood and Never Lost a Dime*.

191. Morris, "Roger Corman," 63.

192. Interview with Roger Corman in *Kings of the Bs*, 308.

193. King, "'Just like Back Home—Only Different!,'" 48.

194. Mayne, *Framed*, 116; Zalcock, *Renegade Sisters*, 19. See Cromwell, *Caged*. The first women-in-prison film, according to Zalcock, was Cecil B. DeMille's *The Godless Girl* and William A. Seiter's *Prisoners*, both released in 1929.

195. Nashawaty, *Crab Monsters, Teenage Cavemen, and Candy Stripe Nurses*, 107.

196. Yeatter, *Cinema of the Philippines*, 124–25. See De Leon, *Women in Cages*; Hill, *The Big Bird Cage*; Viola, *The Hot Box*; Romero, *Black Mama, White Mama*; Meyer, *Night of the Cobra Woman*; Romero, *The Woman Hunt*; Santiago, *T.N.T. Jackson*; Romero, *Savage Sisters*; Santiago, *The Muthers*.

197. Corber, *Cold War Femme*, 28. See also Russo, *The Celluloid Closet*.

198. King, "'Just like Back Home—Only Different!,'" 51.

199. See Lake and Reynolds, *Drawing the Global Colour Line*.

200. Mayne, *Framed*, 115. See also Jenkins, *The Wow Climax*.

201. Nashawaty, *Crab Monsters, Teenage Cavemen, and Candy Stripe Nurses*, 109.

202. Nashawaty, *Crab Monsters, Teenage Cavemen, and Candy Stripe Nurses*, 109–13.

203. Drenner, *From Manila with Love*.

204. See Hartley, *Machete Maidens Unleashed!*; Drenner, *From Manila with Love*.

205. Hill, *Big Doll House*.

206. Hill, *The Big Bird Cage*. See Roberts, *Killing the Black Body*, 31.

207. Hartley, *Machete Maidens Unleashed!*

208. See *The Best of Charlie's Angels*.

209. For discussions on lesbianism in these films, see Mayne, *Framed*.

210. Collins, *Black Sexual Politics*, 96–97.

211. Cook, "Film Culture," 125.

212. Derounian-Stodola, *Women's Indian Captivity Narratives*; Donovan, *White Slave Crusades*.

213. The film *Captain Blood* (1935) also utilizes Caribbean slavery for the white cast of political prisoners.

214. See Davis, "Reflections on the Black Woman's Role in the Community of Slaves"; Giddings, *When and Where I Enter*; Collins, *Black Feminist Thought*; Hines, "Rape and the Inner Lives of Black Women in the Middle West"; Roberts, *Killing the Black Body*; Morgan, *Laboring Women*.

215. For the jungle film genre, see Robinson, *Forgeries of Memory and Meaning*, 298; Segrave, *Drive-In Theaters*; Hartley, *Machete Maidens Unleashed!*

216. See Berenstein, "White Heroines and Hearts of Darkness"; Dunn, "Lights . . . Camera . . . Africa."

217. See Bederman, *Manliness & Civilization*; Wexler, *Tender Violence*; Rosenberg, *Financial Missionaries to the World*; Robinson, *Forgeries of Memory & Meaning*.

218. Robinson, *Forgeries of Memory & Meaning*, 298.

219. Robinson, *Forgeries of Memory & Meaning*, 298.

220. See Lake and Reynolds, *Drawing the Global Colour Line*.

221. Jenkins, *The Wow Climax*, 120.

222. Baldwin, *No Name in the Street*, 46.

223. See Lichtenfeld, *Action Speaks Louder*.

224. Krämer, *The New Hollywood*, 72.

225. See Flamm, *Law and Order*.

226. See Flamm, *Law and Order*; Siegel, *Coogan's Bluff*; Avildsen, *Joe*; Siegel, *Dirty Harry*; Winner, *Death Wish*.

227. See Engelhardt, *The End of Victory Culture*.

228. Haskell, *From Reverence to Rape*, 22.

229. For captivity narratives, Demos, *The Unredeemed Captive*.

230. Haskell, *From Reverence to Rape*, 340.

231. Lasch, *The Culture of Narcissism*, 190.

232. Siegel, *Dirty Harry*; Post, *Magnum Force*; Fargo, *The Enforcer*.

233. Eastwood, *High Plains Drifter*.

234. Hawks, *Red River*.

235. Pateman, *The Sexual Contract*.

236. Foner, *Give Me Liberty!*, 218.

Chapter 7

1. Patterson, *The Eve of Destruction*, 18.

2. See Marcus, *Happy Days and Wonder Years*; Dwyer, *Back to the Fifties*; Hoberman, *Make My Day*.

3. Bob Seger and the Silver Bullet Band, *Night Moves*.

4. See Kazin, *The Populist Persuasion*; Berlot and Lyons, *Right-Wing Populism in America*.

5. Lumet, *Network*.

6. Phillips, *The Emerging Republican Majority*.

7. For men and masculinity as the universal, see Cavarero, "Equality and Sexual Difference."

8. For femme fatale, see Kaplan, *Women in Film Noir*; Wager, *Dames in the Driver's Seat*; Hanson, *Hollywood Heroines*.

9. Wager, *Dames in the Driver's Seat*, 4.

10. Fitzpatrick, "*Network*: The Other Cold War," 38.

11. Lumet, *Network*.

12. For the popular image of Angela Y. Davis, see Davis, "Afro Images," 37–39, 41–43, 45.

13. Brown, *Undoing the Demos*, 21. The paraphrase of Brown is a paraphrase of: Schwartz, "You Look Good Wearing My Future," 382.

14. See Sandbrook, *Mad as Hell*.

15. Higgins, *9 to 5*; Borden, *Born in Flames*.

16. Kessler-Harris, *Out to Work*, 303.

17. See Schein, "Women in Management."

18. See Barger, "Backlash."

19. For work on women coalitions during this period, see Gilmore, *Feminist Coalitions*.

20. Cavarero, "Equality and Sexual Difference," 41.

21. Davies, *The Limits of Neoliberalism*, 27.

22. Sargent, *Women and Revolution*; Hull et al., *All the Women Are White, All the Blacks Are Men, but Some of Us Are Brave*.

23. "The Corporate Image: PR to the Rescue," 47.

24. Davies, *The Limits of Neoliberalism*, 27.

25. Echols, *Daring to Be Bad*, 291.

26. See hooks, *Ain't I a Woman*; Hull et al., *All the Women Are White, All the Blacks Are Men, but Some of Us Are Brave*; hooks, *Feminist Theory*; Giddings, *When and Where I Enter*; Lorde, *Sister Outsider*; Roth, *Separate Roads to Feminism*; Springer, *Living for the Revolution*.

27. Lorde, *Sister Outsider*, 119.

28. For discussions of this master-slave dialectic, see Davis, *The Problem of Slavery in the Age of Revolution*; Robinson, *Black Marxism*; Trouillot, *Silencing the Past*; Beckles, "Capitalism, Slavery and Caribbean Modernity"; Buck-Morss, *Hegel, Haiti, and Universal History*; Trouillot, "The Otherwise Modern"; Fischer, *Modernity Disavowed*; Scott, *Conscripts of Modernity*; Horne, *The Counter-revolution of 1776*.

29. Lennon, *Sometime in New York City*; Smith, *Easter*. See also Mailer, "The White Negro."

30. See Davis, *Women, Race & Class*; Friedan, *The Feminine Mystique*.

31. Cooper, *Stand Up and Be Counted*; Scorsese, *Alice Doesn't Live Here Anymore*; Forbes, *The Stepford Wives*; Mazursky, *An Unmarried Woman*. See also Haskell, *From Reverence to Rape*; Kuhn, *Women's Pictures*; Dow, *Prime-Time Feminism*; Lehman, *Those Girls*.

32. Reddy, *The Woman I Am*.

33. Bradley, *Mass Media and the Shaping of American Feminism*, 219.

34. The New Haven and Chicago Women's Liberation Rock Band, *Mountain Moving Day*. See also the work of Near, *Simply Love* and Fire, *Songs of Fire*, who represented an important voice for women and lesbians in the 1970s, recording albums throughout the rest of the century.

35. Liner notes to The New Haven and Chicago Women's Liberation Rock Band, *Mountain Moving Day*.

36. Liner notes to The New Haven and Chicago Women's Liberation Rock Band, *Mountain Moving Day*.

37. Liner notes to The New Haven and Chicago Women's Liberation Rock Band, *Mountain Moving Day*.

38. Liner notes to The New Haven and Chicago Women's Liberation Rock Band, *Mountain Moving Day*.

39. The New Haven and Chicago Women's Liberation Rock Band, *Mountain Moving Day*.

40. The New Haven and Chicago Women's Liberation Rock Band, *Mountain Moving Day*.

41. See Roberts, *Killing the Black Body*; Solinger, *Wake Up Little Susie*; Stern, *Eugenic Nation*; Washington, *Medical Apartheid*. For Black feminism, see Collins, *Black Feminist Thought*; Smith, "Black Feminism and Intersectionality."

42. See Trouillot, "North Atlantic Universals."

43. See Crenshaw, "Demarginalizing the Intersection of Race and Sex"; Smith, "Black Feminism and Intersectionality."

44. Cavarero, "Equality and Sexual Difference," 37.

45. Cavarero, "Equality and Sexual Difference," 37.

46. See Pateman, *The Sexual Contract*.

47. Roth, *Separate Roads to Feminism*, 3.

48. hooks, *Ain't I a Woman*; Hull et al., *All the Women Are White*; hooks, *Feminist Theory*; Giddings, *When and Where I Enter*; Lorde, *Sister Outsider*.

49. Giddings, *When and Where I Enter*, 308.

50. See Beale, "Double Jeopardy"; hooks, *Feminist Theory*.

51. Rosen, *The World Split Open*, 136–37. See also Roth, *Separate Roads to Feminism*.

52. See Gilmore, *Feminist Coalitions*; Bradley, *Mass Media*; Lehman, *Those Girls*.

53. See May, *Homeward Bound*; Cooper, *Family Values*.

54. Lorde, *Sister Outsider*, 110–11.

55. See Roediger, *The Wages of Whiteness*.

56. This transaction, of course, points to an entire set of colloquialisms—from "working like a n****r" to "Free, white, and 21"—utilizing Blackness as the weight of oppressive treatment across the history of American culture, including its use by the Founding Fathers to justify the American Revolution. While those using the slave-master dialectic might not have been consciously trafficking anti-Black sentiment, from a *longue durée* systemic viewpoint, we see the depth of the intersectional psychology that masks imagery associated with Black degradation as color blind and universal, and thus invisible as a norm. See Citron, "The 'Rightness of Whiteness'"; Robbins, "Social awareness and semantic change"; Horne, *The Counter-revolution of 1776*.

57. Bradley, *Mass Media*, 244.

58. For example, see Delton, *Racial Integration in Corporate America*.

59. "For Women, a Difficult Climb to the Top," 42.

60. "For Women, a Difficult Climb to the Top," 42.

61. "How Bosses Feel about Women's Lib," 18.

62. "How Bosses Feel about Women's Lib," 18.

63. "Secretaries Play Hard to Get," 24.

64. "Why Women's Stock Is Rising on Wall Street," 114.

65. "The Corporate Woman: Up the Ladder, Finally," 58.

66. "The Corporate Woman: The 100 Top Corporate Women," 56; "The Corporate Woman: Stress Has No Gender," 73; "The Corporate Woman: When Career Couples Have Conflicts of Interest," 86; "How Men Adjust to a Female Boss," 90.

67. "A Double Standard for Women Managers' Pay," 61.

68. Lorde, *Sister Outsider*, 119.

69. Pateman, *The Sexual Contract*, 2; hooks, *Feminist Theory*, 9. See also Trouillot, "North Atlantic Universals."

70. hooks, *Feminist Theory*, 16.

71. Cowie, *The Great Exception*, 151.

72. Hallin, "Neoliberalism, Social Movements and Change in Media Systems," 52.

73. See Fraser, "Feminism, Capitalism and the Cunning of History."

74. Fraser, "Feminism, Capitalism and the Cunning of History," 103–4.

75. For examples of business language engaging with diversity, see Gundling and Zanchettin, *Global Diversity*; Greene and Kirton, *The Dynamics of Managing Diversity*.

76. For post-1970s wealth, and racial wealth inequality, see Conley, *Being Black, Living in the Red*; Congressional Budget Office, "Trends in the Distribution of Household Income"; Piketty, *Capital in the Twenty-First Century*.

77. Snipp and Cheung, "Changes in Racial and Gender Inequality since 1970"; Brown, "The Intersection and Accumulation of Racial and Gender Inequality."

78. See Ward, *Women Workers and Global Restructuring*; Hong, *The Ruptures of American Capital*; Wright, *Disposable Women and Other Myths of Global Capitalism*.

79. Fraser, "Feminism, Capitalism and the Cunning of History," 99.

80. Fraser, "Feminism, Capitalism and the Cunning of History," 108.

81. For the "Great Compression," see Goldin and Margo, "The Great Compression," 1; Piketty and Saez, "Income Inequality in the United States"; Stein, *Pivotal Decade*. For "family wage," see Cooper, *Family Values*.

82. For "corporate multiculturalism," see Marable, *Beyond Black and White*.

83. Rosen, *The World Split Open*, 275.

84. Mellen, "The Return of Women to Seventies Films," 525.

85. Gordon, "Moralizing Doesn't Help," 30. See also Rosen, *The World Split Open*, 269; Baxandall and Gordon, *America's Working Women*, 318–20.

86. Higgins, *9 to 5*.

87. Cowie, *Stayin' Alive*, 351.

88. Dow, *Prime-Time Feminism*, xvi, xxiii, 26.

89. See Bradley, *Mass Media*; Faludi, *Backlash*.

90. Barger, "Backlash," 341.

91. "The Corporate Woman: Why So Few Women Have Made It to the Top," 99.

92. Higgins, *9 to 5*.

93. See Washington State Commission on African American Affairs, *Affirmative Action, Who's Really Benefitting?*

94. See MacLean, *Freedom Is Not Enough*.

95. "The New Pay Push for Women," 66.

96. MacLean, *Freedom Is Not Enough*, 315.

97. "Sexual Harassment Lands Companies in Court," 120.

98. Corporate adaptation after the 1960s to demands for greater worker control, or sense of control, over their workplace environment is discussed in Boltanski and Chiapello, *The New Spirit of Capitalism*.

99. Cowie, *Stayin' Alive*, 352.

100. For work on *Born in Flames*, see Oxenberg and Winer, "Born in Flames"; De Lauretis, "Aesthetic and Feminist Theory"; MacDonald and Borden, "Interview with Lizzie Borden"; Kuhn, *Women's Pictures*; Foster, *Women Film Directors*; Lane, *Feminist Hollywood*; Sherwood, "Anarcha-Filmmaker." See also the transcription of the film *Born in Flames*.

101. See Hung, *The Ruptures of American Capital*. See "Feminism Takes a Backseat at Women's Banks," 125–30.

102. "An 'Old Girl Network' Is Born," 154.

103. For contemporary studies, see Gregory, "'Talking Sports.'"

104. Lane, *Feminist Hollywood*, 127.

105. Lane, *Feminist Hollywood*, 129.

106. See Echols, *Daring to Be Bad*.

107. *New York Magazine*, November 21, 1983, 121.

108. Jaehne, "Born in Flames by Lizzie Borden," 22.

109. See Randolph, "Not to Rely Completely on the Courts."

110. For the connection between Islam and the Black freedom struggle, see Daulatzai, *Black Star, Crescent Moon*.

111. See Gilmore, "Thinking about Feminist Coalitions."

112. Jaehne, "*Born in Flames* by Lizzie Borden," 24.

113. Sherwood, "Anarcha-Filmmaker," 316.

114. De Lauretis, "Aesthetic and Feminist Theory," 165; Foster, *Women Film Directors*, 46. See also Stein, *Rethinking the Gay and Lesbian Movement*.

115. See Hull et al., *All the Women Are White*; Springer, *Living for the Revolution*, 137; Lane, *Feminist Hollywood*, 131.

116. See Larson, *Television's Window on the World*; Donovan and Scherer, *Unsilent Revolution*; Bradley, *Mass Media*; Postman, *Amusing Ourselves to Death*.

117. Oxenberg and Winer, "Born in Flames," 17.

118. Borden, *Born in Flames*.

119. Cowie, *Stayin' Alive*, 238–39; Kessler-Harris, *Out of Work*, 309–10; Baxandall and Gordon, *America's Working Women*; "The New Pay Push for Women."

120. Mies, *Patriarchy & Accumulation on a World Scale*, 27.

121. Borden, *Born in Flames*.

122. Faludi, *Backlash*, 388–93.

123. Schwarz, *America's Hidden Success*, 28.

124. See Cooper, *Family Values*.

125. Borden, *Born in Flames*.

126. Borden, *Born in Flames*.

127. Rosen, *The World Split Open*, 78–79. See also Fousekis, *Demanding Child Care*.

128. Borden, *Born in Flames*.

129. Lorde, *Sister Outsider*, 152.

130. Postman, *Amusing Ourselves to Death*, 7, 102.

131. Postman, *Amusing Ourselves to Death*, 131.

132. Kruse and Zelizer, *Fault Lines*, 214.

133. Rosen, *The World Split Open*, 337.

134. Rosen, *The World Split Open*, 339. See also Kessler-Harris, *Out to Work*, 318.

135. "Women: The New Venture Capitalists," 100.

136. Lind, "Conservative Elites and the Counterrevolution against the New Deal," 258.
137. Garrison, "U.S. Feminism-Grrrl Style!"; Gillis et al., *Third Wave Feminism*.
138. See Fanon, *Wretched of the Earth*.
139. Friedman, *Capitalism and Freedom*, xiv.
140. Jayne Cortez and the Firespitters, *There It Is*. See also Cortez, *Coagulations*. Originally from *Firespitter*.
141. Brown, "Of Poststructuralist Fallout, Scarification, and Blood Poems," 76.
142. Brown, "Of Poststructuralist Fallout, Scarification, and Blood Poems," 75.
143. Jayne Cortez and the Firespitters, *There It Is*.
144. Cortez, *Coagulations*, 63.
145. Cortez, *Coagulations*, 63–64.
146. Lester, *Look Out, Whitey!*, x.
147. Baldwin, *Conversations with James Baldwin*, 194.

Chapter 8

1. Scott-Heron, *I'm New Here: Gil Scott-Heron*.
2. Guralnick, *Searching for Robert Johnson*, 43; Johnson, *King of the Delta Blues Singers*.
3. See Peck, *Constructions of Neoliberal Reason*; Phillips-Fein, *Fear City*.
4. "Why U.S. Mayors Plead Poverty," 46; "The Financial Noose Draws Tighter," 31; Rhoalyn, "New York City Mirrors the U.S.," 12. See also Lankevich, *New York City*, 209–29; Beauregard, *When America Became Suburban*, 82–83.
5. Sites, *Remaking New York*, 37, author's italics. See also Greenberg, *Branding New York*.
6. Sites, *Remaking New York*, 39.
7. Carson-Parker, "The Options ahead for the Debt Economy," 120.
8. Shapiro et al., "The Roots of the Widening Racial Wealth Gap."
9. Frank, "Income Inequality."
10. Davies, *The Limits of Neoliberalism*, 27.
11. Sites, *Remaking New York*, 39.
12. Scott-Heron, *Small Talk at 125th and Lenox*.
13. Cooper, *Africa since 1940*; Singh, "Resistance, Essentialism, and Empowerment in Black Nationalist Discourse in the African Diaspora"; Austin, "All Roads Led to Montreal"; Gaines, "Locating the Transnational in Postwar African American History"; Plummer, *In Search of Power*; Quinn, *Black Power in the Caribbean*.
14. See Du Bois, *Black Reconstruction in America*; James, *The Black Jacobins*; Du Bois, *The World and Africa*; Jones, "Women in the Struggle for Peace and Security." See also Robinson, *Black Marxism*; Gilroy, *The Black Atlantic*; Taylor, "'Read[ing] Men and Nations'"; James, *Holding Aloft the Banner of Ethiopia*; Kelley, *Freedom Dreams*; Moten, *In the Break*; Bogues, *Black Heretics, Black Prophets*; Davies, "Sisters Outside"; Rabaka, *Africana Critical Theory*; Bay et al, *Toward an Intellectual History of Black Women*.
15. Bush, *We Are Not What We Seem*; Steinberg, *Turning Back*.
16. For Black arts movement, see Smethurst, *The Black Arts Movement*; Clarke, "After Mecca"; Widener, *Black Arts West*.
17. Fraser, "Rethinking the Public Sphere," 67. See O'Reilly, *"Racial Matters"*; Churchill and Wall, *The COINTELPRO Papers*; Bush, *We Are Not What We Seem*; Countryman, *Up South*.

18. Gilroy, *The Black Atlantic*; Bush, *We Are Not What We Seem*, 20. For "age of diminishing expectations," see Lasch, *The Culture of Narcissism*.

19. Baker, "Critical Memory and the Black Public Sphere," 7.

20. Young, *Soul Power*, 9.

21. See Wacquant, "From Slavery to Mass Incarceration."

22. Marable, *How Capitalism Underdeveloped Black America*, xxxviii. Originally published in 1984.

23. Van Deburg, *New Day in Babylon*; Woodard, *A Nation within a Nation*; Ogbar, *Black Power*; Joseph, *Waiting 'Til the Midnight Hour*; Thörn, *Anti-Apartheid and the Emergence of a Global Civil Society*; The Watts Prophets, *The Black Voices*; *The Definitive Groove Collection Grandmaster Flash, Melle Mel and the Furious Five*. See Kitwana, *The Hip Hop Generation*, viii. The movement against globalization often cites the New Left as a model for activism. The rise of Black Power, in the wake of an already transnational critique of modernity emanating from Black Atlantic scholars such as Aimé Césaire and Frantz Fanon, played an important role in theorizing Eurocentrism, including a *longue durée* view of slavery and colonialism. As this chapter asserts, Black Power advocates such as Scott-Heron and Cortez expanded these ideas into critiques of globalization taking shape in the 1970s while simultaneously focusing on the racial oppression that often emanated from the policies of multinationals and their nation-state sponsors. For anti-globalization, see Juris, *Networking Futures*.

24. See Gale Reference Team, "Biography"; Geesling, "The First Minute of a New Day"; Scott-Heron, *The Last Holiday*.

25. Scott-Heron utilized "Coming from a Broken Home" to bookend *I'm New Here*. For "welfare queen," see Hancock, *The Politics of Disgust*.

26. Scott-Heron, *I'm New Here*; Scott-Heron, *Now and Then*, 1–6.

27. See Wilkinson, "New York Is Killing Me."

28. See Neal, "The Black Arts Movement," 272; Joyce, "Gil Scott-Heron." This essay originally appeared in *Drama Review* in the summer of 1968.

29. Gale Reference Team, "Biography."

30. See Isoardi, *The Dark Tree*.

31. See Ford, *Gender and the Poetics of Excess*; Brown, "Of Poststructuralist Fallout, Scarification, and Blood Poems"; Page, *Encyclopedia of African American Women Writers*.

32. Garrett, "Cortez, Jayne." See also Widener "The Art of Creative Survival."

33. See Widener, *Black Arts West*, 130–32.

34. Anderson, *Notes to Make the Sound Come Right*, 122. See also Isoardi, *The Dark Tree*.

35. Anderson, *Notes to Make the Sound Come Right*, 122.

36. Melhem, *Heroism in the New Black Poetry*, 203.

37. Melhem, *Heroism in the New Black Poetry*, 200.

38. Anderson, *Notes to Make the Sound Come Right*, 119. See also Wallenstein, "The Jazz-Poetry Connection."

39. Anderson, *Notes to Make the Sound Come Right*, 120.

40. Melhem, *Heroism in the New Black Poetry*, 201.

41. Nielsen, *Black Chant*, 221.

42. Melhem, *Heroism in the New Black Poetry*, 182.

43. Garrett, "Cortez, Jayne."

44. For "supersurrealism," see Melhem, *Heroism in the New Black Poetry*, 181. Kelley, *Freedom Dreams*, 187.

45. See *Manifestoes of Surrealism*. For discussion on Black surrealism, see Kelley, *Freedom Dreams*.

46. Kelley, *Freedom Dreams*, 160.

47. Kelley, *Freedom Dreams*, 160.

48. Melhem, *Heroism in the New Black Poetry*, 205–6.

49. Nielsen, *Black Chant*, 189. See also Palmer, "The Poetry of Three Revolutionaries"; Smethurst, *The Black Arts Movement*; Isoardi, *The Dark Tree*. Clarke, "*After Mecca*"; Widener, *Black Arts West*.

50. Ogbar, *Black Power*, 94–95. For vernacular and African American poetry, see Brown, *Performing the Word*.

51. Ongiri, *Spectacular Blackness*, 98.

52. James, *Holding Aloft the Banner of Ethiopia*, 80; Jackson, *Get Your Ass in the Water and Swim like Me*. See also Levine, *Black Culture and Black Consciousness*; Floyd, *The Power of Black Music*; Brown, *Performing the Word*.

53. James, *Holding Aloft the Banner of Ethiopia*, vii.

54. Brown, *Performing the Word*, 83.

55. Jackson, *Get Your Ass in the Water and Swim like Me*, 5.

56. Anderson, *Notes to Make the Sound Come Right*, 121.

57. Melhem, *Heroism in the New Black Poetry*, 200.

58. See The Watts Prophets, *The Black Voices*; Angelou, *The Poetry of Maya Angelou*; Crouch, *Ain't No Ambulances for No Nigguhs Tonight*; The Last Poets, *The Last Poets*; Scott-Heron, *Small Talk at 125th and Lenox*; The Original Last Poets, *Right On!*; The Last Poets, *This Is Madness*; Kain, *Blue Guerrilla*; Sanchez, *A Sun Lady for All Seasons Reads Her Poetry*; Giovanni, *Truth Is on Its Way*; Giovanni, *Like a Ripple on a Pond*; Giovanni, *The Way I Feel*; Robinson, *The Soul Jazz of Wanda Robinson*; The Watts Prophets, *Things Gonna Get Greater*; The Last Poets, *At Last*. See also Thomas, *Listen, Whitey!*

59. Boyd, *The Notorious PH.D.'s Guide to the Super Fly '70s*. See also Van Deburg, *New Day in Babylon*.

60. Widener, *Black Arts West*, 114. For my own work on this, see McClure, "'Have You Understood Anything I've Said?'" For work on suggesting the liberal–Black Power connection dampened Black Power advocacy in a positive way, see Fergus, *Liberalism, Black Power, and the Making of American Politics*.

61. Scott-Heron, *Small Talk at 125th and Lenox*.

62. Beauregard, *When America Became Suburban*, 41–51. See also Katznelson, *When Affirmative Action Was White*; Freund, *Colored Property*; Marable, *Race, Reform and Rebellion*, 121–23.

63. Hartman, *Lose Your Mother*, 6. Scott-Heron, *Small Talk at 125th and Lenox*. When possible, my quotations follow the form from his book of poetry, with the alterations during the recording of the album in brackets. See Scott-Heron, *Small Talk at 125th and Lenox: A Collection of Black Poems*. See also Scott-Heron's *So Far, So Good* and *Now and Then*.

64. Scott-Heron, *Small Talk at 125th and Lenox*.

65. Scott-Heron, *Small Talk at 125th and Lenox*.

66. Marable, *Blackwater*, 74.

67. Scott-Heron, *Small Talk at 125th and Lenox*.

68. See Patterson, *Freedom and the Making of Western Culture*, xiii.

69. See Muse, *The American Negro Revolution*; Allen, *Black Awakening in Capitalist America*.

70. Bush, *We Are Not What We Seem*, 31.

71. Liner notes to Scott-Heron, *Pieces of a Man*.

72. Scott-Heron, *Pieces of a Man*.

73. Cortez, *Celebrations and Solitudes*.

74. Scott-Heron and Jackson, *Winter in America*. The following quotations are from this album, unless noted otherwise.

75. Daulatzai, *Black Star, Crescent Moon*, 36. See also Malcolm X, *By Any Means Necessary*; Marable, *Race, Reform and Rebellion*, 87–88.

76. See also Cortez, *Scarifications*, 32.

77. Cortez, *Scarifications*, 56.

78. Scott-Heron and Jackson, *Winter in America*. The following quotations are from this album, unless noted otherwise.

79. Scott-Heron and Jackson, *Winter in America*.

80. Scott-Heron and Jackson, *Winter in America*.

81. Scott-Heron and Jackson, *Winter in America*.

82. Scott-Heron and Jackson, *Winter in America*.

83. See Blum, *Years of Discord*, 368, 385, 386–87, 415.

84. For ITT involvement in Chile, see http://foia.state.gov/Reports/HincheyReport.asp#17. See also Klein, *The Shock Doctrine*.

85. See Blum, *Killing Hope*; Grandin, *Empire's Workshop*; Westad, *The Global Cold War*.

86. See Panitch and Gindin, *The Making of Global Capitalism*; Latin American Bureau, *The Poverty Brokers*; Grandin, *Empire's Workshop*; Westad, *The Global Cold War*.

87. See Osterhammel and Petersson, *Globalization*; Adelman, dir., *Controlling Interest*.

88. See Peck, *Constructions of Neoliberal Reason*; MacLean, *Democracy in Chains*; Klein, *The Shock Doctrine*.

89. For example, the infamous Kirkpatrick, "Dictatorships and Double Standards." See also Clark and Worger, *South Africa*; Berger, *South Africa in World History*.

90. Gilmore, "Globalisation and US Prison Growth"; Wacquant, "From Slavery to Mass Incarceration"; Davis, *Are Prisons Obsolete?*; Wacquant, *Punishing the Poor*; De Jong, *Invisible Enemy*; Daulatzai, *Black Star, Crescent Moon*.

91. Koh, *The National Security Constitution*; Marshall, Scott, and Hunter, *The Iran Contra Connection*; Wacquant, *Punishing the Poor*; Alexander, *The New Jim Crow*.

92. Koh, *The National Security Constitution*, 63.

93. See Cunningham, *There's Something Happening Here*; O'Reilly, *"Racial Matters"*; Churchill and Wall, *Agents of Repression*.

94. Scott-Heron and Jackson, *Midnight Band: The First Minute of a New Day*. See also Scott-Heron, *Now and Then*, 69.

95. See Killen, *1973 Nervous Breakdown*.

96. See Bradley, *This Is Reggae Music*; Chang and Chen, *Reggae Routes*; Collins, "A Social History of Ghanaian Popular Entertainment since Independence"; Olaniyan, *Arrest the Music!*; Gilbert, "Singing against Apartheid."

97. Gilroy, *"There Ain't No Black in the Union Jack,"* 157. See also Chrisman and Hare, *Pan-Africanism*; Marable, *Blackwater*, 102–15.

98. For a description of the early era of record distribution, see Denning, *Noise Uprising*.

99. Gilroy, "There Ain't No Black in the Union Jack," 172. See also Bradley, *This Is Reggae Music*; Grant, *The Natural Mystics*; Alleyne, *Roots of Jamaican Culture*.

100. See Bob Marley and the Wailers, *Catch a Fire*; *The Harder They Come*; Henzell, *The Harder They Come*. See also Hoberman and Rosenbaum, *Midnight Movies*.

101. For Black Power in Jamaica and the link between reggae and Rastafarianism, see Campbell, *Rasta and Resistance*; Palmer, "Identity, Race, and Black Power in Independent Jamaica." See also Rodney, *The Groundings with My Brothers*.

102. See Hebdige, *Cut 'n' Mix*, 55–58; Johnson, "African Consciousness in Reggae Music"; *Trojan Nyahbinghi Box Set*; Price, *Maroon Societies*.

103. Campbell, *Rasta and Resistance*, 139; James, "The IMF and Democratic Socialism in Jamaica." See also Kaufman, *Jamaica under Manley*.

104. Bob Marley and the Wailers, *Catch a Fire*.

105. James, *Holding Aloft the Banner of Ethiopia*, 78–80, 124.

106. The Last Poets, *The Last Poets*; Big Youth, *Chi Chi Run*.

107. Big Youth, *Chi Chi Run*. The Last Poets' version goes: "when the revolution comes / jesus christ is gonna be standing / on the corner of Malcolm X Blvd. and 125 St. / trying to catch the first gypsy cab out of Harlem." See Oyewole and Hassan, *The Last Poets*, 47.

108. See Chang, *Can't Stop Won't Stop*.

109. Chang, *Can't Stop Won't Stop*, 78.

110. Nuriddin's release was a follow-up to his earlier 1969 explorations of traditional toasts accompanied with musical backing by guitarist Jimi Hendrix and drummer Buddy Miles ("Doriella Du Fontaine"). See Lightnin' Rod, *Hustlers Convention*; Hendrix/Lightnin' Rod/Miles, *Doriella Du Fontaine*.

111. For Black action films, see Guerrero, *Framing Blackness*; Massood, *Black City Cinema*; Sims, *Women of Blaxploitation*; Dunn, *"Baad Bitches" & Sassy Supermamas*.

112. Toop, *The Rap Attack*, 119.

113. For hip-hop and postindustrialism, see Shonk and McClure, *Historical Theory and Methods through Popular Music*, 111–40.

114. Rose, *Black Noise*, 63. See also Reeves, *Somebody Scream!*

115. See Bagdikian, *The Media Monopoly*.

116. Scott-Heron and Jackson, *Midnight Band: The First Minute of a New Day*; Scott-Heron and Jackson, *From South Africa to South Carolina*.

117. Skinner, *The Foundations of Anti-Apartheid*, 201. See also Thörn, *Anti-Apartheid and the Emergence of a Global Civil Society*; Parrott, "Boycott Gulf!"

118. Liner notes to Scott-Heron, *The Mind of Gil Scott-Heron*.

119. Cortez, *Mouth on Paper*.

120. Cortez, *Unsubmissive Blues*.

121. See Wilson, *Steve Biko*; Ross, *A Concise History of South Africa*; Abraham, *Politics of Black Nationalism*.

122. Cortez, *Unsubmissive Blues*.

123. Scott-Heron, *The Mind of Gil Scott-Heron*.

124. Liner notes to Scott-Heron, *The Mind of Gil Scott-Heron*.

125. Marable, *Race, Reform, and Rebellion*, 148.

126. Marable, *Blackwater*, 116.

127. Marable, *Blackwater*, 117.

128. Scott-Heron and Jackson, *Winter in America*.
129. Wilson, *The Declining Significance of Race*.
130. See Porter, "Affirming and Disaffirming Actions," 69; Lipsitz, *The Possessive Investment in Whiteness*, 18.
131. Toop, *The Rap Attack*, 19.
132. See Rose, *Black Noise*; Chang, *Can't Stop Won't Stop*.
133. See George, *Hip Hop America*; Kitwana, *The Hip Hop Generation*; Reeves, *Somebody Scream!*
134. Chang, *Can't Stop Won't Stop*, 85.
135. Chang, *Can't Stop Won't Stop*, 15–19.
136. Liner notes to *Big Apple Rappin'*.
137. Spoonie Gee, *Godfather of Hip-Hop*.
138. For example, see Blow, *Kurtis Blow*.
139. Sugrue, *The Origins of the Urban Crisis*; Self, *American Babylon*; Beauregard, *Voices of Decline*; Freund, *Colored Property*.
140. See Johnson, *Street Justice*; Taylor, *Fight the Power*.
141. Chang, *Can't Stop Won't Stop*, 99.
142. Smiley and Fakunle, "From 'Brute' to 'Thug.'" See also Van Deburg, "Villains, Demons, and Social Bandits"; Robinson, *Forgeries of Memory and Meaning*.
143. See Flamm, *Law and Order*.
144. Wacquant, *Punishing the Poor*, xiii. For the death penalty, see Ellsworth, and Gross. "Hardening of the Attitudes."
145. Watkins, *Representing*, 30.
146. Watkins, *Representing*, 30. The song was released as a single: Brother D, "Dib-Be-Dib-Be-Dize"/"How We Gonna Make the Black Nation Rise." Jamaican connections continued as the hip-hop era unfolded. Reggae producer Joe Gibbs worked with emerging hip-hop groups (including female vocalist Xanadu), while some signposted the island nation (Jamaica Girls). Crossover between reggae and hip-hop also emerged, including General Echo's "Rapping Dub Style." The Clappers label started distributing reggae music in the United States while also releasing one of the first tracks combining a rapper and a DJ (reggae singer/toaster): Sons of Creation "Feeling Down a Yard" (1982). Finally, dance hall (reggae's dominant style after roots reggae) and hip-hop increasingly blended together through the 1980s, with crossover successes like Shabba Ranks, Sean Paul, and Lumidee. See *Big Apple Rappin'*; Cooper, "'Ragamuffin Sounds.'"
147. Davis, *Prisoners of the American Dream*, 136.
148. Gilmore, "What Is to Be Done?," 250.
149. Scott-Heron, *Reflections*.
150. See Jacobson, "Resistance to Affirmative Action."
151. Scott-Heron, *Reflections*.
152. Clymer, "Black Influence Is Lowest in Two Decades."
153. Stein, *Pivotal Decade*, 262–69.
154. Scott-Heron, *Reflections*.
155. Stein, *Pivotal Decade*, 267.
156. Urquhart and Hewson, "Unemployment Continued to Rise in 1982 as Recession Deepened," 3.

157. Chang, *Can't Stop Won't Stop*, 90.

158. Chang, *Can't Stop Won't Stop*, 178.

159. Wonder, *Innervisions*.

160. Chang, *Can't Stop Won't Stop*, 179.

161. See "The Message" from *Grandmaster Flash, Melle Mel and the Furious Five: The Definitive Groove Collections*.

162. See Conley, *Being Black, Living in the Red*; Feagin, "Excluding Blacks and Others from Housing"; Katznelson, *When Affirmative Action Was White*; Freund, *Colored Property*.

163. Chang, *Can't Stop Won't Stop*, 15.

164. Barnett, "The US Farm Financial Crisis of the 1980s."

165. Pinkney, *The Myth of Black Progress*, 76.

166. For "counterrevolution against the New Deal," see Lind, "Conservative Elites and the Counterrevolution against the New Deal."

167. See Phillips, *The Politics of Rich and Poor*.

168. Jayne Cortez and the Firespitters, *There It Is*.

169. See also Cortez, *Coagulations*, 68.

170. See Eagleton-Pierce, "Historicizing the neoliberal spirit of capitalism."

171. Jayne Cortez and the Firespitters, *There It Is*. See also Cortez, *Coagulations*, 68.

172. See Anderson, *White Rage*; Baldwin, *The Devil Finds Work*, 562.

173. Steinberg, *Turning Back*, 112–15.

174. Scott-Heron, *The Mind of Gil Scott-Heron*.

175. See Cowie and Salvatore, "The Long Exception."

176. Mugge, *Black Wax*.

177. Scott-Heron, *Free Will*.

178. See Jong, *Invisible Enemy*.

179. Trattner, *From Poor Law to Welfare State*, 368.

180. See Lind, *Up from Conservatism*; Carter, *From George Wallace to Newt Gingrich*; Lowndes, *From the New Deal to the New Right*; Perlstein, *Nixonland*.

181. See Kruse and Zelizer, *Fault Lines*.

182. See Scott-Heron, *Spirits*.

183. Daulatzai, *Black Star, Crescent Moon*, xvi.

184. Harvey, *A Brief History of Neoliberalism*, 6.

185. Harvey, *A Brief History of Neoliberalism*, 17.

Conclusion

1. Carson-Parker, "The Options ahead for the Debt Economy," 120.

2. Carson-Parker, "The Options ahead for the Debt Economy," 120.

3. See Brantlinger, *Dark Vanishings*.

4. See Lake and Reynolds, *Drawing the Global Colour Line*.

5. Baldwin, *The Devil Finds Work*, 562–63.

6. Kendi, *Stamped from the Beginning*, 410.

7. Kendi, *Stamped from the Beginning*, 426.

8. Hayek, *The Constitution of Liberty*, 99.

9. Piketty and Saez, "Income Inequality in the United States, 1913–1998."

10. See Brown, *Strain of Violence*.

11. Burns, Martin, and Haberman, "G.O.P. Alarmed by Trump's Comments on Extremist Group."

12. See Hayden and Bejarano, *Trump's Immigration Order Was Drafted by Officials with Ties to Hate Groups, According to Report*; Serwer, "Jeff Sessions's Unqualified Praise for a 1924 Immigration Law."

13. See Griffith, *God's Daughters*; Shaw, "Gracious Submission"; Padgett, "The Bible and Gender Troubles." For example, on the website for Focus on the Family (https://www.focusonthefamily.com/family-qa/submission-of-wives-to-husbands), it states: "Unfortunately, 'male bashing' in our culture makes it too easy to forget about the importance of masculine leadership altogether. We can't swing so far one way trying to avoid male domination that we go to the other extreme and strip husbands of their authority."

14. Pew Research Center, February 7, 2020. https://www.pewresearch.org/fact-tank/2020/02/07/6-facts-about-economic-inequality-in-the-u-s/ft_2020-02-07_inequality_05/.

15. Zammito, "Are We Being Theoretical Yet?," 800.

16. Kellner, *Language and Historical Representation*, 207–8.

17. Baldwin, *The Devil Finds Work*, 562.

18. Kellner, *Language and Historical Representation*, 8.

19. Trouillot, "North Atlantic Universals," 847.

Bibliography

Aanerud, Rebecca. "Now More than Ever: James Baldwin and the Critique of White Liberalism." In *James Baldwin Now*. Dwight A. McBride, ed. New York: New York University Press, 1999.

Abraham, Kinfe. *Politics of Black Nationalism: From Harlem to Soweto*. Trenton, NJ: Africa World Press, 1991.

Acham, Christine. *Revolution Televised: Prime Time and the Struggle for Black Power*. Minneapolis: University of Minnesota Press, 2004.

Adelman, Larry, dir. *Controlling Interest: The World of the Multinational Corporation*. California Newsreel, 1978.

"A Classical Look at the 'Real Cost' of Money." *Business Week*, June 28, 1969.

"A Consensus for a Tax Cut." *Business Week*, January 13, 1975.

"A Counterattack in the War between the States." *Business Week*, June 21, 1976.

Adams, John. *The Works of John Adams*, vol. 6. Boston: Charles C. Little and James Brown, 1851.

"A Double Standard for Women Managers' Pay." *Business Week*, November 26, 1977.

"A Draconian Cure for Chile's Economic Ills?" *Business Week*, January 12, 1976.

"Advice and Dissent on Monetary Policy." *Business Week*, December 13, 1969.

Akard, Patrick J. "Corporate Mobilization and Political Power: The Transformation of U.S. Economic Policy in the 1970s." *American Sociological Review* 57, no. 5 (October 1992): 597–615.

Aleiss, Angela Maria. *Making the White Man's Indian: Native Americans and Hollywood Movies*. Westport: Praeger, 2008.

Alexander, Michelle. *The New Jim Crow: Mass Incarceration in the Age of Colorblindness*. Rev. ed. New York: The New Press, 2011.

Allen, James. *Without Sanctuary: Lynching Photography in America*. Santa Fe, NM: Twin Palms, 2000.

Allen, Robert L. *Black Awakening in Capitalist America: An Analytic History*. New York: Anchor Books, 1970.

Alleyne, Mervyn C. *Roots of Jamaican Culture*. London: Pluto, 1988.

Aloisi, Antonio. "Commoditized Workers: Case Study Research on Labor Law Issues Arising from a Set of On-Demand/Gig Economy Platforms." *Comparative Labor Law and Policy Journal* 37 (2015): 1–31.

"A Loud Dissent from Blue Collars." *Business Week*, February 10, 1975.

Altschuler, Glenn C., and David I. Grossvogel. *Changing Channels: America in* TV Guide. Urbana: University of Illinois Press, 1992.

American Women: The Report of the President's Commission on the Status of Women and Other Publications of the Commission. New York: Scribner's, 1965.

"America's Growing Antibusiness Mood." *Business Week*, June 17, 1972.

"America's New Financial Structure." *Business Week*, November 17, 1980.

Amott, Teresa, and Julie Matthaei. *Race, Gender, and Work: A Multi-cultural Economic History of Women in the United States*. Rev. ed. Boston: South End, 1996.

"A Nation Builds under Fire." 1967 episode TV-695 of *The Big Picture*. U.S. Department of Defense/Armed Forces Information & Education, 1952–71.

Anderson, Benedict. *Imagined Communities: Reflections on the Origin and Spread of Nationalism*. Rev. ed. London: Verso, 1991.

Anderson, Carol. *White Rage: The Unspoken Truth of Our Racial Divide*. New York: Bloomsbury, 2017.

Anderson, Steve. "History TV and Popular Memory." In *Television Histories: Shaping Collective Memory in the Media Age*. Gary R. Edgerton and Pater C. Rollins, eds. Lexington: University Press of Kentucky, 2001.

Anderson, T. J. III. *Notes to Make the Sound Come Right: Four Innovators of Jazz Poetry*. Fayetteville: University of Arkansas Press, 2004.

"A New Breed of Company Has Sprung Up with the Boom." *Business Week*, June 23, 1956.

Angelou, Maya. *The Poetry of Maya Angelou*. GWP Records, 1969. LP ST 2001.

"An Interview with James Baldwin." *Esquire*, July 1968, 52.

"An 'Old Girl Network' Is Born." *Business Week*, November 20, 1978.

Antiliff, Allan, ed. *Only a Beginning: An Anarchist Anthology*. Vancouver: Arsenal Pulp, 2004.

"An Urgent Need for New Ties to Government." *Business Week*, March 12, 1979.

Apple, Michael W. "Rebuilding Hegemony: Education, Equality, and the New Right." In *Views beyond the Border Country: Raymond Williams and Cultural Politics*. Dennis L. Dworkin and Leslie G. Roman, eds. New York: Routledge, 1993.

Appleby, Joyce. *The Relentless Revolution: A History of Capitalism*. New York: Norton, 2010.

"Are Government Programs Worth the Price?" *Business Week*, June 30, 1975.

Armitage, David. "What's the Big Idea? Intellectual History and the Longue Durée," *History of European Ideas* 38, no. 4 (2012): 493–507.

Armstrong, Philip, Andrew Glyn, and John Harrison. *Capitalism since 1945*. Oxford: Blackwell, 1991.

"A Rougher Road for Multinationals." *Business Week*, December 19, 1970.

Arrighi, Giovanni. *The Long Twentieth Century: Money, Power and the Origins of Our Times*. London: Verso, 2010.

"A Steelmaker Pushes into Lending." *Business Week*, March 5, 1979.

"A Surprising Rally for Profits." *Business Week*, November 20, 1978.

Austin, David. "All Roads Led to Montreal: Black Power, the Caribbean, and the Black Radical Tradition in Canada." *Journal of African American History* 92, no. 4 (2007): 516–39.

Avila, Eric. *Popular Culture in the Age of White Flight: Fear and Fantasy in Suburban Los Angeles*. Berkeley: University of California Press, 2004.

Avildsen, John G., dir. *Joe*. Cannon Film Distributors, 1970.

Badger, Anthony J. *The New Deal: The Depression Years, 1933–40*. Chicago: Ivan R. Dee, 1989.

Bagdikian, Ben H. *The Media Monopoly*. 6th ed. Boston: Beacon, 2000.

Bailey, Beth. *Sex in the Heartland*. Cambridge, MA: Harvard University Press, 1999.

———. "She 'Can Bring Home the Bacon': Negotiating Gender in Seventies America." In *America in the Seventies*. Beth Bailey and David Farber, eds. Lawrence: University Press of Kansas, 2004.
Bailey, Beth, and David Farber, eds. *America in the Seventies*. Lawrence: University Press of Kansas, 2004.
Baker, Houston A. Jr. "Critical Memory and the Black Public Sphere." In *The Black Public Sphere: A Public Culture Book*. The Black Public Sphere Collective, eds. Chicago: University of Chicago Press, 1995.
Baldwin, James. *No Name in the Street*. New York: Vintage Books, 1972.
———. *The Devil Finds Work*. In *Collected Essays*. New York: The Library of America, 1998.
———. *The Fire Next Time*. In *James Baldwin: Collected Essays*. New York: The Library of America, 1998.
Baldwin, James, and Nikki Giovanni. *A Dialogue*. Philadelphia: Lippincott, 1973.
Baldwin, James, and Margaret Mead. *A Rap on Race*. New York: Dell Publishing, 1971.
Baldwin, Richard. *The Great Convergence: Information Technology and the New Globalization*. Cambridge, MA: Belknap Press, 2016.
Balfour, Lawrie. *The Evidence of Things Not Said: James Baldwin and the Promise of American Democracy*. Ithaca, NY: Cornell University Press, 2001.
Balibar, Etienne. "Is There a 'Neo-Racism'?" In *Race, Nation, Class: Ambiguous Identities*. Etienne Balibar and Immanuel Wallerstein, eds. Chris Turner, trans. London: Verso, 1991.
Bancroft, Hubert Howe. "A Historian's View of the Negro." In *The Development of Segregationist Thought*. I. A. Newby, ed. Homewood: Dorsey, 1968.
Baptist, Edward E. *The Half Has Never Been Told: Slavery and the Making of American Capitalism*. New York: Basic Books, 2014.
Barger, Lilian Calles. "Backlash: From *Nine to Five* to *The Devil Wears Prada*." *Women's Studies* 40, no. 3 (2011): 336–50.
Barker, Martin. *The New Racism: Conservatives and the Ideology of the Tribe*. London: Junction Books, 1981.
Barnett, Barry J. "The US Farm Financial Crisis of the 1980s." *Agricultural History* 74, no. 2 (2000): 366–80.
Baxandall, Rosalyn. "Re-visioning the Women's Liberation Movement's Narrative: Early Second Wave African American Feminists." *Feminist Studies* 27, no. 1 (Spring 2001): 225–45.
Bay, Mia. *To Tell the Truth Freely: The Life of Ida B. Wells*. New York: Hill & Wang, 2009.
Bay, Mia, Farah J. Griffin, Martha S. Jones, and Barbara D. Savage, eds. *Toward an Intellectual History of Black Women*. Chapel Hill: University of North Carolina Press, 2015.
Beale, Frances. "Double Jeopardy: To Be Black and Female." *The Black Woman: An Anthology*. Toni Cade Bambara, ed. New York: Washington Square, 1970.
Beauregard, Robert A. *Voices of Decline: The Postwar Fate of US Cities*. Cambridge, MA: Blackwell, 1993.
———. *When America Became Suburban*. Minneapolis: University of Minnesota Press, 2006.
Beckert, Sven. *Empire of Cotton: A Global History*. New York: Knopf, 2014.

Beckles, Hilary McD. "Capitalism, Slavery and Caribbean Modernity." *Callaloo* 20, no. 4 (Autumn 1997): 777–89.

Bederman, Gail. *Manliness & Civilization: A Cultural History of Gender and Race in the United States, 1880–1917.* Chicago: University of Chicago Press, 1995.

Beisner, Robert L. *Twelve against Empire: The Anti-imperialists, 1898–1900.* New York: McGraw-Hill, 1968.

Bell, Daniel. *The Coming of Post-industrial Society: A Venture in Social Forecasting.* New York: Basic Books, 1973.

Belton, John. *American Cinema/American Culture.* 2nd ed. Boston: McGraw Hill, 2005.

Beman, Lewis B. "The Democrats Go Over to the Supply Side." *Business Week*, April 27, 1981.

Benton, Robert, dir. *Kramer vs. Kramer.* Columbia Pictures, 1979.

Berenstein, Rhona J. "White Heroines and Hearts of Darkness: Race, Gender and Disguise in 1930s Jungle Films." *Film History* 6, no. 3 (Autumn 1994): 314–39.

Berg, Manfred. "Black Civil Rights and Liberal Anticommunism: The NAACP in the Early Cold War." *Journal of American History* 94, no. 1 (2007): 75–96.

Berger, Iris. *South Africa in World History.* Oxford: Oxford University Press, 2009.

Berger, Martin A. *Sight Unseen: Whiteness and American Visual Culture.* Los Angeles: University of California Press, 2005.

Berkowitz, Edward D. *Something Happened: A Political and Cultural Overview of the Seventies.* New York: Columbia University Press, 2006.

Berle, Adolf A. Jr. *The 20th Century Capitalist Revolution.* New York: Harcourt, Brace & World, 1954.

Berlin, Ira. *Many Thousands Gone: The First Two Centuries of Slavery in North America.* Cambridge, MA: Belknap Press, 1998.

Berlot, Chip, and Matthew N. Lyons. *Right-Wing Populism in America: Too Close for Comfort.* New York: Guilford, 2000.

Berman, Marshall. *All That Is Solid Melts into Air: The Experience of Modernity.* New York: Penguin, 1982.

Bernstein, Irving. *The Lean Years: A History of the American Worker, 1920–1933.* Baltimore: Penguin, 1960.

Berwanger, Eugene H. *The Frontier Against Slavery: Western Anti-Negro Prejudice and the Slavery Extension Controversy.* Urbana: University of Illinois Press, 1967.

Best, Joel, ed. *Images of Issues: Typifying Contemporary Social Problems.* 2nd ed. New York: Aldine de Gruyter, 1995.

Bevins, Vincent. *The Jakarta Method: Washington's Anticommunist Crusade and the Mass Murder Program that Shaped Our World.* New York: PublicAffairs, 2020.

Big Apple Rappin': The Early Days of Hip-Hop Culture in New York City 1979–1982. Soul Jazz Records, 2006. CD SJR CD 125.

Big Youth. *Chi Chi Run.* Melodisc Records, 1973. LP MS 8.

Bilteryst, Daniel, and Roel Vande Winkel, eds. *Silencing Cinema: Film Censorship around the World.* London: Palgrave Macmillan, 2013.

Birch, Kean. "Financial Economics and Business Schools: Legitimating Corporate Monopoly, Reproducing Neoliberalism?" In *The Handbook of Neoliberalism.* Simon Springer, Kean Birch, and Julie MacLeavy, eds. New York: Routledge, 2016.

Biskind, Peter. *Easy Riders, Raging Bulls: How the Sex-Drugs-and-Rock 'n' Roll Generation Saved Hollywood.* New York: Touchstone, 1998.

Bivens, Josh, and Lawrence Mishel. *Understanding the Historic Divergence between Productivity and a Typical Worker's Pay: Why It Matters and Why It's Real.* Washington, DC: Economic Policy Institute, September 5, 2015.

Black, Brian C. *Crude Reality: Petroleum in World History.* Lanham, MD: Rowman & Littlefield, 2012.

Black, Gregory D. *Hollywood Censored: Morality Codes, Catholics, and the Movies.* New York: Cambridge University Press, 1994.

Blackhawk, Ned. *Violence over the Land: Indians and Empires in the Early American West.* Cambridge, MA: Harvard University Press, 2006.

"Black Power." *Firing Line*, March 7, 1967.

"Black Unemployment: Bad, and No Quick Fix." *Business Week*, August 4, 1980.

Blair, M. Elizabeth, and Eva M. Hyatt. "Meanings of the Home in Popular Song Lyrics: A Feminist Critique Examining Rock and Country Music." *Consumption, Markets and Culture* 1, no. 3 (1997): 272–96.

Blight, David W. "Decoration Days: The Origins of Memorial Day in North and South." In *The Memory of the Civil War in American Culture.* Alice Fahs and Joan Waugh, eds. Chapel Hill: University of North Carolina Press, 2004.

Block, Sharon. *Rape & Sexual Power in Early America.* Chapel Hill: University of North Carolina Press, 2006.

Blow, Kurtis. *Kurtis Blow.* Mercury, 1979. CD 314 558 200-2.

Bluestone, Barry, and Bennett Harrison. *The Deindustrialization of America: Plant Closings, Community Abandonment, and the Dismantling of Basic Industry.* New York: Basic Books, 1982.

———. *The Great American Job Machine: The Proliferation of Low Wage Employment in the US Economy.* Washington, DC: Joint Economic Committee, December 1986.

Blum, John Morton. *Years of Discord: American Politics and Society, 1961–1975.* New York: Norton, 1991.

Blum, William. *Killing Hope: U.S. Military and CIA Interventions since World War II.* Monroe, ME: Common Courage Press, 1995.

Blyth, Mark. *Great Transformations: Economic Ideas and Institutional Change in the Twentieth Century.* Cambridge: Cambridge University Press, 2002.

Bob Marley and the Wailers. *Catch a Fire.* Island Records, 1973. LP ILPS 9241.

———. *Catch a Fire (Deluxe Edition).* Island, 2001. CD 314 548 635-2.

Bob Seger and the Silver Bullet Band. *Night Moves.* Capitol, 1976.

Bock, Gisela, and Susan James, eds. *Beyond Equality and Difference: Citizenship, Feminist Politics and Female Subjectivity.* New York: Routledge, 1992.

Bogle, Donald. *Toms, Coons, Mulattoes, Mammies, & Bucks: An Interpretive History of Blacks in American Films.* New York: Continuum, 2009.

Bogues, Anthony. *Black Heretics, Black Prophets: Radical Political Intellectuals.* New York: Routledge, 2003.

Bogus, Carl T. *Buckley: William F. Buckley Jr. and the Rise of American Conservatism.* New York: Bloomsbury, 2011.

Boltanski, Luc, and Eve Chiapello. *The New Spirit of Capitalism.* Gregory Elliott, trans. London: Verso, 2007.

Borden, Lizzie, dir. *Born in Flames.* First Run Features, 1983.

Born in Flames. Belgium: Occasional Papers, 1983.

Borstelmann, Thomas. *1970s: A New Global History from Civil Rights to Economic Inequality.* Princeton, NJ: Princeton University Press, 2012.

Boston, Thomas D. *Affirmative Action and Black Entrepreneurship.* London: Routledge, 2002.

Boyd, Herb. *Baldwin's Harlem: A Biography of James Baldwin.* New York: Atria Books, 2008.

Boyd, Todd. *The Notorious PH.D.'s Guide to the Super Fly '70s.* New York: Harlem Moon, 2007.

Bradley, Lloyd. *This Is Reggae Music: The Story of Jamaica's Music.* New York: Grove, 2000.

Bradley, Patricia. *Mass Media and the Shaping of American Feminism, 1963–1975.* Jackson: University Press of Mississippi, 2003.

Brands, H. W. *American Colossus: The Triumph of Capitalism, 1865–1900.* New York: Anchor Books, 2010.

Brantlinger, Patrick. *Dark Vanishings: Discourse on the Extinction of Primitive Races, 1800–1930.* Ithaca: Cornell University Press, 2003.

Braudel, Fernand. *Civilization and Capitalism, 15th–18th Century, Volume II: The Wheels of Commerce.* Siân Reynolds, trans. New York: Harper & Row, 1979.

———. *On History.* Sarah Matthews, trans. Chicago: University of Chicago Press, 1980.

Breen, T. H. "A Changing Labor Force and Race Relations in Virginia 1660–1710." *Journal of Social History* 7, no. 1 (Autumn 1973): 3–25.

Brenner, Robert. *The Boom and the Bubble: The US in the World Economy.* London: Verso, 2002.

Briley, Ron. "John Wayne and *Big Jim McLain* (1952): The Duke's Cold War Agency." *Film and History* 31, no. 1 (2001): 28–33.

Brine, Kevin R. and Mary Poovey. *Finance in America: An Unfinished Story.* Chicago: University of Chicago Press, 2017.

Brother D. "Dib-Be-Dib-Be-Dize"/"How We Gonna Make the Black Nation Rise." Clappers, 1980. 12" CL12-0001.

Brown, Fahamisha Patricia. *Performing the Word: African American Poetry as Vernacular Culture.* New Brunswick, NJ: Rutgers University Press, 1999.

Brown, James. *It's a New Day—So Let a Man Come In.* Polydor, 1970. LP PD 1095.

Brown, Kimberly N. "Of Poststructuralist Fallout, Scarification, and Blood Poems: The Revolutionary Ideology behind the Poetry of Jayne Cortez." In *Other Sisterhoods: Literary Theory and U.S. Women of Color.* Sandra Kumamoto Stanley, ed. Urbana: University of Illinois Press, 1998.

Brown, Richard Maxwell. *Strain of Violence: Historical Studies of American Violence and Vigilantism.* Oxford: Oxford University Press, 1975.

Brown, Tyson. "The Intersection and Accumulation of Racial and Gender Inequality: Black Women's Wealth Trajectories." *Review of Black Political Economy* 39, no. 2 (2012): 239–58.

Brown, Wendy. *Undoing the Demos: Neoliberalism's Stealth Revolution.* Brooklyn: Zone Books, 2015.

Brownmiller, Susan. *Against Our Will: Men, Women and Rape.* New York: Simon & Schuster, 1975.

Bruff, Ian. "The Rise of Authoritarian Neoliberalism." *Rethinking Marxism* 26, no. 1 (2014): 113–29.

Buccola, Nicholas. *The Fire Is upon Us: James Baldwin, William F. Buckley Jr., and the Debate over Race in America*. Princeton, NJ: Princeton University Press, 2019.

Buckley, William F. Jr. "Desegregation: Will It Work? No." *Saturday Review*, November 11, 1961, 21–22.

———. "Our Mission Statement." *National Review*, November 19, 1955.

———. "The Brownsville Affair and Old Discrimination Policy." *Lawrence Journal-World*, December 19, 1968, 4.

Buckley, William F. Jr., ed. *American Conservative Thought in the Twentieth Century*. New York: Bobbs-Merrill, 1970.

Buck-Morss, Susan. *Hegel, Haiti, and Universal History*. Pittsburgh, PA: University of Pittsburgh Press, 2009.

Bufwack, Mary A., and Robert K. Oermann. *Finding Her Voice: Women in Country Music, 1800-2000*. Nashville, TN: Country Music Foundation and Vanderbilt University Press, 2003.

Burgin, Angus. *The Great Persuasion: Reinventing Free Markets since the Depression*. Cambridge, MA: Harvard University Press, 2012.

Burke, Peter. *The French Historical Revolution: The Annales School 1929-2014*. 2nd ed. Stanford, CA: Stanford University Press, 2015.

Burns, Alexander, Jonathan Martin, and Maggie Haberman. "G.O.P. Alarmed by Trump's Comments on Extremist Group, Fearing a Drag on the Party." *The New York Times*, September 30, 2020; updated January 20, 2021. https://www.nytimes.com/2020/09/30/us/politics/trump-debate-white-supremacy.html

Bush, Rod. *We Are Not What We Seem: Black Nationalism and Class Struggle in the American Century*. New York: New York University Press, 1999.

"Business and the Urban Crisis." *Business Week*, February 3, 1968.

Business Week, April 17, 1971.

Business Week, January 17, 1977.

Business Week, March 12, 1979.

Business Week, June 23, 1980.

Calder, Lendol. *Financing the American Dream: A Cultural History of Consumer Credit*. Princeton, NJ: Princeton University Press, 1999.

Campbell, Horace. *Rasta and Resistance: From Marcus Garvey to Walter Rodney*. Trenton, NJ: Africa World Press, 1987.

Campbell, Joseph. *The Hero with a Thousand Faces*. New York: Pantheon, 1949.

Campney, Brent M. S. *Hostile Heartland: Racism, Repression, and Resistance in the Midwest*. Urbana: University of Illinois Press, 2019.

Capino, José B. *Dream Factories of a Former Colony: American Fantasies, Philippine Cinema*. Minneapolis: University of Minnesota Press, 2010.

"Capital Spending: Flat at Home, Up Abroad." *Business Week*, September 10, 1960.

Carmichael, Stokely, with Ekwueme Michael Thelwell. *Ready for Revolution: The Life and Struggles of Stokely Carmichael (Kwame Ture)*. New York: Scribner, 2003.

Carmody, Pádraig. *The New Scramble for Africa*. Cambridge: Polity Press, 2011.

Carroll, Hamilton. *Affirmative Reaction: New Formations of White Masculinity*. Durham, NC: Duke University Press, 2011.

Carroll, Peter N. *It Seemed Like Nothing Happened: America in the 1970s*. New Brunswick, NJ: Rutgers University Press, 1990.

Carson-Parker, John. "The Options Ahead for the Debt Economy." *Business Week*, October 12, 1974.

Carter, Dan T. *From George Wallace to Newt Gingrich: Race in the Conservative Counterrevolution, 1963–1994*. Baton Rouge: Louisiana State University Press, 1996.

———. *The Politics of Rage: George Wallace, The Origins of the New Conservatism, and the Transformation of American Politics*. 2nd ed. Baton Rouge: Louisiana State University Press, 2000.

Cavanagh, Edward, and Lorenzo Veracini, eds. *The Routledge Handbook of the History of Settler Colonialism*. London: Routledge, 2017.

Cavarero, Adriana. "Equality and Sexual Difference: Amnesia in Political Thought." In *Beyond Equality and Difference: Citizenship, Feminist Politics and Female Subjectivity*. Gisela Bock and Susan James, eds. New York: Routledge, 1992.

Caves, Richard E. *Multinational Enterprise and Economic Analysis*. 3rd ed. Cambridge: Cambridge University Press, 2007.

"Challenge of Ideas." 1960 episode TV-512 of *The Big Picture*. U.S. Department of Defense/Armed Forces Information & Education, 1952–71.

Chambers, John Whiteclay II. *The Tyranny of Change: America in the Progressive Era, 1890–1920*. 2nd ed. New York: St. Martin's, 1992.

Chandler, Alfred D. Jr. *The Visible Hand: The Managerial Revolution in American Business*. Cambridge, MA: Belknap Press, 1977.

Chandler, Alfred D. Jr., and Bruce Mazlish, eds. *Leviathans: Multinational Corporations and the New Global History*. Cambridge: Cambridge University Press, 2005.

Chang, Ha-Joon. *Bad Samaritans: The Myth of Free Trade and the Secret History of Capitalism*. New York: Bloomsbury, 2008.

Chang, Jeff. *Can't Stop Won't Stop: A History of the Hip-Hop Generation*. New York: St. Martin's Press, 2005.

Chang, Kevin O'Brien, and Wayne Chen. *Reggae Routes: The Story of Jamaican Music*. Philadelphia: Temple University Press, 1998.

"Chicago School Builds a Model." *Business Week*, November 30, 1968.

Chrisman, Robert, and Nathan Hare, eds. *Pan-Africanism*. New York: Bobbs-Merrill, 1974.

Churchill, Ward, and Jim Vander Wall. *The COINTELPRO Papers: Documents from the FBI's Secret Wars against Dissent in the United States*. 2nd ed. Cambridge, MA: South End, 2002.

Citron, Abraham F. "The 'Rightness of Whiteness': The World of the White Child in a Segregated Society." *Michigan-Ohio Regional Education Lab* (January 1969): 1–16.

Clark, Nancy L., and William H. Worger. *South Africa: The Rise and Fall of Apartheid*. 2nd ed. Harlow, UK: Pearson, 2011.

Clarke, Cheryl. *"After Mecca": Women Poets and the Black Arts Movement*. New Brunswick, NJ: Rutgers University Press, 2007.

Clarke, Gerald. "The Meaning of Nostalgia." *Time*, May 3, 1971.

Clover, Carol J. *Men, Women, and Chain Saws: Gender in the Modern Horror Film*. Princeton, NJ: Princeton University Press, 1992.

Clymer, Adam. "Black Influence Is Lowest in Two Decades." *New York Times*, June 3, 1981, B8.

Coates, Ta-Nehisi. "Slavery Made America." *The Atlantic*, June 24, 2014.

Cobble, Dorothy Sue. *The Other Women's Movement: Workplace Justice and Social Rights in Modern America*. Princeton, NJ: Princeton University Press, 2004.

Cohen, Lizabeth. *A Consumers' Republic: The Politics of Mass Consumption in Postwar America*. New York: Vintage, 2004.

Collier-Thomas, Bettye, and V. P. Franklin, eds. *Sisters in the Struggle: African American Women in the Civil Rights–Black Power Movement*. New York: New York University Press, 2001.

Collins, John. "A Social History of Ghanaian Popular Entertainment since Independence." *Transactions of the Historical Society of Ghana* 9 (2005): 17–40.

Collins, Patricia Hill. *Black Feminist Thought: Knowledge, Consciousness, and the Politics of Empowerment*. New York: Routledge, 1990.

———. *Black Sexual Politics: African Americans, Gender, and the New Racism*. New York: Routledge, 2005.

"Conglomerates Start Looking Good Again." *Business Week*, June 23, 1975.

"Conglomerates: The Corporations That Make Things Jump." *Business Week*, November 30, 1968.

Congressional Budget Office. *Trends in the Distribution of Household Income between 1979 and 2007*. Pub. No. 4031. Washington, DC: Congressional Budget Office, October 2011.

Conley, Dalton. *Being Black, Living in the Red: Race, Wealth, and Social Policy in America*. Berkeley: University of California Press, 1999.

Cook, David A. *Lost Illusions: American Cinema in the Shadow of Watergate and Vietnam, 1970–1979*. Berkeley: University of California Press, 2000.

Cook, Pam. "Film Culture: 'Exploitation' Films and Feminism." *Screen* 17, no. 2 (1976): 122–27.

Cook, Pam, ed. *The Cinema Book*. London: BFI, 1994.

Cooper, Carolyn. "'Ragamuffin Sounds': Crossing Over from Reggae to Rap and Back." *Caribbean Quarterly* 44, nos. 1–2 (March–June 1998): 153–68.

Cooper, Frederick. *Africa since 1940: The Past of the Present*. Cambridge: Cambridge University Press, 2002.

———. *Colonialism in Question: Theory, Knowledge, History*. Berkeley: University of California Press, 2005.

Cooper, Jackie, dir. *Stand Up and Be Counted*. Columbia Pictures, 1972.

Cooper, Melinda. *Family Values: Between Neoliberalism and the New Social Conservatism*. New York: Zone Books, 2017.

Corber, Robert J. *Cold War Femme: Lesbianism, National Identity, and Hollywood Cinema*. Durham, NC: Duke University Press, 2011.

Corkin, Stanley. "Cowboys and Free Markets: Post–World War II Westerns and U.S. Hegemony." *Cinema Journal* 39, no. 3 (Spring 2000): 66–91.

Corman, Roger, with Jim Jerome. *How I Made a Hundred Movies in Hollywood and Never Lost a Dime*. New York: Da Capo, 1990.

"Corporate Planning: Piercing Future Fog in the Executive Suite." *Business Week*, April 28, 1975.

"Corporations: Where the Game Is Growth." *Business Week*, September 30, 1967.

Cortez, Jayne. *Celebrations and Solitudes*. Strata-East, 1974. LP SES-7421.

———. *Coagulations: New and Selected Poems*. New York: Thunder's Mouth Press, 1984.

———. *Firespitter.* New York: Bola Press, 1982.
———. *Mouth on Paper.* New York: Bola Press, 1977.
———. *Scarifications.* New York: Bola Press, 1978.
———. *Unsubmissive Blues.* Bola Press, 1980. LP BP-8001.
Cott, Nancy F. *The Bonds of Womanhood: "Woman's Sphere" in New England, 1780–1835.* 2nd ed. New Haven, CT: Yale University Press, 1997.
Countryman, Matthew J. *Up South: Civil Rights and Black Power in Philadelphia.* Philadelphia: University of Pennsylvania Press, 2006.
Cowie, Jefferson. *Capital Moves: RCA's Seventy-Year Quest for Cheap Labor.* Ithaca, NY: Cornell University Press, 1999.
———. "Nixon's class struggle: Romancing the New Right worker, 1969–1973." *Labor History* 43, no. 3 (2002): 257–83.
———. *Stayin' Alive: The 1970s and the Last Days of the Working Class.* New York: New Press, 2010.
———. *The Great Exception: The New Deal & the Limits of American Politics.* Princeton, NJ: Princeton University Press, 2016.
Cowie, Jefferson, and Nick Salvatore. "The Long Exception: Rethinking the Place of the New Deal in American History." *International Labor and Working-Class History* 74 (2008): 1–32.
Cox, Oliver Cromwell. *Caste, Class, & Race: A Study in Social Dynamics.* New York: Monthly Review Press, 1959.
Crane, Andrew, Abigail McWilliams, Dirk Matten, Jeremy Moon, and Donald Siegel, eds. *The Oxford Handbook of Corporate Social Responsibility.* Oxford: Oxford University Press, 2008.
Creedence Clearwater Revival. *Willy and the Poor Boys.* Fantasy, 1969.
Crenshaw, Kimberlé. "Demarginalizing the Intersection of Race and Sex: A Black Feminist Critique of Antidiscrimination Doctrine, Feminist Theory and Antiracist Politics." *University of Chicago Legal Forum* 1989, no. 1 (1989): 139–67.
Cromwell, John, dir. *Caged.* Warner Bros, 1950.
Crouch, Stanley. *Ain't No Ambulances for No Nigguhs Tonight.* Flying Dutchman, 1969. LP FDS-105.
Crozier, Michel, Samuel P. Huntington, and Joji Watanuki, eds. *The Crisis of Democracy: Report on the Governability of Democracies to the Trilateral Commission.* New York: New York University Press, 1975.
Cruse, Harold. *Rebellion or Revolution?* New York: Morrow, 1968.
Cunningham, David. *There's Something Happening Here: The New Left, the Klan, and FBI Counterintelligence.* Berkeley: University of California Press, 2004.
Cuordileone, K. A. *Manhood and American Political Culture in the Cold War.* New York: Routledge, 2005.
Curran, Andrew S. *The Anatomy of Blackness: Science & Slavery in an Age of Enlightenment.* Baltimore: Johns Hopkins University Press, 2011.
Curtis, Jesse. "'Will the Jungle Take Over?' *National Review* and the Defense of Western Civilization in the Era of Civil Rights and African Decolonization." *Journal of American Studies* 53, no. 4 (2018): 1–27.
Dailey, Jane. "Sex, Segregation, and the Sacred after Brown." *The Journal of American History* 91, no. 1 (June 2004): 119–44.

Daulatzai, Sohail. *Black Star, Crescent Moon*. Minneapolis: University of Minnesota Press, 2012.

David Hesmondhalgh, and Jason Toynbee, eds. *The Media and Social Theory*. New York: Routledge, 2008.

Davies, Carole Boyce. "Sisters Outside: Tracing the Caribbean/Black Radical Intellectual Tradition." *Small Axe* 13, no. 1 (March 2009): 217–29.

Davies, William. *The Limits of Neoliberalism: Authority, Sovereignty and the Logic of Competition*. Rev. ed. Los Angeles: Sage, 2017.

Davis, Angela Y. "Afro Images: Politics, Fashion, and Nostalgia." *Critical Inquiry* 21, no. 1 (Autumn, 1994): 37–39, 41–43, 45.

———. *Are Prisons Obsolete?* New York: Seven Stories Press, 2003.

———. "Joan Little: The Dialectics of Rape." *Ms.*, June 1975.

———. "Reflections on the Black Woman's Role in the Community of Slaves." *Massachusetts Review* 13, nos. 1–2 (Winter–Spring, 1972): 81–100.

———. *Women, Race & Class*. New York: Vintage Books, 1981.

Davis, David Brion. *Inhuman Bondage: The Rise and Fall of Slavery in the New World*. Oxford: Oxford University Press, 2006.

———. *Slavery and Human Progress*. New York: Oxford University Press, 1986.

Davis, Mike. *City of Quartz: Excavating the Future in Los Angeles*. London: Verso, 2006.

———. *Prisoners of the American Dream: Politics and Economy in the History of the US Working Class*. London: Verso, 1986.

Davis, Ronald L. *Duke: The Life and Image of John Wayne*. Norman: University of Oklahoma Press, 1998.

Dawley, Alan. "The Abortive Rule of Big Money." In *Ruling America: A History of Wealth and Power in a Democracy*. Steve Fraser and Gary Gerstle, eds. Cambridge, MA: Harvard University Press, 2005.

Debate: Baldwin vs. Buckley. National Educational Television Network, February 1965.

De Beauvoir, Simone. *The Second Sex*. H. M. Parshley, trans. New York: Bantam, 1949.

De Grazia, Victoria. *Irresistible Empire: America's Advance through 20th-Century Europe*. Cambridge, MA: Belknap Press, 2005.

De Jong, Greta. *Invisible Enemy: The African American Freedom Struggle after 1965*. Malden, MA: Wiley-Blackwell, 2010.

De Lauretis, Teresa. "Aesthetic and Feminist Theory: Rethinking Women's Cinema." *New German Critique* 34 (1985): 154–75.

De Leon, Gerardo, dir. *Women in Cages*. New World Pictures, 1971.

Delton, Jennifer. *Racial Integration in Corporate America, 1940–1990*. Cambridge: Cambridge University Press, 2009.

Demme, Jonathan, dir. *Caged Heat!* New World Pictures, 1974. DVD SF 12289.

Demme, Ted, and Richard LaGravenese, dirs. *A Decade under the Influence*. IFC Films, 2003.

Demos, John. *The Unredeemed Captive: A Family Story from Early America*. New York: Vintage, 1994.

Denisoff, R. Serge, and Richard A. Peterson, eds. *The Sounds of Social Change: Studies in Popular Culture*. Chicago: Rand McNally, 1972.

Denning, Michael. *Noise Uprising: The Audiopolitics of a World Musical Revolution*. London: Verso, 2015.

———. *The Cultural Front: The Laboring of American Culture in the Twentieth Century.* London: Verso, 1998.

"'Deregulation' Is off to a Halting Start." *Business Week*, November 13, 1971.

Derounian-Stodola, Kathryn Zabelle, ed. *Women's Indian Captivity Narratives.* New York: Penguin, 1998.

De Santis, Vincent R. *The Shaping of Modern America: 1877–1920.* 3rd ed. Wheeling, IL: Harlan Davidson, 2000.

De Stefano, Valerio. "The Rise of the Just-in-Time Workforce: On-Demand Work, Crowdwork, and Labor Protection in the Gig-Economy," *Comparative Labor Law and Policy Journal.* 37 (2015): i–37.

Dick, Bernard F. *The Star-Spangled Screen: The American World War II Film.* Lexington: University Press of Kentucky, 1985.

DiMaggio, Paul, Richard A. Peterson, and Jack Esco Jr. "Country Music: Ballad of the Silent Majority." In *The Sounds of Social Change: Studies in Popular Culture.* R. Serge Denisoff and Richard A. Peterson, eds. Chicago: Rand McNally, 1972.

Di Silvestro, Rino, dir. *Women in Cell Block 7* (*Diario segreto da un carcere femminile*). Angry Film, 1973. DVD SO-3009.

"Diversification That Offsets the Slack in Steel." *Business Week*, December 12, 1977.

Dmytryk, Edward, dir. *Back to Bataan.* RKO Radio Pictures, 1945.

Doherty, Thomas. *Pre-code Hollywood: Sex, Immorality, and Insurrection in American Cinema, 1930–1934.* New York: Columbia University Press, 1999.

———. *Teenagers and Teenpics: Juvenilization of American Movies.* Philadelphia: Temple University Press, 2002.

"Donald Cook Takes on the Environmentalists." *Business Week*, October 26, 1974.

Donovan, Brian. *White Slave Crusades: Race, Gender, and Anti-vice Activism, 1887–1917.* Champaign: University of Illinois Press, 2010.

Donovan, Robert J., and Ray Scherer. *Unsilent Revolution: Television News and American Public Life, 1948–1991.* Cambridge: Cambridge University Press, 1992.

Dow, Bonnie J. *Prime-Time Feminism: Television, Media Culture, and the Women's Movement since 1970.* Philadelphia: University of Pennsylvania Press, 1996.

Drenner, Elijah, dir. *From Manila with Love.* Shout! Factory, 2011.

Dubois, Laurent. "An Enslaved Enlightenment: Rethinking the Intellectual History of the French Atlantic." *Social History* 31, no. 1 (2006): 1–14.

Du Bois, W. E. B. *Black Reconstruction in America, 1860–1880.* New York: Free Press, 1935.

———. *The World and Africa.* New York: International Publishers, 1946.

Dudziak, Mary L. *Cold War Civil Rights: Race and the Image of American Democracy.* Princeton, NJ: Princeton University Press, 2000.

———. "The Little Rock Crisis and Foreign Relations: Race, Resistance, and the Image of American Democracy." *Southern California Law Review* 70 (September 1997): 1–56.

Duggan, Lisa. *The Twilight of Equality? Neoliberalism, Cultural Politics, and the Attack on Democracy.* Boston: Beacon, 2003.

Duménil, Gérard, and Dominique Lévy. *Capital Resurgent: Roots of the Neoliberal Revolution.* Derek Jeffers, trans. Cambridge, MA: Harvard University Press, 2004.

———. *The Crisis of Neoliberalism.* Cambridge, MA: Harvard University Press, 2011.

Dunn, Kevin. "Lights . . . Camera . . . Africa: Images of Africa and Africans in Western Popular Films of the 1930s." *African Studies Review* 39, no. 1 (1996): 149–75.

Dunn, Stephane. *"Baad Bitches" and Sassy Supermamas: Black Power Action Films.* Urbana: University of Illinois Press, 2008.
Dursteler, Eric R. "Fernand Braudel (1902–1985)." In *New Historical Writing in Twentieth-Century France: French Historians, 1900–2000.* Philip Daileader and Philip Whalen, eds. Malden, MA: Wiley-Blackwell, 2010.
Dwan, Allan, dir. *Sands of Iwo Jima.* Republic Pictures, 1949.
Dworkin, Dennis L., and Leslie G. Roman, eds. *Views beyond the Border Country: Raymond Williams and Cultural Politics.* New York: Routledge, 1993.
Dwyer, Michael D. *Back to the Fifties: Nostalgia, Hollywood Film, and Popular Music of the Seventies and Eighties.* Oxford: Oxford University Press, 2015.
Eagleton-Pierce, Matthew. "Historicizing the neoliberal spirit of capitalism." In *The Handbook of Neoliberalism.* Simon Springer, Kean Birch, and Julie MacLeavy, eds. New York: Routledge, 2016.
Eastwood, Clint, dir. *High Plains Drifter.* Universal Pictures, 1973. DVD.
Ebert, Teresa L. "The Romance of Patriarchy: Ideology, Subjectivity, and Postmodern Feminist Cultural Theory." *Cultural Critique* 10 (1988): 19–57.
Echols, Alice. *Daring to Be Bad: Radical Feminism in America, 1967–1975.* Minneapolis: University of Minnesota Press, 1989.
———. "Nothing Distant about It: Women's Liberation and Sixties Radicalism." In *The Sixties: From Memory to History.* David Farber, ed. Chapel Hill: University of North Carolina Press, 1994.
"Economically the Negro Gains but He's Still the Low Man." *Business Week,* December 18, 1954.
Edgerton, Gary R. *The Columbia History of American Television.* New York: Columbia University Press, 2007.
Edsall, Thomas Byrne, and Mary D. Edsall. *Chain Reaction: The Impact of Race, Rights, and Taxes on American Politics.* New York: Norton, 1991.
Edwards, Brent Hayes. *The Practice of Diaspora: Literature, Translation, and the Rise of Black Internationalism.* Cambridge, MA: Harvard University Press, 2003.
Edwards, Paul N. *The Closed World: Computers and the Politics of Discourse in Cold War America.* Cambridge, MA: MIT Press, 1996.
"Egalitarianism: Threat to a Free Market." *Business Week,* December 1, 1975.
Eley, Geoff, and Ronald Grigor Suny. "Introduction: From the Moment of Social History to the Work of Cultural Representation." In *Becoming National: A Reader.* Geoff Eley and Ronald Grigor Suny, eds. New York: Oxford University Press, 1996.
Elkins, Caroline, and Susan Pedersen, eds. *Settler Colonialism in the Twentieth Century: Projects, Practices, Legacies.* New York: Routledge, 2005.
Ellsworth, Phoebe C., and Samuel R. Gross. "Hardening of the Attitudes: Americans' Views on the Death Penalty." *Journal of Social Issues* 50, no. 2 (1994): 19–52.
Elson, Diane, and Ruth Pearson. "'Nimble Fingers Make Cheap Workers': An Analysis of Women's Employment in Third World Export Manufacturing." *Feminist Review* 7, no. 1 (1981): 87–107.
Engelhardt, Tom. *The End of Victory Culture: Cold War America and the Disillusioning of a Generation.* Amherst: University of Massachusetts Press, 1998.
Engelhardt, Tom, and John Brown. "The War on Terror as an Indian War." *LewRockwell.com,* January 21, 2006.

Erenberg, Lewis A., and Susan E. Hirsch, eds. *The War in American Culture: Society and Consciousness during World War II*. Chicago: University of Chicago Press, 1996.

Erskine, Hazel. "The Polls: Negro Housing," *Public Opinion Quarterly* 31, no. 3 (Autumn 1967): 482–98.

———. "The Polls: Politics and Law and Order." *Public Opinion Quarterly* 38, no. 4 (Winter 1974–75): 623–34.

———. "The Polls: Recent Opinion on Racial Problems." *Public Opinion Quarterly* 32, no. 4 (Winter 1968–69): 696–703.

Erskine, Hazel Gaudet. "The Polls: Race Relations." *Public Opinion Quarterly* 26, no. 1 (Spring 1962): 137–48.

"Eurodollar Works for Both Sides." *Business Week*, July 28, 1962.

Fahs, Alice. "Remembering the Civil War in Children's Literature of the 1880s and 1890s." In *The Memory of the Civil War in American Culture*. Alice Fahs and Joan Waugh, eds. Chapel Hill: University of North Carolina Press, 2004.

Fahs, Alice, and Joan Waugh, eds. *The Memory of the Civil War in American Culture*. Chapel Hill: University of North Carolina Press, 2004.

Fairbanks, Brian W. *Writings: Film*Literature*Music*Society*. Morrisville, NC: Lulu.com, 2005.

Falicov, Tamara L. "U.S.-Argentine Co-productions, 1982–1990: Roger Corman, Aries Productions, 'Schlockbuster' Movies, and the International Market." *Film & History* 34, no. 1 (2004): 31–38.

Faludi, Susan. *Backlash: The Undeclared War against American Women*. New York: Crown, 1991.

Fanon, Frantz. *Wretched of the Earth*. Constance Farrington, trans. New York: Grove, 1963.

Farber, David. *The Age of Great Dreams: America in the 1960s*. New York: Hill & Wang, 1994.

Farber, David, ed. *The Sixties: From Memory to History*. Chapel Hill: University of North Carolina Press, 1994.

Farber, David. "The Silent Majority and Talk about Revolution." In *The Sixties: From Memory to History*. David Farber, ed. Chapel Hill: University of North Carolina Press, 1994.

Fargo, James, dir. *The Enforcer*. Warner Bros. Pictures, 1976. DVD.

Farrow, John, dir. *Hondo*. Batjac/Warner Bros., 1953.

Faulkner, William. *Requiem for a Nun*. New York: Random House, 1951.

Feagin, Joe R. "Excluding Blacks and Others from Housing: The Foundations of White Racism." *Cityscape* 4, no. 3 (1999): 79–91.

"Feminism Takes a Backseat at Women's Banks." *Business Week*, October 9, 1978.

Fergus, Devin. *Liberalism, Black Power, and the Making of American Politics, 1965–1980*. Athens: The University of Georgia Press, 2009.

Ferguson, James. *Global Shadows: Africa in the Neoliberal World Order*. Durham, NC: Duke University Press, 2006.

Ferguson, Niall, Charles S. Maier, Erez Manela, and Jeremy Adelman, eds. *The Shock of the Global: The 1970s in Perspective*. Cambridge, MA: Belknap Press, 2010.

Ferguson, Thomas. "Industrial Conflict and the Coming of the New Deal." In *The Rise and Fall of the New Deal Order, 1930–1980*. Steve Fraser and Gary Gerstle, eds. Princeton, NJ: Princeton University Press, 1989.

Ferrara, Abel, dir. *Ms. 45*. Rochelle Films, 1981.

Field, Douglas. *All Those Strangers: The Art and Lives of James Baldwin*. Oxford: Oxford University Press, 2015.

Finkelman, Paul, ed. *Encyclopedia of African American History, 1896 to the Present: From the Age of Segregation to the Twenty-First Century*. Oxford: Oxford University Press, 2009.

Fire, Kathy. *Songs of Fire*. Folkways Records, 1978. LP FS 8585.

Firing Line. "The Economic Crisis." Taped on January 8, 1968. Hoover Institution Video Library, 2010.

Fischer, Kirsten. *Suspect Relations: Sex, Race, and Resistance in Colonial North Carolina*. Ithaca, NY: Cornell University Press, 2002.

Fischer, Sibylle. *Modernity Disavowed: Haiti and the Cultures of Slavery in the Age of Revolution*. Durham, NC: Duke University Press, 2004.

Fitzpatrick, Kathleen. "*Network*: The Other Cold War." *Film & History* 31, no. 2 (2001): 33–39.

Flamm, Michael W. *Law and Order: Street Crime, Civil Unrest, and the Crisis of Liberalism in the 1960s*. New York: Columbia University Press, 2005.

Fligstein, Neil. "States, Markets, and Economic Growth." In Jürgen Kocka and Marcel van der Linden, eds. *Capitalism: The Reemergence of a Historical Concept*. London: Bloomsbury, 2016.

Flowers in the Wildwood: Women in Early Country Music. Trikont, 2003. CD.

Floyd, Samuel A. Jr. *The Power of Black Music: Interpreting Its History from Africa to the United States*. Oxford: Oxford University Press, 1995.

Foner, Eric. *Give Me Liberty! An American History, Volume 1: To 1877*. 5th ed. New York: Norton, 2017.

Foner, Eric, ed. *The New American History*. Philadelphia: Temple University Press, 1990.

Fones-Wolf, Elizabeth A. *Selling Free Enterprise: The Business Assault on Labor and Liberalism, 1945–1960*. Urbana: University of Illinois Press, 1994.

Forbes, Bryan, dir. *The Stepford Wives*. Palomar Pictures, 1975.

Ford, John, dir. *Fort Apache*. RKO Pictures, 1948.

———. *Judge Priest*. Fox Film Corporation, 1934.

———. *She Wore a Yellow Ribbon*. RKO Pictures, 1949.

———. *Stagecoach*. United Artists, 1939.

———. *The Searchers*. Warner Bros., 1956.

———. *The Man Who Shot Liberty Valance*. Paramount Pictures, 1962.

Ford, Karen Jackson. *Gender and the Poetics of Excess: Moments of Brocade*. Jackson: University of Mississippi Press, 1997.

"For Women, a Difficult Climb to the Top." *Business Week*, August 2, 1969.

Foster, Gwendolyn Audrey. *Women Film Directors: An International Bio-critical Dictionary*. Westport, CT: Greenwood, 1995.

Foster, Hal, ed. *The Anti-aesthetic: Essays on Postmodern Culture*. Seattle: Bay Press, 1983.

Foucault, Michel. *The Birth of Biopolitics: Lectures at the Collège de France, 1978–1979*. Graham Burchell, trans. New York: Picador, 2008.

Fousekis, Natalie M. *Demanding Child Care: Women's Activism and the Politics of Welfare, 1940–1971*. Chicago: University of Illinois Press, 2011.

Franco, Jesus, dir. *Women behind Bars* (*Des diamants pour l'enfer*). Brux International Pictures, 1975.

Frank, Andre Gunder. "The Post-war Boom: Boon for the West, Bust for the South." *Millennium* 7 (1978): 153–61.

Frank, Robert H. "Income Inequality: Too Big to Ignore." *New York Times*, October 16, 2010.

Frank, Thomas. *The Conquest of Cool: Business Culture, Counterculture, and the Rise of Hip Consumerism*. Chicago: University of Chicago Press, 1997.

Frantzen, D. J. *Growth and Crisis in Post-war Capitalism*. Worcester, UK: Billing, 1990.

Fraser, Nancy. "Feminism, Capitalism and the Cunning of History." *New Left Review* 56 (March–April 2009): 97–117.

———. *Fortunes of Feminism: From State-Managed Capitalism to Neoliberal Crisis*. New York: Verso, 2013.

———. "Rethinking the Public Sphere: A Contribution to the Critique of Actually Existing Democracy." *Social Text*, nos. 25–26 (1990): 56–80.

Fraser, Nancy, and Linda Gordon. "A Genealogy of Dependency: Tracing a Keyword of the US Welfare State." *Signs* 19, no. 2 (1994): 309–36.

Fraser, Steve. "The 'Labor Question.'" In *The Rise and Fall of the New Deal Order, 1930–1980*. Steve Fraser and Gary Gerstle, eds. Princeton, NJ: Princeton University Press, 1989.

Fraser, Steve, and Gary Gerstle, eds. *Ruling America: A History of Wealth and Power in a Democracy*. Cambridge, MA: Harvard University Press, 2005.

———. *The Rise and Fall of the New Deal Order, 1930–1980*. Princeton, NJ: Princeton University Press, 1989.

Fredrickson, George M. *Racism: A Short History*. Princeton, NJ: Princeton University Press, 2002.

———. *The Black Image in the White Mind: The Debate on Afro-American Character and Destiny, 1817–1914*. New York: Harper and Row, 1971.

"Free Enterpriser—without Any Strings." *Business Week*, October 6, 1962.

Freund, David M. P. *Colored Property: State Policy & White Racial Politics in Suburban America*. Chicago: University of Chicago Press, 2007.

Frey, William H. *Diversity Explosion: How New Racial Demographics Are Remaking America*. Rev. ed. Washington, DC: Brookings Institution Press, 2018.

Friedan, Betty. *The Feminine Mystique*. New York: Norton, 1963.

Frieden, Jeff. "The Trilateral Commission: Economics and Politics in the 1970s." In *Trilateralism: The Trilateral Commission and Elite Planning for World Management*. Holly Sklar, ed. Montreal: Black Rose Books, 1980.

Frieden, Jeffry A. *Global Capitalism: Its Fall and Rise in the Twentieth Century*. New York: Norton, 2006.

Friedkin, William, dir. *The French Connection*. Twentieth Century Fox, 1971.

Friedman, Gerald. "Workers without Employers: Shadow Corporations and the Rise of the Gig Economy." *Review of Keynesian Economics* 2, no. 2 (2014): 171–88.

Friedman, Milton. *Capitalism and Freedom*. Chicago: University of Chicago Press, 1962.

———. "Neo-liberalism and Its Prospects." *Farmand*, February 17, 1951, 89–93.

———. "Which Way for Capitalism." *Reason*, May 1978.
Gaddis, John Lewis. *The United States and the Origins of the Cold War, 1941–1947*. New York: Columbia University Press, 1972.
Gaines, Kevin. "Locating the Transnational in Postwar African American History." *Small Axe* 13, no. 1 (March 2009): 192–202.
Gale Reference Team. "Biography—Scott-Heron, Gil." In *Contemporary Authors*. Farmington Hills, MI: Thomson Gale, 2002.
Gans, Herbert J. *Deciding What's News: A Study of* CBS Evening News, NBC Nightly News, Newsweek, *and* Time. Evanston, IL: Northwestern University Press, 2004.
Garrett, Van G. "Cortez, Jayne." In *Encyclopedia of African American History, 1896 to the Present: From the Age of Segregation to the Twenty-First Century*. Paul Finkelman, ed. Oxford: Oxford University Press, 2009.
Garrison, Ednie Kaeh. "U.S. Feminism-Grrrl Style! Youth (Sub)cultures and the Technologics of the Third Wave." *Feminist Studies* 26, no. 1 (Spring 2000): 141–70.
Gay, Peter. *The Enlightenment: An Interpretation: The Rise of Modern Paganism*. New York: Norton, 1966.
Gayle, Addison Jr., ed. *The Black Aesthetic*. Garden City, NY: Doubleday, 1971.
Geertz, Clifford. *The Interpretation of Cultures*. New York: Basic Books, 1973.
Geesling, Donald. "'The First Minute of a New Day': The Politics, Poetics, and Legacy of Gil Scott-Heron." MA thesis, University of Tulsa, 2007.
Genovese, Eugene D. *From Rebellion to Revolution: Afro-American Slave Revolts in the Making of the Modern World*. Baton Rouge: Louisiana State University Press, 1979.
———. *Roll, Jordan, Roll: The World the Slaves Made*. New York: Vintage, 1976.
George, Nelson. *Hip Hop America*. New York: Penguin, 1998.
Gerson, Joseph. "US Foreign Bases and Human Rights." *Peace Review* 2, no. 1 (1990): 38–41.
Gerstle, Gary. *American Crucible: Race and Nation in the Twentieth Century*. Princeton, NJ: Princeton University Press, 2001.
Gibson, Donald B., ed. *Modern Black Poets: A Collection of Critical Essays*. Englewood Cliffs, NJ: Prentice-Hall, 1973.
Gibson, James William. *Warrior Dreams: Paramilitary Culture in Post-Vietnam America*. New York: Hill and Wang, 1994.
Giddings, Paula. *When and Where I Enter: The Impact of Black Women on Race and Sex in America*. New York: Quill William Morrow, 1984.
Gilbert, James. *Men in the Middle: Searching for Masculinity in the 1950s*. Chicago: University of Chicago Press, 2005.
Gilbert, Shirli. "Singing against Apartheid: ANC Cultural Groups and the International Anti-Apartheid Struggle." *Journal of Southern African Studies* 33, no. 2 (2007): 421–41.
Gilder, George. *Wealth and Poverty*. New York: Basic Books, 1981.
Gill, Stephen. *American Hegemony and the Trilateral Commission*. Cambridge: Cambridge University Press, 1990.
Gillis, Stacy, Gillian Howie, and Rebecca Munford, eds. *Third Wave Feminism: A Critical Exploration*. 2nd ed. New York: Palgrave Macmillan, 2007.
Gilmore, Glenda Elizabeth. *Gender and Jim Crow: Women and the Politics of White Supremacy in North Carolina, 1896–1920*. Durham: University of North Carolina Press, 1996.

Gilmore, Ruth Wilson. "Globalisation and US Prison Growth: From Military Keynesianism to Post-Keynesian Militarism." *Race & Class* 40, nos. 2–3 (March 1999): 171–88.

———. "What Is to Be Done?" *American Quarterly* 63, no. 2 (June 2011): 245–65.

Gilmore, Stephanie. "Thinking about Feminist Coalitions." In *Feminist Coalitions: Historical Perspectives on Second-Wave Feminism in the United States*. Stephanie Gilmore, ed. Urbana: University of Illinois Press, 2008.

Gilmore, Stephanie, ed. *Feminist Coalitions: Historical Perspectives on Second-Wave Feminism in the United States*. Urbana: University of Illinois Press, 2008.

Gilroy, Paul. *The Black Atlantic: Modernity and Double Consciousness*. Cambridge, MA: Harvard University Press, 1993.

———. *"There Ain't No Black in the Union Jack": The Cultural Politics of Race and Nation*. Chicago: University of Chicago Press, 1987.

Gingrich, Newt, and Richard M. Pious. *To Renew America*. New York: HarperCollins, 1995.

Giovanni, Nikki. *Like a Ripple on a Pond*. Collectables, 1993 [1973]. COL-CD-6505.

———. *The Way I Feel*. Collectables, 1995 [1975]. COL-6507.

———. *Truth Is on Its Way*. Right On Records, 1971. RR 05001.

Gitlin, Todd. *The Sixties: Years of Hope, Days of Rage*. New York: Bantam, 1993.

Glazer, Nathan. *Affirmative Discrimination: Ethnic Inequality and Public Policy*. Cambridge, MA: Harvard University Press, 1975.

Glazer, Nathan, and Daniel P. Moynihan. *Beyond the Melting Pot: The Negroes, Puerto Ricans, Jews, Italians, and Irish of New York City*. Cambridge, MA: MIT Press, 1963.

Gleick, James. *The Information: A History, A Theory, A Flood*. New York: Vintage Books, 2012.

Go, Julian. *Patterns of Empire: The British and American Empires, 1688 to the Present*. Cambridge: Cambridge University Press, 2011.

Goldberg, David Theo. *The Threat of Race: Reflections on Racial Neoliberalism*. Malden, MA: Wiley-Blackwell, 2009.

"Gold Fever Rises to Record Heat." *Business Week*, March 16, 1968.

Goldin, Claudia, and Robert A. Margo. "The Great Compression: The Wage Structure in the United States at Mid-Century." *Quarterly Journal of Economics* 107, no. 1 (February 1992): 1–34.

Goodwyn, Lawrence. *The Populist Moment: A Short History of the Agrarian Revolt in America*. Oxford: Oxford University Press, 1978.

Gordon, Linda. "Moralizing Doesn't Help." *International Labor and Working-Class History*, no. 67 (Spring 2005): 26–32.

———. *Pitied but Not Entitled: Single Mothers and the History of Welfare*. New York: Free Press, 1994.

Gordon, Linda, ed. *Women, the State, and Welfare*. Madison: University of Wisconsin Press, 1990.

Gordon, Robert J. *The Rise and Fall of American Growth: The U.S. Standard of Living since the Civil War*. Princeton, NJ: Princeton University Press, 2016.

"Government Intervention." *Business Week*, April 4, 1977.

"Government Intervention: Regulation." *Business Week*, September 14, 1974.

Grandin, Greg. *Empire's Workshop: Latin America, the United States, and the Rise of the New Imperialism*. New York: Holt, 2006.

———. "Living in Revolutionary Times: Coming to Terms with the Violence of Latin America's Long Cold War." In *A Century of Revolution: Insurgent and Counterinsurgent Violence during Latin America's Long Cold War*. Greg Grandin and Gilbert M. Joseph, eds. Durham, NC: Duke University Press, 2010.

———. *The End of the Myth: From the Frontier to the Border Wall in the Mind of America*. New York: Metropolitan Books, 2019.

Grant, Colin. *The Natural Mystics: Marley, Tosh, and Wailer*. New York: Norton, 2011.

Grateful Dead. *Europe '72*. Warner Bros., 1972. LP.

Green, Alfred E., dir. *Babyface*. Warner Bros. Pictures, 1933.

Greenberg, Amy S. *Manifest Manhood and the Antebellum American Empire*. Cambridge: Cambridge University Press, 2005.

Greenberg, Miriam. *Branding New York: How a City in Crisis Was Sold to the World*. New York: Routledge, 2008.

Greene, Anne-Marie, and Gill Kirton. *The Dynamics of Managing Diversity: A Critical Approach*. London: Routledge, 2015.

Gregory, Michele Rene. "'Talking Sports': Sports and the Construction of Hegemonic Masculinities at Work." In *Equality, Diversity and Inclusion at Work: A Research Companion*. Mustafa F. Özbilgin, ed. Cheltenham, UK: Edward Elgar, 2009.

Griffith, R. Marie. *God's Daughters: Evangelical Women and the Power of Submission*. Berkeley: University of California Press, 1997.

Grossberg, Lawrence. "Does Cultural Studies Have Futures? Should It? (Or What's the Matter with New York?): Cultural Studies, Contexts and Conjunctures." *Cultural Studies* 20, no. 1 (January 2006): 1–32.

Grossman, Rachael. "Women's Place in the Integrated Circuit." *Radical America Sommerville, Ma* 4, no. 1 (1980): 29–49.

"Group Management to Control Diversity." *Business Week*, September 15, 1975.

Guerrero, Ed. *Framing Blackness: The African American Image in Film*. Philadelphia: Temple University Press, 1993.

"Guiding Growth toward a Global Economy." *Business Week*, December 19, 1970.

Guldi, Jo, and David Armitage, *The History Manifesto*. Cambridge: Cambridge University Press, 2014.

Gundling, Ernest, and Anita Zanchettin. *Global Diversity: Winning Customers and Engaging Employees within World Markets*. London: Nicholas Brealey, 2006.

Guralnick, Peter. *Searching for Robert Johnson*. New York: Plume, 1989.

Habermas, Jürgen. "Modernity—an Incomplete Project." In *The Anti-aesthetic: Essays on Postmodern Culture*. Hal Foster, ed. Seattle: Bay Press, 1983.

Hacker, Jacob S., and Paul Pierson. *Winner-Take-All Politics: How Washington Made the Rich Richer—and Turned Its Back on the Middle Class*. New York: Simon & Schuster, 2010.

Hahn, Peter L., and Mary Ann Heiss, eds. *Empire and Revolution: The United States and the Third World since 1945*. Columbus: Ohio State University Press, 2001.

Hall, Stuart, Dorothy Hobson, Andrew Lowe, and Paul Willis, eds. *Culture, Media, Language*. London: Routledge, 1980.

Hall, Stuart, Don Hubert, David Held, and Kenneth Thompson, eds. *Modernity: An Introduction to Modern Societies*. Cambridge, MA: Blackwell, 1996.

Hallin, Daniel C. "Neoliberalism, Social Movements and Change in Media Systems in the Late Twentieth Century." In *The Media and Social Theory*. David Hesmondhalgh and Jason Toynbee, eds. New York: Routledge, 2008.

Halloran, S. Michael. "Aristotle's Concept of Ethos, or If Not His Somebody Else's." *Rhetoric Review* 1, no. 1 (September 1982): 58–63.

Hancock, Ange-Marie. *The Politics of Disgust: The Public Identity of the Welfare Queen*. New York: New York University Press, 2004.

Hanson, Helen. *Hollywood Heroines: Women in* Film Noir *and the Female Gothic Film*. New York: I. B. Tauris, 2007.

Harrington, Michael. *The Other America: Poverty in the United States*. New York: Touchstone, 1962.

Harris, Cheryl I. "Whiteness as Property." *Harvard Law Review* 106, no. 8 (June 1993): 1707–91.

Harris, Mark. *Five Came Back: A Story of Hollywood and the Second World War*. New York: Penguin, 2014.

———. *Pictures at a Revolution: Five Movies and the Birth of the New Hollywood*. New York: Penguin, 2008.

Harris, Stan. *Swing Out, Sweet Land*. November 28, 1970. Batjac/NBC.

Hartley, Mark, dir. *Machete Maidens Unleashed!* Bionic Boy Productions and Fury Productions, 2010.

Hartman, Saidiya V. *Lose Your Mother: A Journey along the Atlantic Slave Route*. New York: Farrar, Straus and Giroux, 2007.

———. *Scenes of Subjection: Terror, Slavery, and Self-Making in Nineteenth-Century America*. Oxford: Oxford University Press, 1997.

Harvey, David. *A Brief History of Neoliberalism*. Oxford: Oxford University Press, 2005.

———. *The Condition of Postmodernity: An Enquiry into the Origins of Cultural Change*. Cambridge, MA: Blackwell, 1990.

Haskel, Jonathan, and Stian Westlake. *Capitalism without Capital: The Rise of the Intangible Economy*. Princeton, NJ: Princeton University Press, 2018.

Haskell, Molly. *From Reverence to Rape: The Treatment of Women in the Movies*. 2nd ed. Chicago: University of Chicago Press, 1987.

Hassan, Ihab. *The Postmodern Turn: Essays in Postmodern Theory and Culture*. Columbus: Ohio State University Press, 1987.

Hathaway, Henry, dir. *True Grit*. Paramount Pictures, 1969.

Hawks, Howard, dir. *Hatari*. Paramount Pictures, 1962.

———. *Red River*. United Artists, 1948.

Hawley, Charles V. "You're a Better Filipino than I Am, John Wayne: World War II, Hollywood, and U.S.-Philippines Relations." *Pacific Historical Review* 71, no. 3 (August 2002): 389–414.

Hawley, Ellis W. *The Great War and the Search for a Modern Order: A History of the American People and Their Institutions, 1917–1933*. New York: St. Martin's, 1992.

Hayden, Michael Edison, and Eddie Bejarano. *Trump's Immigration Order Was Drafted by Officials with Ties to Hate Groups, according to Report*. Montgomery, AL: Southern Poverty Law Center, April 24, 2020.

Hayek, F. A. *The Constitution of Liberty*. Chicago: University of Chicago Press, 1960.
———. *The Road to Serfdom: Text and Documents*. Bruce Caldwell, ed. Chicago: University of Chicago Press, 2007; orig. 1944.
———. "The Use of Knowledge in Society." *American Economic Review* 35, no. 4 (September 1945): 519–30.
Hazlitt, Henry. *Man vs. the Welfare State*. New Rochelle, NY: Arlington House, 1969.
Hebdige, Dick. *Cut 'n' Mix: Culture, Identity and Caribbean Music*. New York: Routledge, 1987.
Heilbroner, Robert L., and Aaron Singer. *The Economic Transformation of America: 1600 to the Present*. 2nd ed. San Diego, CA: Harcourt Brace Jovanovich, 1984.
Heisel, Andrew. "The Rise and Fall of an All-American Catchphrase: 'Free, White, and 21.'" *Jezebel*, September 10, 2015.
Heller, Henry. *The Birth of Capitalism: A Twenty-First Century Perspective*. London: Pluto, 2011.
Heller-Nicholas, Alexandra. *Rape-Revenge Films: A Critical Study*. Jefferson, NC: McFarland, 2011.
Hendershot, Heather. *Open to Debate: How William F. Buckley Put Liberal America on the Firing Line*. New York: Broadside Books, 2016.
Hendrix/Lightnin' Rod/Miles. *Doriella Du Fontaine*. Metrotone Records, 1984. CD 7 72663-2.
Henzell, Perry, dir. *The Harder They Come*. New World Pictures, 1972.
Herbes-Sommers, Christine, Tracy Heather Strain, and Llewellyn Smith, dirs. *Race: The Power of an Illusion*. Episode 3 (PBS).
Higgins, Colin, dir. *9 to 5*. Twentieth Century Fox Film Corporation, 1980.
Hill, Herbert. "Racism within Organized Labor: A Report of Five Years of the AFL-CIO, 1955–1960." *Journal of Negro Education* 30, no. 2 (1961): 109–18.
———. "The Problem of Race in American Labor History." *Reviews in American History* 24, no. 2 (1996): 189–208.
Hill, Jack, dir. *Big Doll House*. New World Pictures, 1971. DVD.
———. *Coffy*. American International Pictures, 1973. DVD 4001653.
———. *Foxy Brown*. American International Pictures, 1974. DVD 4001655.
———. *Switchblade Sisters*. Centaur Pictures Inc., 1975.
———. *The Big Bird Cage*. New World Pictures, 1972.
Hilmes, Michele. *Only Connect: A Cultural History of Broadcasting in the United States*. Belmont, CA: Wadsworth/Thomson Learning, 2002.
Hinckley, Story. "Texas: We Don't Need Academics to Fact-Check Our Textbooks." *Christian Science Monitor*, November 19, 2015.
Hines, Darlene Clark. "Rape and the Inner Lives of Black Women in the Middle West." *Signs* 14, no. 4 (Summer 1989): 912–20
Hixson, Walter L. *American Settler Colonialism: A History*. New York: Palgrave Macmillan, 2013.
Hoberman, J. *Make My Day: Movie Culture in the Age of Reagan*. New York: New Press, 2019.
———. *The Dream Life: Movies, Media, and the Mythology of the Sixties*. New York: New Press, 2003.
Hoberman, J., and Jonathan Rosenbaum. *Midnight Movies*. New York: Da Capo, 1983.

Hodgson, Godfrey. "The Foreign Policy Establishment." *Ruling America: A History of Wealth and Power in a Democracy.* Steve Fraser and Gary Gerstle, eds. Cambridge, MA: Harvard University Press, 2005.

Hoefle, Scott William. "Bitter Harvest: The Frontier Legacy of US Internal Violence and Belligerent Imperialism." *Critique of Anthropology* 24 (2004): 277–300.

Hoerr, John. "An Argument against Preferential Hiring." *Business Week*, March 22, 1976.

Hoff, Joan. *Law, Gender, and Injustice: A Legal History of U.S. Women.* New York: New York University Press, 1994.

Hofstadter, Richard. *The Paranoid Style in American Politics and Other Essays.* Cambridge, MA: Harvard University Press, 1965.

Hole, Judith, and Ellen Levine. *Rebirth of Feminism.* New York: Quadrangle Books, 1971.

Hong, Grace Kyungwon. *The Ruptures of American Capital: Women of Color Feminism and the Culture of Immigrant Labor.* Minneapolis: University of Minnesota Press, 2006.

hooks, bell. *Ain't I a Woman: Black Women and Feminism.* Boston: South End, 1981.

———. *Feminist Theory: From Margin to Center.* Boston: South End, 1984.

Hooks, Gregory. "The Rise of the Pentagon and U.S. State Building: The Defense Program as Industrial Policy." *American Journal of Sociology* 96, no. 2 (September 1990): 358–404.

Hooks, Gregory, and Leonard E. Bloomquist. "The Legacy of World War II for Regional Growth and Decline: The Cumulative Effects of Wartime Investments on U.S. Manufacturing, 1947–1972." *Social Forces* 71, no. 2 (December 1992): 303–37.

Horeck, Tanya. *Public Rape: Representing Violation in Fiction and Film.* New York: Routledge, 2004.

Horne, Gerald. *The Counter-revolution of 1776: Slave Resistance and the Origins of the United States of America.* New York: New York University Press, 2014.

"How 1,200 Companies Performed in 1978." *Business Week*, March 19, 1979.

"How Bosses Feel about Women's Lib." *Business Week*, September 5, 1970.

"How Men Adjust to a Female Boss." *Business Week*, September 5, 1977.

Hughey, Matthew W. "White Backlash in the 'Post-racial' United States." *Ethnic and Racial Studies* 37, no. 5 (2014): 721–30.

Hull, Gloria T., Patricia Bell Scott, and Barbara Smith, eds. *All the Women Are White, All the Blacks Are Men, but Some of Us Are Brave: Black Women's Studies.* New York: Feminist Press, 1982.

Hunt, Michael H., and Steven I. Levine. *Arc of Empire: America's Wars in Asia from the Philippines to Vietnam.* Durham: University of North Carolina Press, 2014.

Hunter, James Davison. *Culture Wars: The Struggle to Define America.* New York: Basic Books, 1991.

Huyssen, Andreas. *After the Great Divide: Modernism, Mass Culture, Postmodernism.* Bloomington: Indiana University Press, 1986.

Hyman, Louis. "Rethinking the Postwar Corporation: Management, Monopolies, and Markets." In *What's Good for Business: Business and American Politics since World War II.* Kim Phillips-Fein and Julian E. Zelizer, eds. Oxford: Oxford University Press, 2012.

Incredibly Strange Films. San Francisco: RE/Search Publications, 1986.

"Industry Still Needs Updating." *Business Week*, December 7, 1968.

"Interview: Russ Meyer." In *Incredibly Strange Films*. San Francisco: RE/Search Publications, 1986.

"Interview with Friedrich von Hayek: Recession as Inflation's Only Cure." *Business Week*, December 15, 1980.

Interview with John Wayne. *The Great American Picture Star*. BBC, 1976.

Isenberg, Nancy. *White Trash: The 400-Year Untold History of Class in America*. New York: Penguin, 2016.

Isoardi, Steve. *The Dark Tree: Jazz and the Community Arts in Los Angeles*. Berkeley: University of California Press, 2006.

"Is the Merger Fever Really Cooling Off?" *Business Week*, June 21, 1969.

Jackson, Bruce. *Get Your Ass in the Water and Swim like Me: African American Narrative Poetry from Oral Tradition*. New York: Routledge, 2004.

Jacob, Margaret C. *Scientific Culture and the Making of the Industrial West*. Oxford: Oxford University Press, 1997.

Jacobs, Lea. *The Wages of Sin: Censorship and the Fallen Woman Film, 1928–1942*. Berkeley: University of California Press, 1997.

Jacobs, Margaret D. *White Mother to a Dark Race: Settler Colonialism, Maternalism, and the Removal of Indigenous Children in the American West and Australia, 1880–1940*. Lincoln: University of Nebraska Press, 2009.

Jacobson, Cardell K. "Resistance to Affirmative Action: Self-Interest or Racism?" *Journal of Conflict Resolution* 29, no. 2 (1985): 306–29.

Jacobson, Matthew Frye. *Barbarian Virtues: The United States Encounters Foreign Peoples at Home and Abroad, 1876–1917*. New York: Hill & Wang, 2000.

———. *Roots Too: White Ethnic Revival in Post–Civil Rights America*. Cambridge, MA: Harvard University Press, 2006.

———. *Whiteness of a Different Color: European Immigrants and the Alchemy of Race*. Cambridge, MA: Harvard University Press, 1998.

Jaehne, Karen. "*Born in Flames* by Lizzie Borden." *Film Quarterly* 37, no. 4 (Summer 1984): 22–24.

James, C. L. R. *The Black Jacobins: Toussaint L'Ouverture and the San Domingo Revolution*. 2nd ed. rev. New York: Vintage, 1963.

James, Harold, "Finance Capitalism." In *Capitalism: The Reemergence of a Historical Concept*. Jürgen Kocka and Marcel van der Linden, eds. London: Bloomsbury, 2016.

James, Winston. *Hold Aloft the Banner of Ethiopia: Caribbean Radicalism in Early Twentieth-Century America*. London: Verso, 1998.

———. "The IMF and Democratic Socialism in Jamaica." In *The Poverty Brokers: The IMF and Latin America*. London: Latin America Bureau, 1983.

Jameson, Fredric. *Postmodernism, or, the Cultural Logic of Late Capitalism*. Durham, NC: Duke University Press, 1991.

Jayne Cortez and the Firespitters. *There It Is*. Bola Press, 1982. LP BP8201.

Jenkins, Henry. "Exploiting Feminism: An Interview with Stephanie Rothman." *Confessions of an ACA-Fan* blog, October 15, 2007.

———. *The Wow Climax: Tracing the Emotional Impact in Popular Culture*. New York: New York University Press, 2007.

Jenkins, Philip. *Decade of Nightmares: The End of the Sixties and the Making of Eighties America*. Oxford: Oxford University Press, 2006.

Johnson, David K. *The Lavender Scare: The Cold War Persecution of Gays and Lesbians in the Federal Government*. Chicago: University of Chicago Press, 2004.

Johnson, Linton Kwesi. "African Consciousness in Reggae Music: Some Examples." *Black Renaissance* 15, no. 1 (2015): 40–43.

Johnson, Marilynn S. *Street Justice: A History of Police Violence in New York City*. Boston: Beacon, 2004.

Johnson, Robert. *King of the Delta Blues Singers*. Sony Music. LP 65746.

Johnson, Victoria E. *Heartland TV: Prime Time Television and the Struggle for U.S. Identity*. New York: New York University Press, 2008.

Johnson, Walter. *River of Dark Dreams: Slavery and Empire in the Cotton Kingdom*. Cambridge, MA: Belknap Press, 2013.

Jones, Claudia. "Women in the Struggle for Peace and Security." *Political Affairs* (March 1950): 107–23.

Jones, Daniel Stedman. *Masters of the Universe: Hayek, Friedman, and the Birth of Neoliberal Politics*. Princeton, NJ: Princeton University Press, 2012.

Jones, Geoffrey. "Multinationals from the 1930s to the 1980s." In *Leviathans: Multinational Corporations and the New Global History*. Alfred D. Chandler Jr. and Bruce Mazlish, eds. Cambridge: Cambridge University Press, 2005.

Jones, Jacqueline. *Labor of Love, Labor of Sorrow: Black Women, Work, and the Family from Slavery to the Present*. New York: Vintage, 1985.

Jordan, Winthrop D. *White Over Black: American Attitudes toward the Negro, 1550–1812*. Durham: University of North Carolina Press, 1968.

Joseph, Peniel E. *Waiting 'til the Midnight Hour: A Narrative History of Black Power in America*. New York: Holt, 2006.

Joyce, Joyce. "Gil Scott-Heron: Larry Neal's Quintessential Artist." In Gil Scott-Heron, *So Far, So Good*. Chicago: Third World Press, 1990.

Judis, John B. *The Nationalist Revival: Trade, Immigration, and the Revolt against Globalization*. New York: Columbia Global Reports, 2018.

Juhn, Chinhui, Kevin M. Murphy, and Brooks Pierce. "Wage Inequality and the Rise in Returns to Skill." *Journal of Political Economy* 101, no. 3 (1993): 410–42.

Juris, Jeffrey S. *Networking Futures: The Movements against Corporate Globalization*. Durham, NC: Duke University Press, 2008.

Kain. *Blue Guerrilla*. Collectables Records, 1990. CD COL-CD-6501.

Kaplan, Cora, and Bill Schwarz, eds. *James Baldwin: America and Beyond*. Ann Arbor: University of Michigan Press, 2011.

Kaplan, E. Ann. *Women and Film: Both Sides of the Camera*. New York: Routledge, 1983.

Kaplan, E. Ann, ed. *Women in Film Noir*. London: BFI Publishing, 1998.

Kaplan, Jonathan, dir. *Truck Turner*. American International Pictures, 1974. DVD.

Katznelson, Ira. *When Affirmative Action Was White: An Untold History of Racial Inequality in Twentieth-Century America*. New York: Norton, 2005.

Kaufman, Michael. *Jamaica under Manley: Dilemmas of Socialism and Democracy*. Westport, CT: Lawrence Hill, 1985.

Kazin, Michael. *The Populist Persuasion: An American History*. Ithaca, NY: Cornell University Press, 1995.

Kelley, Robin D. G. *Freedom Dreams: The Black Radical Imagination*. Boston: Beacon, 2002.

———. *Race Rebels: Culture, Politics, and the Black Working Class.* New York: Free Press, 1994.
———. *Yo' Mama's Disfunktional! Fighting the Culture Wars in Urban America.* Boston: Beacon, 1997.
Kelljan, Bob, dir. *Rape Squad* (aka *Act of Vengeance*). American International Pictures, 1974.
Kellner, Hans. *Language and Historical Representation: Getting the Story Crooked.* Madison: University of Wisconsin Press, 1989.
Kendi, Ibram X. *Stamped from the Beginning: The Definitive History of Racist Ideas in America.* New York: Nation Books, 2016.
Kennedy, Burt, dir. *Hannie Caulder.* Paramount Pictures, 1971.
Kerr, Robert L. "Creating the Corporate Citizen: Mobil Oil's Editorial-Advocacy Campaign in *The New York Times* to Advance the Right and Practice of Corporate Political Speech, 1970–80. *American Journalism* 21, no. 4 (2004): 39–62.
Kerssens, Niels. "The Database 'Revolution': The Technological and Cultural Origins of the Big-Data-Based Mindset in American Management, 1970s–1980s." *Journal for Media History* 21, no. 2 (2018): 7–29.
Kessler-Harris, Alice. *Out to Work: A History of Wage-Earning Women in the United States.* Oxford: Oxford University Press, 2003.
Keynes, John Maynard. *The General Theory of Employment, Interest, and Money.* New York: Harvest Book, 1964.
Killen, Andreas. *1973 Nervous Breakdown: Watergate, Warhol, and the Birth of Post-Sixties America.* New York: Bloomsbury, 2006.
Kilpatrick, Jacquelyn. *Celluloid Indians: Native Americans and Film.* Lincoln: University of Nebraska Press, 1999.
Kimmel, Michael. *Manhood in America: A Cultural History.* 4th ed. Oxford: Oxford University Press, 2018.
King, Amy K. "'Just like Back Home—Only Different!': Plantation Exploitation in 1970s Women-in-Prison Movies Filmed in the Philippines." *The Global South* 10, no. 2 (Fall 2016): 48–69.
Kinzer, Stephen. *Overthrow: America's Century of Regime Change from Hawaii to Iraq.* New York: Times Books, 2006.
Kirk, Russell. "The Problem of the New Order." In *American Conservative Thought in the Twentieth Century.* William F. Buckley Jr., ed. New York: Bobbs-Merrill, 1970.
Kirkpatrick, Jeanne. "Dictatorships and Double Standards." *Commentary,* November 1979.
Kirshner, Jonathan. *Hollywood's Last Golden Age: Politics, Society, and the Seventies Film in America.* Ithaca, NY: Cornell University Press, 2012.
Kitwana, Bakari. *The Hip Hop Generation: Young Blacks and the Crisis in African American Culture.* New York: Civitas, 2002.
Klein, Christina. *Cold War Orientalism: Asia in the Middlebrow Imagination, 1945–1961.* Berkeley: University of California Press, 2003.
Klein, Naomi. *The Shock Doctrine: The Rise of Disaster Capitalism.* New York: Metropolitan Books, 2007.
Kluge, P. F. "First and Last, a Cowboy." *Life,* January 28, 1972.
Knauft, Bruce M., ed. *Critically Modern: Alternatives, Alterities, Anthropologies.* Bloomington: Indiana University Press, 2002.

Knight, Franklin W., and Colin A. Palmer, eds. *The Modern Caribbean*. Chapel Hill: University of North Carolina Press, 1989.

Kocka, Jürgen, and Marcel van der Linden, eds. *Capitalism: The Reemergence of a Historical Concept*. London: Bloomsbury, 2016.

Koh, Harold Hongju. *The National Security Constitution: Sharing Power after the Iran-Contra Affair*. New Haven, CT: Yale University Press, 1990.

Kolko, Gabriel. *Main Currents in Modern American History*. New York: Pantheon, 1984.

Konings, Martijn. "The Construction of US Financial Power." *Review of International Studies* 35, no. 1 (2009): 69–94.

Kopacsi, Rosemarie, and Audrey Olsen Faulkner. "The Powers That Might Be: The Unity of White and Black Feminists." *Affilia* 3, no. 3 (1988): 33–50.

Krämer, Peter. *The New Hollywood: From Bonnie and Clyde to Star Wars*. New York: Wallflower, 2005.

Krehbiel, Randy. *Tulsa 1921: Reporting a Massacre*. Norman: University of Oklahoma Press, 2019.

Kruse, Kevin M. *White Flight: Atlanta and the Making of Modern Conservatism*. Princeton, NJ: Princeton University Press, 2005.

Kruse, Kevin M., and Julian E. Zelizer. *Fault Lines: A History of the United States since 1974*. New York: Norton, 2019.

Kuhn, Annette. *Women's Pictures: Feminism and Cinema*. 2nd ed. New York: Verso, 1994.

Kunz, William M. *Culture Conglomerates: Consolidation in the Motion Pictures and Television Industries*. Lanham, MD: Rowman & Littlefield, 2007.

Kuznick, Peter J., and James Gilbert, eds. *Rethinking Cold War Culture*. Washington, DC: Smithsonian Institution Press, 2001.

"Labor Seeks Less." *Business Week*, December 21, 1981.

"Labor Woes Cloud Outlook for Economy." *Business Week*, October 14, 1967.

La Chapelle, Peter. *Proud to Be an Okie: Cultural Politics, Country Music, and Migration to Southern California*. Berkeley: University of California Press, 2007.

Ladd, Everett Carll Jr., Marilyn Potter, Linda Basilick, Sally Dantels, and Dana Suszkiw. "The Polls: Taxing and Spending." *Public Opinion Quarterly* 43, no. 1 (Spring 1979): 126–135.

LaFeber, Walter. *The New Empire: An Interpretation of American Expansion, 1860–1898*. Ithaca, NY: Cornell University Press, 1963.

Lahart, Justin. "U.S. Firms Build Up Record Cash Piles." *Wall Street Journal*, June 10, 2010.

Lake, Marilyn, and Henry Reynolds. *Drawing the Global Colour Line: White Men's Countries and the International Challenge of Racial Equality*. Cambridge: Cambridge University Press, 2008.

Lane, Christina. *Feminist Hollywood: From* Born in Flames *to* Point Break. Detroit, MI: Wayne State University Press, 2000.

Lankevich, George J. *New York City: A Short History*. New York: New York University Press, 2002.

Larson, James F. *Television's Window on the World: International Affairs Coverage on the United States Networks*. Norwood, NJ: Ablex, 1984.

Lasch, Christopher. *The Culture of Narcissism: American Life in an Age of Diminishing Expectations*. New York: Norton, 1979.

Lassiter, Matthew D. *The Silent Majority: Suburban Politics in the Sunbelt South.* Princeton, NJ: Princeton University Press, 2006.

Latham, Michael E. *Modernization as Ideology: American Social Science and "Nation Building" in the Kennedy Era.* Chapel Hill: University of North Carolina Press, 2000.

———. *The Right Kind of Revolution: Modernization, Development, and U.S. Foreign Policy from the Cold War to the Present.* Ithaca, NY: Cornell University Press, 2011.

Latour, Bruno. *We Have Never Been Modern.* Catherine Porter, trans. Cambridge, MA: Harvard University Press, 1993.

Lauck, Jon K., and Catherine McNicol Stock, eds. *The Conservative Heartland: A Political History of the Postwar American Midwest.* Lawrence: University Press of Kansas, 2020.

Lawrence, Errol. "Just Plain Common Sense: The 'Roots' of Racism." In Centre for Contemporary Cultural Studies, *The Empire Strikes Back: Race and Racism in 70s Britain.* London: Routledge, 1982.

Lears, T. J. Jackson. "A Matter of Taste: Corporate Cultural Hegemony in a Mass-Consumption Society." In *Recasting America: Culture and Politics in the Age of the Cold War.* Lary May, ed. Chicago: University of Chicago Press, 1989.

———. *No Place of Grace: Antimodernism and the Transformation of American Culture, 1880–1920.* Chicago: University of Chicago Press, 1981.

Lee, Richard E., ed. *The Longue Durée and World-Systems Analysis.* Albany: State University of New York Press, 2012.

Leeming, David. *James Baldwin: A Biography.* New York: Knopf, 1994.

Leff, Leonard J., and Jerold L. Simmons. *The Dame in the Kimono: Hollywood, Censorship, and the Production Code.* 2nd ed. Lexington: University Press of Kentucky, 2001.

Lehman, Katherine J. *Those Girls: Single Women in Sixties and Seventies Popular Culture.* Lawrence: University Press of Kansas, 2011.

Leitner, Helga, Eric S. Sheppard, Kristin Sziarto, and Anant Maringanti. "Contesting Urban Futures: Decentering Neoliberalism." In *Contesting Neoliberalism: Urban Frontiers.* Helga Leitner, Jamie Peck, and Eric S. Sheppard, eds. New York: Guilford, 2007.

Lemann, Nicholas. *Transaction Man: The Rise of the Deal and the Decline of the American Dream.* New York: Farrar, Straus and Giroux, 2019.

Lennon, John. *Sometime in New York City.* Capitol, 1972. LP.

Lentin, Alana, and Gavan Titley. *The Crises of Multiculturalism: Racism in a Neoliberal Age.* London: Zed, 2011.

Lepore, Jill. *The Name of War: King Philip's War and the Origins of American Identity.* New York: Vintage, 1998.

———. *The Whites of Their Eyes: The Tea Party's Revolution and the Battle over American History.* Princeton, NJ: Princeton University Press, 2010.

Lerner, Gerda. *The Creation of Patriarchy.* Oxford: Oxford University Press, 1986.

Leshem, Dotan. *The Origins of Neoliberalism: Modeling the Economy from Jesus to Foucault.* New York: Columbia University Press, 2016.

Lester, Julius. *Look Out, Whitey! Black Power's Gon' Get Your Mama!* New York: Grove, 1968.

Levine, Lawrence W. *Black Culture and Black Consciousness: Afro-American Folk Thought from Slavery to Freedom.* Oxford: Oxford University Press, 1977.

Levine, Mark. *Overthrowing Geography: Jaffa, Tel Aviv, and the Struggle for Palestine.* Berkeley: University of California Press, 2005.

Lewis, George. *Massive Resistance: The White Response to the Civil Rights Movement.* London: Hodder Education, 2006.

Lewis, Jon. "'American Morality Is Not to Be Trifled With': Content Regulation in Hollywood after 1968." In *Silencing Cinema: Film Censorship around the World.* Daniel Biltereyst and Roel Vande Winkel, eds. London: Palgrave Macmillan, 2013.

———. *Hollywood v. Hard Core: How the Struggle over Censorship Created the Modern Film Industry.* New York: New York University Press, 2002.

———. "Money Matters: Hollywood in the Corporate Era." In *The New American Cinema.* Jon Lewis, ed. Durham, NC: Duke University Press, 1998.

Lewis, Jon, ed. *The New American Cinema.* Durham, NC: Duke University Press, 1998.

Lichtenfeld, Eric. *Action Speaks Louder: Violence, Spectacle, and the American Action Movie.* Westport, CT: Praeger, 2004.

Lightnin' Rod. *Hustlers Convention.* Celluloid, 1984. CD CELD6107.

Lim, Bliss Cua. "American Pictures Made by Filipinos: Eddie Romero's Jungle-Horror Exploitation Films." *Spectator* 22, no. 1 (Spring 2002): 23–45.

Lim, Linda Y. C. "Women's Work in Export Factories: The Politics of a Cause." In *Business, Government and Labor: Essays on Economic Development in Singapore and Southeast Asia.* Linda Y. C. Lim, ed. New Jersey: World Scientific, 2018.

Lim, Linda Y. C., ed. *Business, Government and Labor: Essays on Economic Development in Singapore and Southeast Asia.* Hackensack, NJ: World Scientific, 2018.

Limerick, Patricia Nelson. *The Legacy of Conquest: The Unbroken Past of the American West.* New York: W.W. Norton & Company, 1986.

Lind, Michael. "Conservative Elites and the Counterrevolution against the New Deal." In *Ruling America: A History of Wealth and Power in a Democracy.* Steve Fraser and Gary Gerstle, eds. Cambridge, MA: Harvard University Press, 2005.

———. *Land of Promise: An Economic History of the United States.* New York: HarperCollins, 2012.

———. "The Five Worldviews That Define American Politics." Salon.com, January 11, 2011. http://www.salon.com/2011/01/12/lind_five_worldviews/.

———. *Up from Conservatism: Why the Right Is Wrong for America.* New York: Free Press, 1996.

Lindsay, Brendan C. "Humor and Dissonance in California's Native American Genocide." *American Behavioral Scientist* 58, no. 1 (2013): 1–27.

Linethal, Edward T., and Tom Engelhardt, eds. *History Wars: The* Enola Gay *and Other Battles for the American Past.* New York: Holt, 1996.

Lippmann, Walter. *An Inquiry into the Principles of the Good Society.* Boston: Little, Brown, 1938.

Lipsitz, George. *Rainbow at Midnight: Labor and Culture in the 1940s.* Urbana: University of Illinois Press, 1994.

———. *The Possessive Investment in Whiteness: How White People Profit from Identity Politics.* Rev. ed. Philadelphia: Temple University Press, 2006.

Litwack, Leon F. *Trouble in Mind: Black Southerners in the Age of Jim Crow.* New York: Vintage, 1998.

Lloyd, Christopher, Jacob Metzer, and Richard Sutch, eds. *Settler Economies in World History*. Boston: Brill, 2013.

Lopez, Ian Haney. *Dog Whistle Politics: How Coded Racial Appeals Have Reinvented Racism and Wrecked the Middle Class*. Oxford: Oxford University Press, 2015.

Lorde, Audre. *Sister Outsider: Essays & Speeches*. Freedom: The Crossing Press, 1984.

Lott, Eric. *Love and Theft: Blackface Minstrelsy and the American Working Class*. Oxford: Oxford University Press, 1993.

Lowndes, Joseph E. *From the New Deal to the New Right: Race and the Southern Origins of Modern Conservatism*. New Haven, CT: Yale University Press, 2008.

Ludwig, Edward, dir. *Big Jim McLain*. Warner Bros., 1952.

Lumet, Sidney, dir. *Network*. United Artists, 1976. DVD.

Lumpkins, Charles L. *American Pogrom: The East St. Louis Race Riot and Black Politics*. Athens: Ohio University Press, 2008.

Lundberg, Ferdinand, and Marynia F. Farnham. *Modern Woman: The Lost Sex*. New York: Harper, 1947.

Lyotard, Jean-François. *The Postmodern Condition: A Report on Knowledge*. Geoff Bennington and Brian Massumi, trans. Minneapolis: University of Minnesota Press, 1979.

MacCabe, C., ed. *High Theory/Low Culture: Analyzing Popular Television and Film*. Manchester, UK: Manchester University Press, 1986.

MacDonald, J. Fred. *Who Shot the Sheriff? The Rise and Fall of the Television Western*. New York: Praeger, 1987.

MacDonald, Scott, and Lizzie Borden. "Interview with Lizzie Borden." *Feminist Studies* 15, no. 2 (Summer 1989): 327–45.

MacLean, Nancy. *Democracy in Chains: The Deep History of the Radical Right's Stealth Plan for America*. New York: Penguin, 2017.

———. *Freedom Is Not Enough: The Opening of the American Workplace*. Cambridge, MA: Harvard University Press, 2006.

Maier, Charles S. "'Malaise': The Crisis of Capitalism in the 1970s." In *The Shock of the Global: The 1970s in Perspective*. Niall Ferguson, Charles S. Maier, Erez Manela, and Daniel J. Sargent, eds. Cambridge, MA: Belknap Press, 2010.

Mailer, Norman. "The White Negro." *Dissent* (Fall 1957).

Malcolm X. *By Any Means Necessary*. New York: Pathfinder, 1992.

Maloney, Thomas N., and Warren C. Whatley. "Making the Effort: The Contours of Racial Discrimination in Detroit's Labor Markets, 1920–1940." *Journal of Economic History* 55, no. 3 (1995): 465–93.

Mandel, Ernest. *The Second Slump: A Marxist Analysis of Recession in the Seventies*. London: Verso, 1980.

Mandel, Robert. *Global Data Shock: Strategic Ambiguity, Deception, and Surprise in an Age of Information Overload*. Stanford, CA: Stanford University Press, 2019.

Manifestoes of Surrealism. Richard Seaver and Helen R. Lane, trans. Ann Arbor: University of Michigan Press, 1972.

Mann, Geoff. "Why Does Country Music Sound White? Race and the Voice of Nostalgia." *Ethnic and Racial Studies* 31, no. 1 (2008): 73–100.

Mannheim, Karl. *From Karl Mannheim*. 2nd ed. Kurt H. Wolff, ed. New Brunswick, NJ: Transaction, 1993.

Marable, Manning. *Beyond Black and White: Transforming African-American Politics*. London: Verso, 1995.

———. *Black Liberation in Conservative America*. Boston: South End, 1997.

———. *Blackwater: Historical Studies in Race, Class Consciousness, and Revolution*. Niwot: University Press of Colorado, 1993.

———. *How Capitalism Underdeveloped Black America*. Cambridge, MA: South End, 2000.

———. *Race, Reform, and Rebellion: The Second Reconstruction and beyond in Black America, 1945–2006*. 3rd ed. Jackson: University Press of Mississippi, 2007.

Marcus, Alan I., and Howard P. Segal. *Technology in America: A Brief History*. 3rd ed. London: Palgrave, 2018.

Marcus, Daniel. *Happy Days and Wonder Years: The Fifties and the Sixties in Contemporary Cultural Politics*. New Brunswick, NJ: Rutgers University Press, 2004.

Marin, Edwin L., dir. *Tall in the Saddle*. RKO, 1944.

Markusen, Ann. "Cold War Workers, Cold War Communities." In *Rethinking Cold War Culture*. Peter J. Kuznick and James Gilbert, eds. Washington, DC: Smithsonian Institution Press, 2001.

Marshall, Johnathan, Peter Dale Scott, and Jane Hunter. *The Iran Contra Connection: Secret Teams and Covert Operations in the Reagan Era*. Boston: South End Press, 1987.

Martin, Bradford. *The Other Eighties: A Secret History of America in the Age of Reagan*. New York: Hill & Wang, 2011.

Martinez, Gerald, Diana Martinez, and Andres Chavez. *What It Is . . . What It Was! The Black Film Explosion of the '70s in Words and Pictures*. New York: Hyperion, 1998.

Martinot, Steve, and Jared Sexton. "The Avant-Garde of White Supremacy." *Social Identities* 9, no. 2 (2003): 169–81.

Massey, Doreen. "Flexible Sexism." *Environment and Planning D: Society and Space* 9, no. 1 (1991): 31–57.

Massood, Paula J. *Black City Cinema: African American Urban Experiences in Film*. Philadelphia: Temple University Press, 2003.

May, Elaine Tyler. *Homeward Bound: American Families in the Cold War Era*. New York: Basic Books, 2008.

May, Lary. "Introduction." In *Recasting America: Culture and Politics in the Age of the Cold War*. Lary May, ed. Chicago: University of Chicago Press, 1989.

———. "Making the American Consensus: The Narrative of Conversion and Subversion in World War II Films." In *The War in American Culture: Society and Consciousness during World War II*. Lewis A. Erenberg and Susan E. Hirsch, eds. Chicago: University of Chicago Press, 1996.

———. "Movie Star Politics: The Screen Actors' Guild, Cultural Conversion, and the Hollywood Red Scare." In *Recasting America: Culture and Politics in the Age of the Cold War*. Lary May, ed. Chicago: University of Chicago Press, 1989.

May, Lary, ed. *Recasting America: Culture and Politics in the Age of the Cold War*. Chicago: University of Chicago Press, 1989.

Mayer, Martin. *The Bankers: The Next Generation*. New York: Truman Talley, 1997.

Mayer-Schönberger, Viktor, and Thomas Ramge. *Reinventing Capitalism in the Age of Big Data*. New York: Basic Books, 2018.

Mayne, Judith. *Framed: Lesbians, Feminists, and Media Culture*. Minneapolis: University of Minnesota Press, 2000.

Mazursky, Paul, dir. *An Unmarried Woman*. Twentieth Century Fox Film Corporation, 1978.

McBride, Dwight A., ed. *James Baldwin Now*. New York: New York University Press, 1999.

McCarthy, Andrew C. "John Wayne to the Rescue." *National Review Online*, April 14, 2009.

McCarthy, Todd, and Charles Flynn, eds. *Kings of the Bs: Working within the Hollywood System*. New York: Dutton, 1975.

McClendon, McKee J. "Racism, Rational Choice, and White Opposition to Racial Change: A Case Study of Busing." *Public Opinion Quarterly* 49, no. 2 (Summer 1985): 214–33.

McClintock, Anne. *Imperial Leather: Race, Gender and Sexuality in the Colonial Contest*. New York: Routledge, 1995.

McClure, Daniel R. "'Have You Understood Anything I've Said?': The *Dick Cavett Show*, Jimi Hendrix, and the Framing of the Black Counterculture in 1969." *The Sixties* 5, no. 1 (June 2012): 23–46.

———. "The Possession of History and American Innocence: James Baldwin, William F. Buckley, Jr., and the 1965 Cambridge Debate." *James Baldwin Review* 2 (2016): 49–74.

McConahay, John B., Betty B. Hardee, and Valerie Batts. "Has Racism Declined in America? It Depends on Who Is Asking and What Is Asked." *Journal of Conflict Resolution* 25, no. 4 (December 1981): 563–79.

McCurdy, Charles W. "Justice Field and the Jurisprudence of Government-Business Relations: Some Parameters of Laissez-Faire Constitutionalism, 1863–1897." *Journal of American History* 61, no. 4 (March 1975): 970–1005.

McCusker, Kristine M., and Diane Pecknold, eds. *A Boy Named Sue: Gender and Country Music*. Jackson: University Press of Mississippi, 2004.

McElvaine, Robert S. *The Great Depression: America, 1929–1941*. New York: Three Rivers Press, 2009.

McGirr, Lisa. *Suburban Warriors: The Origins of the New American Right*. Princeton, NJ: Princeton University Press, 2001.

McLaglen, Andrew V., dir. *McLintock!* United Artists, 1963.

McMath, Robert C. Jr. *American Populism: A Social History, 1877–1898*. New York: Hill & Wang, 1992.

McQuaid, Kim. *Uneasy Partners: Big Business in American Politics, 1945–1990*. Baltimore: Johns Hopkins University Press, 1994.

Medovoi, Leerom. *Rebels: Youth and the Cold War Origins of Identity*. Durham, NC: Duke University Press, 2005.

Meeuf, Russell. *John Wayne's World: Transnational Masculinity in the Fifties*. Austin: University of Texas Press, 2013.

Melhem, D. H. *Heroism in the New Black Poetry*. Lexington: University Press of Kentucky, 1990.

Mellen, Joan. "The Return of Women to Seventies Films." *Quarterly Review of Film & Video* 3, no. 4 (1978): 525–43.

"Merger Pot Is Boiling Over." *Business Week*, September 23, 1961.

"Merger Tide Is Swelling." *Business Week*, May 29, 1965.

Mervosh, Sarah, and Niraj Chokshi. "Reagan Called Africans 'Monkeys' in Call with Nixon, Tape Reveals." *New York Times*, July 31, 2019.

Meyer, Andrew, dir. *Night of the Cobra Woman*. New World Pictures, 1972.

Meyer, Frank S. "The Recrudescent American Conservatism." In *American Conservative Thought in the Twentieth Century*. William F. Buckley Jr., ed. New York: Bobbs-Merrill, 1970.

Meyers, Richard. *For One Week Only: The World of Exploitation Films*. Guilford, UK: Emery Books, 2011.

———. *For One Week Only: The World of Exploitation Films*. Piscataway, NJ: New Century, 1983.

Mieczkowski, Yanek. *Gerald Ford and the Challenges of the 1970s*. Lexington: University Press of Kentucky, 2005.

Mies, Maria. *Patriarchy & Accumulation on a World Scale: Women in the International Division of Labour*. London: Zed, 1986.

Milanovic, Branko. *Global Inequality: A New Approach for the Age of Globalization*. Cambridge, MA: Belknap Press, 2016.

Miller, H. Laurence Jr. "On the 'Chicago School of Economics.'" *Journal of Political Economy* 70, no. 1 (February 1962): 64–69.

Miller, Michael, dir. *Jackson County Jail*. New World Pictures, 1976. DVD SF 12289.

Mirowski, Philip. "Hell is Truth Seen Too Late." *boundary 2* 46, no. 1 (2019): 1–53.

———. *Never Let a Serious Crisis Go to Waste: How Neoliberalism Survived the Financial Meltdown*. London: Verso, 2013.

———. "Postface: Defining Neoliberalism." In *The Road from Mont Pèlerin*. Philip Mirowski and Dieter Plehwe, eds. Cambridge, MA: Harvard University Press, 2009.

Mirowski, Philip, and Dieter Plehwe, eds. *The Road from Mont Pèlerin: The Making of the Neoliberal Thought Collective*. Cambridge, MA: Harvard University Press, 2009.

Mishel, Lawrence. "Huge Disparity in Share of Total Wealth Gain since 1983." *Economic Policy Institute*, September 15, 2011.

Mitchell, J. Paul. *Race Riots in Black and White*. Englewood Cliffs, NJ: Prentice-Hall, 1970.

Modleski, Tania. "Femininity as Mas(s)querade: A Feminist Approach to Mass Culture." In *High Theory/Low Culture: Analyzing Popular Television and Film*. C. MacCabe, ed. Manchester, UK: Manchester University Press, 1986.

Mohawk, John C. "The 'Disappearing Indian': 20th Century Reality Disproves 19th Century Prediction." *Native Americas* 19, no. 1 (2002): 40.

Monaco, Paul. *The Sixties: 1960–1969*. Berkeley: University of California Press, 2001.

"Monetarists Dent Conventional Wisdom." *Business Week*, June 14, 1969.

"Money Theory Comes Back in Style." *Business Week*, September 18, 1965.

Moreau, Joseph. *Schoolbook Nation: Conflicts over American History Textbooks from the Civil War to the Present*. Ann Arbor: University of Michigan Press, 2010.

Morgan, Jennifer L. *Laboring Women: Reproduction and Gender in New World Slavery*. Philadelphia: University of Pennsylvania Press, 2004.

Morgan, Robin, ed. *Sisterhood Is Powerful: An Anthology of Writings from the Women's Liberation Movement*. New York: Vintage Books, 1970.

Morris, Chris. "Roger Corman: The Schlemiel as Outlaw." In *Kings of the Bs: Working within the Hollywood System*. Todd McCarthy and Charles Flynn, eds. New York: Dutton, 1975.

Morris, Gary. "Roger Corman on New World Pictures: An Interview from 1974." *Bright Lights*, no. 2 (Spring 1975).

Morrison, Toni. *Playing in the Dark: Whiteness and the Literary Imagination*. New York: Vintage, 1992.

Morton, J., V. Vale, and H. Cross. "Russ Meyer: Biography." In *Incredibly Strange Films*. San Francisco: RE/Search Publications, 1986.

Moten, Fred. *In the Break: The Aesthetics of the Black Radical Tradition*. Minneapolis: University of Minnesota Press, 2003.

"Mounting a Long War on Inflation." *Business Week*, February 2, 1968.

Moye, J. Todd. *Let the People Decide: Black Freedom and White Resistance Movements in Sunflower County, Mississippi, 1945–1986*. Durham, NC: University of North Carolina Press, 2006.

Mugge, Robert, dir. *Black Wax*. Mug-Shot, 1983. DVD.

Muhammad, Khalil Gibran. *The Condemnation of Blackness: Race, Crime, and the Making of Modern Urban America*. Cambridge, MA: Harvard University Press, 2010.

Mulargia, Edoardo, dir. *Escape from Hell*. Arturo González Producciones Cinematográficas, 1980. DVD SO-3009.

Müller, Jan-Werner. *What Is Populism?* Philadelphia: University of Pennsylvania Press, 2016.

Muller, Jerry Z. *The Mind and the Market: Capitalism in Western Thought*. New York: Anchor Books, 2002.

"Multinationals: The Public Gives Them Low Marks." *Business Week*, June 9, 1973.

Mulvey, Laura. "Visual Pleasure and Narrative Cinema." *Screen* 16, no. 3 (1975): 6–18.

Murrin, John, Paul Johnson, James McPherson, Alice Fahs, and Gary Gerstle. *Liberty, Equality, Power: A History of the American People*. 7th ed. Boston: Cengage, 2007.

Muse, Benjamin. *The American Negro Revolution: From Nonviolence to Black Power, 1963–1967*. Bloomington: Indiana University Press, 1968.

Nasaw, David. "Gilded Age Gospels." In *Ruling America: A History of Wealth and Power in a Democracy*. Steve Fraser & Gary Gerstle, eds. Cambridge, MA: Harvard University Press, 2005.

Nashawaty, Chris. *Crab Monsters, Teenage Cavemen, and Candy Stripe Nurses: Roger Corman: King of the B Movie*. New York: Abrams, 2013.

Navasky, Victor S. *Naming Names*. New York: Hill & Wang, 2003.

Neal, Larry. "The Black Arts Movement." In *The Black Aesthetic*. Addison Gayle Jr., ed. Garden City, NY: Doubleday, 1971.

Near, Holly. *Simply Love: The Women's Music Collection*. Calico Tracks Music, 2000.

Pieterse, Jan Nederveen. *White on Black: Images of Africa and Blacks in Western Popular Culture*. New Haven, CT: Yale University Press, 1992.

Nelson, Bruce. *Divided We Stand: American Workers and the Struggle for Black Equality*. Princeton, NJ: Princeton University Press, 2002.

"New Look in Mergers Frowned on by FTC." *Business Week*, March 13, 1965.

"New View: Build Here and Export." *Business Week*, January 1, 1972.

"New World Economic Order." *Business Week*, July 24, 1978.

New York Magazine, November 21, 1983.

New York Magazine, December 19, 1983.
New York Magazine, May 21, 1984.
New York Magazine, July 15, 1985.
Newby, I. A., ed. *The Development of Segregationist Thought*. Homewood, IL: Dorsey, 1968.
Ngai, Mae M. *Impossible Subjects: Illegal Aliens and the Making of Modern America*. Princeton, NJ: Princeton University Press, 2004.
Nickel, John. "Disabling African American men: Liberalism and Race Message Films." *Cinema Journal* 44, no. 1 (2004): 25–48.
Nielsen, Aldon Lynn. *Black Chant: Languages of African-American Postmodernism*. Cambridge: Cambridge University Press, 1997.
Nik-Khah, Edward, and Robert Van Horn. "The ascendency of Chicago neoliberalism." In *The Handbook of Neoliberalism*. Simon Springer, Kean Birch, and Julie MacLeavy, eds. New York: Routledge, 2016.
Noah, Timothy. "The United States of Inequality: Introducing the Great Divergence." *Slate*, September 3, 2010.
Norwood, Stephen H. *Strikebreaking & Intimidation: Mercenaries and Masculinity in Twentieth-Century America*. Chapel Hill: University of North Carolina Press, 2002.
"Not Much Pain for Big Business." *Business Week*, January 6, 1968.
Novick, Peter. *That Noble Dream: The "Objectivity Question" and the American Historical Profession*. Cambridge: Cambridge University Press, 1988.
Ogbar, Jeffrey O. G. *Black Power: Radical Politics and African American Identity*. Baltimore: Johns Hopkins University Press, 2004.
Olaniyan, Tejumola. *Arrest the Music! Fela and His Rebel Art and Politics*. Indianapolis: Indiana University Press, 2004.
Omi, Michael, and Howard Winant. *Racial Formation in the United States: From the 1960s to the 1990s*. 2nd ed. New York: Routledge, 1994.
Ongiri, Amy Abugo. *Spectacular Blackness: The Cultural Politics of the Black Power Movement and the Search for a Black Aesthetic*. Charlottesville: University of Virginia Press, 2010.
"Only Mergers Can Bail out the Airlines." *Business Week*, January 9, 1971.
O'Reilly, Kenneth. *"Racial Matters": The FBI's Secret File on Black America, 1960–1972*. New York: Free Press, 1989.
Osterhammel, Jürgen, and Niels P. Petersson. *Globalization: A Short History*. Princeton, NJ: Princeton University Press, 2009.
Oxenberg, Jan, and Lucy Winer. "Born in Flames." *The Independent*, November 1983, 17.
Oyewole, Abiodun, and Umar Bin Hassan. *The Last Poets: On a Mission*. New York: Holt, 1996.
Özbilgin, Mustafa F., ed. *Equality, Diversity and Inclusion at Work: A Research Companion*. Cheltenham, UK: Edward Elgar, 2009.
Padgett, Alan G. "The Bible and Gender Troubles: American Evangelicals Debate Scripture and Submission." *Dialog* 47, no. 1 (2008): 21–26.
Page, Yolanda Williams, ed. *Encyclopedia of African American Women Writers*. Westport: Greenwood, 2007.
Paige, Jeffery M. "Conjuncture, Comparison, and Conditional Theory in Macrosocial Inquiry." *American Journal of Sociology* 105, no. 3 (November 1999): 781–800.
Painter, Nell Irvin. *The History of White People*. New York: Norton, 2010.

Palmer, Colin A. "Identity, Race, and Black Power in Independent Jamaica." In *The Modern Caribbean*. Franklin W. Knight and Colin A. Palmer, eds. Chapel Hill: University of North Carolina Press, 1989.

Palmer, R. Roderick. "The Poetry of Three Revolutionaries: Don L. Lee, Sonia Sanchez, and Nikki Giovanni." In *Modern Black Poets: A Collection of Critical Essays*. Donald B. Gibson, ed. Englewood Cliffs, NJ: Prentice-Hall, 1973.

Panitch, Leo, and Sam Gindin. *The Making of Global Capitalism: The Political Economy of American Empire*. London: Verso, 2012.

Parenti, Michael. "More Bucks from the Bang." *The Progressive*, July 1980.

Parks, Gordon Jr., dir. *Shaft*. Metro-Goldwyn-Mayer, 1971. DVD 67840.

———. *Super Fly*. Warner Brothers Studios, 1972.

Parrott, R. Joseph. "Boycott Gulf! Angolan Oil and the Black Power Roots of American Anti-Apartheid Organizing." *Modern American History* 1, no. 2 (2018): 195–220.

Pascoe, Peggy. *What Comes Naturally: Miscegenation Law and the Making of Race in America*. Oxford: Oxford University Press, 2009.

Pateman, Carole. *The Sexual Contract*. Stanford, CA: Stanford University Press, 1988.

Patterson, James T. "A Conservative Coalition Forms in Congress, 1933–1939." *Journal of American History* 52, no. 4 (1966): 757–72.

———. *The Eve of Destruction: How 1965 Transformed America*. New York: Basic Books, 2012.

Patterson, Orlando. *Freedom and the Making of Western Culture*. New York: Basic Books, 1991.

———. *Slavery and Social Death: A Comparative Study*. Cambridge, MA: Harvard University Press, 1982.

Patterson, Thomas C. *Inventing Western Civilization*. New York: Monthly Review Press, 1997.

Peck, Jamie. *Constructions of Neoliberal Reason*. Oxford: Oxford University Press, 2010.

Perlstein, Rick. *Before the Storm: Barry Goldwater and the Unmaking of the American Consensus*. New York: Hill & Wang, 2001.

———. "Exclusive: Lee Atwater's Infamous 1981 Interview on the Southern Strategy." *The Nation*, November 13, 2012.

———. *Nixonland: The Rise of a President and the Fracturing of America*. New York: Scribner, 2008.

———. *The Invisible Bridge: The Fall of Nixon and the Rise of Reagan*. New York: Simon & Schuster, 2014.

"Petrodollars: Easing the Pressure on Western Banks." *Business Week*, January 20, 1975.

Philips, Lee, dir. *The Girl Most Likely to . . .* ABC Circle Films, 1973.

Phillips, Kevin P. *The Emerging Republican Majority*. New Rochelle, NY: Arlington House, 1969.

———. *The Politics of Rich and Poor: Wealth and the American Electorate in the Reagan Aftermath*. New York: HarperPerennial, 1990.

———. *Wealth and Democracy: A Political History of the American Rich*. New York: Broadway Books, 2002.

Phillips-Fein, Kim. *Fear City: New York's Fiscal Crisis and the Rise of Austerity Politics*. New York: Metropolitan Books, 2017.

———. *Invisible Hands: The Businessmen's Crusade against the New Deal*. New York: Norton, 2009.

Piercy, Marge. "The Grand Coolie Damn." In *Sisterhood Is Powerful: An Anthology of Writings from the Women's Liberation Movement*. Robin Morgan, ed. New York: Vintage Books, 1970.

Piketty, Thomas. *Capital in the Twenty-First Century*. Arthur Goldhammer, trans. Cambridge, MA: Belknap Press, 2014.

Piketty, Thomas, and Emmanuel Saez. "Income Inequality in the United States, 1913–1998." *Quarterly Journal of Economics* 118, no. 1 (February 2003): 1–39.

Pinkney, Alphonso. *The Myth of Black Progress*. Cambridge: Cambridge University Press, 1984.

Platt, Anthony M., ed. *The Politics of Riot Commissions*. New York: Collier Books, 1971.

"*Playboy* Interview: John Wayne." *Playboy*, May 1971.

Plehwe, Dieter. "Introduction." In *The Road from Mont Pèlerin: The Making of the Neoliberal Thought Collective*. Philip Mirowski and Dieter Plehwe, eds. Cambridge, MA: Harvard University Press, 2009.

Plummer, Brenda Gayle. *In Search of Power: African Americans in the Era of Decolonization, 1956–1974*. Cambridge: Cambridge University Press, 2013.

Polanyi, Karl. *The Great Transformation: The Political Economic Origins of Our Time*. Boston: Beacon, 2001.

Pollard, Tom. *Sex and Violence: The Hollywood Censorship Wars*. Boulder, CO: Paradigm, 2009.

Popkin, Jeremy D. *From Herodotus to H-Net: The Story of Historiography*. Oxford: Oxford University Press, 2016.

Porter, Eric. "Affirming and Disaffirming Actions: Remaking Race in the 1970s." In *America in the Seventies*. Beth Bailey and David Farber, eds. Lawrence: University Press of Kansas, 2004.

Porter, Horace A. *Stealing the Fire: The Art and Protest of James Baldwin*. Middletown, CT: Wesleyan University Press, 1989.

Porter, Roy. *The Creation of the Modern World: The Untold Story of the British Enlightenment*. New York: Norton, 2000.

Post, Ted, dir. *Magnum Force*. Warner Bros. Pictures, 1973. DVD.

Postman, Neil. *Amusing Ourselves to Death: Public Discourse in the Age of Show Business*. New York: Penguin Books, 1985.

Prasad, Monica. *The Politics of Free Markets: The Rise of Neoliberal Economic Policies in Britain, France, Germany, and the United States*. Chicago: University of Chicago Press, 2006.

Price, Richard, ed. *Maroon Societies: Rebel Slave Communities in the Americas*. 3rd ed. Baltimore: Johns Hopkins University Press, 1996.

"Profits Hold Up under a Threat of Recession." *Business Week*, July 30, 1979.

"Profits Set Still Another Record." *Business Week*, November 11, 1972.

"Profits Stay Surprisingly Strong." *Business Week*, November 19, 1979.

Quinn, Kate, ed. *Black Power in the Caribbean*. Gainesville: University Press of Florida, 2013.

Rabaka, Reiland. *Africana Critical Theory: Reconstructing the Black Radical Tradition, from W. E. B. Du Bois and C. L. R. James to Frantz Fanon and Amilcar Cabral*. Lanham, MD: Lexington Books, 2010.

Raheja, Michelle H. *Reservation Reelism: Redfacing, Visual Sovereignty, and Representations of Native Americans in Film*. Lincoln: University of Nebraska Press, 2010.

Randolph, Sherie M. "Not to Rely Completely on the Courts: Florynce Kennedy and Black Feminist Leadership in the Reproductive Rights Battle." In *Toward an Intellectual History of Black Women*. Mia E. Bay, Farah J. Griffin, Martha S. Jones, and Barbara D. Savage, eds. Chapel Hill: University of North Carolina Press, 2015.

Ray, Robert B. *A Certain Tendency of the Hollywood Cinema, 1930–1980*. Princeton, NJ: Princeton University Press, 1985.

"Reagan's Plan: Sidestep Unions, Woo Workers." *Business Week*, September 15, 1980.

Reddy, Helen. *The Woman I Am: The Definitive Collection*. Capitol Records, 2006. CD 09463-57613-2-0.

Reeves, Marcus. *Somebody Scream! Rap Music's Rise to Prominence in the Aftershock of Black Power*. New York: Faber and Faber, 2008.

Reich, Robert B. "The Executive's New Clothes." *New Republic*, May 13, 1985.

Reid, Mark A. *Redefining Black Film*. Berkeley: University of California Press, 1993.

Reinarman, Craig, and Harry G. Levine. "The Crack Attack: America's Latest Drug Scare, 1986–1992." In *Images of Issues: Typifying Contemporary Social Problems*. Joel Best, ed. 2nd ed. New York: Aldine de Gruyter, 1995.

Reiss, Albert J. "Police Brutality—Answers to Key Questions." *Trans-action* 5, no. 8 (1968): 10–19.

Report of the National Advisory Commission on Civil Disorders. New York: Bantam, 1968.

Reynolds, Simon, and Joy Press. *The Sex Revolts: Gender, Rebellion, and Rock 'n' Roll*. Cambridge, MA: Harvard University Press, 1995.

Rhoalyn, Felix G. "New York City Mirrors the U.S." *Business Week*, March 27, 1978.

Robbins, Rossell Hope. "Social awareness and semantic change." *American Speech* 24, no. 2 (1949): 156–58.

Roberts, Dorothy E. *Killing the Black Body: Race, Reproduction, and the Meaning of Liberty*. New York: Vintage, 1997.

Roberts, Randy, and James S. Olson. *John Wayne: American*. New York: Free Press, 1995.

Robin, Corey. *The Reactionary Mind: Conservatism from Edmund Burke to Sarah Palin*. Oxford: Oxford University Press, 2011.

Robins, Nick. *The Corporation that Changed the World: How the East India Company Shaped the Modern Multinational*. 2nd ed. London: Pluto, 2012.

Robinson, Cedric J. *Black Marxism: The Making of the Black Radical Tradition*. Chapel Hill: University of North Carolina Press, 1983.

———. *Black Marxism: The Making of the Black Radical Tradition*. 2nd ed. Chapel Hill: University of North Carolina Press, 2000.

———. *Forgeries of Memory and Meaning: Blacks and the Regimes of Race in American Theater and Film before World War II*. Chapel Hill: University of North Carolina Press, 2007.

Robinson, Wanda. *The Soul Jazz of Wanda Robinson*. Castle Music, 2002. CD 06076 81220-2.

Robyn, Dorothy. *Braking the Special Interests: Trucking Deregulation and the Politics of Policy Reform*. Chicago: University of Chicago Press, 1987.

Rodgers, Daniel T. *Age of Fracture*. Cambridge, MA: Belknap Press, 2011.

Rodney, Walter. *The Groundings with My Brothers*. London: Bogle-L'Ouverture Publications, 1969.

Rodríguez, Dylan. "Goldwater's Left Hand: Post-raciality and the Roots of the Post-racial Racist State." *Cultural Dynamics* 26, no. 1 (2014): 29–51.

———. *White Reconstruction: Domestic Warfare and the Logics of Genocide*. New York: Fordham University Press, 2020.

Roediger, David R. *The Wages of Whiteness: Race and the Making of the American Working Class*. London: Verso, 1999.

Romero, Eddie, dir. *Black Mama, White Mama*. American International Pictures, 1972.

———. *Savage Sisters*. American International Pictures, 1974.

———. *The Woman Hunt*. New World Pictures, 1973.

Rose, Tricia. *Black Noise: Rap Music and Black Culture in Contemporary America*. Hanover, NH: Wesleyan University Press, 1994.

Rosen, Ruth. *The World Split Open: How the Modern Women's Movement Changed America*. New York: Penguin, 2000.

Rosenberg, Emily S. *A Date Which Will Live: Pearl Harbor in American Memory*. Durham, NC: Duke University Press, 2003.

———. *Financial Missionaries to the World: The Politics and Culture of Dollar Diplomacy, 1900–1930*. Durham, NC: Duke University Press, 2003.

———. *Spreading the American Dream: American Economic and Cultural Expansion, 1890–1945*. New York: Hill & Wang, 1982.

Ross, Robert. *A Concise History of South Africa*. Cambridge: Cambridge University Press, 1999.

Roth, Benita. *Separate Roads to Feminism: Black, Chicana, and White Feminist Movements in America's Second Wave*. Cambridge: Cambridge University Press, 2004.

Roth, William V. Jr. "How Tax Cuts Can Pay for Themselves." *Business Week*, September 11, 1978.

Rothman, Adam. "The 'Slave Power' in the United States, 1783–1865." In *Ruling America: A History of Wealth and Power in a Democracy*. Steve Fraser and Gary Gerstle, eds. Cambridge, MA: Harvard University Press, 2005.

Rothman, Stephanie, dir. *Terminal Island*. Dimension Pictures, 1973. DVD CRD 2036.

Roush, Lana. "Don't Liberate Me." RCA, 1972. 45rpm BWKM-1640.

Rowe, Daniel. "Local and Regional Countercurrents: Reagan Democrats and the Politics of the Rust Belt, 1976–1988." In *The Conservative Heartland: A Political History of the Postwar American Midwest*. Jon K. Lauck and Catherine McNicol Stock, eds. Lawrence: University Press of Kansas, 2020.

Russo, Vito. *The Celluloid Closet: Homosexuality in the Movies*. Rev. ed. New York: Harper and Row, 1987.

Ryan, Mary P. *Cradle of the Middle Class: The Family in Oneida County, New York, 1790–1865*. Cambridge: Cambridge University Press, 1981.

Ryan, Michael, and Douglas Kellner. *Camera Politica: The Politics and Ideology of Contemporary Hollywood Film*. Bloomington: Indiana University Press, 1988.

Safa, Helen I. "Runaway Shops and Female Employment: The Search for Cheap Labor." *Signs* 7, no. 2 (Winter 1981): 418–33.

Sala-Molins, Louis. *Dark Side of the Light: Slavery and the French Enlightenment*. John Conteh-Morgan, trans. Minneapolis: University of Minnesota Press, 2006.

Sanchez, Sonia. *A Sun Lady for All Seasons Reads Her Poetry*. Folkways Records, 1971. LP.
Sandbrook, Dominic. *Mad as Hell: The Crisis of the 1970s and the Rise of the Populist Right*. New York: Knopf, 2011.
Santiago, Cirio H., dir. *The Muthers*. Dimension Pictures, 1976.
———. *T.N.T. Jackson*. New World Pictures, 1974.
Sargent, Lydia, ed. *Women and Revolution: A Discussion of the Unhappy Marriage of Marxism and Feminism*. Boston: South End, 1981.
Saunders, Frances Stonor. *The Cultural Cold War: The CIA and the Worlds of Arts and Letters*. New York: New Press, 1999.
Sayre, Nora. *Running Time: Films of the Cold War*. New York: Dial Press, 1982.
Schaefer, Eric. *"Bold! Daring! Shocking! True!": A History of Exploitation Films, 1919–1959*. Durham, NC: Duke University Press, 1999.
Schein, Virginia E. "Women in Management: Reflections and Projections." *Women in Management Review* 22, no. 1 (2007): 6–18.
Schenk, Catherine R. "The Origins of the Eurodollar Market in London: 1955–1963." *Explorations in Economic History* 35, no. 2 (1998): 221–38.
Schrecker, Ellen W. *No Ivory Tower: McCarthyism and the Universities*. Oxford: Oxford University Press, 1986.
Schui, Florian. *Austerity: The Great Failure*. New Haven, CT: Yale University Press, 2014.
Schulman, Bruce J. *From Cotton Belt to Sunbelt: Federal Policy, Economic Development, and the Transformation of the South, 1938–1980*. Durham, NC: Duke University Press, 1994.
———. *The Seventies: The Great Shift in American Culture, Society, and Politics*. New York: Da Capo, 2002.
Schultz, Kevin M. *Buckley and Mailer: The Difficult Friendship That Shaped the Sixties*. New York: Norton, 2015.
Schumach, Murray. *The Face on the Cutting Room Floor: The Story of Movie and Television Censorship*. New York: Picador, 1964.
Schwartz, Danielle B. "You Look Good Wearing My Future": Resisting Neoliberalism in John Hughes's *Pretty in Pink* and *Some Kind of Wonderful*. *The Journal of Popular Culture* 51, no. 2 (2018): 379–98.
Schwarz, John E. *America's Hidden Success: A Reassessment of Public Policy from Kennedy to Reagan*. Rev. ed. New York: Norton, 1988.
Scorsese, Martin, dir. *Alice Doesn't Live Here Anymore*. Warner Bros. Pictures, 1974.
Scott, David. *Conscripts of Modernity: The Tragedy of Colonial Enlightenment*. Durham, NC: Duke University Press, 2004.
Scott-Heron, Gil. *Free Will*. Bluebird, 2001. CD 09026-63843-2.
———. *I'm New Here: Gil Scott-Heron*. XL Recordings, 2010. CD XLCD471.
———. *Now and Then: The Poems of Gil Scott-Heron*. New York: Canongate U.S., 2000.
———. *Pieces of a Man*. Flying Dutchman, 1971. CD 66627-2.
———. *Reflections*. Arista, 1981. CD 254 094.
———. *Small Talk at 125th and Lenox*. Flying Dutchman, 1970. LP 10131.
———. *Small Talk at 125th and Lenox: A Collection of Black Poems*. New York: World Publishing, 1970.
———. *So Far, So Good*. Chicago: Third World Press, 1990.
———. *Spirits*. TVT, 1994. CD 4310-2.

———. *The Last Holiday: A Memoir.* New York: Grove, 2012.

———. *The Mind of Gil Scott-Heron: A Collection of Poetry and Music.* TVT Records, 2000. CD TVT 4360-2.

Scott-Heron, Gil, and Brian Jackson. *From South Africa to South Carolina.* TVT Records, 1998. CD 4340-2.

———. *Midnight Band: The First Minute of a New Day.* TVT Records, 1998. CD 4350-2.

———. *Winter in America.* Strata East 1973. LP 19742.

"Secretaries Play Hard to Get." *Business Week*, June 24, 1972.

Segrave, Kerry. *Drive-In Theaters: A History from Their Inception in 1933.* Jefferson, NC: McFarland, 1992.

Self, Robert O. *All in the Family: The Realignment of American Democracy since the 1960s.* New York: Hill & Wang, 2012.

———. *American Babylon: Race and the Struggle for Postwar Oakland.* Princeton, NJ: Princeton University Press, 2003.

Sennett, Richard. *The Culture of the New Capitalism.* New Haven, CT: Yale University Press, 2006.

Serwer, Adam. "Jeff Sessions's Unqualified Praise for a 1924 Immigration Law." *The Atlantic*, January 10, 2017.

Sexton, Jared. *Amalgamation Schemes: Antiblackness and the Critique of Multiracialism.* Minneapolis: University of Minnesota Press, 2008.

———. *Black Masculinity and the Cinema of Policing.* New York: Palgrave Macmillan, 2017.

———. "The Ruse of Engagement: Black Masculinity and the Cinema of Policing." *American Quarterly* 61, no. 1 (2009): 39–63.

"Sexual Harassment Lands Companies in Court." *Business Week*, October 1, 1979.

Shammas, Carole. "Re-assessing the Married Women's Property Acts." *Journal of Women's History* 6, no. 1 (1994): 9–30.

Shannon, Bobby. "Women's Liberation's for the Birds." Major Recording Co., n.d. 45rpm NR3870-2.

Shapiro, Thomas, Tatjana Meschede, and Sam Osoro. *The Roots of the Widening Racial Wealth Gap: Explaining the Black-White Economic Divide.* Waltham, MA: Institute on Assets and Social Policy, 2013.

Shaw, Susan M. "Gracious Submission: Southern Baptist Fundamentalists and Women." *NWSA Journal* 20, no. 1 (2008): 51–77.

Shear, Barry, dir. *Across 110th Street.* United Artists, 1972.

Sherwood, Glynis. "Anarcha-Filmmaker: An Interview with Lizzie Borden." In *Only a Beginning: An Anarchist Anthology.* Allan Antiliff, ed. Vancouver: Arsenal Pulp Press, 2004.

Shlaes, Amity. *The Forgotten Man: A New History of the Great Depression.* New York: HarperCollins, 2007.

"Shock Treatment for Inflation." *Business Week*, March 3, 1980.

Shonk, Kenneth L. Jr., and Daniel Robert McClure. *Historical Theory and Methods through Popular Music, 1970–2000: "Those Are the New Saints."* London: Palgrave Macmillan, 2017.

Siegel, Don, dir. *Coogan's Bluff.* Universal Pictures, 1968.

———. *Dirty Harry.* Warner Bros. Pictures, 1971.

Sieving, Christopher. *Soul Searching: Black-Themed Cinema from the March on Washington to the Rise of Blaxploitation*. Middletown, CT: Wesleyan University Press, 2011.

Sigler, Jay A., ed. *The Conservative Tradition in American Thought*. New York: Capricorn Books, 1969.

Silk, Leonard, and David Vogel. *Ethics and Profits: The Crisis of Confidence in American Business*. New York: Simon & Schuster, 1976.

Silver, Alain, and James Ursini, eds. *Film Noir Reader*. New York: Limelight Editions, 1996.

Simmon, Scott. *The Invention of the Western Film: A Cultural History of the Genre's First Half Century*. Cambridge: Cambridge University Press, 2003.

Sims, Yvonne D. *Women of Blaxploitation: How the Black Action Film Heroine Changed American Popular Culture*. Jefferson, NC: McFarland, 2006.

Singh, Nikhil Pal. *Black Is a Country: Race and the Unfinished Struggle for Democracy*. Cambridge, MA: Harvard University Press, 2004.

Singh, Simboonath. "Resistance, Essentialism, and Empowerment in Black Nationalist Discourse in the African Diaspora: A Comparison of the Back to Africa, Black Power, and Rastafari Movements." *Journal of African American Studies* 8, no. 3 (Winter 2004): 18–36.

Sirota, David. "The Legend of the Persecuted White Guy." Salon.com, April 18, 2011.

Sites, William. *Remaking New York: Primitive Globalization and the Politics of Urban Community*. Minneapolis: University of Minnesota Press, 2003.

Skinner, Rob. *The Foundations of Anti-Apartheid: Liberal Humanitarians and Transnational Activists in Britain and the United States, c. 1919–64*. New York: Palgrave Macmillan, 2010.

Sklar, Holly, ed. *Trilateralism: The Trilateral Commission and Elite Planning for World Management*. Montreal: Black Rose Books, 1980.

Sklar, Robert. *Movie-Made America: A Cultural History of American Movies*. Rev. ed. New York: Vintage, 1994.

Skrentny, John David. "The Effect of the Cold War on African-American Civil Rights: America and the World Audience, 1945–1968." *Theory and Society* 27, no. 2 (1998): 237–85.

Slatzer, Robert F., dir. *No Substitute For Victory*. Alaska Pictures, 1970.

Slobodian, Quinn. *Globalists: The End of Empire and the Birth of Neoliberalism*. Cambridge, MA: Harvard University Press, 2018.

Slotkin, Richard. *Gunfighter Nation: The Myth of the Frontier in Twentieth-Century America*. Norman: University of Oklahoma Press, 1998.

———. *Regeneration through Violence: The Mythology of the American Frontier, 1600–1860*. Middletown, CT: Wesleyan University Press, 1973.

Smethurst, James Edwards. *The Black Arts Movement: Literary Nationalism in the 1960s and 1970s*. Chapel Hill: University of North Carolina Press, 2005.

Smiley, Calvin John, and David Fakunle. "From 'Brute' to 'Thug': The Demonization and Criminalization of Unarmed Black Male Victims in America." *Journal of Human Behavior in the Social Environment* 26, nos. 3–4 (2016): 350–66.

Smith, Adam. *The Wealth of Nations*. Edwin Cannan, ed. New York: Bantam Classic, 2003.

Smith, Andrea. "Not an Indian Tradition: The Sexual Colonization of Native Peoples." *Hypatia* 18, no. 2 (2003): 70–85.

Smith, Anthony D. "The Origins of Nations." *Ethnic and Racial Studies* 12, no. 3 (1989): 340–67.

Smith, Jason Scott. "The Liberal Invention of the Multinational Corporation: David Lilienthal and Postwar Capitalism." In *What's Good for Business: Business and American Politics since World War II*. Kim Phillips-Fein and Julian E. Zelizer, eds. Oxford: Oxford University Press, 2012.

Smith, Patti. *Easter*. Arista Records, 1978. LP 4171.

Smith, Sharon. "Black Feminism and Intersectionality." *International Socialist Review* 91, no. 11 (2013). https://isreview.org/issue/91/black-feminism-and-intersectionality.

Smukler, Maya Montañez. *Liberating Hollywood: Women Directors and the Feminist Reform of 1970s American Cinema*. New Brunswick, NJ: Rutgers University Press, 2018.

Snipp, C. Matthew, and Sin Yi Cheung. "Changes in Racial and Gender Inequality since 1970." *The ANNALS of the American Academy of Political and Social Science* 663, no. 1 (2016): 80–98.

Sobel, Robert. *The Age of Giant Corporations: A Microeconomic History of American Business, 1914–1992*. 3rd ed. Westport, CT: Praeger, 1993.

Solinger, Rickie. *Wake Up Little Susie: Single Pregnancy and Race before Roe v. Wade*. 2nd ed. New York: Routledge, 2000.

"Special Report: Multinational Companies." *Business Week*, April 20, 1963.

Spiro, David E. *The Hidden Hand of American Hegemony: Petrodollar Recycling and International Markets*. Ithaca, NY: Cornell University Press, 1999.

Spoonie Gee. *Godfather of Hip-Hop: Classic Old-School Hip-Hop 1979–1988*. Tuff City Records, 2004. CD OSF CD 4014.

Springer, Kimberly. *Living for the Revolution: Black Feminist Organizations, 1968–1980*. Durham, NC: Duke University Press, 2005.

Springer, Simon, Kean Birch, and Julie MacLeavy, eds. *The Handbook of Neoliberalism*. New York: Routledge, 2016.

Standing, Guy. "Global Feminization through Flexible Labor." *World Development* 17, no. 7 (1989): 1077–95.

———. "Global Feminization Through Flexible Labor: A Theme Revisited." *World Development* 27, no. 3 (1999): 583–602.

Standley, Fred L., and Louis H. Pratt, eds. *Conversations with James Baldwin*. Jackson: University Press of Mississippi, 1989.

Stanley, Sandra Kumamoto, ed. *Other Sisterhoods: Literary Theory and U.S. Women of Color*. Urbana: University of Illinois Press, 1998.

Starrett, Jack, dir. *Cleopatra Jones*. Warner Brothers Studios, 1973. DVD 11275.

Stearns, Linda Brewster, and Kenneth D. Allan. "Economic Behavior in Institutional Environments: The Corporate Merger Wave of the 1980s." *American Sociological Review* 61, no. 4 (August 1996): 699–718.

Steigerwald, David. *The Sixties and the End of Modern America*. New York: St. Martin's, 1995.

Stein, Judith. *Pivotal Decade: How the United States Traded Factories for Finance in the Seventies*. New Haven, CT: Yale University Press, 2010.

Stein, Marc. *Rethinking the Gay and Lesbian Movement*. New York: Routledge, 2012.

Steinberg, Stephen. "'Race Relations': The Problem with the Wrong Name." *New Politics* 8, no. 2 (Winter 2001). https://archive.newpol.org/issue30/steinb30.htm#.

———. *Turning Back: The Retreat from Racial Justice in American Thought and Policy.* Boston: Beacon, 1995.

Steinmetz, Jay Douglas. *Beyond Free Speech and Propaganda: The Political Development of Hollywood, 1907–1927.* Lanham, MD: Lexington Books, 2018.

Stepan-Norris, Judith, and Maurice Zeitlin. *Left Out: Reds and America's Industrial Unions.* Cambridge: Cambridge University Press, 2003.

Stern, Alexandra Minna. *Eugenic Nation: Faults and Frontiers of Better Breeding in Modern America.* Berkeley: University of California Press, 2005.

Stiglitz, Joseph E. *Globalization and Its Discontents Revisited: Anti-globalization in the Era of Trump.* New York: Norton, 2017.

Stoler, Ann Laura. *Carnal Knowledge and Imperial Power: Race and the Intimate in Colonial Rule.* Berkeley: University of California Press, 2002.

Sugrue, Thomas J. *The Origins of the Urban Crisis: Race and Inequality in Postwar Detroit.* Princeton, NJ: Princeton University Press, 1996.

———. *Sweet Land of Liberty: The Forgotten Struggle for Civil Rights in the North.* New York: Random House, 2008.

Sundstrom, William A. "The Color Line: Racial Norms and Discrimination in Urban Labor Markets, 1910–1950." *Journal of Economic History* 54, no. 2 (1994): 382–96.

Tansel, Cemal Burak. *States of Discipline: Authoritarian Neoliberalism and the Contested Reproduction of Capitalist Order.* Lanham, MD: Rowman & Littlefield, 2017.

Taylor, Clarence. *Fight the Power: African Americans and the Long History of Police Brutality in New York City.* New York: New York University Press, 2019.

Taylor, Ella. *Prime-Time Families: Television Culture in Postwar America.* Berkeley: University of California Press, 1989.

Taylor, Ula Y. "'Read[ing] Men and Nations': Women in the Black Radical Tradition." *Souls* 1, no. 4 (1999): 72–80.

"The American Dream and the American Negro." *New York Times*, May 7, 1965, SM32.

The Best of Charlie's Angels. Columbia Tristar Home Entertainment, 2003. DVD 00660.

The Black Public Sphere Collective, eds. *The Black Public Sphere: A Public Culture Book.* Chicago: University of Chicago Press, 1995.

"The Corporate Image: PR to the Rescue." *Business Week*, January 22, 1979.

"The Corporate Woman: Stress Has No Gender." *Business Week*, November 15, 1976.

"The Corporate Woman: The 100 Top Corporate Women." *Business Week*, June 21, 1976.

"The Corporate Woman: Up the Ladder, Finally." *Business Week*, November 24, 1975.

"The Corporate Woman: When Career Couples Have Conflicts of Interest." *Business Week*, December 13, 1976.

"The Corporate Woman: Why So Few Women Have Made It to the Top." *Business Week*, June 5, 1978.

"The Deadlock over the Dollar." *Business Week*, September 25, 1971.

"The Debt Economy." *Business Week*, October 12, 1974.

"The Decline of U.S. Power." *Business Week*, March 12, 1979.

The Definitive Groove Collection Grandmaster Flash, Melle Mel & the Furious Five. Rhino, 2006. CD R2 74081.

"The Financial Noose Draws Tighter." *Business Week*, January 2, 1971.

The Harder They Come. Mango Records, 1972. LP SMAS-7400.
"The Implications of Oil Company Profits." *Business Week*, August 18, 1980.
The Last Poets. *At Last.* Blue Thumb Records, 1973. LP BTS 52.
———. *The Last Poets.* Fuel 2000 Records, 2002. CD 302 061 226 2.
———. *This Is Madness.* Celluloid, 1984. LP CELL 6105.
"The Multinationals Reap a Windfall." *Business Week*, February 17, 1973.
"The Neo-liberals Push Their Own Brand of Reform." *Business Week*, January 31, 1983.
"The New Banking." *Business Week*, September 15, 1973.
"The New Diversification Oil Game." *Business Week*, April 24, 1978.
The New Haven and Chicago Women's Liberation Rock Band. *Mountain Moving Day.* Rounder Records, 1972. LP 4001.
"The New Pay Push for Women." *Business Week*, December 17, 1979.
The Original Last Poets. *Right On!* Collectable Records, 1990. CD COL-6500.
"Theorizing for Goldwater?" *Business Week*, November 23, 1963.
"The Payoff of Wage Moderation." *Business Week*, January 18, 1982.
The Poverty Brokers: The IMF and Latin America. London: Latin America Bureau, 1983.
"The Race Crisis Coming to a Head." *Business Week*, June 8, 1963.
"The Regulators Can't Go on This Way." *Business Week*, February 28, 1970.
"The Reindustrialization of America." *Business Week*, June 30, 1980.
"The Right Way to Spur R&D." *Business Week*, July 3, 1978.
The Rolling Stones. *Aftermath.* ABKCO Records, 1966. LP 7476-1.
The Rolling Stones. "Brown Sugar/Bitch/Let It Rock." Rolling Stones Records, 1971. 7" RS-19100.
"The Second War between the States." *Business Week*, May 17, 1976.
"The U.S. Can't Afford What Labor Wants." *Business Week*, April 11, 1970.
"The Warning of the Riot Commission." *Business Week*, March 9, 1968.
The Watts Prophets. *The Black Voices: On the Streets in Watts.* ALA, 1969. LP ALA 1970.
———. *Things Gonna Get Greater: The Watts Prophets 1969–1971.* Water, 2005. CD water157.
"The Week." *National Review*, August 24, 1957, 149.
The Willis Brothers. "Women's Liberation." Starday, n.d. 45rpm S-9259.
"The World Economy." *Business Week*, July 6, 1974.
"The World Tests Friedman's Theories." *Business Week*, November 1, 1976.
Thomas, Pat. *Listen, Whitey! The Sights and Sounds of Black Power, 1965–1975.* Seattle: Fantagraphics Books, 2012.
Thörn, Håkan. *Anti-Apartheid and the Emergence of a Global Civil Society.* New York: Palgrave Macmillan, 2006.
Thrower, Stephen. *Nightmare USA: The Untold Story of the Exploitation Independents.* 2nd ed. Godalming, UK: FAB Press, 2008.
"Time of Testing for Conglomerates." *Business Week*, March 2, 1968.
Toffler, Alvin. *Future Shock.* New York: Bantam Book, 1970.
Tohill, Cathal, and Pete Tombs. *Immoral Tales: European Sex and Horror Movies 1956–1984.* New York: St. Martin's Griffin, 1994.
Tolnay, Steward E., and E. M. Beck. *A Festival of Violence: An Analysis of Southern Lynchings, 1882–1930.* Chicago: University of Illinois Press, 1992.
Toop, David. *The Rap Attack: African Jive to New York Hip Hop.* Boston: South End, 1984.

Trachtenberg, Alan. *The Incorporation of America: Culture and Society in the Gilded Age.* New York: Hill & Wang, 1982.

Trattner, Walter I. *From Poor Law to Welfare State: A History of Social Welfare in America.* New York: Simon & Schuster, 2007.

Trojan Nyahbinghi Box Set. Trojan Records, 2003. CD TJETD094.

"Trouble Plagues the House of Labor." *Business Week*, October 28, 1972.

Trouillot, Michel-Rolph. *Global Transformations: Anthropology and the Modern World.* New York: Palgrave Macmillan, 2003.

———. "North Atlantic Universals: Analytical Fictions, 1492–1945." *South Atlantic Quarterly* 101, no. 4 (Fall 2002): 839–58.

———. *Silencing the Past: Power and the Production of History.* Boston: Beacon, 1995.

———. "The Otherwise Modern: Caribbean Lessons from the Savage Slot." In *Critically Modern: Alternatives, Alterities, Anthropologies.* Bruce M. Knauft, ed. Bloomington: Indiana University Press, 2002.

United States. *Catalog of the Big Picture Films.* Washington, DC: Department of the Army, Office of the Chief of Information, 1965.

Urquhart, Michael A., and Marillyn A. Hewson. "Unemployment Continued to Rise in 1982 as Recession Deepened." *Monthly Labor Review* 106 (February 1983): 3.

"U.S. Industry Migrates Abroad to Tap Markets of the World." *Business Week*, January 3, 1959.

Van Deburg, William L. *New Day in Babylon: The Black Power Movement and American Culture, 1965–1975.* Chicago: University of Chicago Press, 1992.

———. "Villains, Demons, and Social Bandits: White Fear of the Black Cultural Revolution." In *Media, Culture, and the Modern African American Freedom Struggle.* Brian Ward, ed. Gainesville: University Press of Florida, 2001.

Van Horn, Rob. "Reinventing Monopoly and the Role of Corporations: The Roots of Chicago Law and Economics." In *The Road from Mont Pèlerin: The Making of the Neoliberal Thought Collective.* Philip Mirowski and Dieter Plehwe, eds. Cambridge, MA: Harvard University Press, 2009.

Van Horn, Rob, and Philip Mirowski. "The Rise of the Chicago School of Economics and the Birth of Neoliberalism." In *The Road from Mont Pèlerin: The Making of the Neoliberal Thought Collective.* Philip Mirowski and Dieter Plehwe, eds. Cambridge, MA: Harvard University Press, 2009.

"Vanishing Innovation." *Business Week*, July 3, 1978.

Vatter, Harold G. *The U.S. Economy in the 1950s: An Economic History.* Chicago: University of Chicago Press, 1963.

Veracini, Lorenzo. *Settler Colonialism: A Theoretical Overview.* New York: Palgrave Macmillan, 2010.

———. *The Settler Colonial Present.* New York: Palgrave, 2015.

Vincent, Rickey. *Funk: The Music, the People, and the Rhythm of the One.* New York: St. Martin's Griffin, 1996.

Viola, Joe, dir. *The Hot Box.* New World Pictures, 1972.

Von Eschen, Penny M. *Race against Empire: Black Americans and Anticolonialism, 1937–1957.* Ithaca, NY: Cornell University Press, 1997.

Von Mises, Ludwig. "How Liberty Defined Western Civilization." In *Money, Method, and the Market Process.* Richard M. Ebeling, ed. Norwell, MA: Kluwer Academic, 1990.

Wacquant, Loïc. "From Slavery to Mass Incarceration: Rethinking the 'Race Question' in the US." *New Left Review* 13 (January–February 2002): 41–60.

———. *Punishing the Poor: The Neoliberal Government of Social Insecurity.* Durham, NC: Duke University Press, 2009.

Wade, Michael. "Johnny Rebel and the Cajun Roots of Right-Wing Rock." *Popular Music & Society* 30, no. 4 (October 2007): 493–512.

Wager, Jans B. *Dames in the Driver's Seat: Rereading Film Noir.* Austin: University of Texas Press, 2005.

Wallace, Michele. "Race, Gender and Psychoanalysis in Forties Film: *Lost Boundaries, Home of the Brave* and *The Quiet One.*" In *Black American Cinema.* Manthia Diawara, ed. New York: Routledge, 1993.

Wallenstein, Barry. "The Jazz-Poetry Connection." *Performing Arts Journal* 4, no. 3 (1980): 122–34.

Wallerstein, Immanuel, ed. *The Modern World-System in the Longue Durée.* Boulder, CO: Paradigm, 2004.

Walsh, Francis R. "The Films We Never Saw: American Movies View Organized Labor, 1934–1954." *Labor History* 27, no. 4 (1986): 564–80.

Wambeke, Ann Marie. "Politics Makes for Strange Bedfellows: Republican Feminists Fight for Abortion Rights in Michigan, 1968–1982." In *The Conservative Heartland: A Political History of the Postwar American Midwest.* Jon K. Lauck and Catherine McNicol Stock, eds. Lawrence: University Press of Kansas, 2020.

Wanniski, Jude. *The Way the World Works.* Washington, DC: Regnery, 1978.

Wapshott, Nicholas. *Keynes Hayek: The Clash That Defined Modern Economics.* New York: Norton, 2011.

Ward, Brian. *Just My Soul Responding: Rhythm and Blues, Black Consciousness, and Race Relations.* Berkeley: University of California Press, 1998.

Ward, Brian, ed. *Media, Culture, and the Modern African American Freedom Struggle.* Gainesville: University Press of Florida, 2001.

Ward, Kathryn, ed. *Women Workers and Global Restructuring.* Ithaca, NY: ILR Press, 1990.

Washington, Harriet A. *Medical Apartheid: The Dark History of Medical Experimentation on Black Americans from Colonial Times to the Present.* New York: Doubleday, 2006.

Washington State Commission on African American Affairs. *Affirmative Action, Who's Really Benefitting? Part I: State Employment & Part III: State Contracting.* Olympia: Washington State Commission on African American Affairs, 1995/1996.

Waterhouse, Benjamin C. *The Land of Enterprise: A Business History of the United States.* New York: Simon & Schuster, 2017.

Watkins, S. Craig. *Representing: Hip Hop Culture and the Production of Black Cinema.* Chicago: University of Chicago Press, 1998.

Wayne, John, dir. *The Alamo.* United Artists, 1960.

Wayne, John, and Ray Kellogg, dirs. *The Green Berets.* Batjac/Warner Bros., 1968.

Weatherby, W. J. *James Baldwin: Artist on Fire.* New York: Donald I. Fine, 1989.

Weaver, Richard M. *Ideas Have Consequences.* Chicago: University of Chicago Press, 1948, 2013.

Webb, Clive, ed. *Massive Resistance: Southern Opposition to the Second Reconstruction.* Oxford: Oxford University Press, 2005.

Webber, Michael J., and David L. Rigby. *The Golden Age Illusion: Rethinking Postwar Capitalism.* New York: Guilford, 1996.

Weiss, Carol H. "What America's Leaders Read." *Public Opinion Quarterly* 38, no. 1 (Spring 1974): 1–22.

Weiss, Linda. "Globalization and the Myth of the Powerless State." *New Left Review* 225 (September–October 1997): 3–27.

Welter, Barbara. "The Cult of True Womanhood: 1820–1860." *American Quarterly* 18, no. 2 (Summer 1966): 151–74.

Werner, Craig. "The Economic Evolution of James Baldwin." In *Critical Essays on James Baldwin.* Fred L. Standley and Nancy V. Burt, eds. Boston: G. K. Hall, 1988.

Westad, Odd Arne. *The Global Cold War: Third World Interventions and the Making of Our Times.* Cambridge: Cambridge University Press, 2007.

Western, Bruce, and Jake Rosenfeld. "Unions, Norms, and the Rise in US Wage Inequality." *American Sociological Review* 76, no. 4 (2011): 513–37.

"What Price Will Whites Pay?" *Business Week*, May 4, 1968.

Wheeler, Billy Edd. *Love.* RCA, 1971. LP LSP-4491.

———. "Woman's Talkin' Liberation Blues"/"Little Lucy." RCA, 1971. 45rpm ZWKM-1901.

"When a World Money System Is Out of Date." *Business Week*, February 22, 1968.

"Where the Recession Really Hurts." *Business Week*, April 19, 1982.

"White Business Balks at Sharing the Work." *Business Week*, November 17, 1975.

"White House Eyes Deregulation Route." *Business Week*, November 21, 1970.

Whitfield, Stephen J. *The Culture of the Cold War.* 2nd ed. Baltimore: Johns Hopkins University Press, 1996.

"Why Business Needs Two Tax Cuts." *Business Week*, August 28, 1978.

"Why Foreign Companies Are Betting on the U.S." *Business Week*, April 12, 1976.

"Why Joblessness May Stay High." *Business Week*, April 15, 1972.

"Why the Cash Piles Up." *Business Week*, September 18, 1978.

"Why U.S. Mayors Plead Poverty." *Business Week*, February 10, 1968.

"Why U.S. Technology Lags." *Business Week*, January 15, 1972.

"Why Women's Stock Is Rising on Wall Street." *Business Week*, November 10, 1975.

Widener, Daniel. *Black Arts West: Culture and Struggle in Postwar Los Angeles.* Durham,, NC: Duke University Press, 2010.

———. "The Art of Creative Survival." From the digital archive of the exhibition Now Dig This! Art and Black Los Angeles 1960–1980 at the Hammer Museum, 2016. hammer.ucla.edu/now-dig-this/essays/the-art-of-creative-survival/

Wiebe, Robert H. *Self Rule: A Cultural History of American Democracy.* Chicago: University of Chicago Press, 1995.

———. *The Search for Order, 1877–1920.* New York: Hill & Wang, 1967.

Wilderson, Frank B. III. "Gramsci's Black Marx: Whither the Slave in Civil Society?" *Social Identities* 9, no. 2 (2003): 225–40.

———. *Red, White & Black: Cinema and the Structure of U.S. Antagonisms.* Durham, NC: Duke University Press, 2010.

Wight, David M. *Oil Money: Middle East Petrodollars and the Transformation of Us Empire, 1967–1988.* Ithaca: Cornell University Press, 2021.

Wilentz, Sean. *The Age of Reagan: A History, 1974–2008.* New York: Harper Perennial, 2009.

Wilkins, Mira. "Multinational Enterprise to 1930: Discontinuities and Continuities." In *Leviathans: Multinational Corporations and the New Global History*. Alfred D. Chandler Jr. and Bruce Mazlish, eds. Cambridge: Cambridge University Press, 2005.

Wilkinson, Alec. "New York Is Killing Me." *New Yorker* 86, no. 23 (August 9, 2010): 26–32.

Williams, Daniel K. *God's Own Party: The Making of the Christian Right*. Oxford: Oxford University Press, 2010.

Williams, Lee E. *Anatomy of Four Race Riots: Racial Conflict in Knoxville, Elaine (Arkansas), Tulsa, and Chicago, 1919–1921*. Jackson: University Press of Mississippi, 2008.

Williams, Oscar, dir. *Final Comedown*. New World Pictures, 1972.

Williams, Raymond. *Marxism and Literature*. Oxford: Oxford University Press, 1977.

———. *Television: Technology and Cultural Form*. London: Routledge, 1974.

Williams, William Appleman. *The Tragedy of American Diplomacy*. New York: Norton, 1959.

Willman, Chris. *Rednecks & Bluenecks: The Politics of Country Music*. New York: New Press, 2005.

Wills, Garry. *John Wayne's America*. New York: Simon & Schuster, 1997.

Wilson, Lindy. *Steve Biko*. Johannesburg: Jacana, 2011.

Wilson, Mark R. "The Advantages of Obscurity: World War II Tax Carry-Back Provisions and the Normalization of Corporate Welfare." In *What's Good for Business: Business and American Politics since World War II*. Kim Phillips-Fein and Julian E. Zelizer, eds. Oxford: Oxford University Press, 2012.

Wilson, William Julius. *The Declining Significance of Race*. Chicago: University of Chicago Press, 1978.

Winner, Michael, dir. *Death Wish*. Paramount Pictures, 1974.

Wittern-Keller, Laura. "All the Power of the Law: Governmental Film Censorship in the United States." In *Silencing Cinema: Film Censorship around the World*. Daniel Biltereyst and Roel Vande Winkel, eds. London: Palgrave Macmillan, 2013.

Wolfe, Audra J. *Competing with the Soviets: Science, Technology, and the State in Cold War America*. Baltimore: Johns Hopkins University Press, 2013.

Wolfe, Patrick. *Settler Colonialism and the Transformation of Anthropology: The Politics and Poetics of an Ethnographic Event*. London: Cassell, 1999.

"Women: The New Venture Capitalists." *Business Week*, November 2, 1981.

Wonder, Stevie. *Innervisions*. Motown, 1973. CD 012 157 355-2.

Woodard, Komozi. *A Nation within a Nation: Amiri Baraka (LeRoi Jones) and Black Power Politics*. Chapel Hill: University of North Carolina Press, 1999.

Wright, Melissa W. *Disposable Women and Other Myths of Global Capitalism*. New York: Routledge, 2006.

Wright, Will. *Sixguns & Society: A Structural Study of the Western*. Berkeley: University of California Press, 1975.

Wynette, Tammy. "Don't Liberate Me (Love Me)." On *We Sure Can Love Each Other*. Epic, 1971. SEPC64502.

Yeatter, Bryan L. *Cinema of the Philippines: A History and Filmography, 1897–2005*. Jefferson, NC: McFarland, 2007.

Yergin, Daniel. *The Prize: The Epic Quest for Oil, Money, and Power*. New York: Free Press, 1991.

Young, Cynthia A. *Soul Power: Culture, Radicalism, and the Making of a U.S. Third World Left*. Durham, NC: Duke University Press, 2006.

Young, Marilyn B. *The Vietnam Wars, 1945–1990*. New York: HarperPerennial, 1991.

Zalcock, Bev. *Renegade Sisters: Girl Gangs On Film*. N.d.: Creation Books, 1998.

Zammito, John H. "Are We Being Theoretical Yet? The New Historicism, the New Philosophy of History, and 'Practicing Historians.'" *Journal of Modern History* 65, no. 4 (December 1993): 783–814.

Zaniello, Tom. *Working Stiffs, Union Maids, Reds, and Riffraff: An Expanded Guide to Films About Labor*. Ithaca, NY: ILR, 2003.

Zarchi, Meir, dir. *I Spit on Your Grave* (aka *Day of the Woman*). Cinemagic Pictures, 1978.

Zaretsky, Natasha. *No Direction Home: The American Family and the Fear of National Decline, 1968–1980*. Chapel Hill: University of North Carolina Press, 2007.

Zuboff, Shoshana. *The Age of Surveillance Capitalism: The Fight for a Human Future at the New Frontier of Power*. New York: PublicAffairs, 2019.

Zucker, Seymour. "Reaganomics II: More Keynes than Laffer." *Business Week*, March 21, 1983.

———. "The Fallacy of Slashing Taxes without Cutting Spending." *Business Week*, August 7, 1978.

Index

Abel, J. W., 191
abortion, 213, 214, 239, 260, 277, 278. *See also* women's rights
accumulation, historical cycles of, 90–91, 116, 211
Acheson, Dean, 182
Across 110th Street (film), 233
action films, 192–93, 242, 243. *See also* exploitation films; film industry
Adams, Emmie Schrader, 213
Adams, John, 2, 19, 247, 309, 326
affirmative action, 8, 54, 138, 154, 189, 263, 264, 309. *See also* racial inequality
Affirmative Discrimination (Glazer), 43, 139, 189
African Americans. *See* Black Americans
Afrika Bambaataa, 310
Against Our Will (Brownmiller), 230
agency, 64, 229. *See also* self-determination
Agnew, Spiro, 199
"Ain't No New Thing" (Scott-Heron), 293–94
airline industry, 115, 154, 155
The Alamo (film), 175–76
Alcoa, 134
Alice (television show), 259
Alice Doesn't Live Here Anymore (film), 220, 259
Altschuler, Glenn C., 92
American Bankers Association, 82
American Business Consultants, 168
American dream, 37–47, 304–5. *See also* defense of Western civilization trope; frontier myth; nostalgia; settler colonialism; white innocence
American exceptionalism, 2, 24, 36, 47, 164–65, 174–75, 177, 180, 325. *See also* frontier myth; settler colonialism; white innocence; white supremacy

American Graffiti (film), 249
American Indians. *See* Native Americans
American Legion, 168
American Liberty League, 134
American myth. *See* frontier myth
American Revolution, 190
American Women: The Report of the President's Commission on the Status of Women and Other Publications of the Commission (Kennedy administration), 212
Anderson, Carol, 3, 312
Anderson, T. J., 292
anger, 279, 280–81
Anthony, Paul, 125
anti-Blackness: Baldwin on, 18, 37–38; by Buckley, 18–19, 44–46, 47, 55–56, 83–84; in films, 307; individualism and, 76–77; of John Wayne, 159, 189–92, 201; "Negro problem" trope, 44, 45, 47, 83; N-word as, 153, 191, 233–34, 258, 363n162, 367n56; welfare programs and, 140, 308. *See also* Black Americans; Blackness; color blindness; erasure; racial capitalism; racism; slavery; violence against Black Americans
anti-segregation movement, 332n39
antiwar movement, 170–71, 175, 179
Apartheid, 190, 302, 303–4
Apple, Michael W., 177
Armitage, David, 16, 330n75
Arrighi, Giovanni, 90, 107, 116, 120, 211
assimilation:—immigrant narrative, 183, 189, 206; of people of color, 257, 304–5, 313, 320; of white ethnics, 37, 44; of women, 223, 230, 256–57, 261–62, 270. *See also* difference; diversity, as term
Atlantic slave trade. *See* slavery

Atwater, Lee, 153, 156, 202–3
Austrian school of economics, 63
authoritarianism, 6, 105, 106, 141, 142, 156, 235, 261. *See also* communism
automobile industry, 119

Baby Face (film), 217
Back to Bataan (film), 235
Bacon's Rebellion (1676), 81, 87
Baker, Elaine DeLott, 213
Baker, Ella, 212–13
Baker, Houston A., Jr., 287–88
Baldwin, James: background of, 29; on civil rights movement, 283; *The Devil Finds Work*, 16, 34; *The Fire Next Time*, 40, 127; on freedom, 209; influence of, 290, 292; *Nobody Knows My Name*, 45; *No Name in the Street*, 48, 161; political framework of, 29–30; on possession of history, 32–33, 34, 36, 37, 48, 54–55; on racial capitalism, 25, 30, 38; on racial inequality and anti-Blackness, 17–18, 37–38, 158–59; on victimhood, 34, 36, 207, 215, 225, 312, 319; on whiteness, 199. *See also Baldwin vs. Buckley* (Cambridge Debate, 1965)
Baldwin vs. Buckley (Cambridge Debate, 1965): cultural framework of, 17–19, 26–27, 30–32, 47–48, 249, 314; on "ethos" and the American dream, 37–47; framing of, 32–37; transcript of, 331n18. *See also* Baldwin, James; Buckley, William F., Jr.
Bancroft, Hubert Howe, 173
Bank Holding Company Act (1970), 117
Bank of America, 150
Bank of International Settlements, 142
Baraka, Amiri, 290, 291, 292
Batjac Productions, 183
The Battle of Algiers (film), 282
Beard, Charles, 199
Beauvoir, Simone de, 212
Bechtel Corp., 148
Beebe, N. Lorraine, 213
benign neglect policies, 10, 43, 124, 157, 286, 300
Berger, Martin, 198
Berle, Adolf A., 93, 101, 105

Beyond the Melting Pot (Glazer and Moynihan), 42, 43, 45, 139
The Big Bird Cage (film), 237, 238, 240
big data, 112
The Big Doll House (film), 236, 237, 238, 239–40
Big Jim McLain (film), 170
Big Youth, 302
Biko, Steve, 304
Birmingham, Alabama, bombing (1963), 30–31
Birth of a Nation (film), 56, 175
Black action films (Blaxploitation), 192–93, 222, 233, 244, 303, 307. *See also* film industry
Black Americans: assimilation of, 257, 304–5, 313, 319; BAM, 288–92; BLM, 298; radical tradition of, 29–30, 228, 254, 283, 287; simplistic film representations of, 197–98, 219, 221. *See also* anti-Blackness; Blackness; Black womanhood; *names of specific persons*; racial inequality; racism; slavery; violence against Black Americans
"Black Art" (Baraka), 292
Black arts movement (BAM), 288–92
Black Consciousness Movement (South Africa), 304
"Black Dada Nihilismus" (Baraka), 292
Black internationalism, 297, 298, 301, 303
Black Lives Matter (BLM) movement, 298
Blackness: Baldwin on, 38; Buckley on, 39–40, 41, 44–45; portrayed in films, 197–98. *See also* anti-Blackness; racial inequality; racism
Black Panther Party, 228
Black Reconstruction of America (Du Bois), 33–34, 35
Black surrealism, 291
Black Wax (film), 313, 314
Black womanhood: *Born in Flames* film on, 17, 21, 248, 256, 267, 268, 272–79; feminist politics on, 212, 258–65; hypersexualization of, 222, 232, 238–39; intersectionality of, 222–23, 225, 228, 230–32, 268; mammy caricature of, 175–76; in *Nine to Five* film, 270; patriarchal violence to, 261. *See also*

430 Index

Black Americans; white womanhood; women
Blow, Kurtis, 307
Bluestone, Barry, 118, 136
"B' Movie" (Scott-Heron), 309, 314
B movies, 217. *See also* film industry
Bob Marley and the Wailers, 301
Bonnie and Clyde (film), 218
Borden, Lizzie, 268, 272–78. See also *Born in Flames* (film)
Born in Flames (film), 17, 21, 248, 256, 267, 268, 272–79
Bradley, Patricia, 215
Braudel, Fernand, 1, 14, 35, 88, 122, 287
Brazil, 135, 145, 150
Bread and Roses (organization), 268–69
Bretton Woods Agreement (1944), 102, 107, 108, 110
Brides of Blood (film), 235
Bronson, Charles, 194
"Brooding" (Cortez), 288–89
Brother D with Collective Effort, 308
Brown, James, 228, 260
Brown, Kimberly N., 282
Brown, Richard Maxwell, 15
Brown, Sterling, 291
Brownmiller, Susan, 230
"Brown Sugar" (song), 226, 228
Buccola, Nicholas, 28
Buckley, William F., Jr.: background of, 18, 26, 27; on civil rights movement, 37, 40; *Firing Line* show of, 27, 43, 83, 333n102; on Hentoff and Black Power, 333n102; on individualism, 28, 31, 42–43; on the Moynihan Report, 228; political framework of, 12, 27–29; "Pro-Negro Discrimination Encouraged," 23; on racial inequality, 18, 44–46, 47, 55–56, 83–84, 124, 192; as victim, 41; on whiteness *vs*. Blackness, 39–40, 41, 44–45. See also *Baldwin vs. Buckley* (Cambridge Debate, 1965); *National Review* (publication); New Right
Buckley v. Valeo, 134
buried history. *See* possession of history
Burroughs Corp., 98–99
Bush administration (G. H. W.), 6

Bush administration (G. W.), 6, 203
Bush Mama (film), 307
business conservatism, 2, 93–94, 99–100, 138, 140–42. *See also* conservatism; corporations; financial institutions; populist conservatism; privatization
business news publications, 91, 92, 339n15, 339n17. See also *Business Week* (publication)
Business Week (publication): about, 91–92, 132, 339n15; Carson-Parker on rise of neoliberalism in, 317–18; on conglomerates and MNCs, 98, 99, 107, 114–16, 119, 161–63, 257; on corporations and women, 21, 263–64, 266, 272, 281; on currency fluctuation, 108, 109; on decline of U.S. power, 148–49; on economic policies, 82, 110, 151; on federal redistribution policies, 140–41; on federal regulation, 137, 144, 152–53; on feminism, 213–14, 266; on Friedman's economic theories, 82, 85; on frontier capitalism, 204; on immigration, 152; on labor movements, 121, 133, 154–55; on overproduction, 106; on racial inequality, 124–26, 139–40; on rapid changes to business environment, 143–44; sexist advertising in, 339n17; on U.S. debt economy, 128, 129, 130
busing, 153–54

Cabral, Amilcar, 297
Caffaro, Cheri, 238
California, 61, 144
Calley, William, 299
Cambodia, 183
Cambridge Debate. See *Baldwin vs. Buckley* (Cambridge Debate, 1965)
campaign contributions, 134
Canby, Vincent, 197
Cane, Paul W., 148
capitalism: Braudel on, 1; corporate woman and, 22, 257–58, 266–67; of film industry, 204; frontier individualism as form of, 204–6; historical cycles of accumulation in, 90–91, 116, 211; industrial, 65, 97; in postwar America, 100–106; Scott-Heron on, 298–99, 309. *See also* financial

capitalism (cont.)
  institutions; globalization; laissez-faire capitalism; multinational corporations (MNCs)
Capitalism and Freedom (Friedman), 75, 79–80, 81–82, 123, 156–57
Capital Resurgent (Duménil and Lévy), 128
captivity narratives, 210–11, 240, 358n11. *See also* frontier myth; white innocence
Carlson-Parker, John, 129–30, 135, 317
Carmichael, Stokely, 228
Carson-Parker, John, 285, 296, 310
Carter, Jimmy, 113
Carter administration, 134–35, 144, 145, 150, 308
Carter Family (band), 226
Catch a Fire (Bob Marley and the Wailers), 301
Catholic Church, 182
Cato Institute, 134
Cavarero, Adriana, 229–30, 257, 261
Cayman Islands, 137
Celebrations and Solitudes (Cortez), 297
censorship in films. *See* film industry; Hays Production Code
Césaire, Aimé, 291, 371n23
Chandler, Alfred, 97–98
Chang, Jeff, 306, 310
Charlie's Angels (television show), 238–39
Chayefsky, Paddy, 249
Chicago school of economics, 6, 66, 67, 82. *See also* neoliberalism
Chicago Women's Liberation Rock Band, 260–61
Chile, 110, 117, 142–43, 150, 297, 300
Chinatown (film), 252
Christianity, 30, 36, 227
Civilization and Capitalism, 15th–18th Century (Braudel), 1, 88
Civil Rights Act (1964), 10, 80, 121, 208, 212, 215
civil rights movement: Baldwin on, 18, 29; Buckley on, 37, 40; *Business Week* on, 124–25; Cortez in, 290; cultural framework of, 170–71, 175, 220; feminism and, 212, 258; Friedman on, 79–80; SNCC, 213, 228, 283, 290; violence of, 24, 175, 187, 219; white backlash to, 106, 140, 167. *See also* Black Americans; racial inequality; white supremacy
Civil War, 5, 96, 186
classical liberalism, 3, 5, 66–69, 77, 162. *See also* free market economics; neoliberalism
Claudine (film), 220
Cleopatra Jones (film), 222
Cliff, Jimmy, 301
Clinton, Bill, 155
Clinton administration, 6, 314
Coffy (film), 222
Cold War: film representations and, 167–74, 180–82; global spending in the, 314; settler colonialism and, 174–91
collectivism, 73, 77, 94, 104, 105, 168, 176–77
Collins, Addie Mae, 30
Colloque Walter Lippmann (1938), 66
colonialism. *See* settler colonialism; U.S. colonialism in Philippines
color blindness: Buckley on, 39–40, 41, 62–63; of conservatism, 28–29, 262; feminism and, 258, 262–63; in housing policies, 140; King on, 80, 313; polls on, 60–62; of Reagan, 61; residential segregation and, 19; rhetoric of, 3, 8–9, 13, 55. *See also* anti-Blackness; invisibility of whiteness; racism; universalism; whiteness
Combahee River Collective, 274
"Coming from a Broken Home" (Scott-Heron), 289
communism, 94, 95, 168, 178, 180, 181. *See also* authoritarianism; social equality
Comte, Auguste, 56
conglomeration, 96, 113–18; Beale on, 89; *Business Week* on, 98, 99, 107, 114–16, 119, 161–63, 257; film and, 211, 250; music and, 303. *See also* corporations; multinational corporations (MNCs)
Congo, 150, 300
conjuncture, defined, 327n1
conservatism: in business, 2, 93–94, 99–100, 138, 140–42; color blindness of, 28–29; on defense of Western civilization, 14, 18, 19, 53, 55–59; defined, 331n23; GOP politics of

432 Index

post-war era, 3–4; sociology of racial differences in, 44–45. *See also* neoliberalism; New Right; populist conservatism; white nationalism
conservative culture war. *See* culture war, overview
The Constitution of Liberty (Hayek), 74
consumerism, 95, 100, 296. *See also* capitalism; mass production
Coogan's Bluff (film), 244, 245
Cook, Donald C., 137
Cook, Pam, 221
Cooper, Anna J., 287
Cooper, Melinda, 215
Cooper, Richard, 102
Corkin, Stanley, 162
Corman, Roger: films by, 222, 234, 236, 238, 239; film subjects of, 220, 221, 222; on public interest in B movies, 217; on reason for filming in Philippines, 236–37
corporate woman, 21, 257–58, 266; *Business Week* on, 21, 263–64, 267, 272, 281; in film *Born in Flames*, 17, 21, 248, 256, 267, 268, 272–79; in film *Network*, 229, 248, 249–57, 263, 268, 273; in film *Nine to Five*, 17, 21, 248, 256, 268–73. *See also* capitalism; corporations; feminist politics; women
corporations, 96–106; monopolies, 66–68, 93, 98, 114, 116, 168–69; personhood of, 5, 162; structural adjustment of, 132–48. *See also* business conservatism; conglomeration; corporate woman; foreign direct investments; multinational corporations (MNCs)
Cortez, Jayne, 290–93; "Brooding," 288–89; on globalization, 22, 371n23; "If the Drum Is a Woman" (Cortez), 282–83; "Rape" (poem), 283; *There It Is*, 311–12; "They Came Again in 1970 in 1980," 296–97; *Unsubmissive Blues*, 303–4; "Watching a Parade in Harlem 1970," 284
cotton industry, 185, 232
"Cotton is King" (Hammond), 56–57
country music, 226–27, 249. *See also* music
Cowie, Jefferson, 8, 95, 272, 313

crime films, 192, 194–98, 321. *See also* film industry
critical memory, 287–88, 295
Crockett, Davy, 355n73
Crouch, Stanley, 290
Cruse, Harold, 78
cultural diversity. *See* diversity, as term
culture, defined, 11–12, 326
The Culture of the New Capitalism (Sennett), 88
culture war, overview, 1–4, 13–15, 31, 317–26, 327n12
Culture Wars (Hunter), 1, 327n12
Cuordileone, K. A., 174
currency fluctuation, 107–13

Damas, Léon, 291
dance hall, 375n146. *See also* music
Davies, William, 52, 69, 86, 257
Davis, Angela Y., 230, 232, 253
Davis, Michael, 155
Davison, Jon, 235
Death Wish (film), 244, 321
debt economy, 128–30
The Declining Significance of Race (Wilson), 305
defense industry, 100
defense of Western civilization trope, 14, 18, 19, 53, 55–59, 69–70, 78–79. *See also* American dream; nationalism; settler colonialism; "silent majority" strategy; white innocence; white nationalism
Deliverance (film), 223
Democratic Party, 93, 157, 312–13. *See also* neoliberalism; New Left
Depository Institutions Deregulatory and Monetary Control Act (1980), 153
Depression. *See* Great Depression
"deviant culture" rhetoric, 45, 46, 54, 194, 230, 237
The Devil Finds Work (Baldwin), 16, 34
difference, 207, 211–12, 234, 279. *See also* assimilation; diversity, as term; multiculturalism, as term
Diller, Phyllis, 185
The Dirty Dozen (film), 218

Index 433

Dirty Harry (film), 195, 244, 321
Dita Beard scandal, 299
diversification, economic, 116–17
diversity, as term, 16, 211, 281. *See also* assimilation; difference
domesticity, 214, 229. *See also* suburbanization
Douglass, Frederick, 187, 188, 287
Dred Scott v. Sandford, 25, 26, 77, 152, 231
Du Bois, W. E. B., 33, 35, 125, 186, 287
Dunn, Stephane, 222

Eastwood, Clint, 194, 195, 244, 246
economic depression. *See* Great Depression
economic recessions, 89, 92, 96
economics and racial oppression. *See* racial capitalism
The Economist (publication), 91, 156
education, 3, 34, 45, 187
EEOC (Equal Employment Opportunity Commission), 212, 213
Eisenhower, Dwight D., 103
Eley, Geoff, 33
Ellender, Allen J., 56, 57
The Emerging Republican Majority (Phillips), 251
The Empire Strikes Back: Race and Racism in 70s Britain (Lawrence), 44
Employment Act (1946), 100
The Enforcer (film), 246, 251
enslaved African Americans, 26, 358n11. *See also* Black Americans; slavery
Eppert, Ray R., 98–99
Equal Employment Opportunities Act (1964), 263
Equal Employment Opportunity Commission (EEOC), 212, 213
Equal Rights Amendment, 227
erasure, 39–42. *See also* anti-Blackness
ethnic cleansing. *See* genocide
"ethos" argument, 46–47, 63, 85, 154, 332n45. *See also* American dream
Eurocentrism, 371n23
Eurodollars, 107–8
The Eve of Destruction (Patterson), 24
exceptionalism. *See* American exceptionalism

exploitation films, 209–12; Blaxploitation, 192, 222, 233, 244, 303, 307; regulation and realism in, 217–34; women-in-prison, 229, 237–41. *See also* film industry
exports, U.S., 98–99, 111, 118–19, 151
Exxon, 117
"Eye to Eye" (Lorde), 279

Faludi, Susan, 225
family values, 4, 188, 227, 322. *See also* patriarchy
family wage, 8, 11–12, 25, 77. *See also* white masculinity
Fanon, Frantz, 282, 371n23
farming industry, 65
Faster, Pussycat! Kill! . . . Kill! (film), 218
Faulkner, William, 36, 48, 100
federalism, 97
Federal National Mortgage Association, 130
federal overreach, 64–65, 73, 79, 244, 308–9. *See also* individualism
Federal Reserve, 64, 83, 108, 117, 128–29, 155
The Feminine Mystique (Friedan), 212
feminist politics: of Abigail Adams, 247; of Black vs. white womanhood, 258–59, 261–62; civil rights movement and, 212, 258; films and television and, 17, 185, 217, 229, 237–41; of first-wave feminism, 212; of Lorde, 259; in music, 226–27, 366n34; Schaffer on, 207; of second-wave feminism, 59, 212–16, 267–68. *See also* corporate woman; patriarchy; women; women's rights
femme fatale, 229, 252, 253. *See also* corporate woman; women
"Festivals and Funerals 1970" (Cortez), 297
fetishization of difference, 234
film industry: Black action films (or Blaxploitation), 192–93, 222, 233, 244, 303, 307; B movies, 217; capitalism of, 204; conglomerates in, 114; crime films, 192, 194–98, 321; exploitation films, overview, 209–12; *film noir*, 192, 229, 252; overseas production of, 21, 234–37; populist rage in, 88; portrayals of Native Americans in, 171, 172–73, 194, 320; regulation and

deregulation of, 168–70, 209, 217–34; Western films, 167–76, 193; women-in-prison films, 229, 237–41. *See also* corporate woman; *names of specific films*; television; Wayne, John
film noir, 192, 229, 252
The Final Comedown (film), 236, 307
financial institutions: bailout of, 86; globalization and, 111, 142, 300; innovation in, 111–13; as MNCs, 117, 119; reawakening of, 12; regulation of, 2, 116–17, 150; trade journals on, 91–92. *See also* business conservatism; capitalism; neoliberalism
The Fire Next Time (Baldwin), 40, 127
Firing Line with William F. Buckley Jr. (television show), 27, 43, 83, 333n102
First Minute of a New Day (Scott-Heron), 301
First National City Bank, 116
first-wave feminism. *See* feminist politics
First Women's Rights Convention (1848), 212
flexible accumulation, 211
flexible feminism, 237–38
flexible misogyny (or flexible sexism), 210–11
Focus on the Family, 377n13
Forbes (publication), 91
Ford, Gerald, 129
Ford, Henry, 101
Ford administration, 111, 129
Ford Company, 119
foreign direct investments, 107–8, 112, 118–19, 135, 147, 235. *See also* globalization; multinational corporations (MNCs)
Fort Apache (film), 178, 307
"Fortunate Son" (song), 158
Fortune (publication), 91, 92, 339n15. *See also* business news publications
Fourteenth Amendment, 5, 162
Foxy Brown (film), 222
Frank, Robert H., 286
Franklin, Benjamin, 30
Frantzen, D. J., 143
Fraser, Nancy, 266, 267
Freedom Is Not Enough (MacLean), 23
freedoom, Scott-Heron on, 295

free market economics, 64, 67, 74–75, 85, 142–43, 163–64. *See also* classical liberalism; individualism; neoliberalism
French colonial occupation of Vietnam, 178
The French Connection (film), 233, 243–44
Freund, David M. P., 9, 123
Friedan, Betty, 212, 229
Friedman, Milton, 53, 318; *Capitalism and Freedom*, 75, 79, 81–82, 123, 156; debates on economic logic of, 82–83; debate with Buckley by, 83–85; on federal overreach, 79–80; on free market capitalism, 49, 115, 136, 142–43, 163, 206; "Neoliberalism and Its Prospects," 67–68, 69; Nobel Prize for, 85, 142
From South Africa to South Carolina (Scott-Heron), 303
frontier capitalism, 204–6. *See also* racial capitalism
frontier myth, 15–16, 161–66, 171–72, 182–84. *See also* American dream; American exceptionalism; captivity narratives; Native Americans; patriotism; settler colonialism; Wayne, John
Future Shock (Toffler), 317

Gans, Herbert J., 91
Gee, Spoonie, 306–7
gender discrimination. *See* women's rights
General Agreement on Tariffs and Trade (GATT), 106
General Electric, 119, 134
General Motors, 119
The General Theory of Employment, Interest, and Money (Keynes), 64
Geneva school of economics, 63
genocide, 172–73, 177, 186, 319. *See also* Native Americans; white supremacy; white terrorism
GI Bill, 95
Gilder, George, 10
Gilmore, Ruth Wilson, 308
Gilroy, Paul, 30
Gingrich, Newt, 49–50, 51, 53, 54, 158
Giovanni, Nikki, 25, 54, 290
Glass-Steagall Act (1933), 112, 117

Index 435

Glazer, Nathan, 42, 43, 45, 139
globalization: corporations and, 96–100; financial institutions and, 111, 142, 300; populist rage against, 74–75, 89, 248–49, 371n23; regulation of, 96. *See also* capitalism; foreign direct investments; multinational corporations (MNCs)
Glover, Clifford, 298
Go, Julian, 90
The Godfather (film), 233
The Golden Age Illusion (Rigby), 88
Goldwater, Barry, 75, 103, 130, 131, 143
Gone with the Wind (film), 51, 175
Good Society (Lippman), 99
Good Times (television show), 229
GOP (Grand Old Party), 3. *See also* Republican Party
Gordon, Robert J., 91
The Graduate (film), 218
Grandin, Greg, 15, 190
Grandmaster Caz, 306
Grandmaster Flash, 288, 307, 310–11
Grapes of Wrath (film), 169–70
Grateful Dead (band), 226
Grazia, Victoria de, 103
Grease (film), 249
Great Compression, 101, 103, 268
Great Depression, 2, 64–65, 82, 105, 214
Great Society policy, 106
The Great Transformation (Polanyi), 71–72
The Green Berets (film), 178, 179, 180
Grier, Pam, 222–23, 239
Grossvogel, David I., 92
Guatemala, 110, 150, 300
Guillén, Nicolás, 291

"H2O Gate (Watergate) Blues" (Scott-Heron), 298–99
Hamer, Fannie Lou, 290
Hamilton, Alexander, 97
Hammond, James Henry, 56–57
Happy Days (television show), 249
The Harder They Come (film), 301, 302
Harris, Cheryl, 76, 139
Harrison, Bennett, 118, 136
Hartman, Saidiya, 294

Harvey, David, 101, 113, 118, 211
Haskell, Molly, 244–45
Hatari! (film), 190
hatred, 24, 265, 279. *See also* misogyny; racism
Hawley, Ellis W., 64
Hayden, Casey, 213
Hayek, Friedrich August von: background of, 63; *The Constitution of Liberty*, 74; on market as information processor, 6–7, 85, 205, 216; Mont Pèlerin Society by, 69; neoliberal economics of, 53, 64, 69–71, 85, 105, 318, 322; Nobel Prize for, 85; *The Road to Serfdom*, 49, 70, 71, 72–74
Hays, Will H., 169
Hays Production Code, 169, 204, 217–18, 231, 234. *See also* film industry
Hazlitt, Henry, 2, 12
Heckscher, Eli F., 63
"The Hell He Is Equal" (Kilpatrick), 30
heroism trope, 16, 20–21, 194. *See also* frontier myth; white male authority and privilege; white masculinity
Higgins, Colin, 268, 269
High Plains Drifter (film), 246
Hill, Jack, 237–38, 239
hip-hop, 293, 302–12, 375n146. *See also* music; spoken word
histoire événementielle framework, 14
history and its effects. *See* possession of history
Hoberman, J., 165
Ho Chi Minh, 178, 181–82
Hoerr, John, 139
Hofstadter, Richard, 103
Hollywood. *See* film industry
homeownership. *See* residential segregation; suburbanization
Homestead Act (1862), 21
"Homicide 1973" (Cortez), 298
homophobia, 36, 229, 275, 294. *See also* lesbianism
Hong, Grace Kyungwon, 234
Hoover, Herbert, 28, 64, 65
Horne, Gerald, 38
horror exploitation films, 234–41. *See also* film industry

House of Un-American Activities Committee (HUAC), 168, 170
housing discrimination. *See* residential segregation; suburbanization
Hughes, Langston, 289, 290, 291
Hunter, James Davidson, 1, 4, 327n12
Hustlers Convention (Nuriddin), 303
hypersexualization of Black women, 222, 232, 238–39. *See also* Black womanhood

"I Am Woman" (song), 259
"If the Drum Is a Woman" (Cortez), 282–83
immigrant-assimilationist narrative, 183, 189, 206. *See also* difference; diversity, as term
immigration, 151–52, 182, 183, 310
Immigration Act (1924), 200, 324
Immigration and Nationality Act (1965), 152, 200
The Immoral Mr. Teas (film), 218
I'm New Here (Scott-Heron), 284–85, 316
income inequality. *See* wealth inequality
Indian Removal Act (1830), 21
Indians. *See* Native Americans
individualism: Buckley on, 28, 31, 42–43; Friedman on, 79–80; Hoover on, 65; racism on film and, 233–34; rugged individualism, 8, 21, 28; white privilege and, 77, 141–42. *See also* defense of Western civilization trope; federal overreach; free market economics; white male authority and privilege
industrial capitalism, 65, 97
inegalitarian libertarianism, as term, 28. *See also* libertarianism
innocence trope. *See* white innocence
(An Inquiry into the Principle of) The Good Society (Lippmann), 65–66
Intel Corporation, 235
International Monetary Fund, 111, 142, 300
intersectionality, 223, 225, 228, 230–32, 262. *See also* Black womanhood; homophobia; racism; sexism
In the Heat of the Night (film), 198
invisibility of whiteness, 10, 18, 104, 125–27, 206. *See also* color blindness; universalism; whiteness

Iran, 148–49, 150, 180, 300
Iraq, 150, 180, 315–16
Irish Americans, 26, 37, 43, 46, 124, 262
iron industry, 119
I Spit on Your Grave (film), 231
Italian Americans, 37, 43, 46
Italy, 90
ITT (corporation), 110, 132, 299

Jackson, Maynard H., Jr., 138
Jackson Bruce, 292
Jackson County Jail (film), 231
Jacobs, Harriet, 287, 358n11
Jacobson, Matthew Frye, 42, 44
Jamaica: music of, 22, 301–3, 306, 308, 375n146; political economy of, 110, 155
James, Harold, 94
Japan: colonial occupation by, 181, 235; economic markets of, 89, 106, 108, 116, 119, 122, 134, 144, 150; WWII and, 179, 182
Jaws (film), 88, 307
jazz, 290, 291, 292, 297, 303, 306. *See also* music
Jenkins, Henry, 235, 236
Jewish Americans, 37, 46, 124
Jezebel (caricature), 222, 232, 239. *See also* Black womanhood; racism
Jim Crow welfare state, defined, 12–13, 325. *See also* welfare state, overview
"Joan Little" (Davis), 230
Joe (film), 243, 244, 245
John Birch Society, 176
Johnson, Robert, 285
Johnson administration, 43, 106, 107, 180
Johnston, Eric, 169, 185
Jones, Geoffrey, 90
journals, 92. *See also* business news publications
Joyce, Joyce, 289
Judge Priest (film), 176
judicial discrimination, 154

Kael, Pauline, 252
Katznelson, Ira, 123
Kaye, Lenny, 258
Kefauver, Lee, 213
Kelley, Robin D. G., 291

Index   437

Kellner, Douglas, 99, 194
Kellner, Hans, 325
Kendi, Ibram X., 10, 42
Kennedy administration, 212
Kerner Commission, 124, 125, 126, 195, 233
Keynes, John Maynard: debates on economic logic of, 82–83, 85; failure of economic logic of, 2, 3, 6; overview of economic logic of, 64
Killer of Sheep (film), 307
Kilpatrick, James J., 28, 30, 80
King, Amy K., 237
King, Martin Luther, Jr., 30, 80, 308, 313
King, Mary, 213
King Kong (film), 241
Kirk, Russell, 30, 58, 214
Koch, Charles, 134
Koh, Harold Hongju, 300
Kondracke, Morton, 202
Kool Herc (or Clive Campbell), 302, 306, 310
Krämer, Peter, 218, 219, 222, 242
Kramer v. Kramer (film), 229
Kruse, Kevin, 144
Kucinich, Dennis, 156
Kuhn, Annette, 218

labor movements, 94, 96, 100, 105–6, 121, 133, 143, 154–55. See also *names of specific industries*
laissez-faire capitalism, 3, 7, 47, 64–65, 72, 76, 141, 156, 162, 214. See also capitalism; free market economics; neoliberalism
land, as concept, 33
land dispossession, 171–72
Landis, John, 235
Lasch, Christopher, 245
Lassiter, Matthew D., 13, 321
Last Poets, 289, 293, 294, 302
Latham, Michael, 105
Latour, Bruno, 224
"law and order" framework, 54, 60, 85, 181, 196–97, 243–44, 280. See also "rule of law" rhetoric
"Learning from the 60s" (Lorde), 259
Lears, T. J. Jackson, 168
Lee, Don L., 292
Lennon, John, 258

Leon, Gerardo de, 235
lesbianism, 229, 237, 239, 274, 278. See also homophobia
Lester, Julius, 283
Lewis, Jon, 169
liberalism. See classical liberalism; neoliberalism
liberation gauntlets: about, 21, 224; corporations and, 256, 269; films and, 221–23, 236–37, 242–47, 251, 255; mainstream masculinity and, 242–47; Reddy on, 260; sexual violence in, 216, 229, 283; women's empowerment and, 223, 231, 233, 256
liberation music, 366n34
libertarianism, 12, 27–28, 170. See also New Right
Lichtenfeld, Eric, 192, 195
Life (publication), 190
Lilienthal, David E., 97
Limerick, Patrick Nelson, 24
Lincoln, Abraham, 13, 159, 186
Lind, Michael, 199, 281
Lippmann, Walter, 65–66, 67, 99
Lipsitz, George, 41, 171
lobbying, 134
Lockwood, Belva, 185
longue durée, overview, 4–5, 6, 14–15, 36, 297, 298
Lorde, Audre: on difference, 207, 211; "Eye to Eye," 279; on intersectional feminism, 262; "Learning from the 60s," 259; "Poetry Is Not a Luxury," 311; on white *vs.* Black feminist politics, 258, 264–65
Louisiana Purchase, 186
Lumumba, Patrice, 297, 300
lynching, 21, 26, 56, 189. See also violence against Black Americans
lynch law, 232
Lynn, Kane, 235
Lynn, Loretta, 227

MacArthur, Douglas, 180
MacLean, Nancy, 23, 138
Maier, Charles S., 150
Malaysia, 235
Malcolm X, 24, 30, 297

male gaze, 219–21, 229–30. *See also* white male authority and privilege
mammy (caricature), 175–76. *See also* Black womanhood; racism
Manhattan Institute, 134
Mannheim, Karl, 199
The Man Who Shot Liberty Valance (film), 194
Marable, Manning, 304–5
Marley, Bob, 301, 302
Married Women's Property Acts, 212
Marshall Plan, 12, 89, 102–3, 108
The Mary Tyler Moore Show (television show), 229, 259
masculinity. *See* white masculinity
Massey, Doreen, 210
mass incarceration, 124, 154. *See also* prison-industrial complex
mass production, 101–2, 113–14. *See also* capitalism; consumerism
Maude (television show), 229, 259
Mayfield, Curtis, 301
Mazlish, Bruce, 97–98
McConahay, John, 81
McGovern, George, 132
McLintock! (film), 194, 208, 209
McNair, Denise, 30–31
McQ (film), 192, 194–98, 243
McQuaid, Kim, 102
"Me and the Devil Blues" (song), 285, 286, 316
media representation. *See* film industry; television
Meeuf, Russell, 165, 166
Mellon, Andrew, 64
mergers. *See* conglomeration
"The Message" (Grandmaster Flash and the Furious Five), 310–11
Mexican Americans, 177, 320. *See also* immigration
Mexican people, 171–72, 186, 194, 319. *See also* settler colonialism
Meyer, Frank S., 193
Meyers, Richard, 221, 242, 361n91
Mies, Maria, 230
The Mind of Gil Scott-Heron (Scott-Heron), 304
Miranda v. Arizona, 243, 244

Mirowski, Philip, 7, 75
miscegenation, 45, 56, 62, 70, 169, 182, 214
Mises, Ludwig von, 65, 73
misogyny, 210–11, 220–23, 243. *See also* patriarchy; sexism; violence against women; women's rights
Miss American pageant, 213
Mississippi, 45, 202
mixed economy, 72–73, 92, 94–96, 100–106, 129. *See also* corporations
MNCs. *See* multinational corporations
Mobil Oil Corporation, 117
mob violence. *See* white terrorism
The Modern Corporation and Private Property (Berle), 93
Modern Woman: The Lost Sex (Lundberg), 214
Monaco, Paul, 193
monopolies, 66–68, 93, 98, 114, 116, 168–69. *See also* corporations; free market economics; multinational corporations (MNCs)
Mont Pèlerin Society, 66, 69–70, 71
Moreau, Joseph, 177
Morrison, Toni, 23, 24–25, 28, 35, 37
Motion Picture Association of America (MPAA), 218
Motion Picture Producers' Association, 169
Motor Carrier Act (1980), 115
Mountain Moving Day (New Have and Chicago Women's Liberation Rock Band), 260
Moynihan, Daniel P., 42, 43, 45, 124, 139, 228
The Moynihan Report (Moynihan), 43, 139, 228
Mudhoney (film), 218
Muller, Jerry Z., 74–75
multiculturalism, as term, 16, 211
multinational corporations (MNCs): Berle on, 93; conglomerates and global capitalism, 113–19; currency fluctuations and, 106–13; defined, 97–98; discontent of, 149–50; foreign direct investments by, 107–8, 112, 118–19, 147, 235; frontier myth and, 161–64; new global economy of, 90, 95, 97–100; populist rage against, 88–89; reawakening of, 1, 2, 12. *See also* conglomeration; globalization; monopolies

Index 439

music: country, 226–27, 249; on feminism and women's liberation, 259–61, 366n34; hip-hop, 293, 302–13, 375n146; of Jamaica, 22, 301–3, 306, 308, 375n146; jazz, 290, 291, 292, 297, 303, 306; rap, 305–6; R&B, 228, 301; reggae, 301–2, 375n146; rock, 226; sexism and racism in, 226–29; soul, 301

Nashville (film), 88
National Conference for a New Politics (1967), 213
National Equal Rights Party, 185
nationalism, 33, 46, 94. *See also* defense of Western civilization trope; white nationalism; white supremacy
National Mobilization Committee, 226
National Organization for Women (NOW), 213, 229, 278
National Review (publication), 27, 28, 30, 37, 46, 204. *See also* Buckley, William F., Jr.
A Nation Builds under Fire (tv program), 178–79, 180
Native Americans: attempted genocide of, 172–73, 177, 186, 319; film and television portrayals of, 171–73, 184–85, 193–94, 320; John Wayne on, 173, 174–75; violence against, 231. *See also* frontier myth; racism; settler colonialism
Naturalization Act (1790), 25, 77, 152, 232
natural laws: on economics, 64, 68, 215; on women and people of color, 214, 224
"The Negro Family," or the Moynihan Report (Moynihan), 139, 228
"Negro problem" trope, 44, 45, 47, 83
neoliberalism: overview of rise of, 1–13, 67, 90, 317–18; Chicago school of economics on, 6, 66, 67, 82; exploitation films and, 209–11; Friedman on, 68, 69, 79–85; Hayek on, 53, 64, 69–71, 85, 104–5, 318, 322; modernity and, 13–15, 318–19; Plehwe on, 63; Scott-Heron on, 285, 286; as term, 63; through benign neglect policies, 10, 43, 124, 157, 286, 300. *See also* classical liberalism; conservatism; culture war, overview; free market economics; laissez-faire capitalism

"Neoliberalism and Its Prospects" (Friedman), 67–68, 69
"neo-liberals," defined, 157
Netherlands, 90
Network (film), 21, 88–89, 229, 248, 249–57, 263, 268, 273
New Deal, 1, 2, 102, 138, 203. *See also* Roosevelt, Franklin; welfare state, overview
"The New Deal" (song by Scott-Heron), 284, 304
New Haven (band), 260–61
New Left, 159, 213, 226, 228, 371n23. *See also* Democratic Party
New Right: color blindness of, 321; criticisms on welfare state by, 104–5; rise of, 2, 4, 12, 54, 130. *See also* Buckley, William F., Jr.; Republican Party
New York City, 285–86, 302–3, 305, 306, 310–11, 316
9/11 attacks (2001), 316
Nineteenth Amendment, 212
Nine to Five (film), 17, 21, 248, 256, 268–73
Nine to Five (organization), 269
Nixon, Richard, 146, 177, 189, 243, 321
Nixon administration, 78; benign neglect policies of, 10, 43, 124, 157, 286, 300; economic policies of, 85, 108, 111, 128–29, 137; populist conservatism of, 130; Watergate corruption by, 146, 194, 248
Nkrumah, Kwame, 297
Nobel Prize in Economics, 85
Nobody Knows My Name (Baldwin), 45
No Name in the Street (Baldwin), 48, 161
normalized violence. *See* violence against Black Americans; violence against Native Americans; violence against women
North Atlantic universals, 11, 50, 261
nostalgia, 8, 104, 166, 249, 308, 318–19, 330n80. *See also* American dream; frontier myth; possession of history; settler colonialism; white innocence
No Substitute for Victory (film), 178, 179–81
n****r, as term. *See* N-word

nuclear warfare, 181
Nuriddin, Jalal, 303, 374n110
N-word, 153, 191, 233–34, 258, 363n162, 367n56. *See also* anti-Blackness; Black Americans; racism

Obama administration, 6, 204
OECD (Organisation for Economic Co-operation and Development), 112
O'Hara, Maureen, 208
oil industry, 89, 97, 111, 117, 128, 133–34, 144–45, 148
Old and New Economic Liberalism (Heckscher), 63
Omi, Michael, 15
One Day at a Time (television show), 259
Ongiri, Amy Abugo, 292
Ono, Yoko, 258
OPEC (Organization of Petroleum Exporting Countries), 111, 144
Operation Iraqi Freedom, 315–16
Opinion Research Corporation (ORC), 132, 133
Orwell, George, 70

PACs (political action committees), 134, 148
"Paint It Black" (Scott-Heron), 293
Pan-Africanism, 297, 298, 301, 302, 303
Parenti, Michael, 149
Pateman, Carole, 224, 246
paternalism, 2, 40, 164, 191, 355n77. *See also* white male authority and privilege
patriarchy, 157, 171; family wage, 8, 12, 25, 77; gender hierarchy, 208–9; music on, 226–29; in Walt Disney Productions, 355n73. *See also* feminist politics; misogyny; sexism; violence against women; white male authority and privilege; women's rights
patriotism, 152, 170–71, 180, 183, 188, 316. *See also* frontier myth; white masculinity; white nationalism
Patterson, James T., 23, 24
Pax Americana, 102, 105
"Peace Go with You, Brother" (Scott-Heron), 305

Perlstein, Rick, 79
personhood of corporations, 5, 162. *See also* corporations
Philippines, 21, 222, 223, 234–41
Phillips, Kevin, 121, 203, 205–6, 251
Phillips-Fein, Kim, 23
Pieces of a Man (Scott-Heron), 296
Piketty, Thomas, 323
Pinochet, Augusto, 117
Pissstained Stairs and the Monkey Man's Wares (Cortez), 291
Playboy (publication), 173, 200, 241
Playing in the Dark (Morrison), 23
Plehwe, Dieter, 63
Plessy v. Ferguson, 25, 26, 77
poetry, 282–84, 288–89. *See also* Cortez, Jayne; Scott-Heron, Gil; spoken word
"Poetry Is Not a Luxury" (Lorde), 311
Poitier, Sidney, 197, 198
Polanyi, Karl, 71–72
police brutality, 196–97, 233, 298, 307
police state, 300, 307–8
polyglots, as term, 98. *See also* conglomeration
populist conservatism, 6, 8, 130, 163–64; of John Wayne, 164, 166–67, 198–202, 207–8; Lears on, 168; against multinational corporations, 88–89; of Reagan, 202–3. *See also* business conservatism; conservatism
Portuguese colonialism, 297
"Position Paper 24" (or Waveland memo), 213
Posner, Richard, 206
possession of history, 32–36, 48, 54–55, 75, 177, 306, 319, 323. *See also* defense of Western civilization trope; frontier myth; nostalgia; settler colonialism
Postman, Neil, 280
Post-Reconstruction, 18
poverty: Buckley on, 83, 85; federal programs on, 140, 154, 314; Kirk on, 58; rates of, 108, 157, 314; Scott-Heron on, 293–94, 296; of women, 281. *See also* wealth inequality
Powell, Lewis, 132
predator lesbian (caricature), 237

Index   441

prison films, 229, 237–41. *See also* film industry
prison-industrial complex, 300, 307–8. *See also* mass incarceration
privatization, 3, 7, 95–96, 300. *See also* business conservatism; financial institutions; multinational corporations (MNCs)
Program for Conservatives (Kirk), 58
"Pro-Negro Discrimination Encouraged" (Buckley), 23
Proposition 13 (California), 144
Proposition 14 (California), 61
prostitution, 195, 218, 222, 239
Psycho (film), 218

racial capitalism, 25, 30, 38, 42, 321. *See also* anti-Blackness; frontier capitalism; neoliberalism; racism; slavery
racial coding, 13, 214. *See also* racial inequality
racial hierarchy, 57–59, 80–81, 158, 209. *See also* racism; social Darwinism; white supremacy
racial inequality: of the 1980s, 154–55; affirmative action on, 8, 54, 138, 154, 189, 264, 309; Atwater on, 153–54; Baldwin on, 17–18; Buckley on, 18, 44–46, 47, 55–56, 83–84; in business and economic opportunities, 138–39, 270; *Business Week* on, 124–26, 139–40; Kerner Commission on, 124, 125, 126; in military, 179; "Negro problem" trope on, 44, 45, 47, 83; poverty rates, 157; regeneration of, 191–98; residential segregation, 10, 19, 123. *See also* Black Americans; social equality; wealth inequality
racial violence. *See* genocide; slavery; violence against Black Americans; violence against Native Americans
racism: Apartheid system, 190, 302, 303–4; of Atwater, 153–54; deregulation of, 80–81; in federal policies, 10, 18, 104; in film, 51, 165–66, 171–73, 175–76, 182–85; Kerner Commission on, 124, 125; in language, 16, 153–54, 191, 233–34, 258, 363n162, 367n56; public polling on, 60–62, 126; of Reagan, 61, 140, 189, 202; residential segregation and suburbanization, 10, 19, 122–24; in school textbooks, 34, 177; scientific justification for, 19, 37, 44–45, 232, 321; using caricatures, 40, 41, 51, 126, 161, 175–76, 188. *See also* anti-Blackness; Black womanhood; color blindness; settler colonialism; slavery; violence against Black Americans; white fear; whiteness; white womanhood
railroad corporations, 96–97
Rand, Ayn, 170
rap, 305–6. *See also* hip-hop; music
The Rap Attack (Toop), 305–6
rape. *See* violence against women
"Rape" (poem by Cortez), 283
Rape Squad (film), 231
Rastafarianism, 302
rationality: of Buckley, 39–40, 46; of Enlightenment era, 7, 64, 65; Weaver on, 57–58. *See also* scientific racism
Raye, Martha, 182
R&B music, 228, 301. *See also* music
RCA, 121, 133
Reagan, Ronald, 140; involvement in SAG and Red Scare, 169; presidential campaigns of, 130, 151, 152, 314; racism of, 61, 140, 189, 202
Reagan administration: anti-labor policies of, 121, 152, 156, 169; economic policies of, 6, 47–48, 98, 146, 157, 202–3, 308; foreign policies of, 300; nostalgia and racist policies of, 309, 311
Reconstruction, 3, 18, 33–34. *See also* White Reconstruction
Redding, J. Saunders, 290
Reddy, Helen, 259–60, 261
redface, 184
Red River (film), 171, 172, 173, 203
Red Scare, 94, 168–69, 170
Red Sea piracy incident (2009), 204
Reflections (Scott-Heron), 308
reggae, 301–2, 375n146. *See also* music
Reich, Robert, 204–5
religious liberty, 36
reparations, 47, 54, 138. *See also* slavery

442 Index

reproductive rights, 209, 213, 214, 239, 260, 278. *See also* women's rights
Republican Party, 130, 213, 314. *See also* GOP (Grand Old Party); neoliberalism; New Right
Republic Steel, 144
residential segregation, 10, 19, 122–25. *See also* segregationists; suburbanization
Revenue Act (1978), 146
"The Revolution Will Not Be Televised" (Scott-Heron), 296
Rigby, David L., 88, 102, 108, 112
"rights of property" rhetoric, 3, 9, 54, 139, 212
Rio Grande (film), 178
The Road to Serfdom (Hayek), 49, 70, 71, 72–74
Roberts, Dorothy, 55
Robertson, Carole, 31
Robinson, Cedric, 29, 241
Rockefeller, David, 134
rock music, 226, 260. *See also* music
Rocky (film), 307
Rodgers, Daniel, 146
Rodríguez, Dylan, 4, 15
Roe v. Wade, 260
Rogers, Bob, 297
Rohrabacher, Dana, 180
Rolling Stones (band), 226, 260
Romero, Eddie, 234, 235
Roosevelt, Franklin, 93, 180. *See also* New Deal
Roosevelt, Theodore, 73, 161, 172–73, 205
Rosen, Ruth, 281
Roth, Benita, 261
Rothman, Stephanie, 217, 221
Roush, Lana, 227
rugged individualism, 8, 21, 28, 78, 165, 183, 204–8. *See also* frontier myth; individualism; settler colonialism; white male authority and privilege; white masculinity
"rule of law" rhetoric, 54, 67, 70–71, 77, 85–86. *See also* "law and order" framework
Ryan, Michael, 99, 194

Saez, Emmanuel, 323
Saint-Just, Louis Antoine de, 279
Salvatore, Nick, 95, 313
Sambo (caricature), 40, 51, 126, 161, 175–76, 188. *See also* Black Americans; racism
Sanchez, Sonia, 292, 293
Sands of Iwo Jima (film), 173–74
Santiago, Cirio, 235
Schaffer, Jane, 207, 238
Schlafly, Phyllis, 227
Schulman, Bruce, 151
Schultz, Theodore W., 82
Schwartz, Anna J., 82
Schwarz, John E., 121
scientific racism, 19, 37, 44–45, 232–33, 321. *See also* Black Americans; racism; white supremacy
Scott-Heron, Gil: "Ain't No New Thing," 293–94; *Black Wax* film on , 313, 314; "B' Movie," 309, 314; "Coming from a Broken Home," 289; death of, 284; early life of, 289–90; *First Minute of a New Day,* 301; on globalization, 22, 371n23; "H2O Gate (Watergate) Blues," 298–99; *I'm New Here,* 284–85, 316; "Me and the Devil Blues"/"Your Soul and Mine," 285, 286, 287, 316; *The Mind of Gil Scott-Heron,* 304; "The New Deal," 284, 304; *The N****r Factory,* 290; "Paint It Black," 293; *Pieces of a Man,* 296; on racism, 51, 313; *Reflections,* 308; "The Revolution Will Not Be Televised," 296; *Small Talk at 125th and Lenox,* 289, 294; *From South Africa to South Carolina,* 303; *Spirits,* 315; "The Vulture" (song), 285, 286, 287, 316; *The Vulture* (book), 289; "Whitey on the Moon," 296, 313; *Winter in America* (album), 17, 157, 298, 305; on Winter in America (concept), 5, 6, 297, 298
Screen Guide for Americans (Rand), 170
The Searchers (film), 199
Second Gulf War, 315–16
The Second Sex (Beauvoir), 212
second-wave feminism. *See* feminist politics
Securities and Exchange Commission, 115
Seger, Bob, 249
segregationists, 3, 12, 28, 80, 124. *See also* Buckley, William F., Jr.; New Right; racism; residential segregation

self-determination, 45–46, 287, 291. *See also* agency
Selma, Alabama, protests (1965), 24
Sennett, Richard, 88, 109, 120
"separate but equal" policies, 3
Servicemen's Readjustment Act (1944), 95
settler colonialism: American dream and, 37–44, 304–5; Cold War and, 174–91; Engelhardt on, 33; immigration and, 151; modern forms of, 157; portrayed in film and television, 165–66, 171–73, 183–85, 231, 355n73. *See also* American exceptionalism; frontier myth; rugged individualism; slavery; Wayne, John; white nationalism
sexism: in Black Power movements, 213, 228; by Bob Hope, 185; in *Business Week* (publication), 339n17; in cultural language, 17; in films, 196, 219–20; flexible sexism, 210; in music, 226–28; welfare state and, 8. *See also* misogyny; patriarchy; white male authority and privilege; women
Sexton, Jared, 25
sexuality. *See* homophobia; lesbianism
sexual violence. *See* violence against women
She Wore a Yellow Ribbon (film), 172, 178, 200
"silent majority" strategy, 78–79, 164–65, 176, 184, 195, 243, 313. *See also* white supremacy
Simmons, William J., 56, 57
Singh, Nikhil Pal, 41
Singlaub, John K., 180
slave narratives, 358n11. *See also* enslaved African Americans; slavery
slave plantation films, 186, 237, 240, 241. *See also* women-in-prison films
slavery: in Caribbean, 365n213; film portrayals of, 175–76, 186–87; Hammond on, 56–57; memory and legacy of, 62, 157, 186, 319; music about, 226; paternalism and, 355n77; reparations for, 47, 54, 138; Scott-Heron on, 294–95. *See also* anti-Blackness; enslaved African Americans; racial capitalism; settler colonialism; violence against Black Americans
Slobodian, Quinn, 52, 66, 110
Slotkin, Richard, 168, 171, 218

Small Talk at 125th and Lenox (Scott-Heron), 289, 294
Smith, Adam, 7, 66–67, 82
Smith, Anthony D., 166
Smith, Howard, 212
Smith, Patti, 258
Sobel, Robert, 137
social Darwinism, 68. *See also* racial hierarchy; scientific racism
social equality: color blindness rhetoric on, 3, 8; Ellender on, 56; Kilpatrick on, 30; legislation on, 14–15; post-1950s era and, 2–4; rights of property policies on, 3, 9; Scott-Heron on, 295–96. *See also* communism; culture war, overview; racial inequality; wealth inequality; white innocence; women's rights
socialism, 94
Soldier Blue (film), 193
"Song for Kwame 1972" (Cortez), 297
soul music, 228, 229, 290, 301, 306. *See also* music
South Africa, 119, 190, 300, 302, 303–4
South Carolina, 135
Southern Segregationist Democratic Party, 130
Southern strategy, 13, 78, 153–54, 321
South Korea, 145
Soviet Union, 72, 78, 314
space program, 100
Spain, 90
Spencer, Herbert, 205
Spirits (Scott-Heron), 315
spoken word, 22, 289–92, 293, 302–3. *See also* hip-hop; poetry
The Spook Who Sat by the Door (film), 282
Stagecoach (film), 165, 167, 199
Stand Up and Be Counted (film), 259–60
Stanwyck, Barbara, 217
Star Wars (film), 307
state-sanctioned violence. *See* violence against Black Americans; violence against Native Americans
steel industry, 117, 119–20, 144
Stein, Judith, 111, 116, 135, 140, 146
The Stepford Wives (film), 259

St. John-Stevas, Norman, 26–27, 37. See also *Baldwin vs. Buckley* (Cambridge Debate, 1965)
Stock Market crash (1929), 64–65. *See also* Great Depression
The Strenuous Life (Roosevelt), 161
Student Nonviolent Coordinating Committee (SNCC), 213, 228, 283, 290. *See also* civil rights movement
Studies in Classic American Literature (Lawrence), 161
suburbanization, 9–10, 13, 18, 59, 100, 122–23, 140. *See also* domesticity; residential segregation; white flight
suburban strategy, 13, 321
Sugar Hill Gang, 306, 310
Sumner, William Graham, 205
Sun Belt, 99, 104, 122, 136
Suny, Ronald, 33
supersurrealism, 291
supply-side economics, 82–83, 85
surrealist poetry, 291
surveillance capitalism, 100
Swing Out Sweet Land (television show), 183–89
Switchblade Sisters (film), 221

Taft-Hartley Act (1947), 94, 100
Tall in the Saddle (film), 172
Taney, Roger B., 231
Tanganyika, 190
Tarzan the Ape Man (film), 241
taxation: education and, 3; increase of, 144; of MNCs, 137, 145, 150; reduction of, 82–83, 130, 135, 136, 146, 154; of wealthy, 122, 147, 322
Taxi Driver (film), 321
technological innovation, 111–12, 143–44
television: Buckley's *Firing Line*, 27, 43, 83, 333n102; feminist politics in, 229, 259; nostalgia by, 249; portrayals of Native Americans in, 184–85, 320. See also *Baldwin vs. Buckley* (Cambridge Debate, 1965); film industry
Terminal Island (film), 221
textbooks and historical education, 34, 177
*The N****r Factory* (Scott-Heron), 290

There It Is (Cortez), 311–12
"They Came Again in 1970 in 1980" (Cortez), 296–97
Thomas, Lowell, 181
Time (publication), 161
Toffler, Alvin, 100, 317
To Renew America (Gingrich), 49–50
"traditional values" rhetoric. *See* family values
transfer pricing, 118
transtemporal history, 16, 330n75
Trattner, Walter I., 202
Trends of Economic Ideas (Honegger), 63
Trilateral Commission, 134
Trouillot, Michel-Rolph, 11, 50, 57, 261, 326
trucking industry, 115
Truck Turner (film), 222
True Grit (film), 194
Trump, Donald, 323–24
Truth, Sojourner, 287
Tulsa Massacre (1921), 191, 320. *See also* violence against Black Americans
Tuskegee syphilis experiment, 261
Twain, Mark, 187

unemployment rates, 64, 83, 121–22, 129, 143, 148. *See also* wealth inequality
unions. *See* labor movements
United Fruit, 110
universalism, 11, 14, 50, 261–62. *See also* invisibility of whiteness
University Professors Conference (1965), 82
An Unmarried Woman (film), 259
Unsubmissive Blues (Cortez), 303–4
Up Tight! (film), 218, 307
U.S. Capitol siege (2021), 323
U.S. colonialism in Philippines, 235
U.S. Constitution, 5, 162, 212
U.S. Department of Defense, 178, 179
U.S. Department of Homeland Security, 324
U.S. imperialism in film, 234–41
U.S. Steel Corporation, 119, 144
U.S. v. Paramount Pictures, Inc., 168–69

Van Horn, Rob, 75
Variety (publication), 170

Vatter, Harold G., 94–95
victimhood: Baldwin on, 34, 36, 207, 215, 225, 312, 319; of white people, 41, 55, 72, 127, 166, 195, 233
Vietnam, 178
Vietnam War: antiwar movement, 170–71, 175, 179, 182; conclusion of, 297; defense of Western civilization and, 59, 60; economic effects of, 89, 106; initial invasion of, 24; John Wayne's trilogy on, 178–80; public opinion on, 146, 158, 183, 194, 242
vigilantes. *See* white terrorism
A Vindication on the Rights of Woman (Wollstonecraft), 212
violence against Black Americans: during civil rights movement, 24, 175, 187, 219; in film, 222–23, 231, 233; lynchings, 21, 26, 56, 189; media display of, 59; music on, 226, 294; scientific racism as justification of, 19, 37, 44–45, 232, 321; Tulsa Massacre, 191, 320, 323; "white right" to commit, 56. *See also* anti-Blackness; Black Americans; slavery; white terrorism
violence against Native Americans, 172–73, 177, 186, 231, 319. *See also* Native Americans
violence against women: in captivity narratives, 210–11, 358n11; in film and television, 208, 209, 210, 216–42, 355n73; music on, 226; poetry on, 282–83; by Trump, 324; witch burning, 232. *See also* misogyny; patriarchy; women
virility cult, 244–47. *See also* white masculinity
Volcker, Paul, 111, 128, 150, 151, 153, 155
Volker Fund, 67, 68, 69
voting rights, 55–46, 212
Voting Rights Act (1965), 24, 154
"The Vulture" (song by Scott-Heron), 285, 266, 287, 316
The Vulture (book by Scott-Heron), 289

Wacquant, Loïc, 307
wage discrimination, 81, 228, 272. *See also* wealth inequality
wage-price controls, 151
Wager, Jans B., 252

Walker, David, 287
Walker, Margaret, 291
Wallace, George, 177
Walls, Chaka, 228
Wall Street. *See* capitalism
Wapshott, Nicholas, 64
Ward, Brian, 228
Warner Bros., 170, 179
war on drugs, 124, 154
War on Terror, 180, 203
wartime economics, 89, 94, 95, 105, 106, 315–16
wartime films, 178–83
Washington, Booker T., 45
"Watching a Parade in Harlem 1970" (Cortez), 284
Watergate, 146, 194, 248. *See also* Nixon, Richard; Nixon administration
Waterhouse, Benjamin C., 113
Watts Prophets, 288, 290, 293, 294
Watts riots (1965), 24
Waveland memo, 213
Wayne, John: anti-Blackness of, 159, 189–92, 201; background and career of, 164–66; legacy of, 160, 204; in Philippines, 234; populist conservatism of, 164, 166–67, 198–202. *See also* frontier myth; *names of specific films and television shows*; Western films
The Way the World Works (Wanniski), 144, 152
wealth inequality, 65, 86, 203, 286, 322. *See also* poverty; racial inequality; social equality; unemployment rates; wage discrimination; welfare state, overview
Weaver, Richard M., 57–58
Webb, Marilyn Salzman, 226
Webber, Michael J., 88, 102, 108, 112
Weinberger, Caspar W., 141
Weiss, Carol H., 92
Welch, Robert, 176–77
"welfare queen" trope, 140
welfare state, overview, 1–13, 317–26
Wells, Ida B., 287
Wesley, Cynthia, 31
West, Mae, 217

Westad, Arne, 105
Western films, 167–76, 193. *See also* film industry; *names of specific films;* Wayne, John
Wheeler, Billy Edd, 227
"Which Way for Capitalism" (Friedman), 49
white backlash, 3, 15, 30, 140–41, 332n39. *See also* violence against Black Americans; violence against Native Americans; white male authority and privilege; white terrorism
white fear, 40, 85, 125, 176, 229, 307. *See also* racism; white terrorism
white flight, 62, 83. *See also* suburbanization
white innocence: American dream and, 37–47, 304–5; of individualism, 79; Morrison on, 23, 24–25; on racist and sexist past, 8, 18, 31, 75, 138–39, 152, 175, 227; Scott-Heron on, 295; Trouillot on, 50. *See also* American exceptionalism; color blindness; defense of Western civilization trope; nostalgia; possession of history; settler colonialism; white nationalism
white liberalism, 43, 55, 293, 296, 332n39
white male authority and privilege: Baldwin on, 16; Buckley on, 41–42; erosion of, 15–16, 30, 50–51, 203, 324; federal redistribution policies and, 140–42; John Wayne and, 167, 208; male gaze in film, 219–21, 229–30; as patriotism, 152, 170–71, 180, 182–83, 188, 316; political systems of, 21. *See also* culture war, overview; individualism; patriarchy; sexism; violence against women; white backlash; white supremacy
white masculinity, 15–16; family wage and, 8, 12, 25; Focus on the Family on, 377n13; global economics and, 96; heroism trope, 15–16, 20–21, 194; historical overview of, 231; of John Wayne, 165, 166, 172, 173; liberation gauntlets and, 242–47; as rugged individualism, 8, 21, 28, 78, 165, 183, 204–8; virility cult, 244–47; women's liberation and, 213–14, 216. *See also* patriotism; violence against women; white male authority and privilege

white nationalism, 53, 166. *See also* conservatism; defense of Western civilization trope; patriotism; settler colonialism; white innocence
whiteness: affirmative action for, 8, 264; Baldwin on, 38; Buckley on, 39–40, 41, 44–45; individualism and, 76–77; invisibility of, 10, 18, 104, 125–27, 206; media portrayal of, 165–66, 171–73, 182–85; victimhood and, 41, 55, 72, 127, 166, 195, 210, 233. *See also* anti-Blackness; color blindness; universalism; white liberalism; white nationalism; white womanhood
white rage, 3, 15, 125, 312. *See also* white terrorism
White Reconstruction, 4, 15, 26, 48. *See also* Reconstruction
white supremacy: by attempted genocide of Native Americans, 172–73, 177, 186, 319; in business and economic opportunities, 138–39; neoliberal economics and, 86; post-1950s era challenges to, 2–3; scientific racism on, 19, 37, 44–45, 232, 321; silent majority, 78–79, 164–65, 176, 184, 195, 243, 313; Trump and, 323–24. *See also* American exceptionalism; color blindness; nationalism; racial hierarchy; racism; scientific racism; white male authority and privilege; white nationalism
white terrorism, 3, 9, 15, 125, 323. *See also* anti-Blackness; genocide; slavery; violence against Black Americans; violence against Native Americans; white backlash; white fear
white womanhood: captivity narratives of, 358n11; domesticity of, 214; feminist politics on Black womanhood *vs.*, 212, 258–65; gender hierarchy and, 208–9; *Nine to Five* film on, 17, 21, 248, 256, 268–73. *See also* Black womanhood; whiteness; women
"Whitey on the Moon" (Scott-Heron), 296, 313
Whitney, Eli, Jr., 185
Wight, David M., 111
The Wild Bunch (film), 193, 218

Willis Brothers, 227
Winant, Howard, 15
The Winning of the West (Roosevelt), 172–73
Winter in America (album by Scott-Heron), 17, 157, 298, 305
Winter in America, as concept, 5, 6, 14–15, 36, 297, 298
witch burning, 232
Wollstonecraft, Mary, 212
"Woman's Talkin' Liberation Blues" (song), 227
women: assimilation of, 223, 230, 256–57, 261–62, 270; captivity narratives on, 210–11, 240, 358n11; as femme fatale, 229, 252, 253; violence against (*See* violence against women); white womanhood, 208–9, 214, 358n11. *See also* Black womanhood; corporate woman; feminist politics; white womanhood; women's rights
women-in-prison films, 229, 237–41. *See also* film industry; slave plantation films
"Women's Liberation" (song), 227
women's liberation films, 217
women's liberation movement. *See* feminist politics
women's liberation music, 366n34
women's rights: conservatism on, 156; country music on, 226–27; in employment, 263–64; John Wayne on, 208; as property, 31, 212; to reproduction, 209, 213, 214, 239, 260, 278; second-wave feminism on, 59, 212–16; Wollstonecraft on, 212. *See also* feminist politics; misogyny; patriarchy; sexism; violence against women; white womanhood
World Bank, 300
World War II, 178, 181–82, 214
Wright, Richard, 290

xenophobia, 51, 325

"Your Soul and Mine" (song), 285, 286, 287, 316

Zelizer, Julian, 144
Zip Coon (caricature), 41. *See also* Black Americans; racism
Zuboff, Shoshana, 100